Communication and Interpersonal Relations
Text and Cases

❋
❋
❋

Communication and Interpersonal Relations
Text and Cases

William V. Haney, Ph.D.
Wm. V. Haney Associates
Wilmette, Illinois 60091

Sixth Edition

IRWIN

Homewood, IL 60430
Boston, MA 02116

This symbol indicates that the paper in this book is made from recycled paper. Its fiber content exceeds the recommended minimum of 50% waste paper fibers as specified by the EPA.

Sponsoring editor: Craig Beytien
Project editor: Karen Smith
Production manager: Ann Cassady
Designer: Hiedi Fieschko
Compositor: Alexander Typesetting, Inc.
Typeface: 10/12 Century Schoolbook
Printer: R. R. Donnelley & Sons Company

Library of Congress Cataloging-in-Publication Data

Haney, William V.
  Communication and interpersonal relations   text and cases /
William V. Haney. — 6th ed.
    p.   cm.
  Includes bibliographical references and index.
  ISBN 0-256-06974-3
  1. Communication—Psychological aspects.   2. Communication in
organization.   3. Interpersonal relations.   I. Title.
HM258.H355   1992
658.4'5'019—dc20   91–20955

Printed in the United States of America
2 3 4 5 6 7 8 9 0 DOC 8 7 6 5 4 3 2

＊
＊
＊

Every writer is a product of his experiences. In the case of this book, so much is due to the author's contact with one outstanding personality that special mention must be made of it. The author is deeply grateful for eight years of study and friendship with the late **Professor Irving J. Lee** of Northwestern University. Those who have been stimulated by his writings and inspired by his person will recognize his influence. It is to the continuation of his teachings and values that this book is respectfully dedicated.

Preface

❋
❋
❋

Communication is the process by which we give and receive information, signals, or messages by talking, writing, listening, reading, gesturing, and so on. It's associated with the Latin *communicatio*—literally, to make common.

Accordingly, this book about communication and interpersonal relations is intended for people who deal with other people in organizations such as business, government, military, hospital, and educational institutions. It was written for use in college courses, management-development seminars, supervisory training programs, adult education classes, and individual self-study.

This sixth edition of the book attempts to reflect the evolutions and, in some cases, revolutions that have occurred in this vital field in the past five years.

Among the new features of this edition:

- The "World of Change" is back in Chapter 1 after its absence in the previous edition. Note how quickly the headline names and places become obsolete. Which, of course, is the point of the "World of Change." Our lives are replete with change.
- The Table of Contents has been augmented with sub-titles. Readers suggested that the Contents would be more helpful if the chapter headings included a brief description of their content. This seemed particularly relevant to the chapters in Part Three, "Patterns of Miscommunication." After all, terms such as *intensional orientation, blindering,* and *indiscrimination* are hardly household labels.
- The chapters have been edited, updated, and—in some cases—substantially altered. Chapter 2, "Trust and Communication," is wholly new—reflecting the growing concern for a climate of trust and trustworthiness in our organizations.

- New cases have been included to stay abreast of some of the changes in organizational life.

One evolution is that women increasingly occupy responsible executive and technical positions. So to existing cases "Nancy Sawyer" and "Pat's Story," "Janet Is Looking," "Lynn Barfield," and "Tommie Sanders (A and B)" have been added. "Janet," a young woman, is contemplating leaving her current position as a design engineer, largely because of difficulties with her boss. "Lynn Barfield," a woman in her mid-thirties, describes her experiences as a supervisor in a university's management development adjunct. "Tommie Sanders" relates some of her activities and feelings leading to and including her role as a hotel executive.

Another development concerns corporate takeovers. They have been going on for years, of course, but only recently have they become front-page news. The leveraged buyouts, or attempts at them, have captured a good deal of public attention. But the more subtle consequences of such organizational upheavals are rarely chronicled. "Merger Mania" suggests some of the tensions that invade an organization when top management changes. And in "Tommie Sanders–B," the title character makes some interesting comments about such an impact. "The Logan Company," an existing case, is another example of the human stress that often accompanies gross reorganization.

Minorities increasingly have made their marks on organizations. "Tom Rollins," a black university professor, and "Tommie Sanders," a Mexican-born hotel executive, exemplify, to an extent, such changes. In addition, black female employees play a role in "Lynn Barfield." But the most poignant example of the burden many minority members bear as they try to ascend in an organization appears in "Janet Is Looking." Although we never hear from him directly, it is clear that George Barrow, a black supervisor, is striving diligently to build a successful career in a high-tech firm. Janet's encounter with him suggests some of the stress he is enduring.

Still another change has been occurring for some time but is now accelerating. For economic, technical, political, and psychological reasons, managing—especially the managing of people in an organization—has become markedly more demanding. Small wonder that the skills of managing are increasingly being *taught* rather than merely assumed. Educational institutions as well as private firms have been offering such training and development. "MTC," short for Management Training Center, is a case about a consultant's appraisal of the supervisory practices and morale of such a unit. "Lynn Barfield," incidentally, is a staff member of MTC.

And we can hardly ignore the changes that have accompanied the incredible advances in communication technology we've enjoyed in the last few years. Thanks to the microchip and the omniscience of aids such as computers, fax machines, and E-mail, our communication facility has been greatly enhanced. But there has been a human cost for such technical progress. "Tommie Sanders–B" reflects some of these repercussions.

The world grows ever smaller. That's a cliché, but it is also true. Many young people find themselves working in a culture other than their own. Their rewards can be substantial—psychologically as well as economically. However, living and succeeding in an environment that seems so alien to the one to which one is accustomed can also be highly challenging. It is hoped that "Cultural Pitfalls" will be helpful. "Tommie Sanders–A" depicts a young woman for whom the United States represents another culture.

Relatedly, world affairs in recent months have changed at a dizzying pace. Hopefully, *glasnost* is here to stay, and the Cold War between East and West is finally at an end. If so, I will be delighted to consider some cases obsolete and delete them.

Finally, the bibliography has been pruned and renewed. A systematic review of recent literature leads to an inescapable conclusion. The body of knowledge in the broad areas of communication and organizational behavior is dramatically increasing. In terms of *quantity*—which is overwhelming—*and quality*—which is impressive if not uniform—there has probably been more solid development in these areas in the last half-decade alone than in the entire previous history of their study. And well there might for we are being drawn inexorably into "the race between education and destruction." To paraphrase William F. Buckley, Jr.: "Communication may not save us but without communication we will not be saved."

This book continues to consider communication in the *organizational* setting and in terms of a broad *behavioral* base for the communicative act. The communicator, after all, is a complex being with feelings, values, attitudes, perceptions, needs, goals, expectations, and motives. To examine communication behavior apart from the whole person and apart from interpersonal relations is not only artificial but misleading. Moreover, society is becoming progressively *organized*—thus an inspection of the impact of the organization on the individual's communication is necessary.

According to its title, this book is about *communication*. The title will appear appropriate or inappropriate, I suppose, to the extent that the reader's visualization of communication coincides with the author's. Perhaps it would be helpful to indicate what this book is *not* about. It does not, for example, deal with much of the subject matter usually developed in texts of public, conversational, conference, business, and professional speaking. It does not serve the purposes of texts of composition or of business writing, reports, and letters. Nor is it a book on reading or listening. These vital aspects, phases, and media of communication are treated skillfully and thoroughly in many fine works. Some of them are listed in the bibliography at the end of this book.

This book is concerned with the less familiar but equally critical phases of communication common to all of the modes of human interchange. It focuses on what it is that happens *inside* a communicator *before* talking and writing and *after* listening, reading, and so forth. Some might call these processes thinking and dissociate them from the communication experience. Others, including this writer, have felt no need to make such a distinction and, indeed, question the wisdom of drawing an arbitrary line between thinking and communicating. I feel perceiving, evaluating, visualizing, and interpreting are as involved in the communication process as are phonation, articulation, spelling, and grammar.

The book is also about *interpersonal relations in organizations*. That interpersonal relations and communication are inextricably interwoven is a major thesis of the opening chapters.

Accordingly, the book is organized as follows:

Part One deals with the organizational setting in which communication occurs. Part Two discusses the behavioral basis of the communicative act with special reference to the roles that perception and motivation play in communication. A basic model of communication is detailed in Chapter 8, "The Process of Communication." The model describes communication as a serial process involving the phases of encoding, sending, medium, receiving, and decoding. Each step, like a link in a chain, is crucial. Because they are by far the least understood, this book focuses on the encoding and decoding phases.

Each chapter in Part Three deals with one or more patterns of miscommunication that arise in the encoding and/or decoding phases. These miscommunications stem largely from various fallacious assumptions unconsciously held by the communicators—be they speakers or writers, listeners, or readers. The usual chapter format in Part Three includes a definition of the miscommunication pattern(s), the range and types of their consequences, some of their probable causes, and finally, suggestion of techniques for correcting the miscommunications and for preventing their recurrence.

Part Four, Overview (Chapter 19), is a digest of each of the preceding chapters. Some readers use this chapter as a preview of the book's scope, content, and organization.

THE CASES

If the book's purpose were only to provide the reader with a body of information and theory about communication, it would seem sufficient to restrict it to the textual material. I hope, however, that readers will use the book to move beyond the level of acquaintance with content to the improvement of their own communication performance. And this is the function of the cases. Some suggestions on using the cases are in Chapter 1, "Introduction."

INSTRUCTOR'S MANUAL

A manual for teachers is also available from the publisher. Its intent is to assist instructors to help students obtain more value from the textbook. It is organized chapter-by-chapter to correspond with the text. Typical chapter format of the manual is:

Discussion Questions—answers to the questions appended to the chapter.

Objective Questions—provides numerous agree-disagree, fill-in, or multiple-choice questions that pertain to the chapter.

Case Analyses—a synopsis of each case is offered plus responses and comments relevant to the questions following the cases.

Additional Activities—suggestions that individual students or, in some instances, the entire class may wish to pursue.

ACKNOWLEDGMENTS

I want to thank the students of Northwestern and DePaul Universities and the executives, supervisors, and professionals of numerous business, academic, government, and military organizations in management development seminars here and abroad who permitted me to share and test theories and techniques with them.

Principal among these organizations are Aetna Life and Casualty, Abbott Laboratories, Agway, Alcoa, Allegheny Ludlum, Allis Chalmers, the American Business Communication Association, The American Group of CPA Firms, American Medical Association, Anaconda, Anderson Community Hospital, Army Corps of Engineers, Ashland Oil, Carter Oil, Caterpillar Tractor (domestic and international), Chemplex, Cities Service, Copeland, The Executive Committee, Firestone, Hamilton Memorial Hospital, IBM (domestic and international), Inland Steel, Internal Revenue Service, International Nickel, Liberty Mutual Insurance Management and Business Services, Management Services, McCann-Erickson, MacNeal Memorial Hospital, Mead Johnson, Metropolitan Life, Mobil Oil (domestic and international), Montgomery Ward, Motorola, New York Life, Northwest Industrial Council, Northrop, Official Airline Guides, Otter Tail Power, Pillsbury, Presidents' Association (American Management Association), Price-Waterhouse, Prudential Life, RCA,

Rockwell International, Sentry Insurance, Standard Oil of Indiana, Swift, Teletype, the Travellers, Unocal (domestic and international), U.S. Departments of Air Force, Army, Health Education and Welfare, NASA, Navy, Public Health, and State, U.S. Gypsum, Weiss Memorial Hospital, Western Electric, Westfield Insurance, Zenith Radio, the Ministry of Lands, Tasmania, Australia, and the Ecole des Hautes Etudes Commerciales. In addition there were the executive development programs conducted by the American College, the American Hospital Assn., the American College of Hospital Administrators, the American Institute of Baking, the Bank Marketing Association, the Battelle Memorial Institute, the Brookings Institution, the College of Insurance, Cornell University, DePaul University, Edison Electric Institute, Emory University, Kentucky State University, Louisiana State University, Loyola University, Management and Business Services, Miami University, National Association of Mutual Savings Banks, National Management Association, Northwestern University, Northwestern's Traffic Institute, Notre Dame University, the Ohio State University, Oklahoma State University, Pepperdine University, UCLA, the University of Arkansas, the University of Chicago, the University of Illinois, the U.S. International University, the University of Richmond, the University of Tennessee, and the University of Wisconsin.

My particular thanks go to Caterpillar Tractor, IBM, Mobil Oil, the Presidents' Association, and Unocal for sending me to Europe, Africa, South America, Asia, Australia, and New Zealand to work with management groups in other parts of the world.

I am especially indebted to Standard Alliance Industries, Inc., which, with wholehearted cooperation, has permitted me in the roles of director, researcher, and consultant to explore without inhibition organizational communication and relationships.

I am grateful to the Ford Foundation for a research fellowship that, with the assistance of the Graduate School of Industrial Administration, Carnegie-Mellon Institute of Technology, enabled me to do some of the behavioral research.

Many people have aided me with their reviewing and editing of this book. Among my benefactors for this and earlier editions were M. Kendig, cofounder and former director of the Institute of General Semantics; Robert R. Hume, National Science Foundation; and Warren G. Bennis (M.I.T.); and also Ann Baxter (University of North Carolina); John F. Mee (Indiana University); Joseph S. Moag (Northwestern University); Victor H. Vroom (Carnegie-Mellon Institute of Technology); Karl F. Weick (Cornell University); Ogden H. Hall (University of New Orleans); Jon M. Huegli (Eastern Michigan University); James M. Lahiff (University of Georgia); Raymond V. Lesikar (North Texas State University); James E. Wade (California State University at San Jose); James T. Watt (Corpus Christi State University); Michael Giallourakis (Mississippi State University).

Reviewers who assisted in this edition by providing valuable editing and organization feedback were Michael Peich (University of Pennsylvania–West Chester); Jeffrey G. Phillips (Northwood Institute); and Gary Keele (California State Polytechnic University). Special thanks goes to Ross Figgins (California State Polytechnic University).

And for this, the sixth edition of *Communication and Interpersonal Relations,* I am especially indebted to Irwin's sponsoring editor, Craig S. Beytien, and to editorial assistant Jeanne Warble.

Much appreciation goes to my wife, Arlene, who—when revision times occurred—somehow managed to shield me from our five wonderful but active sons and daughters. That protection is no longer necessary. But she is still my best friend—and for that I am indeed grateful.

Finally, it should be clear that any errors and shortcomings in this book are uniquely my own and undoubtedly result from good advice unheeded.

William V. Haney

Contents

❋
❋
❋

PART TWO

The Behavioral Basis of Communication   67

4 Perception and Communication
1. The Process of Perception   69

Communication and Interpersonal Relations
Text and Cases

❋
❋❋
❋

PART ONE

Communication in Organizations

❋
❋
❋

CHAPTER ONE

Introduction

✳
✳
✳

Whenever people deal with one another they communicate. Even the studious avoidance of explicit communication communicates something.

When people lived in caves their communication might not have consisted of much more than grunts, gestures, and facial expressions but they had to have some way of expressing such messages as: "I'm not intending to bash your brains in—I hope you feel the same" or "You take that side of the mammoth and I'll take this side and let's hope we get him before he gets us."

Today's interrelations are more complex, of course, and so are the messages but the coexistence remains: Communication and interpersonal relations are inextricably entwined.

Nowhere is this more obvious than in organizations such as business, governmental, military, hospitals, schools, communities, families, and so forth. The emphasis on communication in organizations is growing rapidly.[1]

And well it might, for we are in a new age; that is, a postindustrial age. Smokestack industries are declining rapidly. Twenty years ago, manufacturers of American automobiles employed 676,000 persons. Today, the figure is approximately 400,000. Steel and rubber producers are shrinking also.

According to futurists, heavy industry is giving way to services and the processing of information. The "fungible" (i.e., the worker considered interchangeable with and indistinguishable from any other) is vanishing. Individuals must be considered as just that—individuals.

Moreover, the efficiency of a group depends largely on how well the efforts of its individual members are coordinated. But coordination doesn't just happen. Satisfactory communication is necessary if people are to achieve understanding and cooperation; if they are to cope with the

---

[1] Currently, the United States has 72 *associations*—not *organizations* but *associations* of *organizations*—concerned with organizational communication!

problems that come with functional change, geographic decentralization, and departmental specialization; if they are to present a desirable image of their organization to its various publics. In dealing with these and many other concerns, people in organizations have become, characteristically, *communicators*.

And the higher one is on the organizational ladder, the more time and energy he or she will likely devote to communication. Studies indicate that aside from communicating—speaking, writing, listening, reading, and thinking (intrapersonal communication)—an organization's top administrator does virtually nothing! The typical executive spends about 75 percent of the time communicating and about 75 percent of that time in individual, face-to-face situations. Even middle- and lower-management personnel devote the bulk of their working hours to the processes and problems of communication.

With all this increased interest, one might expect improvements in the communicative process. And, indeed, there has been fantastic advancement—in some areas. With the aid of modern electronic equipment, it is possible to send, receive, process, store, retrieve, and reproduce prodigious amounts of information with mind-numbing speed—and to reach huge numbers of people in the process.

The advent of microchips (computers) and optic fibers (telephonic transmission) has enormously increased the versatility and availability of these means of information processing and communication.

And the ramifications are being felt at all levels. Telecommunications innovations, for example, are not only changing the ways people get information and communicate with friends and colleagues—but how they shop, invest, work, and are educated.[2] With electronic mail, letters may be sent, read, and filed in on-line storage much faster than by long-distance telephone, express delivery, or facsimile transmission. Subscribers can choose from 56 huge databases in numerous categories including business news, financial services, and medical information. Computerized conferencing permits immediate access to everything on file including changes and challenges. Thus, any member of a project can review the entire transcript at a moment's notice.

Sometimes our communication technology yields benefits in most unexpected ways:

In August 1990, a horrendous tornado tore through some suburbs southwest of Chicago leaving titanic destruction. Twenty-nine people died, hundreds were injured, and the property damage approached $1 billion.

---

[2] A quick comment on education: Experts assert that with the aid of computers, children would be reading and writing at age three. A Canadian study contends that with computer assistance, a student could be *intellectually* prepared for college in 7 rather than 12 years. Just how *emotionally* ready for college a 10- or 12-year-old might be is another matter.

Among the heroes and heroines, and gratefully there were many, was the ubiquitous fax machine. Two little girls (age three and six) from two different families were quickly reunited with their heartsick parents because of the widespread faxing of the children's photos.

Hi-tech improvements are occurring at an incredible rate; for example, computers. In his BBC television series, "Making the Most of the Micro," Ian McNaught-Davis analogizes: "In the early postwar years when computers were very large and ponderously slow (by today's standards), the Volkswagen Beetle began to appear on American streets. Had the Bug developed at the same rate as the computer, it would currently blaze about at 600 miles per hour, get 30,000 miles per gallon, and need no service for 10,000 years. Its price? About 65 cents!"

Of course, the Beetle didn't make that progress—in fact, it is virtually extinct, at least in the United States. But the computer did and continues to do so at an astonishing pace. Your digital watch, by the way, contains more logic than that huge, old clunker. As for miniaturization, in the 1960s and 1970s a computer mainframe could fill a room. Today it can fit into a filing cabinet. Prediction: Within five years it will be the size of a cigarette pack!

Continuing in the predicting mode, we are told that by the year 2000 engineers will be able to put 100 million transistors on a one-inch square semiconductor. This chip will operate at 250 megahertz and execute 2 billion instructions every second.

And for a truly awesome development, consider the current effort to create an *optical* computer. It will use pulses of light rather than electrical signals to process data and will be 100 to 1,000 times more powerful than the present-day *supercomputers*!

I am personally delighted with these technical developments. One reason: I happen to be an amateur radio operator. But even if I were not, there would still have been a catch in my throat when I read this:

Good Vibrations

What do a personal computer, a shoe, and the Morse code have in common? Combined, they enable Raymond Boduch, WA2GXI, of Buffalo, New York, to lead a fuller life. Having lost his sight and hearing at a very early age, Boduch relies on a computer to keep personal files. To use his computer, he activates a device inside his shoe. The device, developed by a New Jersey electronics expert and a student at Rensselaer Polytechnic Institute, transforms the words and numbers that appear on the PC screen into Morse code impulses that Boduch can "read" with his foot.[3]

My modern solid-state, high-frequency transceiver, by the way, is not only more versatile and powerful, but it is only about ¹⁄₂₀th the weight and

---

[3] *QST: The Official Journal of the American Radio Relay League,* 58, no. 5 (May 1984), p. 85.

size of the 1950's equipment my wife had (she was a ham, too). Moreover, all five of our children are involved more or less directly with computer technology. And the competition for my PC is intense.

Because of modern technology we can now receive audiovisual signals from any place on earth[4] almost instantaneously. We saw and heard the horror of the Tiananmen Square Massacre *as it was happening*. If Motorola has its way (at the cost of $2.3 billion to build and launch a network of seventy-seven 700-pound satellites) you'll soon be able to make a cellular phone call anywhere. Say you're touring the Machu Picchu ruins in Peru and you feel you'd like to chat with a friend who is trekking through a rain forest in Southern Nigeria. Well, pick up your 24-ounce phone, punch a few buttons, and there you are. Just *why* you would want to make that call is beyond the province of this book, but the technology will make it possible.

But in our awe of communication science, let us not ignore one somber but compelling thought. Quantity, speed, and coverage are not the only requirements of communication. It is also imperative that we communicate clearly and precisely. But progress toward greater *understandability* has come much more slowly than the technological improvements. It is still quite possible for persons to fail to understand one another, even though they speak the "same" language; for firms to snarl orders and lose customers' confidence; for nations to break off diplomatic relations and even declare wars because of distortions in communication.

This is partly because we live in a state of *flux*. Consider the World of Change in Figure 1.1. Those words were in the news at the time of this writing. But given the requirements of manuscript submission, publication, printing, distribution, etc., you are reading this book *at least* several months after it was written. Note how many of those people, places, things, and events are already obsolete—no longer part of common parlance.

Indeed, we live in a milieu of change. But it isn't just change; it's the *acceleration* of change which has so sorely tested our ability, and our willingness, to communicate with one another.

Another factor is that we may have allowed our technological advances to lull us into complacency. We apparently have lost sight of the fact that the ultimate senders and receivers of messages, regardless of the sophisticated intervening apparatus, are frail, fallible human beings.

Here's a sober statement that Mortimer Adler made 30 years ago:

> How far can we overcome the imperfections of language?
> Only slightly.

---

[4] And *beyond* Earth, considering the excellent telephotos and the mountain of data we've received via *Voyager 2* from Jupiter, Saturn, Uranus and, more recently, Neptune and its icy moon, Triton. "Instantaneous," however, is hardly the proper adjective for such communications. Even at the speed of light, a message from Neptune (2.8 billion miles away) requires over four hours to reach us!

FIGURE 1.1
A World of Change

How far can we keep the relations of our thoughts and our feelings in good order?

Very slightly.

How far can we go to create a common background of knowledge and experience for all men?

Not very far.

How much can we attain the ideal of each man perfectly understanding himself without psychosis or neurosis to any degree?

Not very much.

How many of us are willing, every time we talk to another human being, to expend the effort to really do it well?

Few of us or, if ever, few times.

How many of us are free from all neurosis and in perfect possession of the moral and the intellectual virtues?

As you answer that question you will see that I am not exaggerating when I say that a fifty percent success in the process of communication would be very good, indeed. We probably do not come near that now.[5]

Regrettably, that assessment seems as valid today as it did then. And there's a price to be paid for such nonprogress. Over the past several years, I have been asking top executives to calculate the cost of miscommunication in their respective organizations. In addition to the dollars lost in waste and duplication clearly induced by miscommunication, I asked them to include the difficult-to-quantify but very real costs of miscommunications that contribute to:

loss of customer confidence	absenteeism
hurt feelings	turnover
grudges and retaliations	grievances
office feuds	strikes
baseless rumors	sabotage
malicious obedience	production retardation

Their estimates range from 25 to 40 percent of budget! Consider just the costs associated with poor labor-management relations. As the veteran federal mediator Douglas Brown put it: "At least 99 percent of the union-company difficulties I deal with either start with or are complicated by poor, inadequate, or omitted communication."

Just what happens when people talk together, when they write, when they read? Why are they sometimes so unsuccessful in exchanging their thoughts clearly, understandably, and effectively? When Green speaks, why does White fail to "get" him, even though White tries to understand? How is it possible for an executive, earnestly wanting to communicate with his or her employees, to make costly errors in terms of money and morale? How is it that a military commander can issue orders that can be misinterpreted so as to lead to incalculable disasters? This is the nature of the problems that concern us in this book.

PLAN OF THE BOOK

The book's "shape" is similar to a funnel's—beginning broadly and progressively tapering down.

---

[5] Mortimer Adler, "Challenges of Philosophies in Communication," *Journalism Quarterly*, 40, no. 3 (Summer 1963), p. 452.

The book consists of four parts. Part One, "Communication in Organizations," is the most comprehensive. The first of its three chapters, "Introduction," begins with a discussion of communication as a whole, suggesting the gap between communication *technology* and interpersonal communication *practice*. It ends with a description of the book's "plan" and a rationale for using its cases. The next two chapters concern communication within the organization. Chapter 2 focusses on *trust* and the key role it plays when people communicate—or attempt to. When trust is considered in terms of the entire organization, it is more appropriate to speak of a *climate*, the overall atmosphere that affects—and is affected by—the interpersonal relationships that exist within the organization. This is the province of Chapter 3, "Organizational Climate and Communication."

Despite the popularity of such phrases as "the company maintains . . .," "the union states . . .," and "the government reports . . .," organizations, as a whole, do not communicate. Ultimately, only *individuals* do. Therefore, the focus of Part Two, "The Behavioral Basis of Communication," is on the individual. Accordingly, the person is depicted as a complex organism whose behavior can be profoundly influenced by his or her *perceptions* (Chapters 4, 5, and 6) and *motivations* (Chapter 7). Chapter 8, "The Process of Communication," examines that special critical behavior called *communication* and also serves as a transition between what has gone before and what is to come.

What is to come is Part Three, "Patterns of Miscommunication." This is the largest part of the book, Chapters 9 through 18. Each chapter describes a pattern of miscommunication (a definitive mode of self-deception and/or inaccuracy that often leads to misunderstanding, confusion, and conflict), examines its prime causes, and recommends strategies and techniques for preventing or correcting its occurrence.

Part Four, which is also Chapter 19, is an "Overview" consisting of a concluding rationale for the book and a synopsis of each of the preceding 18 chapters.

THE CASES

The late communication authority Irving J. Lee used to say that the road to becoming a competent practitioner of communication (and of the prevention and correction of miscommunication) was marked by five milestones. First, you acquaint yourself with the subject matter—the studies, the theories, and the methods. In other words you acquire the current knowledge of the field. Second, you develop the ability to recognize and learn from proficiencies and shortcomings in the communication of others. Third, and more difficult, you come to perceive and understand them in your own behavior. Fourth, you strengthen your own communication skills. Fifth, and by far the most formidable accomplishment you learn to prescribe for the communicative problems of others.

Lee listed these steps in their order of difficulty rather than suggesting that they be strictly adhered to chronologically. He never insisted, for example, that Step One had to be mastered before Step Two was practiced, and so fourth. Nor did he discourage developing skills on two or more levels simultaneously. However, some accomplishment at Step One should facilitate development at Step Two; learning at Step Two should aid in accomplishing Step Three; and so on.

Explorations into Steps Three and Four may be within grasp for some at this point. It is recommended, however, that Step Five be approached with considerable caution and constraint. In all candor, Step Five may be something of a will-o'-the-wisp. Communication habits are often so deeply rooted that change may take place only at the volition of the individual. For one to attempt to change another may arouse the other's defenses and lead to resistance. (Defense against change is discussed more fully in Chapter 4.) Change, if any, would probably be superficial and temporary at best.

Given the requisite of volition, perhaps the best that one can do is to try to provide a nonthreatening environment in which the other person can perform Step Four (see Carl Rogers and Richard E. Farson, *Active Listening,* at the end of Chapter 6 in this regard).

The textual part of this book can only contribute to your realization of Step One. The cases that follow each of the succeeding chapters,[6] however, give you the opportunity to practice at the level of Step Two and, to some extent, Steps Three and Four.

Most of the cases are reports of actual happenings in which communications somehow went awry. They are offered because there is often a decided gap between one's *intellectual acquaintance* with a subject matter and one's *internalization* of it. The cases afford the opportunity to move beyond a superficial knowledge of the patterns of miscommunication to a more profound and enduring awareness and understanding of them.

You will benefit from the cases to the extent that you bore into them. Here is a good list of questions to impose on each case:

What is going on in the case? What has happened?

Why did it occur? What are the *underlying assumptions* of the communicators involved?

What could have been done to prevent the communication failure or at least to diminish its consequences?

What can be done now? By whom? When? Where? How?

What procedures, techniques, measures would you suggest to prevent a *recurrence* of this type of miscommunication?

---

[6] Except Chapter 8, the transition chapter.

The cases were allocated to the chapters because they appear to this writer and to many of his students (all of the cases have been class- and/or management seminar-tested) to exemplify in some manner the content of the chapters to which they are appended. This is not to suggest that other patterns of miscommunication (including those described elsewhere in this book or in other works) cannot or should not be perceived in the cases. On the contrary, you are encouraged to probe, to examine, to analyze, and to dissect as far as your insights and skills will permit.

In sum, the purpose of this book is not unlike that of medical training. Although there is no pretense of turning out Doctors of Communication, there is the earnest hope that, after acquiring some background from a given chapter, you will proceed to develop a heightened sensitivity to the communicative processes of others and also your own. I genuinely hope that you will begin to acquire or reinforce awarenesses and techniques for avoiding and coping with these patterns of miscommunication in real life.

Discussion Questions

1. "... it is not just change, but the *acceleration* of change, which has so sorely tested our ability—and our willingness—to communicate with one another." How do you react to that statement? What do you anticipate for the future? Will the situation improve, worsen? Why? How?

2. Some people feel that Adler's assessment is unnecessarily gloomy. What do you think?

3. In view of Chapter 1, "Introduction," and the Preface, what is this book about? What is it *not* about? What value might the book have for you?

4. What do you think of Lee's five-step procedure toward becoming a more competent practitioner of communication? Why might Step Five be considered a will-o'-the-wisp?

5. "... there is often a decided gap between one's *intellectual acquaintance* with a subject matter and one's *internalization* of it." Do you agree? Why or why not?

6. What is the best way to get maximum value from the use of the cases in this book?

7. "The souls of emperors and cobblers are cast in the same mold. ... The same reason that makes us wrangle with a neighbor causes a war twixt princes."
—*Michel de Montaigne*

"We are in such great haste to construct an electric telegraph between Maine and Texas. But it may be that Maine and Texas have nothing to communicate."
—*Henry David Thoreau*

What bearing might these statements have on Chapter 1?

CHAPTER TWO

Trust and Communication

❋
❋
❋

One of the main themes of Chapter 1 was that despite incredible technological communication advances, our *interpersonal* communication practices often leave a great deal to be desired. A significant factor in this anomaly lies in the fascinating concept of *trust*.

My dictionary defines trust as "a firm belief or confidence in the honesty, integrity, reliability, justice, . . . of another person. . . ." Kreitner and Kinicki write of the *mutuality* of trust, seeing it as the "reciprocal faith in others' intentions and behavior."[1] They conclude by asserting that "we tend to give what we get: trust begets trust; distrust begets distrust."[2]

That seems straightforward enough, but let us consider trust in the context of an *organization*. Imagine the smallest organization possible— just two people. Say, you and I.

Now, imagine that we want a large pane of glass moved from Point A to Point B. It is too unwieldy for either of us to carry individually. But if you take one end and I take the other, we could manage it easily. So it is agreed that's what we'll do.

On the way to Point B, I, for some reason, drop my end and the glass smashes. Let's quickly make the happy twin assumptions that neither of us was injured and that neither of us will have to pay for the glass.

---

[1] Robert Kreitner and Angelo Kinicki, *Organizational Behavior* (Homewood, Ill.: Irwin BPI, 1989), p. 350.

[2] Ibid., p. 351. See also J. David Lewis and Andrew Weigert, "Trust as a Social Reality," *Social Forces,* June 9, 1985, p. 971:

When we see others acting in ways that imply that they trust us, we become more disposed to reciprocate by trusting in them more. Conversely, we come to distrust those whose actions *appear* to violate or *to distrust us.*

The italics are mine. This "contagion" of trust (and distrust) is particularly relevant to the trust and performance cycles discussed in Chapter 3.

Nevertheless, you surely will have some feelings about the event, and probably strong ones: anger, dismay, fear, disappointment, shock, and so forth. You might try to ascertain *why* I failed to hold up (literally) my end of the bargain. You might decide to punish, counsel, or even forgive me. But in any event you'll probably find it difficult to trust me again to help you carry a pane of glass. In fact, your distrust might extend even into other areas of our relationship.

Now, why were you so upset? After all, you were not harmed physically or financially. But my unexpected behavior did cost you something— namely, your ability to predict my future behavior, to trust me.

If a two-person relationship is to thrive, or even to survive, each party must be able to predict and rely on the other. This is a crucial requirement of any organization whether it consists of two persons—or 200,000.

ORGANIZATION

Let us examine some of the key characteristics of an organization, with special emphasis upon trust and communication.

Interdependence

An organization is an *interdependent* phenomenon. If you had 1,000 employees and *each* person designed a product, purchased materials, manufactured, sold, shipped, and serviced that product, then you would not have *an organization*; you would have 1,000 enterprises.

But if those 1,000 people were interdependent (i.e., if each one did things that affected and were affected by what other people, within that 1,000, did), then you would indeed have the makings of an organization.

Collaboration

If an organization is to succeed in a competitive environment, its members will have to do more than just *interdepend*—they will have to *collaborate* and to work together as a team.

Within many firms technological skills are critical, and grow more so everyday. But these skills alone will not guarantee the organization's success. After all, a collection of superstars does not automatically constitute a superteam. The stars must collaborate to assure that.

To express that in a formula, I offer: $OS = f(TS + CS)$. That's short for: Organizational success in terms of human skills is a function of technological skills *and* collaborative skills.

Above all, the members of an organization must not "undo" each other. They must avoid a very destructive form of competition.

Competition

It is dictionary time again. *Competition* is defined as a "rivalry, match, or contest." Win-lose contests (sometimes called *zero-sum games*) can be healthy and constructive. However, the parameters must be drawn carefully.

For example, fair competition between firms within an industry supposedly keeps everyone sharp and productive and provides the consumer a good product at a reasonable price. As a sports fan I support competition between individuals, or between teams within a league.

In another vein, I enthusiastically endorse intra-individual competition which leads to the individual pursuit of excellence. On the job, for example, I believe a person should be able to reach his or her best potential (through performance and merit) irrespective of discrimination by sex, age, race, nationality, and creed.

However, when that win-lose competition occurs *within* an organization, including that special organization called a *family*, the consequences are usually mutually destructive. If *within* an organization an individual or group succeeds at the expense of one or more members of that organization then the sure loser is the organization.

Admittedly, some organization members are better infighters, backstabbers, bad-mouthers, rumor mongers, or atmosphere poisoners than others. Such members, at least in the short run, may "win." However, an organization which tolerates, or even rewards, such behavior generally ends by paying a horrendous cost—the long-term deterioration of its human asset.

Nevertheless, we face a formidable challenge here because win-lose is almost bred into us. Consider the sports and games kids engage in. The only time one wins a boxing, wrestling, or tennis (assuming singles) match is when the opponent loses.

If one's tastes are more sedentary, that person only wins at chess, checkers, or Othello when, again, the other player loses.

That often goes for grades as well. Grading "on the curve" involves a sort of win-lose contest. One can achieve an excellent grade only if there are sufficient mediocre and even failing grades.

Sometimes the "win-win" mentality is taught and reinforced. It is found, for example, in team sports such as football, basketball, and hockey, where individuals are asked to sacrifice in the interests of the team.

But on the whole, the notion of "win-lose" seems more effectively programmed into most people than "win-win."

Trust

How, then, can an organization create a collaborative, "win-win" atmosphere and avoid the destructive, competitive "win-lose" (which usually eventuates in a "lose-lose") climate?

The basic answer is *trust.*

Members of an organization must genuinely believe that the best way to help themselves *and their organization* is by being trusting of others, and by being trustworthy themselves. I must believe that others will not abuse my trust for their short-range gain. Conversely, I must be trustworthy, recognizing that to take advantage of another's trust usually leads to defensiveness, retaliation, and the escalating conflict called *the Vicious Pendulum* (see Chapter 13).

Communication

The next question—How do you build trust in an organization? The same way one builds it anywhere else, by *communication*. Here is a commonplace example:

If you drive, this may already have happened to you (see Figure 2.1). Let's say that A has just gassed up and wants to join the string of autos heading north. Currently stopped at a traffic light, the cars are bumper to bumper and stretch as far back as A can see. Suppose that A considers two methods for entering the queue:

Noncommunication mode: As soon as B clears the inlet, A will dart in ahead of C. A *might* make it without a fender bender. But in any event he will probably have infuriated C, and who knows what C will do now!

Communication mode: A will turn on his right directional signal. But that might not be enough. C may be unable to or *unwilling* to notice the flashing light. But if A could establish eye contact and gesture with a pointing forefinger, C will be more likely to understand and accede to A's desire.

Will that eye contact and finger-pointing routine work? Will C permit A to squeeze in? I can offer no airtight guarantee, but it has never failed me.

The point of the illustration is to underscore the importance of communication, including nonverbal communication, in establishing trust. But it also suggests how noncommunication or poor communication can lead to *dis*trust and animosity.

Parenthetically, consider the relationship of non- or faulty communication at the international level. Is it not tragic that so often just before wars begin, the ambassadors are called back or sent home? The very moment when communication is most imperative, the communicators cease to function. Small wonder, then, that in such an atmosphere, bullets, bombs, and missiles replace the exchange of words.

Back to the main issue. Good communication is essential in building trust within an organization. But it is also crucial in the *maintenance*

FIGURE 2.1

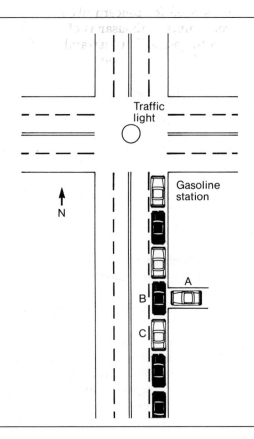

of that trust. Trust, after all, is a precious but fragile commodity. It can often be very challenging to create; but it can be easily weakened and even destroyed. Once that happens, trust can be extremely difficult to restore. Recall the episode we had regarding the pane of glass.

Another point about communication: If an organization is to accomplish its objectives, its members must pull together. But their *willingness* to collaborate is not enough. They must know in *which direction* to pull. An organization's objectives must be universally understood and accepted by its members. So here again communication excellence is vital.

Many authorities have underscored the importance of communication and trust in an organization's successful pursuit of its goals.[3]

_____

[3] See, for example, W. Ouchi, *Theory Z: How American Business Can Meet the Japanese Challenge* (Reading, Mass.: Addison-Wesley Publishing, 1981); and T. J. Peters and R. H. Waterman, Jr., *In Search of Excellence* (New York: Warner Books, 1988).

Finally, is there a need for concern about trust in organizations? Judging from the complaints of thousands of organizational members I have encountered over the years, there certainly is. This excerpt from *The Wall Street Journal* emphasizes that point:

> Most workers don't trust their bosses, a study finds.
>
> Fully 78 percent of American workers are suspicious of management, developing an "us-against them" syndrome that interferes with their performance, contend Boston University's Donald Kanter and Philip Mirvis. These workers, the psychologists say, "spurn innovation and create unrest. Their first loyalty is to themselves, not the firm."[4]

SUMMARY

An *interdependent* organization succeeds in attaining its objectives in direct relation to its technical *and* collaborative skills. *Collaboration* is impeded by zero-sum (win-lose) *competition* between members *within* the organization. Organizations which fail to penalize this type of *intra*-organizational competition and, in some cases, reward the "winners," usually suffer long-term deterioration of their human assets.

Thus, win-win relationships must be encouraged and rewarded. Such relationships are most likely to occur in an atmosphere of mutual *trust*, wherein open, receptive, nondeceptive, and nondefensive *communication* prevails.

In the next chapter we will examine that organizational climate in more detail.

Discussion Questions

1. Regarding the dropping of my end of the glass pane, if you weren't injured or out of pocket, why were you upset?

2. True or false: The author is clearly anticompetition. Discuss.

3. $OS = f(TS + CS)$. What does the equation stand for? Do you agree or disagree?

4. In our society win-lose is more effectively taught than win-win. Discuss.

5. What does communication have to do with trust?

6. Trust is fragile. Discuss.

---

[4] Excerpted from "Labor Letter: Special News Report on People and Their Jobs in Offices, Fields, and Factories," *The Wall Street Journal*, February 10, 1987, p. 1.

C A S E S

CASE 2.1

A Crude Misunderstanding*

Les Lammers

Red Thurston, 45, is the nearest thing to a first sergeant I've seen outside the Marines. He runs our oil refinery with an iron fist. We all hate his guts, but top management likes him because, frankly, he gets results.

That is, he did until the day he pushed a little too hard. That was when he walked into our crude unit and found it acutely out of kilter. According to the operating board readings, the temperatures were all wrong and the system was surging. Henry Koehler, 64, was frantically trying to correct the imbalance.

Red blew his stack and screamed at Henry: "If you can't run this God-damned system any better than this, shut it down!"

Henry stopped dead in his tracks for a few seconds. Then he looked Red squarely in the eyes and calmly said; "What did you say?"

"What the hell's the matter with you—are you deaf, too? I said you might as well shut the God-damned thing down if you can't control it any better than this!"

"Well, OK, if that's what you want." Henry walked over to the board and proceeded to shut down the system.

Red couldn't believe his eyes. "What the hell are you doing?!"

"Shutting down the line just like you told me."

Since the crude unit was the first in line, the restart took 40 hours and cost about a half-million dollars. Henry's union got him off scot-free claiming he had just followed orders. He's now enjoying his retirement. Red, on the other hand, was severely reprimanded. Needless to say, he is no longer top management's fair-haired boy.

Discussion Questions

1. How do you size up this case?
2. How might Red Thurston have perceived the situation?
3. How do you account for Koehler's action?
4. What part does *trust* play in this case?

---

* All names, including the author's, have been disguised.

CASE 2.2

Janet Is Looking*

Sandra Cummings

I'm an associate professor of interpersonal communication in the School of Business Administration of our university. Our students, typically, have never had full-time jobs. Granted, many have worked in the summer and know what it's like to work from 8 to 5 for 8 or 10 weeks or so. But they've never had positions which go on month after month after month.

Understandably, they're curious about what will be in store for them once they leave the university. So I thought it might be interesting to follow up on "Janet." She's the daughter of some friends, and I regard her as a bright and articulate young woman.

I explained my motive for the "interview" and she agreed to cooperate.

Sandra: Pretend we don't know each other. What's your background?
Janet: I'll be 26 next month. I was graduated from a large midwestern university about four years ago.
Sandra: Your major?
Janet: Mechanical engineering.
Sandra: Isn't that a little unusual for a woman?
Janet: Not anymore. Dad said that when he was an undergrad in the late forties there wasn't a single woman in the entire tech school of his university.
Sandra: Was he supportive of your choice?
Janet: Both of my parents were—they were always proud of my academic accomplishments.
Sandra: You were a good student?
Janet: It sounds conceited to say so but I believe I was. Virtually straight A's and I made a number of honorary fraternities such as Tau Beta Pi, Phi Kappa Phi, Golden Key, Pi Tau Sigma. . . .
Sandra: Did you join a social sorority?
Janet: Yes.
Sandra: So what happened after graduation?
Janet: I got a nice break from a high-tech firm. The plan was that I'd work a couple of months immediately after graduation. Then I'd go back to school, get a master's in mechanical engineering, and the firm would foot the bill.
Sandra: That sounds like a nice break for you.
Janet: Yes, but now I'm thinking of leaving. I've been here ever since the master's—about 2½ years ago.

---

* All names are disguised.

Sandra: Has your current supervisor been your boss during all that time?

Janet: I was married last October and unknown to me I got this new boss while I was on my honeymoon. So George Barrow has been my boss only since last November—about nine months ago.

Sandra: And he supervises whom?

Janet: Well, physical designers, device qualification people, software writers—six people all told.

Sandra: What is your title and work?

Janet: I'm a design engineer and I design computer cabinets.

Sandra: And this was a new group for everyone? Barrow was new to the group and the employees were all new to each other?

Janet: Right.

Sandra: What was your experience with Barrow?

Janet: My activity remained the same but now I had a boss whose style of supervision was very different.

Sandra: How?

Janet: My old boss was very relaxed, nondemanding—very loose supervision. Perhaps too much so. But in any event he would just give me a job and let me get it done.

Sandra: And the new boss?

Janet: Just the opposite. From the very beginning he was quite uptight. He would ask very detailed questions about my work. He obviously didn't trust me—didn't have confidence in me.

Sandra: So what did you do about that?

Janet: About two weeks after I came back to work I confronted him with it. I said: "I want our relationship to evolve to the point where you don't have to ask me so many questions—where you will have the confidence that I'll get the job done on time."

Sandra: And his reaction?

Janet: Very positive. He agreed with my comments and seemed very excited that we could attain such a relationship.

Sandra: And then?

Janet: Well, for a while it went well, then slowly the situation deteriorated again.

Sandra: Again he displayed his lack of trust in you?

Janet: Either that or he didn't realize how bogged down in technical minutiae he was getting. I thought he should be spending more of his time in management activities such as making sure our checks were arriving on time, that we were happy on the job, and so forth.

Sandra: Did you talk to him again about this?

Janet: I don't remember ... but I do recall another incident. A new assignment came along and George gave it to me. He told me I'd need some help, so he broke the job down into seven specific activities and selected Keith Robins to be my assistant.

Sandra: And Robins reported to you?

Janet: No, to George.

Sandra: What's Keith's background?

Janet: He has a bachelor's in mechanical engineering from my school and a master's in mechanical engineering from a West Coast university and I think he's working on an M.B.A. right now. Anyway, Keith was to be my assistant, but he didn't have any experience *at all* in design. Well, George, Keith, and I had a meeting and George laid out the seven parts of the assignment and asked Keith and me to each send him a memo of the parts each of us preferred and what parts we didn't like.

Sandra: And . . .?

Janet: Well, I tried to be a positive employee so I sent in a list of my preferences but made no comment about the parts I didn't want. Keith, on the other hand, indicated his preferences and that he didn't care for the others, but that he'd do them if necessary, but that I'd probably be a better match for them. The upshot was that Keith got all of his preferences and none of his unpreferreds. I got one of my preferences and all of the parts I didn't like.

Sandra: Your reaction?

Janet: Very angry. I met George privately and told him how unhappy I was with the situation. I said the subassignments given to me totally mismatched my career-growth pattern. For example, I was not given the design work—in fact, I was listed as the secondary designer on the project even though I had a lot more design experience than Keith.

Sandra: George's response?

Janet: Well, he did make me co-designer on the main design work and he massaged the other subassignments so I was a bit happier with them. Later, though, I made it clear how unhappy I was, and he responded: "But everything is fine *now*, isn't it?" And I said: "Yeah, and if I were a robot that would be one thing—but the bottom line is that I was hurt by what had happened." He gave some lame excuse about how Keith had given him some negatives and that I hadn't and he figured my blanks could be interpreted as positives—a real bogus alibi. At any rate, I thought I had heightened his awareness about our relationship, about who I was and that I was to be taken seriously. Well, things improved for a while but then they really deteriorated.

Sandra: How was that?

Janet: Here's an example. I wrote a letter to a customer. It was supposed to be signed by me and my supervisor; namely, George. Well, he wouldn't sign it because it contained a proprietary notice.

Sandra: What's a "proprietary notice"?

Janet: Information that should be kept within the company and not shared with outsiders. Well, I made it clear in the letter that that info was to go no farther than the letter's recipient.

Well, anyway, I offered to remove the notice from the copy the customer received but that it should remain on the copy we retained for our files.

Well, he still wouldn't sign it and, in fact, wanted to line out his name on the letter.

Actually, the copy would probably go into the garbage anyway. It's really unimportant.

Sandra: Then why make an issue of it?

Janet: I interpreted all that to mean that he didn't trust me to do what I had promised to do. I felt insulted. I think he handled the matter very childishly.

To make a long story short . . . he became more and more critical of me. He became competitive with me on technical matters. Sometimes I'd show him that he was wrong (*laughing*) and that wasn't very appealing to him. And he wouldn't support me in front of upper management. If he suspected his own superiors had reached some conclusion he would immediately agree with them.

Sandra: Things weren't going well . . . .

Janet: You got that right. He and I had a merit appraisal meeting recently. He asked me what motivated and demotivated me. For motivators I said: "Teamwork, working with sharp people, management that gives me a lot of freedom." For demotivation I mentioned the three points above and gave him concrete examples of each.

Sandra: How did he react?

Janet: He was very receptive and surprised that I was so frank with him and asked me to continue to be open with him in the future. Then he said a very interesting thing. He said that before he became a supervisor he had been proud of his ability to conceal his feelings. His boss could never decipher how he was feeling. But now that he was a supervisor he realizes that's the opposite of how he ought to be. He said: "I need to communicate my emotions and I'm shocked that I have not communicated to you how much I value you. At the same time I've spent my entire life trying to be very objective, very impartial. But I know I should support you more."

Sandra: That sounds promising.

Janet: Yes, but he admits he won't support me in front of his superiors until he knows I'm right. Thus he has to ask me a lot of questions to be sure that I'm right.

In contrast, my first boss would support me to the ends of the earth whether I was right or wrong to make himself and me look good. Now, that's not all good—but it's not all bad, either. I believe that giving people support when they need it is more important than being absolutely sure they're right.

Sandra: So where does it stand now?

Janet: Well, I think George is beginning to realize that he has to be more supportive of his people. He has to go to bat for them, defend them, give constructive criticism and positive feedback, and ease up on the I-need-to-know-every-single-detail-of-what-you're-doing attitude. The last few weeks he's signed a lot more of my documentations without asking a lot of questions. That's a big milestone because I've been doing these documents for 2½ years and I'm very good at it and I don't make mistakes.

Sandra: It sounds as if things are improving—why are you looking?

Janet: Well, it looks like there might be a good chance with the HQ operation of a fast-food outfit—really a quality firm. One of my best friends works for them and she gives me glowing reports of how well people are managed over there.

Sandra: I should have asked this before but can you give something of Barrow's background?

Janet: He's about 30 and comes originally from Mississippi. He has a bachelor's, double major, in math and mechanical engineering. And he has a master's in mechanical engineering.

Sandra: His degrees came from where?

Janet: The bachelor's is from an all-black university in the Southeast and his master's is from the West Coast.

Sandra: He's black, then?

Janet: Yes. He's been with the company about eight years full-time.

Sandra: Had his master's been subsidized as was yours?

Janet: I think so.

Sandra: His being black—do you think that played a part in any of this?

Janet: Not as far as I am concerned. I'm white, obviously, but I can honestly say that I have no racial prejudices. But I'm sure George feels it. He probably feels he has to work harder to realize his ambitions. That's typical of minorities. For example, women feel they have to work twice as hard to be considered equal to men.

He's fanatical about always being right and never being caught at being wrong or messing up. They call him "Mr. Clean." He makes sure nothing is ever pinned on him.

He works from 7 A.M. till 6 P.M. He works on weekends. He works very hard to achieve his goals. Someone told me that he's scared because our division is not doing well and he could lose his job.

Sandra: Was he previously a supervisor before taking on the unit you're in?

Janet: Yes, for about 1½ years. I don't think he clicked very well with that group. There were about 20 of them—nontechnical people.

For them it was a job—not a career. Apparently, it wasn't very important to them that they received his approval. I think he encountered a fair amount of rebelliousness. All in all I think it was very stressful for him.

Sandra: There are a few more questions I'd like to ask.

Janet: Shoot.

Sandra: One—is there a position elsewhere in your current organization that you would consider?

Janet: Well, yes. I consider myself a broad-based person and I believe I could find a niche elsewhere here. Mechanical engineering is a very small part of this operation and there's a lot more to computer science here than just the M.E. part of it. Therefore, I could take more classes and prepare myself for a job elsewhere in the company.

Sandra: Does that mean that you might stay on here?

Janet: Not really. I don't feel too good about this company. I don't think this is the greatest outfit around. They don't make the wisest decisions. They make a lot of mistakes. Mostly, they don't always treat their people the way they should.

Sandra: Can you give an example of that?

Janet: Sure. A week before Christmas last year they laid off a third of their people: 50 out of 150. What a time of year! That was bad enough but the way they went about it . . . !

Sandra: How was that?

Janet: Well, first, the announcement came out that some people were going to be laid off—no names, no numbers . . . just that people were going to be laid off. Then the number came out . . . then the number grew. Talk about tension! The first thing people would do every morning was to ask their supervisors if they (the people) would be let go. Finally, those who were to leave were notified. And then the big bosses decided to have a meeting and everyone, including those who were leaving, was to attend.

At the meeting the names of those people were projected on a screen by an overhead projector. So, in effect, there's the list for everyone to see as if the message was: "Here are the people that are not up to snuff or who don't have the right skills for the company." A public humiliation. That's just one example.

Sandra: I guess you have already answered this question in a way— but how do you feel about leaving the company in view of the fact that they sponsored your master's degree?

Janet: That's no problem for me. From the very beginning they made it clear that there were no strings attached. They never asked me to sign a contract—or even promise to spend a year with them. The only constraint was that they requested that we not interview with other companies while we were in the master's program.

But some of my colleagues broke even this promise, they traveled to interviews with other companies while they were working on their degrees.

Sandra: How did you feel about that?

Janet: Shocked. My original plan was to work for the company at least one year. They gave me one year. So I figured I'd give them one year. Well, I've been here for 2½ years so I feel that I more than kept my part of the bargain.

Sandra: So . . . where do you stand now?

Janet: The question that I have to resolve is this—I can see the imperfections in this company but is this typical? Are these defects unique with this firm—or are they par for the course in large outfits. I just don't know. If it's the former then I don't want to settle down here if there are better situations elsewhere.

Discussion Questions

1. What are Janet's perceptions of the situation?

2. We have only Janet's account, but what might George Barrow's perceptions be of Janet? Of his job?

3. What should Janet do now?

4. What should Barrow do now?

5. What do you think of Janet's view of the company's sponsorship of her master's program?

CASE 2.3

The Monfield Public Library*

Jane Everson, 33, has a B.A. and an M.L.S. from a large western university. At the time she joined Monfield she had 11 years of library experience. She was hired to be a cataloger and an audiovisual librarian. Her cataloging skills were deemed well above average. Moreover, she was very knowledgeable about music, having had a good deal of experience as a vocal and instrumental performer.

Part of her responsibilities in audiovisuals involved the library's burgeoning videocassette collection. Her duties in that respect included the ordering and processing of the new tapes. In the five months that Jane had been with Monfield the number of videos tripled. In fact, the videotape activity became so demanding that she had been unable to keep up with her cataloging.

Betty Connelly, 45, director of the library, became increasingly concerned with the cataloging backlog and called Jane into her office. The

---

* All names in this case have been disguised.

conference lasted about 10 minutes. Jane assured Betty that she would, indeed, meet her cataloging responsibilities and that within a month she would be entirely caught up.

The month came and went but Betty saw no appreciable improvement in the cataloging status. She was disappointed. She decided that the job was just too large for one person and, accordingly, assigned the video collection to Nancy Hollander, 24, who had recently joined the library. Betty reasoned that Nancy, who was well-versed in films, would do well in that area and ease Jane's burden.

A formal announcement of the change was posted but Jane received no further information from Betty Connelly.

Jane was deeply distressed and requested a meeting with Betty. Jane stated that she felt she could indeed fulfill all the requirements of her original assignment. Betty requested that Jane submit a written summary of her feelings and aspirations and that in the meantime Jane was to provide training for Nancy in managing the video collection. The summary was to be due in two weeks.

It is now three weeks later and Betty has received no written report from Jane. The latter is visibly upset and uncommunicative and has provided virtually no training for Nancy.

Discussion Questions

1. What has happened in this case?

2. What are Jane's perceptions?

3. What are Betty's perceptions and how do you evaluate her managerial performance?

4. What does this case have to do with *trust* and *communication*?

CASE 2.4

Merger Mania*

My name is Kevin Parisi and I'm an assistant professor of business administration at the School of Business in a large midwestern university. I live in Evanston, Illinois, a suburb immediately north of Chicago.

I received the Ph.D. four years ago and I've been teaching since then— summers, too. An assistant professor's salary isn't so great that you can afford to take summers off, especially if you and your wife have two small children.

However, last summer was an exception. I received a fellowship from a charitable institution to study a particular company for eight weeks. The fellowship was to pay me a stipend and cover my expenses so I considered it a good deal. Our dean was very supportive, too. He didn't come

---

* All names are disguised.

right out and say it but I sensed what he was feeling: "If you're going to teach business administration you'd better go out and learn about it in the flesh!"

The "Stillwell Company" manufactures steel cabinets, tables, shelves, and so forth. They'd been bought out by the XYZ Corporation back in March. By May, that's when the fellowship came through, no changes had occurred in Stillwell; at least none that I was aware of.

To be honest, I was more concerned about how I was going to get out to the factory. Stillwell is located in the Clearing District, south of Midway Airport. If you know Chicago you know that would be difficult to reach by public transportation, especially from Evanston. Then I got a lucky break.

Two weeks before I was to start the fellowship I received a phone call from Ned Espinosa, Stillwell's personnel manager. He explained that he'd be setting up my interviews with executives and managers and that he thought it would be best to start me off with first-line supervisors and gradually work up. The plan was that I would finally meet with the president in the last week.

I wasn't so sure about his bottom-up method, but I figured he knew what he was doing so I agreed.

Then came the big break. He mentioned that he lived in Evanston, too, and he'd be happy to pick me up and drive me to and from Stillwell. Well, that was great! We have a car (a 1976 Buick station wagon, a real beater), but my wife needs it to get around during the day.

Ned turned out to be a fine guy and I truly enjoyed those trips we took. He started me off with his own department. In the first few days I had long conversations with the personnel people: Marty, who was in charge of employee insurance; Evelyn, who handled the various labor contracts and did the negotiating with the unions; Sharon, who was in charge of training; Wendell, who was in charge of hiring and placement; and several others.

Marty, Evelyn, Sharon, Wendell, and I hit it off quite well. We were all about the same age (in the late twenties), so that might have been a factor. In the first weeks I had almost every lunch with one or more or all of them. Oftentimes, Ned would join us. He was probably 40 or so but he fitted right in with the group.

I was really impressed with how open everyone was, even when Ned was present. The morale of that gang was excellent and they would good-naturedly needle each other.

Ned was the leader of the group but Marty was definitely number two. Ned obviously thought of him that way, too. Whenever Ned was absent Marty was in charge. Everyone accepted that.

Let me tell you about the two women. Both were very nice. Sharon and Evelyn helped me a lot especially in the early weeks. However, they also were very competent. On a number of occasions Ned told me privately that they were the best at their respective positions he had ever seen.

I probably identified most closely with Marty. We had a lot in common. He was also married, with a two-year-old and another baby on the way. He'd already received the M.B.A. and was thinking about going back to school for a Ph.D. He thought he'd like teaching at the college level.

* * * * *

Well, after a few days, I began to interview people in other departments. I talked with foremen and supervisors in production, marketing, R&D, finance—you name it. Some meetings were more interesting than others, but that might have been a function of my own interests more than anything else.

One session really stands out in my memory. I was talking to the head guy in the plating department. He showed me the various vats of chemicals and explained how his department electroplated certain products. The man obviously had very little formal education and he had a thick accent. He referred to "cadium" and "aluninum." Memories of undergrad chemistry told me that he was mispronouncing those words and I was about to correct him. But thankfully I kept my big mouth shut and thought: "This man knows more about plating than I ever will. And who cares about how he pronounces the names as long as the job gets done?"

Speaking of pronunciation, I noticed something peculiar as I worked through management. A number of people interviewed pronounced the word *issue* as "iss-yew." I think the English say it that way but as far as I knew Americans always say "ish-yew." And these people weren't English!

Well, anyway, I was now in the fourth week of the fellowship and I began to sense that something was wrong. I was now interviewing managers at about the third level up from the bottom. Some of them seemed suspicious. One man in particular kept asking me who I was and why I was talking to him. I kept explaining about the fellowship but I could tell he wasn't convinced. I didn't learn much from that meeting.

In the fifth week I had a meeting scheduled with Steve Waltz, the manager of industrial engineering. I had looked forward to this because the industrial engineers are usually the people who do those ingenious things to make the manufacturing more efficient, less costly.

I still recall the conversation I had with his secretary:

Me: I'm here to see Mr. Waltz. I think he's expecting me.
Secretary: He's not here.
Me: That's OK. I'm a little early. I'll just wait here if I may.
Secretary: You don't understand . . . Mr. Waltz is no longer with us. (She seemed to choke and tear up a bit.)
Me: You mean he's no longer working here?
Secretary: That's right.
Me: Oh . . . has there been a . . . uh . . . replacement?
Secretary: That's not been announced. (And with that she got up and walked into Waltz's office and closed the door.)

That was the first of a series of no-longer-with-us experiences I was to have. In the next week I counted seven interviews that had to be canceled because he or she "was no longer with us."

I had to see Ned and find out what was going on. By the way, I should have explained something. For the last week or so, I had rarely seen Ned. He had to get to work early and leave late and he seemed to be spending most of his time at some meeting or other.

That meant that I had to drive myself and that was nerve-wracking. I kept fearing the old clunker would break down at any moment. Also my wife had to mooch off of friends and neighbors for transportation.

Well, I finally got hold of Ned and he laid it on the line:

Ned: You remember when Bill Beatty was replaced a month ago?

Me: Sure. (I should have mentioned this also. I think it was right after I started the fellowship that Mr. Beatty, he was Stillwell's president, resigned. He was replaced by a Mr. Grenzebach who had been with XYZ. Mr. G was called "general manager" but according to Ned he assumed all of the duties and authority that Mr. Beatty had had.)

Ned: Well, that "retirement" wasn't entirely Bill's idea. (Now the pieces were beginning to fit together. Mr. Beatty was only about 50 and I thought that was kind of young to retire. Ned had mentioned that XYZ had bought out Beatty's employment contract and gave him a "Golden Parachute"—namely a generous pension. So I just assumed that the retirement idea was so attractive that he couldn't pass it up.) It really wasn't Bill's doing. He could see what was happening and thought he'd better get out the easy way.

Me: You mean he was fired, actually?

Ned: Well, just about. XYZ was in charge and they wanted their own guy running the show.

Me: And that's why they brought in Grenzebach?

Ned: Exactly. Incidentally, do you know that he commutes on weekends to his home in Connecticut?

Me: No. What do you make of that?

Ned: What *can* you make of it? Either the man is here as a temporary hatchet man or he figures his days are numbered as well. In either event he doesn't want to commit his family to moving out here.

Me: What do you mean "hatchet man"?

Ned: You heard that Waltz left?

Me: Yes.

Ned: And those other people?

Me: Yes.

Ned: Well, they didn't "leave"—they were canned!

Me: Fired?

Ned: Most of them were. Grenzebach is cleaning house. Since he's been here a good half of top management has gone (most of them were let go)—a few saw the handwriting on the wall and resigned. These new people, their replacements, all come from outfits that are part of XYZ.

Two days later Ned was gone!

After the initial shock I began to wonder who would replace him. I thought it might be Marty. He had the most seniority and the others looked up to him. But that wasn't to be. Mr. Grenzebach brought in another XYZ man, Peter Schroeder.

I really don't know what I can tell you about Mr. Schroeder. I almost never saw him. He spent a great deal of time meeting with Mr. Grenzebach and the other XYZ people Grenzebach had brought in.

I did learn two things, though: One, Schroeder had formerly reported to Grenzebach in their previous jobs. Two, Schroeder, like Mr. G, commuted on weekends to Connecticut. I gather they lived pretty close to each other.

Another change occurred when Ned left. I began to see less and less of the personnel people. They'd still come to work but there were no more group lunches. Some of them brought lunches in brown paper bags and ate alone in their respective offices. I almost felt that they were avoiding me. Even Marty seemed to have little time for me. That hurt but I guess they were all kind of uneasy by then.

My interviewing schedule was shot and frankly I spent the last two weeks goofing off. No meetings were arranged for me and everyone seemed too busy to see me. I think the fellowship just fell through the cracks as far as Stillwell was concerned.

I did get to see Mr. Grenzebach in the last week—for about five minutes. What was he like? Well, very, very busy. I did learn one thing, though. I learned where "iss-yew" came from!

* * * * *

A comment about the title of my case: TV and the papers often carry big stories about the corporate raiders and their attempts to take over other corporations. Sometimes the raiders succeed, and that's usually where the news story ends. As I think back, my case is about the *aftermath* of a takeover. The takeover itself may make *economic* sense (although in this case it's too early to tell), but I wonder if anyone ever calculates the *human* cost, the erosion of an organization's human asset.

Discussion Questions

1. What seems to be going on in this case?

2. Any reaction to how Parisi dealt with the plating department foreman?

3. If the personnel department people were avoiding Parisi as he concluded, why would they do so?

4. Your reaction to Parisi's comment regarding the aftermath of a merger?

5. Why is this case appended to a chapter on *Trust*?

CHAPTER THREE

Organizational Climate and Communication

❀
❀
❀

The previous chapter extolled the virtues of trust within an organization. It may seem that an organization characterized by mutual trust and trust worthiness would be a nice place in which to work.

It probably would, but there is much more at stake than the creation of a pleasant organizational atmosphere. It relates directly to the issues of productivity and even organizational survival. Consider these trends in organizations.

TRENDS

1. They are becoming more complex. The simple line organization of authority and responsibility is often inadequate to cope with the growing complexities of many of today's organizations, in which an individual reports to one superior for one function, to another for another activity, and so on. Complicated? Yes, but necessary. For when the organization's objectives become more demanding, a more complex grouping of its skills and resources may be imperative.

2. A closely related trend is the increasing demand, due to international as well as domestic competition, for even greater efficiency and quality in the production of goods and the provision of services.

And that competition is accelerating—especially from extranationals. Consider a few of the markets in which the Japanese, for example, have become a factor (in some cases, a dominant factor): cameras, watches, television and radio equipment, VCRs, personal computers, appliances, autos, motorcycles, trucks, tractors, ships, and even pianos and violins!

3. Society is beginning to impose other requirements on its organizations. For one, there has been growing concern about mental health in our country. Some feel that the structure and climate of today's organizations are in many respects inimical to the emotional health and development of its members. They call for a serious reappraisal of and, where advisable, significant changes in our organizations.

4. Another of society's intensifying demands upon organizations concerns the environment. Tolerance for toxic waste dumping, air and water pollution, excessive radiation, petroleum spills, and so on, is rapidly diminishing.

5. Moreover, the organization's members, particularly its younger participants, are expecting more of their employers. They insist upon higher compensation, yes, but they also demand greater satisfaction on the job for their psychological needs.[1]

In sum, when we consider the nature of an organization and the growing trends of complexity, demands for efficiency, and so on, one conclusion is eminently clear: Modern-day organization requires communication performance at an unprecedented level of excellence. Prominent among the demands made upon organizations is the increasing necessity for an organizational climate compatible with the psychic needs of its members.

Perhaps an organizational climate seems like some ethereal abstract. It is not; it is very real. One may not be able to see it but one can certainly *feel* it. It is both cause and effect.

The overall atmosphere of an organization is created by the people in that organization, but it also has tremendous bearing on the behavior (especially the communication behavior) of those people. The point is that an organization's climate is not a magical product; it can be determined and altered.

In this we-can-call-our-own-shots mentality, we turn to a managerial philosophy that is designed to establish and maintain a constructive, positive, organizational climate.

SUPPORTIVE CLIMATE

"I know I'm supposed to 'know my people,' but business is just too good. Pressure for output is tremendous, the labor market is drum-tight, and turnover is high. I simply don't have time to know my people." The complaint is pervasive in many of our fast-growing sectors.

---

[1] A key provision in a recent contract negotiated by the UAW and the auto manufacturers was the workers' right to *refuse* overtime—even though they would be paid time and a half or double time. One suspects that older generations, who had suffered through the Great Depression, would regard such a clause as utterly incomprehensible.

Even supervisors who have the time insist that people are more difficult to understand, more complex, that their needs are less directly satisfiable by the boss. Moreover, employees' expectations of their employers are high and growing higher—in terms of psychic as well as material rewards.

In consequence of these changes a new, more subtle postindustrial revolution is in process, and it is leading to a serious reexamination of the role of the manager and of the organization.

I would express that emerging relationship as follows:

> The leadership and overall atmosphere of an organization must be consistent with the needs of its individual members. The organization must provide a supportive climate. The essential element is trust. Management must trust that subordinates will (or can) be capable of and indeed will contribute to the attainment of organizational objectives.
>
> And employees must trust that the organization, mostly in the form of their respective managers, will reward individuals fairly and provide for the gratification of their relevant needs as they help the organization achieve its goals.

Trust and Communication

The key, then, is *trust*. Of course, we have already discussed trust in Chapter 2. But the thesis there was that good communication is essential in building trust—or, conversely, that faulty communication can prevent the formation of trust or erode the trust that already exists.

The correlation between trust and communication cuts both ways, however. The nature and degree of trust in an organization's climate can have a decided bearing on the interpersonal communication within that organization. When the climate is basically trusting and supportive, communication practices are usually good. There are a number of reasons for this.

First, the members of such an organization tend to have no ax to grind or nothing to be gained by miscommunicating deliberately or by malicious obedience. The aura of openness makes possible candid expressions of feelings and ideas. Even faulty communication does not lead immediately to retaliation, for others are not prone to presume malice on the offenders' part, but instead carry them; that is, compensate for their errors. Moreover, a lapse in communication is viewed not as an occasion for punishment but as an opportunity to learn from mistakes. Obviously, effective communication will do much to reinforce and enhance an existing trusting climate. But if communication performance begins to falter repeatedly, the trusting relationship may be jeopardized. People begin to wonder whether the slipups are inadvertent or whether the other person has something in mind. When self-fulfilling prophecies of intrigue and suspicion emerge, the organization may be in for trouble.

When the climate is hostile and threatening, communication tends to suffer. Not only is there a tendency toward miscommunication with malice aforethought, but in such an atmosphere, true feelings are suppressed lest one be punished for revealing them. When an organization member slips, no one carries that person. On the contrary, the individual may serve as a useful scapegoat for others who seek temporary relief from criticism of themselves. By and large, one's communication (as well as one's behavior in general) is dominated by the need to protect oneself rather than the desire to serve the interests of the organization. Unfortunately, when the climate is unhealthy, even letter-perfect communication practice can be inadequate, because if people wish to misunderstand or to be misunderstood they can do so readily, as will be demonstrated in Chapter 10, "Bypassing."

Good communication, however, is usually only a *means*—not an end in itself. The *end* in most organizations is productive *performance*—behavior which contributes to the achievement of the organization's objectives. Accordingly, let us examine the relationship between *trust* and *performance*.

Trust and Performance

By and large, high trust tends to stimulate high performance—so say the overwhelming majority of more than 9,500 people-managers I have questioned in 64 organizations of varying kinds and sizes. These managers feel that subordinates generally respond well to their superiors' genuine confidence in them. They try to justify their bosses' good estimate of them. And, axiomatically, high performance will reinforce high trust, for it is easy to trust and respect a person who meets or exceeds your expectations. (See Figure 3.1.)

"But how can I develop trust under today's pressures and complexities?" Too frequently the circle is vicious rather than virtuous. Unable to "know their people," supervisors are unwilling to trust them and fail to provide for a supportive relationship. More often than not subordinates respond with minimal compliance and maximum resentment. "If that's all they think of me, I might as well give it to them. I won't get credit for doing any more." Low performance, under these circumstances, reinforces low trust, and the system is self-perpetuating. (See Figure 3.2.) A supervisor's assumptions about his or her workers can readily become a self-fulfiling prophecy.

Breaking the Cycle.   There are two general ways of breaking the destructive cycle and converting it to the constructive cycle of Figure 3.1. First, if the subordinates can respond to a low-trusting superior with high performance, if they can resist performing down to the supervisor's low

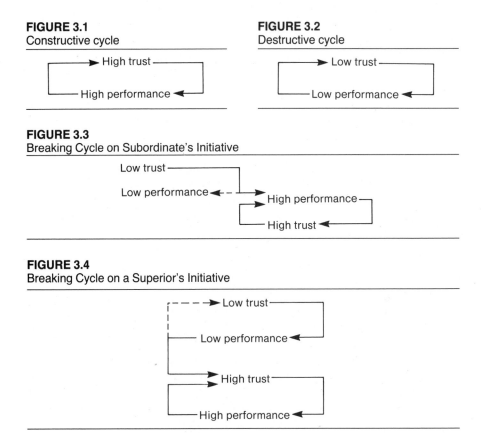

FIGURE 3.1
Constructive cycle

FIGURE 3.2
Destructive cycle

FIGURE 3.3
Breaking Cycle on Subordinate's Initiative

FIGURE 3.4
Breaking Cycle on a Superior's Initiative

regard, they stand a chance of eventually winning the boss's respect. (See Figure 3.3.)

However, the ability to withstand a low-trust atmosphere for a prolonged period requires considerable strength and maturity on the subordinate's part. Consider also that the subordinate is already psychologically disadvantaged simply by being in the subordinate role. Under these conditions, persistent high performance, though possible, does not seem very probable.

Parenthetically, if the superior's low-trusting attitude is primarily a function of external conditions, such as temporary pressure for production, rather than one's own personality, say, a tendency toward paranoia, the prognosis is more favorable.

The other approach lies in the superior's ability to respond to low performance with high (or at least *higher*) trust. (See Figure 3.4.)

This presents a paradox. How, indeed, can you trust someone who has not demonstrated trustworthiness? And can you con low producers into high performance by making believe that you regard them highly? Or, will the subordinates conclude that they are being manipulated?

It was this seeming contradiction that the supportive climate was designed to confront.

A RECONCILIATION

The trend toward this mutual trust system took shape in the 1950s. One of the first of the behavioral scientists to articulate it was the late Douglas McGregor.[2]

He contrasted two general modes of thought about how a manager should manage people. Theory X was his term for the traditional and still largely current philosophy of management. Theory Y was the emerging concept that promised to integrate the goals of the organization and its members.

Theory X

The *theory* of Theory X holds that the so-called average person is inherently (and therefore unalterably) immature, that he or she is innately lazy, irresponsible, gullible, resistant to change, self-centered, and thus indifferent to organizational needs. The managerial practice in dealing with such persons is to apply external controls (harshly or paternalistically or firmly but fairly). External control is clearly appropriate for dealing with truly immature individuals. We externally control infants, for example, and without such management, they would perish.

While conceding that people are quite capable of immature behavior, McGregor argued that such behavior and attitudes are not manifestations of their inborn nature but the product of their experiences. Treat people as if they were children, he said—and thus chronically underestimate them, distrust them, refrain from delegating authority—and they will respond as children.

Thus, in reacting to a myth (people are unchangeably immature) with external controls, managers have stimulated subordinates' behavior, and this in turn perpetuated the myth and seemingly justified their practice, for the more one controls, the more one *has* to control; and, as goes the old Chinese expression, "Whoever rides a tiger can never dismount."

The Hierarchy of Needs

What, then, is the nature of the "average person"? Very much the same as any other person's, and McGregor drew on Abraham Maslow's "hierarchy of needs"[3] to support his case.

---

[2] Douglas McGregor, *The Human Side of Enterprise* (New York: McGraw-Hill, 1960).

[3] Abraham H. Maslow, *Motivation and Personality* (New York: Harper & Row, 1954).

Maslow held that we are all constituted in such a way that we normally seek satisfaction (and thus are motivated) through a sequence of needs:

Physiological needs—the needs to have oxygen, eat, drink, rest, be protected from the elements, and so forth—the "tissue needs."

Security and safety needs—respectively, the needs to be free of the fear of physiological deprivation and of the fear of physical danger.

Social needs—the needs to belong, to be accepted, to be loved, and so forth.

Ego needs—the needs to be respected, to be somebody, to gain recognition, prestige, status, and so forth.

Self-fulfillment needs—the needs to realize one's fullest potential in whatever guise it may take. Among the modes of self-fulfillment are religion, altruism, education, power, and artistic expression.

Two propositions pertain: The upper-level needs (social, ego, self-fulfillment) ordinarily will have little or no motivating effect on individuals until their lower-level needs (physiological and safety-security) have been reasonably[4] satisfied. This suggests that there is little point in running off to developing nations to preach democracy and free enterprise (or any other abstraction) to people who are literally starving, as they can't listen *at that level.* George Bernard Shaw in *Major Barbara* noted: "I can't talk religion to a man with bodily hunger in his eyes."

Conversely, once the lower-level needs are at least reasonably fulfilled, they become inoperative on the premise that a satisfied need is no longer a motivator of behavior. The individual is thus open to motivation from the upper-level needs, or, in the words of Will Rogers, "It is easy to be a gentleman when you are well fed."

And the latter state of affairs is precisely what prevails today in the United States, asserted McGregor. For the first time in history, the masses of a nation, except depressed minority groups, pockets of depression, and so on, have had their physiological and safety-security needs at least reasonably satisfied and are now susceptible to motivation from their higher level-needs.

But American management, according to McGregor, could not thwart these upper-level needs more if it tried. He felt that managers were failing

---

[4] The word *reasonably* is used deliberately. Note the caution of Kreitner and Kinicki:

We must be careful not to misinterpret Maslow's theory by characterizing the hierarchy of needs as a fixed and rigid structure.

Robert Kreitner and Angelo Kinicki, *Organizational Behavior* (Homewood, Ill.: Irwin/ BPI, 1989), p. 152.

to understand the change that has occurred in people. Many managers still insist on attempting to motivate in the ways that were quite effective when people were preoccupied with their physiological and safety-security needs.

The Utility of Money.   Take the dollar, for example. Let it be clear, first of all, that neither McGregor nor any other behavioral scientist has claimed that money is an unimportant motivator. Consider, however, that no one has a need for dollars as such, that money is a *tool*, a most versatile tool, which can be used to satisfy needs. However, the utility of a given dollar amount to satisfy diminishes as one ascends the hierarchy of needs. (See Figure 3.5.)

The A-B curve represents the degree of need satisfaction hypothetical Joe Single[5] could obtain on $70 a day. Line C-D represents the minimal satisfaction level for each of his needs. If satisfaction falls below this line, Joe is hurting.

Seventy dollars is more than enough to satisfy Joe's physiological needs—to have sufficient food to subsist, protection from the elements, warm clothes, and so forth. Let us now imagine that some benefactor steps in and says: "Don't worry, Joe, I'll pay for your physiological needs." Joe can now spend his $70 exclusively for his security needs. If he conservatively invests his daily $70, he'll soon have a sizable nest egg, which should do a fair job of alleviating his security needs unless they are unusually extensive. Enter again Joe's munificent patron and *voilá!* he's free to spend his $70 at the third level. How well his social needs are met is largely dependent on how much Joe needs to belong and upon the dues of the group from which he desires acceptance. If Joe insists on "buying" ego satisfaction, say, through the purchase of a new BMW every other year, he will probably find the price exorbitant, and thus his $70 will leave him somewhat frustrated in this department. And as for self- fulfillment . . . .

Perhaps you felt that as Joe moved into the upper levels of the need hierarchy, the notion of using money to *buy* satisfaction was singularly inappropriate. How can one *buy* genuine respect, for example? Which is precisely the point. Even with unlimited funds, Joe will find it impossible to *buy* all of his satisfaction; the higher he goes in the need hierarchy, the more he will have to *earn* his satisfactions, and money becomes increasingly irrelevant.

Thus a management that relies largely or exclusively on monetary rewards to coax productivity from its employees is using an increasingly ineffectual means of motivation, provided that its people have their lower-level needs basically satisfied.

---

[5] Joe With-a-Family would be a more complex example.

FIGURE 3.5
Utility of Money for Need Satisfaction

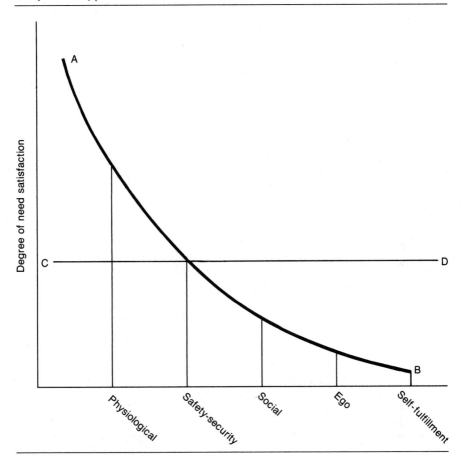

The Ford Story.   There is a distinct irony in all of this. Consider the case of Henry Ford. Ford became eminently successful by implementing the concepts of assembly-line operation and interchangeable parts. Jobs became highly specialized portions of larger, more complex tasks. How did Ford entice a grown man to work for him, screwing in bolt 14 all day long? Simple: if the man was living marginally—and many were—just pay him $5 a day (almost twice as much as the going rate) and he would be delighted to put in his purgatory time to gain a bit of financial breathing room. But workers were not the only ones who had to play restrictive, externally controlled roles. Managers, generally, were deprived of the freedom to manage, to exercise authority, to make decisions.

Ford has been characterized as the arch-authoritarian, but no one can deny his success—two-thirds of the automobile market by the early 1920s.

But he was to pay a price for his one-man-showmanship. The story of the near collapse of the company is a long and involved one, but the moral is clear. People will submit to strict external control when there is no effective escape and when the controller has the power to satisfy their needs. In Ford's case, dollars proved highly successful in motivating people when their predominant needs were at the lower end of the hierarchy. But as the base of wealth broadened, as the dollars came in, these needs began to be satisfied to the extent that they were no longer the individual's exclusive preoccupation. Ironically, the very success of the methods—external controls and good wages—eventually undermined their utility as motivating agents as the needs to which they were eminently suited became fulfilled. The Ford story differs only in degree from the story of industry in general.

Theory Y

Thus a new management theory was necessary, one based on more valid premises about human nature and motivation. Whereas Theory X held that the average person was unalterably immature, the *theory* of Theory Y is essentially that humans are at least *potentially* [6] mature. Managerial practice, therefore, should be geared to the subordinate's current level of maturity with the overall goal of helping him/her to develop, to require progressively less external control, and to gain more and more self-control. And why would a person want this? Because under these conditions, one achieves satisfaction on the job at the levels, primarily the ego and self-fulfillment levels, at which one is most motivatable.

Thus, Theory Y would lead to management practices that would work with rather than against the grain of human nature. The goal of management under Theory Y, then, is to provide circumstances so that people can achieve their own goals best by directing *their own* efforts toward organizational objectives. (See Figure 3.6 for summaries of Theory X and Theory Y.)

Flexibility.   For a time, Theory Y was misconstrued by some as the soft version of Theory X, a sort of sugarcoated or manipulative system.

Theory Y permits access to the full range of management approaches from external to self-control. Where on the spectrum to peg one's approach

---

[6] Even at this late date, occasional writers ignore that key word, *potentially*. Consequently, they oversimplify and assess Theory Y erroneously.

... other managers (the "Theory Y" types) view their employees as near-perfect winners, office dynamos full of selfless dedication to the organization.

John K. Clemens and Douglas F. Mayer, *The Classic Touch: Lessons in Leadership from Homer to Hemingway* (Homewood, Ill.: Dow Jones-Irwin, 1987), p. 80.

FIGURE 3.6

Theory	Resulting Practice
Theory X—The "average person" is inherently (unalterably) immature.	Therefore, it is necessary to control and motivate him or her *externally*. While the manager may have a range of modes by which to apply controls, he or she has no choice as to *whether* external control will be imposed. The *theory* of Theory X precludes anything other than external control.

Modes of external control:
— Hard, strong
— Firm, but fair
— Soft, weak

However, external controls tend to perpetuate themselves, for they keep people immature, emotionally undeveloped, unable to shoulder responsibility, etc.

Theory Y—The "average person" is *potentially* mature.

External control

Individual growth

Self-control

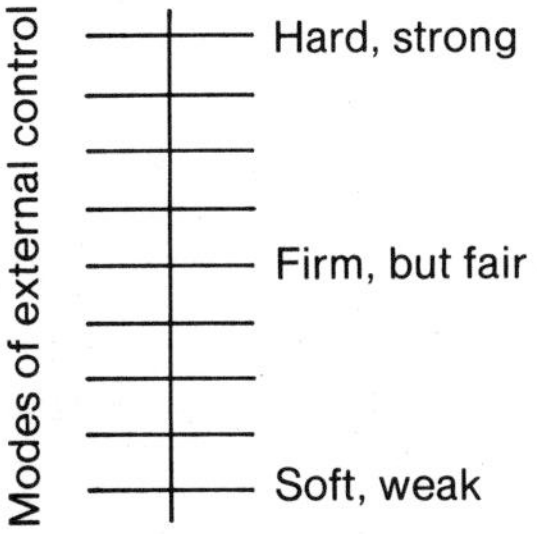

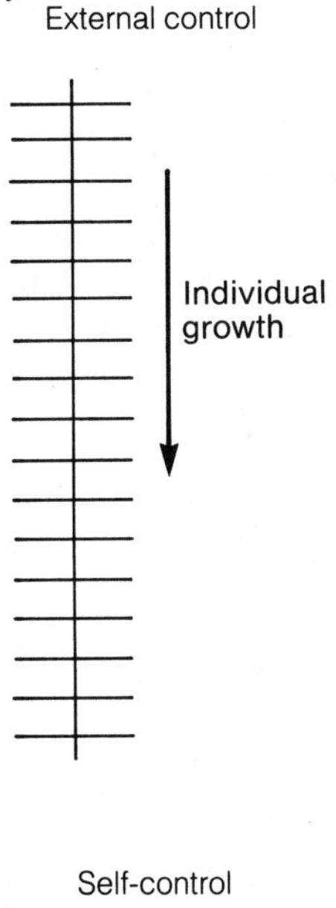

Balance of external control and self-control

Therefore, select the *appropriate balance* between external control and individual freedom commensurate with the individual's *current stage* of development. A new dimension is now open. It is no longer only a question of *how* to administer external control but of *how much* external control is desirable.

The overall objective is to build the constructive cycle (see Figure 3.1): Given skillful coaching and the opportunity to grow (less external control; more freedom to exercise his/her initiative, to make decisions, etc.), the individual will indeed be motivated to grow (because growth renders satisfactions particularly at the ego and self-fulfillment need levels).

By growing, he or she will become more capable of responsible, more self-controlled behavior which serves the best interests of his or her organization as well as his or her own best interests. In sum, the more growth—the more self-control; the more self-control—the more growth; etc.

---

depends on the supervisor's judgment of the subordinate's current state of development. For example, if the subordinate is new and inexperienced, rather close supervision and guidance may be necessary initially. But external control gradually decreases as the individual learns to make decisions and takes independent action. The two theories might be epitomized as follows:

Theory X: John, I want you to be able to swim. However, you cannot swim. Therefore, do not go into the water until you can swim.

The illustration is absurd but relevant. The net result is that John does not learn to swim, remains undeveloped and dependent upon his superior, which is what the superior may have intended, at least unconsciously, in the first place.

Theory Y: John, I want you to be able to swim. However, you cannot swim. Therefore, I shall teach you and let you practice in three feet of water. If you show some prowess there, you may try five feet, and so on.

The key to the art of managing under Theory Y is the ability to *trust appropriately.* Chronic undertrusting leads to apathy or resentment and the conditions that generally prevail under Theory X. Overtrusting can be equally destructive. To carry the swimming analogy further, the over-trusting manager throws John into 10 feet of water. Since John is currently incapable, he begins to sink and the boss must rescue him. There tend to be two destructive consequences: (1) John's self-confidence has been destroyed or at least badly battered; (2) the boss's confidence in John may be destroyed, and thus the boss may be sorely tempted to run back to rigorous external control—"You'll never get a chance to fail me again!"—with the ensuing pattern of John's nondevelopment. Ironically, the boss fails to recognize that it was faulty judgment that triggered the fiasco.

THE FREEDOM-ORDER DICHOTOMY

Prior to McGregor, some traditional management philosophers and managers seem to have been burdened with a myth—that freedom (of the individual to satisfy his or her needs) and order (coordination to achieve the organization's objectives) existed as polar opposites on a single continuum, and that freedom would be attained only at the expense of order, and vice verse. (See Figure 3.7.)

Business management had attempted to work out its role at various points along the continuum—hard, soft, firm but fair (See Figure 3.6), but has generally gravitated toward the high order-low freedom end. The rationale appears to have been essentially as follows:

1. Free enterprise has been demonstrably effective in motivating high quality and quantity performance: "No one works harder than the self-employed."
2. But economic and technological reasons require complex, interdependent, well-ordered organizations.

FIGURE 3.7
The Freedom-Order Dichotomy

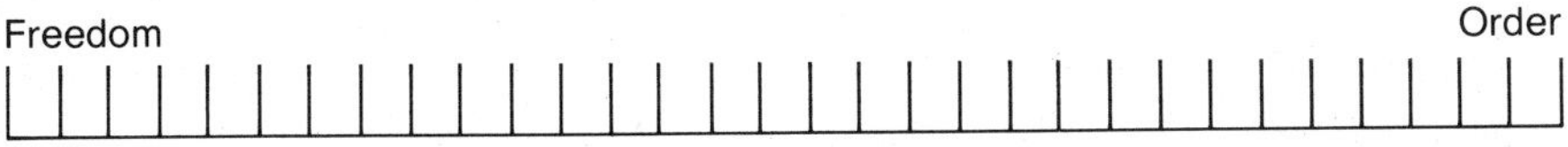

Freedom   Order

3. Nos. 1 and 2 appeared to be in conflict, and 2 usually prevailed: "Let people work for themselves when and in the manner they wish, and the result is usually *chaos!*"
4. Thus the institution has generally striven for coordination, often at the cost of passivity and antagonism on the part of its employees.

On first analysis, we are faced with a dilemma. On one side, there is the force for logic, order, and control; on the other, the drive for individual expression and need satisfaction. The immediate necessity in industry seems to be for logical planning, executing, and controlling. Accordingly, the concepts of organizational structure, job simplification, and control systems seem mandatory. Unfortunately, they tend to develop submissive and dependent performance on the part of employees. Occasionally, such measures generate active or passive revolt. More frequently the outcome is simply overwhelming dullness and minimal compliance.

But the dilemma is more apparent than real. It has become increasingly clear that freedom and order are not necessarily extremes on a single continuum but can exist as two distinct dimensions. (See Figure 3.8.)

Real-life counterparts for the four quadrants in Figure 3.8 might be: (A) In some unfortunate Third World nations where terrorism is rampant, low order and very little freedom in the sense that citizens could not walk down the street without extreme danger. (B) The stereotypical Polynesian idyll, where life is presumably sublime but little is accomplished. (C) Stalin's Russia, Hitler's Germany, and Mao's China. And (D)? There is increasing evidence that it or something approaching it is a possibility in organizations.

Integration of Goals

D will be possible, according to Theory Y, when there is an alliance of individual and organizational goals. The prospect: the organization will encourage individuals to participate more fully in decision making, in determining the destiny of the organization—to provide them significantly more freedom to be in business for themselves—that is, to satisfy their needs but in such a way as to maintain the order necessary to achieve the goals of the organization. Thus they will simultaneously work at satisfying their own psychic needs and at contributing maximally to

FIGURE 3.8

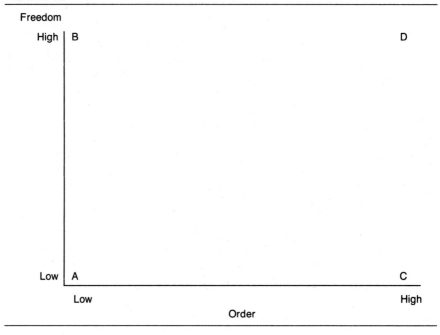

Freedom

High | B   D

Low | A   C
     Low   High
                          Order

their organization's objectives, in McGregor's words, a true "integration of goals."

> The concept rests on a philosophy of management that emphasizes an integration between external control (by managers) and self-control (by subordinates). It can apply to any manager or individual, no matter what his/her level or function, and to any organization, regardless of size. . . . The extent that individuals and groups perceive their own goals as being satisfied by the accomplishment of organizational goals is the degree of integration of goals.[7]

Through *participatory management* (the broader sharing of authority), workers will identify more closely with the firm for basically the same reason that top management identifies with it now. The organizational setting will offer them more opportunity for satisfying their needs, especially those at the ego and self-fulfillment levels. And this, by and large, has been the open secret of motivating anyone at any time, offering the opportunity to satisfy needs. It follows, however, that when needs change, so should the means for satisfying them.

---

[7] Paul Hersey and Kenneth Blanchard, *Management of Organizational Behavior*, 5th ed. (Englewood Hills, N.J.: Prentice-Hall, 1988); see the section "Integration of Goals and Effectiveness," pp. 137–39.

IMPLEMENTATION PROBLEMS

To be sure, there have been problems associated with the implementation of changes growing out of the Theory Y rationale. One is the inevitable expense of transition. The installation of a participative management approach at one company exacted a toll. The initial consequences of their changes were to boost morale sky high . . . and disrupt production! It took three months to return production to its former rate. Subsequently, though, output increased 30 percent, rejects dropped to virtually nil, the job of inspector became unnecessary and was eliminated, customer complaints fell 70 percent, and the increased flexibility of the firm permitted retooling in 2 to 3 weeks, whereas in the past it had required 8 to 10 weeks to crank up for a new model.

Another problem arises when behavioral changes are attempted in the middle and lower echelons of an organization without reinforcement from above. "How can I be a Theory Y manager when I report to a Theory X boss?" or, "How can I delegate authority when the boss doesn't delegate it to me?" These are the plaintive cries of many managers participating in management seminars at which Theory Y or any of its more recent manifestations are suggested.

A message to the complainers:

> Your frustration is understandable. But it might be best not to overpersonalize your feelings. Is it not possible that *your* boss doesn't delegate[8] because *his* or *her* boss doesn't delegate? And, of course, in our hierarchical organizations, everyone has a boss—even the chief executive officer. In a typical publicly owned corporation, that boss might be called the board—or the board's chairperson—or the shareholders. And the latter, judging from my experience as a corporate director, can be distinctly Theory X in their orientation!

In the final analysis, though, the full implementation of Theory Y depends upon *faith*. Here's an old joke which epitomizes the point:

> Little Johnny went to summer camp, got lost in the forest, and fell over a precipice. After tumbling 10 or 15 feet he managed to grab hold of a small tree. He looked down and saw a sheer drop of a hundred feet to the rocks below. He looked up and shouted:
>
> **Johnny:** Is there anyone up there who can help me?
> (*A voice from the heavens responded*): Johnny?
> **Johnny:** Yes?
> **Voice:** Do you believe?
> **Johnny:** Oh, yes . . . I believe!

---

[8] Substitute "trust" for "delegate," and we come closer to the heart of the matter.

Voice: Well, then . . . let go of the tree.
Johnny (*after a long pause*): Is there anyone *else* up there who can help me?

A good number of today's managers share Johnny's fear of "letting go." Incidentally, I have no quarrel with Johnny's attempt to find alternative aid. But the managers are concerned with "letting go" of something else—authority.

They have two primary apprehensions. We have already addressed the first one: They fear that the sharing of authority would lead to gross inefficiency, grievous errors, lack of control, and organizational chaos. They find it difficult to accept the notion that people, if given the opportunity, would *grow up* and share the authority maturely and enthusiastically.

Their second misgiving is more personal. Consider our current system of progression. Is it not, other factors being equal, the power-oriented individual who rises in our organizations? Participative management approaches, however, are asking such individuals to relinquish the very means of need satisfaction they strove so diligently to acquire. Maslow's hierarchy of needs suggests that a solution to this seeming dilemma lies in the prospect of the executives finding even greater need fulfillment in the sharing of power and the development of their own skills and the skills of their subordinates.

I would add that making Theory Y work is everyone's business. Hence this chapter on organizational climate; that is, that all-pervading atmosphere in which a working group is immersed. Odiorne speaks of excellence:

> *Excellence results from a climate in which the search for excellence goes on at all levels, at all times.*
>
> Keen attention must be paid to maintaining an organizational climate which respects excellence, which tries for it, which holds it up as its standard, and which impresses the desire for it upon everyone on the payroll.[9]

Developments

Hundreds of behavioral scientists and thousands of practicing executives have challenged, confirmed, updated, and extended McGregor's initial work.

Rensis Likert, for example, on the basis of considerable experimental and empirical evidence on supportive climates, devised his System 4[10] style of managing organizations.

---

[9] George S. Odiorne, *The Effective Executive's Guide to Managerial Excellence* (Westfield, Maine: MBO, 1983), p. 3. See also Thomas Peters and Robert Waterman, Jr., *In Search of Excellence: Lessons from America's Best-Run Companies* (New York: Harper & Row, 1982).

[10] Systems 3, 2, and 1 were progressively more authoritarian approaches.

System 4—Management is seen as having complete confidence and trust in subordinates. Decision making is widely dispersed throughout the organization, although well integrated. Communication flows not only up and down the hierarchy but among peers. Workers are motivated by participation and involvement in developing economic rewards, setting goals, improving methods, and appraising progress toward goals. There is extensive, friendly superior-subordinate interaction with a high degree of confidence and trust. There is widespread responsibility for the control process, with the lower units fully involved. The informal and formal organizations are often one and the same. Thus, all social forces support efforts to achieve stated organizational goals.[11]

One interpersonal concept that received a substantial boost from Theory Y is *situational leadership*—or, more broadly speaking, the *contingency approach*. This view of management is based on the premise "that there is no one best way to manage in every situation but that managers must find different ways that fit different situations."[12]

Recall that "the key to the art of managing under Theory Y is the ability to *trust appropriately*." Thus, the best way to lead depends upon the specific situation—including the characteristics of the subordinates, the task, organizational policy and climate, superiors, peers, the leader's own characteristics and traits, and the responses of the subordinates.

Leadership is not a simple one-way street in which the leader influences the group. Rather it is determined by many forces outside (as well as inside) the leader. The upshot, then, is that the leader may not be able to have it his or her way. This is the premise that Cohen et al. accept:

We assume that each person is likely to have a *preferred* leadership style, which he/she will opt for whenever possible, but that this should be tempered by what is *appropriate* to the organizational situation.[13]

Another important outgrowth of McGregor's pioneering has been the concept of *goal setting*. This is Reitz's view:

One aspect of the organizational environment which has received considerable attention in behavior-change programs is the setting of goals toward which individuals and groups can strive. Much of this interest developed from

---

[11] Hersey and Blanchard, *Management of Organizational Behavior*, pp. 95–96.

[12] John M. Ivancevich and Michael T, Matteson, *Organizational Behavior and Management* (Homewood, ILL.: Irwin/BPI, 1987), p. 754. For other examinations of the contingency theory of management, see: Laurence Siegle and Irving M. Lane, *Personnel and Organizational Psychology*, 2nd ed. (Homewood, Ill.: Richard D. Irwin, 1987), pp. 546–57, and James L. Gibson, John M. Ivancevich, and James H. Donnelly, Jr., *Organizations: Behavior, Structure, Processes*, 6th ed. (Homewood, Ill.: Irwin/BPI, 1988), pp. 9, 755–56.

[13] Allan R. Cohen, Stephen L. Fink, Herman Gadon, and Robin D. Willits, *Effective Behavior in Organizations*, 4th ed. (Homewood, Ill.: Richard D. Irwin, 1988), p. 344.

empirical studies which showed that individuals tend to perform at higher or more effective levels when they are working toward specific goals than when they are not.[14]

One variation of goal setting that has attracted a great deal of attention in organizations has been *management by objectives* (MBO). The essence of MBO is that it combines specific goal setting, participation, and feedback into a performance appraisal system.

MBO can be properly defined as: A managerial process whereby organizational purposes are diagnosed and met by joining superior and subordinates in the pursuit of mutually agreed-upon goals and objectives, which are specific, measurable, time-bounded, and joined in an action plan; progress and goal attainment are measured and monitored in appraisal sessions which center on mutually determined objective standards of performance.[15]

The key characteristics of MBO are:

1. Effective goal setting and planning by top levels of the managerial hierarchy.
2. Commitment of the organization to this approach.
3. Participation of subordinates in setting goals.
4. Frequent performance review (feedback).
5. Some freedom in developing means for achieving objectives.[16]

Under companywide MBO programs, objectives at all levels of management and employees are set with reference to the overall organizational goal. Goal setting starts at the top and works down, with each level setting goals consistent with those of the next highest level.

In this system, the supervisor and employee to be evaluated jointly set objectives in advance for the employee to try to achieve during a specified period. The technique encourages if not requires, them to phrase these objectives primarily in quantitative terms. The evaluation consists of a joint review of the degree of achievement of the objectives.[17]

---

[14] H. Joseph Reitz, *Behavior in Organizations*, 3rd ed. (Homewood, Ill.: Richard D. Irwin, 1987), p. 580. See E. A. Locke and G. P. Latham, *Goal Setting: A Motivational Technique That Works!* (Englewood Cliffs, N.J.: Prentice-Hall, 1984) for a comprehensive appraisal of the goal-setting process.

[15] M. L. McConkie, "A Clarification of the Goal Setting and Appraisal Processes in MBO," *Academy of Management Review*, 1979, p. 37.

[16] S. J. Carroll, Jr., and H. L. Tosi, Jr., *Management by Objectives: Applications and Research* (New York: Macmillan, 1973), p. 3.

[17] George T. Milkovich and John W. Boudreau, *Personnel/ Human Resource Management: A Diagnostic Approach*, 5th ed. (Homewood, Ill.: Irwin/BPI, 1988), p. 202.

MBO often requires a good amount of time to implement and it is not without other difficulties.[18] At the same time it has been successful in changing behavior.

In one production firm productivity had been *declining* at an average rate of 0.4 percent per month. After MBO was instituted productivity *increased* at an average rate of 0.3 percent per month. Managers involved in the program attributed the improved productivity to performance appraisal, better planning, and better communications resulting from MBO.[19]

Still another emphasis for which McGregor's Theory Y is a logical antecedent is organization development (OD). OD's principal objective is "to uncover and remove attitudinal, behavioral, procedural, policy, and structural barriers to effective performance across the entire sociotechnical system, gaining in the process increased awareness of the system's internal and external dynamics so that future adaptations are enhanced."[20]

The chief aspects of OD include the following:

1. It is planned and long term.
2. It is problem oriented.
3. It reflects a systems approach.
4. It is action oriented.
5. It involves change agents.
6. It involves learning principles.

These characteristics of contemporary organizational development indicate that managers who implement OD programs are committed to making fundamental changes in organizational behavior. At the heart of the process are learning principles that enable individuals to unlearn old behaviors and learn new ones.[21]

---

[18] Most behavioral scientists believe that such difficulties stem from misunderstanding and faulty practice of MBO's tenets rather than from an inherently invalid concept. . . . Many organizations have lost the elementary insight into the essential functions of a manager. Their managers go through the motions of managing by living up to set procedures; for example, watching time clocks, granting everyday personnel requests, selecting replacements when someone quits, focusing on minor elements while not seeing the big picture.

Advice: Costly programs with attractive packages and procedures (sort of paint-by-number sets) to reinstitute the traditional managerial funtions are unnecessary. Once corporate objectives are ascertained and competent managers hired, MBO becomes a natural function. (From Leonard R. Sayles, "Management by Objectives: A Reappraisal," *Boardroom Reports* 7, no. 11 (June 15, 1978), p. 7.)

[19] Reitz, *Behavior in Organizations*, p. 582.

[20] R. E. Miles, *Theories of Management: Implications for Organizational Behavior and Development* (New York: McGraw-Hill, 1975), p. 191.

[21] James L. Gibson, John M. Ivancevich, and James H. Donnelly, Jr., *Organizations: Behavior, Structure, Processes*, 6th ed. (Homewood, Ill.: Irwin/BPI, 1988), pp. 695–96.

Japanese manufacturers have been phenomenally successful in some areas. One of their practices, *quality circles*, has become increasingly popular in American organizations. Theory Y, again, is its philosophic underpinning. Teams of employees meet periodically to determine ways of improving quality and productivity. The record for reducing defects and unnecessary work procedures has often been impressive.[22]

This technique has obvious implications for motivation. After all, when people have a voice in *how* something is produced they generally have more interest in producing it well (quality control) and efficiently.[23]

One potential hazard, though, is that management sometimes focuses on the technical developments and insufficiently appreciates the motivational implications of bringing employees together and allowing them to influence the way the work is done.

But a broader caution is in order. There is no doubt that Japanese industrial experiences have attracted a great deal of attention worldwide. Two books in particular, which compare Japanese and American management practices, are certainly worthy of serious study.[24] But we must guard against the temptation to assume that that which works well for the Japanese will, ipso facto, work equally well in American organizations.

We must remind ourselves that the two cultures differ substantially. Rehder offers an insightful contrast of the two traditional organizational and management systems.[25] And Schermerhorn's advice is warranted:

> The final answer on how well management practices such as lifetime employment, the ringi system, and even quality-control circles work in the United States and other countries remains to be determined. For now, it appears that we should use books like *Theory Z* and *The Art of Japanese Management* for provocation and dialogue . . . . Their function, like much of the writing on Japanese management, is to help develop creative and critical thinking about the way we do things and about whether or not we can and should be doing them better.[26]

Clearly Theory Y management, eupsychian (meaning "good vibes") management, enlightened management, or whatever one cares to call it,

---

[22] Robert I. Patchin, *The Management and Maintenance of Quality Circles* (Homewood, Ill.: Dow Jones-Irwin, 1983).

[23] See Donald A. Ball and Wendell H. McCulloch, Jr., *International Business: Introduction and Essentials*, 4th ed. (Homewood, Ill.: Irwin/BPI, 1990), pp. 597–98, 636–38.

[24] William Ouchi, *Theory Z: How American Business Can Meet the Japanese Challenge* (Reading, Mass.: Addison-Wesley, 1981), and Richard Tanner Pascale and Anthony G. Athos, *The Art of Japanese Management: Applications for American Executives* (New York: Simon & Schuster, 1981).

[25] Robert R. Rehder, "What American and Japanese Managers Are Learning from Each Other," *Business Horizons*, 24 (March–April 1981), p. 67.

[26] John R. Schermerhorn, Jr., *Management for Productivity* (New York: John Wiley & Sons, 1984), pp. 646–48.

and its descendants (situational leadership, goal setting, MBO, OD, and quality circles) have exciting potentials. But they also place markedly greater demand upon managers' abilities to analyze and predict human behavior (their own included), to know their people, and to communicate (encode and decode messages). The strengthening of these skills is this book's principal purpose.

We have considered the organization and the climate it generates. We will now turn to the individual and examine some of the perceptual and motivational aspects of communication behavior.

Discussion Questions

1. "Some feel that the structure and climate of today's organization are in many respects inimical to the emotional health and development of its members." Do you agree or disagree? More specifically, what might be the objection?

2. "A new, more subtle postindustrial revolution is in process." What was intended by that statement? What is contributing to this revolution? Is it broader than just industrial?

3. The author asserts: "The leadership and overall atmosphere . . . achieve its goals." How does this strike you as a managerial philosophy? Is it too idealistic? Will it work? Does it have sufficient regard for organizational needs? If you were employed in an organization which adhered as closely as possible to these ideals, would you be effectively motivated to produce? If you were the boss, how would this philosophy affect your people?

4. Re: the constructive and destructive cycles. Are they valid, that is, do high trust and high performance generally tend to reinforce each other? Do low trust and low performance generally tend to reinforce each other? If high performance tends to follow high trust, why don't managers simply start "high-trusting" their subordinates, even if they don't mean it?

5. What is the relationship between *trust* and *communication* in an organization?

6. "Whoever rides a tiger can never dismount." How does that statement relate to this chapter?

7. Maslow's *hierarchy of needs*: Does it explain and predict human behavior to your satisfaction?

8. According to McGregor, most employees in the United States have had their physiological and safety-security needs at least reasonably satisfied. Do you agree? If so, what are the implications of this for managers and others who are concerned with the motivation of people?

9. "A management which relies largely or exclusively on monetary rewards . . . is using an increasingly ineffectual means of motivation, provided that its people have their lower-level needs basically satisfied." Discuss. How does the Ford story relate to the above statement?

10. In accordance with Theory Y, managerial practice "should be geared to the subordinate's current level of maturity with the overall goal of helping him/her to develop, to require progressively less external control, and to gain more and more self-control." Is this realistic? Will it work? Does it have limitations?

11. Discuss the freedom-order dichotomy. Under what conditions could these qualities coexist?

12. What are some of the problems associated with the implementation of the changes called for by Theory Y?

13. What does this chapter on *organizational climate* have to do with *communication*? What special challenges confront the manager who attempts to implement Theory Y?

14. Write an essay on organizational climate discussing the relationships among the destructive and constructive cycles, Theories X and Y, external and internal control, the hierarchy of needs, the freedom-order dichotomy, and the integration of goals.

C A S E S

CASE 3.1

Drexel Electronics Company*

The Drexel Electronics Company, a nationally known firm, special-ized in the manufacture of communications equipment. One of its larger plants was located in a nearby suburb of a large West Coast city. Some 800 people were employed in this plant, engaged in the production and minor assembly of metal parts from sheet and bar stock. Finished parts were sent to another plant for final assembly. Local sales, public relations, and general office departments were maintained on the premises in addition to the personnel, time study, engineering, and maintenance departments. Ninety percent of the employees were engaged in the 10 production and materials handling departments.

One of the production departments, small parts, was supervised by Fred Schultz, assisted by two supervisors. Some 40 men and women worked in small parts on the day shift. Another 35 on the night shift were supervised by the night supervisor. Workers in this department were clas-sified into 12 grades, according to skill and seniority. The lower grades, 1 through 3, were composed mainly of younger workers who had little expe-rience or technical skills. Their work consisted of deburring, straighten-ing, and assembling small parts with simple hand tools. The middle grades, 4 through 6, consisted of skilled workers who did more complex work, while grades 7 through 12 were reserved for inspectors, setup peo-ple, assistant supervisors, and supervisors.

Although production in this department was on an individual or job order basis, a weekly bonus determined by the total production of the department was added to the base wage for each job grade. This group bonus plan was employed wherever feasible throughout the plant.

In July, Jack Marcell, 18, a recent high school graduate, applied for employment at Drexel Electronics. The personnel manager told Jack that the prime factor in advancement was ability and that superior workers had been known to make grade 7, the lowest grade of inspector, after five years of service. Seniority, he said, played only a secondary role and was generally rewarded with pay increases rather than with advancement in rank.

---

* All names and organizational designations have been disguised. Northwestern Uni-versity cases are reports of concrete events and behavior, prepared for class discussion. They are not intended as examples of good or bad administrative practice. Copyrighted by North-western University. Reprinted by permission.

Marcell was assigned to the small parts department. The day he reported for work, Schultz took him aside for a brief interview and confirmed the personnel manager's statements about advancement. He explained that all new workers were hired on a trial, or probationary, basis.

The maximum probationary period was five months. If a worker had attained the department standards of quantity and quality of production before the end of this period, he or she was considered to be on a permanent basis with the firm. Otherwise, the employee was released. An exceptional producer could be promoted to grade 3 anytime after a minimum probationary period of five weeks. Grade 3 represented a raise in base pay and work of a more complex, less monotonous nature. Schultz said the company's probation policy was designed to give ample opportunity for the late bloomer to develop and yet permit the unusual worker to advance as rapidly as ability and production warranted.

Each worker was required to turn in a "factor time summary" at the end of each working day. This sheet showed the job orders on which the employee had worked, actual hours worked on each job, the standard rate for each, the number of parts finished, and the standard hours produced. Jack soon learned that management expected the average worker to produce 8 to 10 standard hours[1] per day, while a superior worker produced 10 to 12 standard hours per day.

Most of the job rates seemed hard to make to Jack, but he learned quickly and was soon producing seven to eight standard hours per day. Within several weeks, he learned from other workers that there were certain gravy jobs that came through the department quite often. These jobs carried unusually low standard rates in relation to the amount of hand finishing necessary to complete the part. Low rates were often caused by improved manufacturing procedures in one or more of the departments which processed the parts before they reached Small Parts, thus making certain small parts jobs easier, although the rates remained unchanged. On such jobs, it was possible to produce 18 or 20 standard hours per day. Furthermore, these hours could be saved up and turned in anytime during the week. A worker who had a gravy job on Monday, for example, might turn out 20 standard hours of work but would report only 12 hours and save the other 8 hours to spread over the remaining days of the week.

---

[1] A standard hour was a measure of production. For example, if the standard rate for a particular piecework job had been set at 100 pieces per hour, then a standard hour on that job would be 100 pieces. A worker who turned out 120 pieces would have produced 1.2 standard hours of work. The group bonus was computed at the end of the week. A worker who produced 50 standard hours for the week was paid his or her base hourly wage for the 40 hours. The worker's standard hours over 8 per day (10 in this case) were thrown into the pot along with the excess hours of the other workers. The pot hours were divided equally each week among the workers, regardless of grade. Pay for these hours varied with the bonus rate for each worker's grade (approximately 80 percent of his or her base rate).

Thus, it would be possible to report 12 hours for each of the five days of the week even though producing only 10 standard hours on each of the other four days.

It became obvious to Jack that the saving technique was designed to conceal the gravy jobs from the time study department. It was clear that only the supervisors and Fred Schultz were in a position to detect these jobs. The actual starting and stopping times on each job were not revealed by the time cards sent to the payroll department but only by the route sheets or individual and group productivity reports which were forwarded to the production department. But he never heard Schultz or any supervisor mention the soft touches to anyone except their older workers.

> **Foreman:** Elaine [a senior employee], I got a light one coming up. Do you need it?
>
> **Elaine:** Well, no—I've had a few of them already this week, so I don't need it. Why don't you give it to Tom [a younger employee]? He's had some rough ones. He'll need the hours.

In order to even up for the week, it seemed to Jack that many gravy jobs were given workers who handled a series of jobs with tighter rates. However, the distribution of the easier jobs was not entirely determined by worker need. Although all workers received gravy jobs occasionally, those closest to the senior workers and supervisors were assigned appreciably more than average. This group appeared to be favored over eight younger people who ate and took their breaks together, without much contact with Schultz, the supervisors, and the other workers. One of the supervisors expressed what he said was the general feeling toward the out group. "They're our poorest workers. They're always complaining. The only thing they're looking for on this job is the almighty buck. They have the lowest output in the department, and if you turn your back for two minutes, they're off sneaking a smoke or goofing off in some other way. They're just punks and wise guys in my book."

Not all young workers were in the out group. Jack Marcell found no difficulty in making friends with his co-workers and supervisors. Before long, he was getting his share of gravy jobs, which made it possible for him to turn in 12 standard hours per day much of the time.

At the end of the fifth week of Jack's employment at Drexel Electronics, Fred Schultz called him aside to tell him that he was pleased with his work and that he was being promoted to grade 3. As Jack expressed his gratitude, Schultz added, "You'd better keep this under your hat. There are two other men in the department who have been with the company four months but are still in grade 2."

Jack did not mention his promotion to his co-workers, but they soon noticed that Jack was doing more advanced work. Carson and Welles, young grade 2 men with more seniority than Jack, went to see Schultz in his office and complained bitterly.

Schultz drew a breath and said acidly, "You men knew the rules when you came in here. If you don't like it, you know where the door is."

Discussion Questions

1. What were the frames of reference, respectively, of Marcell, Schultz, the in-group, and the out-group?

2. What were the major problems in this case?

3. Since Schultz seems unlikely to take any action on Carson's and Welles' complaints, assume that Carson and Welles go to a Mr. Brown, Schultz's superior, and register their complaints. As Brown, what would you do, step by step?

CASE 3.2

"My Case against Paul Brown"*

Jimmy Brown and Myron Cope

In the summer of 1957, when I first arrived in the Cleveland Browns' training camp in the town of Hiram, Ohio, a burly man named Lenny Ford took me aside and gave me a few words of advice.

"Rookie," he said to me, "if you want to get along here, listen to what I'm telling you.

"First," he said, "when you're running through plays in practice, always run 20 yards downfield. Don't just run through the hole and then jog a few steps and flip the ball back. The man doesn't like that. Run hard for 20 yards, even if you feel silly."

"Second," Lenny Ford told me, "keep your mouth shut when he speaks to you. When he tells you how to run a play, run it the way he tells you. If you have an idea for improving the play, keep it to yourself. Suggestions make the man mad. If you're pretty sure you can make more ground by changing the play, change it in the *game.* Don't change it in practice. Run it your way in the game and hope it works, and if it does, don't say anything. Just make your yardage and act like it was a mistake."

Lenny was telling me to behave in a way that sounded kind of childish to me, but I wasn't about to mistake him for an idiot. He was a feared man in professional football. I kept listening.

"Also," he went on, "don't start any conversations with the man. Don't *initiate* anything. You see something wrong, let it go. He does all the talking here."

The man being described by Lenny Ford was, of course, Paul Brown, our head coach. Working for Paul Brown in the ensuing years, I became

---

* From *Off My Chest* by James N. Brown and Myron Cope. Copyright © 1964 by James N. Brown and Myron Cope. Reprinted by permission of Doubleday & Company, Inc.

the highest-salaried player in the history of football and have continued upward. My salary this season is more than $50,000. And thanks in part to my football reputation, I've earned substantial money in business, in broadcasting, and in the movies. So I suppose I should be able to say some nice things about Paul, and the truth is, I can. But I'm afraid I'll never rank as one of his leading admirers.

In 1962, I told Cleveland clubowner Art Modell that if Paul Brown remained as head coach in '63 I wanted out. Trade me, I told Modell, or I'll quit. I was not the only player to make such a threat. Nor did I relish taking a stand against Paul. I don't think it can be seriously questioned that among all of America's coaches this pale, tight-lipped, little man was far and away the genius of modern postwar football. He was the Browns' first coach, and they were named for him. His teams thoroughly dominated the old All-America Conference, then won six straight divisional titles in the National Football League. An original thinker and painstaking organizer, Paul Brown made the Cleveland Browns one of the most astonishingly successful organizations in the history of commercial sports. Then, sadly, they declined. My six years under Paul were as much as I could stomach. . . .

Although I was billed as Paul's star performer, I had no relationship with him. I wanted to, but his aloofness put him beyond approach. Yet curiously, during my rookie season I thought Paul was a great guy. Far from being the grim man Lenny Ford warned me about, Paul dazzled me with compliments and solicitude. I led the league in rushing that year with 942 yards, and we won the Eastern Division title. I had every reason to expect that I would always be happy working for Paul. But I didn't realize at the time that Paul followed a pattern in his handling of men—a pattern in which, at an almost predictable moment, he would turn off his amiability as decisively as a plumber turns off the warm water with a twist of his wrench.

Given a rookie who had outstanding promise, Paul would flatter and cajole him. But after the rookie proved himself and got acclimated in his first season, he became little more than a spoke in the wheel. I became Paul's big brute, the man who would slug out yardage for him. It seemed to me that he thought of me as nothing more than a weapon. I felt he had no interest in me as an individual.

Fair enough, I did not hanker to be babied. Yet in the atmosphere that Paul created, his players inevitably became robots. You played hard, but you concerned yourself almost entirely with your own performance. "I've done *my* job," you told yourself. When a teammate scored a touchdown, you didn't go out of your way to hug him or pat him on the fanny. When the ball changed hands, you went to the bench and sat there in silence. You cared, but the action on the field moved you to no demonstration of emotion. You were as close to being a mechanical man as a football player can get.

And as the NFL developed a balance of power that made every game a tough one, it became obvious that robots no longer would do. The Browns lacked spirit. It is my honest opinion that in Paul Brown's last five years as coach—five years in which we were also-rans every season—every one of those five squads, given its fair share of breaks and a feeling of enthusiasm, could have won the championship.

Discussion Questions

1. What are Jimmy Brown's allegations against Paul Brown?

2. Accepting Jimmy's charges at face value, what do you think of Paul's philosophy of coaching?

3. The author of this case is also its chief protagonist. How do you feel about his dual role?

CASE 3.3

Atlas Publishing Co.*

All improvements and changes at Atlas Publishing Company had, for years, been initiated and directed by Mr. Arthur Dalton, the business manager. Atlas published a variety of monthly trade and general business periodicals. It was Dalton's practice to make most of the decisions personally on problems that arose during the day's work. Some of his associates said that they often suggested changes and improvements in the various magazines but, they felt, Dalton rarely listened. One of the department heads said, "Arthur believes, because of his experience in directing the business, that he knows what should be done, what shouldn't, and when."

When Dalton wanted any change made, he simply requested that it be done. He often explained in some detail how it could be done expeditiously and effectively. As a rule, his action was taken with a minimum of discussion with the people immediately affected. Some executives felt the timing of changes was unpredictable.

For the past two years, the company's net profit had been below the industry's figures. During the 59 years of its existence, Atlas Publishing Company had consistently shown a profit, but the net profit percentage of both sales and investment had gradually decreased during the past decade. Several Atlas publications had doubled their advertising volumes in the last 10 years, but competitors had "stolen" large advertising accounts from others. Junior executives believed some of these publications had not kept up

---

to date with developments in the interests, habits, and attitudes of their readers. In their judgment, competitors had recognized these changing trends and had revised their periodicals to meet readers' needs.

The record showed that Mr. Dalton was by no means opposed to change. He had personally initiated many modifications in editorial policy. Several staff people, however, told Arthur Dalton's son, Ben, that the reasons for these changes were not always clear to others in the business.

The consolidated balance sheet and P&L reports of Atlas Publishing were prepared monthly by the controller and distributed to the president, the business manager, and members of the board of directors. Arthur Dalton told his management group that he knew when the expenditure of money was justified and when it was not. Since he had a substantial personal investment in the business, he felt that "frills," as he called them, should be kept to a minimum. For example, advertisements occupied a large portion of the front covers of several Atlas publications, reducing the amount of space available for the title and contents of the publication. In the opinion of many in the trade, some of these ads were unsightly and gave a negative impression to readers. Most competitors had abandoned this practice long ago in favor of attractive four-color illustrations relevant to the contents of the issue. Their covers were designed to create a favorable "publication image," a term used frequently in the trade. It was Dalton's opinion that his competitors were wasting space and money on window dressing, with loss of potential advertising revenue. Discussion and documentation by other executives had not succeeded in convincing Dalton that Atlas should give the prevalent trade practice a try.

Mr. Dalton often said that he maintained an open-door policy. His executives could come to see him on problems whenever necessary. He didn't have to agree with them, he said, but they could secure his opinion on any subject at any time.

When some of the younger, college-trained executives met at luncheon, they often discussed their feelings about Dalton's arbitrary behavior. It seemed to them that substantive changes in the magazines might be accomplished more effectively through long-range planning. When decisions were made on a day-to-day basis, many areas, they felt, received no attention, while others were treated almost as pet projects.

Arthur Dalton had often said, "When we have the money, we'll spend it on things that are necessary. When we haven't the money, even important projects will just have to wait." One of the executives, who had studied modern magazine business methods, thought that some improvements could be considered capital items, to be depreciated over a period of years rather than charged wholly against current income. He held the opinion that, in some instances, it might be wise for the company to borrow money for improvements instead of postponing them indefinitely merely because working capital was needed for day-to-day operations.

Dalton's son, Ben, started work with Atlas Publishing upon graduation from Yale. On the eighth anniversary of his employment with the organization, Ben was named business manager, and his father became president. Arthur Dalton told Ben that, from then on, the operating responsibilities of the publishing company were his job. Arthur Dalton planned to concern himself primarily with broad matters of policy and community affairs.

Ben realized he had moved up swiftly through the organization. He was only superficially acquainted with many of the magazines' operating problems. He decided that he needed a firmer basis than his own experience on which to start to make major decisions. He told one of his friends that he intended to make use of the know-how of other, more seasoned executives.

Ben also recalled the opinions younger executives had expressed from time to time at luncheon meetings. He decided to encourage his staff to participate in decision making. He began to consult regularly with his associates and encouraged them in turn to consult with him. To give this idea more than lip service, he appointed a Management Committee, consisting of major heads of departments, including editorial, circulation, production, advertising, and sales promotion.

After several meetings, Ben proposed that the committee develop a long-range program for improving the business. He asked each committee member to submit projects which, in his judgment, should be initiated within the coming 12 months, plus other projects which he thought were desirable but could be deferred until the following year.

Within a month, the Management Committee agreed on a consolidated list of projects which they felt were important enough to be given top priority. The estimated cost of these improvements for the next fiscal year was in excess of $1,500,000. The program included:

1. Changing magazine formats to achieve a modern appearance.
2. Hiring additional writers and upgrading salary scales.
3. Maintaining a Washington sales office and editorial correspondent.
4. Using more pictures, which would require additional and more up-to-date photographic equipment.
5. Using four-color pictures, as well as selling four-color advertising.
6. Offering more merchandising services to back up advertising sales.
7. Conducting research on readership, magazine image, and buyer motivation.
8. Creating a new magazine to meet growing needs in a related industry.

Ben was shocked by the report. He was sure that no more than $900,000 could be appropriated for the coming 12-month period and that it would be difficult to persuade his father and the board of directors to go along with even this amount. He did not believe he could or should decide personally which items should be deferred for another year or two. All the items had been marked by the Management Committee as high priority. As he studied the list, Ben himself agreed that all were important.

Ben finally decided against launching a new magazine at this time. This alone would require an outlay of $750,000 the first year. If this project were implemented now, other urgent improvements would necessarily be tabled.

Ben explained to the committee, "Perhaps we have set our sights too high." He asked them to review the list again to determine which items should be given top priority so that a final decision could be made at the next meeting, one week later.

The committee readily accepted this assignment to prune the original proposals. They agreed on a special priority list of projects totaling $600,000. The group also concluded that all of the work could not be included in the allocations for the next 12 months. However, if $300,000 were authorized for each of the next two years, most of the recommended actions could be initiated. This plan met with unanimous approval. The business manager decided he was ready to discuss it with his father.

The following day, Ben presented to his father the $600,000 program of improvements for the next two years. Arthur Dalton exploded, "We simply can't afford it, Ben. Why is this necessary now? Some of these things may need attention, but we just can't tackle them with our working capital situation in the shape it is. What else have you been dreaming up, Ben?"

Ben explained that he was not alone in feeling that these improvements were necessary. He told his father about the Management Committee he had set up to work with him in planning the needs of the business. Mr. Dalton sputtered, "How long has this Management Committee been going on? Why take the valuable time of all these people? How long did it take the group to arrive at these recommendations? If you had come to me in the first place, we could have worked this out in less than an hour and at a much lower cost than $600,000."

Arthur Dalton studied the complete list more carefully. He concluded that it might be reasonable to spend $300,000 for several items that he agreed were urgently needed. He blue-penciled the remaining proposals as he said, "Some of the other directors may be more liberal, but I personally can't justify spending more than $300,000 for improvements."

Ben went back to his office. He looked out the window and pondered the future effectiveness of his Management Committee and his own future with Atlas Publishing.

Discussion Questions

1. How is business at Atlas Publishing?

2. How do you account for this state of affairs?

3. What is Arthur Dalton's philosophy of managing people?

4. What is Ben Dalton's philosophy of managing people?

5. Arthur epitomized Theory X and Ben, Theory Y. Do you agree? Why, or why not?

6. How do you appraise Ben's actions?

7. What should Ben do now?

CASE 3.4

Mayhem House*
Keith Grayson

Mayhall House is an independent men's dormitory on the campus of a large midwestern university. The grade average of the dorm was one of the lowest of any house on campus. This was mainly because almost all of our 65 residents were majoring in either engineering or business—generally acknowledged as the most difficult schools in the university. And, of course, we had our share of goof-offs—five or six fellows who had ability but had never been able to apply themselves to their studies. We chalked them up as immature and hoped they would see the light before their academic probation ran out. But as long as they didn't disturb anyone, we felt we could get along with them.

As a matter of fact, there was very little horsing around in the house. I had visited a number of the other dorms and was surprised to see college men, or rather boys, running up and down the halls yelling and chasing one another and playing silly pranks. As I said, I had always considered our house remarkably calm and dignified—until this year. Now, you wouldn't know it. Everyone's calling it Mayhem House.

The situation has become so out of hand that it's difficult to know how to describe it, but I'll try to start at the beginning.

When we started school in September, two important events (at least to me) occurred. I was elected president of Mayhall House, and a new counselor moved in. His name was John Morrison, 23, a graduate student in theology. John seemed to be very pleasant but made it clear in his first meeting with the residents of the house that he had heard our grade average was low and hoped we could raise it. He gave quite a pep talk and said if we would all pull together, we might put Mayhall near the top of the list.

I agreed with this, but I didn't see how there could be much improvement, in view of the fact that most of us were in the toughest schools.

The first evidence that John meant what he said occurred when he established his closed-door policy. The fellows had the custom of leaving

---

* All names, including the author's (an undergraduate student), have been disguised.

the doors of their rooms open and occasionally talking across the corridor to one another. If John happened to be passing by, he would simply close the doors without saying a word. I suppose he thought the fellows would take the hint, but they only got sore about the situation and started doing more transcorridor communicating. It got to be quite a joke. John would start at one end of the corridor and close 10 sets of doors as he walked to the other end. Two minutes after John was gone, all the doors would be open, and the talking would start in again—only louder and more of it. On one occasion, a student yelled, "Go to hell, John!" after John had closed his door. John opened the door again and put the student on formal warning.

Next was the stereo episode. About the middle of November, John posted a notice:

> In order to provide proper study conditions,
> no stereos will be turned on after
> 7 P.M.; effective this date.

This seemed high-handed and unnecessary to me. Stereos had never been a problem in the house before. A few students liked to study with some soft music in the background. But if anyone objected, they would turn their stereos off.

The fellows seemed to accept this as a challenge. The same night the notice was posted, about seven or eight men turned on their stereos to get them warmed up but not loud enough for anyone to hear.

Then one stereo blared full blast for a second and was quickly snapped off. John came bolting down the corridor to find the culprit. When he got near the room, another stereo blared for a moment at the opposite end of the hall. John wheeled and streaked back. At this moment, two other stereos opened up, and John started twirling around in circles! It was the most ridiculous thing you ever saw, and the fellows couldn't help bursting out laughing.

John was furious. "All right, *children*! If you can't take proper care of your *toys*, someone will have to take care of them for you!"

He then started moving from one room to the next, confiscating the stereos. It took him about three hours, but he picked up every stereo—minus speakers—in the house, put them in a storeroom, and locked the door. Maybe the seven or eight pranksters deserved this, but he took *all* the stereos, mine included!

Well, that was the sign for open warfare. What happened then was one continuous nightmare. The next night, somebody brought some firecrackers into the house, and the mayhem started! Someone tied a firecracker to a burning cigarette and laid it in front of John's door. A few minutes later, the cigarette burned down and ignited the firecracker, John threw open his door, and not a soul was to be seen. He was fit to be tied. That was a night to be remembered! All night long, about every 10 minutes, a firecracker went off somewhere—outside the dorm, in the corridor, in somebody's room, or outside John's door! John didn't even come out.

The next day it snowed, and that night it was snowballs. I won't go into the gory details, but the end result was the damage of property, including five broken windows!

This, of course, brought in the dean of men. I was surprised that he hadn't come in before. I guess John never mentioned our situation to him. The rest is history. John has been transferred to another house, and we are on social probation for the rest of the semester.

Discussion Questions

1. How do you size up John Morrison? The author of this case? The dean of men?
2. How should John Morrison have handled his assignment at Mayhall?

CASE 3.5

The Man and the Desk*
F. J. Roethlisberger and William T. Dickson

The personnel of one of the departments interviewed was moved from one building to another. In the new location, because of lack of space, it was found necessary to seat four people across the aisle from the remainder of the group. It happened that there were three women in the department who were to be transferred to other work. These women were given desks across the aisle so that their going would not necessitate a rearrangement of desks. The fourth person, a man, was given a desk there simply because there was no other place for him to sit. In choosing the fourth person, the supervisor was undoubtedly influenced by the fact that he was older than the rest of the group and was well acquainted with the three women. But, beyond that, nothing was implied by the fact that he was chosen.

Now see how this employee interpreted the change in his seating position. He felt that his supervisor evaluated him in the same way in which he evaluated the women. The women were being transferred to other types of work; consequently, he felt that he too would be transferred before long. Two of the women were being returned to jobs in the shop. He felt that he himself might be transferred to the shop; and there was nothing he dreaded more. Having dwelt on speculations like these for a while, the employee recalled with alarm that his name had been omitted from the current issue of the house telephone directory. This omission had been

---

* *Management and the Worker* (Cambridge, Mass.: Harvard University Press, 1939), pp. 544-45. Reprinted by permission.

accidental. The house telephone directory, however, constituted a sort of social register. Names of shop people below the rank of assistant foreman were not printed unless they were employed in some special capacity requiring contacts with other organizations. With the exception of typists and certain clerical groups, the names of all office people were listed. The fact that his name had been omitted from the directory now took on new significance for the employee. It tended to reinforce his growing conviction that he was about to be transferred to a shop position. He became so preoccupied over what might happen to him that for a time he could scarcely work.

Discussion Questions

1. There is no indication that the supervisor informed the man (let's call him Joe) of the reasons for seating him with the three women on the other side of the aisle. Why might he have failed to explain his motives for the seating arrangement?

2. Apparently, Joe failed to question his boss about the seating arrangement. Why?

3. What does this case have to do with this chapter?

4. How should the supervisor have handled the situation?

5. Assume the supervisor has observed the falloff in Joe's work. What should he do now?

PART TWO

The Behavioral Basis of Communication

❋
❋
❋

CHAPTER FOUR

Perception and Communication
1. The Process of Perception

❄
❄
❄

"This is nothing. When I was your age the snow was so deep it came up to my chin!"
Reprinted from Redbook with the permission of the cartoonist, Gerry Marcus.

Dad is right—as he perceives it. And in this seemingly innocuous self-deception lies one of the most interesting and awesome aspects of human experience: We never really come into direct contact with reality. Everything we experience is a manufacture of our nervous systems.

Although there is never a perfect match between reality and one's perception of it, the range of disparity between reality and perception is considerable. When engineers are measuring, analyzing, testing, and the like, usually with the aid of precise gauges and instruments, their perceptions may be extremely close approximations of reality. This is basically why bridges, tunnels, and skyscrapers not only get built but generally stay built.

But when engineers, or anyone else, are relating to and communicating with other human beings—when they are operating in a world of feelings, attitudes, motives, values, aspirations, ideals, and emotions—they are playing in a very different league, and the match between reality and perceptions may be far from exact.

THE PROCESS OF PERCEPTION

The role of perception in the practice of communication is critical, so let's examine the perceptual process more closely.

To reword the basic premise: When one deals with people—for example, when you are coping with your professors, classmates, parents, relatives, friends, neighbors, spouse, children, boss, subordinates, colleagues, customers, strangers, enemies, and so forth—one never deals directly with *reality*.

Reality

I don't pretend to get any closer to whatever it is that we call "reality," but I do presume that it exists. And it does so largely independent of us. It occurs, for the most part, outside our skins.

Stimuli

Now this reality may give off certain *stimuli*—audible vibrations, visible lightwaves, smellable smells, and so on. But most stimuli never reach us. At this instant, there may be loud noises occurring—a tree falls, two cars collide, a dynamite charge is detonated. But if these events occur beyond our ken, then we are oblivious of them.

Sensation

But suppose we are in the right place, at the right time, and with appropriate sensory equipment; that is, properly functioning auditory systems, in this case. The stimuli impact upon our respective nervous systems and we sense, hear, in this instance. But *sensation*, itself, is a thoroughly meaningless experience. William James described it as a "great, blooming, buzzing mass of confusion." The infant in the crib is bombarded by all sorts of stimuli but is unable to make much meaning out of the barrage of sounds, sights, odors, and so forth.

Perception

It is only when we are able to and, indeed, do take the next step that the experience becomes meaningful: We perceive—we create meaning out of the sensory experiences we are having. Kreitner and Kinicki define *perception* as "a mental and cognitive process that enables us to interpret and understand our surroundings."[1]

That describes what perception does, but how does it get that way? Why do we perceive as we do? What is it that determines how you will perceive a given event—in addition to the event itself?

What about your mood at the moment of perception? Elated? Depressed? Relaxed? Tense? Apathetic? Angry? Wistful? Fearful? Embarrassed? Hopeful?

How about your physical state? Weary? Rested? Ill? Under the influence?

Does it make a difference who is present during the event—your boss, your spouse, your peers, your professor, your parents?

What do you have at stake? What do you stand to gain or lose by this event?

And your values? What have you come to consider as more or less important?

These are some of the potential influences on how one might perceive a given event. We can put virtually all of them under one broad heading—learning.[2]

Learning

This is *learning* in the broadest conceivable sense. I am talking not only about formal, classroom learning experiences—but about any experience, which can occur anywhere and at any time, that somehow teaches one how to perceive. Moreover, this teaching or conditioning or programming can occur at any level of consciousness—including nonconsciousness. A great deal of what we have learned, then, we have not been aware of learning.

I can demonstrate this if you will play a little word game with me. I'll make a statement and deliberately omit a word. Then you quickly jot down a word that pops into your head.

---

[1] Robert Kreitner and Angelo Kinicki, *Organizational Behavior* (Homewood, Ill.: Irwin/BPI, 1989), p. 109.

[2] One may argue that a physical state is not learned. But how we react to it certainly is. The hypochondriac may regard a cold as pneumonia, a headache as brain cancer, and so on.

Here's the scene: A young parent has just entered the living room and has discovered the four-year-old son with a large, black, permanent ink felt pen drawing pictures on the wall. The parent says: "Johnny! You've been a _____ boy!" Supply a word for the blank.

According to cultural anthropologists, play this game with English-speaking people and the large percentage of the responses will be the words "bad" or "naughty." The issue is seen as one of morality and the usual admonition is "don't be bad" or, conversely, "be good." Greek-speaking and Italian-speaking people similarly respond. However, this perception is not universal. In lieu of "Johnny, be good," the French say: "Jean, sois sage"—be wise—or, by implication, don't be stupid or foolish or imprudent. Scandinavians speak differently. A Swede would typically say: "Jan, var snel," while a Norwegian says: "Jen, ble snil." They mean the same—be kind—don't be mean. In Germany, it is still different—at least in the so-called Prussian part of Germany—where the usual expression is "Hans, sei artig"—get back in line, conform.

Let these people observe the youngster decorating the wall and you can confidently predict that they will all disapprove—but they will do so for differing reasons. And they have been *taught* these reasons—these perceptions—subtly but effectively by their respective cultures.

Travel has tremendous potential for self-learning. When you are suddenly deposited in another culture, you can become aware of some of the lessons you have unconsciously absorbed from your own. When you recognize what other cultures are incessantly teaching their respective residents, you can become more sensitive to what has been subtly but effectively programmed into you.

And the learning need not stop when you return home. Your heightened awareness will help you identify the unique, unchallenged, and often arbitrary nature of your own culture as your teacher. According to G. K. Chesterton, "The whole object of travel is not to set foot on foreign land; it is at least to set foot on one's own country as a foreign land."

Response

Thus, it is one's self-made meaning—this personalized perception that can be so extraordinarily affected by one's prior programming—that one most directly responds to or, more specifically, acts, thinks, or feels about.

PERCEPTUAL MODEL

The perceptual model is shown in Figure 4.1. It is simple but valid in that it depicts human response as only an *indirect* reaction to reality. That premise may be disquieting enough, but there is more to come. Because there are multiple stages between reality and response, there

FIGURE 4.1

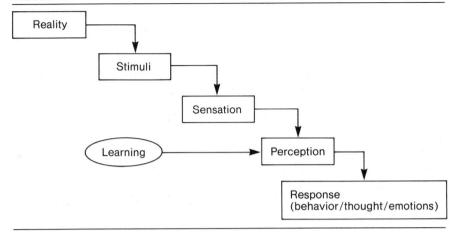

are also multiple opportunities for us to *differ* from each other as we go from step to step.

Differing Responses

To illustrate the latter proposition, consider a social unit—say, an industrial organization. Just as relevantly we could have selected other units—such as your college, your sorority or fraternity, or club, or even your family. But back to the industrial firm—just what is it? In addition to its physical and financial resources, the firm is basically a collection of individual human beings. Now let us consider how these individuals might differ among themselves as they move through the perceptual process.

Differing Stimuli.   Immediately, at the stimuli level, differences can occur. In fact, we decree them. We create elaborate organization charts with all sorts of boxes and layers and lines (solid and dotted) whereby we divide the reality. We say to various groups (and individuals):

"You people are in R&D, so you'll deal with this hunk of reality (these stimuli)."

"You're in our industrial engineering department, so here's your province (another set of stimuli)."

"You're in PR, so here's what you'll cope with (still other stimuli)."

"You're responsible for cost accounting so we want you to focus on these stimuli."

And on and on and on.

And this is one of the key dilemmas of organizations—task specialization and isolation. To be fair, it isn't really feasible for General Motors to employ 100,000 individual artisans—each of whom generates the requisite capital, designs a unique car, purchases or manufactures the parts for it and assembles them, tests and sells the cars, and arranges for customer financing. Parenthetically, there is some tendency to put the job back together again (or at least to enlarge it) as discussed in Chapter 3, but it is difficult to imagine an advanced ecomony without specialization. Unfortunately, specialization divides people, requires them to deal with particular stimuli, and the net results, too often, are sizable abysses between people who supposedly work in the same organization.

Without mentioning any names I can report that I have seen great gulfs between major functions in some companies. Here's a recent candid conversation:

> **Me:** I don't mean to be offensive but I get the impression that you folks here in the shop producing this product don't really work in quite the same firm as those people out there in the field who are selling it and servicing it and otherwise dealing with the customer.
>
> **Them:** Well, that's right. We don't really appreciate their embarrassment and tension when we fail to deliver on their promises. But at the same time, they don't really see what happens here—our pressures and frustrations and deadlines.

We already have discussed some of the ways organizations might bridge such chasms in Chapter 3, so let's leave the stimuli level for now and move on to the next phase.

Differing Sensations.   Let's be optimistic and say that the members of our mythical firm are "even," so far. That is, they have all been exposed to the same stimuli. Still they could *sense* them differently. There could be sensory variations among them. Suppose they all look at the cover of this book. If the group is typical, most of them will have normal color vision. Even so, will any two of them share an identical color experience? This is ultimately a subjective, inside-the-head experience and we simply do not know. Now add the more obvious sensory differences such as those that emanate from various forms of "color blindness" and from disease and injury. In my case, for example, I get different color experiences depending on which eye I'm using. One eye was banged up in what Archie Bunker lovingly calls WW II. And from it I get—not different colors—but much grayer, dimmer hues than from my good eye.

There is a fun way to demonstrate differing sensory equipment. Sometimes I will give each member of a class or seminar a small bit of paper. Each person is to chew it up and register any taste sensations. Typically, about 20 percent of the group will start looking for water, coffee, a Coke—

anything to wash away a distinctly bitter taste. Others will be puzzled by this, because for them the paper will be sweet. Still others find the paper to be sour, and a small percentage taste it as salty. And for about half the group, the paper is tasteless. So what is happening? The paper is impregnated with a chemical—phenylthiocarbamide (PTC)—which geneticists use to trace hereditary traits. Their contention: We may inherit varying sensory equipment, at least when it comes to tasting PTC.

There are indeed sensory variations among us but they probably aren't too pertinent for most of us unless, for example, one happens to be operating a restaurant, a perfumery, or a brewery.

Differing Perceptions.   In a sanguine mood, let us suppose that all of the members of our hypothetical organization have not only received the same stimuli—the same chunk of reality—but have similarly sensed them. However, they have one more hurdle and it is a formidable one—the very act of perceiving—of *imputting meaning to experience*. We have already considered some of the factors, under the comprehensive heading of learning, which can influence how one perceives. If the learning had differed, the perceiving is likely to differ as well.

For example, superiors and subordinates in organizations usually learn to perceive themselves and each other quite differently. A person looking downward in an organization may perceive very differently from a person below looking up. Rensis Likert of the Institute for Social Research (University of Michigan) reported that 85 percent of a sampling of supervisors estimated that their employees felt very free to chat about important aspects concerning the job with the boss. However, only 51 percent of their people shared this view. Seventy-three percent of the supervisors felt that they "always or almost always" solicited subordinates' thoughts regarding solution of job problems. Only 16 percent of their subordinates agreed with this appraisal. Ninety-five percent of the supervisors said they understood their people's problems, but only 34 percent of the latter felt they did.

Norman Maier, also of the University of Michigan, arrived at a similar conclusion that would be humorous, if it weren't so poignant. He studied 35 pairs of people from four large firms. A pair consisted of a manager, third echelon from the top, and an immediate subordinate. Each partner in each pair was questioned regarding the subordinate's job. On only one aspect was there substantial agreement—the content of the subordinate's duties. However, there was little agreement on the order of importance of these duties. There was only fair agreement on the job's requirements and almost complete disagreement on their priority ranking of these requirements. Finally, there was virtually no agreement on the problems and obstacles of the subordinate. These findings were discussed with all participants. Several months later, a questionnaire was sent to each participant, asking whether the superior and the respective subordinate had gotten together to discuss their differences. Only 22 pairs replied. Six of them agreed that they had gotten together; nine agreed that they had not; and seven pairs could not agree on whether they had or had not gotten together!

Unacknowledged Differences

So far we have two disturbing premises: (1) We never respond directly to reality and, consequently, (2) we can differ from each other at one or more of the steps (stimuli-sensation-perception) between reality and our response to it. This is why two or more people can respond differently to the same situation. Now, add a third element—lack of awareness and/or lack of acceptance of these two propositions—and we have a truly explosive potential for problems in interpersonal relations.

DEFENSIVENESS

So it is the failure to *acknowledge* these differences (differences between reality and one's perception of it . . . and differences of perceptions from person to person) that induces so much defensiveness within organizations and elsewhere. The prevailing, albeit largely unconscious, assumption is that "the world is as I see it." One who harbors this notion will find life continuously threatening, for there are many others who share this notion but **not the same world!** Such people find it perpetually necessary to protect *their* worlds and to deny or attack the other person's.

Admittedly, the premise that one deals only indirectly and often unreliably with reality can be upsetting. To those who crave a certain, definite, and dependable world (and that includes all of us in varying degrees), the admission that we respond only to what a thing appears to be rather than what it is necessarily lessens our ability to predict about the real world. Even those who intellectually accept the perception model and the roles that stimuli, sensation, learning, and so on play in determining responses may still have difficulty converting the concept into performance. A good test of the extent to which we have truly internalized such awareness occurs when we become emotionally involved with others.

For instance, suppose that A and B work in the same organization and that they observe Joe, one of their colleagues, taking home such company supplies as paper pads, paper clips, and pencils, not in large quantities, but more than he will need for official purposes. He will let the children have them, use them for his private affairs, and so on.

Now, let us say that A is the product of a rigorous, religious upbringing. He may regard Joe as dishonest. But suppose that B has none of that training and that the only part of his background that is particularly relevant is the time he spent in the Army—in particular, the months in the Middle East as part of Operation Desert Shield/Storm. There he discovered a code that was unwritten but very pervasive. It was, in effect, "You may rob the Army blind!—but you must not steal a nickel from another serviceman." He might regard Joe as honest and could readily consider his acquisitions as normal perquisites.

Let us examine the communication issue. (Permit me to disregard the moral issue without denying that there is one.) Consider the tremendous difficulty that A and B would have in discussing Joe if in their increasingly vehement statements, "Joe's dishonest!" "No, he's not!" they failed to realize that neither of them was talking about Joe. They were talking about A and B and their respective inside-the-skin experiences. Their respective worlds were different from the outset, and there was no reason to expect them to be identical—and no rational reason to have to protect them. Why, then, did they defend them so ardently?

Let us begin with an assertion: Most reasonably mature people can tolerate fairly well differences in value judgments, opinions, attitudes, points of view—as long as they can recognize them as such. If I can realize that your "reality" is not the same as mine, then your statement about *your* reality is no threat to *mine.*

But no one can tolerate differences on matters of objectivity—matters that can be submitted to corroborative measurement and are capable of general agreement. To illustrate, suppose that you and I have a mutual superior who comes to us and says: "This may sound silly, but I'm serious. I want you two to estimate the length of that two-by-four over there (about 20 feet away) on the ground. You have to estimate because you can't use any kind of measuring device and you can't get any closer to it than you are now. I want a good estimate and only one between you, so get to it!"

Now suppose the piece of lumber is actually seven feet long but neither of us knows that. So we start sizing up the situation, and you say, "Looks about 6-1/2 or 7 feet." And I say, "No, no—you're way short—that's a lot closer to 14 feet." Unless you have admirable constraint you would probably blurt out, "You're crazy!"

Now, why were you moved to feel that I was crazy?

Was it not partly because my statement was at least a slight threat to your sense of reality and, therefore, your sanity? In other words, if I were indeed right—that is, if the board actually were 14 feet and everything were actually twice as big as you perceive it—would you not begin to have serious misgivings about *your* contact with reality? Thus, "You're crazy!" is your understandable if impulsive way of defending yourself against an attack on your sanity.

Actually, we are unlikely to have such a disparity (unless one or both of us were indeed losing touch with reality) because our perceptual lessons, when we initially learned to perceive the inch, the foot, and the yard, were likely to have been very similar, regardless of where or when we learned them. And even if we were to disagree on such matters as distance, speed, and weight, we could resolve our differences by using standardized measuring devices.

But when we encounter Cézanne and Grandma Moses, Ernest Hemingway and Barbara Cartland, Wolfgang Mozart and Paul McCartney,

Enrico Caruso and Madonna, we are unlikely to have had identical learning experiences, and where are the standardized measuring devices? Will someone resolve a controversy with "Why, that Van Gogh is 87 percent beautiful"? Even professional critics are unable to provide universally acceptable and applicable criteria.

The point is that not only can we not tolerate differences in matters of objectivity (although what differences there may be are generally minor or resolvable by objective measurement), but we cannot accept differences on matters of subjectivity (value judgments, opinions, and so on) if we unconsciously treat them as matters of objectivity. Many important aspects of our lives such as art, music, architecture, religion, politics, morals, fashions, food, and economic and political theory, (1) are not taught to us in standardized lessons and (2) are not, by and large, measurable by standardized scales or gauges. It is in such areas that we find it easiest to threaten one another. And when we are threatened we tend, if we do not run, to fight back—the threatener is now threatened, and the stage is set for an escalation of conflict. This progressive conflict, the "vicious pendulum," is discussed in Chapter 13.

Defensiveness appears to be so pervasive and potentially so destructive to organizational communication and interpersonal relationships that we shall examine it in the next chapter in terms of the communicator's *frame of reference* and then again in Chapter 6 in connection with increasing the validity of one's *self-image*.

SUMMARY

We have depicted human behavior as most immediately determined by the individual's programmed perception of experience. Behavior, then, is only indirectly a response to reality. One who cannot tolerate this basic uncertainty of life and who assumes that his or her world is the only real world may find that "world" in almost constant jeopardy. Closed and defensive, one may respond to the threats with irrational attack and/or flight.

We have conceded that many organizations are populated to some extent with more or less defensive (and thus often aggressive) people. Therefore, the challenge to anyone who aspires to be an effective leader or member of an organization (or, more broadly, wishes to live an emotionally mature and deeply satisfying life) might be phrased as follows:

1. Can one come to accept the fact that his/her and everyone else's "reality" is subjective, incomplete, unique, and to some extent, distorted? Can one, therefore, muster the courage to become open and nondefensive—to permit even contrary cues to reach one and to begin to revise, update, and make more valid one's concept of reality?

2. Having clarified one's own perceptions, can one learn to assess accurately the worlds of others? Can the manager, for example, realize the simple but profound truth that his/her subordinates' worlds have him/her in it as a boss, whereas the manager's world does not?

In Chapter 5, we will examine how we can meet these challenges.

PERCEPTUAL ILLUSIONS

The following illusions illustrate the role of *learning* in distorting perception.

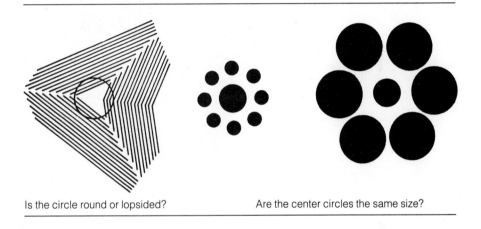

Is the circle round or lopsided?   Are the center circles the same size?

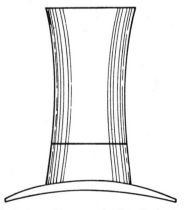

Is the vertical dimension of the hat equal to or greater than the horizontal?

Are the letters parallel?

Are the checkers parallel?

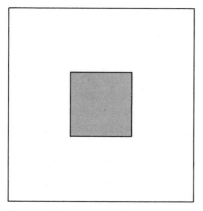

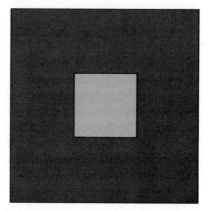

Note how the backgrounds determine set in perceiving the center squares, which are the same shade of gray.

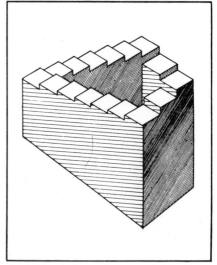

In these illusions we perceive the *two-dimensional depictions* as *three-dimensional objects*. The impossible staircase is disturbing because we have been programmed to accept the shading of the walls as representing depth.

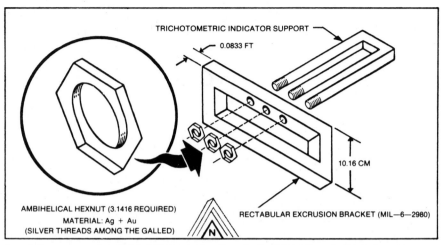

An article was recently published listing instructions for the fabrication of a Trichotometric Indicator. However, it seems that some difficulty is being experienced with the brackets which attach the indicator. As an aid toward fabricating the indicator brackets, the above illustration has been provided. It will be noted that in attaching the bracket to the indicator, a special ambihelical hexnut is used. The application of this nut is rather unique in that any attempt to remove it in the conventional manner only tightens it. Because of this design, the nut must be fully screwed on before it can be screwed off.

Sources: The illusions on pp. 79–80 are reprinted with permission from *Observation . . . Perception* published by E.I. du Pont de Nemours & Co., Wilmington, Delaware.

The "impossible staircase" is reprinted with permission from L.S. Penrose and R. Penrose. "Impossible Objects: A Special Type of Illusion." *British Journal of Psychology*, 49, 31 (1958).

The "Trichotometric Indicator Bracket" is courtesy of NAA "Operations & Service News." From *Approach*, May 1965.

REPERCEIVING

Some simple drawings are shown on the next page. Chances are the moment you look at them, you will traverse the perceptual process in an instant: The *stimuli* in the form of light waves will bounce off the page into your eyes and you will *sense*—you will see—then, almost immediately, you will *perceive*—create a meaning for each of the drawings.

Then glance below the drawings for labels for each of them. If any label, not that it is any better or worse, happens to differ from your original perception, note how quickly you reorganize the pictorial data inside your own head and arrive at another perception. Keep in mind, though, that you are creating the new meaning; you are *reperceiving*. The stimuli and the sensing, after all, remain the same.

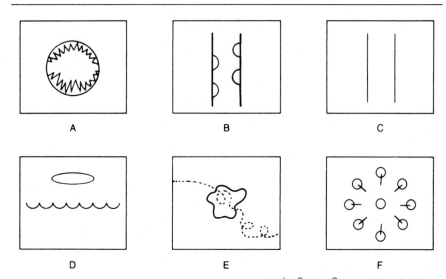

A—a vicious circle; B—large bear climbing a tree; C—small bear climbing a tree; D—a saint who thought he could walk on water; E—column of ants marching through a puddle of scotch; F—not too bright firing squad.

Discussion Questions

1. What is the point of the cartoon at the beginning of this chapter?

2. "We never really come into direct contact with reality"? What is meant by that statement? Do you agree?

3. Perception has been described as leading to "a meaningful and coherent picture of the world." Does that suggest that meaning does not exist until perception has taken place?

4. Recalling the example of the child with the black felt pen being perceived by people from differing cultures, what special problems confront United Nations members, or the personnel of multinational organizations who live and work in a foreign culture, or others who communicate cross-culturally?

5. What does the *acknowledgment of differences* have to do with *defensiveness?*

6. At this writing, 25 wars are in process. Most of them, gratefully, are small, although that doesn't make their victims any less homeless, maimed, or dead. How does the perception model help explain this mutually ruinous behavior?

7. To communicate well with someone, you must agree with that person's perceptions. How do you respond to that assertion?

C A S E S

Case 4.1

Lynn Barfield*

Lynn: My name is Lynn Barfield and I'm 36. I'm single now but there's a 50-50 chance I'll be married within six months.

Interviewer: Had you been married before?

L: Once. I was 19. My father was dying; my sister had cancer; and my mother was a basket case. I suffered, too—a bleeding ulcer. I needed a strong shoulder to lean on and Bob seemed ideal.

He turned out to have an alcohol problem. I should have recognized it—big man in the frat, and so on. And there was also verbal and physical abuse toward the end. But don't get me wrong. He's basically a fine man.

At any rate we were divorced after eight years of marriage. But I can honestly say that we are still friends.

I: Any children?

L: None.

Education

I: How about your collegiate background?

L: I received a bachelor's in Upper Elementary Education from a university in California. I then taught 7th and 8th grades for six years in various locations in California. During that time I got a master's in Administration/Supervision from a large California university. That was 12 years ago.

I: Then what?

L: Nine years ago I moved here (another large state university on the West Coast) and started on a Ph.D. I had an assistantship in the College of Education. My major interest was Curriculum and Instruction. My collateral was Continuing Education and Management. Researchwise my focus was on Survey Research and Computer Programming.

I: How far along are you on the doctorate?

L: I completed all my course work and prelims and I've written three chapters on my dissertation. The dissertation has been on the back burner for the past five years but I've started up on it again.

I: So all that remains is part of a dissertation?

L: Right. The research is completed; only the writing remains.

I: The subject?

---

* All names are disguised.

L: Internal management training for industry. I'm trying to deter-mine the critical components of planning, implementing and eval-uating successful managment training.

I: An the emphasis is on internal as opposed to external training?

L: Correct.

I: You say the dissertation has been on the back burner. Why?

L: Well, partly because I've got this job which takes all my time and energy. But to be utterly honest it partly traces back to my gradu-ate committee. One member was clearly against me. I think of it as sex discrimination more than anything else.

I: Care to elaborate?

L: Privately, he made it clear to me that women weren't supposed to get doctorates—not as long as *he* had anything to say about it.

I: How did the other committee members feel about that?

L: I really don't think they realized just how prejudiced he was. He was a cagey old bastard. (*Pause.*) Well, following my Ph.D. course work I took a job as management trainer in the university's Per-sonnel Department. I was there about four years. Then I came here to the Management Training Center, which is part of the university's College of Business Administration.

Management Training Center

I: What was MTC's organization at that time?

L: That was five years ago. I'll draw you a chart:

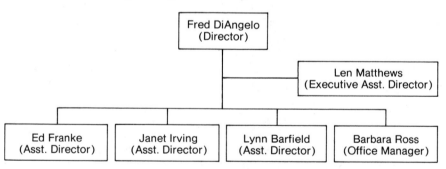

Six months later, Fred left and Len replaced him. Nobody filled Len's old job. Then a year after that Janet left and was replaced by Dave Munson. At that point Ed, Dave, and I were named associate directors.

I: Was that only a name change—or were there changes in authority, responsibility, salary, personnel, and so forth?

L: Let me back up. When I first joined MTC I had no one reporting to me. I was strictly a bureaucrat. My concern was solely with such things as making sure that my courses were marketed well, that participants were properly registered, that my programs went well, and so on. There were training assistants who rotated among Ed, Janet, and me but they actually reported to the office manager. They were paid by the hour.

I: Then you, Ed, and Dave were named associate directors?

L: That's right. By this time, MTC was expanding greatly—more courses. Courses were offered more frequently. At this point teams were created. I now head up a team. Currently, I have three course administrators and a registrar reporting to me.

I: So now you're a boss?

L: Yes, and I don't like it. For one thing I tend to deal with my CAs as friends rather than as subordinates. If they're not performing up to par I tend to say nothing until the situation really gets out of hand. By that time the problem has become severe. If I had dealt with it earlier it could have been handled more constructively.

I: And your CAs are. . . ?

L: Evelyn, Sandra, and Susan. Ninety percent of my people-problems come from my dealings with them or with other internal people. When it comes to dealing with my clients or the faculty I have had virtually no problems. There are two other CAs—Jackie who reports to Ed, and Erin who reports to Dave.

I: Any problems there?

L: For me there are. Jackie was already here when I arrived and she had applied for the job that I got. So she's been resentful ever since. Jackie and Erin share an office and they're very close. So when one is mad at you, they're both mad at you.

I: How have you dealt with them?

L: By keeping our relationship strictly on a business level. In the past year I have refrained from all *personal* contact with them.

I: How's it been going with your own three CAs?

L: Better than it's been. Let me take them one at a time. First, Evelyn. We've always been close friends. And if anything goes wrong she tells me immediately and we sit down and sort it out. We're friends outside of work, too. I help her with her child, I give her clothes, and I help her out financially because she needs help from time to time. I've never had problems with Evelyn and she seems very honest with me.

Sandra has been very difficult to deal with. She doesn't joke or take a joke well. She tends to take literally something I only meant in jest. We've made a real effort in the last six months to understand each other better. And she is now more willing to question me when she's not sure about something.

I really have no problems with Susan, now. We're good friends. For a while, though, she sort of teamed up with Jackie and Erin. Then they hurt her feelings badly six months ago, so she left them and joined our team.

I: For the record, what are the office assignments?

L: Jackie and Erin share an office, Evelyn and Susan share an office, and Sandra is by herself. And, of course, Ed, Dave, and I each have our own office.

I: Evelyn and Sandra are black; everyone else you mentioned is white. Does that make a difference?

L: Not at all. They are both extraordinarily competent, and I respect each of them as individuals. Sandra has an outstanding character. She is very logical and organized and buttoned-down, whereas I tend to be more flighty. Maybe that's one of the reasons we've had difficulty with one another.

At this point Lynn had to excuse herself because of a previous appointment. She returned two hours later.

* * * * *

L: Can you tell me how this interview came about? Did Len ask you to talk to me?

I: No, it was entirely my idea. I explained to him that I wanted to talk to a woman who had achieved considerable status and I specifically mentioned you. He said that was great—he was very supportive.

L: That's fine. Where do we go from here?

I: Anything more on dealing with Jackie and Erin?

L: Well, Jackie wouldn't even talk to me for the first six months I was here. She apparently blamed me for taking the job that she had her heart set on. She ignored the fact that my job calls for a master's degree and she doesn't even have a bachelor's. Nevertheless, she still feels she could do the job—and she probably could.

And, of course, she and Erin are a unit. I like them but I don't trust them. For one thing, they're tremendous gossips. But that's a problem with the whole MTC, and Len is the biggest gossip of all. He doesn't mean to be malicious but he just loves to talk. And because he gossips, the culture of our organization has come to OK gossiping.

I: Anything more on Jackie and Erin?

L: Recall that period when Susan seemed to be teaming up with them against me? Do you know what they were telling her? That I was being unfair in distributing authority and responsibility—that she, Susan, was getting the short end of the stick.

I: And that was not true?

L: Not at all. Now, I do admit that to manage three is more difficult than to manage only one. Recall that Ed and Dave each have one CA to supervise.

I: You mentioned jealousy. Did that extend to salaries?

L: I'm sure it does. I make $46,500—so does Dave, I think. Ed, who has a doctorate and has been here longer than any of us, makes about $48,000. Barbara makes about $38,000.

I: And the CAs?

L: In the mid- to upper-20s. Everybody knows pretty much what everybody else makes. That information shouldn't have been shared but it was.

I: By whom?

L: Len. Back to the jealousy angle—Jackie reports to Ed and it doesn't seem to bother her that he and Dave make $20,000 more than she does. But I'm a woman so it does bother her there. Of course, we're close in age, too.

I: How are the salaries determined?

L: Yearly, Len submits a list for the Dean's approval.

I: How do you feel about your salary?

L: No complaint. But the major boost came through the efforts of Len's predecessor, Fred. He wasn't much as a director but he sure fought for us salarywise. We received a $10,000 raise one year because of Fred. Len isn't nearly as strong as Fred. In fact, I think he was chosen to replace Fred simply because it was felt that he could be controlled.

I: Len wouldn't have fought for you?

L: No. About three years ago we did an evaluation, and the two main things about Len that came through were that he could not be trusted to protect confidences and that he was gutless as a boss. He was horrified to find out how he was being perceived. But in fairness Len has made a real effort to change since that time. Of course, it's very difficult to change those early perceptions.

I: Until now we've been looking mostly down and up—how do you feel about your peers?

L: Let's begin with Ed. Rarely have I had any problems with Ed. We've had our disagreements but we've always worked them out.

   With Barbara, though, I have had some problems—at least in the past. She tends to make unilateral decisions and fails to take into account how those decisions will affect other people. When she would do that to me I'd go in and raise holy hell. All I can say is that I've not had a single problem with her in the past two years.

   Dave—I've had very few problems with him. By the way, he's got a master's—I forgot to mention that. The only problem I had with him was when we were restructuring management systems. At that point I believe he was trying to screw Ed and me to get ahead of us.

   The good part in dealing with Dave is that we've always been extremely honest with each other. For example, at that time I went into his office and shut the door and said: "Dave, you're try-ing to screw us." He was horrified, I'm sure he didn't perceive it that way.

So anytime one of us feels that the other is doing something wrong, we tell the other party and clear the air.

I: Can we return to your dealings with Len?

L: Well, we've gotten angry with each other but that's normal given the hours we work and the intense situations we've had to deal with. But we apologize later and everything is OK. It's just that I don't feel free to say things to Len because I don't trust that he'll keep things to himself. But when it comes to work matters I tell him very frankly the way I see it.

L: I gather you feel Len is not malicious—but indiscreet.

L: Exactly. Some people just like to talk. Incidentally, I don't think I mentioned it but Len is about 45, Ed is in his early 50s, Dave and Barbara are both about my age. Oh, one more thing about Len. When I first arrived, Janet warned me confidentially: "Len is very sweet and easy to work for. But don't ever get him mad at you because he will get revenge."

I: I'm aware the MTC has grown enormously in the last several years. I've heard that it currently does about six times the business it did just eight years ago. How would you express MTC's basic objective?

L: Our mission is to create and disseminate a framework of knowledge to industry; to enable them to enhance their effort toward more efficient and higher quality productivity. In short, to enable them to be more competitive. We're an advanced learning center with a research base.

I: Fair to say that MTC has a symbiotic relationship with industry?

L: Sure, they send executives and managers here and pay the freight. And we do a good job for them. But, of course, our "alums" then become salespeople for us and convince others that MTC is a good place to come to or to send people to.

Another point: Corporations frequently make contributions to the university, and we like to think that our efforts had something to do with their largesse.

Discussion Questions

1. How do you size up Lynn Barfield?
2. What are her perceptions?
3. How do you think Jackie and Erin regard Lynn?
4. What, if anything, should Len Matthews do now?

CASE 4.2

On a Certain Blindness in Human Beings*
William James

Some years ago, while journeying in the mountains in North Carolina, I passed by a large number of "coves," as they call them there, or heads of small valleys between the hills, which had been newly cleared and planted. The impression on my mind was one of unmitigated squalor. The settler had in every case cut down the more manageable trees, and left their charred stumps standing. The larger trees he had girdled and killed, in order that their foliage should not cast a shadow. He had then built a log cabin, plastering its chinks with clay, and had set up a tall zigzag rail fence around the scene of his havoc, to keep the pigs and cattle out. Finally, he had irregularly planted the intervals between the stumps and trees with Indian corn, which grew among the chips; and there he dwelt with his wife and babes—an axe, a gun, a few utensils, and some pigs and chickens feeding in the woods, being the sum total of his possessions.

The forest had been destroyed; and what had "improved" it out of existence was hideous, a sort of ulcer, without a single element of artificial grace to make up for the loss of Nature's beauty. Ugly, indeed, seemed the life of the squatter, scudding, as the sailors say, under bare poles, beginning again away back where our first ancestors started, and by hardly a single item the better off for all the achievements of the intervening generations.

Talk about going back to nature! I said to myself, oppressed by the dreariness, as I drove by. Talk of a country life for one's old age and for one's children! Never thus, with nothing but the bare ground and one's bare hands to fight the battle! Never, without the best spoils of culture woven in! The beauties and commodities gained by the centuries are sacred. They are our heritage and birthright. No modern person ought to be willing to live a day in such a state of rudimentariness and denudation.

Then I said to the mountaineer who was driving me, "What sort of people are they who have to make these new clearings?" "All of us," he replied. "Why, we ain't happy here, unless we are getting one of these coves under cultivation." I instantly felt that I had been losing the whole inward significance of the situation. Because to me the clearings spoke of naught but denudation, I thought that to those whose sturdy arms and obedient axes had made them they could tell no other story. But, when *they* looked on the hideous stumps, what they thought of was personal victory. The chips, the girdled trees, and the vile split rails spoke of honest sweat, persistent toil, and final reward. The cabin was a warrant of safety for self and wife and babes. In short, the clearing, which to me was a mere

---

* From *Essays in Faith and Morals*, by William James (New York: Longmans, Green, 1943). Reprinted by permission.

ugly picture on the retina, was to them a symbol redolent with moral memories and sang a very paean of duty, struggle, and success.

I had been as blind to the peculiar ideality of their conditions as they certainly would also have been to the ideality of mine, had they had a peep at my strange indoor academic ways of life at Cambridge.

Discussion Questions

1. How do you account for James's initial perception of the *improved coves?*

2. How was it possible for him to grasp the perceptions of the mountaineers?

3. Why might the Highlanders have found it difficult to appreciate or to feel comfortable in James's Cambridge surroundings?

4. How might the moral of this essay be applied elsewhere?

CASE 4.3

Is This Man Mad?*

Imagine that the individual described in the following brief case history came to you for treatment. How would you diagnose his ailment and what therapy would you recommend?

All through childhood, K. qas extremely meditative, usually preferred to be alone. He often had mysterious dreams and fits, during which he sometimes fainted. In late puberty, K. experienced elaborate auditory and visual hallucinations, uttered incoherent words, and had recurrent spells of sudden coma. He was frequently found running wildly through the countryside or eating the bark of trees and was known to throw himself with abandon into fire and water. On many occasions he wounded himself with knives or other weapons. K. believed he could "talk to spirits" and "chase ghosts." He was certain of his power over all sorts of supernatural forces.

The Actual Diagnosis

Believe it or not, K. was not found insane, nor was he committed to the nearest institution for the mentally ill. Instead, in due course, he became one of the leading and most respected members of his community.

How this strange turn of events could come about may become more plausible to you if we supply an important bit of information that was purposely left out of the case history above.

K., we should have told you, was a member of a primitive tribe of fishermen and reindeer herders who inhabit the arctic wilderness of Eastern Siberia. In this far-off culture the same kind of behavior that we regard as symptomatic of mental illness is considered evidence of an individual's fit-

---

* *State of Mind*, published by Ciba Pharmaceutical Products, Inc., Summit, N.J., 1, no. 1. Reprinted by permission.

ness for an important social position—that of medicine man or shaman.

The hallucinations, fits, manic episodes, and periods of almost complete withdrawal that marked his early years were considered signs that he had been chosen by some higher power for an exalted role. His behavioral eccentricities were, in fact, prerequisite to his becoming a shaman, just as balance, solidity, self-confidence, and aggressiveness are prerequisites for the young person who hopes to be successful in American business.

Sociologists and anthropologists explain that shamanism serves two socially useful purposes in Siberian society. In the first place, it provides an approved outlet for the person of unstable temperament. It allows him to let off steam through an emotionally satisfying dramatic performance in which he summons spirits and manipulates the supernatural. In the second place, shamanism provides entertainment for other tribesmen and welcome relief from the monotony of their bleak environment.

Discussion Questions

1. What is the main point of this case?
2. Does this case have broader implications for us?

CASE 4.4

Cultural Pitfalls

A good deal of Chapter 4 was concerned with how one's *learning* influences one's *perceptions* of and therefore one's *reaction* to experience.

A tremendous amount of this learning is programmed into us by our culture. Because we are constantly immersed in that culture we are rarely aware of what it has been—or is—teaching us.

Consequently, if we are to deal effectively with someone in—or from—another culture, it behooves us to understand not only our own culture but that of the other person, as well. At the very least we should be aware of some of the potential pitfalls in intercultural contacts. The following may be helpful.

Be Attuned to Business Etiquette[1]

The proverb, "When in Rome, do as the Romans do," applies to the business representative as well as the tourist. Being attuned to a country's business etiquette can make or break a sale, particularly in countries where thousand-year-old traditions can dictate the rules for proper behavior. Some of the considerations anyone interested in being a successful marketer should be aware of include:

---

[1] Source: *Foreign Agriculture*, U.S. Department of Agriculture, February 1987, pp. 18–19.

Local customer, etiquette, and protocol. (An exporter's behavior in a foreign country can reflect favorably or unfavorably on the exporter, the company, and even the sales potential for the product.)

Body language and facial expressions. (Often, actions do speak louder than words.)

Expressions of appreciation. (Giving and receiving gifts can be a touchy subject in many countries. Doing it badly may be worse than not doing it at all.)

Choices of words. (Knowing when and if to use slang, tell a joke, or just keep silent is important.)

The following informal test will help exporters rate their business etiquette. See how many of the following you can answer correctly. (Answers follow the last question.)

1. You are in a business meeting in an Arabian Gulf country. You are offered a small cup of bitter cardamom coffee. After your cup has been refilled several times, you decide you would rather not have any more. How do you decline the next cup offered to you?
   a. Place your palm over the top of the cup when the coffee pot is passed.
   b. Turn your empty cup upside down on the table.
   c. Hold the cup and twist your wrist from side to side.

2. In which of the following countries are you expected to be punctual for business meetings?
   a. Peru.
   b. Hong Kong.
   c. Japan.
   d. China.
   e. Morocco.

3. Gift giving is prevalent in Japanese society. A business acquaintance presents you with a small wrapped package. Do you:
   a. Open the present immediately and thank the giver?
   b. Thank the giver and open the present later?
   c. Suggest that the giver open the present for you?

4. In which of the following countries is tipping considered an insult?
   a. Great Britain.
   b. Iceland.
   c. Canada.

5. What is the normal workweek in Saudi Arabia?
   a. Monday through Friday.
   b. Friday through Tuesday.
   c. Saturday through Wednesday.

6. At a business meeting in Seoul, your Korean business associate hands you his calling card, which states his name in the traditional Korean order: Park Chul Su. How do you address him?

a. Mr. Park.

b. Mr. Chul.

c. Mr. Su.

7. In general, which of the following would be good topics of conversation in Latin American countries?

   a. Sports.

   b. Religion.

   c. Local politics.

   d. The weather.

   e. Travel.

8. In many countries, visitors often are entertained in the homes of clients. Taking flowers as a gift to the hostess is usually a safe way to express thanks for the hospitality. However, both the type and color of the flower can have an amorous, negative, or even ominous implication. Match the country where presenting them would be a social *faux pas.*

   a. Brazil.   1. Red roses.

   b. France.   2. Purple flowers.

   c. Switzerland.   3. Chrysanthemums.

9. In Middle Eastern countries, which hand does one use to accept or pass food?

   a. Right hand.

   b. Left hand.

   c. Either hand.

10. Body language is just as important as the spoken word in many countries. For example, in most countries, the thumbs-up sign means "OK." But in which of the following countries is the sign considered a rude gesture?

    a. Germany.

    b. Italy.

    c. Australia.

Answers: 1—*c.* It is also appropriate to leave the cup full. 2—*a, b, c, d,* and *e.* Even in countries where local custom does not stress promptness, overseas visitors should be prompt. 3—*b.* 4—*b.* 5—*c.* 6—*a.* The traditional Korean pattern is surname, followed by two given names. 7—*a, d* and *e.* 8—*a* and 2. Purple flowers are a sign of death in Brazil, as are chrysanthemums in France (*b* and 3). In Switzerland (*c* and 1), as well as in many other north European countries, red roses suggest romantic intentions. 9—*a.* Using the left hand would be a social gaffe. 10—*b.*

How's Your Business Etiquette?

8–10 Congratulations—you have obviously done your homework when it comes to doing business overseas.

5–7   While you have some sensitivity to the nuances of other cultures, you still might make some social errors that could cost you sales abroad.

1–4   Look out—you could be headed for trouble if you leave home without consulting the experts.

Where to Turn for Help

Whether you struck out completely in the business etiquette department of just want to polish your skills, there are several sources you can turn to for help.

Books. While two years ago business etiquette information may have been difficult to locate, most good bookstores today carry a variety of resource materials to help the traveling business representative.

Workshops and seminars. Many private business organizations and universities sponsor training sessions for the exporter interested in unraveling the mysteries of doing business abroad.

State marketing specialists. In some states, your first contact should be your state agriculture department, where international specialists there can pass on their expertise or put you in touch with someone who can.

* * * * *

For readings designed to help avoid cultural pitfalls, I suggest:

"Blunders Abroad," *Nation's Business*, March 1989, pp. 54–55.

"Capitalist Chic," *The Wall Street Journal*, June 10, 1988, p. A1.

Chesanow, Neil, "The Importance of Being Fluent—Or at Least Knowing a Few Words," *Hyatt Magazine*, November–December 1989, pp. 10–11.

Harris, Phillip R., and Robert T. Moran, *Managing Cultural Differences*, 2nd ed. Houston: Gulf Publishing, 1987.

Knotts, Rose, "Cross-Cultural Management: Transformations and Adaptations" *Business Horizons*, January–February 1989, pp. 29–33.

"Regulations Direct Ad Traffic Differently around the World" *Advertising World*, April–May 1988, pp. 39–40.

For an overall text on doing business internationally, I enthusiastically recommend:

Ball, Donald A., and Wendell H. McCulloch, Jr., *International Business: Introduction and Essentials*, 4th ed. Homewood, Ill.: Irwin/BPI, 1990.

CHAPTER FIVE

Perception and Communication
2. The Frame of Reference and the Self-Image

❄
❄
❄

We have examined the perceptual process in which we relate indirectly and imperfectly to reality. We now turn to the *frame of reference* concept: a singularly useful tool for helping one not only to understand and communicate with others, but also to understand and communicate with oneself.

YOUR SOLITARY CONFINEMENT CELL

Visualize that each person lives continuously in an individual, solitary, confinement cell. This person never gets out and no one ever comes to visit. The somber point is that no one ever gets inside your head and has experiences exactly as you do. At this highly personalized level, we are all isolated from one another. The most we can do is to *represent* what we are thinking or wishing or believing or dreading, and so on, by some form or other of communication.

The Stained-Glass Window

Let's get more optimistic. In your cell, there is a window—one aperture through which you have all of your contact with the rest of the world—including the people you deal with. The window is what behavioral scientists call your *frame of reference*.

Unfortunately, the window is not a pane of clear glass. If it were clear glass for everyone, I would anticipate a paradise on Earth in which we would all perceive reality realistically and deal with it appropriately. Thus there would be no wars, little if any crime or emotional disturbance, no hurt feelings or grudges or feuds or sabotage or strikes, no riots or mass burnings or pogroms, and certainly no prejudice.

Regrettably, what we have is much more like a stained-glass window filled with a variety of peculiarly tinted, distorting lenses. And the lenses are the products of the past. They represent the programmed—acquired— ways by which we distort our perceptions of reality. Having a stained- glass window is inevitable. After all, everyone has to be born in some par- ticular place at some particular time and thus will be exposed to and programmed by some special people. The earliest ones were probably called Momma and Daddy. Later came friends, other relatives, neighbors, classmates, instructors, and so forth. And each of these "teachers" had a unique stained-glass window.

The question, then, is not whether or not we have such windows but can we do anything about them? Are we destined to live out our lives peer- ing through such spurious media? Emphatically, no! We can cope with these delusions essentially the same way we deal with any distortion. Stick a pencil into a glass of water. The pencil will appear to bend abruptly. But if we can understand the nature of the deception—refrac- tion, in this case—we can learn to compensate for it. Thus, we can aim at where the pencil appears not to be and hit it.

To repeat: We can cope with distortion provided we can understand it and correct for it. This principle applies, albeit more profoundly, to the distortions in our respective frames of reference, as well.

The Self-Image. But here we must face up to a formidable challenge. In the center of one's frame of reference is a huge lens. More accurately, it's a complex of lenses. It is known as one's self-image.

The psychology of the self-image goes like this: When a human being is born (some would say *before* one is born) he or she begins to create an increasingly complicated, multifaceted, ambivalent, dynamic picture or concept or image of self. This image-manufacture is wholly unconscious at the onset, gradually becomes more conscious as the person matures, but probably never becomes a fully conscious activity.

Your self-image is your most precious possession. You never leave it behind. And you protect it accordingly. Some authorities contend that the most basic drive of humans is not self-preservation but self-image preservation.

Perhaps so, but let me raise another question. If your self-image is so all-fired important that you will protect it at virtually any cost, what, then, are you protecting it against? What is the most fundamental, grevi- ous threat to your, or anyone's, self-image?

Failure? Ridicule? Rejection? These can be quite painful, especially if you feel rather good about yourself. But there are people who are self- admitted losers, who don't and perhaps have never felt very positive about themselves. These are people for whom success, praise, and acceptance can be uncomfortable—even frightening.

The most severe menace to anyone's self-image is *change*—provided three conditions exist. To be truly threatening the change must be: (1) large enough, (2) quick enough, and (3) uncontrolled enough (uncontrolled, that is, by the possessor of the self-image).

So any big, sudden, uncontrolled change of self-image can be unbearably terrifying, regardless of the direction of the change. Perhaps the last part of that assertion seems dubious. Can we actually be appalled by excessively positive change?

Assume that you are a young man or woman, say 22 years old, who was graduated from college six months ago. At that time you took a position with a very large, prestigious organization, say IBM. And suppose that one evening you receive a phone call.

Operator: I have a long distance person-to-person call from Armonk, New York, for (your name).

You: This is he (or she). (To yourself: Armonk? That's IBM's head shed!)

Operator: Go ahead, sir.

Voice: Hello, is this (your name)?

You: Yes, who is this?

Voice: This is John Akers with the company in Armonk.

You: (Gulp! John F. Akers is the chairman of the board! And this voice squares with the one I recall from a videotape I saw during the orientation program!) Why . . . er . . . uh . . . yes, sir?

J.A.: I know this is rather sudden, but the President (another big name!) has just asked me to come to Washington to take over one of the Cabinet positions, and I can't refuse him. The point is, we need a replacement for me here, and the board has decided you're our man [or woman]!

You *(after five seconds of silence)*: I'm your wh-a-a-a-t!!?!?!?!?!

Assuming that you're convinced that this is not a case of mistaken identity or that Mr. Akers has not taken leave of his senses, how much sleep will you get tonight? May I suggest why that call could be highly disturbing for you? If (and try to accept this *if,* for the moment) Mr. Akers is *right*—that is, if, despite your youth and inexperience, you are that brilliant and competent, *so* good that you can go to Armonk and direct that huge, complex, multinational corporation—do you know what that means to you? It means that your *current* self-image is quite unrealistic, that your contact with reality is suspect; in short, your sanity is in question.

I grant that the phone call illustration is an absurd one—but it is absurd only in degree—not in kind. Organizations have frequent examples of individuals passing up promotions, balking at enlarged responsibilities, and in general resisting positive feedback—because those cues, albeit favorable, constituted too great a disparity from the individual's current self-image. In sum, one's self-image is threatened by big, sudden, uncontrolled change—whether the change is negative or positive. The basic threat comes across as: "You are *not* who you think you are—you do not have contact with reality!"

But how big, how sudden, and how uncontrolled must the change be in order to constitute a threat? The answer depends upon one's comfort zone.

The Comfort Zone. Consider the operation of a thermostat. It serenely maintains its status quo—that is, it continues to break or complete an electric circuit—until its comfort zone is violated. At this point the instrument "protects" itself by reversing itself—that is, it either closes or opens the circuit—which returns the temperature of the environment to the instrument's comfort zone.

There is a kind of thermostat in each of us that throws up defenses whenever the comfort zone of one's self-image is exceeded by feedback. This can be illustrated most concretely when the feedback is quantitative—as in a golf score.

Over the years my scores have fallen quite consistently in the 90 neighborhood. Visualizing myself as a 90 (plus or minus 5 strokes) shooter, I could readily accept any score from 85 to 95. 96, 97, 98? Also acceptable, but hardly elating, 99, 100, 101? I'm beginning to feel uncomfortable—am I slipping? And a 130? Unbelievable! That is the precise word for my reaction. That feedback is so discrepant from my self-image that, while I must concede the score, I would be compelled to defend against it—to deny its validity as a reflection of my ability. How? Like most duffers, I have an inexhaustible repertoire of rationalizations—bad weather (gusts up to seven MPH at times), poor groundskeeping (the fairway hadn't been mowed for a good eight hours), headache (how can they expect an invalid to play this game?), evil companions, and so forth.

My comfort zone has a limit in the positive direction, too. Suppose that, suddenly, one day I shoot a 70! Thrilling, worth six years of locker room stories, but again, incredible! And, psychologically, I would have to defend my self-image against this score as well—it just isn't me! My alibis are less developed here because I have had fewer occasions to use them, but "gigantic fluke," "my horoscope was just right," and "an enormous celestial error" come to mind.

There are no *specific* scores that abruptly turn me off—as happens with a thermostat. But there are *regions* of scores (the vicinities of 98 and 82, respectively) above or below which I cannot play without increasing uneasiness.

My self-image, then, is surrounded by a comfort zone—the margin of disparity between my self-image and feedback concerning it that I can currently tolerate without feeling compelled to be defensive. This is not to suggest that comfort zones or, for that matter, self-images do not change.

For example, if I really paid serious attention to my golf game (played every day, took lessons from a pro, and so forth), I am confident that I could significantly lower my scores. And after gradually (perhaps over a period of six months or so) moving into the lower 80s and upper 70s and playing there consistently, suppose that I were now to card a 70. Probably, I could now accept it—it might stretch my comfort zone, but it would not rupture it as it would have done before. The entire comfort zone would have shifted—but note that the change was in *small, gradual,* and above all, *self-controlled* increments—*I engineered my own change.*

Forming Images of Others

How about the images we form of others? How much time and energy do you spend creating, modifying, defending, discarding images of other people—especially of the key people in your life, such as parents, siblings, teachers, fiancé, friends, spouse, offspring, bosses, subordinates, colleagues, and customers? The question is difficult to answer in specific terms. So much of our image-making is a largely unconscious affair. Moreover, it is often a substantially nonrational process. But in addition to how we fashion the images and how much time and energy we spend doing it, the question arises: *Why?* What motives do you have for forming accurate images of others? Is it to:

Determine common ground with them?
Protect your own self-image?
Communicate with them?
Determine whether or not you wish to associate with them?
Use their performance to develop standards?
Win them over to your point of view?
Determine how much to trust them?
Understand them?
Determine how they can help and/or hurt you?
Help them grow?
Be liked, accepted, approved by them?
Please them? Satisfy their expectations of you?
Cooperate with them?
Determine how to compete successfully with them?
Sell to them?
Assign them to roles, duties, responsibilities?
Determine whether you should vote for them?
Know how to interact with them?
Use or manipulate them?
Encourage them?
Impress them favorably?

Evaluate them?

Satisfy your curiosity about them?

Protect yourself from them?

Learn from them? Emulate them?

Win their support?

Deceive them?

Assess their strengths and weaknesses?

Love them?

Be more comfortable with them?

Hone your image-making skills?

Know how to play "games" with them?

Protect the image that you desire them to have of yourself?

Categorize them in order to expedite relationships with them?

All of these motives (and a good many others) may be relevant at various times, depending upon who the other person is and his/her relationship to you. In the interest of manageability, this lengthy list can be compressed into three basic motives. You form an image of the other person because you need or want to:

1. *Predict his/her behavior*—or his/her reaction to your behavior. This, in turn, should enhance your ability to—
2. *Cope or deal with him/her* in whatever manner is required by the situation. Accordingly, you should be better able to—
3. *Satisfy your needs* in respect to the relationship. Needs are defined broadly here as including the kinds of needs you gratify when you do very selfless and altruistic things—as well as needs which are more self-centered.

To check the adequacy of that trimotive concept, consider this question: Do you recall a time when someone extremely important to you abruptly began to behave in ways that quite contradicted your image of that person? If so, do you recall how you felt at that time—what your emotions were? Fear? Disillusionment? Embarrassment? Bewilderment? Sense of betrayal? Rage? Depression? Guilt? Anxiety? Shock?

These are negative sentiments. Does it make a difference if that abrupt shift is in a positive direction; that is, suddenly the individual is behaving in ways that are far more favorable than your image led you to expect?

Suppose that you and I have a boss who is an utter tyrant, an absolute despot. However, one day, for no apparent reason, he or she walks into the office, wreathed in smiles, laughing and joking. You and I and our colleagues would leap to our feet, chirping: "Goody! The boss has finally turned over a new leaf!" Right? **WRONG!** Rampant suspicion reigns: "What's he or she up to?" or, more contemporaneously, "What's he or she *on?*"

We would dearly love to believe that a permanent change is in the offing, but we are not about to accept it on such limited data. The point is: We can work for an SOB—as long as he or she is a *consistent* SOB. That doesn't make it pleasant, but it may make it possible. As long as we can predict the behavior, we have a reasonable chance of coping in such a way as to satisfy our needs concerning the SOB.

Indeed, the individual who is most capable of contributing to your bleeding ulcer, your hypertension, or your emotional breakdown is a key person (such as your parent or boss or spouse) who turns it on and off *unpredictably.* If you are dependent upon this person for the satisfaction of essential needs in your life, you have a real problem. For to satisfy those needs, you must successfully cope with the individual; but to cope you must be able to predict that person's behavior and that is where the sequence breaks down. The prime basis upon which you predict the other person is your image of him or her, and it just isn't holding up.

The Self-Image Threatened

If a sudden, dramatic change of behavior on the part of another can destroy your image of that person, cost you your predictability about that person—and thus your capability regarding that person—and lead to painful, frightening, and destructive consequences, consider what could happen if you were suddenly to have your own self-image challenged.

You stand the risk of losing the ability to predict, control, and *know* yourself. It is difficult to imagine a greater internal upheaval than suddenly not to know oneself—to lose contact with oneself.

Anyone who has suffered through a deeply traumatic experience— whether related to a parent, a spouse, a child, school, religion, vocation, narcotics, alcoholism, job loss, illness, injury, lawsuit, and so forth—will probably find in retrospect that his or her self-image was being severely threatened.

The "Great Chemist."   My own experience is a case in point. As a high school freshman, I hit upon chemical research for a career. I was encouraged by an older boy I admired who also aspired to chemistry. He had built a laboratory in his basement, so of course I had to have one, too. I remember collecting hundreds of jars and bottles and other treasures that might somehow be useful in my lab. I can also recall spending hour after hour thoroughly enjoying mixing potions of every description, and some beyond description. (I recall without quite so much relish the time I brewed some chlorine and nearly gassed myself unconscious!)

I devoured the chemistry course in my junior year. I must admit to having felt rather smug during this period, for I had a ready response to the recurrent question from grown-ups: What are you going to be? Most of my friends had either a hazy answer or none at all. My self-image in this regard was forming and solidifying.

I was graduated from high school during World War II and immediately entered the service. Somehow the Army gave little consideration to young men who were long on aspiration but short on experience, and consequently I had three years of singularly nonchemical activities. In fact, most of my Army career was devoted to protecting our nation from invasion—invasion from Juarez, Mexico. (Let it be recorded that not one Japanese Zero reached El Paso, Texas!)

But none of these nonadventures dissuaded me. Finally, the war ended and I was discharged. I immediately enrolled in a chemical technology program at a university reputed in this field.

Suddenly, reality began to catch up with my self-image. I had not realized that a chemist was also expected to be a pretty fair mathematician. I had done well enough in high school math courses, but the Army years were nonmathematical as well as nonchemical. At any rate, I foolishly disregarded the math refresher course (my self-image said I didn't need a crutch) and charged headlong into college algebra, where I was in competition with students fresh from high school math. While I was rusty, it would be unfair to say that I didn't understand the math; I did get it, but usually about a week *after* the exams—poor timing! The net result was the first *D* I had ever received in my life. What was the consequence, did I trade in my self-image for a new model? Hardly; my comfort zone had been violated. Rather than yield, I fought tenaciously and found a ready explanation for my plight: Aside from the Army's rusting me, the instructor had it in for me. Among other evidences, he had a Scottish name, and I was convinced that he was anti-Irish!

I was practicing what some writers call perceptual defense. Confronted with feedback that challenged my self-image, I managed to distort the incoming data. Result: The feedback, which I misperceived in self-serving ways, was no longer a contradiction to my self-image. As a communication authority, David K. Berlo paraphrased the Bible: "Seek and ye shall find—whether it is there or not!"

The next quarter? I received a *C* in math. The instructor had an Irish name, but he didn't like me either! (I suspected that he was from Northern Ireland!) In the middle of the third quarter and another math *D,* my self-image had withstood all the onslaught from harsh reality that it could. And for two to three weeks (at the time it seemed like six months) I was in a state of unrelenting depression. I became very nervous and had difficulty eating, sleeping, and studying, which only intensified my problem. A large section of my self-image had been shot away. The most appalling aspect of the experience was that I realized that I didn't know myself.

I began to lose the ability to predict my behavior. Increasingly, I found myself exclaiming: "Now, why did I do *that*? That's not *me*!" Then came the hallucinations. I recall that on one or two occasions, I looked into a mirror and glimpsed someone else's face where mine was supposed to be! I was truly frightened, and for the first time sought counsel.

Ultimately, I took a battery of placement and aptitude tests, changed my major, and transferred to another university (closer to comforting home). Gradually, and often painfully, I constructed a revised self-image in which I could place some of that former faith and confidence.

The Great Chemist Debacle, then, is just one example of what can happen when a person undergoes a sudden (a few months versus seven years is sudden), dramatic, and uncontrolled change of self-image. For seven years I had been creating, nurturing, and cherishing a dream—a self-image that pictured me in my immaculate lab coat, inventing world-saving concoctions in my shimmering, crystalline laboratory, the walls of which were adorned with Nobel Prize plaques! Quadratic equations, cosines, and differential calculus were never in that picture!

Far from being a peripheral, avocational aspect, the Great Chemist was the core of my self-image. And when it was finally destroyed, I had nothing to replace it.

Resistance to Image Change. Anyone who has undergone a traumatic experience will understand why the individual generally resists image change—particularly sudden, dramatic, uncontrolled change. And herein lies one of the greatest obstacles to the full development of an effective communicator and, for that matter, an effective person. Psychiatrist Karen Horney contends that the neurotic process is a special form of human development that is the antithesis of healthy growth. Optimally, one's energies are directed toward realizing one's own potentialities. But under inner stress one becomes estranged from the real self and protects oneself by creating and protecting a false, idealized self, based on pride, but threatened by doubts, self-contempt, and self-hate.

Take the case of a high school friend. After graduation he, too, went into the service, but he was more fortunate (in a sense), for the Navy put him through three years of an engineering curriculum. Then the war was over, and he was discharged. But he decided that he did not care for engineering and could not bring himself to take a final year of course work to earn an engineering degree. And yet he could not bear the thought of starting all over again in another field. The net result was that, for all practical purposes, he did nothing. He took a clerical job in a nearby insurance firm and has been there ever since. Through the years, his perhaps largely unconscious philosophy of life has evidently been: "I can't stand another failure [he probably regarded not completing the engineering degree as a failure], and one sure way not to lose a race is not to enter it." In sum, here is a person who has apparently protected his invalid self-image at the cost of a stunted life.

The handicap of inaccurate self-knowledge and the unwillingness to reconstruct a more realistic self-image seem to be very widespread. In 35 years of organizational research and consulting, I have known scores, if not hundreds, of men (and some women), particularly in the middle echelons of their organizations, who seemed to have all the requisites for continued success—intelligence, education, experience, drive, ability, ambition. But they had one vital failing—they did not know themselves. The image they held of themselves was pitifully out of phase with that which they were projecting to others. They seemed chronically annoyed and/or bewildered by the reactions of others to them. What was happening? Because of their unrealistic self-images they found it too threatening to entertain contrary cues from other people. By fending off the reactions of others variously as "those malicious/crazy/misinformed/ornery/perverse/stupid people," they had been successful in perpetuating and even reinforcing their respective self-myths. Thus, they had ineffectualized themselves; squandered their nervous energies. The masterful Robert Burns captured the poignancy of self-deception two centuries ago:

Oh wad some power the giftie gie us
To see oursels as ithers see us!
It wad frae monie a blunder free us,
    An' foolish notion.

The ERSI

Why does this detailed consideration of the self-image appear in a text on communication and interpersonal relations? My principal assumption about most of the readers of this book is that they are currently working—or within a few years will be working—in organizations. I further assume that their positions will be people related, perhaps even people centered. Accordingly, they will probably deal with people from various socioeconomic strata, with differing ethnic, religious, technological, and educational backgrounds, who occupy a variety of positions within and outside of the organization—bosses and colleagues, perhaps subordinates, customers, sales personnel, union representatives, governmental regulatory officials, and so on.

To successfully discharge the responsibilities of a challenging, people-oriented position requires the possession of a more-than-ordinarily-realistic self-image—an exceptionally realistic self-image (ERSI, for short).

The various blessings associated with an ERSI and various approaches by which one can attain and maintain an ERSI are the province of the next chapter.

SUMMARY

The frame of reference concept was likened to a stained-glass window in a solitary confinement cell. Experience is severely limited; the window's size and orientation are finite; thus comparatively few stimuli can enter the cell. Moreover, experience is often distorted; the lenses in the window represent prior programmings—biases, values, preconceptions, and so on.

One can correct for distortion provided that one understands its nature. But the window's most significant lens, the individual's self-image presents a special problem: Self-perpetuation.

The peculiarity of the self-image is that it is can be threatened by *change*—sudden, dramatic, uncontrolled change (even if the change is favorable). The self-image is surrounded by a comfort zone that determines which inputs can be accepted or at least tolerated and which constitute excessive change. The latter inputs (even though they may be valid) are generally resisted and warded off by the individual's defense mechanisms.

The irony is that an unrealistic self-image can not only perpetuate itself but, deprived of corrective intelligence, can grow increasingly invalid.

We also form images of others primarily to predict them in order to cope more effectively with them so as to best satisfy our own needs with respect to them. These three basic motives apply to one's self-image as well. One needs to predict his/her own behavior, and so on. Traumatic image change, as exemplified by the Great Chemist Debacle, generally thwarts these motives and leads to stressful disorientation.

This chapter dwelt on the frame of reference and self-image constructs in order to provide a conceptual foundation by which a person preparing for or currently holding a people-oriented position could purposely strive for a progressively more realistic self-image.

Discussion Questions

1. The stained-glass window is a figurative analogy designed to clarify an aspect of human behavior. In what respect do you feel that it is a valid (or invalid) depiction?

2. The most fundamental threat to one's self-image is *change*. Do you agree? Disagree? Why?

3. Change of self-image is most harrowing if the change is big and fast and uncontrolled. Agree? Disagree? Why? Are there other important characteristics of change? Are they equally critical?

4. What was the point of the illustration involving IBM's John Akers' phone call?

5. A common complaint of the weekend golfer: "Why is it that whenever I burn up the front line, I blow up in the home stretch?" How could this behavior be explained in terms of the self-image and comfort zone concepts?

6. It was asserted that three primary motives for forming an image of others are to *predict* them in order to *cope* with them in order to *satisfy one's needs* with respect to them. Do you agree? Are there basic motives in addition to or in lieu of these three motives?

7. According to Horney, under inner stress, one becomes estranged from one's real self and spends oneself creating and protecting a false, idealized self, based on pride, but threatened by doubts, self-contempt, and self-hate. Does that strike you as a valid assertion? What might it have to do with communicating and relating to others?

8. "To successfully discharge the responsibilities of a challenging people-oriented position requires the possession of . . . an exceptionally realistic self-image." Do you agree or disagree with that assertion? Why? What particular advantages would maintaining an ERSI give someone?

CASES

CASE 5.1

Frank Corbett's Problem*

Frank Corbett, 41, was the managing partner of Corbett & Wilde, a rapidly growing advertising agency serving a large metropolitan area in the eastern United States. Corbett had been instrumental in the establishment of the firm, having merged his firm with that of Gordon Wilde, 36. There were 37 persons in the employ of the partners.

Frank Corbett, clearly the dominant partner in the firm, was a dynamic man, full of ideas and drive. Wilde, an artist, was a quiet person by temperament, content to let Frank Corbett manage the firm. "Frank is a dynamo," said Wilde. "He likes that sort of thing, and I prefer to work on the creative end." Corbett felt that Gordon Wilde was a topnotch commercial artist.

Of the account executives, Carlton Phelps was regarded by Frank Corbett as the most promising partnership material. In fact, Corbett felt that he would either have to make Carl Phelps a partner soon or run the risk of losing him.

Phelps, 35, came to Corbett & Wilde from a large nationwide advertising firm where he had been an account executive. Claiming that he was given no room for independence of action, he had resigned and applied to Frank Corbett for a position. Corbett hired him on the spot. Within three years, Phelps was made a senior account executive responsible for a considerable number of clients.

Some of the accounts which Phelps supervised were those he had brought in himself. And there seemed to be no doubt that he was highly popular with his clients. Corbett was continually hearing of the wonderful service clients were getting from Phelps.

Yet, Frank Corbett had come to believe that Carl Phelps was a very difficult problem indeed. So when he was approached by Alvin Mahoney, a university case writer, he was eager to unburden himself. These are his comments:

> I hired Carl because I thought he would be just the kind of man I wanted in this organization. He has a lot of drive and originality. Furthermore, I know I can trust him and depend on his loyalty. The way I operate, I need a loyal organization who will put my interests first all the time.
>
> He is positively sensational in the way he keeps the clients happy. And he even brings in new clients—quite a number of them.

---

* All names are disguised.

So what's the problem? I'll tell you. Carl has no feeling for the organization. He is the most unpopular man in the firm. My people feel that he pushes them around.

For example, he puts pressure on Harry Klein, the office manager, to get the people he wants, and, of course, those he wants are the topnotchers that everyone else wants, too. If Carl gets a person assigned to him that he doesn't want, he usually just sends him back to Harry. This is hard on the person, and so Harry feels that he can't assign any but our best people to Carl's accounts.

The other account executives claim that Carl doesn't train on the job. Instead he grabs off the people that they have trained. They complain that Carl doesn't pull his own weight.

When a client asks Carl for a special favor, you should see him operate. He is a past master at getting other people to give service to *his* clients. For example, he may get a request from a client to speed up a magazine layout—say, from next week to tomorrow night. He goes straight to the artists, photographers, copywriters, and so on, until he gets *his* work done. Of course, other people's work gets put aside.

It doesn't make any difference to Carl that he has kicked the schedule to pieces and gotten everybody mad at him. Of course, the client is enthusiastic and recommends Carl and the firm to new clients.

Everyone says they like Carl personally, but it is impossible to work with him. I suppose there is some jealousy of him, too.

I have talked with Carl many times about this. I've given him hell, pleaded with him, tried patiently to point out the results of the way he operates. For maybe a week after one of those sessions, he will be better, and I begin to think that things will work out, and then, bang, he's off again and has people mad at him.

I suppose that in many respects Carl is like me. I can appreciate what he is doing and why he is doing it. I didn't get where I am by being a pantywaist. If I wasn't managing partner, with all that that means in getting things done, I suppose I might do just about what Carl does. You see, I have a lot of sympathy for his point of view.

So, I guess you can see my problem. Should I fire Carl? That doesn't make too much sense. In fact, Carl should probably be a partner—if not immediately, then soon. Here is a man who has real talents and abilities. He is valuable. Yet he is a liability, too. Should I order him to work with the organization, or else? What would that do to his enthusiasm and the enthusiasm of the clients who are so crazy about him? And I might find myself in a position where I'd have to fire him.

But if I just let things go, isn't there real danger to my organization? My staff will think I have given Carl the green light, and maybe they will transfer their antagonism to me. I can't afford that.

Having expressed himself, Frank Corbett seemed relieved. He added, "I suppose you are going to have these remarks typed up. I suggest you show them to Harry Klein and get his views."

Mahoney did just that. Klein read through the transcript, thought for a moment, and said:

> Well, it is a difficult thing to put into words, but I feel that basically Carl Phelps is one of the most selfish men I have ever known. He is not selfish in the ordinary sense of the word, but rather in his all-consuming conviction that everything is important only to the extent that it affects him personally. In many ways he is genuinely friendly and generous. On many occasions he has been most considerate and helpful to individuals in this firm. But beneath it all, I'm convinced that each action he takes is unconsciously linked with his own personal progress. I doubt very seriously if he ever realizes it, because he had been brought up that way.
>
> Carl is generally regarded in the firm as the man most likely to be taken into the partnership. Not that this is popular with the staff, but they feel pretty helpless about it because he is Frank's fair-haired boy. It seems to me that if the partners make him a partner, they will be making a mistake. Carl is a man of inherent narrowness of purpose, and the firm will suffer.

Discussion Questions

1. What are the frames of reference of the people in this case? That is, how do they perceive what is going on?

2. Is anyone's self-image being threatened in this case?

3. What should Frank do?

CASE 5.2

The Cocktail Party*

The following conversation occurred between Fred Lyons and William Baird at a cocktail party. Both men were in their early 30s. Lyons had been practicing dentistry for six years, and Baird had just been graduated from law school. Each man had worked part time to supplement his income during his years in college. They had known each other on a casual basis for about a year.

Lyons: Well, Bill, I hear you're about to take your bar examinations. What are your plans if you get by them?

Baird: There's no *if* about it, Fred. But to answer your question, I'm lining up a practice right now.

Lyons: Do you mean to tell me you have no doubts about passing the bar?

---

* Adapted from a case prepared by Eleanor Lynch Roeser. Printed by permission.

Baird: None, really. This is the way I look at it: I attended one of the better law schools in the country, and I was one of the better people in my class. So I really don't have any qualms at all.

Lyons *(Slightly sarcastically):* And I suppose you have no qualms about succeeding in law, in general?

Baird: No, I'm really quite confident that I'll make a go of it.

Lyons: Well, buddy, you've got a lot to learn. [He then began to recount at length some of his own difficulties and disappointments in starting in his profession.] And when you come right down to it, it's a plenty tough uphill climb to establish a reputation and a following. Frankly, Bill, you're going to have trouble attracting a clientele with this superconfidence of yours.

Baird: There's where you're dead wrong. You have to have assurance and confidence in yourself, or no one else will have confidence in you. Do you think a person would want his legal problems handled by a fellow who didn't give the appearance that he was dead certain he knew what he was doing?

Lyons: To be honest, I think the average person would be repelled rather than attracted by this attitude. Here, I'll give you a test. Suppose I come to you with a problem. [He then posed a legal question concerning income tax.] How would you handle it?

Baird: I can't give you an opinion on that. I'd have to have a good many more facts, and I'd have to study them.

Lyons: Now, do you see? Be honest with yourself, Bill. You don't have the experience, and if you parade around with that cocksure attitude of yours, you're not going to get to first base.

Baird *(Both men were somewhat angered by now):* Now listen, Fred. Law is a science of the mind. Dentistry is more of a mechanical science where you might expect to solve some problems immediately. And even in dentistry you can't pass judgment on an oral problem without an examination and maybe even an X ray.

Lyons: Well, all I can say, Bill—if you don't learn a more humble approach; if you don't bring your speaking and attitude down to the level of the average person, you're asking for trouble.

Baird: Well, if you ask me, the "average person" isn't going to have much confidence in anyone who is *too* average.

The afternoon was saved by a third person who broke into the conversation and managed to switch the subject to baseball.

Discussion Questions

1. Why did Baird respond, as he did, to Lyons' original three questions?
2. Why did Lyons disagree with these responses?

3. What might have happened had a third party not distracted the two men?

4. Assuming the absence of the third party, how might either Lyons or Baird have averted a "vicious pendulum"? (See Chapter 13.)

CASE 5.3

The Sally Port Episode

> One of the real questions facing working people is how much to suck up to the boss. Do you give him the treatment he deserves (utter contempt) or the treatment he expects (slavish devotion)? Most people reach a simple solution: You show devotion to his face and contempt to his back.*

That's one way of resolving it. But what do you do when your boss's expectations conflict with getting your job done correctly?

Here's what happened, according to Simon:

Scene: The rear sally port (area between the outer and inner gates) at the Pontiac (Illinois) Correctional Center—a prison.

Principal characters: Michael Lane, director of the Corrections Department. Kevin Finefield, 24, a guard.

Finefield's duties include searching incoming and outgoing vehicles in the sally port. The objective is to prevent guns, drugs, liquor, and so forth from being smuggled into the prison—and, more important, to intercept any prisoners from being smuggled out of it.

On the day in question, Finefield was checking an outgoing truck. Lane approached the gate. He concedes that there was no emergency and that he was in no hurry.

Lane's Version. "I came in the back way. I walked up to the gate where the guard was searching a truck in the sally port. The truck was on its way out of prison. I was not impatient. It was evident to me that the guard noticed me when I was approaching. I was with the Deputy Director of Adult Institutions. We both wore suits.

"I waited. And after a while I said: 'Officer, get the gate.' I asked to be let in. The guard didn't do it. So I identified myself. I said, 'This is Director Lane. Open the gate.'

"The guard did not have a conversation with me. I must have waited a total of six minutes. There were some inmates who were close enough to monitor what was going on. A correctional captain appeared on the scene and got the guy to open the gate. I went in."

---

* Roger Simon, "Guard Does His Job, Gets the Gate," *Chicago Sun Times*, May 17, 1984, p. 7.

Lane immediately complained to the warden and shortly thereafter Finefield was told that he was suspended pending discharge and was escorted out of the prison.

Finefield's Version.   "I had a bread truck coming out and I had to check it. I was doing that when I heard this voice say, 'Open up.' I said: 'Sir, you'll have to wait.'

"Then the guy says, 'I'm Michael Lane and I'm giving you a direct order: Open up.' I said, 'Sir, I can't do that until I'm done searching the truck. A prisoner might escape.'

"I had to go underneath the truck—there's a pit—to make sure nobody was hiding under there and I had to search behind all the racks in the truck. Well, Lane didn't have to wait more than five minutes. But when he came in, he was screaming. Fifteen minutes later, I was escorted out of the prison.

"You know, I was accidentally shot by a tower officer a while ago. He fired his shotgun and it ricocheted and hit me. I didn't sue the state. I just do my job and it's a tough job.

"I have an 18-month-old daughter at home and now I'm fired. All I was doing was trying to make Lane look good. I was trying to keep prisoners from escaping."

Norma Duba's Version.   Norma Duba, representing the American Federation of State, County, and Municipal Employees, spoke in Finefield's behalf:

"The Corrections Department sometimes does check to see if everybody is doing his job. Previously at Pontiac, a correctional official hid in a truck to see if the guard would find him. The guard did. For all Finefield knew, Lane was checking security.

"You can't interrupt a search, because if you do, a prisoner can slip into the area you've already searched.

"This is just an ego thing. Lane's ego was hurt and so he hands down this extreme punishment. The simple question is which is more important: Lane's ego or the security at Pontiac?"

Lane's Response.   "This man was clearly insubordinate to me, his superior. My conduct does not show ego or arrogance. I waited and waited and waited. I am running a paramilitary-type organization and I cannot allow this kind of thing to happen."

Is there a moral in all of this? Simon thinks so:

Take care of the boss before you take care of your job.
And, while you're at it, it wouldn't hurt to click your heels.[1]

---

[1] Ibid.

Sequel. According to a source who did not wish to be identified, Finefield was discharged. In November 1984, his case was appealed. A settlement was reached. Finefield was reinstated but he was placed on suspension for 25 days. He returned to the job, served a few days, then resigned.

Discussion Questions
1. Just what is the problem here?
2. What do self-images have to do with this case?
3. How objective was Simon?
4. How might this type of episode be prevented from recurring?

CASE 5.4

Nancy Sawyer*

Nancy Sawyer had risen rapidly in the Coleridge Corporation, a large insurance company headquartered in Hartford (Connecticut). She had joined the firm immediately after receiving a law degree from a prestigious midwestern university. She was 25 at the time. Previously, she had earned an M.B.A. from the same university.

Sawyer was clearly considered fast-track material. She had moved through several of the major functions of the company: claims, underwriting, and marketing. She had also had brief stints in actuarial, investment, and EDP. Currently, she was the claims department vice president.

Today, President Richard Schramm called her into his office. Schramm tapped his fingers together as he invariably did when he was about to propose an idea.

"Nancy, I have an idea I'd like you to mull over. As you know, we've acquired the Dolton company, a smallish life company, about a month ago."

"Yes, sir. They're in Milwaukee, right?"

"Yes, but what you don't know is that we're thinking about sending you out there to turn that situation around for us."

"You mean as a trouble-shooter?"

Schramm looked out the window briefly, then swung back to Nancy.

"Well, yes, but as a permanent assignment. You'd move out there. You'd be the CEO."

Sawyer was stunned; she hoped it didn't show. Her feelings were mixed.

"Wow! Milwaukee's a long way from Hartford! . . ."

"It is indeed . . . about 850 miles, I should say."

---

* All names are disguised.

Nancy recovered. "Of course, it's my old stomping ground, it's the area where I went to school."

"That's part of the reason we thought of you. You're basically a Midwesterner. Some of our Eastern types might have a little trouble fitting in."

"Well, this is quite a development, Dick. I knew we had Dolton, of course, but it never occurred to me . . . ."

"What about John?" John Swanson was her husband; they had no children. "Think he'd go for it?"

"Well, I really don't know . . . he's a Midwesterner, too . . . we'd have to talk about it."

"Certainly."

"Of course, there are plenty of hospitals in Milwaukee. I just don't know how he'd react to a move."

"Why don't you two talk it over . . . we have some good contacts in Milwaukee who could help him line up something. What is he now, associate administrator at Mercy General?"

"That's right. Another thing, too . . . he's awfully close to finishing up on his M.H.A. here."

"Well, you'd surely want to take that into consideration. So why don't you talk it over with him . . . of course, this assumes that you're interested . . ."

"I'm certainly interested, but this all comes from out of the blue . . . I knew of the acquisition, but I had no idea that I was being considered. . . ."

"I know. Chet (Chester Rizzo, executive vice president) and I have been keeping this under wraps. Frankly, there are people around here who think they should be tapped, and some of them have quite a few years on you. And, of course, most of them are men . . . ."

"Oh, yes . . . I've been wrestling with that one for the last 10 years. I keep trying to remind myself that these are the years I'll be able to tell my granddaughters about!"

"I realize some of the crap you've had to put up with, Nancy. But I think you've handled it beautifully."

Nancy was touched. "Well, thank you, Dick, I appreciate that."

"And, frankly, that's another reason why Chet and I thought of you. We know you can handle yourself. You'd be president of the subsidiary and let's see . . . salary . . . you're what? . . . $60,000?"

"62."

"Okay, let's say you start in Milwaukee at 75 . . . oh, hell! Let's not be chintzy . . . make it 80. And, of course, there'd be increased stock options, profit sharing, pension benefits, and so on. And that's just the start of it if things pan out."

Nancy's face fell. "That's very generous, Dick . . . but do you think there'll be a problem?"

Schramm pursed his lips. "Well, not really . . . but, after all, Dolton is a bit of a bag of worms. Otherwise, we couldn't have bought it at a discount."

Schramm and Sawyer continued to discuss details. A half hour later, Schramm concluded the conference. "So Nancy, why don't you and John hash it over . . . . What would be a reasonable deadline . . . two weeks?"

"Yes, Dick, I'm sure I can give you an answer within that time."

"Excellent. Keep it on the Q.T. and get back to me or Chet if you need any additional fill-in."

They rose and shook hands. Sawyer left the president's office and headed for her own. She was elated, yet troubled. The money—the challenge—they were exciting. But how would John react? Perhaps he would welcome it. He had seemed somewhat restive during the past year. He was basically happy at Mercy but with a young administrator in charge, he recognized he was in a deadend job—at least for the near term.

And how about herself? She had heard rumors about Dolton's "bag of worms." How would they take to a woman—and a young one at that? What if she took the job and flopped? She had never had so much responsibility and autonomy. Milwaukee was a long way from Hartford . . . and Dick. She was acutely aware that Dick had been her informal mentor over the years. He had known Nancy's father intimately and she always felt Dick had had a personal concern for her development and welfare. Could she stand alone?

And what if she turned down the offer? Would that derail her from Coleridge's fast track?

Nancy Sawyer felt she had a great deal of thinking to do.

Discussion Questions

1. What should Nancy Sawyer consider in reaching her decision about the Dolton Company?

2. What does Sawyer's self-image have to do with this case?

CHAPTER SIX

Perception and Communication
3. The Exceptionally Realistic Self-Image

✳
✳
✳

The previous two chapters, by developing the *perceptual* process and the *frame of reference* and *self-image* constructs, laid the foundation for this, the payoff chapter.

The central premise is that in order to communicate with or deal with others—to organize and lead them, motivate them, teach them, aid them, sell to them, collaborate with them, trust them, meet their expectations, discipline them, satisfy their needs, delegate assignments and authority to them, hold them responsible—to do these things (and countless others) and to do them well, one must have an unusually authentic conception of self—an *exceptionally realistic self-image* (ERSI).

ADVANTAGES OF THE ERSI

Depending upon where one begins, the process of attaining and maintaining an ERSI can be an exacting project. But the goal is generally well worth the effort and fortitude required. For with an ERSI, one is more likely to:

1. *Be a liberated person.* To the extent that one's self-image is invalid, it is likely to be challenged by cues from reality—feedback whose basic message is: "In some respect or other you are not who you think you are." If this contradiction exceeds one's comfort zone, the image is threatened and the usual (although not inevitable) response is defense. And defensive behavior requires energy expenditure.

An ERSI will tend not to be attacked—at least not by the cues from reality. On the contrary, they are signaling: "You are basically who you think you are." Therefore, energy-consuming defensiveness is not provoked. Accordingly, energy that would otherwise have been preempted for self-image protection is now freed and available for more constructive pursuits, such as contributing more productively and creatively to one's organization, family, and community.

2. *Maintain and increase self-image validity.* Because the ERSI obviates defensiveness, the individual tends to be more open and receptive to feedback. Thus one is able to receive inputs that can keep this self-image updated and increase its validity.

3. *Read others validly.* Analogically, one can only perceive others through one's own self-image—the central lens in one's frame of reference. If this lens is clouded or distorted, it follows that one's view of the world (including the people one deals with) is prone to be unrealistic. One has a head start in understanding others (forming accurate images of them) if one begins by truly understanding oneself. A person who validly assesses his or her own strengths, weaknesses, feelings, values, and needs is much more likely to accurately perceive those characteristics in others.

4. *Screen inputs accurately.* One of the characteristics of a responsible, integral position in an organization is that the incumbent is constantly barraged with inputs—data, information, feedback, cues—from other people. Some of this influx is garbage—inaccurate, phony material. Part of the trash is deliberately contrived, as in the cases of ax-grinding, special pleading, lobbying, calculated fraud. Some of it is unintentionally misleading, as when the inputer is defending his/her own self-image.

The obvious protection against garbage is simply to close the shutters on one's window and preclude all inputs. This would ward off the fallacious—but it would prohibit the valid inputs as well. And considering the high degree of interdependence required by organizations, playing the hermit would be untenable.

The appropriate stance would be to keep the shutters open so as to receive the inputs but to develop the screening skills by which to separate the wheat from the chaff—the valid from the invalid inputs.

An ERSI is a prerequisite to acquiring such skills. An erroneous self-image can be a serious deterrent to one's learning to read inputs accurately. Suppose that someone makes a decision which is then mildly criticized by the boss. Let us say that the individual has an inaccurate self-image which contributes to insecurity and leads the manager to interpret criticism far more personally than intended. Thus he or she may *over*react to the perceived threat—perhaps by irrational resistance or grovelling acquiescence.

5. *Choose realistic personal goals.* The poet Lew Sarett said: "Everyone needs basically two things: A block of granite to stand on and a star as a guide." In this chapter's terminology, he would probably say that each of us needs a currently realistic self-image partly in order to extrapolate into the future and choose realistic goals to which to aspire.

In the interests of a productive, happy, emotionally healthy life, it is important to have goals. "No wind favors him," wrote Michel de Montaigne, "who has no destined port." But it is also important that those goals be realistic. For if I shoot for an unrealistic star I am likely to pay a price for my inaccuracy. If my goal is extravagantly high, I am courting failure and frustration, which, if chronic, can degenerate to disillusionment and even demoralization.

If my goal is unchallengingly low, I may be settling, perhaps unwittingly, for semivegetation—a psychological stagnation that augurs well for neither health nor happiness.

One of the most important blessings of an exceptionally realistic self-image (the block of granite) is that it enhances one's ability to choose appropriate, attainable growth goals (the star).

The foregoing list is not exhaustive. But it does highlight several of the key values associated with the ERSI—suggesting why it is worth the price of attainment. And it does exact a price in terms of effort, time, honesty, patience, and above all, courage to endure the temporary discomfort sometimes required by image change through reprogramming. I use the term *reprogramming* because one's self-image is a programmed product—that is, it is learned. It follows then that if the self-image is, in some respects, inaccurate, that self-image can be *re*learned. But desirable reprogramming requires that the inputs be both valid and tolerable. Valid—so that the modified self-image will indeed be more realistic. Tolerable—so that one's comfort zone will not be violated by sudden, dramatic, uncontrolled change leading to one's defenses either screening out the inputs or being crushed by overwhelming inputs.

A GAME PLAN

Accordingly, here is a game plan designed to help one gain and maintain an ERSI through reprogramming by valid and tolerable inputs.

1. *Make a commitment.* Considering the aforementioned price of attaining an ERSI, it is evident that if you are to make significant gains in self-discovery and self-understanding, you must truly want to do so. You must adopt the scientific attitude: "Regardless of where the chips may fall, who am I really?"

2. *Identify and reduce your defenses.* The most important single reason most of us do not understand ourselves better lies in our own internal fortifications that seal us off from contrary, disturbing cues from reality. Considering that many of these bastions are rather well formed by the age of seven, the biblical age of reason, it would be astounding if anyone were aware of all his or her defenses.

So the challenge is progressively (it is a lifetime project) to recognize the existence of such defenses and to find ways of reducing them. In more rustic language—to identify the particular shutters on your window, to push them open, and to keep them open.

3. *Receive and evaluate the inputs.* With the shutters open, you are now able to receive the inputs. But not all feedback is authentic, so you must also evaluate, weigh, sift, and analyze it in order to separate the valid from the invalid.

VALID CUES

Input sources can be usefully classed into two categories: Those that originate from outside one's skin (external cues) and those generated from within (internal cues).

The remainder of this chapter will consist of a litany of sources of valid external and internal cues.

Cues from Others

For most of us, the greatest potential source of valid external cues is other people, especially those who have had the opportunity to observe us over a period of time under various circumstances.

This is not to say that everything everyone has to offer will be unfailingly authentic. Garbage is conceded. But it seems safe to assume that some of the feedback some of them could give is quite valid and potentially very helpful—if only we could communicate our receptivity to it. This seems a simple enough nostrum. Indeed, it is simplistic. For being receptive to feedback of any substance—and receiving it—on a continuing basis implies a relationship.

The Johari Grid. An insightful model involving feedback in the context of a relationship has been devised by psychologists Joseph Luft[1] and Harrington Ingham. They called it the Johari (pronounced, uncoincidentally, Joe-Harry) Window. Johari *Grid* seems more appropriate, because their construct represents a *person*, not an opening for air and light or any other conventional usage for "window."

More specifically, the Johari Grid portrays *an individual as he or she relates to others.* To illustrate this construct in simplest terms, let us

---

[1] Joseph Luft, *Of Human Interaction* (Palo Alto, Calif.: National Press Books, 1969); and Joseph Luft, *Group Processes: An Introduction to Group Dynamics* (Palo Alto, Calif.: National Press Books, 1970).

FIGURE 6.1

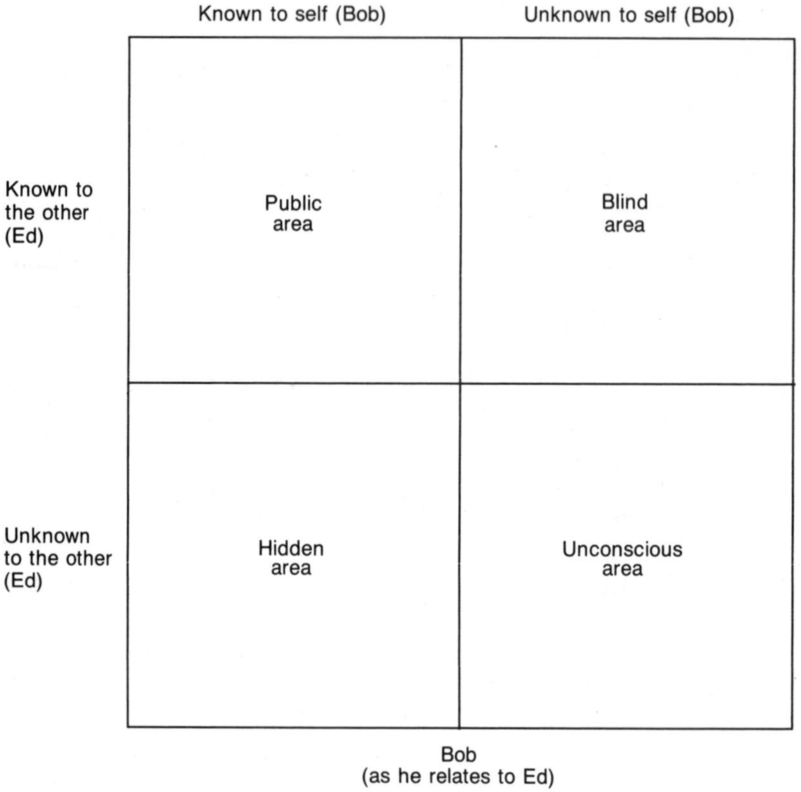

	Known to self (Bob)	Unknown to self (Bob)
Known to the other (Ed)	Public area	Blind area
Unknown to the other (Ed)	Hidden area	Unconscious area

Bob
(as he relates to Ed)

visualize a one-on-one relationship between, say Bob, a boss, and Ed, one of his subordinates.

Figure 6.1 represents *Bob* (we will see Ed's grid later) *as he relates to Ed*. Two premises apply: (1) Everything in the large rectangle is valid information (including feelings, facts, assumptions, beliefs, personal values, prejudices, and needs); and (2) everything in the large rectangle is pertinent to Bob's relationship with Ed. The only distinction the grid purports to make is who has knowledge of which information.

The *public area* represents that part of Bob that relates to Ed and is known to both of them. It includes such details as the fact that Bob is the administrator of the X Memorial Hospital; that Ed is one of his immediate subordinates, along with Sally, Stu, Morris, and Jane; that when Bob is absent (out-of-town meetings, vacations, etc.) he appoints Ed to serve as acting administrator; and so on. Bob's public area with respect to Ed represents common ground. Because it is mutually perceived and acknowledged, it ordinarily presents no unrecognized problem for Bob or for Ed. If difficulties do arise in Bob's public area, Bob and Ed become conscious of them, identify what they are disagreeing about, and have at least the opportunity to reconcile their differences.

The *hidden area* is that part of Bob that relates to Ed of which Bob is aware, Ed is not, and about which Bob may prefer to keep Ed in the dark. For example, despite the fact that Ed serves as administrator in Bob's absence, Bob does not consider him as his crown prince. Bob regards Ed as an excellent director of personnel but feels that he lacks the potential to become a full-time administrator. Bob has been offered the reins of a larger hospital in another city. Should he accept the new position, he plans to recommend Sally to the board as his replacement. But none of this has he confided to Ed.

Bob's hidden area with respect to Ed includes that which he has simply not yet had occasion to reveal to Ed, as well as that which he is deliberately concealing from Ed.

The *blind area* is that part of Bob that relates to Ed of which Ed is aware, Bob is not, and Ed has not as yet seen fit or felt free to bring to Bob's attention. For instance, Bob has an M.B.A., has attended many management seminars, and has read widely in management literature. He feels that he practices a highly participative style of leadership by trusting his subordinates implicitly and delegating freely to them. Ed knows better. He recognizes, as do his colleagues, that Bob is a soft-spoken, beneficent autocrat who merely gives lip service to liberal delegation.

Ed, thus, has knowledge that could reduce Bob's blind area. Whether it actually does reduce it depends upon two interrelated factors: Ed's willingness to share the information and Bob's willingness to receive and accept it. If Bob has consciously (or more likely, unconsciously) communicated his nonreceptivity to Ed's feedback, he is unlikely to have the information proffered to him.

The *unconscious area* is that part of Bob that relates to Ed, and of which neither man is aware. Theoretically, then, they are powerless to change this sector. Thus, if a sufficiently severe problem arises in Bob's unconscious area, psychotherapy may be required.

However, another alternative is possible. When the one-on-one relationship is a very open, trusting, receptive one, the two intimates—husband and wife, parent and child, friend and friend, even boss and subordinate—may sometimes stumble onto something in the unconscious area, thus putting it into one of the other three sectors, depending on whether one or the other party or both parties become aware of it.

Leveling and Feedback Solicitation. The size and shape of the grid's four sectors are determined by the following two basic communication processes:

FIGURE 6.2

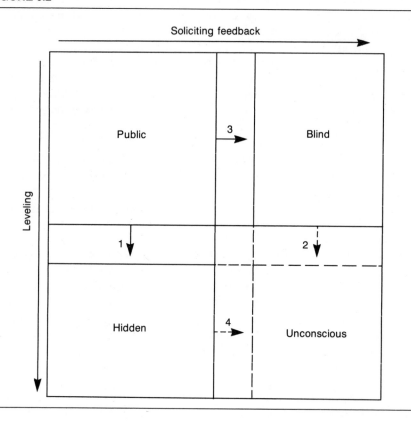

Leveling is synonymous with opening up, coming clean, revealing one's thoughts and feelings, being honest and candid. It is represented by the vertical dimension in Figure 6.2.

Soliciting feedback, the lateral dimension, involves genuinely seeking and requesting feedback from another person, expressing the willingness to receive inputs, even negative ones, without becoming feisty, defensive.

To the extent that Bob levels with Ed, he will be enlarging his public area while reducing his hidden sector (see arrow 1). It does not necessarily follow that the new floor on the public area will be extended across the grid increasing the blind while reducing the unconscious (see arrow 2). This will occur only to the extent that in leveling with Ed, Bob is actually revealing more to Ed than Bob is aware and that Ed does not share this new information with Bob.

Similarly, to the extent that Bob's solicitation of feedback from Ed is successful—that is, he actually receives the feedback—Bob's blind area will be diminished, increasing his public sector (see arrow 3). Again, the new wall will not necessarily extend downward, enlarging the hidden while reducing the unconscious (see arrow 4). This will happen only to the extent that as Ed offers feedback he is giving more information than he thinks he is. If Bob keeps this bonus knowledge to himself, it is considered hidden area material.

We have acknowledged that the public area's new floor and wall do not necessarily extend, respectively, across and down through the grid. Accordingly, in subsequent grids, the blind-unconscious and hidden-unconscious boundaries will be expressed by dotted lines.

Interpersonal Styles.   Note that we have not been discussing Bob in isolation—but in his relationship with a particular person at a particular time. Like most of us, Bob relates differently to different people. He also relates differently to the same person at different times.

Let us examine several interpersonal styles and consider their implications for both parties—the possessor of the grid and the person to whom he or she is relating.

Figure 6.3 shows a Johari Grid characterized by a tiny public area, sizable hidden and blind areas, and a huge unconscious area. Suppose that this grid represents Bob as he deals with Ed. It implies that Bob has been unwilling or unable to level with Ed and has also been unreceptive to feedback from Ed. This hermit style will pose problems for both Bob and Ed.

For Ed's part, there is so much that he does not know about his boss in terms of their relationship (hidden and unconscious areas) that Ed is likely to have a very limited and perhaps inaccurate image of Bob. He will have difficulty in predicting Bob's behavior, coping with him, and satisfying his own (Ed's) needs with respect to Bob. He will have only a fuzzy notion of what Bob expects of him or of how he stands with Bob. Moreover, he will be reluctant to offer candid feedback, for Bob's large blind area implies that he has not been especially receptive to feedback that could have reduced that sector. In addition, since Bob is likely to be quite reserved—maintaining his substantial hidden area would require this—Ed is likely to be cautious as well.

Clearly Ed will be frustrated should Bob assume the hermit posture. But how Ed will be affected *specifically* depends largely upon his own particular needs and motivations.

> Subordinates whose manager employs such a style . . . will often feel that his behavior is consciously aimed at frustrating them in their work. The person in need of support and encouragement will often view a [hermit] manager as aloof, cold and indifferent. Another individual in need of firm directions and plenty of order may view the same manager as indecisive and administratively impotent. Yet another person requiring freedom and

FIGURE 6.3

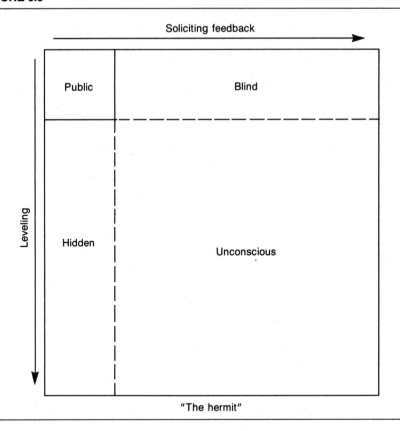

opportunities to be innovative may see the [hermit] interpersonal style as hopelessly tradition-bound and as symptomatic of fear and an overriding need for security.[2]

Bob's plight, if anything, is worse than Ed's. With an enormous unconscious area coupled with a significant blind area, he is unlikely to have a very complete or valid self-image. His faulty self-perception may lead to erratic behavior on his part, which, incidentally, makes him even less predictable to Ed. Moreover, for Bob to protect his hidden area against revelation will require constant security. Indirectly, as suggested above, Bob's maintaining a large hidden area will constrain Ed from offering candid feedback.

The hermit style is particularly troublesome in an organizational context. For it is extremely difficult to report to someone who comes on as a

---

[2] Jay Hall, "Communication Revisited," *California Management Review*, 15, no. 3 (Spring 1973), p. 69.

FIGURE 6.4

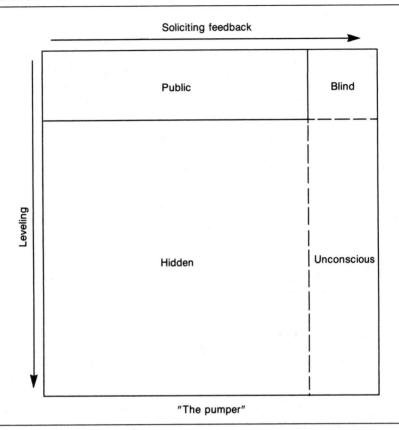

"The pumper"

hermit, or to supervise or attempt to collaborate with a person who manifests this style. It is singularly frustrating to be required to interact with a person who simply will not—or cannot—relate.

The most prominent feature of the Johari Grid in Figure 6.4 is its immense hidden area. This is the pumper style, for it is created when a person is successful in sucking information out of another while giving little if any in return. The motives for pumping could be broadly classed as defensive and offensive.

Defensively, pumpers reveal very little of themselves, thus concealing their inadequacies and vulnerabilities from those who might take advantage of them. Offensively, they gain knowledge which they may be able to use to attack, influence, or manipulate others. If knowledge is power, the pumper may be attempting to build a dynasty.

Maintaining security on one's huge hidden area can be an exhausting compulsion for the pumper. It requires considerable energy to keep secrets, to play "games," to keep people in the dark. An uncomfortable thought: Have you ever told a lie and then had to live with it? Do you recall how it drained you to keep the fiction intact? "Oh, what a tangled web we weave," wrote Sir Walter Scott, "when first we practice to deceive!"

From the pumper's standpoint, another major problem with pumping is that it is often detectable. Once "pumpees" realize that they are involved in a lopsided relationship wherein they are virtually always the givers and rarely the takers, they may grow suspicious and wary. "What's going on here?" ponders the pumpee. "He knows everything about me—my views of our boss, our mutual colleagues, our organization, even of himself—yet he never seems to commit himself. Why does he need all of this from me? What is he going to do with it? Hurt me?"

At this point, the pumpee has turned defensive and may withdraw to the hermit posture by avoiding the pumper. If he or she senses that the pumper is oblivious of the unbalanced relationship, the pumpee may confront the pumper and demand reciprocal leveling. Or the pumpee may come on as a counterpumper. But this usually eventuates in a "You tell me!"—"No, you tell me!" standoff. A more drastic defense is to feed the pumper some false information. Although this tactic may "cure" the pumper of trying to tap this particular source, it may have some destructive by-products. For if the pumper uses the fallacious material, it may harm others—perhaps himself or herself—and the pumpee may have created a vengeful enemy.

In any event, the success of the pumper style tends to be short-lived because when pumpees suspect that they are on a one-way street, they are apt to thwart the pumper's needs for accurate and intimate information.

I call the interpersonal style depicted in Figure 6.5 the blabbermouth. If Bob were playing the blabbermouth with respect to Ed, he would be doing a great deal of talking and very little listening. The net result could be a vast blind area.

Why does Bob talk so much? Among the possibilities: He's on a constant ego trip— needs applause; he's whistling in the dark—to shore up his own flagging spirits; he's venting his spleen—thus forcing the listener into the role of therapist; he's truly arrogant—genuinely assured of his own opinions and values; he has an authoritarian personality—feels that decision making should be centralized in himself; he's paternalistic, dictatorial, and so on.

Why does Bob listen so little? Perhaps he lacks respect for Ed's views; possibly he fears that Ed's views may challenge his own; his obsession with being right brooks no contrary feedback; and so on.

Ed, to the extent that he is not a captive audience, may escape some of Bob's excessive leveling by retreating to a hermit role and simply hiding from him. But this tactic may not suffice for some of the problems that Bob's blabbermouth style presents for Ed.

Bob's tiny hidden area may indicate that he is not very circumspect—"he lets it *all* hang out." Thus, Ed may be justifiably concerned about Bob's discretion regarding the confidences Ed has shared with him.

FIGURE 6.5

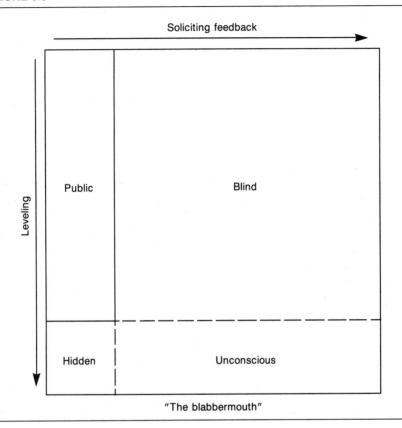

Soliciting feedback

Leveling

Public

Blind

Hidden

Unconscious

"The blabbermouth"

But it is probably Bob's nonreceptivity to Ed's feedback that pains Ed most acutely. Ed may feel disenfranchised and may perceive that Bob has little use for his contributions or little concern for his feelings. As a result, Ed may feel resentful, insecure, and bitter and may retaliate by perpetuating Bob's blind area by "withholding important information or giving only selected feedback . . . this is a reflection of the passive aggressiveness and unarticulated hostility which this style can cause."[3]

But Ed may occasionally resort to active aggression. If Bob is highly authoritarian, this can be perilous for Ed, but it can be dangerous for Bob as well. Since their relationships are dominated by blind areas, blabbermouths, according to Jay Hall, "are destined for surprise whenever people get enough and decide to force feedback upon them, solicited or not."[4]

---

[3] Ibid., p. 61.

[4] Ibid.

FIGURE 6.6

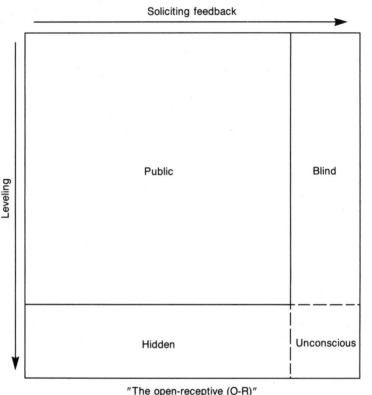

"The open-receptive (O-R)"

The grid in Figure 6.6 represents the open-receptive or O-R style. It occurs when there is a balanced combination of generous leveling and a genuine willingness to receive feedback. The consequence, assuming that feedback is received, is a grid dominated by the public area.

If Bob deals with Ed in the O-R fashion, a number of significant advantages over other styles can accrue. Ed will be able to form a more accurate image of Bob, due largely to Bob's uninhibited leveling—this is in stark contrast with the hermit and pumper styles, in which Bob is largely an unknown quantity for Ed. Ed will not be inhibited for fear of offending or threatening Bob, as is the case in the blabbermouth style, because Bob has made it clear that he welcomes feedback and will not punish Ed for his candor.

The O-R style should enhance Bob's chances of gaining an ERSI, at least in his relationship with Ed, for Bob's receptivity to feedback promises to reduce his blind area to a minor sector. Bob's unconscious area is also likely to be diminished, subject as it is to fortuitous stumbling into by intimates. Not the least of the ERSI benefits that Bob may enjoy is the freedom from having to "play games" with Ed, keeping him in the dark.

The obvious drawback to the O-R style is its vulnerability. Anyone who is this open and receptive could be hurt. Thus, the O-R style is only appropriate (and, indeed, possible) when mutual trust and trustworthiness exist between the parties to the relationship. For a White House staff member to have attempted to relate to others in the O-R manner during the Watergate period would have been naive—he or she would have been devoured.

Your OPA. We have been comparing the advantages and limitations of several interpersonal styles. But is there an *ideal* Johari Grid? Not for all circumstances. To determine the best grid, or more specifically the best public area, for a given situation, I suggest this formula:

$$OPA = f(Y, O, C)$$

Translated, your optimal public area is a function of at least three factors: *you*, the *other* to whom you are relating, and the social or organizational *climate* within which the two of you are interacting.

The most appropriate public area for you depends to a considerable extent on the basic kind of person *you* are. Are you generally a withdrawn, recessive person? Do you find it difficult to reach out to people? to trust them? to share confidences with them? Does intimacy threaten you? If so, this doesn't mean that you can't have open, receptive relationships. But you may require more time, energy, and courage to build them than would a more outgoing person.

And how trusting is the *other* person? There are limits to how intimate you can become with a confirmed recluse. And what of his or her trustworthiness? It would be foolhardy to open up with a person who would abuse your trust.

Even though you and the other person may be basically trusting and trustworthy, the *climate* in which you are interrelating must be considered. An organizational jungle, such as the aforementioned Watergate White House, is no place to let it all hang out.

Suboptimal Public Areas. How do members of organizations normally relate to one another? When the public areas in boss-subordinate, colleague-colleague, or staff-line relationships are less than optimal, in which direction do they usually miss the mark? Are they dangerously open or needlessly closed?

Judging from reports by most managers in my seminars and from my own observations, people in organizations tend to have unnecessarily small public areas. Their dealings with one another are excessively aloof and guarded. An ironic survival of the most defensive seems to be mainly responsible. Visualize two company employees. Considering their environment, each has an inappropriate public area. A's is vulnerably large, whereas B's is overcautiously small. The predictable outcome? A will promptly receive painful feedback clearly signalling: "You're too open and defenseless!" In short, he will be burned. He may leave the organization. If he remains, he will become more self-protective. Indeed, he may over-react—polarize[5]—and shrink his public area excessively.

B, however, will not have his trust abused—he'll never proffer it. He is unlikely to be seared by negative feedback. His defensive posture precludes it. He is even shielded from corrective intelligence which challenges: "You're too closed and insulated!"

In a hostile environment, natural selection favors the best protected. So the Bs remain; the As who stay become Bs; and everyone is obsessed with defense.

Add the collective time and energy spent "playing games," protecting inaccurate self-images, fending off disturbing feedback, bristling against criticism, playing it close to the vest, smoke-screening, passing the buck, scapegoating, and watching out for Number One, and we begin to appreciate the exorbitant price an organization pays when its people are preoccupied with personal defensiveness rather than with organizational objectives and working together to get the job done.

Enlarging the Public Area.   Such organizations would do well to encourage their members to enlarge their public areas. This ultimately occurs at the one-on-one level, so let us examine a method by which Bob and Ed can expand their respective public areas. It consists of gradually and reciprocally increasing the flow of information between the two men—that is, progressive leveling and feedback solicitation.

Suppose that Bob and Ed have maintained a hermit-hermit relationship (see Figure 6.7) for some time and that at least one of them, say Bob, wants to alter it. Bob's first step is to deliberately reveal a bit of his hidden area to Ed—to tell Ed forthrightly something he had been concealing from him: "Look, Ed, this is how I really feel about. . . ." (see arrow 1). Beyond this overt information, Bob is sending a second message covertly: "See, Ed? I'm letting my guard down. I'm taking you into my confidence. Convince me that it's safe to disarm like this with you, so please don't get alarmed or feisty, and don't abuse my trust, and if you want some more candor, then reciprocate, man; let *your* hair down a bit."

---

[5] See Chapter 13.

FIGURE 6.7

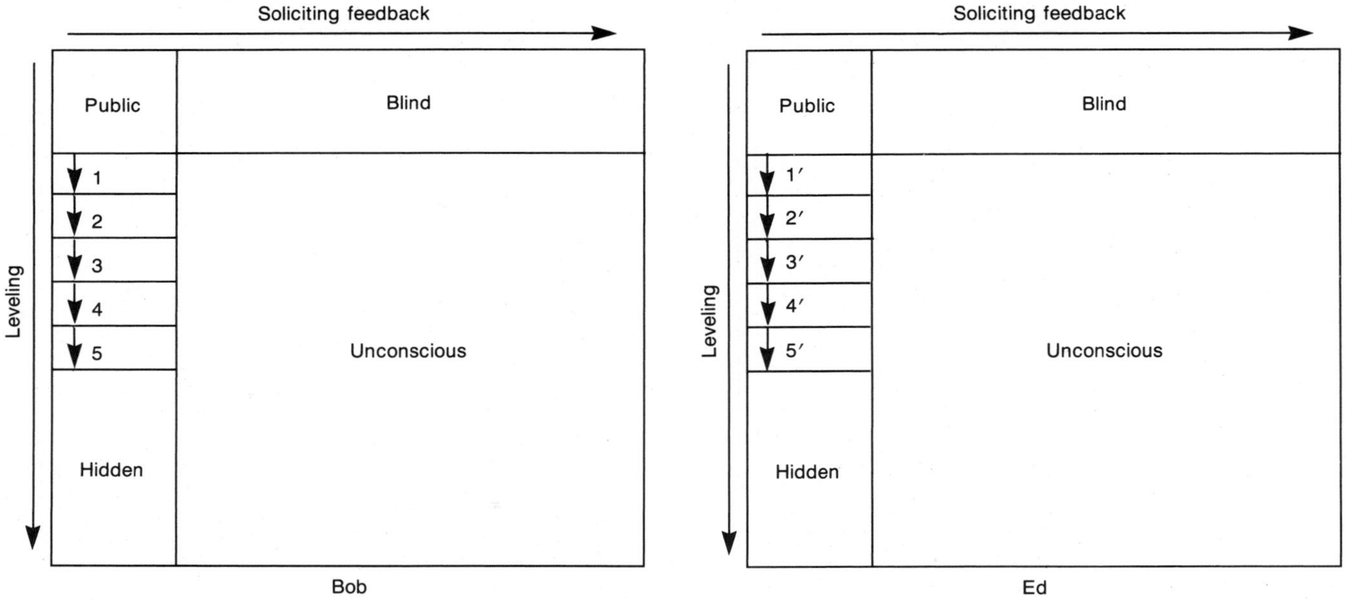

PROGRESSIVE LEVELING

FIGURE 6.8

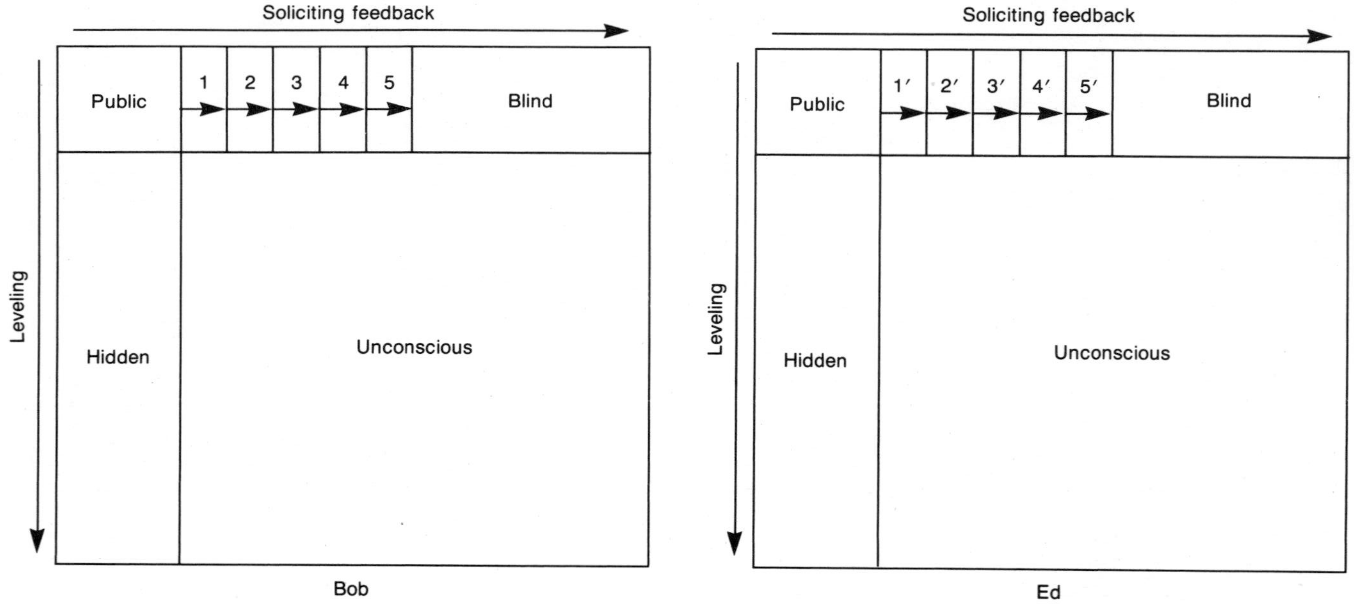

PROGRESSIVE|FEEDBACK|SOLICITATION

FIGURE 6.9

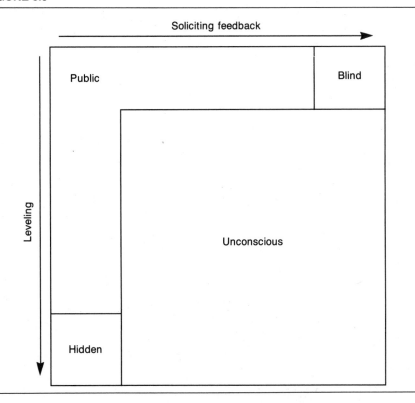

If Ed gets this second message and trusts it, then he reciprocates and shares some intimacy with Bob (arrow 1'), coupled with the same reciprocity plea. Hopefully, Bob will interpret Ed's intent and respond accordingly (arrow 2), and so forth.

Simultaneously with this progressive leveling, mutual solicitation of feedback may occur (see Figure 6.8). Let's say that Bob again initiates the process: "Ed, what is your honest opinion of . . .?" Once more, there is a second veiled message: "Lay it on me, Ed—I can take it. I promise that if you express yourself frankly, I will not make it difficult, unpleasant, or threatening for you."

If Ed takes Bob at his word, he will offer some unvarnished, valid feedback. And suppose that Bob is able to accept it without defensiveness. Thus, Bob has learned something (his blind area is reduced—arrow 1), but so has Ed. "That Bob is a pretty big man," he muses, "he can really take it. Well, maybe I can, too." Through gradual, reciprocating solicitation and reception of feedback, each man's blind area shrinks.

The net result of these two concurrent communication processes is an inverted L-shaped public area (see Figure 6.9) for each man, which is

FIGURE 6.10

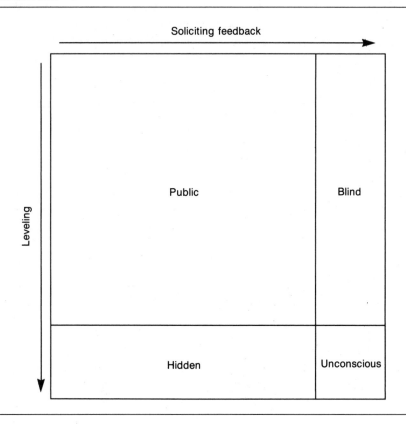

considerably larger than those of the former hermits. But there are two additional prospects for increasing the public area—or, at least, for shrinking the unconscious sector. One is the previously mentioned fortuitous stumbling of intimates. The other is the constant possibility that the sender (be he leveling or offering feedback) may be communicating more than he intends to the receiver. Thus unconscious material may be transferred variously to hidden or blind or public areas, depending upon whether one man or the other or both become aware of the newly developed information. If the transfer is primarily to the public area, Bob's and Ed's grids may approach that depicted in Figure 6.10.

The Johari Grid depicts interpersonal relationships in terms of one's willingness and ability to level with and receive feedback from others. Its relevance for self-image validity is clear. For candid feedback is a prime source (for most of us) of external cues by which one can ascertain and increase the authenticity of his or her self-image.

Our present concern with the Johari Grid is as a vehicle by which one can increase the validity of self-image. But this is not to ignore the wider implications of the concept in terms of interpersonal communication.

Gibson et al., for example, summarizes the four modes discussed above as follows:[6]

> Those managers who persist in the *hermit* style "are frequently poor interpersonal communicators. Often, they are autocratic leaders who are aloof and cold toward others."
>
> *Pumpers* sometimes "seek good relationships with subordinates but are unable to openly express their feelings."
>
> *Blabbermouths* are "interested only in their own ideas and not . . . [those] of others."
>
> Those who characteristically maintain the *open-receptive* style generally are the most effective interpersonal communicatiors . . . .

We will now touch upon some special concepts and approaches by which one can receive useful feedback from others: sensitivity training, group therapy, and transactional analysis.

Sensitivity Training. Uninhibited group interactions, variously termed "sensitivity training," "T-groups," "laboratory education," "group dynamics," "encounter groups," and so on, have gained increasingly enthusiastic supporters and equally energetic detractors in recent years, and the dust has yet to settle.

The format is to create a nonstructured atmosphere in which participants feel free to level with and to seek feedback from one another.

The objectives of sensitivity training have been many and varied. Some have focused on "group process phenomena, attempting to improve the ability of individuals to understand, predict, evaluate, and change the way groups work. Still others have worked on particular aspects of behavior like the use of power and influence, leadership skills, listening ability, and giving and receiving feedback."[7]

Most relevant here, though, is that the approach has considerable potential for helping one to increase the validity of his or her self-image at least insofar as the here-and-now dynamics of the present groups are concerned.

But some precautions seem well advised; there should be, for example, professional leaders and psychologically screened participants. "Sensitivity training," warn some of its critics, "is too rough for sick people."[8]

---

[6] James L. Gibson, John M. Ivancevich, and James H. Donnelly, Jr., *Organizations: Behavior, Structure, Processes*, 6th ed. (Homewood, Ill.: Irwin/BPI, 1988), pp. 551–52.

[7] Allan R. Cohen, Stephen L. Fink, Herman Gadon, and Robin D. Willits, *Effective Behavior in Organizations*, 4th ed. (Homewood, Ill.: Richard D. Irwin, 1988), p. 427.

[8] For a balanced discussion of the pros and cons of sensitivity training, especially as relates to development in people in organizations, see Gibson et al., *Organizations*, pp. 738–39.

Group Therapy. Superficially, group therapy and some forms of sensitivity training are similar. The setting is informal and seemingly unstructured. People speak and are responded to spontaneously, without an apparent agenda. But the most important distinctive characteristic of group therapy is control. The therapist, usually a highly trained professional, realizing that the participants are vulnerable, generally exercises more control on interactions than is ordinarily the case in sensitivity training.

Transactional Analysis. Conceived by the psychiatrist Eric Berne, "TA" was originally used as a tool for psychotherapy. More recently, it has also been used to aid in understanding and coping with interpersonal relations—especially those pertaining to families (spouse-spouse, parent-child, sibling-sibling, and so forth) and organizations (boss-subordinate, colleague-colleague, salesperson-customer).

TA's central premise is that each person consists of three ego states: Parent-Adult-Child. The objective of TA is to assure that the Adult dominates the personality and that neither an excessively critical Parent nor a primitive, self-deprecating Child is permitted to foul up transactions or relationships with others.

The individual, therefore, needs to learn to recognize which of the ego states is controlling his or her thoughts, feelings, and behavior at a given moment. With practice, one can sense who is in charge. For example, let us assume that you have never heard of TA before reading this brief description. Tune in on your current feelings. If your inner voice is saying, "Oh, this is just more drivel those behavioral scientists have cooked up!" this may be your critical, fault-finding Parent reacting. Are you temporarily withholding judgment? "This is the first I've heard of TA—sounds interesting, but I think I'd better learn more about it before passing judgment on it." This sounds like your rational, objective Adult. Or if you are immediately enthusiastic (or turned off): "Gee, this sounds like fun—figuring out who's running me—and using it to psych out others, too!" or "Transactional analysis!—that's just one more term I have to memorize for the exam," your Child seems to be controlling you.

As its name implies, TA is concerned with the transactions or communications between people—each of whom consists of a Parent-Adult-Child. The principal issue as A and B relate is: Which ego state in A is transacting with which ego state in B? Generally, when transactions are *parallel* they are considered constructive, beneficial, or at least harmless. Visualize a mother who needs to know the time (see Figure 6.11). She knows that her 16-year-old son can tell her. Her Adult asks a straight-forward question directed to her son's Adult. And the son responds out of his Adult (assuming that he is giving valid information insofar as he knows it) directed to his mother's Adult.

The key aspect of parallel (complementary) transactions is that the sender receives the expected response.

FIGURE 6.11

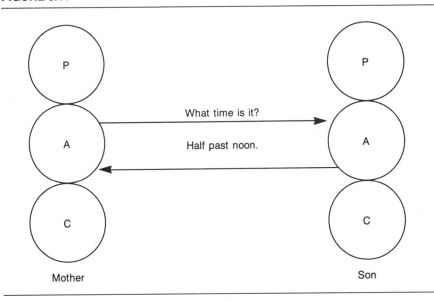

But some transactions are crossed, and the consequences may be undesirable (see Figure 6.12). The sender gets an unexpected response. Imagine the same mother asking the same question with the same intention—that is, learning the correct time.

In neither case does the mother receive the desired information, and in both cases the stage has been set for a rancorous, unprofitable series of exchanges.

Particularly relevant to organizations is the concept of *games*—deceptions that members of the firm and others unconsciously (to some extent) perpetrate on one another. Regardless of who wins these games, the organization is a certain loser. The costs in terms of hurt feelings, retaliations, absenteeism, turnover, and grievances may be difficult to quantify on a profit-and-loss statement but that does not diminish their counterproductivity.

To illustrate games, go back to the mother-son transactions. In each case, there was the potential for a mutually destructive game known as *uproar*. In the first exchange, the mother might have understandably retaliated with, "Don't talk that way to *me*, young man!" with an appropriately fierce facial expression. The problem with that approach is that her son is now likely to be convinced that his original interpretation of her question was correct, and the wedge that divides them has been driven in more deeply.

The mother would have been well-advised to keep her cool and remain in her Adult state. Something like, "I didn't mean it that way, John, but can you tell me what time it is?" might have defused the situation.

FIGURE 6.12

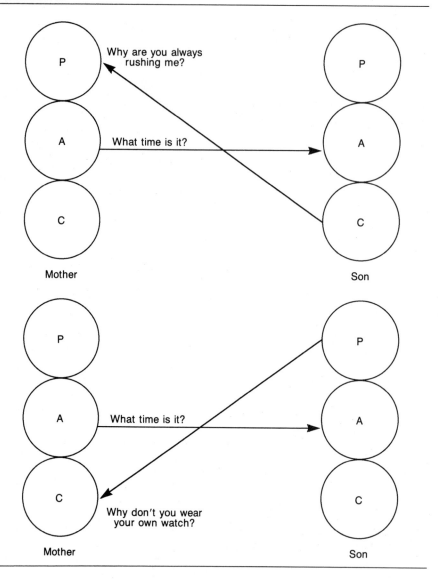

In the second case, again, the advice is for mother to stay in her Adult and not let the other party dictate her response. The idea is not to get into her Child, for example, and to defend or alibi or quibble. Recommendation: "You're right, John, but can you tell me what time it is?"

Granted, neither of these Adult responses is likely to reconcile mother and son, especially if their alienation has been going on for some time. But at least they will not refuel their respective animosities. And, who knows, the mother might even find out what time it is!

There is *much* more to TA:[9] "ulterior transactions," "strokes," "life positions," "trading stamps," "scripts," "persecutor," "victim," "rescuer," and so forth. TA has been amply described in books by Berne, Harris, James and Jongeward, and Meininger. See the annotated references to these books later in this chapter.

Cues from Psychometric Instruments

Another approach for obtaining information by which we can increase the validity of our self-images is through standardized psychometric instruments. Granted that tests in general and intelligence tests in particular have been controversial. (They have rarely been out of controversy in the past three decades!) Nevertheless, it seems reasonable to assume that some instruments, especially if these are selected, administered, and interpreted by professionals, can offer useful feedback in terms of abilities, skills, achievement, aptitudes, attitudes, interests, values, temperaments, motivations, and so on.

I use instruments in my courses and management seminars for a very specialized purpose: To offer potentially useful leads that will aid the test-taker in his or her own self-appraisal. My premise is that a human being is an enormously complex entity and that a major challenge to self-understanding is to select aspects about oneself that are specific enough to observe and study. Therefore, if a modest amount of time and money spent on an instrument or two helps one to reduce his or her area of search, then the investment seems warranted.

The instruments I use must satisfy these criteria:

1. They must have at least face-validity—that is, they must appear to a reasonable, objective observer to measure what they purport to measure.
2. They must measure behaviors or characteristics that the individual can recognize in on-the-job or in-the-home communications with others. Test results should be considered hypotheses to be tested by subsequent observations.
3. They must be capable of *self*-administration and *self*-scoring. The point here is that the results of many instruments are "fudgeable"—

---

[9] For implications of TA for interpersonal relations in organizations, see Paul Hersey and Ken Blanchard, *Management of Organizational Behavior: Utilizing Human Resources,* 4th ed. (Englewood Cliffs; N. J.: Prentice-Hall, 1982), pp. 67–77 and 227–30. See also: Dale A. Level, Jr. and William P. Calle, Jr., *Managerial Communications* (Homewood, Ill.: Irwin/BPI, 1988); and James B. Lau and A. B. Shani, *Behavior in Organizations: An Experiential Approach,* 4th ed. (Homewood, Ill.: Richard D. Irwin, 1988), Chapter 18, "Individual Effectiveness: Personal Growth via TA," pp. 393–416.

that is, capable of being distorted to suit the test-taker's purposes. Self-scoring tests, therefore, assure that the individual *alone* will see the scores and thus will only be doing oneself a disservice by responding less than candidly.

4. They must measure behaviors and characteristics that the individual accepts as truly relevant in dealings with other people, for only then will one be genuinely motivated to learn about oneself in these respects.

The following are a few of the instruments[10] I have found helpful. I assert no particular claim for their validity and reliability, but they have proven useful as focus sharpeners and search-area narrowers.

FIRO-B—

Consulting Psychologists Press, Inc. (Palo Alto, Calif.). Purports to indicate one's characteristic behavior toward other people in the areas of inclusion, control, and affection.

Kolbe Conative Index—

Kolbe Concepts, Inc. (Phoenix, Ariz.). See annotation of Kolbe's *The Conative Connection* (p. 142). The instrument purports to offer feedback in terms of one's insistent versus resistant modes of action.

Management Style Diagnosis Test—

Organizational Test Ltd. (Fredricton, New Brunswick, Canada). Purports to indicate one's management style in terms of task orientation, relationships orientation, and effectiveness.

Myers-Briggs Type Indicator—

Consulting Psychologists Press, Inc. (Palo Alto, Calif.). This instrument purports to offer feedback in terms of four dimensions:

> Introversion .... Extraversion
> Sensing .... Intuition
> Thinking .... Feeling
> Judging .... Perceiving

Orientation Inventory—

Consulting Psychologists Press (Palo Alto, Calif.). Purports to indicate one's tendency to be oriented toward *(a)* self-aggrandizement, *(b)* pleasant relationships with others, and *(c)* the group task at hand.

---

[10] For a comprehensive annotated list or published tests, see Oscar K. Buros, ed., *The Tenth Mental Measurements Yearbook* (Lincoln, Neb.: Buros Institute of Mental Measurements, University of Nebraska, 1989). See also: Louis Aiken, *Psychology Testing and Assessment,* 6th ed. (Newton, Mass.: Allyn & Bacon, 1988).

Personnel Relations Survey—

Teleometrics, International (Conroe, Tex.). Based upon the Johari Grid concept and purports to measure the size and shape of one's public area, that is, one's willingness to level and to solicit feedback as one relates to members of the organization at three levels: employees, colleagues, and supervisors.

Strength Deployment Inventory—

Personal Strengths Assessment Service (Pacific Palisades, Calif.). Purports to assess one's interpersonal orientation when all is going well and then again in the face of conflict and opposition.

Study of Values—

Houghton Mifflin (Boston). Purports to indicate one's value system with respect to six factors: theoretical, economic, aesthetic, social, political, and religious.

Uncritical Inference Test—

William V. Haney Associates (Wilmette, Ill.). Purports to indicate one's tendency to jump to conclusions and, conversely, one's awareness of inferring.

Cues from Readings

Can reading a book or article help a person to better understand oneself? Although readings do not offer feedback, per se, they can provide concepts, insights, tools, and techniques by which we can interpret and learn from the feedback that we do receive from interpersonal experiences. Such readings are almost too abundant. The problem is to choose sound, competent, useful works from the profusion available. Listed below are several books that I and others have found particularly germane and helpful:

George Bach and Herbert Goldberg. *Creative Aggression.* Garden City, N.Y.: Doubleday, 1974. Whereas Freud asserted that the repression of sexual expression was the root of most personal and interpersonal evils, these authors contend that today's counterpart culprit is the repression of aggression. Accordingly, they offer rationale by which aggression can be released in safe, constructive, and even creative ways.

George Bach and Peter Wyden. *The Intimate Enemy: How to Fight Fair in Love and Marriage.* New York: Avon Books, 1968. The operative word is *fair*. The authors offer a sound and sensible approach for resolving or at least diminishing conflict and increasing intimacy. Admittedly couched in terms for the couple, the book is nevertheless highly relevant to on-the-job relationships.

Eric Berne, M.D. *Games People Play.* New York: Grove Press, 1964. A psychoanalyst's application of transactional analysis concepts to interpersonal relationships. The games are the deceptions we employ (at varying levels of consciousness) in our dealings with others in order to satisfy our needs.

Roger M. D'Aprix. *Struggle for Identity.* Homewood, Ill.: Dow Jones-Irwin, 1972. This book focuses on the discrepancy between reality and what we have been programmed to believe about the relationship between the individual and the organization. It discusses the growing resistance to be molded into organization people and the struggle of the individual to maintain a personal identity, integrity, and intellectual freedom against the increasing pressure of organizational forces.

Colette Dowling. *Perfect Women: Hidden Fears of Inadequacy and the Drive to Perfection*. New York: Summit Books, 1988. The relationship between self-esteem and achievement-oriented behavior in women is examined in this book. According to the author: "A 'legacy of self-doubt' is handed down from mother to daughter, one that is disguised—but not cured—by a frantic quest for self-improvement."

David Goleman. *Vital Lies, Simple Truths: The Psychology of Self Deception*. New York: Simon & Schuster, 1985. This book is about blind spots of the mind—certain kinds of experiences we unconsciously blank out by ignoring or forgetting. Some of these repressions protect us from overly painful experience. Others perpetuate our ignorance. Goleman's prescription is to follow "the path to sanity and survival—somewhere between the two poles of living a life of vital lies and speaking simple truths."

Amy Bjork Harris and Thomas A. Harris, M.D. *Staying OK: How to Maximize Good Feelings and Minimize Bad Ones*. New York: Harper & Row, 1985. How to identify and dispel the oppressive voices from the past that undermine us in the present. The authors prescribe specific steps to examine parental messages recorded when we were children along with the often distorted assumptions we made about them.

Thomas Harris, M.D. *I'm O.K., You're O.K.: A Practical Guide to Transactional Analysis*. New York: Avon, 1982. The bestselling translation and application of Berne's transactional analysis. The book's title stems from the most desirable of the four life positions underlying people's behavior and interpersonal relationships.

Muriel James and Dorothy Jongeward. *Born to Win: Trans-actional Analysis with Gestalt Experiments*. Reading, Mass.: Addison-Wesley, 1971. A highly regarded popularization and application of TA and Frederick Peris' interpretation of gestalt therapy. The book's objective is "discovering and fostering awareness, self-responsibility, and genuineness."

Susan Jeffers. *Feel the Fear and Do It Anyway*. San Diego: Harcourt Brace Jovanovich, 1987. Dr. Jeffers states: "Whenever we take a chance and enter unfamiliar territory or put ourselves into a world in a new way, we experience fear. Very often this keeps us from moving ahead with our lives. The trick is to FEEL THE FEAR AND DO IT ANYWAY. Together we will explore the barriers that keep us from experiencing life the way we want to live it."

Kathy Kolbe. *The Conative Connection*. Reading, Mass.: Addison-Wesley, 1990. The author's key premise is that the human mind consists of the cognitive (thought), the affective (emotion), and the conative (action). Contending that the first two parts have been studied extensively, she focuses on the third. She identifies four modes of action: Fact Finding, Following Through, Quick Starting, and Implementing. She asserts that people would profit considerably if they could determine which mode(s) is predominant in them.

Jut Meininger. *Success through Transactional Analysis*. New York: Grosset and Dunlap, 1973. A sound treatment of TA specifically directed to on-the-job relationships. It offers insights and techniques by which one can deal with people problems in organizations and change unsuccessful personal patterns of behavior.

Carl Rogers. *Client-Centered Therapy.* Boston: Houghton Mifflin, 1951. The basic text on the theory and practice of client-centered psychotherapy, from which the ideas of acceptance and active listening were derived.

Also Worthwhile

Linda Adams. *Effectiveness Training for Women.* New York: Wyden Books, 1979.

Joe Alexander. *Dare to Change: How to Program Yourself to Success.* New York: New American Library, 1984.

Eastwood Atwater. *Psychology of Adjustment: Personal Growth in a Changing World.* Englewood Cliffs, N.J.: Prentice-Hall, 1983.

Alban N. Bacchus. *Personal Wellness and Self-Realization.* Washington, D.C.: Oryn Publications, 1985.

Richard Nelson Bolles. *What Color Is Your Parachute? A Practical Manual for Job Hunters and Career Changers.* 3d ed. Berkeley, Calif.: Ten Speed Press, 1988.

Leo Buscaglia. *Living, Loving and Learning.* Thorofare, N.J.: Slack, 1982.

John R. Cheydleur, *How to Find and Be Yourself: Your Personality Portrait.* Anaheim, Calif.: Living Anaheim, 1989.

Daniel Druckman and John A. Swets, eds. *Enhancing Human Performance.* Washington, D.C.: National Academy Press, 1988.

Wayne Dyer. *The Sky's the Limit.* New York: Simon & Schuster, 1980.

―――――. *Your Erroneous Zones.* New York: Avon, 1977.

―――――. *You'll See It When You Believe It.* New York: William Morrow & Co., 1989.

Martha Friedman. *Overcoming Your Fear of Success.* New York: Sea View Press, 1980.

M. Robert Gardner. *Self-Inquiry.* Boston: Little, Brown, 1983.

Herbert Goldberg. *The Inner Male.* New York: New American Library, 1987.

Wendell Johnson. *People in Quandaries: The Semantics of Personal Adjustment.* New York: Harper & Row, 1946.

Dorothy Jongeward et al. *Everybody Wins: Transactional Analysis Applied to Organizations.* Reading, Mass.: Addison-Wesley, 1973.

―――――. and Dru Scott. *Women as Winners.* Reading, Mass.: Addison-Wesley, 1976.

Gordon MacDonald. *Ordering Your Private World.* Chicago: Moody Press, 1984.

Harold W. Noonan. *Personal Identity.* New York: William Morrow & Co., 1989.

Dru Scott. *How to Put More Time in Your Life.* New York: Rowson Wade, 1980.

Hans Selye. M.D. *Stress without Distress.* Philadelphia: J.B. Lippincott, 1974.

Anthony Storr. *Solitude: A Return to the Self,* New York: Ballantine Books, 1989.

Carol Tribe. *Self World Understanding: Analysis and Observation Manual.* Dubuque, Iowa: Kendall Hunt Publishing, 1983.

Maurice F. Villiere. *Transactional Analysis at Work: A Guide for Business and Professional People.* Englewood Cliffs, N.J.: Prentice-Hall, 1981.

Abe Wagner. *The Transactional Manager: How to Solve People Problems with Transactional Analysis.* Englewood Cliffs, N. J.: Prentice-Hall, 1981.

Theodora Wells. *Keeping Your Cool Under Fire: Communicating Non-Defensively.* New York: McGraw-Hill, 1981.

Internal Cues

Let us now examine some of the ways in which one can acquire valid internal cues—that is, information and insights which originate within the individual.

Cues from Psychotherapy.   Although psychotherapy is conducted in a wide variety of ways, its basic purpose is to help the patient (or client) to better understand how his/her self-image, on the one hand, and his/her self, on the other, may be out of alignment. For when the map and the territory are out of sync, the individual's ability to function—to perform adequately as a spouse, parent, student, manager, employee—and to live a creative, productive life can be impaired.

To the extent that the therapy is nondirective or client-centered, it is the individual who engineers any changes in his or her self-image and/or self. Desirably, such changes lead to increased congruity between the two, thus liberating the person from internal conflict. In sum, psychotherapy is a professional mode of reprogramming.

Cues from Active Listening.   But can lay people be helpful to friends and associates? The answer is a guarded yes, provided that the person is not seriously disturbed. But being genuinely helpful sometimes requires a good deal of sensitivity and skill.

Have you ever tried to help someone who seemed unhappy, fearful, angry, envious, guilt-ridden, or insecure, and found yourself drawn rapidly into a quarrel? If so, you have discovered how unhelpful or even downright threatening your well-intentioned aid can be perceived to be by the other person. Incidentally, it is quite likely that your friend was suffering at the self-image level.

The challenge, then, is to help people who really need assistance but cannot accept it directly because they too readily see the helper as a threatening change agent. Carl Rogers and Richard Farson have proposed a safe and sound approach that they call Active Listening. Their article of the same title appears at the end of this chapter. In essence, their method consists of helping beleaguered persons to help themselves. If any change of self-image is necessary, the individual will conduct it—the changer and the changee will be one and the same.

It would be redundant to preview the article here, but these suggestions may increase its value to you:

1. The article's title, "Active Listening," may be misleading. Active listening is not simply attentive, careful listening. Therapeutic or empathic listening would be more apt.

2. The authors distinguish between sympathy and empathy. To keep on their wavelength, you might recall the Greek roots of those terms:

Sym (with) + *pathos* (feeling). When you sympathize with others you feel with them—you literally share their feeling. If they are grief-stricken, you are sad, too. If they are enraged, you are angry as well.

Em (in) + *pathos* (feeling). When you empathize with others you do not share their emotion, but you do understand how they feel. You imaginatively project yourself into their solitary confinement cells and accurately perceive what they are experiencing.

3. Probably the most important skill for the listener to develop is the ability to determine whether the speaker needs *external* inputs (information, data, assistance, authority, advice—something that the listener can provide directly or help the speaker find) or *internal* inputs (feedback of the speaker's own thoughts, feelings, values, convictions, which may help the speaker understand oneself better).

One major caveat is to avoid giving internal inputs when external inputs are needed, and vice versa. To wit, these facetious but relevant illustrations:

Scene: A business office
Needed: External input
Provided: Internal input

Sam Salesman, visiting a customer firm for the first time, stops by Oscar Obtuse's open office door: "Pardon me, can you tell me where the men's room is?"

Oscar replies, "If I sense your feelings accurately, sir—you're experiencing some internal pressures, aren't you?"

Even in this liberated age, I fear Sam's response would be unprintable!

Scene: Same
Needed: Internal input
Provided: External input

Bristling with rage, Section D's supervisor, Mary, stomps into Oscar's office and with clenched teeth and obvious restraint says: "Boss, can you tell me precisely who has the responsibility for Section D?"

Oscar rummages through his cluttered desk, pulls out a yellowing organization chart, and benignly smiles: "Well, it looks like your name is in that box, Mary."

Aside from Archie Bunker, also fictional, it is difficult to conceive of anyone as dense as Oscar. But the distinction between internal and external input needs is not always so obvious as in Sam's and Mary's cases—especially when the individual's problems require both kinds of inputs.

Although it is demanding, active listening can be an exceedingly useful communication skill for managers, teachers, parents, spouses, and others who want to help effectively.

Cues from Videotaping. The advent of closed-circuit television taping has opened a unique and exciting avenue for providing cues at the self-image level. Videotaping has important advantages over certain other modes of feedback.

Authenticity. Technically, videotaping offers highly valid and immediate feedback. I blush for the many times TV's instant replay proved my calls incorrect—invariably calls I had made in favor of my team or player.

Visual feedback. Videotape is obviously superior to audiotape (alone) in that it adds the visual dimension.

Objectivity. A major advantage of videotaping over the mirror is that one can monitor oneself other than in real time. Thus, one can study oneself dispassionately and repeatedly as one appeared at previous times. The motion picture has the same capability, but videotape's economy and ease of operation—no film-developing time, simple lighting needs, the operator can be trained in the rudiments in a matter of minutes—places it in a class by itself.

Permanence. Videotapes can be stored indefinitely for replay at a subsequent date. Among other applications, this permits the assessment of skill development by comparisons of a person's performances over intervals of time.

Impact. Videotape gets to you! I am 15 pounds lighter than I used to be. Once I saw how I filled up the screen, my self-deceptions disintegrated. While feedback from others can sometimes be challenged and dismissed as ax-grinding, there is really no defense against videotape.

I recall a public accounting firm for which I conducted a seminar. Following our first video exercise one young CPA, who sported a prominent mustache, watched a replay of himself and promptly disappeared! Twenty minutes later he returned without his bushy appendage! He explained that his wife had repeatedly complained about his adornment but that he had discounted her feedback until he saw the walrus on TV!

Safety. Although videotape makes an impact, it is nontraumatic. Recall that threatening cues are generally those that embody the prospect of big, sudden, uncontrolled change. Videotape feedback involves none of those characteristics. Granted that you may have a few mild surprises concerning your appearance and behavior. But you will be quite able to accept the feedback largely because you (rather than some external agent or event) are providing it, albeit through the aegis of an electronic instrument.

In this vein, I will never forget Big George. Along with a group of fellow bankers, he came to one of my seminars. The group as a whole was splendid, as have been the large majority of the people I have met in my 35 years of teaching courses and conducting seminars. But Big George was a rousing exception. The man was incredibly arrogant and insensitive. The other members of the group were thoroughly disgusted with him. But they were powerless to feedback to him because George's defenses rendered him impervious to insult!

I recall one exchange in particular. George had just made a typically inane remark, and one exasperated participant looked him directly in the eyes and said in a voice dripping with sarcasm: "George, some people are fatheads, aren't they?"

George smiled knowingly, obviously assuming that the comment had been directed elsewhere, and replied earnestly: "You're damned right, Harry!"

Big George had the hide of an elephant—and I was crawling the walls! My job included helping people gain some self-image validity, and nothing seemed to be working with George.

Fortunately, I had four full days with the group and the availability of videotape. I used it generously. And, to be fair, George did participate. But I could detect no change. Finally, the seminar was concluded and many of the participants queued up to say good-bye to me—and Big George was in line!

I waited in some trepidation because George outweighed me by 80 pounds! Eventually he appeared, grasped my hand with both of his (a double handshake must be significant body language!), stared directly into my eyes, and said softly: "Thanks, Bill"—and left . . . leaving me with a folded-up note in my palm.

With superhuman restraint, I pocketed the note and bade farewell to my remaining seminarians. At long last they were all gone and I retrieved the note. It was a poem evidently composed by Big George. In stubby-penciled block letters:

> *There was a man that I knew well.*
> *I knew him to a tee,*
> *His looks, manners, voice, and dress*
> *Until I saw me—on TV.*

That's no Shakespearean sonnet, and I may be guilty of wishful thinking, but that was so much more of a response than I ever expected from
Big George! And if, indeed, he did receive feedback he could accept, that
his marvelous defenses would not shield out, I don't believe they came
from me or even from the group—but from the videotape. *He* put that feedback on the tape, and from himself he could take it!

One need not be a callous boor in order to profit from videotape. If you
are interested in receiving safe, authentic, impactful feedback, I enthusiastically recommend that you grab any opportunities to get before the
camera, particularly as you are interacting with others, and then view the
replay.

These two suggestions may add value to your TV experiences:

Cosmetic Effect.   If you have never or rarely seen yourself on tape,
you will probably have to overcome the do-I-really-look-like-that?
syndrome. You are likely to be quite enthralled with your physical
appearance and mannerisms. Accordingly, I like to give my people the
option of viewing their replays a number of times. Once the cosmetic effect
has been dissipated, they are ready for more challenging exercises in such
areas as conflict resolution, problem solving, decision making,
communication skills, role behavior, and conference leadership and
participation.

Relevant Activity.   Some people who are unaccustomed to videotaping may be initially uneasy and overly aware of the camera. A good
antidote is to be so involved with the activity that one is oblivious to the
taping and free to be oneself. Thus, I try to arrange to have people doing
things that are directly related to their needs and interests.

For example, I recently conducted a seminar for sales managers of
wholesale grocery products from H. J. Heinz, Pillsbury, Coca-Cola, Bea-
trice Foods, Kellogg, General Foods, and so forth. They sell at the district
levels to A&P, National, Ralph's, Safeway, Jewel, Dominick's, Kroger,
and so on. To add reality, I hired three professional buyers. The latter
were real-life customers (or their counterparts) of the salespersons.

Then came the role-playing. A salesperson would enter a buyer's
"office" and proceed to make a pitch. (The salesperson had been asked to
bring his/her tools such as samples, ads, displays, and data.) The buyers
had been requested to be themselves and to respond to the salespersons as
they normally would on the job. A camera recorded the interview while a
small audience—two of the salesperson's colleagues, the other two buyers,
and I—monitored the meeting in another room.

After the session ended, the salesperson joined us in the monitor
room, received our critique (which centered on what to look for in the
replay), and finally saw the replay. The next salesperson then interviewed a second buyer, and the process continued until each salesperson

had interviewed each of the buyers. Postseminar evaluations indicated that the salespersons regarded the videotaping as exceptionally helpful largely because of the realism of the activity. Granted that it was role-playing—a simulated sales interview—but the players were portraying their real-life roles.

An acid test for determining whether those taped have been thoroughly involved and relatively unconscious of the camera? If they heartily resent being cut off at the end of their allotted camera time: "Get lost—we want to finish our business!" I can assume that the videotaping has been unobtrusive.

Cues from Personal Stocktaking. Concluding this list of techniques for gaining a more valid self-image through internal inputs, I recommend two approaches to personal stocktaking. One is periodic—usually annually—and the other is current—as the occasion arises.

The Personal Inventory. Basic requirements: A pen, a pad of paper or a notebook, an hour of solitude, and a generous measure of self-honesty.

Caption page 1 thus: (your name): Who is he (or she)?[11] (date)

Then answer the following questions as objectively as possible:

1. What are his (or her) principal strengths? (In what one, two or three areas are you especially strong and able? This is no time for false modesty—no other people will ever see this document unless you let them. So, what do you do well? Where do you *really shine?*)

2. What are his (or her) principal deficiencies? (No point in pulling your punches here either. Restrain your shame or guilt—in what one, two, or three significant areas do you fall short?)

3. What are his (or her) values? (What do you really treasure? What are your priorities? What comes first with you? Second? Third? Wealth-fame-love-food-education-power-accomplishment-security-health-art-sex-work-religion-family-career-? If you had one week to live—and knew it—what would you be certain to do? Caution: List your values as they are, not as you feel they should be.)

4. What are his (or her) principles? (What do you believe in? What maxims have you gleaned from experience that you truly accept? Again, these are the guidelines that you actually adhere to, not the ideals that you wish you could measure up to. Don't list the golden rule, for example, unless you genuinely buy it and try to abide by it.)

---

[11] Suggestion: Refer to yourself as "he" or "she" rather than "I" to help maintain your role as impartial observer.

5. What "games" does he (or she) play with his (or her):

—boss?	—spouse?	—teachers?
—subordinates?	—children?	—siblings?
—customers?	—parents?	—others?

(What repetitive unconscious deceptions do you attempt to play with other people? Do you feel compelled to keep up the game-playing, or can you risk a gameless, more intimate relationship? Suggest that you review Berne or Harris or James and Jongeward [listed earlier in this chapter] to help you answer this question.)

6. What are his (or her) most important "*hangups*"? And what, if anything, does he (or she) plan to *do about them,* and when and how does he (or she) plan to do it? (This question will be discussed in more detail in the next section.)

7. Within the next year, what one or two attainable things could he (or she) do in order to wind up the year liking himself (or herself) more?

When you have completed the Inventory, lock it up so that no one, especially you, will see it. Then circle a date on your calendar a year hence to the day. When that day finally rolls around, repeat the Inventory, using the same format. Then—but not until then—get out your first edition and compare it with the one you have just written.

I make you two promises: (1) Provided that you were honest with yourself on both inventories, you will find some fascinating comparisons and changes! (2) If you prepare your Inventory twice—that is, two years in a row—you will find this annual assessment so rewarding that you will be sold on continuing it for the rest of your life!

The Personal Inventory is akin to the electrocardiogram in a sense. Cardiologists say that a single EKG has limited value. They would prefer a series of readouts spaced over a period of time to get a more accurate conception of the trends that are occurring. This enhances their ability to predict and thus to prescribe and control.

The objective of the Personal Inventory is similar. If you have a readout on yourself now and another a year from now you will have some basis for predicting rather than blindly, wishfully guessing how that readout will look in the third year. And accurate predictions enable you to control more of your personal development.

What is your philosophy of action? Do you prefer that life more or less happens to you—or do you want to call more of the shots? If you are inclined toward Socrates' sentiment that the "unexamined life is not worth living," you may find the Personal Inventory or your adaptation of it extremely worthwhile.

The Crisis Journal.   The Personal Inventory lends itself to a long-term, periodic self-assessment. But we can also capitalize on the immediate, specific, concrete learning opportunities that we call crises. I don't mean only life-and-death matters, but the times when we are frightened, infuriated, embarrassed, disillusioned, jealous, bewildered, disgusted, depressed, or, in general, roundly upset.

These distressing episodes can be acute learning experiences, provided that we treat them as such—if we can consider them in the dual sense that the Chinese do, as both dangers and opportunities. Accordingly, I recommend the *Crisis Journal* as a technique for gaining self-image knowledge during the periods when we are being tested.

Your only investment is a small notebook that you can carry with you constantly. Then the next time you find yourself in the midst of a crisis—you're uptight, offended, worried, guilt-stricken, angry—get off by yourself, cool off a bit (but not too much), and record[12] your answer to this question: What happened? Who, including myself, said or did what?—or failed to say or do what?—and why?

Important: Do not try to be rational or objective. Because at this moment your passions have taken over. Your IQ has temporarily dropped about 75 points, and you are an analytic imbecile! In transactional analysis terms, your Parent and your Child are having a raging battle and your Adult is out to lunch—powerless, ineffectual.

Do the one thing you can do now—and cannot do later: Record your data. Capture the rampant emotionality, the distorted value judgments, the defensiveness and irrationality erupting within you. Spill your guts as fully and uninhibitedly as you would to a thoroughly trusted confidant. You can expect two important benefits from this disgorging:

1. *Catharsis:* You will feel better immediately. Granted, the ventilating will not dissipate all the bad vibes, but it will allieviate some of the most acute discomfort and tension and, not incidentally, help restore some of your objectivity and judgment.

2. *Authenticity:* The primary objective of answering the what-happened question, however, is to record your current feelings accurately for future analysis. This can rarely be done as validly in retrospect. Who has not been embroiled in a heated argument only to find that later he or she was incapable of reconstructing the chain of events? This is because you are asking your Adult to report on what happened. Sorry, your Adult was probably so contaminated by your Parent or Child or both that it is unable to give an accurate account.

---

[12] Speaking into a tape recorder would be even better, for this would preserve your vocal cues, which could communicate an additional dimension of emotional information to you when you are able to listen dispassionately. I suggested the notebook only because of its portability, for you never know when you will need it.

The next step is to cool off enough for your Adult function to return. This may require anywhere from 10 minutes to a day or longer, depending upon you and the circumstances. Then get out your *Crisis Journal,* read the recorded information, and write answers to two additional questions:

1. *Was I defensive then?* Was my self-image somehow threatened, and accordingly, was I compelled to protect it? If your honest answer is yes (which is highly likely), answer the next question.

2. *What part of my self-image was I defending?* What facet of my self-image was contradicted (threatened with change) by the external cues (usually what others said and did)? To what part of me did the cues say, "No, you're not what you think you are"? Is this aspect of my self-concept, then, so frail and insecure that I simply cannot bear to have it challenged and thus am driven to throw up my defenses?

This completes the project insofar as Crisis Number One is concerned. Just keep your journal at the ready for the next upsetting experience.

The first step of the *Crisis Journal* technique calls for one, in the throes of a crisis, to do something constructive—specifically, to record current emotional data for subsequent processing. This is contrary to how most of us habitually respond to crises. Typically and understandably we immerse ourselves in the passions of the moment. Therefore, for the first few times that you attempt to apply the *Journal* technique, it will seem unnatural—at times you won't feel like doing it.

Thus, you must convince yourself in advance that this is the best and, in fact, the only time that you can capture your feelings and perceptions so accurately. Resolve that you will temporarily resist the urge to indulge yourself. As the *Crisis Journal* begins to produce insights and self-understanding, you will find the technique increasingly easy to use.

When does the payoff occur? That depends—upon the type of person you are, upon the kinds and frequency of your crises, upon your skills in recording and analyzing your behavior and feelings, and so on. (Those skills, incidentally, will sharpen with practice.) A reasonable expectation is that the technique will begin to bear fruit after about a half-dozen episodes.

On a day when you are feeling particularly sturdy and willing to face reality—when your Adult is definitely in charge—read through the half-dozen accounts, looking for patterns, for threads that seem to run through most if not all of the vignettes. The chances are that you will find some. And those recurrent themes can be valuable clues for you because they may reveal some aspects of yourself about which you are *not* totally sure—some fears and shortcomings that you have not recognized or admitted to yourself. Most likely, those feelings have been *repressed.*

The process usually occurs like this: Everyone has his or her own inadequacies and insecurities. There is no Superman or Wonder Woman other than in fiction. Such feelings can be uncomfortable, sometimes decidedly so, especially if one erroneously assumes that he or she is uniquely afflicted. As pain-avoidance organisms we often resort to defense mechanisms such as repression to diminish the discomfort.

Repression (semideliberate forgetting) consists of progressively squeezing the uncomfortable thoughts and feelings down and down until they submerge just below the level of consciousness. Then they just seem to go away and cease to bother us—consciously. But they never do go away—they are still there, lurking in that subterranean cellar, haunting us, gnawing at us in that nebulous, ill-defined, unscratchable-itch kind of way that we experience as vague feelings of guilt, anxiety, irritability, unease, depression, and so on.

These ghosts are our unconscious hangups—the ones we have hidden from ourselves because we have never been quite able to face up to them.

The objective, using the clues gleaned from the *Crisis Journal*, is to dredge up those hangups one at a time; to appraise them in the light of *today's* competence, strength, wisdom, and resources; and to decide what to do about them. They will fall along a continuum ranging from the whippables on over to the acknowledgeables—with many gradations between them.

The whippables are the hangups that we can now overcome because, having grown, we are bigger, stronger, and smarter than we were when the bugbears were too much for us. But if we have concealed our fear of a whippable by suppressing our consciousness of it, we cannot beat it until we bring it to the surface again and comprehend what it is that we must conquer.

For one example of a whippable, I cite my own experience. You may not be afflicted with this particular malady, but I can assure you that innumerable people are. They are the legion of poor souls who have a morbid dread of getting up and giving a talk before other people. Untechnically, this is called stage fright and I was a prime victim.

In my junior year in high school, I pulled every conceivable string to get out of that required public speaking course. And I succeeded! I didn't have to take it—what a narrow escape!

But in my senior year, I made a grievous error. I somehow got elected to class office, then realized I would have to give a 30-second acceptance speech before all 600 of my classmates! On the day of that assembly period, I was very uncoincidentally home and sick, sick both ways to be clinical about it! And I couldn't get better until I personally called the school to be sure that the accursed meeting was past history. The conversation (which should have won me an Academy Award) went like this:

Me: I'm really under the weather today . . . I think I'm going to die . . . but the worst thing is that I guess I'm not going to able to give this terrific speech . . . I've been looking forward to giving. . . .

Voice: You already missed it . . . assembly period's over!
Me: Oh, wow, that's terrible (this is the great acting part). Well, I guess we have our disappointments . . . well . . . (click!)

Only then could I get my stomach back to where it was supposed to be. And that monkey rode my back for six long years—three in the Army and three more in college. Finally, I pulled myself by the scruff of the neck and said, "Haney, when are you going to face up to this idiotic, juvenile fear—when are you going to start to grow up?" And the resounding answer was a feeble, "Well, . . ." and I went out and did perhaps the most courageous thing I've ever done in my life—I enrolled in a public speaking course. And it was terrifying at first. My speeches were horrible and I was quaking in my boots . . . but I was finally beginning to like it! To face up to one of your bugbears, to get a toehold, to make a little progress, that is joy—unadulterated joy.

So that's an example of a whippable. In fact, I've made a lifelong career of getting up and giving talks before groups of people. And in all honesty I have to ask myself, would I be in this profession of meeting with groups and still getting a great deal of satisfaction from doing it, if that stage fright nightmare had not been part of my history?

At the other end of the spectrum are the hangups that the individual still cannot and perhaps never will conquer, but perhaps can *acknowledge* and *accept*. An example of an acknowledgeable is offered by Marie, a 45-year-old mother, who describes an event that occurred 16 years earlier:

We went to the park for a Sunday excursion. I was sitting in a swing with our eight-month-old, Judy. Our two-and-a-half-year-old, Sharon, was climbing on a jungle gym. Our five-year-old, Larry, was on a merry-go-round. My husband was about 15 feet away, watching Sharon as she climbed. She reached the top, stepped across to the center post, slipped, and fell headfirst, landing on rocks at the bottom. She was unconscious; she had several head lacerations; her right shoulder, elbow, and knee were terribly scratched; and we thought she might have a broken neck.

Her father picked her up; we yelled for Larry; I carried Judy, and we ran to the car and on to the hospital. . . . She regained consciousness.

X rays were taken. She was stitched up, and we were told to watch her for any signs of concussion. We all went home. Sharon's only concern was her painful but superficial elbow and knee injuries. She seemed fine.

The next day, however, the doctor called and told us that Sharon had a fine-line skull fracture. But it was in a complete circle, so she would have to be watched carefully so that the area could not be hit again—risking the fracture slipping, chipping, or causing some other type of damage. It would take about six weeks to heal.

She *was* watched carefully. There was no hard playing, no climbing of any kind allowed, including stairs—I carried her. Even poor Larry was restricted from vigorous activity.

Over the next two years I found myself looking for excuses for not going to certain places where the children would climb or be in dangerous areas. And this went on for all three children—not just Sharon. If they looked as if they were going to go up something, I managed to be there and direct them elsewhere. I didn't really realize I was doing this.

One day, while looking through the kitchen window, I saw Sharon heading for the very climbable tree in our backyard, and I headed for the back door to ward her off. Suddenly I stopped as if I had hit a brick wall and heard the words, *"Stop doing that!"* To this day I don't know if I actually said this or heard a voice. But the words were there: "Stop doing that, let those kids grow." I ran back to our bedroom, shut the door, and just sat. I don't recall even thinking at that time. After a while I took a deep breath and went back to the kitchen. I didn't look out the window. Soon Sharon came in, unhurt, very happy, but I didn't ask her if she made it up the tree. I still don't know if she did.

Since then there have been plenty of trees, mountains, and other danger areas that the three have gotten into—and out of—in their manner. *I still haven't lost my fear.* But I have learned that they have their needs to climb and grow and that I can't stop them—nor do I want to.

All that was 16 years ago, but occasionally I have reminders. Larry once called me from boot camp: "Hi, Mom, guess what I'm doing? Skydiving!"

Mom took a deep breath: "That's great, Larry—that's something I've always wanted to do!" It's *not* what I've always wanted to do, and it never will be. But he will never know how that old fear grabbed at my heart again.

Marie, by her own admission, has not conquered her fear. But she has done the next best thing. She has been able to acknowledge its existence and to realize how her overgeneralized fear was causing her to smother her kids.

Let us return to the analogy of the stained-glass window in one's solitary confinement cell. The window, one's frame of reference, is composed of a myriad of colored, distorting lenses. Its most significant lens or, more accurately, complex of lenses is one's self-image. Repressed fears and inadequacies may be the most acutely deceptive lenses of all. I can personally vouch for that assertion. I still recall how that fear of public speaking contaminated my perceptions—my contact with people, my career plans— everything tainted by that one corrupting lens. Thus, when one exposes a hangup, he or she is able at long last to recognize the existence of the lens.

If the bugbear is essentially whippable, and the individual does indeed conquer it, or cut it down to size, this is tantamount to plucking the lens out of one's window. If the best that one can do is to acknowledge and accommodate the bugbear, then one can at least understand how the lens has been coloring his or her perception of reality and learn to compensate for the distortion—as in correcting for a bent pencil in a glass of water.

Whether by removing the lens or correcting for its distortion, one clarifies a frame of reference to that extent. Thus one is able to perceive reality more realistically and to deal with it more appropriately and intelligently. This is the bottom line result for which the foregoing list of external and internal cues have been proposed.

SUMMARY

This chapter began with the premise that a person in a responsible position needs to have an exceptionally realistic self-image (ERSI) in order to function well. With an ERSI, one is liberated from constantly expending energy for self-image defense; more capable of maintaining and increasing the validity of one's self-image; able to understand, predict, and cope with others more effectively; better able to distinguish valid from invalid inputs; and more likely to select realistic personal goals.

For those who wish to make a concerted effort to attain and maintain an ERSI, I offered a three-step program:

1. Make a commitment—decide that you really want to know yourself better and that you are willing to pay the price (time, effort, temporary unease) which may be required.
2. Learn to recognize and to reduce your defenses against the cues from reality.
3. Receive and evaluate those cues in order to assess how your current self-image and your authentic self may be incongruent.

The major categories of external cues (feedback from outside one's skin) included feedback from others (the mechanism of which was discussed in detail in connection with the Johari Grid concept), psychometric instruments, and readings. Internal cues can be acquired through psychotherapy, active listening, videotape playback, and personal stocktaking techniques such as the *Personal Inventory* and the *Crisis Journal*.

The ultimate objective, again, was an exceptionally realistic self-image and a substantial measure of emotional maturity—high rewards. There was no promise that the venture would be without effort or discomfort. For, to augment the Bible, "The truth shall make you free . . . but for a while it may make you a bit miserable."

Discussion Questions

1. The central premise of Chapter 6 is that an ERSI is required in order to communicate with or deal with others well. What is the rationale for this assertion? Do you accept it?

2. What do you think of the five advantages associated with attaining and maintaining an ERSI? Do you agree with them? Are there other advantages that are equally or even more important? Are there disadvantages in possessing an ERSI?

3. Lew Sarett said, "Everyone needs . . . a block of granite to stand on and a star as a guide." What is so important about the star? About the block of granite?

4. "Desirable reprogramming requires that the inputs be both valid and tolerable." Why?

5. "The most important single reason most of us do not understand ourselves better lies in our own internal fortifications that seal us off from contrary, disturbing cues from reality." Do you agree? Disagree? Why?

6. Should the public area dominate the Johari Grid?

7. Is it best to reduce the hidden area of the Johari Grid to nil?

8. Is it best to reduce the blind area of the Johari Grid to nil?

9. Since one's unconscious area is known neither to the Johari Grid's owner nor to the person to whom he or she is relating, can that area be reduced only through psychotherapy?

10. What is the best way to cope with a "pumper?"

11. Your optimal public area depends upon *you*, the *other* person, and the *environment* in which the two of you are interrelating. Do you accept this assertion? Would you delete any of these factors? Add others?

12. What do you think of TA? Is it a valid construct? Do you feel that it might be helpful to you? If so, how?

13. What do you think of the author's use of psychometric instruments? Can they really be helpful as focus sharpeners and search-area-narrowers?

14. The author states that readings, per se, do not provide self-image feedback. How, then, can they be helpful?

15. Psychotherapy's basic purpose is to help the patient (or client) bring his or her self-image and self into greater congruity. What do you think of this view of psychotherapy?

16. Active Listening—in what ways is it like or unlike nondirective psychotherapy?

17. Why is feedback from videotape considered safe?

18. How do you feel about doing the *Personal Inventory*? Eager? Curious? Queasy? Indifferent? Negative?

19. Probably the most difficult step in the *Crisis Journal* technique is answering the first question: *What happened?* How can you develop skill in executing this step?

20. If one cannot overcome a fear or weakness, what is the value of merely acknowledging it?

A R T I C L E

Active Listening*
Carl R. Rogers and Richard E. Farson

The Meaning of Active Listening

One basic responsibility of the supervisor or executive is the development, adjustment, and integration of individual employees. He or she tries to develop employee potential, delegate responsibility, and achieve cooperation. To do so, he must have, among other abilities, the ability to listen intelligently and carefully to those with whom he works.

There are, however, many kinds of listening skills. The lawyer, for example, when questioning a witness, listens for contradictions, irrelevancies, errors, and weaknesses. But this is not the kind of listening skill we are concerned with in this booklet. The lawyer usually is not listening in order to help the witness adjust or cooperate or produce. On the other hand, we will be concerned with listening skills which *will help* employees gain a clearer understanding of their situation, take responsibility, and cooperate with each other.

Two Examples.   The kind of listening we have in mind is called "active listening." It is called "active" because the listener has a very definite responsibility. He does not passively absorb the words which are spoken, but he actively tries to grasp the facts and the feelings in what he hears, to help the speaker work out his own problems.

To get a fuller picture of what is meant by active listening, let us consider two different approaches to the same work problem.

Example No. 1
Foreman: Hey, Al, I don't get this production order. We can't handle this run today. What do they think we are?
Supervisor: But that's the order. So get it out as soon as you can. We're under terrific pressure this week.
Foreman: Don't they know we're behind schedule already because of that press breakdown?
Supervisor: Look, Kelly, I don't decide what goes on upstairs. I just have to see that the work gets out and that's what I'm gonna do.
Foreman: The guys aren't gonna like this.
Supervisor: That's something you'll have to work out with them, not me.

---

* Reproduced by special permission of the authors and The University of Chicago's Industrial Relations Center.

Example No. 2

Foreman: Hey, Ross, I don't get this production order. We can't handle this run today. What do they think we are?

Supervisor: Sounds like you're pretty sore about it, Kelly.

Foreman: I sure am. We were just about getting back to schedule after that press breakdown. Now this comes along.

Supervisor: As if you didn't have enough work to do, huh?

Foreman: Yeah. I don't know how I'm gonna tell the guys about this.

Supervisor: Hate to face 'em with it now, is that it?

Foreman: I really do. They're under a real strain today. Seems like everything we do around here is rush, rush.

Supervisor: I guess you feel like it's unfair to load anything more on them.

Foreman: Well, yeah. I know there must be plenty of pressure on everybody up the line, but—well, if that's the way it is . . . guess I'd better get the word to 'em.

There are obviously many differences between these two examples. The main one, however, is that Ross, the supervisor in the second example, is using the active-listening approach. He is listening and responding in a way that makes it clear that he appreciates both the meaning and the feeling behind what Kelly is saying.

Active listening does not necessarily mean long sessions spent listening to grievances, personal or otherwise. It is simply a way of approaching those problems which arise out of the usual day-to-day events of any job.

To be effective, active listening must be firmly grounded in the basic attitudes of the user. We cannot employ it as a technique if our fundamental attitudes are in conflict with its basic concepts. If we try, our behavior will be empty and sterile and our associates will be quick to recognize this. Until we can demonstrate a spirit which genuinely respects the potential worth of the individual, which considers his rights and trusts his capacity for self-direction, we cannot begin to be effective listeners.

What We Achieve by Listening. Active listening is an important way to bring about changes in people. Despite the popular notion that listening is a passive approach, clinical and research evidence clearly shows that sensitive listening is a most effective agent for individual personality change and group development. Listening brings about changes in people's attitudes toward themselves and others, and also brings about changes in their basic values and personal philosophy. People who have been listened to in this new and special way become more emotionally mature, more open to their experiences, less defensive, more democratic, and less authoritarian.

When people are listened to sensitively, they tend to listen to themselves with more care and make clear exactly what they are feeling and thinking. Group members tend to listen more to each other, become less argumentative, more ready to incorporate other points of view. Because listening reduces the threat of having one's ideas criticized, the person is better able to see them for what they are, and is more likely to feel that his contributions are worthwhile.

Not the least important result of listening is the change that takes place within the listener himself. Besides the fact that listening provides more information than any other activity, it builds deep, positive relationships and tends to alter constructively the attitudes of the listener. Listening is a growth experience.

These, then, are some of the worthwhile results we can expect from active listening. But how do we go about this kind of listening? How do we become active listeners?

How to Listen

Active listening aims to bring about changes in people. To achieve this end, it relies upon definite techniques—things to do and things to avoid doing. Before discussing these techniques, however, we should first understand why they are effective. To do so, we must understand how the individual personality develops.

The Growth of the Individual.   Through all of our lives, from early childhood on, we have learned to think of ourselves in certain, very definite ways. We have built up pictures of ourselves. Sometimes these self-pictures are pretty realistic but at other times they are not. For example, an overage, overweight lady may fancy herself a youthful, ravishing siren, or an awkward teenager regard himself as a star athlete.

All of us have experiences which fit the way we need to think about ourselves. These we accept. But it is much harder to accept experiences which don't fit. And sometimes, if it is very important for us to hang on to this self-picture, we don't accept or admit these experiences at all.

These self-pictures are not necessarily attractive. A man, for example, may regard himself as incompetent and worthless. He may feel that he is doing his job poorly in spite of favorable appraisals by the company. As long as he has these feelings about himself he must deny any experiences which would seem not to fit this self-picture, in this case any that might indicate to him that he is competent. It is so necessary for him to maintain this self-picture that he is threatened by anything which would tend to change it. Thus, when the company raises his salary, it may seem to him only additional proof that he is a fraud. He must hold onto his self-picture, because, bad or good, it's the only thing he has by which he can identify himself.

This is why direct attempts to change this individual or change his self-picture are particularly threatening. He is forced to defend himself or to completely deny the experience. This denial of experience and defense of the self-picture tend to bring on rigidity of behavior and create difficulties in personal adjustment.

The active-listening approach, on the other hand, does not present a threat to the individual's self-picture. He does not have to defend it. He is able to explore it, see it for what it is, and make his own decision as to how realistic it is. And he is then in a position to change.

If I want to help a man reduce his defensiveness and become more adaptive, I must try to remove the threat of myself as his potential changer. As long as the atmosphere is threatening, there can be no effective communication. So I must create a climate which is neither critical, evaluative, nor moralizing. It must be an atmosphere of equality and freedom, permissiveness and understanding, acceptance and warmth. It is in this climate and this climate only that the individual feels safe enough to incorporate new experiences and new values into his concept of himself. Let's see how active listening helps to create this climate.

What to Avoid. When we encounter a person with a problem, our usual response is to try to change his way of looking at things—to get him to see his situation the way we see it, or would like him to see it. We plead, reason, scold, encourage, insult, prod—anything to bring about a change in the desired direction; that is, in the direction we want him to travel. What we seldom realize, however, is that, under these circumstances, we are usually responding to *our own* needs to see the world in certain ways. It is always difficult for us to tolerate and understand actions which are different from the ways in which *we* believe *we* should act. If, however, we can free ourselves from the need to influence and direct others in our own paths, we enable ourselves to listen with understanding, and thereby employ the most potent available agent of change.

One problem the listener faces is that of responding to demands for decisions, judgments, and evaluations. He is constantly called upon to agree or disagree with someone or something. Yet, as he well knows, the question or challenge frequently is a masked expression of feelings or needs which the speaker is far more anxious to communicate than he is to have the surface question answered. Because he cannot speak these feelings openly, the speaker must disguise them to himself and to others in an acceptable form. To illustrate, let us examine some typical questions and the type of answers that might best elicit the feeling beneath each of them.

Employee's question	Listener's answer
Just whose responsibility is the toolroom?	Do you feel that someone is challenging your authority in there?
Don't you think younger able people should be promoted before senior but less able ones?	It seems to you they should, I take it.
What does the super expect us to do about these broken-down machines?	You're pretty disgusted with those machines, aren't you?
Don't you think I've improved over the last review period?	Sounds as if you feel like you've really picked up over those last few months.

These responses recognize the questions but leave the way open for the employee to say what is really bothering him. They allow the listener to participate in the problem or situation without shouldering all responsibility for decision making or actions. This is a process of thinking *with* people instead of *for* or *about* them.

Passing judgment, whether critical or favorable, makes free expression difficult. Similarly, advice and information are almost always seen as efforts to change a person and thus serve as barriers to his self-expression and the development of a creative relationship. Moreover, advice is seldom taken and information hardly ever utilized. The eager young trainee probably will not become patient just because he is advised that, "The road to success in business is a long, difficult one, and you must be patient." And it is no more helpful for him to learn that "only one out of a hundred trainees reach top management positions."

Interestingly, it is difficult lesson to learn that positive *evaluations* are sometimes as blocking as negative ones. It is almost as destructive to the freedom of a relationship to tell a person that he is good or capable or right, as to tell him otherwise. To evaluate him positively "may make it difficult for him to tell of the faults that distress him" or the ways in which he believes he is not competent.

Encouragement also may be seen as an attempt to motivate the speaker in certain directions or hold him off rather than as support. "I'm sure everything will work out OK" is not a helpful response to the person who is deeply discouraged about a problem.

In other words, most of the techniques and devices common to human relationships are found to be of little use in establishing the type of relationship we are seeking here.

What to Do.   Just what does active listening entail, then? Basically, it requires that we get inside the speaker, that we grasp, *from his point of view,* just what it is he is communicating to us. More than that, we must convey to the speaker that we are seeing things from his point of view. To listen actively, then, means that there are several things we must do.

Listen for total meaning.   Any message a person tries to get across usually has two components: the *content* of the message and the *feeling* or attitude underlying this content. Both are important, both give the message *meaning*. It is this total meaning of the message that we try to understand. For example, a machinist comes to his foreman and says, "I've finished that lathe set-up." This message has obvious content and perhaps calls upon the foreman for another work assignment. Suppose, on the other hand, that he says, "Well, I'm finally finished with that damned lathe set-up." The content is the same but the total meaning of the message has changed—and changed in an important way for both the foreman and the worker. Here sensitive listening can facilitate the relationship. Suppose the foreman were to respond by simply giving another work assignment. Would the employee feel that he had gotten his total message across? Would he feel free to talk to his foreman? Will he feel better about his job, more anxious to do good work on the next assignment?

Now, on the other hand, suppose the foreman were to respond with, "Glad to have it over with, huh?" or "Had a pretty rough time of it?" or "Guess you don't feel like doing anything like that again?" or anything else that tells the worker that he heard and understands. It doesn't necessarily mean that the next work assignment need be changed or that he must spend an hour listening to the worker complain about the set-up problems he encountered. He may do a number of things differently in the light of the new information he has from the worker—but not necessarily. It's just that extra sensitivity on the part of the foreman which can transform an average working climate into a good one.

Respond to feelings.   In some instances, the content is far less important than the feeling which underlies it. To catch the full flavor or meaning of the message one must respond particularly to the feeling component. If, for instance, our machinist had said, "I'd like to melt this lathe down and make paper clips out of it," responding to content would be obviously absurd. But to respond to his disgust or anger in trying to work with his lathe recognizes the meaning of this message. There are various shadings of these components in the meaning of any message. Each time the listener must try to remain sensitive to the total meaning the message has to the speaker. What is he trying to tell me? What does this mean to him? How does he see this situation?

Note all cues.   Not all communication is verbal. The speaker's words alone don't tell us everything he is communicating. And hence, truly sensitive listening requires that we become aware of several kinds of communication besides verbal. The way in which a speaker hesitates in his speech can tell us much about his feelings. So too can the inflection of his voice. He may stress certain points loudly and clearly, and may mumble others. We should also note such things as the person's facial expressions, body posture, hand movements, eye movements, and breathing. All these help to convey his total message.

What We Communicate by Listening. The first reaction of most people when they consider listening as a possible method for dealing with human beings is that listening cannot be sufficient in itself. Because it is passive, they feel, listening does not communicate anything to the speaker. Actually, nothing could be farther from the truth.

By consistently listening to a speaker, you are conveying the idea that: "I'm interested in you as a person, and I think that what you feel is important. I respect your thoughts, and even if I don't agree with them, I know that they are valid for you. I feel sure that you have a contribution to make. I'm not trying to change you or evaluate you. I just want to understand you. I think you're worth listening to, and I want you to know that I'm the kind of person you can talk to."

The subtle but most important aspect of this is that it is the *demonstration* of the message that works. While it is most difficult to convince someone that you respect him by *telling* him so, you are much more likely to get this message across by really *behaving* that way—by actually *having* and *demonstrating* respect for this person. Listening does this most effectively.

Like other behavior, listening behavior is contagious. This has implications for all communications problems, whether between two people or within a large organization. To ensure good communication between associates up and down the line, one must first take the responsibility for setting a pattern of listening. Just as one learns that anger is usually met with anger, argument with argument, and deception with deception, one can learn that listening can be met with listening. Every person who feels responsibility in a situation can set the tone of the interaction, and the important lesson in this is that any behavior exhibited by one person will eventually be responded to with similar behavior in the other person.

It is far more difficult to stimulate constructive behavior in another person but far more profitable. Listening is one of these constructive behaviors, but if one's attitude is to "wait out" the speaker rather than really listen to him, it will fail. The one who consistently listens with understanding, however, is the one who eventually is most likely to be listened to. If you really want to be heard and understood by another, you can develop him as a potential listener, ready for new ideas, provided you can first develop yourself in these ways and sincerely listen with understanding and respect.

Testing for Understanding. Because understanding another person is actually far more difficult than it at first seems, it is important to test constantly your ability to see the world in the way the speaker sees it. You can do this by reflecting in your own words what the speaker seems to mean by his words and actions. His response to this will tell you whether or not he feels understood. A good rule of thumb is to assume that one never really understands until he can communicate this understanding to the other's satisfaction.

Here is an experiment to test your skill in listening. The next time you become involved in a lively or controversial discussion with another person, stop for a moment and suggest that you adopt this ground rule for continued discussion: Before either participant in the discussion can make a point or express an opinion of his own, he must first restate aloud the previous point or position of the other person. This restatement must be accurate enough to satisfy the speaker before the listener can be allowed to speak for himself.

This is something you could try in your own discussion group. Have someone express himself on some topic of emotional concern to the group. Then, before another member expresses his own feelings and thought, he must rephrase the *meaning* expressed by the previous speaker to that individual's satisfaction. Note the changes in the emotional climate and the quality of the discussion when you try this.

Problems in Active Listening

Active listening is not an easy skill to acquire. It demands practice. Perhaps more important, it may require changes in our own basic attitudes. These changes come slowly and sometimes with considerable difficulty. Let us look at some of the major problems in active listening and what can be done to overcome them.

The Personal Risk. To be effective at all in active listening, one must have a sincere interest in the speaker. We all live in glass houses as far as our attitudes are concerned. They always show through. And if we are only making a pretense of interest in the speaker, he will quickly pick this up, either consciously or unconsciously. And once he does, he will no longer express himself freely.

Active listening carries a strong element of personal risk. If we manage to accomplish what we are describing here—to sense deeply the feelings of another person, to understand the meaning his experiences have for him, to see the world as he sees it—we risk being changed ourselves. For example, if we permit ourselves to listen our way into the psychological life of a labor leader or agitator—to get the meaning which life has for him—we risk coming to see the world as he sees it. It is threatening to give up, even momentarily, what we believe and start thinking in someone else's terms. It takes a great deal of inner security and courage to be able to risk one's self in understanding another.

For the supervisor, the courage to take another's point of view generally means that he must see *himself* through another's eyes—he must be able to see himself as others see him. To do this may sometimes be unpleasant, but it is far more *difficult* than unpleasant. We are so accustomed to viewing ourselves in certain ways—to seeing and hearing only what we want to see and hear—that it is extremely difficult for a person to free himself from his needs to see things these ways.

Developing an attitude of sincere interest in the speaker is thus no easy task. It can be developed only by being willing to risk seeing the world from the speaker's point of view. If we have a number of such experiences, however, they will shape an attitude which will allow us to be truly genuine in our interest in the speaker.

Hostile Expressions.   The listener will often hear negative, hostile expressions directed at himself. Such expressions are always hard to listen to. No one likes to hear hostile action or words. And it is not easy to get to the point where one is strong enough to permit those attacks without finding it necessary to defend himself or retaliate.

Because we all fear that people will crumble under the attack of genuine negative feelings, we tend to perpetuate an attitude of pseudo-peace. It is as if we cannot tolerate conflict at all for fear of the damage it could do to us, to the situation, to the others involved. But of course the real damage is done to all these by the denial and suppression of negative feelings.

Out-of-Place Expressions.   There is also the problem of out-of-place expressions, expressions dealing with behavior that is not usually acceptable in our society. In the extreme, forms that present themselves before psychotherapists—expressions of sexual perversity or homicidal fantasies—are often found to be blocking to the listener because of their obvious threatening quality. At less extreme levels, we all find unnatural or inappropriate behavior difficult to handle. That is, anything from an "off color" story told in mixed company to seeing a man weep is likely to produce a problem situation.

In any face-to-face situation, we will find instances of this type which will momentarily, if not permanently, block any communication. In business and industry, any expressions of weakness or incompetency will generally be regarded as unacceptable and therefore will block good two-way communication. For example, it is difficult to listen to a supervisor tell of his feelings of failure in being able to "take charge" of a situation in his department because *all* administrators are supposed to be able to "take charge."

Accepting Positive Feelings.   It is both interesting and perplexing to note that negative or hostile feelings or expressions are much easier to deal with in any face-to-face relationship than are truly and deeply positive feelings. This is especially true for the businessman because the culture expects him to be independent, bold, clever, and aggressive and manifest no feelings of warmth, gentleness, and intimacy. He therefore comes to regard these feelings as soft and inappropriate. But no matter how they are regarded, they remain a human need. The denial of these feelings in himself and his associates does not get the executive out of the problem in dealing with them. They simply become veiled and confused. If recognized, they would work for the total effort; unrecognized, they work against it.

Emotional Danger Signals. The listener's own emotions are sometimes a barrier to active listening. When emotions are at their height, when listening is most necessary, it is most difficult to set aside one's own concerns and be understanding. Our emotions are often our own worst enemies when we try to become listeners. The more involved and interested we are in a particular situation or problem, the less we are likely to be willing or able to listen to the feelings and attitudes of others. That is, the more we find it necessary to respond to our own needs, the less we are able to respond to the needs of another. Let us look at some of the main danger signals that warn us that our emotions may be interfering with our listening.

Defensiveness. The points about which one is most vocal and dogmatic, the points which one is most anxious to impose on others—these are always the points one is trying to talk oneself into believing. So one danger signal becomes apparent when you find yourself stressing a point or trying to convince another. It is at these times that you are likely to be less secure and consequently less able to listen.

Resentment of opposition. It is always easier to listen to an idea which is similar to one of your own than to an opposing view. Sometimes, in order to clear the air, it is helpful to pause for a moment when you feel your ideas and position being challenged, reflect on the situation, and express your concern to the speaker.

Clash of personalities. Here again, our experience has consistently shown us that the genuine expression of feelings on the part of the listener will be more helpful in developing a sound relationship than the suppression of them. This is so whether the feelings be resentment, hostility, threat, or admiration. A basically honest relationship, whatever the nature of it, is the most productive of all. The other party becomes secure when he learns that the listener can express his feelings honestly and openly to him. We should keep this in mind when we begin to fear a clash of personalities in the listening relationship. Otherwise, fear of our own emotions will choke off full expression of feelings.

Listening to Ourselves.   To listen to oneself is a prerequisite to listening to others. And it is often an effective means of dealing with the problems we have outlined above. When we are most aroused, excited, and demanding, we are least able to understand our own feelings and attitudes. Yet, in dealing with the problems of others, it becomes most important to be sure of one's own position, values, and needs.

The ability to recognize and understand the meaning which a particular episode has for you, with all the feelings which it stimulates in you, and the ability to express this meaning when you find it getting in the way of active listening, will clear the air and enable you once again to be free to listen. That is, if some person or situation touches off feelings within you which tend to block your attempts to listen with understanding, begin listening to yourself. It is much more helpful in developing effective relationships to avoid suppressing these feelings. Speak them out as clearly as you can, and try to enlist the other person as a listener to your feelings. A person's listening ability is limited by his ability to listen to himself.

Active Listening and Company Goals

"How can listening improve production?"

"We're in business, and it's a rugged, fast, competitive affair. How are we going to find time to counsel our employees?"

"We have to concern ourselves with organizational problems first."

"We can't afford to spend all day listening when there's a job to be done."

"What's morale got to do with production?"

"Sometimes we have to sacrifice an individual for the good of the rest of the people in the company."

Those of us who are trying to advance the listening approach in industry hear these comments frequently. And because they are so honest and legitimate, they pose a real problem. Unfortunately, the answers are not so clear-cut as the questions.

Individual Importance.   One answer is based on an assumption that is central to the listening approach. That assumption is: the kind of behavior which helps the individual will eventually be the best thing that could be done for the group. Or saying it another way: the things that are best for the individual are best for the company. This is a conviction of ours, based on our experience in psychology and education. The research evidence from industry is only beginning to come in. We find that putting the group first, at the expense of the individual, besides being an uncomfortable individual experience, does *not* unify the group. In fact, it tends to make the group less a group. The members become anxious and suspicious.

We are not at all sure in just what ways the group does benefit from a concern demonstrated for an individual, but we have several strong leads. One is that the group feels more secure when an individual member is being listened to and provided for with concern and sensitivity. And we assume that a secure group will ultimately be a better group. When each individual feels that he need not fear exposing himself to the group, he is likely to contribute more freely and spontaneously. When the leader of a group responds to the individual, puts the individual first, the other members of the group will follow suit, and the group comes to act as a unit in recognizing and responding to the needs of a particular member. This positive, constructive action seems to be a much more satisfying experience for a group than the experience of dispensing with a member.

Listening and Production.   As to whether or not listening or any other activity designed to better human relations in an industry actually raises production—whether morale has a definite relationship to production—is not known for sure. There are some who frankly hold that there is no relationship to be expected between morale and production— that production often depends upon the social misfit, the eccentric, or the isolate. And there are some who simply choose to work in a climate of cooperation and harmony, in a high-morale group, quite aside from the question of increased production.

A report from the Survey Research Center at the University of Michigan on research conduct at the Prudential Life Insurance Company lists seven findings relating to production and morale.[1] First-line supervisors in high-production work groups were found to differ from those in low-production work groups in that they:

1. Are under less close supervision from their own supervisors.
2. Place less direct emphasis upon production as the goal.
3. Encourage employee participation in the making of decisions.
4. Are more employee centered.
5. Spend more of their time in supervision and less in straight production work.
6. Have a greater feeling of confidence in their supervisory roles.
7. Feel that they know where they stand with the company.

After mentioning that other dimensions of morale, such as identification with the company, intrinsic job satisfaction, and satisfaction with job

---

[1] Productivity, Supervision, and Employee Morale," *Human Relations*, series 1, report 1 (Ann Arbor: Survey Research Center, University of Michigan).

status, were not found significantly related to productivity, the report goes on to suggest the following psychological interpretation:

> People are more effectively motivated when they are given some degree of freedom in the way in which they do their work than when every action is prescribed in advance. They do better when some degree of decision-making about their jobs is possible than when all decisions are made for them. They respond more adequately when they are treated as personalities [rather] than as cogs in a machine. In short, if the ego motivations of self-determination, of self-expression, of a sense of personal worth can be tapped, the individual can be more effectively energized. The use of external sanctions, or pressuring for production, may work to some degree, but not to the extent that the more internalized motives do. When the individual comes to identify himself with his job and with the work of his group, human resources are much more fully utilized in the production process.

Maximum Creativeness.   There may never be enough research evidence to satisfy everyone on this question. But speaking from a business point of view, in terms of the problem of developing resources for production, the maximum creativeness and productive effort of the human beings in the organization are the richest untapped source of power still existing. The difference between the maximum productive capacity of people and that output which industry is now realizing is immense. We simply suggest that this maximum capacity might be closer to realization if we sought to release the motivation that already exists within people rather than try to stimulate them externally.

This releasing of the individual is made possible first of all by sensitive listening, with respect and understanding. Listening is a beginning toward making the individual feel himself worthy of making contributions, and this could result in a very dynamic and productive organization. Competitive business is never too rugged or too busy to take time to procure the most efficient technological advances or to develop raw material sources. But these in comparison to the resources that are already within the people in the plant are paltry. This is industry's major procurement problem.

The decision to spend time listening to his employees is a decision each supervisor or executive has to make for himself. Executives seldom have much to do with products or processes. They have to deal with people who must in turn deal with people who will deal with products or processes. The higher one goes up the line, the more he will be concerned with human relations problems, simply because people are all he has to work with. The minute we take a man from his bench and make him a foreman, he is removed from the basic production of goods and now must begin relating to individuals instead of nuts and bolts. People are different from things, and our foreman is called upon for a different line of skills completely. His new tasks call upon him to be a special kind of a person. The development of himself as a listener is an important first step.

Discussion Questions

1. What is the purpose of active listening?

2. What is *not* the purpose of active listening?

3. When is active listening appropriate?

4. Why does active listening work?

5. Can active listening help a company in which it is practiced effectively?

6. Note that passing judgment, either critical or favorable, inhibits free expression. Discuss why even positive, favorable evaluations are barriers to communication.

7. Discuss the ways the business culture encourages negative rather than positive feelings—the tendency to view the human need for warmth and intimacy as soft and inappropriate to business.

8. Discuss what the listener communicates when engaged in active listening.

9. Discuss the risk of the listener being changed.

10. Discuss how the group feels more secure when an individual member is listened to with concern and sensitivity.

Motivation and Communication
What Turns Us On and Off

❋
❋
❋

In Chapter 4, we briefly considered the effects of needs, physiological and psychological, upon perception and thus upon communicative behavior. Indeed, the influence of needs[1] is so pervasive and telling that they deserve at least a chapter if we are to adequately consider communication in a behavioral setting.

Whatever these needs and their respective intensities may be at a given moment can affect one's perceptions and therefore one's behavior—even at the physiological level. Market researchers, for example, conclude that one tends to buy significantly more in a supermarket when hungry than directly after a full meal. A bachelor friend tells me that he prepares his breakfast and packs his lunch before going to work. He discovered that he had to make an adjustment because his lunch was either too abundant or too skimpy, depending upon whether he packed it before or after eating breakfast.

The potency of *needs* in affecting *perception* has been demonstrated repeatedly. The early studies in hunger, for example, reported that hungry persons will complete words such as ME_____ more frequently as food words such as MEAT or MEAL than will nonhungry persons. Moreover, hungrier subjects saw more food objects in very unstructured stimuli than did less hungry ones.

---

[1] Need is defined simply but adequately as "something within an individual that prompts that person to action" (Paul Hersey and Kenneth H. Blanchard, *Management of Organizational Behavior: Utilizing Human Resources,* 5th ed. [Englewood Cliffs, N.J.: Prentice-Hall, 1988], p. 19.) Cognitive psychologists define a *need* or *motive* as "an inner force which impels a person to behave in a particular way." See H. Joseph Reitz, *Behavior in Organizations,* 3rd ed. (Homewood, Ill.: Richard D. Irwin, 1987), p. 74.

A MOTIVATION MODEL

Let us consider more specifically the role of *motivation* in human behavior. Motivation is the internal process leading to behavior to satisfy needs.[2] Leavitt[3] provides a model which he derives from three basic premises:

1. Behavior is *caused*. The things we do don't just happen—there are always underlying reasons. This does not mean, necessarily, that these reasons will be apparent even to the individual who is doing those things.
2. Behavior is *directed*. Ultimately, there is no aimless behavior. We are always pursuing some goal or other. Again, there is no necessity to assume that we are conscious of our goals or that we are approaching them most efficiently.
3. Behavior is *motivated*. Underlying what we do are motives, drives that provide us with the energy to attain our goals, or at least to move in the direction of our goals.

Relate these three ideas, says Leavitt, and you have a system for understanding behavior. (This basic model of behavior is illustrated in Figure 7.1.) According to Leavitt:

> With the help of these ideas, human behavior can be viewed as part of a double play from cause to motive to behavior-toward-a-goal. And it is also helpful to think of the three as generally forming a closed circuit. Arrival at a goal eliminates the cause, which eliminates the motive, which eliminates the behavior.[4]

One's empty stomach sends neural impulses which the individual perceives as "feeling hungry"; the hunger feeling is the motive that directs energy toward food seeking; if the effort is successful, the individual is filled with food, thus eliminating the hunger feeling. If that person now ceases to seek food and thus fails to consume food for several hours, the hunger feelings will reappear and the cycle will be repeated.

This cyclical process also applies to other types of needs. Suppose that a person is psychologically "hungry" (e.g., has a need for freedom from fear of physical deprivation or a need for acceptance and/or esteem from others). This individual now has the motive for seeking satisfaction and if

---

[2] Robert N. Lussier, *Human Relations in Organizations* (Homewood, Ill,: Richard D. Irwin, 1990), p. 117.

[3] Leavitt, *Managerial Psychology*, pp. 7–12.

[4] Ibid., p. 8.

FIGURE 7.1
A Basic Model of Behavior

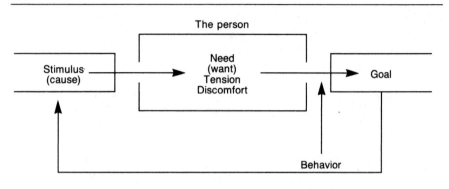

Source: H. J., Leavitt *Managerial Psychology*, 4th ed. (Chicago: University of Chicago Press, 1978), p. 9. See also "The Motivational Process: An Initial Model," in J. L. Gibson, J. M. Ivancevich, and J. H. Donnelly, Jr., *Organizations: Behavior, Structure, Process*, 4th ed. (Homewood, Ill.: Irwin/BPI, 1980), p. 108.

the resultant behavior is successful, the psychological stomach is filled and hunger ceases for the time being. And the same person is quite prone to become hungry in this sense all over again if those psychological appetites are not recurrently appeased.

The analogy breaks down to an extent here, for it is apparent that some psychological appetites, varying with the individual, are rarely if ever fully sated. But they can be momentarily and partially satisfied and the cause-motive-behavior-toward-a-goal cycle decreases in intensity if it does not halt altogether.

This cyclical process involves the concept of *homeostasis,* which assumes a normal state, and when conditions depart from this state, homeostatic mechanisms return the body to its normal level of functioning.[5] Thus equilibrium is protected or pursued if lost.

> ... the ultimate condition of man can be thought of as an equilibrium condition in which he need not behave. This ultimate will be unattainable as long as one fly after another goes on landing on man's rump to stir up some new need and to force him to go on swishing his tail.[6]

There appears, at this writing, to be no dearth of flies in our environment—nor any danger of their extinction.

---

[5] Audrey Haber and Richard P. Runyon. *Fundamentals of Psychology,* 3rd ed. (Reading, Mass.: Addison-Wesley, 1983), p. 192.

[6] Leavitt, *Managerial Psychology,* pp. 10–11.

FRUSTRATION

No discussion of human motivation would be adequate without a consideration of frustration—any interference with goal-directed behavior.[7] The sources of frustrating obstacles include the environment, other people, our personal defects or limitations, and conflict situations.

Generally speaking, when one is confronted with an obstacle he or she becomes aggressive. If a person is confident, this aggression is ordinarily directed toward the obstacle. If unsure and pessimistic about his or her ability, that person tends to direct aggression inwardly and feels blameworthy, inadequate, and so forth. The key to the direction of aggression, then, is the self-concept, as we discussed in the previous chapters.

"Many block situations are depriving rather than frustrating because the obstacles do not seem insurmountable or the goals are not central to the self."[8] That same person will experience fewer frustrations, therefore, if there is a larger repertoire of alternative routes around blocks or if there is sufficient self-confidence within to obviate the need for providing self-worth each time the individual meets a problem. Intimately related to experiences of frustration are aspirations. If they are commensurate with abilities, then frustration will be less frequent. To the extent that aspirations are beyond one's capacities, the person will tend to experience frustration and perhaps ultimately—if the thwarting is chronic—demoralization. Let us remind ourselves that self-confidence is generally a product of repeated success, but that success is what we perceive it to be.

Conflict

A severe species of frustration is conflict—a seemingly escape-proof frustration.

> . . . Conflicts[9] are emotion-producing choice situations, characterized by a pull in two (or more) directions at the same time. The obstacles one meets here are

---

[7] Thomas V. Bonoma and Gerald Zaltman, *Psychology for Management* (Boston: Kent Publishing, 1981), pp. 117–23.

[8] Harold J. Leavitt and Homa Bahrani, *Managerial Psychology: Managing Behavior in Organizations*, 5th ed. (Chicago: University of Chicago Press, 1988), p. 41.

[9] We are currently considering *intra*personal conflict, but *inter*personal conflict has received increasing attention of late. For helpful accounts of this burgeoning concept and of how to deal with conflict constructively, see: Bernard Taylor and Gordon L. Lippitt, eds., *Management Development and Training Handbook* (London: McGraw-Hill, 1975), pp. 379–80, 393–94, 507; Thomas L. Quick, *Person to Person Managing* (New York: St. Martin's Press, 1977), Chapter 7, "Dealing with Conflict"; George Bach and Herbert Goldberg, *Creative Aggression* (Garden City, N.Y.: Doubleday, 1974); A. C. Filley, *Interpersonal Conflict Resolution* (Glenview, Ill.: Scott, Foresman, 1975); the section on "Conflict and Stress in Organizations," in L. L. Cummings and Randall B. Dunham, *Introduction to Organizational*

not brick walls, but internal drags that pull one back even as one goes forward. Conflict situations are frying-pan-and-fire situations, ambivalent situations. They are emotional-choice situations, decision-making situations. And this large class of psychological situations underlies considerable emotional upset and considerable irrationality in everyday life and everyday management.[10]

Conflict situations are generally of three types: *approach-approach*—the individual is between two equally attractive alternatives and to move toward one would pull away from the other; *avoidance-avoidance*—the individual is between two equally unattractive or repulsive alternatives, so that in escaping from one alternative, that person moves closer to the other; *approach-avoidance*—the individual is both attracted and repelled by the same object.[11] Frustration tolerance, the ability to retain normal reactions under stress, varies greatly among individuals. Some are quite capable of maintaining problem-solving actions directed toward constructively resolving the conflict in which they find themselves. Others are more prone toward compensatory or subterfuge reactions. Some of these reactions resemble homeostasis, in the form of physiological compensatory activity that strives to maintain a constant state. Their prime purpose is not to solve problems but to cushion the ego (one's feelings of self-esteem) against threats of deflation. These ego-defensive reactions include: *fantasizing* (wish-fulfilling dreams, daydreaming), *projecting* (inputting one's thoughts and desires to others), *rationalizing* (finding justifiable reasons for behavior or convincing ourselves that the goal is really undersirable—assuming a sour-grapes attitude), *repressing* (attempting to ignore, deny, or forget troublesome things), *regressing* (reverting to childish ways), *identifying* (becoming ego-involved with others), *blaming others* (excusing ourselves by finding others responsible for our failures—scapegoating), *overcompensating* (trying to overcome one's deficiencies, to make up for one's failings—but in an excessive manner), and *sublimating* (getting indirect but socially acceptable satisfaction).

Behavior: Text and Readings (Homewood, Ill.: Richard D. Irwin, 1980), pp. 573–96; and Chapter 17, "Managing Conflict, Change, and Organization Development" in John R. Schermerhorn, Jr., *Management for Productivity* (New York: John Wiley & Sons, 1984); and Robert Kreitner and Angelo Knicki, *Organizational Behavior* (Homewood, Ill.: Irwin/BPI, 1989), pp. 391–400.

[10] Leavitt and Bahrani, *Managerial Psychology*, p. 31.

[11] For a detailed treatment of *intra*personal conflict, see: K. Lewin, *A Dynamic Theory of Personality* (New York: McGraw-Hill, 1935); L. A. Festinger, *A Theory of Cognitive Dissonance* (Stanford, Calif.: Stanford University Press, 1962); David Cohen, *Psychologists on Psychology* (New York: Taplinger, 1977), pp. 126–44; Thomas V. Bonoma and Gerald Zaltman, *Psychology for Management* (Boston: Kent Publishing, 1981), pp. 123–41; and James B. Lau and A. B. Shani, *Behavior in Organizations*, 4th ed. (Homewood, Ill.: Richard D. Irwin, 1988), pp. 201–2, 280–81.

The list is neither inclusive nor mutually exclusive, but it does suggest some of the unconstructive responses to frustration.

How, then, can we really resolve our conflicts? A conflict is a conflict because one *perceives* it to be one. Rather than an external condition, frustration is a state of the organism. A conflict exists for you when certain needs seem mutually exclusive. Therefore, you can resolve a conflict by (1) finding a new way to satisfy both needs simultaneously, (2) reducing your valuation of one need or the other, or (3) reorganizing the situation so that it is perceptually no longer a significant conflict.

Let us now examine in more detail the human need system that is subject to so much frustration and conflict.

MOTIVATION THEORIES

What can we say with confidence about motivation? Is there any rhyme or reason to our needs? Are there any grounds for predicting people's behavior on the basis of their needs?

Let us examine three of the most important theories that purport to answer those questions: Maslow's need hierarchy, Herzberg's two-factor theory, and McClelland's learned needs theory. All three were devised over a generation ago, but they continue to capture management's imagination and spawn further research. They are undoubtedly not the final word but they clearly merit our close attention.

Maslow

There had been need-classifiers long before Abraham Maslow and the earlier models helped sort out the myriad human behaviors. But they did little to aid managers, or anyone else, to predict future behavior. And if managers cannot predict behavior they are powerless to control or influence it—in this case, to channel individual energies in such a way as to achieve organizational objectives. Thus, it was the promise of predictability that was a most attractive feature of Maslow's model. It is one of the more popular of the motivational concepts, so let us examine it carefully.

The model[12] (mentioned in Chapter 3) involves five types of needs: *physiological* (the need for air, water, food, waste elimination, temperature control, sleep); *safety and security* (the need to be free of the fear of physical danger and deprivation); *social* (the need to be accepted and approved, to belong); *ego* (the need for recognition, to be important, to be

---

[12] Abraham H. Maslow, *Motivation and Personality*, 2d ed. (New York: Harper & Row, 1970).

FIGURE 7.2
Maslow's Hierarchy of Needs

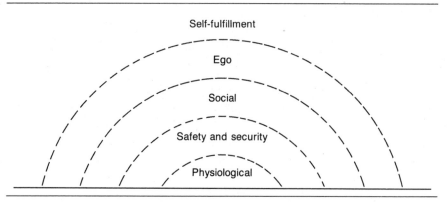

somebody, to have status, fame, reputation);[13] and *self-fulfillment* (the ultimate need—to realize one's fullest potential as a human being; to be creative in the broadest sense of the term).

The principal distinction of Maslow's model is that these needs exist in a prepotency pattern, a hierarchy of needs, as depicted in Figure 7.2.

Maslow's basic propositions are:

1. *The lowest unsatisfied needs must be sufficiently appeased before the needs above them normally become operative, that is, are able to motivate the individual.*

Ordinarily, until a person's physiological needs are reasonably satisfied, none of the higher needs will significantly influence behavior. A desperately hungry man may risk his life, to say nothing of his honor, for food. Even Jesus, who preached, "Man does not live by bread alone," was clearly aware of the importance of bread, and fed the multitudes.

When the physiological needs are sufficiently appeased, one begins to be concerned with future deprivation as well as with present and future danger. Let us say that a hungry person, motivated to work for food, is rewarded with a meal. But now that person continues to work. Clearly working—not for another meal, for it could not be eaten now if available—but for the assurance of the next meal. To stretch the point, it might be argued that some people, particularly those scarred by earlier poverty, are working today predominantly for the assurance of meals 20 or 30 years from now.

And so it is that as the needs at one level are sufficiently satisfied, the level immediately above begins to play a role in one's behavior.

---

[13] Maslow distinguishes between ego needs satisfied privately (self-esteem) and those that are satisfied publicly (esteem from others).

2. *To the extent that needs are satisfied, they will become inoperative, that is, they cease to motivate the individual, for a satisfied need is no longer a motivator of behavior.*

As previously stated, the hungry person who has eaten is no longer hungry. Thus subsequent work efforts are temporarily not motivatable by hunger. And, in fact, if this individual is completely improvident, as many animals are, the person will cease work altogether until hunger feelings reappear sufficiently as a motivation to attain food again. Most of us, of course, are not so casual about the future, and our security needs (e.g., to be free of the fear of hunger) continue to impel us.

Some Qualifications. Perhaps this discussion of the Maslow model suggests that the prediction of human behavior is merely a matter of discovering where a person currently is on the need hierarchy so as to determine where the next jump will be. Unfortunately, the situation is more complex, for the sequence of need occurrence and the sequence of need satisfaction are not necessarily the same.[14] However, if we impose a few qualifications on the need hierarchy, the model gains in applicability.

Multiple Levels. First of all, the dotted lines on Maslow's model, separating the need levels, suggest that the boundaries of the levels are permeable and that one may move up and down the ladder rapidly. Within a typical day, a person working in a factory may be motivated at one time or another by all five need levels. That person certainly becomes physically hungry at least three times a day and concerned about safety when operating a machine—and may experience anxiety about the family's financial security; this individual may do or refrain from doing many things to maintain or gain social acceptance by associates; at the same time there may be a striving for advancement and/or deriving a sense of achievement from the job at hand; there may even be some thoughts about ultimate destiny, a contribution to humanity, and so forth.

Need Conflict. Not only is there considerable mobility up and down the hierarchy of needs during even a relatively short period of time, but it is quite possible for a person to be motivated by two or more need levels simultaneously. When one's needs are sufficiently strong

---

[14] The model has been criticized as simplistic. For example, see: M. A. Wahba and L. G. Birdwell, "Maslow Reconsidered: A Review of Research on the Need Hierarchy Theory," *Organizational Behavior and Human Performance*, April 1976, pp. 212–40; Benjamin Schneider and Clayton P. Alderfer, "Three Studies of Need Satisfactions in Organizations," *Administrative Science Quarterly*, December 1973, pp. 489–505; and Edward L. Lawler, III and J. L. Suttle, "A Causal Correlation Test of the Need Hierarchy Concept," *Organizational Behavior and Human Performance*, April 1972, pp. 265–87.

and/or urgent and yet cannot be satisfied simultaneously, there may be need conflicts. Take the familiar case of an individual bucking for promotion. If the methods used do not coincide with the codes of the peer group, that person is likely to be made aware of his or her deviant behavior in no uncertain terms, with the group threatening various sanctions. Here is the classic conflict of social and ego needs. Will the individual resist the group and if necessary suffer its punishments? Or bow to group pressure and suppress his or her ambitions?[15] Maslow's hierarchy of needs suggests that this person will usually take the latter alternative, for social needs appear to be more primary than ego needs, but the situation is not quite so easily predictable, as we shall presently discuss.

Modifying Factors. There are at least two factors that suggest why the Maslow model cannot be applied literally in every situation. They are the presence of varying appetites, which can be partially accounted for by the concept of dependency, and the role of self-discipline.

1. *Varying appetites.* There is no doubt that physiological needs vary from person to person. Some people simply require less sleep, food, protection from the elements, and the like than do others. There is ample evidence to suggest that our need requirements vary at higher levels as well. Recall the individual striving for promotion? A major determinant of the response to group pressure may be just how much of a social need appetite versus an ego need appetite the person has. If he or she has learned to seek satisfactions primarily within oneself rather than through or from others it may be fairly easy to shrug off the group and proceed.

In addition, we must ask, does the individual have alternative need-satisfaction routes? Can these social needs be satisfied through other groups—on or off the job—and thus, for *this* situation, have limited social needs?

2. *Dependency.* The concept of dependency helps to explain why the appetites, the widths of the need bands, particularly the social and ego bands, seem to vary so much among individuals. Consider that the human infant comes into the world with a fairly well-developed set of needs and an almost completely undeveloped set of means for satisfying them. In

---

[15] Of course, there are often escapes from this seeming dilemma. A person may be able to convince the group that a particular end is acceptable. For example, the need for additional income for extraordinary expenses—family medical bills, and so forth. Or the individual may modify the *means* of approaching a goal so that he or she will be acceptable to the group. The able student often faces a similar peer response with efforts to obtain good grades. A person may be able to justify extra effort by explaining that good grades are required to enter graduate school and by studiously avoiding unacceptable means for attaining good marks, such as apple polishing.

other words, he or she is necessarily dependent upon others to satisfy those needs. What seems to be critical in the personality development of the child is whether dependence is associated primarily with satisfying or with dissatisfying experiences.

If the infant's needs are usually satisfied promptly and sufficiently by others and if this becomes a generalized pattern through the formative years, the child will tend thereafter to rely upon others for need satisfaction—to develop a broad social-needs band. If, however, one's needs are normally *not* thusly satisfied and this pattern is repeatedly reinforced, one will come to rely less upon others and more upon oneself for the satisfaction of needs and thus develop a broad, demanding ego-needs band.

In actuality, the infant's needs can neither be completely frustrated (or it would not survive) nor completely satisfied (mother is only human). As a consequence, that child will develop both social and egoistic needs, but there is likely to be a dominance of one over the other. In any event, it is the internal conflict between the drive to be dependent and the simultaneous drive to be independent that fosters much of the anguish that teenagers (and their parents) experience.

3. *Self-discipline.* Another factor that complicates the use of the model is, in old-fashioned language, willpower. We can refrain from indulging our food and sleep needs to a degree. It is reasonable to assume that we can deny ourselves satisfactions at the subsequent need levels as well. Our friend seeking the promotion may decide to suffer the group's slings and arrows in anticipation of a compensatory reward. This does not mean that this person is without social needs or that they are meager—but that he or she is suppressing them. This may help to explain people such as Albert Schweitzer, Tom Dooley, Mother Teresa, and Mohandas Gandhi—who seemingly lived primarily at the self-fulfillment level. Among possible speculations: Were these people who possessed iron wills capable of deferring or more or less permanently denying the gratification of their more material needs? Were their lower needs relatively narrow bands to begin with? Was the wine of self-fulfillment so heady that the lower need satisfactions became pallid by comparison?

It can be argued that some people seem quite content to obtain a modicum of satisfaction at the lower two or three levels. They seem to have no ambition, no drive to get somewhere or to be somebody. Is it possible that these people were behind the door when the needs were passed out? Not likely. But it is quite possible that they have *learned* not to try to satisfy some of their needs.

I recall dimly an experiment that our undergraduate biology professor described. It involved a tank of water about 12 feet long, 4 feet deep, and 4 feet wide. A glass partition was inserted, separating the tank into two six-foot segments. Then a nothern pike, which had been deprived of food for some time, was placed in one compartment and a bucket of minnows was poured into the other. The pike immediately rushed for the minnows and bumped its nose, which hurt, I assume. But the pike was persistent and continued to bump its nose an average of 165 times. At this point, it stopped trying. It had apparently learned that to seek satisfaction for its needs resulted not only in a thwarting of its hunger drive but in pain as well. The experimenter could now remove the partition, and the minnows (which were evidently more stupid than the pike) swam into the other section, but the pike wasn't having any—it had learned its lesson. And in most cases, it would starve to death midst abundance!

The experiment may be apocryphal, but it does offer a provocative analogy. Substitute a child for the pike and substitute childhood experiences for the tank. Suppose that this child has a skin of a certain color, or a nose of a certain shape, or a certain last name, or a physical impairment, or lives on the wrong side of the tracks. Now suppose that this child tries to achieve some social or ego satisfaction and bumps his or her nose. This is a human being and therefore learns much more rapidly than the pike to stop trying—that way at least. Hopefully, the human learns other ways of dealing with the obstacle, such as were discussed in the sections on frustration and conflict.

But suppose instead that this person generalizes the painful, failing experiences and, by way of defense, denies these needs. In effect, the individual learns to stop trying altogether. Incidentally, since humans learn by concepts as well as by stimuli, they can learn this lesson vicariously from others (parents, older brothers and sisters, friends) who have also learned the lesson—directly or vicariously.

It is likely that when this child has become an adult, the mere opportunity for need satisfaction will often be insufficient to overcome decades of conditioning. The adult may have to undergo a thorough and prolonged process of relearning—of coming to understand that not only are there certain needs, but that there is an acceptable way of satisfying them.

Validity versus Simplicity. The qualifications imposed upon the Maslow model of needs have two consequences: (1) they have, I hope, increased the model's validity in accounting for human behavior; (2) they have complicated the model's use as a predictive tool, suggesting that ordinarily it cannot serve as a simple template to predict the next move. The model in no way enables one who would communicate effectively to dispense with perceptive analysis. But if the trade-off has increased validity even at the cost of simplicity, the bargain would appear to be a good one.

Herzberg et al.

So much for Maslow. Let's move on to another conception of motivation. Herzberg[16] and others don't really contradict Maslow but they have developed an interestingly different way of looking at human needs. Having studied a number of accountants and engineers, they conclude that people have two kinds of drives: growth needs and avoidance needs. They report that certain job factors (motivators) have potency for satisfying growth needs. These include achievement, recognition, the work itself, responsibility, and advancement. Other job factors (hygiene factors) are important largely for their capacity to dissatisfy the individual—and thus trigger avoidance needs. These include company policy and administration, supervision-technical, salary, supervision-interpersonal relations, and working conditions. The motivators are associated with job content, whereas the hygiene factors are related to the job context or environment. The major conclusion of the study was that the job factors capable of satisfying growth needs are largely irrelevant to avoidance needs and that the job factors related to avoidance needs are of little or no consequence with respect to growth needs. For example, management's improvement of substandard working conditions will reduce avoidance needs but will be ineffective in motivating the worker to greater productivity and creativity.

> When these [hygiene] factors deteriorate to a level below that which the employee considers acceptable, then job dissatisfaction ensues. However, the reverse does not hold true. When the job context can be characterized as optimal, we will not get dissatisfaction, but neither will we get much in the way of positive attitudes.[17]
>
> All we can expect from satisfying the needs for hygiene is the prevention of dissatisfaction and poor job performance.[18]

The Expensive Change-Room. Here's an example of overkill in the hygiene department. A friend took a job as an executive with a steel forge company. A day or two before I was to fly to Europe on an

---

[16] F. Herzberg, B. Mausner, and B. Snyderman, *The Motivation to Work*, 2d ed. (New York: John Wiley & Sons, 1962). See also: Frederick Herzberg, "One More Time: How Do You Motivate Employees?" *Harvard Business Review*, 46, no. 1 (January—February 1968) pp. 53–62; Frederick Herzberg, *The Managerial Choice: To Be Efficient and to Be Human* (Homewood, Ill.: Dow Jones-Irwin, 1976); William F. Christopher, *Management for the 1980s* (New York: AMACOM, 1980), pp. 118–19; and George T. Milkovich and John W. Boudreau, *Personnel/Human Resource Management*, 5th ed. (Homewood, Ill.: Irwin/BPI, 1988), p. 168.

[17] Ibid., pp. 113–14.

[18] Ibid., p. 115.

assignment, I drove out to visit him in his new location. He gave me a short tour of the shop.

I had seen many other factories, but the environment in this one was overwhelming. The ear-splitting din, the fumes, the jarring from the huge power hammers, the excruciating temperature from the heat-treat furnaces and the incandescent blooms and billets—what a litany of hygiene factors! There was credence in the old joke about hammersmiths never having to go to hell. They'd already lived there—eight hours a day!

We returned to Bob's office. He was eager.

Bob: Well, what do you think?
Me: What do you mean?
Bob: Any suggestions for us?
Me: Technical improvements? I'm no engineer. . . .
Bob: I know. . . but anything you saw that we could work on?
Me: Well, if you insist. . . it might be a good idea to spruce up the employees' change-room. Frankly, it's a horror now.
Bob: You're dead right! We'll do it.

Three months later, I returned from Europe. There was a note to call Bob . . . he wanted me to come out to the plant again for a big surprise. He was waiting for me when I pulled into the parking lot. "Wait till you see the new change-room!"

I was dumbfounded. The room would have been the envy of most country clubs—completely new plumbing and electrical fixtures, indirect lighting, elegant lockers and benches, wall-to-wall carpeting! The bill, I discovered later, was $37,000!

And what did the company get for its handsome investment? Greater productivity? Less scrap? Fewer pieces needing reworking? Hardly. What they got was simply no complaints about a horrendous change-room. I didn't have the heart to tell Bob—at least not then—that he probably could have achieved the same effect at a fraction of the cost from a thorough paint job and the replacement of a broken commode and a few light fixtures.

Speaking of complaints, now it was management's turn. They were griping that the workers were spending too much time in their luxurious change-room!

Critics.   One of the attractions of the Herzberg model is that it is work-oriented. "There is no need to translate psychological terminology to everyday language."[19] However, his work has had its detractors. For one,

---

[19] James L. Gibson, John M. Ivancevich, and James H. Donnelly, Jr., *Organizations: Behavior, Structure, Process*, 6th ed. (Homewood, Ill.: Irwin/BPI, 1988), p. 121.

its universality has been questioned.[20] His initial study group was made up solely of engineers and accountants. One might wonder if the results would apply equally to such different occupational groups as nurses, medical technologists, salespeople, computer programmers, clerks, and police officers.

Lawler[21] had another reservation. He claimed that little attention had been focused on the motivational and performance implications of the theory.

The jury is still out on the two-factor theory,[22] but the work of Herzberg and his colleagues does effectively squash the old motivational notion that more of something good is only better. Managers are cautioned not to expect too much from expensive office fixtures, Muzak, nicely decorated lounges for breaks, high-base salaries, and other hygiene factors.

Herzberg's distinction between job context and job content reminds managers that there are two important aspects of all jobs: (1) what people do in terms of job tasks—job content and, (2) the work setting in which they do it—job context.[23]

McClelland

A third conception of motivation that merits inspection is David McClelland's *learned needs theory*. We acquire our motives from our respective cultures.[24] He addresses the needs for:

- *Achievement*—to set challenging yet attainable goals for oneself, to work hard to achieve those goals, and to use the skills and abilities needed to do so.
- *Affiliation*—to establish, maintain, and repair social relationships . . . to have warm, friendly associations with others.
- *Power*—to acquire a reputation and to have influence and impact on others. McClelland distinguishes between: *socialized* power used in

[20] Joseph Schneider and Edwin Locke, "A Critique of Herzberg's Dual-Factor Classification System and a Suggested Revision," *Organizational Behavior and Human Performance* (July 1971), pp. 441–58.

[21] Edward E. Lawler, III, *Motivation in Work Organizations* (Monterey, Calif.: Brooks/Cole Publishing, 1973), p. 72.

[22] Steven Kerr, Anne Harlan, and Ralph Stogdill, "Preferene for Motivator and Hygiene Factors in a Hypothetical Interview Situation," *Personnel Psychology*, 27 (Winter 1974), pp. 109–24.

[23] John R. Schermerhorn, Jr., *Management for Productivity* (New York: John Wiley & Sons, 1984), p. 241.

[24] David C. McClelland, *The Achievement Motive* (New York: Appleton-Century-Crofts, 1953).

FIGURE 7.3
Work Preferences of Persons High in Need for Achievement, Power, and Affiliation

Individual Need	Work Preference	Example
High need for achievement	Individual responsibility, challenging but achievble goals; feedback on performance	Field salesperson with challenging quota and opportunity to earn individual bonus
High need for affiliation	Interpersonal relationships; opportunities to communicate	Customer-service representative; member of work unit subject to group wage-bonus plan
High need for power	Control over other persons; attention; recognition	Formal position of supervisory responsibility; appointment as head of special task force or committee

Source: John R. Schermerhorn, Jr., James G. Hunt, and Richard N. Osborn, *Managing Organization Behavior* (New York: John Wiley & Sons, 1982), p. 113.

the interests of the group, the department, the organization, as a whole; and *personalized* power used primarily for self-aggrandizement, often at the expense of the group. Needless to say, he recommends that executives exercise the first kind of power and avoid the second.[25]

Managers find the McClelland theory especially germane on two counts. First, along with the Maslow and Herzberg models, they feel it helps them understand people's behavior on the job. If one's needs are accurately assessed, they may help locate that person in a desirable position. See Figure 7.3.

Second, if needs indeed are acquired, then a person supposedly can learn to adopt a new profile that is required for a given role.

On a much grander scale, McClelland is convinced that entire nations, especially in the "third-world," can buck up their flagging economies by stimulating the achievement motive in their general populations.[26] Of course, McClelland has had his critics, too. Their concern is threefold:

Method—McClelland uses the projective Thematic Apperception Test (TAT) to gather his data. It is difficult to validate this approach.

Learning Decline—The notion that needs can be learned seems at odds with a good deal of research and observation that hold that motives are acquired in childhood and are very difficult to modify

---

[25] David C. McClelland and D. Burnham, "Power Is the Great Motivator," *Harvard Business Review* (March-April 1976), pp. 100–111.

[26] David C. McClelland, "Business Drive and National Achievement," *Harvard Business Review* (July-August 1962), pp. 99–112.

later on. McClelland cites evidence in politics and religion to assert that adult motivation can indeed be altered.

Durability of Change—A third criticism centers on whether needs can be permanently acquired. So far this question is unresolved.

There is a great deal more to motivation. In fact, what we have been examining are three representatives of just one family of motivation conceptions—*content* theories. They have to do with factors within a person that energize, control, sustain, and/or halt behavior. There is another family of theorems—*process* theories. They are certainly worthy of careful study. But since the emphasis is on the *process* of how one's behavior is energized, these theories are more appropriate in a book on organizational behavior than one on interpersonal communication. Accordingly, I will briefly describe a few of the more popular theories and recommend some sources where they be examined in detail.

Some Process Theories

Expectancy theory holds that motivation is a function of *(a) expectancy*—the subjective probability that after a certain behavior, a particular outcome will ensue; *(b) valence*—the value one assigns to work-related outcomes (positive-desired; negative-not desired; zero-indifferent); *(c) instrumentality*—the individual's perception that first-level outcomes will be associated with second-level outcomes.

Equity theory holds that one is motivated to obtain equity between his or her inputs/outputs and those of a comparative person. More simply, we tend to compare our efforts and rewards with those of others in similar work circumstances. We have a desire to be treated equitably, at least as we perceive equity.

Reinforcement theory holds that behavior followed by pleasant outcomes will tend to be repeated whereas behavior followed by unpleasant outcomes will probably not be repeated. Thus, positive reinforcement can be applied to motivate behavior.

These three process theories and others are discussed much more thoroughly in:

Gibson, James L., John M. Ivancevich, and James H. Donnelly, Jr. *Organizations: Behavior, Structure, Processes.* 6th ed. Homewood, Ill.: Irwin/BPI, 1988. Chapter 4, "Motivation: Content Theories and Applications," and Chapter 5, "Motivation: Process Theories and Applications."

Schermerhorn, John R. *Management for Productivity.* New York: John Wiley & Sons, 1984. Chapter 12, "Leading through Motivation."

Dunham, Randall B. *Organizational Behavior: People and Processes in Management.* Homewood, Ill.: Richard D. Irwin, 1984. Part III, "Theories in Organizational Behavior."

Reitz, H. Joseph. *Behavior in Organizations*. 3rd. ed. Homewood, Ill.: Richard D. Irwin, 1987. Chapter 3, "Motivation."

Cohen, Allen R.; Stephen L. Fink; Herman Gadon; and Robin D. Willits. *Effective Behavior in Organizations*. 4th ed. Homewood, Ill.: Richard D. Irwin, 1988. Chapter 7, "Basic Human Needs and Rewards."

THE VALUE OF MOTIVATION THEORY

Much of this discussion of motivation, need models, and conflicts can be broadly categorized as theoretical. So let us pause to consider the practicality, indeed, the inevitability of theory. Theory is a most practical matter. For without theory—without underlying beliefs, assumptions, premises, and so on—we would be unable to act save through our reflex and autonomic responses. Theory and practice are inescapably linked.

If we are to communicate with others, serve as a subordinate, manage others, and the like, we must have some kind of theory—valid or not, conscious or not—about human motivations and relationships. Otherwise we will be unable to function at all. If we are to control or to influence behavior—our own at any rate—we must be capable of predicting reasonably accurately the responses of others—and of ourselves. These are prime reasons for forming images of others and of ourselves, discussed in Chapter 5.

The objective of this chapter is not to sell any particular theory—content or process. Rather its objective is to urge the reader to bring his or her theory to the surface and to examine the premises of that theory consciously and critically—to do this rather than to make decisions, to take action, and to communicate on the basis of unconscious, unexamined, and, possibly, untenable theory.

EPILOGUE

My reason for placing this and the previous chapters in a book on communication is that the act of interpersonal communication never occurs in a vacuum. In its simplest format, that act is one person communicating out of his or her world of feelings, perceptions, values, and needs to another person in his or her world. To treat communication merely at the level of techniques, devices, and media is to imply an unseemly simplicity for a very complex process. To understand human communication as fully as possible, we must attempt to understand the communicator, his or her motivations (and the motivations of others), the relationships between the individual and those with whom that person communicates, and the organizational setting in which they are communicating. Mason Haire summarized the challenge to the communicator almost three decades ago. It is still timely:

There are three outstanding basic facts that we must remember if we are going to be able to understand human behavior. The first is that the environment itself does not provide an organization. If we make a separation between the physical world outside of us, on one hand, and the psychological environment, or the world we see, on the other, we come to see that the order and organization is not in the physical stimulus but in the observer, and that one of man's greatest problems is to make sense of his environment. The second fact is that man's behavior depends, not on what is actually out there, but on what he sees; not on the way the world is actually organized, but on the way he organizes it. This is at first a deceptively simple point, but it is possible that more misunderstanding in human relations arises from this than from any other single factor. The third point is related to the other two: man has a great deal of anxiety attached to his organization of the world. Man's environment is not organized in itself; he must organize it. His organization determines his behavior. His behavior and its appropriateness to the environment determine whether he will be successful or unsuccessful—in many cases, whether he will survive or not. For this reason, he is reluctant to give up any organizations that seem to work, because of the danger that is involved in being lost in a disorganized environment.[27]

The communicator's "behavior and its appropriateness to the environment" are the central concerns of this book. In the next chapter, we will examine that critical form of behavior—the process of human communication.

Discussion Questions

1. Why does this chapter which deals with needs and motivation appear in a book on communication?

2. Leavitt's behavioral model: Does it explain human motivation to your satisfaction? Can you visualize any motivated behavior that would not be accounted for by this model?

3. Give examples of need conflict involving various needs posited by Maslow, for example, conflicts between physiological and safety-security needs, between social and ego needs, between ego and self-fulfillment needs.

4. What does the dependency concept have to do with varying appetites?

5. The Maslow hierarchy of needs—in general, does it account for human behavior? What do you think of the various qualifications imposed upon the model? Are they necessary?

6. Herzberg's major conclusion was that growth needs and avoidance needs were different needs: the need to be happy is different from the need not to be unhappy. Moreover, the two needs are related to different job factors. For example, the elimination of subpar physical working conditions cannot be expected to have a significant impact on productivity. Assuming these conclusions to be valid, what implications do they have for managers in business and industry? For educators?

---

[27] Haire, *Psychology in Management*, 2d ed. (New York: McGraw-Hill, 1964), p. 29.

For the leaders of the executive and legislative branches of federal, state, and municipal governments?

7. Re: Herzberg's motivators and hygiene factors and Maslow's hierarchy of needs. Do these theories regarding needs and motivation appear to be compatible? How or how not?

8. McClelland's central contention is that certain needs are learned rather than inherited. What are the implications for management?

9. What do you think of Haire's "three outstanding basic facts that we must remember if we are going to be able to understand human behavior"?

C A S E S

CASE 7.1

The Accident*
E. C. St. John

The scene is the personnel office of an industrial firm. Bill, the personnel manager, is questioning the second shift printing foreman about an accident that had occurred the previous night. Pete, the printing foreman, is a middle-aged man who has come up through the ranks. He is conscientious, energetic, and proud of his production record.

"Bill, I don't know what makes these guys pull these crazy stunts," Pete said as he lit his cigarette. The cuticles of the fingers holding the match were stained from years of washups and makereadies on the presses. "You front office guys are always harping on this, 'Why do accidents happen?' business too much anyway," he continued. Leaning forward in his chair eager to make his point, he waved a finger under the personnel manager's nose. "Accidents are bound to happen," he stated. "I've been trying to tell you ever since you came to this plant. You take this one you're asking about now. Ross just did a dumb thing, that's all. He knew better than to adjust the gate on the hopper while the press was running, but he just didn't think. Stupid, I guess."

"Stupid?" the personnel manager questioned.

"Oh, I don't mean stupid really," Pete continued. "He's got more education than I have, and when it comes to figuring he's tops, but last night he just didn't care."

"It must have played the devil with your production to have a man almost lose his finger. Besides the time taken getting him to first aid, you had to run the press a man short," Bill said.

"Well, no," Pete said as he tapped his cigarette out. "You see, when they came in, I cornered the whole bunch and told them we had this big beer ad run to get out and I wanted these presses running red hot. I remember telling Ross he wouldn't have time to worry about that baby that's coming soon, cause we were gonna hang up a record for the first shift to shoot at. I had to climb on him a little later for taking so long with his makeready. Then at lunch break he said he was having trouble with his register. I told him not to kid me, I'd run presses when he was reaching for his baby bottle, and I knew he could finish that order if he wasn't too lazy. He didn't get hurt until about an hour and a half after lunch. By then we had two thirds of the order run, so by holding the guys for half an hour, we finished it."

---

* All names have been disguised. Printed by permission.

"You say he hurt his hand because . . . " Bill questioned.

"Cause he's just plain careless," Pete interrupted.

"OK, Pete," the personnel manager said quietly. "I think I understand."

Discussion Questions

1. Why did the accident occur?
2. What role, if any, did the foreman play in the accident?
3. How do you account for the way he is responding to Bill's questions?
4. What does this case have to do with motivation?
5. What did Bill mean by "OK, Pete, I think I understand"?
6. What should Bill do now?

CASE 7.2

Arno Annello, Machinist*

The standards department of the Schoonway Machine Company recommended that Arno Annello, who operated a battery of automatic gear-cutting machines, be discharged for failure to attain required minimum production as set by the standards department. The foreman in whose department Annello was employed objected to the recommendation. The matter was placed before the production manager for final decision.

Arno Annello came to this country from Finland. He had received the equivalent of a grade school education in his native land but had practically no knowledge of the English language. He secured a job as a floor cleaner in the Schoonway plant. He showed himself to be industrious and thorough, and the foreman of the milling and gear-cutting department became interested in him. One day he suggested to one of Annello's friends that the floor sweeper should apply for a better job. When Annello heard this, he signified his desire to become an operative of the automatic sharpening machines. These machines were used to sharpen the teeth of cutters after the cutters were otherwise finished. They were automatic in operation, and with proper setup, there was very little danger of spoiling the work. The foreman or an experienced assistant personally supervised each setup. The operative inserted and removed the work, started and stopped the machines, and dressed the emery wheels when necessary. He operated from four to eight machines, depending on the character of the work.

When a vacancy occurred in the department, the foreman decided to give Annello a chance, and obtained his transfer (on trial) from the

---

* Reprinted by permission from Franklin E. Folts, *Introduction to Industrial Management* (New York: McGraw-Hill, 1949).

cleaning department. Over a period of several months, Annello, with the assistance of the foreman, became proficient in operating the machines, and was given a permanent job. For the next two years, Annello showed steady improvement. He became known in the department as a first-class operative of automatic cutter-sharpening machines and finally developed into a skilled machine setter. While he improved as a machinist, Annello showed no aptitude in mastering the English language, and any extended or involved conversation had to be handled through an interpreter. The foreman, however, believed that Annello had the makings of a first-class machinist and was willing to put up with this inconvenience.

The company decided to install a new battery of gear-cutting machines for milling the teeth in cutters, and the foreman was confronted with the task of getting additional operatives to run these machines. The work of operating the automatic gear-cutting machines required considerably more skill than was necessary to run automatic cutter-sharpening machines. The machine attendant had to set up the indexing mechanism for the cutter blank, set the tooth-milling center at the correct distance off the center line of the blank, see that the cutter was properly sharpened, and set the machine for the correct stroke. The machine fed and indexed automatically, but considerable care was necessary on the part of the operative to keep the indexing at exactly the proper adjustment. The foreman approached Annello with the suggestion that he prepare himself to work on the new machines. Annello was highly pleased and put in all his spare time trying to familiarize himself with the work. He succeeded so well that by the time the machines were finally installed, the foreman felt that Annello was sufficiently qualified and gave him a place on the new battery. Here Annello worked along with the other workers, all of whom had been trained at one time or another by the foreman. He appeared to do average work and was well liked by the other men.

The standards department of the Schoonway Machine Company decided to institute a series of studies relative to the operations of gear-cutting machines for milling teeth in cutters. After the routine research had been made, the standards engineer announced the minimum amount of output that a worker must attain in order to be considered efficient. No bonus could be earned until this standard was exceeded.

During the period in which the studies were made, Annello was nervous. He appeared unable to keep his machine in proper adjustment. The pieces which he turned out were inferior in quality, and the total number gradually fell below the point at which the minimum standard was finally set. Engineers from the standards department, knowing that Annello was a protégé of the foreman, sought to ascertain the cause of his trouble, but he was unable to make an intelligible explanation. They warned him of the seriousness of the situation. For several days there was no change.

Then, at the suggestion of the foreman, time study men retimed Annello, in an endeavor to find the cause of his failure. His showing was worse than ever. The engineers began to question whether or not he had the native ability to do the work. The head of the standards department expressed that doubt to the foreman. The foreman insisted that Annello was a first-class worker. The standards department believed that the foreman was prejudiced because he did not object when they suggested that Joseph Smith be discharged. Smith had been employed on the new battery for about the same length of time as Annello, and his output was not as low.

With their watches concealed in their pockets so as not to arouse Annello's suspicion, the time study men clocked him for a third time. Still he showed no improvement. After that, the standards department became insistent that Annello be discharged. The foreman was obdurate, and the standards department appealed to the production manager for a final decision. The latter listened to the recommendations of the standards department and to the objections which the foreman raised, and then made a ruling that at the end of one week the standards department was to make another clocking of Annello's work. If it still was unsatisfactory, the foreman was to be given an additional week in which he could take any measures he chose in attempting to bring the machinist's work up to standard. If he failed to do this within the allotted period, Annello was to be fired for inability to attain the minimum standard.

At the end of the first week, the new timings were made. Annello showed no improvement. When the foreman received this information, he went to Annello accompanied by a friend who acted as interpreter. The foreman told the machinist that his work was coming along well and that he had no need to fear the time study men, that they would bother him no more. He said he would see to it personally that nothing happened to Annello and that as long as he tried his best, he always could have a job with the Schoonway Machine Company. Annello thanked the foreman profusely and said that he always tried to do his best. The next morning he appeared at work smiling and happy. His output for the day was just at the minimum, but the quality was excellent. The next day his output increased. At the end of the week, he was earning a good bonus. Six months later the standards department, as well as the foreman, rated him as the best worker on the automatic gear-cutting machines.

Discussion Questions

1. What was the relationship between the foreman and Arno before the advent of the standards engineers?
2. Why did Arno become nervous when the standards engineers started their studies?
3. Why did the engineers deal with Arno as they did?
4. How did their behavior affect Arno?

5. Why did the foreman reject the engineers' recommendation that Arno be replaced?

6. What do you think of the way the foreman handled the situation once the production manager declared an ultimatum on Arno?

7. Is it likely that everyone will live happily ever after?

CASE 7.3

MTC*

Len Matthews is director of the Management Training Center, an adjunct of the College of Business Administration. The college is one of several schools that constitute a large university on the West Coast.

Matthews recently hired Dr. Mark James, an organizational consultant, to conduct a survey of MTC's staff. James accordingly interviewed each staff member individually. He assured each person that while general conditions and responses would be reported to Matthews, no specific identification of the interviewee would occur.

After the meetings, James consolidated his findings and submitted them to Matthews. With the latter's approval he then sent a copy of his report to each staff member with the following cover letter:

June 5

Dear MTC Personnel:

The enclosed survey report contains a summary of results from the interviews we recently had. This summary was approved by Mr. Matthews without one change. This has not happened before in all my experience.

Len is setting a meeting of the MTC staff for 1:15 P.M. on June 11. I will be there to answer questions and to clarify any points of interest. Len will continue the meeting after I leave by addressing concerns of interest to MTC.

Thank you for your cooperation. This was a rewarding group with whom to work.

Sincerely,

Mark L. James, Ph.D.

MLJ: bp
ENC

---

* All names have been disguised. Note: You may wish to compare this case with "Lynn Barfield," Case 4.1. Ms. Barfield is an MTC staff member.

Management Training Center Survey

Interviews were conducted with 26 employees of the Management Training Center. This report is a summary of the information gathered in those interviews.

Report on Feelings about Working for the Center

Many people enjoy their work. However, others dislike what they experience here. Negative comments were made regarding the following:

1. Unexplained and unjustified changes.
2. Being punished for not knowing about a change when that change had not been communicated to me.
3. Feeling left out and uninvolved.
4. No recourse against supervisor's judgment.
5. Not feeling free to discuss matters in confidence for fear that they'd be repeated to others.
6. My superior keeping a list of my errors.
7. Unfairness. Some individuals and groups are treated differently.

Working Conditions

Many of you rate working conditions as excellent. You regard stress as a normal part of the work. You view your fellow employees as hardworking, dedicated, and willing to help each other.

Others responded differently. There was concern about:

1. Crowding.
2. Distance between offices.
3. Interruptions.
4. Too many work hours.
5. Storage and delivery problems.
6. Delays.
7. Last-minute changes.
8. Suppression of informal communication—supervisors regard it as "wasting time."
9. Unbalanced work flows.
10. Changes not communicated as they should be.
11. No attempt made to determine effect of changes on jobs an people.
12. Understaffing.
13. Inadequate training of newcomers.
14. Defensiveness.

On Being Spread Out

One comment: "There are pros and cons. If you need anything, it takes longer. But it does separate the functions and people may be better able to control their areas that way." A great many people find that being spread out interferes with accurate and rapid communication. Sometimes it takes a lot of "chasing around" to get things done. "We waste a tremendous amount of time shuffling back and forth. It causes delays and things are lost or misplaced. It would be more convenient if we were closer together—sometimes we can't reach people we need to reach to get answers. We need contact with everyone," was another comment.

Some are quite satisfied with the separate locations, even though recognizing that it might be more convenient to be closer. Some advantages are: freedom to operate, no one looking over your shoulder, and more quiet. In summary, the fact that the Center units are spread out does not seem to be a major problem.

Treatment by Fellow Employees

There were just a few negative comments in this area. Most of them dealt with lack of courtesy, lack of trust, overbearing fellow employees, lack of informal or social interaction, people changing things without telling others about it, being superior, and plans and actions made at the last minute.

It appears that except for some individuals and some isolated problems, relationships with and treatment by fellow employees are generally quite positive.

The Real Reasons People Leave the Center

There are many reasons for turnover in any organization. That appears to be true for the Center as well. The three most frequently mentioned reasons for leaving were better pay and better jobs, reasons associated with managers (no one listens, having favorites, and so on), and the way changes were made.

Opportunity for Growth and Advancement at the Center

Many people see very limited or no opportunities for advancement at the Center. Several mentioned that the Center seemed to favor less qualified outsiders over qualified insiders and that the same standards of education and experience did not seem to apply to outsiders as to insiders, especially if they are friends of managers. A few people indicated that there might be opportunities if one took courses and especially if one earned a degree.

Immediate Supervision, Treatment, Feedback, Training

There were marked differences in your views and comments about your immediate supervisors. Favorable comments were generally made about the same individual supervisors and negative comments were generally made about other individual supervisors. In a few cases, of course, there were mixed comments.

Many employees report that you have excellent supervisors who are helpful, treat you with respect, listen to your opinions, are respected by you, see that you get training and growth opportunities, encourage you, give both positive and corrective feedback as appropriate, and so on.

Others do not like your supervisor. You say your supervisor doesn't listen to you or ignores you, gets panicky, doesn't know your job, gives you no feedback (either positive or negative), won't give answers to questions, applies standards inconsistently to subordinates, doesn't have the ability to do the supervisory job, and that others get blamed because of their supervisor's errors.

It is fair to say that except for a few supervisors and managers, supervision is generally felt to be good.

Center Communications Processes, Difficulties

There were many negative comments about communications which covered a number of topics. About half of the employees made comments such as bad, awful, big problem, key problem, and confusion. Several people mentioned that changes were made and that they were not told of the changes, that people were "assumed" to know, and that rules, regulations, and policies were not consistently enforced after they were communicated. Three people made comments such as lots of breakdowns in communications, we are losing information, difficult to get materials such as letters out on time, have to hunt to get needed information, information mostly comes through the grapevine, no notice of openings, too much bypassing, and don't know who does what.

It is clear that most of the people believe that communications could be improved considerably and that everyone really needs to be informed when things are changed. One person said we operate pretty well in spite of communications. Maybe that is a good summary in itself.

Freedom to Make Suggestions, Point Out Errors

Over half indicated that you feel free to make suggestions, and so on, to either your supervisor or to others. "Sometimes they even listen," a few people said. For others the comments were critical. "They won't listen" or "Suggestions won't be used" were the most frequent comments here. A few people said they would be put down by sarcasm, comments would be misinterpreted, or that confidence would not be maintained if they made comments.

It has been my experience that what happens between making a suggestion and getting feedback about why it is or is not used is a major problem. Sometimes suggestions really don't register, sometimes they are forgotten, but mostly feedback is lacking. Either not listening or no feedback produces the same effect, the belief that people are not heard.

How People Feel about Job Security and Why

Most of you indicate that you feel reasonably secure in your jobs if you perform well. Some recognize that "soft" money and an educational setting may hold some risk of continuation of programs although most of you realize that this is a minor consideration. There is evidence of some resentment from past handling of some people who have left. There is a moderate-sized group of people with feelings of insecurity and threat about their jobs. Another group indicates that managers make it hard on you, use smart alec and sarcastic treatment with you, and pressure you so you want to leave and others are afraid they will be added to the "hit list."

What the Management Development Center Is Doing Well

It is clear that you are proud of what the Center does and that you think it is done well. Most people mentioned the programs and/or the atmosphere of support for the programs and making them top quality. You indicated that where there may be problems in the organization of one sort or another, you never let the participants become aware that everything is not just right. You say you are proud to be a part of the quality programs that are offered. Several mentioned that the opportunity for training and education was another plus.

One or Two Changes Important to Your Work and the Center

There were no consistent, frequent comments made in response to this question. The three most frequently suggested changes were improve the facilities, change a manager, and reduce the pressures on support staff. One concern mentioned in different ways was for backbiting, tattling, going to others before coming to the person involved, and going over the head of the person involved. Another, approached in several ways, addressed the problem of changes being made without the involvement of those who would ultimately be affected and without announcement or communication of the changes. Some would like to have more knowledge about where the Center is headed, what plans are being made, is there to be expansion, and so on.

James's Comments to All Employees

I have tried to provide a representative summary of what you told me in the interviews. Every effort has been made to protect the identity of individuals, either from comments made in the interviews or in comments made about others in the interview.

It appears to me that "then" and "now" differ because of changes in management, personnel, and the situation. As you grew rapidly, those of you who remain from "then" have been shaken by all the changes, the way in which you perceive changes were made (little attention to your experience and input), new authority figures, and continued unease about why things are being done as they are. New personalities have set new kinds of standards and practices. Many of you are anxious because you feel you have no place to turn to voice your concerns in confidence. You feel that when you speak up the response will be, "If you don't like it here, we will help you find another job." That is what you tell me, that you don't trust management and administrators, at least some of them, and that you are not sure what is going on (you feel uninformed). My question is, "Is it really that bad?"

Why do I ask that question? It is clear that there are some problem spots in staff, supervision and management, and administration. Some things have happened which need to be examined carefully for why they happened. For example, change was inevitable, and the need was pressing. Change by nature, if introduced perfectly, is disruptive. When sudden series of changes are introduced with relatively little perceived effort to involve those concerned, stress and troubles can arise in any organization. Then when turnover occurs, little training is done, and the organization is functioning as best *you* can make it function under a lot of new policies and procedures, resentment can arise. Some bitterness and rigidity of behavior occurs even among people of good spirit like the Center employees. In no way is this suggested as an apology or excuse. Mistakes were made and will probably continue to be made. But by working with management and administrators, with supervisors, and with other employees, I am certain that much of the discomfort currently found in this organization can be alleviated and dissipated. The organization, as I see it, is a very healthy one with relatively minor problems that can be overcome by trust, honesty, involvement, and effort. After all, it would be better to produce those excellent programs with less turmoil and fewer problems, wouldn't it?

I thank each of you for your willingness to meet with me and discuss the Management Training Center and its people. You were helpful and cooperative and I have tried to respond by representing your views to management as clearly a possible. I know you will have good success in solving any problems which have been identified.

Sincerely,

Mark

Discussion Questions
1. How do you feel about Matthews hiring James to conduct the survey?
2. What do you see as the major problems associated with MTC?
3. Is *motivation* one of them?
4. What recommendations do you have for Matthews now?

CASE 7.4

"He's Really Coming!"*

Charlie Thorp, with 15 years of management experience with the Darron company, was regarded as company-minded, cooperative with associates, and a good operator. When his bookkeeper retired, Thorp hired John Pasek to replace her. It soon became apparent that Pasek's ambition was to become a salesman. John was a likable young man; so when an opening occurred, Charlie recommended to Bob Norlach, district manager, "that John, given the opportunity and the leadership, has the qualities that could be developed to make him a successful salesman in my area."

Norlach, Thorp, and Pasek met to discuss the job and its performance standards and to arrive at a mutually acceptable budget. Pasek was installed as a salesman.

Norlach asked for periodic progress reports on John, and Charlie invariably responded: "He's really coming! He is ahead of budget in both new accounts and volume of sales during the period. He's right on target."

After six months of favorable reports on young Pasek, Charlie visited Norlach and complained: "We gotta get rid of John. His production stinks. He has not performed up to standard or budget."

Norlach was astounded: "But haven't you been reporting to me how well John has been doing? Why the sudden change in your evaluation of his performance?"

Charlie answered: "I just wanted to encourage him. I figured that if I reported his real output he'd be getting a lot of pressure and he might never shape up. So I was crediting him with all my own new sales and reporting that to you."

Discussion Questions

1. Why did Charlie Thorp behave as he did?

2. What did you think of Charlie's rosy reports on Pasek? Would you appraise them differently if John *had* shaped up?

3. What should Bob Norlach do now?

---

* All names have been disguised.

CASE 7.5

Pat's Story*

Early Promotions

Considering that I had only a high school education and no business experience, I think I did pretty well at the bank, at least at the beginning. After three years, I was made a branch manager. Three years later I became assistant treasurer, but still stayed at the branch as manager.

During this time, my home life and work life were happy and it was rare when I wasn't smiling. In fact, most of the customers would comment if I wasn't kidding or laughing. They'd think I was sick.

Promoted to Treasurer

Still another three years passed—then I got a shock! On February 1st, Mr. Stockton, the president of our Mutual Savings bank, came over for his usual weekly visit. Over the years, we had become close friends. He was sometimes very unreasonable, but knowing him and his good qualities, I grew to love him. If something were to happen to him tomorrow, I would feel as badly as if it were my own dad.

He said he had a problem and could I spare a few minutes. I assumed it was the usual gab and proceeded to the lunchroom with him. There he told me that Ted Roberts, our treasurer, had given one month's notice, at which time he would go to a competitor.

I thought to myself, "God help us. We'll have to close the doors." I asked Mr. Stockton if he had tried to get Ted to stay. He said he did, but I can't imagine him trying very hard, knowing he would be too proud to admit to Ted that the bank needed him.

Mr. Stockton said frankly he didn't know what he should do. Mr. Wirtz, with all his years at the bank, couldn't qualify. Six years ago, when our senior assistant treasurer, died, and he tried it, he was out for five months with a nervous breakdown. Juan Balboa, our other assistant treasurer in the mortgage department, was new and Stockton hadn't much confidence in him yet.

The vice president, who was being groomed to take Stockton's job when he retired, had been let go in January because of lack of aggressiveness and productivity, and there was no one else but me!

"Me? I don't know, Mr. Stockton, I just don't know!" Ted was always crabbing about how he got everyone's operational problems, how stupid his help was, and how bad his ulcers were getting, and besides, I still depended on Ted for certain technical questions.

---

* All names have been disguised.

Mr. Stockton said he had approached the board of investment and really built me up, and he and they decided I could do it. Well, I don't know how these men could evaluate my capabilities. I've known me for 27 years, and I don't know what they are.

But here was a man who didn't care that I was only a 21-year-old female when he made me branch manager and at 24 made me an assistant treasurer, telling me that he needs me. I couldn't live with myself if I didn't at least try. I made up my mind in 10 minutes that I'd try to get as much knowledge from Ted as possible before he left.

Learning the Job

The next day I arrived at the main office, where Ted informed me as to his duties and tried to teach me the things I didn't know.

Well, I discovered there was a hell of a lot I didn't know. And being so content in my own little world at the branch, I never bothered to learn things that didn't pertain to branch operations.

After one day, I went home very depressed and immediately went to bed. I laid there for six or seven hours, telling myself to throw in the towel and at the same time giving myself all the reasons why I couldn't.

What would my folks think! They were so excited about the idea of me as treasurer. And my kid sisters and brothers all patting me on the back, saying, "We know you can do it, Pat." And last, but not least, I will have failed my boss. ("God, I can't throw in that towel; I'd rather die first.")

My second day was worse. While Ted is explaining, I'm not really getting it because I'm constantly thinking, "I've got to get this in a month, I've got to cram 35 years' experience into one month."

When I returned home that evening, I went to my room, closed the door, and had a damn good cry. Not only did it seem there were 3 million jobs being funneled through Ted's desk, but 3 million questions from the tellers. It seemed like they couldn't blow their own noses without checking with Ted first.

I couldn't help thinking that if these interruptions didn't stop, I'd never catch on to anything.

After one week of depression, tears, and frustration, I decided to tell Mr. Stockton to forget it. I don't want to go nuts like Mr. Wirtz, and I don't want to lie awake nights tossing and turning.

I marched into Mr. Stockton's office the next day and said, "Mr. Stockton, I . . . !" and with this he said, "Well, how's my girl doing? You certainly haven't smiled much this week, but you're a worrywart . . . take your time, be yourself, you're smart, and you'll get it."

Well, what could I say but, "One thing good that's happened to me is I've lost 9 pounds this week, and I could stand to lose about 20 more." We both laughed, and I marched out, undetermined and unconvinced.

My morale was fairly good, at least for one day.

Three weeks of lying in bed every night, going over the day's instructions, saying, "What the hell is this amortization all about? Depreciation on the buildings and the furniture and amortizing our insurance over the life of the policy. God help me, when he leaves, I'm going to look like the world's biggest jerk! With me running the show, in two months' time we'll have to close down."

Ted didn't help very much, telling me goodies like, "Forget it, kid, when bookkeeping is out, you won't get anything done. That goof in the back room has been doing this job for 16 years, and she still doesn't know where to look when she's out."

Gee, bookkeeping was out practically every day. When do I do my work? And I don't know where to look myself. I don't know a thing about the general ledger except which column to put the amortization and accrued interest in, and that's providing I know what the hell amortization and accrued interest is by the time he leaves.

By the final week, even my folks were discouraging me, saying: "The money and the job aren't worth it!" "You look awful; you better tell Mr. Stockton you can't handle it."

At this time I owned my own house. Keeping house, and all, the whole business was getting me down. I was too tired to even wash my face before going to bed, let along take care of the problems of a house. I decided to sell.

Well, that was a doozy of an idea! Now I had people bothering me with phone calls, plus selling furniture. Boy, I was beginning to look like death warmed over. Now, I no longer dreaded going to work, but home, too.

In the final week, Ted showed me how to reconcile the computer sheets, payroll, trustee reports, state tax computation, recording new securities, report for estimated earnings, who to collect rent from on our parking lot, and when to pay the board of investment and the board of trustees. Prior to my arrival, both Ted and Mr. Wirtz had handled it, along with our vice president, who had been fired, and Mr. Wirtz was managing our new branch.

I was now making noontime visits to the nearest church. I don't really know if I was praying for success or just to keep from going nuts. I don't think I smiled once during the entire training. Little did I know, I wouldn't be smiling for some time to come.

Ted seemed touched when I started crying when he said goodbye. I don't think he knew I was crying for me.

The weekend prior to my being on my own was spent in bed. If I didn't know better, I would have thought I was pregnant. I was having morning sickness (which lasted for several weeks).

The First Day on My Own

The first day on my own was hell. All the young help decided that Pat was a soft slob, so let's hit her with gripes we were afraid to mention to Ted.

It was the first of the month and we were getting all our coupons and interest checks in, which had to be recorded on the bookkeeping sheet and checkbooks, plus the usual monthly reports, all of which I was supposed to do on my own.

Mr. Stockton left at 11 A.M. for his usual Monday meeting.

As soon as he was gone, Ann from the mortgage department came in.

Ann: Gee, Pat, I was wondering about our Blue Cross.
Me: Wondering about what?
Ann: How come the bank pays the family plan for the guys but not the girls?
Me: That's our policy, I guess.
Ann: When I get married in four months, my husband'll still be in school. I'll be the main support, so why won't they pay?
Me: Did you ask Ted? I really don't know very much about it. It's one thing he didn't mention.
Ann: Well, he was always so busy, I didn't want to bother him.

This kid had insulted me! What does she think I've been doing, sitting here picking my nose?

Me: Well, I can talk it over with Mr. Stockton and see about it.
Ann: It isn't a fair policy. If they can spend $72.80 a month on David, who's a jerk, why can't they spend it on me? I do more than my share.
Me: Ann, I've got 9,000 things piling up. Please let's not discuss this any further. I will find out for you.

Well now, I can get back to work!

Maria: Pat?
Me: (*Now what?*) Yes, Maria?
Maria: Do you suppose we could have a suggestion box?
Me: Sure, why not, it sounds great.

Flora then asked me if she could keep a dentist appointment that was scheduled in three more weeks. She had already gotten Ted's consent. I answered, "If I'm still alive in three weeks, you have my permission. If I don't make it, you'll have to check with the next guy."

By this time it's 11:30 A.M. and everyone seems to be puzzled as to what lunch hours they were to take. Everyone wants to eat with their friends. I was thinking, "If I went in the vault and took those guns out of joint control, these people wouldn't have to worry about eating."

As everyone bickered over the schedule, I decided that when I got home, I'd make one up and post it, but that wasn't helping me today. I decided to let them work it out themselves, provided some of them stayed to wait on the counter.

Every item I put on the bookkeeping sheet was questionable. I kept running to check with Flora. But Flora went and got last month's work to check. I thought: This is the blind leading the blind.

It was now 12:15 P.M., and my desk looked worse. Everything that these people got that seemed a little different was thrown on my desk, plus both inter-office envelopes from the branches were lying there for the contents to be distributed among the help. After sorting the stuff from the envelopes, it was now 12:30. Well, at least I've gotten two things off this desk.

Boy, when Mr. Stockton get back at 1:00, he's going to think I was goofing off for two hours.

At 12:30 P.M. the janitor appeared.

Ernie: Pat, I've got this can of 30W oil, and the paper on the boiler calls for 20W oil. Think it would make much difference?

Me: Ernie, about the only difference in oil that I know of is real olive oil and corn oil, and that difference to me is the taste. Maybe we should taste the oil and see.

Ernie: You made a funny!

Me: Did I? That's the first one in a month.

Ernie: All kidding aside, what do you think?

Me: I think there are two people in this bank who know very little about oil, so you buy whatever oil the boiler calls for. I doubt that it will bankrupt us.

Ernie: OK. Can you give me the money? I'll bring back the receipt.

Me: Sure. Tell Charlie what you need, and he'll give it to you.

God, it's 1:00 and I've accomplished practically nothing.

Then Flora makes the grand announcement of the day: "Pat, bookkeeping is out $1.67."

A fantastic thought: Maybe I could put Flora in the boiler room and get Ernie to do the bookkeeping.

I gave Flora a consoling half smile. If I could smile, she might watch for my crow's-feet and not see my tears. "Well, let's start hunting."

I at least had Charlie to rely on. Ted seemed to have fed him a lot of info that the rest of the help didn't get.

Me: Hey, Charlie, would you mind helping us look for $1.67?

Charlie: Cripe, I've got my own crap sitting here to do, and besides, when the heck are you going to take my teller window away so I can devote my time to this important stuff?

Me: Look, Charlie, we'll consider that possibility later, but unless we can find $1.67, we'll never leave here tonight.

Charlie: Well, in that case I'll help out.

I thought, "If I didn't need this bratty 24-year-old, I'd kick his a--."
It was now 1:15 and Mr. Stockton popped in.

Stockton: Having problems?
Me: I really don't know, we've just started looking.
Stockton: What have you checked?
Me: Well, I've started adding the checkooks, but I don't know what Charlie has checked. He's out front.
Stockton: I guess you've got everything under control.
Me: Yes, more or less.

As Charlie did the directing (which, I might add, was his bag), we checked just about every possibility. It was now 2:15, and neither Flora nor myself had had lunch.

I decided we should leave for a few minutes just to clear our heads.

Me: Charlie, keep looking. Flora and I are going to lunch. Check with the mortgage department again. Ask Juan to do it. We're running out of places to look in savings.
Charlie: If he'd get off his butt instead of having those idiot kids checking for him, we might get results.

As I was thinking the very same thing myself, I kept my mouth shut and proceeded toward the door.

Teller #1: Pat, the coin machine's jammed. I can smell burning.
Me: You're right, its the motor. Is it shut off?
Teller #1: No, I didn't think it would make a difference!

God, what did I ever do to deserve such a fate?
By the time I handcranked the cylinder, it was 2:45, and I finally got out the door.
I didn't eat with Flora. Instead I went to Saint Mary's Church six blocks away. On my way back I grabbed a sandwich. At 3:15 I returned—no change. We looked and looked and finally I threw in the towel.
The help usually get out at 4:00, and it's 3:55.
I'll have to tell Mr. Stockton we can't find it.

Me: Mr. Stockton, we've checked everything. I don't know where else to look.
Stockton: Everybody will be fresh tomorrow; we'll look then.

Fresh? Is he kidding? The way I've been sleeping, I'll be dead tomorrow. (For a moment, I thought that might be a blessing.)

That night on my way home, I bought a bottle of rum. By 9:00 I was soused. I crawled into bed and finally got a good night's sleep.

The Next Two Days

I wasn't tired the next morning, but I sure as hell was nauseated. I arrived at work early.

As cocky as Charlie was—he was early, too.

We started from scratch, checking everything step by step. I had accomplished a bank first! Never before had the daily statement been out for two days. In fact, it had never been out for one.

Plus two days' work still sitting on my desk. Finally, on the third morning, after Flora finished blocking her mortgage cards, she announced that the cards were $1.67 out. Juan had made a wrong correction on the back of the control sheet.

I was so happy at the moment, I couldn't really be mad with Juan. Then it hit me that none of his work had been interrupted and nothing was piled on his desk, plus he left on time with everyone else!

I decided then I would take one day at a time and stop worrying.

The next day I started off in a pretty good mood. I decided this place was not going to get the best of me.

My problem this day was Mr. Stockton. He must have gotten up on the wrong side of the bed. It seemed that everything he looked at was fouled up. As he proceeded to tell me how messy everything was, I noticed the item to which he was referring had been wrong for two years.

"Look, Mr. Stockton, I don't mind being bawled out for my own mistakes, and I make plenty. That's something that has been handled wrong for two years, and I'll try to correct it, but I do not wish to be criticized for it."

This didn't set too well, as he grabbed his hat and coat and mumbled about no one having any respect for his authority and walked out.

I felt crushed. I don't believe he realized just what I was feeling. I thought I'd never catch on to all the detailed things.

Showdown with Stockton

After two months I was slowly gaining confidence, then it hit the fan!

The third week of June, Charlie gave two weeks' notice. Maria, our secretary, got a better paying job. Another teller was being sent to our branch, and another teller from our new branch quit on the spot.

In one month's time, I had five new savings tellers, three of whom had less than one month's experience.

I had to train the new help in as short a time as possible. Their instruction was very poor, as I was now being interrupted every two minutes with questions.

Another two months of turmoil. Mr. Stockton was getting complaints that the help in his organization was giving out wrong information to customers, both over the counter and the telephone. I was certainly bawled out.

I finally got up enough nerve to lay the cards on the table.

"Mr. Stockton, I am not a miracle worker. Just an average person. Before I arrived, things were pretty mixed up. At that time, you had an assistant treasurer making $20,000, a treasurer making $27,000, and a vice president making $35,000. They all leave, and I replace them for $23,000. I'm not complaining about the money, but I only have one head, two hands, and a limited amount of time in the day. I have come to the conclusion that I haven't complained enough for you to recognize all of our problems. I ask nothing of you except consideration. Before screaming, look at the entire picture. I realize we're preparing to merge with another bank and that's why we're not replacing our officers, but the load is getting me down. Especially in that you think this place can run just as efficiently now as it has in the past."

He smiled and said I was right and that he was irritable lately because he was doing a lot more, too.

My little speech cleared the air and has made it a lot easier on both of us.

The Pressure Eases

In October, Juan gave two weeks' notice. He had worked for the bank we were to merge with and wasn't too crazy about going in that direction. He left for a competitive bank.

Things have been looking better the last three months. However, the commissioner refused our merger, so many changes will be needed.

I have some ideas for improvement that I hadn't tried due to the anticipation of a change anyway. Now I want to move.

There are two things which I have come to realize. Most important is the realization that these people are not goofs or idiots.

For example, in 16 years, when bookkeeping was out, it was taken away from Flora and the officers would do the search. She could never look for herself and broaden her knowledge. If it hadn't been for Flora I probably would have fallen on my face when I came to the general ledger. She has become more independent and less of a burden on me.

The moral is—let them think for themselves.

The second thing is make everyone feel his job is important. Through staff meetings, I find that the kids are volunteering a tremendous amount of their ideas and time. Morale has really picked up.

And now that I've stopped fumbling around in the dark, I want to make as many changes as possible to make our organization as smooth-running and as pleasant as possible.

I feel should any great change occur, I will face it, and should I fall, be able to pick myself up and start again.

I really love banking and am now enjoying every minute of it. I have a small ulcer, acquired five months ago, but it's all worth it.

Discussion Questions

1. What makes Pat run?
2. What do you make of Mr. Stockton?
3. What should Pat do now?
4. What do you think of Pat's management philosophy?

CASE 7.6

Tommie Sanders–B*

Interviewer: To recap our previous chat, you are Tommie Sanders, you and your husband live in Oak Park which is a suburb west of Chicago, you are currently the assistant director of sales here at the hotel which is near O'Hare Airport, you've been involved in virtually all aspects of hotel keeping and you've been in this field for nine years—seven at an L.A. hotel and two years here. All is going well except for a few "clouds."

Sanders: Good summary. Before we got the "clouds," it might be helpful if I give you a sketch of the sales department's organization:

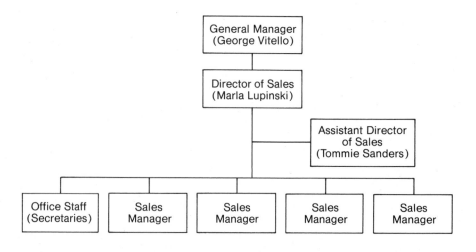

---

* All names have been disguised. Note: You may wish to compare this case with "Tommie Sanders–A," Case 12.2.

Marla reports to the hotel's general manager. He's the top gun here. Everyone else on the chart reports to Marla.

Now, here's Marla's job: She leads the sales effort of the hotel to book groups and individuals; she puts together weekend packages; she's responsible for total marketing for the hotel including advertising.

Interviewer: How is her performance evaluated?

Sanders: There are two criteria and these are calculated monthly: Occupancy and average daily rate. Occupancy is determined by the percentage of rooms actually rented out of the rooms available. Average daily rate, as the name implies, is the average of the rates that were charged during that month.

Hotels, generally, have a great variety of rates. For instance, if you come in off the street and stay one night you'll usually be charged the rack rate, the top rate, $150. But if you have a volume contract with us and use us every night of the year, or if you're a group, you'll get a lower rate. Airline personnel, for example, pay $36 a night.

Interviewer: Then she's measured by both *criteria*. If she's high on occupancy and low on the daily rate—or vice versa, that's not too good.

Sanders: That's right, she must measure up well on both counts.

Interviewer: And what's your job?

Sanders: That chart I showed you is a little misleading. For example, even though the four sales managers report to Marla, she usually doesn't deal with them on a daily basis. Rather, they come to me for a lot of decisions and for training. I do a lot of the reports. I'm in the trenches with these men and woman.

Also, I attend some of the executive meetings along with Marla so I'm considered more as an executive.

Interviewer: Then, in some respects the sales managers report to you?

Sanders: That's right.

Interviewer: Who determines their salaries and other rewards?

Sanders: Salaries and salary increases are determined by Marla with input from me. These matters are based on performance reviews.

Interviewer: Who does these?

Sanders: I do. Now, the bonuses, as distinguished from salaries, come mostly from the occupancy and daily rate criteria that I mentioned before.

Interviewer: Is it fair to say that the performance evaluations would be a least somewhat subjective whereas the bonuses would be largely a matter of arithmetic?

Sanders: Correct. The major portion of the hotel's profit comes from the sleeping rooms. A distant second would be beverages and then food. For example, if we pour a drink it may cost us 20 cents, but we charge $2.50. Food, on the other hand, is not very profitable—maybe 20 to 30 percent profit. That's because labor and material costs are both very high.

Interviewer: So percentagewise you make out quite well on beverages and to a lesser extent on food but the volume just isn't there.

Sanders: That's right. We may make a 75 percent profit on a $150 room and that's $112.50. So even though we might make a 1,000 percent profit on a drink, you'd have to sell a ton of drinks to amass a $112.50 profit.

Interviewer: I appreciate the background on hotel management. How about your "clouds"?

Sanders: Among the ones that bug me the most would be dealing with the office staff, specifically those who operate computers. You'll recall from the organization chart that these people supposedly report to Marla because they type the sales contracts, and so on. But I have a lot of dealings with them, too. Here's what happens:

Some of the office staff are selected to go through computer training. Well, the pattern is very predictable. For the first month or two they're thoroughly enthused; the learning curve is very steep; they're very creative. If they run into a problem they'll sleep on it and usually wind up finding a better way of handling the situation.

Then they sort of level out and perform the day-in and day-out activities on the computer. And somewhere along the line they sort of burn out on computers and become locked into whatever they've been doing.

And at that point, say nine months or a year later, I go down and ask them to massage the computer to come up with a slight modification to print up a slightly different report.

Well, the usual response is that the computer can't do that. And if you didn't know better you'd accept that as gospel and give up trying for a change.

Interviewer: But you did know better?

Sanders: In a way. I learned about the computer. I taught myself. Although I didn't go through the burning-out process. I may not know the solution to a given problem but I know generally how to go about finding it. So I walk the person through it. I try to be real gentle and not make the person feel like an idiot but I do say something like: "Hey, you're not being real helpful here. What if you did this—or that—and so forth?"

Interviewer: And the response?

Sanders: A kind of grudging "Well OK." It's more of a resignation rather than a "Eureka—I see the light!" kind of enthusiasm.

Interviewer: What about their motivation? Do they get more pay as a computer operator?

Sanders: Not really. It's not considered hazardous duty so it doesn't affect their income very much.

Interviewer: Is it a stepping-stone to something else?

Sanders: No, in fact, for some it's a dead-end job.

Interviewer: Could you give a specific example of how people resisted modification?

Sanders: Sure. Initially, we asked them to use the computer to type out contracts for the groups that we had coming into the hotel. The contract would have the group's name, their arrival and departure dates, the number of rooms they needed for each night, what specifications were involved, the date the contract was typed, and the option date—usually, there were two weeks during which the client was to sign the contract and return it to us. In addition, we needed a weekly report of the contracts we had and whose contract was coming due. In regard to the latter the computer would spit out the contracts with cover letters, and so on.

Then about nine months later we felt we needed to know which sales managers had booked which groups for a given month. Now, that information was already in the computer but we had never asked that question of the computer before. But it sure took a lot of pushing to get the operator to think of a way to ask a question of the computer or to program the computer in order to get that information.

Interviewer: Why did you want this information?

Sanders: It would help us evaluate the performance of the sales managers. Now, to be fair this did make the computer operator's job more taxing. We were asking her to do things she hadn't done before.

Interviewer: You mentioned "she"—are all the computer operators women?

Sanders: Yes.

Interviewer: The fact that you are a woman—did that help or hinder you here—or have no bearing?

Sanders: I really don't know. Let me give you another example of how it was difficult to work with the computer operators.

Interviewer: Fine.

Sanders: Hotels are beginning to practice "yield management." The airlines have been doing it for years but hotels are just getting into it.

Interviewer: How does "yield management" work for you?

Sanders: OK. For example, we need to know what bookings do we have now (February) for next December. And how does that compare with last year's February view of last year's December?

Interviewer: I follow.

Sanders: Well, our computers have that information so I'd go to the operators and ask them for it. And they'd say: "No, the computer can't do that."

Interviewer: And you couldn't accept that?

Sanders: That's right. Maybe because I hadn't gone through the burnout or maybe because my mind is more nimble but I'd say: "Oh yes it can, I don't know exactly how to do it but somehow we can get the computer to supply that information." So I'd sit down with the operator and work it out with her and find a way of getting that information.

Interviewer: I gather that your conversance with the computer allowed you to contradict the operator. Without that background would you have had to accept whatever she told you?

Sanders: Undoubtedly. If I hadn't been familiar with the computer the operators could have snowed me very easily. The point is you don't know what's in the future—a new technology, perhaps a new way of looking at things may come along. Maybe a new boss comes in and makes different demands. You simply have to know what the computer can and cannot do.

Interviewer: You originally spoke of "clouds" in the plural. Anything else bothering you?

Sanders: Yes. It has to do with change of ownership.

Interviewer: Has your hotel been through such a change?

Sanders: No, but we came close and it got me thinking about the ramifications of an ownership change. You hear a lot these days about LBOs (leveraged buyouts) and corporate raiders, and so on. Well, that's the glamorous side of it. You rarely hear about the hidden costs, including what happens to the people down here in the trenches.

Interviewer: And your thoughts?

Sanders: During the process of purchase or potential purchase the top gun, the general manager, is simply unavailable to his people. He's the one who has to provide information to the prospective buyers, to answer their questions. If he is going to be replaced—and, by the way, if the purchase goes through he's likely to be the first to lose his job because the new owners will want their own person on the scene to oversee their investment.

So if he's going to be replaced then he'll be out interviewing, finding out what's available. All in all, he's unable to provide the leadership the hotel needs.

Submanagers then become very territorial. They don't help other submanagers and they become very defensive of their own bailiwicks. And those attitudes quickly permeate the entire organization. The notions of trust and teamwork fly out the window.

Another point. Let's say the general manager is replaced by someone from the purchasers. Then watch how slowly the sub-managers relinquish the power they have been protecting. Self-defensiveness rather than hotel profitability becomes the central thrust.

Interviewer: But you said your hotel did not go through an ownership change.

Sanders: That's right, but we came close enough so I could read the handwriting on the wall.

Discussion Questions

1. What do you make of Tommie Sanders' remarks concerning hotel management?

2. Your analysis of the office staff and their reaction to computer training—and computer practice?

3. What suggestions do you have for how Tommie might deal with this situation?

4. Tommie's hotel narrowly escaped an LBO. However, the impact on hotel personnel was felt. Your views?

CHAPTER   EIGHT

The Process of Communication
The Transition Chapter

❊
❊
❊

Now to focus on that critical, challenging, sometimes agonizing human process—communication. Let us begin by examining a very simple, mundane communication experience. Imagine two people, A and B, in an office. A feels warm and asks B to open a window, which B does. We can discuss these events in terms of a model of the communication process.[1]

A COMMUNICATION PROCESS MODEL

Encoding

Consider the steps in this incident. First, A had a need—she felt warm, uncomfortable. Next, she went through a remarkable (for such a simple situation) problem-solving sequence in which she decided, among other things, how best to satisfy her need without thwarting other people's needs; whether to take the action herself or to ask another to take it; and, if she decided to enlist the aid of another, how best to approach that person—when to communicate; what communication medium to use; what choice of words, tone of voice, rate, and loudness of speaking; and so forth.

---

[1] See Figure 8.1. For more detailed models of the communication process, see D. K. Berlo, *The Process of Communication* (New York: Holt, Rinehart & Winston, 1960); C. Shannon and W. Weaver, *The Mathematical Theory of Communication* (Urbana: University of Illinois Press, 1962), p. 5; and W. Schramm, "How Communication Works," in *The Process and Effects of Mass Communication* (Urbana: University of Illinois Press, 1954), pp. 3–26. See also Robert S. Goyer, "Definitions of Communications," special report no. 25, Center for Communication Studies, Ohio University, September 1970; Norman B. Sigband, *Communication for Management and Business*, 5th ed. (Glenview, Ill.: Scott, Foresman, 1989); and Raymond V. Lesikar and John Pettit, Jr., *Business Communication: Theory and Application*, 6th ed. (Homewood, Ill.: Richard D. Irwin, 1989), Chapter 2, "A Model of the Communication Process."

FIGURE 8.1

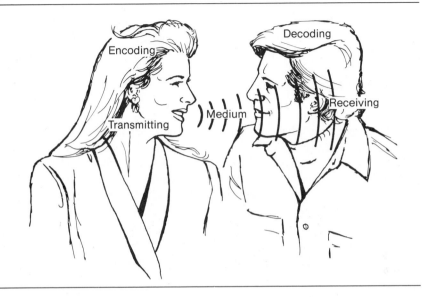

Let's suppose the experience is a familiar one and that B is well known to A, much of A's choice-making is routinized, carried on by conditioned responses—that is, A need not be conscious of making many of those choices.

A has been going through the process of *encoding* a message—perceiving her experiences and formulating a series of symbols with which to express her desire. The *code* part of encoding is important, for the term *code* as we are using it is a system of symbols, and a symbol is something that stands for something else.

The most that the communicator can do is to *represent* feelings, ideas, desires, values, and the like with symbols.

Experiential Isolation.   In other words, each of us is experientially isolated from all others. Recall your individual, solitary confinement cell (page 95). Thomas Wolfe, from the viewpoint of a baby in a crib, captured this insularity.

> He understood that men were forever strangers to one another, that no one ever comes really to know any one, that imprisoned in the dark womb of our mother, we come to life without having seen her face, that we are given to her arms a stranger, and that, caught in that insoluble prison of being, we escape it never, no matter what arms may clasp us, what mouth may kiss us, what heart may warm us. Never, never, never, never, never.
> He saw that the great figures that came and went about him, the huge leering heads that bent hideously into his crib, the great voices that rolled

incoherently above him, had for one another not much greater understanding than they had for him; that even their speech, their entire fluidity and ease of movement were but meagre communicants of their thought or feeling, and served not to promote understanding, but to deepen and widen strife, bitterness, and prejudice.[2]

Complacency.   Considering our state of isolation, communication is indeed a challenge. And yet there appears to be a general denial, albeit unconscious, of this. For several years I have been asking people in organizations how they assessed their communication performance as compared to that of others. Specifically, I asked, by anonymous questionnaire: "In terms of the abilities to understand others and to be understood by others, how do you compare with *(a)* your superior? *(b)* your subordinates? *(c)* people at your rank? *(d)* your department as a whole? *(e)* your organization as a whole?" I have questioned over 13,000 people in universities, business firms, military units, government agencies, hospitals, and so on, and in some cases every individual in the organization was included. The main conclusion of the study was that virtually everyone felt that he or she was communicating at least as well as and, in many cases, better than almost everyone else in the organization!

Most people readily admit that their organization is fraught with faulty communication, but it is almost always *those other people* that they hold responsible. With such complacency about personal communication practices, it is small wonder that communication performance in organizations remains depressingly mediocre. The term *complacency* may suggest a superficial condition that can be ameliorated by just getting people to become a little more humble.

Actually, however, the problem is a function of the individual, the organizational structure, and the nature of communication itself. Many individuals find the admission of communication inadequacy tantamount to admitting inadequacy as a person. And recalling our previous discussion of the self-image, it is clear how threatening such an admission can be. Moreover, organizational processes are generally such that it is often very hard to pinpoint responsibility for a miscommunication. Indeed, it is likely that a number of people cumulatively contributed to the breakdown. Accordingly, it is extremely difficult to assess cause accurately; few, if any, are aware of their full contribution to the confusion. Thus the motivation to upgrade communication performance is generally lacking.

Still another factor inducing complacency about one's communication is the nature of the communication process itself. Consider these aspects, among others: First, communication success (or failure) is a product of the behavior of two (or more) people. Since no one person totally controls the

---

[2] Thomas Wolfe, *Look Homeward, Angel* (New York: Charles Scribner's Sons, 1929), p. 37. Reprinted by permission.

communication process, its success cannot be measured solely in terms of how well one speaks or writes, or how well the other person listens or reads. Conversely, it is generally very difficult to isolate and thus to measure an individual's communication performance because it is so intertwined with that of another.

Second, there is often no objective or clear-cut criterion for communication success. If I try to jump a crossbar at five feet, I will receive immediate and unequivocal feedback (if I am still conscious) as to my success, or lack of it. But in communication, the feedback from my recipient, may not necessarily be either immediate or unequivocal (e.g., even if the other person does not understand me he or she may be reluctant to admit it).

Finally, consider the false assurance that wishful *intra*personal communication (the talking we do to ourselves) can generate: "It's clear, logical, acceptable to me, so she's bound to see it the same way!"

In sum, people in organizations generally seem to be unwarrantedly and dangerously complacent about their communication performance. This is partially because of factors in the individual, the organization, and the communication process that tend to shield the individual from recognizing and/or accepting how deficient his or her performance actually is. And when people are unable or unwilling to acknowledge a deficiency, they are hardly in a position to do anything constructive about it.

But even if we recognized these great barriers to communication—experiential isolation and complacency—and took pains to overcome them, we would still not be assured of an adequate communication. There are four critical steps to go.

Transmission

A's message has been or is being encoded. The next step is to make it available to B. Let's say that A chooses to speak (a memo—"Dear B: Re: Window. Please open. . ." doesn't seem quite appropriate here, unless A and B were not on speaking terms).

Some neural impulses are sent from the brain to the abdominal muscles (for air power), the larynx (for phonation), and the articulatory organs (jaw, teeth, tongue, glottis, lips, and so forth), and A is now *transmitting*. Transmitting what? Words? Thoughts? Meanings? Ideas? Feelings? A message? No, vibrations, simply compressions and rarefactions of molecules in the air.

Parenthetically, why not say that words are coming out of A's mouth? And just what is a word? Consider this: hydroherphamorphastyklebackasoriumperpendercularosis. Is that a word?

It is (or was) a word, and here is the silly but true story to support it: This happened when I was 12 years old. About 100 of us had arrived at summer Boy Scout camp in southern Michigan. The campmaster assigned us to tents, eight boys to the A tent, eight boys to the B tent, and so on, and instructed us to choose a name for our tent (patrol) that began with the letter of the tent. We were supposed to use those names at the evening retreat ceremony.

Retreat came, and each patrol leader, in turn, strode out in front of his patrol and reported in: "All members of the Armadillo Patrol present or accounted for"; "All members of the Bear Patrol. . . ."; and so forth. H tent (ours) had been unable to agree on a name for our patrol, so when his turn came, our patrol leader stepped forward and out of desperation and disgust reported: "All members of the *Herphamorpha* Patrol present or accounted for!" A nonsense word, of course, but it received something we hadn't expected, a loud, appreciative guffaw from the other patrols! (They were 12 years old, too.)

The following morning, at reveille, it was the Hydroherphamorpha Patrol—another chortle—and on it went getting a new syllable or so at each retreat and reveille. It probably would have gotten longer, but camp was only for two weeks.

The point is that that noise became a word, nonsense became sense. When that noise was made or heard, meaning was occurring—people were understanding something—*communication* was taking place. A word, after all, is a subjective matter. When one is born into a particular linguistic culture, he or she acquires (without knowing it at the time) a host of previous agreements as to what would be meant or understood when certain sounds are made or heard or when certain marks are put on a piece of paper or are seen there. (In Chapter 10 on *bypassing*, we shall discuss the sometimes grim and costly consequences of the fact that many of the agreements are hardly airtight.)

The Medium

The vibrations occur in a *medium*, usually air. Of course, there are numerous modes of transmitting—speaking, writing, gestures, drawings, magnetically charged particles on floppy disks, raised dots on Braille cards, smoke signals, flags, and so on with media to match.

Reception

The vibrations now reach B's ears, and B receives these physical stimuli, which, in turn, are relayed to the brain via an intricate combination of processes in the form of electrochemical-neurological impulses.

Decoding

We do not fully understand what happens at the reception stage, but we understand even less what is yet to happen. Somehow B converts these impulses into symbols and the symbols into meaning. B decodes. How successful has the communication been? The prime criterion for judging the success of a deliberate communication is the extent to which *B's decoding matches A's encoding*.

Feedback

Let us assume that B has decoded A's message as intended. Technically, the communication is now complete. But A will not know there is a match, or mismatch, unless B proceeds to provide feedback, to say or do something or even fail to say or do something by which A can ascertain how B decoded and perhaps felt about A's message.

COMMUNICATION: A SERIAL PROCESS

Mismatches can occur, sometimes with extremely costly, even fatal, consequences.

The process of communication is extremely susceptible to distortion and disruption because, among other reasons, it is a *serial process*, a step-by-step process. If you are interested in interfering with or preventing a communication, you need attack it at only one phase. As a chain, the entire process is as strong as its weakest link. Broadly speaking, you would create *noise*, a deterioration of effectiveness, at that particular link.

A's communication to B could be faulty if: A did not transmit adequately, for example, did not speak distinctly or slowly or loudly enough; or if A and B were trying to communicate in an environment where there were competing vibrations, such as in a forge shop or around a jet engine (B could scarcely distinguish A's feeble vocal vibrations from the barrage of noise assaulting his tympanic membranes); or if B had reception difficulty, for example, a hearing loss.

Transmission, medium, and reception are critical phases of the communication process, but this book will not deal with them. I am presuming that the great majority of my readers do not have horrendous problems in the physiological transmission and reception of communication stimuli.[3] I presume, too, that they do not ordinarily encounter serious barriers in the physical media they use.

Even when we have difficulties in the middle three phases of the communication process, we generally have one or two important advantages. First, we are usually *aware* that we are indeed having a problem in our communications, and furthermore we have a good idea of where it lies.

---

[3] There are skilled practitioners in the areas of speech and audiological therapy, ophthalmology, and so on, available to deal with difficulties in these functions.

Thus we usually have the opportunity to cope with the problem—to avoid it or prevent it or correct it or compensate for it.

Encoding and Decoding—The Subtle Phases

But when we have problems in our *encoding* and *decoding*, we often have neither of the advantages mentioned above. We know relatively little about what really happens *inside* a communicator as he or she sends or receives messages, and herein lies the irony I alluded to in Chapter 1.

While investing billions in communication research—and receiving commensurate returns—we have virtually ignored the equally critical end processes. Ultimately, there are *human* encoders and decoders no matter how much sophisticated instrumentation we place between them. The computer people have a phrase for it: GIGO, garbage in, garbage out.

The incongruity is hardly a new one, as evidenced by the wry Josiah Stamp of England's Inland Revenue Department, 1896–1919:

> The government are very keen on amassing statistics. They collect them, add them, raise them to the nth power, take the cube root and prepare wonderful diagrams. But you must never forget that every one of these figures comes in the first instance from the village watchman, who just puts down what he damn pleases.

We have been constructing the communication chain with enormously strong, forged links in the center and paper clips at the ends.

And so, the emphasis in this book is on encoding and decoding, mainly because they are the least understood. To set the stage, examine Figure 8.2 for a superimposition of the perceptual model on the communication process.

Let's return to the example of A trying to get B to open a window. A *encoded* her message on the basis of her *perception* of the situation—

FIGURE 8.2

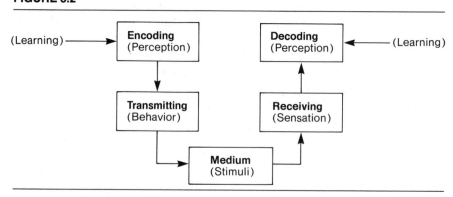

including her assessment of the problem to be solved, her anticipation of B's response to her request, and so forth.

Her subsequent transmission (speaking) was her *behavioral response* to that perception. Then the consequences of her behavior—audible vibrations (*stimuli*)—were conveyed via the medium to be received in the form of auditory *sensations* (B was hearing). But those sensations became meaningful only when B decoded—that is, *perceived* them—created meaning from them.

The roles may switch very quickly. Suppose B replies: "Sure, I'll open the window," or "Can't do it—my back's bothering me" or "No way! It's already too cold in here!" Suddenly B has become the encoder transmitting for A's consumption.

The one element we've disregarded so far is *learning*. Our prior programming, as discussed in Chapter 4, can have a direct bearing on how we perceive (and encode and decode). For example, read the phrases in the triangles shown in Figure 8.3. Almost everyone reads them as "Snake in the grass," "Busy as a bee," and "Once upon a time." But look again—it's "Snake in the *the* grass," and so on. Why do we read them incorrectly? What programmings might have caused us to miss the repeated *the* and *a*?

For one, they are enormously familiar expressions. We often read what we anticipate will be there rather than what *is*.

Another factor, consider the reading ability you've developed through years of practice. You no longer read word by word but in clusters of words. Give the triangles to youngsters who are just learning to read—laboriously working out each letter, syllable, and word—and they'll catch the repetitions. This is no condemnation of speed reading, but it does make us easy prey for the triangle stunt.

Would the trick have worked as well if *snake* or *grass* or *bee* had been repeated? Probably not. The articles *the* and *a* are extraordinarily frequently used words. In fact, in written English, they are respectively the first and fourth most common words.[4] But it's not only English. Use *el* and *la* or *le* and *la* and the Spaniard or Frenchman, respectively, will be equally vulnerable.

FIGURE 8.3

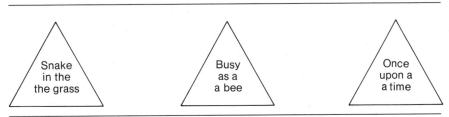

---

[4] Lest your curiosity deprive you of sleep, *of* and *and* are second and third.

Again, the separation of the repeated words, which is seemingly legitimated by triangles, probably threw us off. The same words stretched out on a straight line don't fool as many people. We could have been misled, too, by our predisposition to gloss over apparent typographical errors.

The Role of Assumptions.   Learning provides our memory content including our values, goals, attitudes, habits, and most relevantly here, our *assumptions*. Let us return to A and B to examine the role of individual assumptions.

Suppose that in expressing her desire about opening the window, A chose to say: "Let's get a breath of fresh air in here." By this, she intends to express simply that she feels warm and that she would like B to open the window. Now note some of the assumptions that may be underlying A's remark and of which she may be quite unaware. She could be assuming that because she is warm, B also feels warm and will welcome the idea of opening a window. She could be assuming that because B is closer to the window, B is the logical one to open it and that B will understand and agree with this. She could be assuming that because she means something by her words, B will understand them as A intends them.

Actually, none of these assumptions is necessarily warranted. B may be quite comfortable or even chilly with the window closed and thus be offended by A's apparent selfishness. Furthermore, he may fail to see A's logic about B's proximity to the window and instead resent A's pushing him around. B may even fail to interpret A's words as they were intended. He may, conceivably, hear A's remark as an indictment against B's failure to have opened the window previously. It is even possible that B may feel that A is not interested in opening a window at all but is sarcastically alluding to B's habits of personal hygiene! B as the receiver is, of course, just as prone to contribute to a misunderstanding, influenced as he is by his own assumptions.

Consider these three propositions:

1. Everyone has assumptions—certain underlying beliefs, premises, notions, suppositions, rationales, generalizations, principles.
2. Some of these assumptions are false; they are not borne out by reality.
3. The individual is partially or, in some cases, totally unaware that he or she is laboring under fallacious notions. Many of them are primitive postulates, acquired before the age of reason. They have been semiconsciously learned at best and have never been examined critically.

The third proposition should not be difficult to accept, for does it not stand to reason that most people would not tolerate false assumptions, that they would supplant them with more valid premises. But if they are not *aware* that the assumptions are false or even that they hold them, what will prompt them to do anything about them? As the 19th-century humorist, Artemus Ward put it: "It ain't the things we don't know that hurt us. It's the things we do know that ain't so."

We are all victims, more or less, of unconsciously holding certain fallacious assumptions, which in turn materially, destructively, and insidiously affect our encoding and decoding. The frequent result is miscommunication, sometimes with grievous consequences.

Since our concern is expressly with communication, one category of fallacious assumptions, in particular, merits our attention. These are the assumptions that we develop partially or largely from our language system. For example, one of these fallacies is that words, rather than being merely labels for things, are somehow inextricably linked with what they represent.[5] This is false, of course, but we do not always behave as if it were. In fact, our reaction to a thing is sometimes distinctly colored by its label.

An incident occurred while the late Professor Irving J. Lee was giving his exceedingly popular course, Language and Thought, at Northwestern University. Dr. Lee had several graduate assistants who were occasionally given the opportunity to lecture before a class of 200 to 300 undergraduates. On one such occasion, an assistant set out to dramatize the tendency to react to labels rather than to the objects that the labels represented. He distributed bits of food that resembled dried biscuit and assured the class that the food was sanitary and nutritious and added that most of them had probably never eaten this type of food before. Each student was to taste the food and decide how much he or she liked or disliked it. Most of the students found it relatively tasteless and reported an indifferent reaction. A few said that they liked it slightly and even fewer expressed a mild dislike. Not *one* said that he or she liked or disliked it extremely.

The assistant tabulated the results on the blackboard and suggested that perhaps the food would be tastier with cream and sugar. He added that it was quite inexpensive and readily available. At this point, he reached behind his desk and held up a large, distinctly labeled box and said, "Just go to your grocer's and ask for _____ Dog Biscuits!" The reaction was precisely what he had hoped for—a great deal of groaning, shrieking, laughing, feigned nausea (and some not so feigned). Whereupon he triumphantly cried out: "Now just what are you reacting to— those innocuous bits of food or to the words on this box?"

Elated by his success, the assistant repeated his dramatization during the next term. But the word had spread, and the students had come to expect such things from the course "where they served dog biscuits." Undiscouraged, he changed his tactic. For the third term, he baked some

---

[5] This particular fallacy is developed more fully in Chapter 16.

special cookies, passed them out to the class, and tabulated the results. The cookies were sweet, and the reactions were unanimously favorable.

"Glad you liked them. I'll give you the recipe," he volunteered, "so you can bake some at home if you wish." The recipe: So much flour, sugar, shortening . . . and two cups of carefully cleaned grasshoppers!

He admitted later that even had he been able to restore order, he would not have dared to ask: "Now, what are you throwing up about . . .?"

The Map-Territory Analogy. For focusing attention on the subtle role that language plays in influencing human behavior we are primarily indebted to the late Alfred Korzybski.[6] Korzybski contended that the relation of our assumptions, unconscious or otherwise, to the phenomena with which they are concerned (people, things, theories, processes, relationships, and so on) is analogous to the relation of maps to the territories they represent. Geographic maps are pictures, or abstractions, of their territories. Our assumptive maps, similarly, are pictures of the territories they are used to represent. We rely on both kinds of maps as guides in our dealings with their respective territories.

But there is an essential difference between our geographic and our assumptive maps. Cartography has advanced to the point that most geographic maps can be followed with great confidence. On the other hand, our assumptive maps are often inadequate and distorted representations of their territories. And we are misled by them because we rely upon them so unquestioningly.

Korzybski felt that we are largely *unaware* of the power the structure of our language has over us. Unconscious of such influence, we are in an unlikely position to take action against it. As the biologist J. H. Woodger put it, "Man makes metaphysics just as he breathes, without willing it and above all without doubting it most of the time."

Perhaps this book appears to be at least as much about thinking as it is about communicating. Actually, it is about thinking-communicating, for the two processes are inseparable.

SUMMARY

The first eight chapters have attempted to prepare a foundation for the balance of the book, to delineate its scope, and to set out a rationale. In subsequent chapters, we focus on the encoding and decoding of a perceiving, need-satisfaction-seeking individual communicating in an organizational setting.

---

[6] Alfred Korzybski's *Sicence and Sanity: An Introduction to Non-Aristotelian Systems and General Semantics* (Lancaster, Penn.: Science Press 1933).

The approach to communication here is a "psychosemantic" one, the basic premises of which can be summarized as follows: Behavior, including communication behavior, is largely the product of one's perceptions, which in turn are acutely affected by one's prior learning. And a most critical part of that programming stems from the individual's language system. A major contention is that one's language system spawns certain fallacious, and often unconsciously held, assumptions.[7] Such assumptions pave the way for miscommunication and other forms of foolish, immature, dangerous, unsane behavior. Indeed, our chief concern will be with *self-deception* for, in the words of Goethe: "We are not deceived; we deceive ourselves."

Thus, the remaining chapters explore a number of recurrent, delineable patterns of miscommunication. The patterns are not mutually exclusive. Rather they might be considered as so many handles with which to grasp and cope with some of the most prevalent and serious anomalies of a complex and vital function—communication.

Discussion Questions

1. Anatole Rapaport has said: "Experience cannot be transmitted as *experience:* it must first be translated into something else. It is this something else which is transmitted. When it is received it is translated back into something that resembles experience."

Do you agree with the above statement? What are its implications—for communicators? For the mass media? For organizational communication? Or for any form of communication which goes through a series of people?

2. Compare the model of communication with those of Berlo, Shannon and Weaver, Schramm, and Lesikar and Pettit (see footnote 1). What are the relative strengths and weaknesses of these models? In what ways are they different, similar? Does their adequacy and validity depend to some extent on what kind of communication experience is represented? What are the underlying premises for each model?

3. The issue of communication complacency: Do you agree that most people are unrealistically confident about their communication ability? What do you think of the various reasons offered to account for this attitude? Can you suggest others?

---

[7] *General Information Bulletin,* no. 6, of the International Society for General Semantics asserts the influence of language:

Nor do we realize how grammar warps our "thinking." When we make sentences, we force symbols (words) into certain set relationships. Yet the things which these symbols represent often have quite different relationships. This happens because our grammar preserves many ancient wrong guesses about the world we live in, such as: similar things may be treated as identical; the "essences" of things never change; parts may be considered without relation to the whole; qualities are properties of "things"; an event has "a cause." Such notions once fit man's knowledge of the world. But our century has seen the birth of the relativity theory and atomic fission. Today, primitive language habits serve only to widen the frightening chasm between our lagging civilization and our leaping technology.

4. The Boy Scouts and the "Hydroherpha . . . Patrol." Can literally any nonsense syllable (or polysyllable) become a word? Under what conditions? How do words get to *be* words? Suppose that you invent a gadget and contrive a brand-new word to represent it. What potential communication problems do you foresee?

5. This book focuses on the encoding and decoding phases of the communication process. Why?

6. What "advantages"are there for having problems in the transmission, medium and reception phases as opposed to having them in the encoding and decoding phases?

PART THREE

Patterns of Miscommunication

❋
❋
❋

CHAPTER NINE

The Inference-Observation
Confusion
Jumping to Conclusions

❋
❋
❋

Who has deceiv'd thee as oft as thy self?
—Benjamin Franklin
Poor Richard's Almanac, 1738

Let me begin the first of these patterns of miscommunication by inviting you to test yourself.

Instructions

Read the following story. Assume that all the information presented in it is definitely accurate and true. Read it carefully because it has ambiguous parts designed to lead you astray. No need to memorize it, though. You can refer to it whenever you wish.

Next read the statements about the story and indicate whether you consider each statement true, false, or "?". "T" means that the statement is *definitely true* on the basis of the information presented in the story. "F" means that it is *definitely false*. "?" means that it may be either true or false and that you cannot be certain which on the basis of the information presented in the story. If any part of a statement is doubtful, make it "?". *Answer each statement in turn, and do not go back to change any answer later, and don't reread any statements after you have answered them. This will distort your score.*

To start with, here is a sample story with correct answers.

Sample Story

You arrive home late one evening and see that the lights are on in your living room. There is only one car parked in front of your house, and the words "Harold R. Jones, M.D." are spelled in small gold letters across one of the car's doors.

Statements about Sample Story

1. The car parked in front of your house has lettering on one
   of its doors.   (T) F   ?
   (This is a "definitely true" statement because it is directly corroborated by the story.)
2. Someone in your family is sick.   T F (?)
   (This could be true, and then again it might not be. Perhaps Dr. Jones is
   paying a social call at your home, or perhaps he has gone to the house
   next door or across the street, or maybe someone else is using the car.)
3. No car is parked in front of your house.   T (F) ?
   (A "definitely false" statement because the story directly contradicts it.)
4. The car parked in front of your house belongs to a woman
   named Johnson.   T F (?)
   (May seem very likely false, but can you be sure? Perhaps the car has
   just been sold.)

So much for the sample. It should warn you of some of the kinds of traps to
look for. Now begin the actual test. Remember, mark each statement *in
order*—don't skip around or change answers later.

The Story[1]

A businessman had just turned off the lights in the store when a man
appeared and demanded money. The owner opened a cash register. The
contents of the cash register were scooped up, and the man sped away. A
member of the police force was notified promptly.

Statements about the Story

1. A man appeared after the owner had turned off his store
   lights.   T F ?
2. The robber was a *man*.   T F ?
3. The man who appeared did not demand money.   T F ?
4. The man who opened the cash register was the owner.   T F ?
5. The store owner scooped up the contents of the cash register
   and ran away.   T F ?
6. Someone opened a cash register.   T F ?
7. After the man who demanded the money scooped up the
   contents of the cash register, he ran away.   T F ?
8. While the cash register contained money, the story does *not*
   state *how much*.   T F ?
9. The robber demanded money of the owner.   T F ?
10. A businessman had just turned off the lights when a man
    appeared in the store.   T F ?
11. It was broad daylight when the man appeared.   T F ?
12. The man who appeared opened the cash register.   T F ?

---

[1] The story and statements are a portion of the "Uncritical Inference Test," copyrighted
1955 and 1983 by William V. Haney.

13. No one demanded money.		T F ?
14. The story concerns a series of events which only three persons are referred to: the owner of the store, a man who demanded money, and a member of the police force.		T F ?
15. The following events occurred: someone demanded money; a cash register was opened; its contents were scooped up; and a man dashed out of the store.		T F ?

If you would permit me to withhold the answers for a few pages, I would like to describe a classic study.[2] It is the oldest of its kind I could find and has been repeated in many forms since then, but always, to the best of my knowledge, the results of the Otto experiment have been corroborated.

The scene is a University of Wisconsin classroom (Figure 9.1). A carefully planned incident is about to occur. Of the 75 students present, only four, A, B, C, and D (and the instructor), are in on the stunt. At a given signal the following events occur: (1) While the instructor is collecting papers from students in the front row, A suddenly hits B with his fist, and B retaliates by striking A with a book, and the two fall to quarreling very loudly; (2) at the same time, C throws two silver dollars into the air, permits them to fall to the floor, scrambles after them as they roll away from him, and picks them up; (3) the instructor now orders A, B, and C from the room; (4) as he does so, D simply gets up and walks from the room at a normal gait; (5) as A, B, and C are preparing to leave, the instructor walks to the blackboard at the front of the room, glances at his watch, writes "9:45" on the blackboard, erases it, and writes it again; (6) A, B, and C leave the room, and the instructor turns to the class and says, in effect: "You have all seen what has happened, and you know that you may very well be called upon to give testimony.[3] Let us now take time to write out reports of what we have observed." And with the instructor's assistance the class composes a series of questions to give order to their reports. The following are some of those questions and some of the answers to which these eyewitnesses were willing to testify.

Q: Where was the instructor when the disturbances began?

Twenty-two of the students reported that he was near the front of the room; 20 that he was about in the middle; and 21 that he was in the rear. A number of students scattered all over the room said they would have testified under oath that the instructor was at his (the student's) desk collecting his paper!

---

[2] M. C. Otto, "Testimony and Human Nature," *Journal of Criminal Law and Criminology*, 9 (1919), pp. 98–104.

[3] At this time the university was on a student self-governing basis. This meant that any student disciplinary case, as this incident was to all appearances, would be submitted to a student court and testimony would be taken. In other words, it is most likely that the students saw the situation as quite real and one for which they might very well be asked to appear in court to give testimony.

FIGURE 9.1

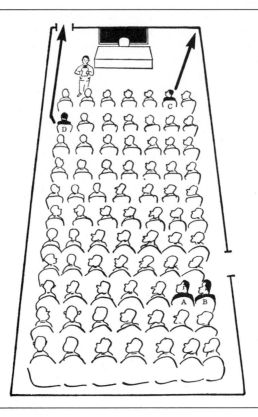

Q: Where was the instructor, and what was he doing when the students left the room?

Only 5 of the 75 reported the "9:45 business" with any accuracy. The attention of the others was obviously fixed elsewhere. However, only six said they did not know. The others gave very definite testimony. Three said the instructor was holding the door open for the students to pass through. One said he was standing in the middle of the room muttering, "I'll break this up, or know the reason why." Three remembered him sitting dejectedly at his desk with his face buried in his hands. The consensus of the remaining students was that he was sitting at his desk nervously toying with, variously, the papers he had collected, class cards, his watch chain, a piece of chalk, etc. He appeared "as if not knowing what to do," and "his face wore an expression of embarrassment and uneasiness."

Q: What did C do?

You will recall that C had thrown two silver dollars into the air. They fell to the floor, and he hurried to pick them up. Some students reported that either A or B, in their fighting, had dropped some money; that these coins had rolled to the front of the room; and that C had scrambled to pick them up. Other students said that an adjustable desk arm from one of the classroom seats had been broken off (and A, incidentally, had tried to poke B with it) during the fighting; that the little ratchet ball inside had fallen out and had rolled to the front; and that it was this ball that C had rushed to pick up. The student sitting next to C, ironically enough, insisted that he had seen a little steel ball come rolling out between C's feet and that C grabbed it and put it in his pocket.

Q: How did A, B, and C look as they left the room?

The reports corresponded directly with the observer's attitude toward the instructor's action. If the student felt that the instructor had been fair and justified in sending the men from the room, then they tended to look "embarrassed" and "ashamed." If, however, the student thought the instructor too severe, the men looked "angry," "injured," and "abused." C's neighbor, who had perceived C do nothing more heinous than pocket a steel ball, reported that C had looked "very angry," while A and B appeared "sheepish."

Q: What did D do?

This question was accidental. While the class was deciding the questions to be answered for their reports, one student asked: "Are we to include the fact that D rushed from the room at the beginning of the disturbance?" The instructor replied noncommittally: "Please report what you saw as completely as you can, but report no more."

It seems highly likely that, with a vociferous struggle having just been waged in an opposite section of the room, only a few at most would have noticed D's casual departure. Yet the suggestion of the student's question plus the obvious fact that D was now absent was apparently enough to convince over 85 percent of the students that they *had* seen D leave, and most of them were quite confident about the specific manner in which he left —saying, variously, that he had "rushed," "hurried," "bolted," or "made a wild dash" from the room.

Otto, who was concerned with the bearing of this sort of behavior on the taking of legal testimony, seemed amply justified in his alarm:

The importance of these facts is obvious. If it is impossible for a witness to reproduce an occurrence as it took place in his presence, even when asked to do so directly after the occurrence; if it is his very nature to demand consistency in such items as he does get, to the point of rejecting some and creating others; if such a thing as sending three men from a room at the same time may act as a suggestion around which is built up what the witness believes himself to have observed concerning them; what are the chances of arriving at the truth under conditions[4] which often obtain where testimony is taken?[5]

It may seem incredible that people could be capable of observing, remembering, and reporting an incident so distortedly—that they could fail so utterly to distinguish between what they had observed and what they only inferred.

THE UNCALCULATED RISK

We need to dig deeper into what we call the inference-observation confusion.

"Taking a calculated risk" is a phrase that we ordinarily use to describe a situation in which a person has decided to take an action that may have undesirable consequences—embarrassment, loss of money, injury, and so forth. But we imply that he or she is aware of these potential effects and, furthermore, has assessed the likelihood that they will occur. Generally speaking, when we take calculated risks, we are apt to be in a better position to avoid the hazards, or at least to cope with them should they occur.

The inference-observation confusion, on the other hand, involves taking *uncalculated* risks. Let's examine an actual traffic accident case.[6] In Figure 9.2, diagram A shows Driver White halted at a stop sign. Driver Black is approaching the intersection from the south. His right directional signal is blinking. White *assumes* that Black is going to turn right at the intersection and, acting on this inference *as if* it were fact, starts to cross the intersection. Black does *not* turn but continues northward and is unable to avoid a costly collision with White (diagram B). The directional signal? Black had intended to turn right into a driveway—20 yards beyond the intersection. Who is liable for the personal injuries and property damage? Usually White, for failing to yield the right-of-way.

---

[4] Referring to such factors as the time lapse between the observation and the giving of testimony (involving sometimes hours, days, weeks, or even years); the third-degree tactics of examining authorities; the leading, confining, and suggestive questions of cross-examining attorneys; and so on.

[5] Otto, "Testimony and Human Nature," p. 104. Perhaps you are concerned that the Otto study, after all, was conducted over 70 years ago. Aren't people more reliable observers today? I wish they were, but one of my colleagues regularly conducts a similar episode in her classroom. The latest portrayal was only a short time ago, and the results were just as dismal!

[6] See William V. Haney, "Are Accident-Prone Drivers Unconscious-Inference-Prone?" *General Semantics Bulletin*, nos. 20 and 21 (1957). Reprinted in *Traffic Digest and Review* 5 (March 1957).

FIGURE 9.2

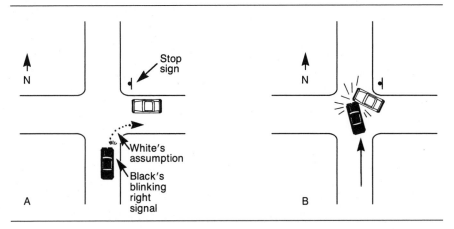

Let us go back and examine White's response more closely. We shall presume that he saw Black approaching and that he noted the blinking directional signal. At about this time he must have made his key assumption that Black was going to turn right at the intersection. Somehow in the process, however, this inference became fused with his observations. Perhaps he forgot that he had, in fact, guessed—or perhaps he was never fully aware that he was in the realm of inference. At any rate, his crucial error occurred at the moment he treated the inference as if it were not an inference.

It was at this point that he took his uncalculated risk. White, in entering the intersection with Black approaching, was taking a very definite risk. But, since he apparently failed to perceive his inference as an inference—that is, as a situation involving a degree of uncertainty—he did not realize the risk he was taking and thus was hardly prompted to calculate its probability.[7]

In sum, the inference-observation confusion usually occurs as follows: (1) Someone makes an inference, (2) fails to recognize or remember that he or she has done so, (3) thus does not calculate the risk involved, (4) proceeds to act upon the assumption as if it were certain, and (5) ends by taking an unrecognized and uncalculated risk that may prove costly, dangerous, or even fatal.

---

[7] Thomas Fansler, of the National Safety Council, described the phenomenon in this manner: "In checking over case histories of traffic accidents, an observer cannot help being impressed with the number of times the idea of suddenness or unexpectedness occurs. After the accident, the driver will report, 'Suddenly the man ran in front of my car,' or 'I expected the other fellow to stop but instead . . .' The inference that may be drawn from this is that there was an *expected* pattern of circumstances in the minds of the drivers and that the change from the *expected* pattern to a 'sudden' or 'unexpected' pattern was partly responsible for the accident." Howard Pyle, National Safety Council, has attributed 90 percent of traffic accidents to *driver error.*

This is the pattern that appears to be responsible for the worst disaster in aviation history: the collision of two 747s in Santa Cruz de Tenerife, Canary Islands, on March 27, 1977. A Pan Am plane had landed but had not yet cleared the runway when a KLM plane inexplicably attempted to take off, ramming into the Pan Am plane. The complete explanation may never be known because the KLM pilot perished along with almost 600 others. But according to one safety official: "The key to the investigation is why did not the captain [KLM pilot] verify the assumption that he had takeoff clearance, expecially after being questioned by another crewmember, or did he *not realize that it was an assumption?*"[8]

So much for how the uncalculated risk occurs. But why does it happen, and what can be done to prevent it?

OBSERVATIONAL AND INFERENTIAL STATEMENTS

Why, after all, does the inference-observation confusion and thus the uncalculated risk happen? Clearly, emotions often play an important role. Consider this incident.

> It happened in Hayward, California. It was there that two police officers, field training officer Eric Ristrim and trainee Marie Yin, observed a man standing at a bus stop. The man was later identified as David St. John, 27, who is blind.
>
> Ristrim reported that St. John put what appeared to be a set of numchukas into his pocket. (Numchukas, an illegal martial arts weapon, consist of two wooden cylinders connected by a chain.)
>
> The officers approached St. John and demanded that he give them the contents of his pockets. Since they were in uniform they felt it was unnecessary to identify themselves as police officers.
>
> St. John thought he was about to be mugged and began to struggle. "I did what my self-defense training and instincts told me to do," he said. The officers hit him twice on the legs with their batons, and when St. John pulled out his collapsible cane they struck him on the forearm to get him to drop it. It was at this point that someone shouted, "He's blind!" and the officers identified themselves.
>
> It's a very regrettable incident," said acting Chief Dick Dettmer.[9]

If there is a prize for understatements, Chief Dettmer's conclusion has an excellent chance of winning it.

---

[8] *Aviation Week & Space Technology*, May 2, 1977.

[9] Adapted from an Associated Press article that appeared in the *Chicago Tribune*, May 17, 1989, sec. 1, p. 10. Subsequently, St. John filed a claim for $200,000 against the city. As of this writing, no adjudication has been made.

Here is an even more tragic example of the emotion-laden inference:

> Life has not been easy for Chicago West Sider Carey Epkins, a deaf mute since birth. Relying upon the intricate system of sign language, even simple communications were a struggle.
>
> Recently, however, things took a decided turn for the better. Epkins, 25, married his childhood sweetheart, Phyllis, also a deaf-mute. Naturally, the ceremony was conducted in sign language.
>
> But on a cold night in March, Carey's short and painful life came to an end. Accosted by an 18-year-old gang member, Epkins tried to signal that he meant no harm. Instead, police said, the gang member *thought* Epkins was using signs to say he was a member of a rival gang. So the street tough drew a .38-caliber handgun and shot Epkins twice.[10]

But emotions constitute only one broad category of variables provoking uncalculated risks. I devoted a lengthy chapter in my Ph.D. dissertation to merely listing and documenting some of the factors that appear to contribute to the inference-observation confusion. They include limited and impaired senses; physiological conditions, such as those associated with hunger, thirst, and fatigue and those incurred with the ingestion of alcohol and narcotics; and a host of psychological factors, including emotion and stress, habit and set, values and needs, and group and social influences. In a category by itself was a seldom suspected agent: *our language!*

A central theme running through the various patterns of miscommunication covered in this part of the book is that how we think and behave is influenced in no small measure by our language—the linguistic tool by which we reason and communicate.

But what does language have to do with the inference-observation confusion? Practically speaking, there are two kinds of declarative statements that I can make about what I observe (see, hear, smell, taste, and so forth). Assuming that my vision and the illumination are normal, I can look at a man wearing a tie and say: "That man is wearing a tie." This is called a statement of observation because it corresponds directly to what I have observed. On the other hand, I can look at the same man and say just as confidently: "That man bought that tie." But unless I actually observed him purchasing the tie, this statement is for me a statement of inference. I *infer* that he bought the tie because (1) he's wearing it; (2) he looks honest; (3) he appears to be the kind of person who would select his own ties; and so on. I may be right—but I may be wrong. Perhaps someone gave him the tie—or loaned it to him. Perhaps he found it. The point is that, since I did not *observe* him buying the tie, the statement for me is necessarily an inferential one.

---

[10] Tom Maier and Mark Brown, "Sign Language Fails. Deaf-Mute Slain," *Chicago Sun-Times*, March 7, 1983, p. 4. (Italics added for emphasis.)

Observational and inferential statements are often extremely difficult to distinguish. Certainly the structure of our language offers no indication of their differences. There may be no grammatical, syntactic, orthographic, punctuational, or pronunciational distinctions between them whatsoever. Moreover, the tones or inflections in which they are uttered may sound equally certain.

You and I can point to this page, and each of us can say: "William Haney wrote this material." Your statement was inferential; mine was observational. Yet the *statements* were the same.

In other words, nothing in the nature of our language (or any other language to my knowledge) makes it inescapable that we discriminate between inferential and observational statements. Our failure to distinguish on these verbal levels contributes appreciably to the difficulty that we have on *nonverbal* levels, namely, our propensity to confuse inference and observation. Thus, we find it enticingly easy to make inferences and to utter inferential statements with the false assurance that we are dealing with fact—and the consequences of acting upon inferences as if they were observations are often less than pleasant.

> "Mother, I wish I didn't look so flat-chested," said my 15-year-old daughter as she stood before the mirror in her first formal dress.
>
> I remedied the matter by inserting puffs of cotton in strategic places. Then I hung around Mary's neck a string of seed pearls—just as my grandmother had done for my mother and my mother for me.
>
> At midnight her escort brought her home. The moment the door closed behind him Mary burst into tears.
>
> "I'm never going out with him again," she sobbed. "Mother, do you know what he said to me? He leaned across the table and said, 'Gee, you look sharp tonight, Mary. Are those real?'"
>
> "I hope you told him they were," I said indignantly. "They've been in the family for three generations!"
>
> My daughter stopped sobbing. "Oh, the pearls. Good heavens, I'd forgotten all about them."
>
> —Mrs. J. L. H. (*Alabama*)[11]

Lest the reader feel that the inference-observation confusion pertains only to teenage girls and University of Wisconsin students of 1919, let us bring the matter somewhat closer to home. Here are the answers to the test that I trust you took at the beginning of the chapter (pages 232-33).

---

[11] From "Life in These United States," *Reader's Digest*. Reprinted by permission.

1. ? Do you *know* that the "businessman" and the "owner" are one and the same?
2. ? Was there necessarily a robbery involved here? Perhaps the man was the rent collector—or the owner's son—they sometimes demand money.
3. F An easy one to keep up the test-taker's morale.
4. ? Was the owner a *man?*
5. ? May seem unlikely, but the story does not definitely preclude it.
6. T The story says that the owner opened the cash register.
7. ? We don't know who scooped up the contents of the cash register or that the man necessarily *ran* away.
8. ? The dependent clause is doubtful—the cash register may or may not have contained money.
9. ? Again, a robber?
10. ? Could the man merely have appeared *at* a door or a window without actually entering the store?
11. ? Stores generally keep lights on during the day.
12. ? Could not the man who appeared have been the owner?
13. F The story says that the man who appeared demanded money.
14. ? Are the businessman and the owner one and the same—or two different people? The same goes for the owner and the man who appeared.
15. ? "Dashed?" Could he not have "sped away" on roller skates or in a car? And do we know that he actually left the store? We don't even know that he entered it.

CORRECTIVES

An effective technique for avoiding the inference-observation confusion is a five-step process:

1. Detect the inference.
2. Calculate the risk.
3. Get more data—if the risk is a poor one.
4. Recalculate the risk.
5. Label your inferences.

Detect the Inference

There is an apocryphal story that goes something like this:

The Case of the Raging River

Four men—Adams, Baker, Carson, and Dawson—are camped alongside a raging river, as diagrammed below:

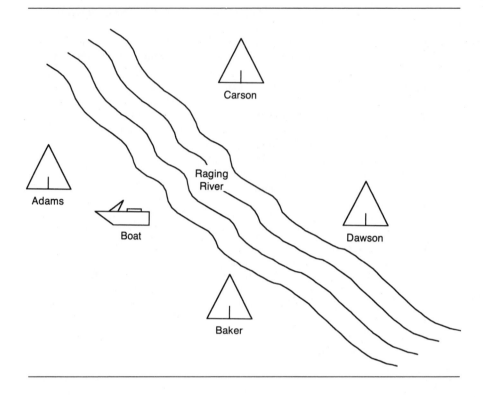

It is dangerous to cross the river in a boat and impossible to swim it. Aside from a boat, which Adams owns, there are no means of crossing within 50 miles of this point on the river.

One day a young woman, Elaine, approaches Adams and asks him to transport her across the river to Carson, her lover. Adams agrees to do so, but only on the condition that she sleep with him. Elaine refuses and asks Baker to intercede for her with Adams. Baker says that he does not want to become involved. Desperate, Elaine returns to Adams and agrees to his terms. Afterward, Adams takes her across to Carson. Elaine immediately tells Carson what happened, and he becomes furious and throws her out. Desolate, she walks to Dawson and explains her plight, and he takes her in.

The usual challenge is to rank the five persons in the order of their morality—who behaved the most morally, the next most morally and so forth. Anyone who accepts this chore would necessarily make a host of assumptions because the case is loaded with ambiguities and information gaps. So to make the story an exercise in detecting inferences I would propose this question: What additional information would you need in order to feel more competent about ranking the five? In other words, what relevant things do you *not* know about the case?

Among other things you would probably want to know a good deal more about:

1. *Relationships.* Were any of the people related to each other in the past? If so, how? Were any of them married? If so to any one in the case?

2. *Motives.* Why did Elaine want to reach Carson? How would you evaluate her if she were on an errand of mercy, for example? Why did Baker refuse to become involved? Is it conceivable that Baker is on bad terms with Adams and that Baker's intercession would be the kiss of death for Elaine's chances of crossing the river on Adams' boat? What were the motives of Adams' bargain with Elaine? Why did Carson throw Elaine out? What were Dawson's motives for taking her in?

3. *Circumstances.* When and where did this case occur? Would it matter to you if the setting were puritanical Salem, Massachusetts, in 1690? Or modern-day America? Or some aboriginal culture whose mores differed greatly from ours? What were the ages of these people? Eight? Eighteen? Eighty? What were the physical features of the situation? For example, how viable an option was the next crossing? Would Elaine have had to wade 50 miles up and back hip-deep in alligators and water moccasins? Or was there a convenient highway and readily available transportation?

4. *Ambiguity.* Precisely what was meant by such phrases as "sleep with him" and "takes her in"? What actually happened between Elaine and Adams? Between Elaine and Dawson?

5. *The Criterion.* The key issue is, what is meant by morality? Ranking the five persons is tantamount to evaluating or judging them. So what is the measuring rod? How do you define morality? For example, do you prefer an orthodox conception, such as the Ten Commandments? Or do you lean toward a more humanistic view, such as doing the most good and the least harm to people? (How, then, do you define good and harm?) Clearly, how one defines morality can greatly influence how he or she ranks the five.

Each of the above questions highlights an awareness of something we don't know. Detecting the inference is easily the most critical phase of our five-step process. For if we are *unaware* that we are inferring, we are hardly likely to take any of the other three steps.

Here are three simple checkpoints for heightening and maintaining your inference-detecting ability.[12] Memorize, practice, and habituate them so that they occur to you almost automatically:

---

[12] Studies indicate clearly that we can indeed increase our inference awareness. See William V. Haney, "Measurement of the Ability to Discriminate between Inferential and Descriptive Statements," unpublished Ph.D. dissertation, Northwestern University, 1953. A précis of this dissertation appeared in *General Semantics Bulletin*, nos. 16 and 17 (1955). See also my article "Police Experience and Uncritical Inference Behavior," *General Semantics Bulletin*, nos. 22 and 23 (1958).

1. (Source) Did *I* make the observation?

What someone else tells you about his or her observation remains hearsay—inferential—for you if you have not personally observed it.

2. (Scope) Did my statement stay with and not exceed my observation?

Back to the aforementioned man and the tie he is wearing. I can make observational statements about the tie's length, width, color, design, and so on, but a statement about its *purchase* would exceed my observation and thus be inferential.

3. (Timing) Did I make the statement *during* or *after* but *not before* my observation?

Again the man with the tie: Two minutes *before* I saw him, I could have said that he was wearing the tie. The statement might very probably have been correct, but it would nevertheless have been inferential.

If you can say *yes* confidently to each of these questions, you are likely to have an observational statement. If you have to say no or even maybe to any one of them, then be alert. You are probably inferring, which is why you need Step 2—and possibly Steps 3 and 4.

Calculate the Risk

Once I recognize that I am dealing with an inference I am ready for Step 2, the calculation of the risk, that is, the assessment of the probability that the inference is correct.

Visualize a continuum with an infinite number of gradations. Label one end "the extremely probable," and the other "the extremely improbable." We are constantly going through the process of pegging our infereneces (provided that we recognize them as such and try to assess their probability) somewhere on this scale. For instance, the inference that the earth will continue to turn on its axis tomorrow seems so extremely probable that we literally bet our lives on it. Or we stake our lives on the improbability of the inference that the sun will be destroyed within a week.

To return to my inference about the man with the tie—that he bought it. I might peg this guess at the 50-50 mark. Why? It's just my judgment. Ties are very popular gifts. Moreover, wives often buy them for their husbands. And who knows? Maybe the man does his shopping after the stores have closed!

I might be willing to wager a quarter that he bought the tie, but probably not a dollar and certainly not five. I consider this a poor risk in need of Steps 3 and 4.

Get More Data

To improve the quality of my risk, I need more data. Suppose that in answer to my question the man says in all apparent sincerity and confidence: "Yes, I clearly remember buying this tie." This still does not make it an observation for me, of course, but I may now be willing to revise the point on the probability scale.

Recalculate the Risk

If I know and trust the man, I may now feel that the risk is a very good one and be willing to wager a considerable sum on my inference. A fifth step applies when we are dealing with other people.

Label Your Inferences

When I am communicating with others, do I label my inferences as such and try to get them to label theirs? I was recently discussing this fifth point with a group of industrial engineers. After the seminar one of the group came up and said: "Am I glad you made that fifth point! That's the core of my problem. I have a man who is constantly giving me his inferences *as if* they were his observations. Maybe he's afraid to tell me they are only guesses, but in any event I go upstairs and report them as certainties to my superior—and sometimes they're wrong and then *I'm* in hot water. I think I know now how to deal with this fellow. I'll tell him: 'Look, management doesn't expect us to *know or see* everything, but they do expect us to know the *difference* between what we know and what we're only guessing at.' "

TWO QUESTIONS

Two particular questions sometimes arise when the inference-observation confusion is discussed. They concern creativity on the one hand and decisiveness on the other.

Creativity

What bearing does inference awareness have on creativity? Wouldn't the rigor required to distinguish inference from observation tend to curtail the imagination?

I see no incompatibility between rigor and creativity. Suppose that Officer Jones observes a motorist racing through a stoplight. As the police officer gives chase he will very probably be trying to infer the driver's motive in order to determine the manner by which to apprehend him. Suppose that the officer assumes the driver was simply in a hurry and felt that he could get away with it. And suppose that Jones fails to recognize this as an inference but blithely treats it as an observation. That probably ends the policeman's analysis of the situation, and we can only hope that in his interest, at least, his inference is correct.

On the other hand, if Jones is aware and remains aware that his first inference was just that—his first inference—he is more likely to try to imagine other possible motives for the motorist's action. Is the driver ill or under the influence of drugs or alcohol? Is he preoccupied and unaware that Officer Jones has seen the violation? Is the car out of control, for example, is the accelerator jammed? Is the driver taking a sick or injured person to the hospital? Is he deliberately flouting the law and egging the officer on? Has he committed a felony, and is he now attempting to escape his pursuers? And so on.

Aware that he is inferring, the officer will be continuously alert for signs that may help him calculate the probability of these various motives and perhaps suggest additional ones. Thus, he will be prepared to deal more appropriately with the situation.

The point is that had Jones confused inference for observation at the outset—had he treated his first inference as observation—he would hardly have been prompted to invent and test the additional alternatives.

Decisiveness

In urging the distinction between inference and observation, do I appear to be saying: "Don't take risks. Stay away from inferences. They are dangerous. They only get you into trouble"? Am I advocating analysis paralysis—the sort of academic impotence that George Bernard Shaw scorned when he asserted that "if all the economists in the world were laid end to end, they still wouldn't reach a conclusion"? Nothing could be further from my purpose. In the first place, we could not avoid inferences if we tried. We assume incessantly. You and I are assuming that the chairs we are seated on (I am assuming that you are sitting on one) will not collapse beneath us. We are assuming that our next inhalation will not be noxious and kill us. When we eat, we make a host of inferences about the source, content, and preparation of the food. Whenever we post a letter, we make inferences about the speed and safety of our mail. Whenever we take advice from a doctor, attorney, or cleric, and whenever we read a newspaper, magazine, or book (this one included), we make inferences about the credibility of the statements we hear and read. We might be able to reduce the number of our inferences by resigning from life and living in bed as a vegetable. But, even so, we would have to make inferences about those who attended us.

In sum, one must deal with inferences. Visualize a woman who is the chief executive officer of her firm. How much does she know from *her* own direct observation about her employees, her products, her markets, her competition, her suppliers, her stockholders, the governmental agencies that may regulate her enterprise, her firm's financial status? And to what extent must she rely upon the observations and inferences of others, who in turn rely upon the observations and inferences of still others, ad infinitum?

Inferring and risking are inescapable parts of living in an active world. The semanticist Stuart Chase once stated: "We cheerfully trust our lives to total strangers in the persons of locomotive engineers, subway motormen, airplane pilots, elevator operators, steamship captains, taxi drivers, traffic cops, and unhesitatingly consign all our worldly goods to bankers and insurance companies."

In short, we live in a world of risk; some risks we can avoid, many we cannot or should not avoid. This chapter does not advocate inaction and indecision. The capacity to infer, after all, is essential in the arts and in the sciences. Analysis, problem solving, planning—all involve inference. Think of any creation—a skyscraper, a portrait, a computer, or a picnic—without inferences, none of these would have been possible.

Your success (or lack of it) in life will depend largely upon your ability—and upon your willingness—to risk . . . to make inferences. A decision invariably involves risking.

> *The mark of an educated man [or woman] is the ability to make a reasoned guess on the basis of insufficient information.*
>
> —A. Lawrence Lowell
> Late president of Harvard University

The point is this: Since we must make inferences anyway, is it not better (1) to be aware that we are making them so that (2) we will be prompted to calculate the risk involved and, if necessary, (3) get more data to upgrade the quality of the risk? This story of a dining-car waiter makes the point:

> It seems that a prosperous-looking man walked into the train's diner, sat down, and ordered a doughnut and coffee. When he finished, he was presented with a check for $1.45. He fished two one-dollar bills out of his wallet and handed them to the waiter. Shortly afterward the waiter returned with his change on a plate—a half-dollar and a nickel. The man gave a grunt of annoyance, pocketed the half-dollar, and looked up, expecting to see a resentful waiter. Instead the waiter grinned widely: "That's all right, sir—I just gambled and lost!"

Aside from miscalculating his risk, the waiter showed considerable maturity. There is a world of difference between professional and novice inferrers. The novice goes out to the racetrack, say, and bets his life's savings on what he is completely convinced is a dead-sure thing. The pro may bet the same amount (which he can just as ill afford to lose), but he knows the odds against him. Both may lose their money, but the novice is likely to lose a great deal more than money.

Let me add an important adjunct here. Much of our risk-taking is not of the simple, one-chance, win-or-lose, horse-racing variety. A good deal of it occurs in a process—a flow of events—which can be modified (or to which our behavior can be adapted) in midstream, so to speak. Few of our decisions are intrinsically irrevocable. Take the automobile collision of White and Black, for instance. If sometime during the process, beginning with White's noting of Black and ending with the crash, White had become aware that he was taking a bad risk, there were numerous actions that he could have taken to avoid, or at least diminish, the consequences. He might, for example, have speeded up to get through the intersection before Black reached it, sounded his horn or arm-signaled to alert Black of the danger, braked his car sooner, veered off to his right, and so forth. In other words, even a poor decision is not necessarily an injurious one if we stay alert to the effect of changing circumstances upon our inferences and risk calculations.

The objective, then, is not the *avoidance* but the *awareness* of risking, of inferring. And to suggest the occasional absurdity of refusing to risk I pass along a letter that was purportedly written by a corporation attorney.

It seems that the attorney's company had purchased some land in Louisiana and was now seeking a loan on it from a federal agency. Before granting the loan, the agency asked for a record of the titles to the land. The attorney sent in titles dating back to 1803. The agency's response: "Who owned the land before that?" to which the lawyer replied:

> Your letter regarding titles in Case #2515619 received. I note that you wish titles to extend farther than I have presented them.
>
> I was unaware that any educated person in the world failed to know that Louisiana was purchased from France by the United States in 1803.
>
> The title to the land was acquired by France by right of conquest from Spain. The land came into the possession of Spain by right of discovery in 1492 by an Italian sailor named Christopher Columbus, who had been granted the privilege of seeking a new route to India by the then reigning monarch, Queen Isabella.
>
> The good queen, being a pious woman and careful about titles (almost as careful, I might say, as your agency), took the precaution of securing the blessings of the Pope of Rome upon the voyage before she sold her jewels to help Columbus. Now the Pope, as you know, is considered by some as the emissary of Jesus Christ, who is regarded by many to be the Son of God, and God, it is commonly accepted, made the world.
>
> Therefore, I believe, it is safe to presume that God also made that part of the United States called Louisiana. And I hope to hell you're satisfied.

To recognize what things you know,
*   And what things you do not know—*
This is wisdom.

—Confucius

Discussion Questions

1. When one jumps to a conclusion, what really happens?

2. Precisely what is involved in the concept of inference-observation confusion?

3. How can one avoid the inference-observation confusion?

4. How can one help others to avoid taking the uncalculated risk—without offending them?

5. List five occupations in which inference awareness would be especially important.

6. List five occupations in which inference awareness would be unimportant.

7. About inferences—how do you go about calculating your risk?

8. What do you think of the five-step process for avoiding the inference-observation confusion? The author feels Step 1—detecting the inference—is the most critical of the five steps. Do you agree? Disagree? Why?

9. Regarding the three checkpoints for heightening and maintaining your inference-awareness: Are there exceptions to these recommendations? Can you make additional recommendations?

10. Are there limits to the extent to which one should become inference-aware? Could preoccupation with inferences lead to indecision, inaction? To stultification of one's imagination? Explain.

11. Describe an incident, possibly involving yourself, in which the inference-observation confusion occurred. Analyze specifically why it occurred, what might have been done to prevent its occurrence, and what measures would prevent its recurrence.

C A S E S

CASE 9.1

Tyler Industries, Inc.*

Len Williams, manager of the Export Parts order section of Tyler's North European division, was puzzled and troubled. Something had obviously gone sour, but what?

Len had always prided himself on the relaxed, friendly atmosphere in the section. Good-natured bantering had been the order of the day, and employees would frequently stop by his desk for an informal chat.

Suddenly, things were different. Len hadn't had a "visitor" for over a week, and everyone seemed too busy for intraoffice needling. With his people becoming more taciturn, Len felt himself growing progressively uneasy and unwilling to go out of his way to initiate conversations.

The change had occurred shortly after young Paul Brock had joined the section. But how could there be a connection? Paul seemed eager to learn and gave every indication of wanting to be a good "team player," but the group had clearly not accepted him.

Tyler Industries, Incorporated, was a large multidivision organization headquartered in Cleveland and operating in the Americas, Europe, Africa, the Far East, and Australia. The service functions of the corporation were organized by geographic areas such as the Great Britain division, the North European division, and so on. Some of these functions were located in the regions they served. Others, such as Export Parts, were centralized in Cleveland.

The North European division's Export Parts order section consisted of Williams and seven order interpreters. Their eight desks were arranged in a straight line. Williams' desk was at the head of the line, and Brock's was second. This desk had been vacated by Lou DeWitt, who had just been promoted to chief of another section. Williams assigned the desk to Brock because Paul was new to the corporation as well as to the section and would probably need considerable coaching. Moreover, Len confided to a friend, "I want to avoid that silly desk reshuffling two years ago when Sheila Rosen was promoted out of the section." Coincidentally, Rosen had occupied the second desk.

Discussion Questions

1. What is your analysis of what has happened?
2. What should Williams have done?
3. What should he do now?

---

* All names have been disguised.

CASE 9.2

56 Minutes before Pearl Harbor*
Hugh Russell Fraser

My task was to investigate the 56 minutes of warning we had of the Jap air attack on Pearl Harbor, December 7, 1941. What I learned amazed me. I reported every detail to the Assistant Chief Signal Officer—specifically, Maj. Gen. James A. Code.

Now, nearly 17 years later, I can tell that story. The facts, incredible as they are, became a part of my history of the U.S. Signal Corps in World War II. To most Americans, who know merely that we had some radar warning of the sneak Jap attack on the "Day of Infamy," the history of those 56 minutes will come as a shock.

Radar could, and did, detect the approach of the Jap air fleet. But not, of course, as it should have been detected, and not as it would have been detected if authorized radar equipment had been installed. Actually, the island of Oahu was to have been ringed with permanent radar-warning installations. It was not. As early as November of the year before, the Corps of Engineers was directed to install six permanent radar-warning sets to be operating around the clock beginning July 1, 1941.

These sets were not installed by July 1. They were not installed by December 1, nor by December 7. Four mobile radar-warning units, mounted in trucks, were provided in their place. Regarded generally by the men assigned to them as toys to experiment with, they were in operation only from 4:00 A.M. to 7:00 A.M. Why were those hours chosen? Probably it was because those were the 3 hours out of the 24 when the enemy—any enemy—was most likely to attack. If this was the theory, then it came very close to being 100 percent right!

The Opana mobile radar set, manned by Privates Joseph Lockard and George Elliott, was the one that detected the approach of the Jap air armada. Singularly enough, it was supposed to be shut down promptly at seven o'clock on the morning of December 7, but, by one of those fortunate accidents of history, the truck coming at that time to take the two men back to base camp and to breakfast was late. So Lockard and Elliott decided to leave the set on until it arrived.

Thus, after 7:00 A.M., the Opana unit was the only radar unit on this island operating. The other mobile sets, also mounted in trucks, had shut down promptly. One was located at Punaluu on Kahana Bay, 20 miles to the southeast; another on the extreme west side of the island near Makua; and the fourth near Waipahu on the southwest coast, 11 miles west of Pearl Harbor itself.

---

* *American Mercury,* August 1957, pp. 80-85. Reprinted by permission.

The Opana unit, which made history, was located about 22 miles due north of Pearl Harbor and about 28 miles northwest of the city of Honolulu. In other words, it was north of the mountains on the island of Oahu, which itself is about 43 miles long and 30 miles wide.

As the seconds after seven o'clock ticked off, Lockard, who kept his eye idly on the machine, noted nothing unusual until, suddenly, at 7:02 A.M., there appeared what he later described as a "huge blip of light—bigger than anything I had even seen before on the set—moving slowly from the extreme left side of the scope to the right. It was, you might call it, a pillar of light. It startled me, for the flight of one plane is represented by a mere dot, several planes a collection of white dots, but here was something different. The whole left side of the scope suddenly took on light!

"My natural reaction," he continued, "was to infer the radar unit was out of order. So I asked the mechanic, Elliott, to check it. He did so in a couple of minutes and reported it was working all right. By then it was 7:04 A.M. Something unusual, I knew, was before my eyes. Elliott thought so, too, although neither of us could imagine what it might be.

"Quickly we plotted it. The calculations were easily made, and it appeared to be definitely a large flight of planes approaching from due north, three points east, and about 137 miles away.

"We looked at each other, and Elliott was the first to reach for the phone. At first he couldn't get anybody at the Army Information Center at Fort Shafter. The line was dead. Then he tried another line. It was open, and soon Private Joseph McDonald at the switchboard answered. Tersely, Elliott told him what we were seeing on the scope. McDonald's answer was: 'Well, what do you expect me to do about it? There's nobody around here but me.' Elliott told him to find somebody and then hung up.

"What happened here, I learned later, was that there was an officer reading a book in the next room. McDonald had supposed he had gone. He was Lt. Kermit Tyler.[1] McDonald told him what Elliott had reported. Lieutenant Tyler looked up from his book, thought awhile as if to take it all in, then said: 'It's all right, never mind.'

"Joe McDonald then called back, and I answered the phone. He told me what Tyler had said. I thereupon insisted on talking to the officer myself. I was a little excited and puzzled and didn't want to let the matter end with McDonald. Joe then asked the lieutenant if he would be good

---

[1] A report of the Army Pearl Harbor Board which was published in the *Army and Navy Journal*, September 15, 1945, reads in part: "The Navy was supposed to have detailed officers in the Information Center to be trained as liaison officers, but had not yet gotten around to it. In the Information Center that morning was a Lieutenant Kermit A. Tyler, a pursuit officer of the Air Corps, whose tour of duty thereat was until 8 o'clock. It was Tyler's second tour of duty at the Center, and he was there for training and observation, but there were no others on duty after 7 o'clock except the enlisted telephone operator. He was the sole officer there between 7 and 8 o'clock that morning; the rest of the personnel that had made the Center operative from 4:00 to 7:00 had departed." (Reprinted by permission.)

enough to talk to me. The officer then came on the phone and said, 'What is it?'

"I made my reply as brief as possible. 'The scope,' I said, 'indicates a large flight of planes approaching Oahu from due north, three points east, about 137 miles away at the last reckoning.'

"There was a pause for a few seconds. Then Tyler said, 'That is probably our B-17s coming in from San Francisco.' I knew there was such a flight coming in, but I knew also those planes would hardly be approaching us from due north.

"At once I made this point clear, and he replied, 'Well, there is nothing to worry about. That is all.' The last words he said with some emphasis, and I judged he didn't want to hear anything further about it, so I said: 'All right, sir,' and hung up.

"Meanwhile, somewhat startled by the whole business, although not alarmed, as now the matter was out of my hands, I continued to watch the set. The pillar of light, or 'blip,' as I call it, continued to move steadily from left to right, and the truck still had not arrived. At 7:25 A.M. we made a quick computation, and the flight of planes, whatever it consisted of, was 62 miles out. At 7:39 A.M., just as we heard the truck arriving outside, I made my last computation, and the flight was 22 miles away!

"It was at 7:39 A.M. that we closed down the radar unit and climbed into the truck for a long ride back to base. I was still turning over in my mind what we had seen on the scope as the truck bounced over the badly rutted road. I said anothing to the driver about it, nor did Elliott—not because we were alarmed but because I knew that what didn't make sense to us would hardly make sense to him.

"After we had been driving about 20 minutes, the driver called our attention to a heavy black pall of smoke that lay on the Pearl Harbor horizon to the south. 'Looks like oil smoke,' he commented. Soon we were hearing what sounded like explosions and even antiaircraft fire. It was all very puzzling, and somebody suggested it was a practice raid on Pearl Harbor.

"However, on we went over the rugged road. Actually, it was only 20 miles back to base camp, but because of the road it took almost 40 minutes. As we drove into view of the camp and the truck slowed down, we saw a lot of soldiers running toward us, shouting questions the words of which I couldn't quite at first make out. Finally, it was plain they were asking, 'What happened?' 'Did you report it?' and the like. I never saw a camp so collectively excited.

"As we started to get out of the truck, a major came elbowing his way through the group of men surrounding us and said, sharply, to us: 'Shut up! Don't say a word! I'll talk to you.'

"With that he took us off to his office and questioned us for 15 minutes. It was not until then I realized the Japs were at that very moment attacking Pearl Harbor, and that what we had seen on the screen was the Jap air fleet approaching.

"Now, as I look back, the position of the flight, the vast number of planes, made sense. I learned later the enemy aircraft carriers had sailed far to the north so that when the planes took to the air they would be coming in from an unexpected direction."

Lockard at one point told me that except for the brief questioning by the major on the island of Oahu on the morning of December 7, 1941, I was the first to interrogate him in detail as to those 56 minutes—namely from 7:04 A.M., when Elliott reported the set was not out of order, to the time the first bomb fell on Pearl Harbor.

The tracing of the history of these 56 minutes, however, led me into a further investigation of why the permanent radar sets had not been installed on the island of Oahu by July 1. Here I ran into a curious and amazing story which I tried in vain to have the Congressional Investigating Committee explore.

My investigation disclosed that the colonel in the Corps of Engineers, who was charged with the duty of having these permanent radar sets installed and operated around the clock by July 1, 1941, had spent most of his time in the summer of 1941 drinking. His entire record demonstrates incredible negligence of duty. Not only did he fall down on his job, but the toll in lives and ships that we had to pay for his failure was heartbreaking.

I tried to bring my evidence before the committee. To that end I prepared a long memorandum, setting forth the facts as I saw them. I requested that this colonel be summoned and be cross-examined under oath.

To my surprise, the Democratic members of the committee, whom I knew personally and regarded highly, handled my request—made in my capacity as a citizen—as if it were a hot potato. They not only refused to act on it in any way, or request that he be summoned, but they told me in essence "to forget it"!

Amazed that members of my own party would take this view, I turned to the Republicans. I knew only one personally. He was Representative Bud Gearhart of California. Mr. Gearhart read my memorandum carefully and promised to do his best to get the colonel summoned. Later he reported back he had failed, but he had tried his best.

"Why won't they go into this question of radar units?" I asked. "Surely, you know their importance!"

"Yes," he said, "of course. My opinion is that somebody failed and failed terribly, but I ran up against a stone wall. The chairman flatly refused me, and when I asked one of my Democratic friends what was the real reason for what I thought, and still think, was an obvious runaround, he said, 'Look, Bud, you can do what you please and maybe you can get somewhere, but don't forget I'm a Democrat and a loyal one, and I take my orders from my commander in chief, and my commander in chief happens to be president of the United States!'"

Discussion Questions

1. Analyze the series of blunders and miscalculations that rendered Oahu's defense system so ineffectual and that squandered the 56-minute warning of the Japanese air attack.

2. Why was this case placed in the inference-observation confusion chapter?

CASE 9.3

The Case of the Ledgers*
W. C. Lohse

Alfred Gregory, bank examiner, and his two assistants were making a routine examination of a country bank. The procedure in such bank examinations is to see that all the various bank ledgers are proved by adding machine to see that they reflect the same figures as those shown on the bank's statement for that particular day. In examination circles, it is customary to refer to the loan ledger as a liability ledger and to checking accounts as commerical ledgers; the general books, in which all entries ultimately arrive and from which the daily statement is made, are called the general ledger. One of the two assistant examiners had been on the examination force for only two or three months, and since he was a novice, he did most of the machine work.

Mr. Gregory and his two assistants, Bill, the recruit, and Lois, the experienced assistant, entered the bank promptly at 7:30 A.M. as Leonard Brace, the cashier and vice president, was opening the bank for business. The examiners' credentials were shown to Brace, and the examination proceeded as scheduled. At this point it might be pointed out that no banker is ever aware of when an examination might take place.

> **Gregory:** Bill, as soon as you have counted the cash, run the liability ledger and then report to Lois.
> **Bill:** OK! *(Bill was elated because he had been put on his own for the first time.)*

Bill succeeded in counting the cash and balancing it in a fairly short time, and proceeded to hunt up the liability ledger. This bank was considerably different from those Bill had been in before. Here, they kept all the ledgers in one place and they were not labeled. Bill picked up a ledger and proceeded to run it on an adding machine.

Gregory and Lois were working in the directors' room, whose open door faced the open door of Brace's office. Bill entered the directors' room and went over to Lois with the total he had on his adding machine tape.

---

* All names have been disguised. Printed by permission.

Bill: Here you are, Lois. I ran the liability ledger, and this is the total that should be on the statement.

Lois: (*looking at the statement*) Boy, you sure goofed. This isn't even close. Run it over again.

Bill: OK!

Gregory: Say, Lois, you better have him stick with it; good experience.

Bill returned to his work, tabulated the ledger again, reported to Lois, and was again dismissed as having the wrong total. This procedure was repeated several times more before the morning was over. From where he sat in his office, Brace could see the repeated trips Bill made between Lois and the ledger. At noon, Mr. Gregory explained to Brace that the examiners would have to leave for lunch and that since Bill had been unable to strike a balance with the liability ledger, the ledger would have to be sealed until they could check it out after lunch.

After lunch the examiners came back to the bank and Bill was sent to Mr. Brace's office to pick up the liability ledger that Brace had sealed. Bill returned to the directors' room, apparently distressed.

Gregory: What's the matter, boy?

Bill: Boy, I've really messed this up.

Gregory: What do you mean?

Bill: I have been running the wrong ledger all morning. I was running the commercial ledger—no wonder I couldn't balance.

Gregory: That's all right, son, no harm done. Here, take this liability ledger back and run it now.

Bill was passing Mr. Brace's door with the ledger, when Brace called to him.

Brace: Wait a minute. I'd like to talk to Mr. Gregory.

Bill and Brace walked back to the directors' room.

Brace (*perspiring heavily*): Well, I guess the jig's up, Mr. Gregory.

Gregory: (*thinking Brace was joking, as most bankers do with examiners*): Yep.

Brace: I didn't think that some young fellow would catch me. If I had to be caught I hoped it would be an old-timer like yourself.

Gregory (*now that it is clear that Mr. Brace is serious*): Well, now that we know of this situation, would you please aid us in ascertaining how far it has gone?

Mr. Brace readily agreed and proceeded to show the examiners where, over the past eight years, he had embezzled $128,000 and the methods used to perpetuate the defalcation. Gregory asked what had given him the idea that the examiners had discovered the defalcation. Mr. Brace said that when he had seen Bill repeatedly going to the ledger, he figured that something was wrong, because in all the years that he had been under various examinations, it had never taken an examiner more than an hour to run and balance his ledger.

Brace was subsequently tried and convicted. Despite his family's reimbursement of the major portion of the emezzlement, he was fined $125,000 and sentenced to 10 years.

Gregory admitted privately that it was quite unlikely that the defalcation would have been detected by the routine examination.

Discussion Questions

1. How do you analyze Mr. Brace's behavior?
2. What is the moral of this case?

CASE 9.4

General Patton and the Sicilian Slapping Incidents*
Henry J. Taylor

> Headquarters Seventh Army
> APO #758, U.S. Army
> 29 August, 1943

My Dear General Eisenhower:

Replying to your letter of August 17, 1943, I want to commence by thanking you for this additional illustration of your fairness and generous consideration in making the communication personal.

I am at a loss to find words with which to express my chagrin and grief at having given you, a man to whom I owe everything and for whom I would gladly lay down my life, cause for displeasure with me.

I assure you that I had no intention of being either harsh or cruel in my treatment of the two soldiers in question. My sole purpose was to try and restore in them a just appreciation of their obligation as men and soldiers.

In World War I, I had a dear friend and former schoolmate who lost his nerve in an exactly analogous manner, and who, after years of mental anguish, committed suicide.

Both my friend and the medical men with whom I discussed his case assured me that had he been roundly checked at the time of his first misbehavior, he would have been restored to a normal state.

Naturally, this memory actuated me when I inaptly tried to apply the remedies suggested. After each incident I stated to officers with me that I felt I had probably saved an immortal soul. . . .

> Very Respectfully,
> *(Signed)* G. S. Patton, Jr.
> *Lieut. General, U.S. Army*

General D. D. Eisenhower
Headquarters, AFHQ
APO #512—U.S. Army

When General Patton gave me a copy of this letter he lay back on the bed in his field-trailer and said, "What does that sound like to you?"

"It sounds to me like only half of the story," I said.

So, first, let's see what actually happened.

Private Charles H. Kuhl (in civilian life a carpet layer from South Bend, Indiana), ASN 35536908, L Company, 26th Infantry, 1st Division, was admitted to the 3d Battalion, 26th Infantry aid station, in Sicily on August 2, 1943, at 2:10 P.M.

He had been in the Army eight months and with the 1st Division about thirty days.

A diagnosis of exhaustion was made at the station by Lieutenant H. L. Sanger, Medical Corps, and Kuhl was evacuated to C Company, 1st Medical Battalion, well to the rear of the fighting.

There a note was made on his medical tag stating that he had been admitted to this place three times during the Sicilian campaign.

He was evacuated to the clearing company by Captain J. D. Broom, M.C., put in quarters, and given sodium amytal, one capsule night and morning, on the prescription of Captain N. S. Nedell, M.C.

On August 3d, the following remark appears on Kuhl's Emergency Medical Tag: "Psychoneurosis anxiety state—moderately severe. Soldier has been twice before in hospital within ten days. He can't take it at front evidently. He is repeatedly returned. *(signed)* Capt. T. P. Covington, Medical Corps."

By this route and in this way Private Kuhl arrived in the receiving tent of the 15th Evacuation Hospital where the blow was struck that was heard around the world.

"I came into the tent," explains General Patton, "with the commanding officer of the outfit and other medical officers.

"I spoke to the various patients, especially commending the wounded men. I just get sick inside myself when I see a fellow torn apart, and some of the wounded were in terribly ghastly shape. Then I came to this man and asked him what was the matter."

The soldier replied, "I guess I can't take it."

"Looking at the others in the tent, so many of them badly beaten up, I simply flew off the handle."

Patton squared off in front of the soldier.

He called the man every kind of a loathsome coward and then slapped him across the face with his gloves.

The soldier fell back. Patton grabed him by the scruff of the neck and kicked him out of the tent.

Kuhl was immediately picked up by corpsmen and taken to a ward.[1]

Returning to his headquarters, Patton issued the following memorandum to corps, division, and separate brigade commanders two days later:

Headquarters Seventh Army
APO #758 U.S. Army
5 August, 1943

It has come to my attention that a very small number of soldiers are going to the hospital on the pretext that they are nervously incapable of combat.

Such men are cowards, and bring discredit on the Army and disgrace to their comrades whom they heartlessly leave to endure the danger of a battle while they themselves use the hospital as a means of escaping.

You will take measures to see that such cases are not sent to the hospital, but are dealt with in their units.

Those who are not willing to fight will be tried by Court-Martial for cowardice in the face of the enemy.

(Signed) G. S. Patton, Jr.
Lieut. General, U.S. Army
Commanding

Five days later General Patton, not a medical man, again took matters into his own hands.

He slapped another soldier.

Private Paul G. Bennett, ASN 70000001, C Battery, Field Artillery, was admitted to the 93d Evacuation Hospital on August 10th at 2:20 P.M.

Bennett, still only 21, had served four years in the Regular Army. He had an excellent record. His unit had been attached to the II Corps since March, and he had never had any difficulties until four days earlier, when his best friend in the outfit, fighting nearby, was wounded in action.

Bennett could not sleep that night and felt nervous. The shells going over bothered him. "I keep thinking they're going to land right on me," he said. The next day he became increasingly nervous about the firing and about his buddy's recovery.

A battery aid man sent him to the rear echelon, where a medical officer gave him some medicine which made him sleep. But he was still nervous, badly disturbed.

---

[1] There Kuhl was found to have a temperature of 102.2° F, gave a history of chronic diarrhea, and was shown by a blood test to have malaria.

On August 10th the medical officer ordered him to the 93d Evacuation Hospital, although Bennett begged not to be evacuated because he did not want to leave his unit.

General Patton arrived at the hospital that day.

Bennett was sitting in the receiving tent, huddled up and shivering.

Patton spoke to all the injured men. He was solicitous, kind, and inspiring. But when he and Major Charles B. Etter, the receiving officer in charge, reached Bennett and Patton asked the soldier what his trouble was, the soldier replied, "It's my nerves," and began to sob.

Patton turned on him like a tiger, screaming at him:

"What did you say?"

"It's my nerves," sobbed Bennett. "I can't take the shelling anymore."

In this moment Patton lost control of himself completely. Without any investigation of the man's case whatever, he rushed close to Bennett and shouted: "Your nerves, hell. You are just a . . . coward, you yellow b_____."

Then he slapped the soldier hard across the face.

"Shut up that . . . crying," he yelled. "I won't have these brave men here who have been shot seeing a yellow b_____ sitting here crying."

Patton struck the man again. He knocked his helmet liner off his head into the next tent. Then he turned to Major Etter and yelled, "Don't admit this yellow b_____, there's nothing the matter with him. I won't have the hospitals cluttered up with these SOB's who haven't got the guts to fight."

Patton himself began to sob. He wheeled around to Colonel Donald E. Currier, the 93d's commanding medical officer. "I can't help it," he said. "It makes me break down to see brave boys and to think of a yellow b_____ being babied."

But this was not all. In his blind fury, Patton turned on Bennett again. The soldier now was managing to sit at attention, although shaking all over.

"You're going back to the front lines," Patton shouted, "You may get shot and killed, but you're going to fight. If you don't, I'll stand you up against the wall and have a firing squad kill you on purpose.

"In fact," he said, reaching for his revolver, "I ought to shoot you myself, you _____ whimpering coward."

As he left the tent, Patton was still yelling back at the receiving officer to "send the yellow SOB back to the front line."

Nurses and patients, attracted by the shouting and cursing, came from the adjoining tent and witnessed this disturbance.

Patton made no initial report of these affairs to his superior, General Eisenhower, who was then in his headquarters at Tunis on the North African mainland.

"I felt ashamed of myself," General Patton told me, "and I hoped the whole thing would die out."

But an official report by Lieut. Colonel Perrin H. Long, Medical Corps consulting physician, was already on the way to Allied headquarters through Medical Corps channels.

"The deleterious effects of such incidents upon the well-being of patients, upon the professional morale of hospital staffs, and upon the relationship of patient to physician are incalculable," reported Lieut. Colonel Long. "It is imperative that immediate steps be taken to prevent a recurrence of such incidents."

General Eisenhower received this report on August 17th. His communication to General Patton was sent off that night.

In his message, which Patton showed me, the commanding general told Patton of the allegation, told him that he could not describe in official language his revulsion, informed Patton that he must make, on his own initiative, proper amends to the soldiers involved and take steps to make amends before his whole army.

"This all happened practically on the eve of a new attack in which I had been written in for a large part of the plans, already issued," Patton explained, "and General Eisenhower stated therefore that he would temporarily reserve decision regarding my relief of command until he could determine the effect of my own corrective measures.

"Then Eisenhower did four things: He sent Maj. General John Porter Lucas to Sicily to make an investigation of the charges, sent the theater's inspector general to investigate command relationships in my entire army, sent another general officer to interview the two soldiers, and made a trip to Sicily himself to determine how much resentment against me existed in the army.

"Eisenhower's problem was whether what I had done was sufficiently damaging to compel my relief on the eve of attack, thus losing what he described as my unquestioned military value, or whether less drastic measures would be appropriate.

"I went to see both Kuhl and Bennett," Patton continued, "explained my motives, and apologized for my actions.

"In each case I stated that I should like to shake hands with them; that I was sincerely sorry. In each case they accepted my offer.

"I called together all the doctors, nurses, and enlisted men who were present when the slappings occurred. I apologized and expressed my humiliation over my impulsive actions.

"Finally, I addressed all divisions of the 7th Army in a series of assemblies, the last of which was an address before the 3d Division on August 30th.

"I praised them as soldiers, expressed regret for any occasions when I harshly treated individuals, and offered my apologies as their commanding general for doing anything unfair or un-American.

"Beyond that, except to leave the Army and get out of the war, I do not know what I could have done."

Discussion Questions

1. How do you analyze General Patton's behavior?
2. What patterns of miscommunication seemed to have occurred in this case?
3. How do you appraise General Eisenhower's actions?

CASE 9.5

"It Really Hit the Fan"*

I've been in the Civil Services since my college graduation eight years ago. I've been making good progress and I've been very happy with my job. But today, it really hit the fan. It all started a week ago Monday when my boss called me.

Harry: Keith, we got instructions from the Director's office. Your unit's got to have another GS 9.

Me: Why . . . what does that mean?

Harry: It means promote somebody—the organization chart calls for it and it's got to be in place when we finalize our budget next week for the new fiscal year.

Me: Well . . . who do I pick?

Harry: That's up to you. You know your people better than I do. Pick somebody, push him up to GS 9, and make him a first-line supervisor.

Me: A supervisor of what?

Harry: That's up to you, too . . . maybe you need an aide, whatever.

Me: When am I supposed to make this move?

Harry: By Friday at the latest . . . no, sooner than that. I've got to approve it and then Mary's got to approve my approval. Personnel has the final say-so on these things.

Me: So when's the deadline?

Harry: Get it to me by noon sharp, Wednesday. Clear?

Me: Well, it's clear enough . . . I just wish I had a little more lead time. . . .

Harry: You and me, both . . . and so would my other three group managers . . . I just called them . . . all four of you people are in the same boat.

Me: Well . . . okay, Harry . . . I'll do my best . . . Wednesday?

Harry: That's it, buddy. Wednesday noon . . . this is bigger than both of us.

Me: Well . . . I'll get right on it.

---

* All names are disguised. Author's name is withheld at his request.

I really didn't need that right then. I'd been up to my eyeballs preparing for the budget proposal. At any rate it was almost quitting time so I collected a bunch of personnel records and headed home.

Fortunately, my wife is understanding ... at least I hope she is. She had to keep the kids off me all that evening while I was going over the files. By midnight, I had narrowed it down to six people. My head was aching so I called it a night.

I don't think I slept more than an hour that whole night. I was so keyed up. I had promoted people before, but I always had plenty of time to make a choice. This time the pressure was really on.

I finally gave up on trying to sleep at about 5 A.M. I got up and made some coffee and tried to get back to the files. But my head was still spinning. At seven I gave up. Betty had made some french toast, but I just couldn't eat anything. My stomach was in a knot.

Then it was out to the car and on to the office. No chance to think in the car; the traffic was lousy. I was 10 minutes early but my in-basket was already stacked, and I had two meetings that morning and another two in the afternoon.

In a way, it was good that I had so much to do because it got me away from the promotion thing. I really couldn't think about that again until I was driving home after work. Miraculously, my mind was clearer again and with a little more homework, I whittled the list down to three.

There were Susan and Laurie and Scott. They were all in their early 20s. Each had had a good education and each had been with the Department two or three years. They were all good people and I felt any one of them would have made a good supervisor. I thought I had gone as far as the records would take me, so I figured I'd chat with each one of them tomorrow and see if that wouldn't help me make up my mind.

I slept much better that night.

The next morning I got to my office a good half-hour early, but still my in-basket was loaded. They must have little gremlins who run around at night and cram the baskets. Well, anyway, by the time I finally got that stuff squared away, it was almost 10 A.M., so I called all three of them in at the same time.

I told them that I had good news and bad news. The good news was that I was going to make someone a GS 9 and that each of them was being seriously considered. The bad news was that I could only pick one of them.

Well, I guess they were surprised ... and they laughed a little, maybe it was more a nervous laugh. I tried to get them talking, but, I don't know, they seemed so self-conscious with one another. It was getting embarrassing and I was beginning to regret I had gotten all three of them in at the same time. Well, anyway, I decided to call a halt and asked them to keep it under their hats for the time being. I told them I'd make a recommendation to Harry for his approval, then he'd pass it to Mary for her okay, and then I'd get the word to them—probably Friday.

The three of them left and I felt depressed. I knew I had handled it poorly but I just didn't know what to do. Dammit! It's the Department's fault, springing this on a guy at the last minute.

Well, I had to make a decision and have it on Harry's desk by noon. I already knew who it would be. My intuition had me leaning toward Susan from the beginning. She's young and inexperienced, but hell! So are the other two. I just sensed she'd be a good bet. So she was my choice and I made Harry's deadline. Now that I had that out of the way, I could get on with my regular work.

Friday came and went; no word from Harry. But I didn't notice. I had just forgotten about the whole business.

No word on Monday either. Harry finally called me today (Tuesday). He said everything was okay and Susan was in.

So I called her to my office and closed the door and told her the good news. Frankly, I hadn't expected her reaction. She didn't actually cry, but she sure teared up. She explained what a strain the weekend had been—not hearing anything. She was sure that someone else had gotten the promotion and that she hadn't been told anything.

So I told her to dry her eyes and not tell anyone anything until I had a chance to talk to Scott and Laurie. She left the office kind of dabbing at her eyes. I noticed that several people were watching her as she headed for the restroom.

Next, I called in Scott and told him the facts of life. He took it pretty well, I think. I told him I still needed to get to Laurie, so I asked him to put on a smile and pretend nothing had happened.

Well, he put on a smile, all right. He wasn't three steps out of my office when some joker yelled across the main office: "I know what that grin means, Scotty! Congratulations, old boy!" And several other people came over to clap him on the back.

Discussion Questions

1. What uncalculated risks seem to have been taken in this case?
2. What was the purpose of the promotions?
3. How should Keith have handled the promotion?

CASE 9.6

The Stardust Motel

It was 7:15 Saturday morning, and Al, Ben, Charlie, Don, Ed, and Frank were driving up to Lake Winnipaninni for a day's fishing. As they passed the Stardust Motel, they caught sight of their mutual superior, George Gilbert, vice president of public relations, First National Bank, and his secretary, Mrs. Gloria Golden, emerging from the motel.

Curiously, no one said anything, but each was certain that the others had seen George and Gloria.

Subsequently, the men responded as follows:

Al phoned George's wife and said: "Mrs. Gilbert, I know it's none of my business, but in your and the children's interests, I think you ought to know what I saw this morning. . . ."

Ben phoned George and said: "George, I think you ought to know that Al, Charlie, Don, Ed, Frank, and I saw you and Gloria this morning. Of course, I'll keep mum, but I don't know how far you can trust the others."

Charlie was called by George Saturday night. "Charlie, I understand you fellows saw Gloria and me this morning. If the wrong people hear this, my marriage could be threatened and I could be ruined at the bank. I appeal to you, Charlie, you're the leader of that group. Can't you get them to clam up?" Charlie responded: "Sorry, George, I'll keep my own mouth shut, but I just don't want to get involved."

Don caught Harold Hayes, executive vice president and Gilbert's boss, at the coffee machine Monday morning: "Mr. Hayes, I hate to do this. But in the bank's interest I think I should tell you what I saw Saturday morning . . ."

Ed made a red valentine and posted it on the bank's bulletin board.

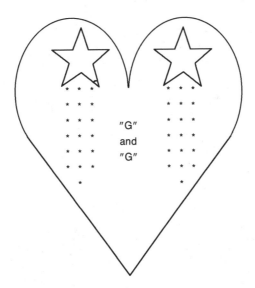

Discussion Questions

1. Rank the people in this case according to the morality of their behavior. That is, identify the person who behaved most morally (or least immorally). Then who would be next, and so on.

2. What inferences would you have to make in order to feel more confident about your ranking?

CASE 9.7

A Slight Breakdown in Communication*
William E. Burrows

At exactly 9:20 on the night of May 8, 1978, National Airlines Flight 193, carrying 52 passengers and a crew of six from Mobile, Alabama, to Pensacola, Florida, turned into its final approach to the Pensacola Regional Airport. The plane was four miles from the edge of the airport's Runway 25 as it eased down rather quickly through the fog and haze that drifted through the darkness over Escambia Bay.

At 9:20 and 11 seconds James Stockwell, the flight engineer, who sat behind the pilot and co-pilot, scanning the final approach checklist—the list of things that had to be done before the jet could safely be landed—called out, "Landing gear and lever."

"Down three green," answered Leonard G. Sanderson, Jr., the co-pilot. Sanderson was telling Stockwell and George T. Kunz, the pilot, that the three green lights on the instrument panel representing the plane's landing gear were glowing green, showing that the gear was down and locked.

At 9:20 and 15 seconds, the Ground-Proximity Warning System, a device that warns when a plane is too close to the ground or to water relative to where it's supposed to be, or is coming down too quickly relative to its altitude, went off with a loud, whooping sound and a flashing red light on the instrument panel. Then, for good measure, it said, "Pull up, pull up!" in recorded English that rang with unmistakable authority and urgency. The warnings continued for nine seconds until Stockwell, believing that he was acting on his pilot's orders, turned off the GPWS.

At 9:20 and 31 seconds Sanderson, the co-pilot, looked out his window and noticed that the Boeing 727 was skimming over Escambia Bay at an alarmingly low altitude. "We're down to 50 feet," he told the others. Two seconds later National 193 hit the water three miles short of Runway 25 and settled in 12 feet of water. Three passengers drowned before the crew of a nearby barge rescued everyone else.

A head-on picture of the 727, lying still and abandoned in water that lapped over its nose and almost up to its windshield, made Page 1 all over the country the next day and has since been used to represent the kind of foul-up that can happen to technological man and his machines despite the best laid of his plans.

The National Transportation Safety Board decided after examining a great deal of evidence that National 193 had crashed because of several errors made by its flight crew. These included the fact that the crew did not monitor the 727's altitude and rate of descent as it approached Pensacola; the

---

* *Psychology Today*, November, 1982, pp. 44–45. Reprinted with permission from *Psychology Today* Magazine. Copyright © 1982 (APA).

co-pilot did not call out the plane's altitude and other indications of perform-ance to the pilot, as he was supposed to do; there was a failure to use all of the instruments available to gauge the plane's altitude; the GPWS was turned off in error; and more. The evidence made a classic case for what is loosely called "pilot error." But that evidence, as described in the NTSB's 46-page report, makes "error" a gross oversimplification.

Were it not for the tragic consequences of that accident, in fact, Flight 193's last 30 seconds could almost be said to have been a comedy of errors. Captain Kunz was descending at a rate of 2,000 feet a minute from an alti-tude of 500 feet. Kunz later testified that he had misread the altimeter, he wasn't wearing his glasses, and thought that it said 1,500 feet. When the alarm went off, it was so loud it made conversation very difficult. Kunz responded to the flashing light, whooping, and "Pull up, pull up!" warning by slowing the plane's rate of descent slightly. At the same time, Flight Engineer Stockwell turned off the alarm because, in all the confusion, he thought that Kunz had ordered him to do so. Then the captain, seeing that the alarm had stopped sounding and flashing, concluded that the situa-tion was again under control. Still, he continued to descend without checking the altimeter, according to the NTSB, until National 193 went in.

The National Transportation Safety Board report went on to note that enough time remained during the four to six seconds after the alarm was turned off for Kunz to level off so that he could have another go at Runway 25.

National 193 plowed in to Escambia Bay because of serious problems in crew communication, integration, operation of the plane's systems, and decision-making.

Discussion Questions

1. This case is appended to the inference-observation confusion chapter. Why?

2. What part did Captain Kunz play in Flight 193's inadvertent ditching?

3. Did Flight Engineer Stockwell contribute?

4. How do you feel about Co-pilot Sanderson's failure to notify the pilot of altitude and other indicators of the plane's performance?

Bypassing
Talking Past One Another

❋
❋
❋

DEFINITION

Belden, West, and Bartell[1] was a medium-sized brokerage firm with approximately 95 employees. The accounting department had 17 employees, of whom 3 were middle-aged women who operated the bookkeeping machines. With an average volume of business, all three were normally finished with their posting about one hour before the usual quitting time.

On February 21 one of the bookkeepers, Elizabeth Morley, phoned in to say she was ill and would be unable to report for duty. The other two, Jane Dover and Catherine Finn, pitched in and completed about 75 percent of the absent woman's posting before the normal quitting time. Supervisor Janet DuFore then approached one of the bookkeepers, Jane Dover, and said: "Elizabeth just called and said she'll be absent again tomorrow, so the balance of her work [25 percent of her normal work load] will have to be completed the first thing in the morning."

Dover, a very conscientious and somewhat unassertive woman, said nothing. The following morning DuFore found that Dover had worked until 8:30 P.M. the previous evening to complete Morley's posting. The supervisor had intended that she and Finn continue with the remainder of Morley's work in the morning before starting on their own posting.

In the preceding instance, there was talking and there was listening. But somehow the communication went awry. The listener presumably heard the same words that the speaker said, but the communicators seem to have *talked past* each other.

This communication phenomenon is called *bypassing* (see Figure 10.1). It is evident that DuFore had one meaning in mind and Dover had

---

[1] All names have been disguised.

FIGURE 10.1

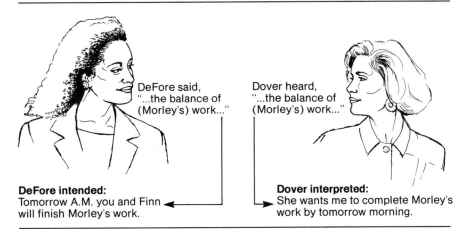

DeFore said,
"...the balance of
(Morley's) work..."

Dover heard,
"...the balance of
(Morley's) work..."

DeFore intended:
Tomorrow A.M. you and Finn
will finish Morley's work.

Dover interpreted:
She wants me to complete Morley's
work by tomorrow morning.

another. Their meanings passed by each other without meeting. *Bypassing,* then, is the name for the miscommunication pattern that occurs when the sender (speaker, writer, and so on) and the receiver (listener, reader, and so forth) *miss each other with their meanings.*

Same Word—Different Things

This bypassing took the form of one person sending and the other receiving the *same words* but attributing *different meanings* to them. This is a very common type of bypassing, but it has an equally prevalent counterpart.

Different Words—Same Thing

Bypassing may occur just as readily when people are using different words to represent the same thing. I once witnessed with thinly disguised amusement a heated and fruitless argument between my 12-year-old nephew and a Massachusetts soda fountain clerk, only a year or two older. Jimmy, born and reared in Illinois, was visiting the East Coast for the first time.

The conversation went something like this:

Jimmy: Do you have pop?
Clerk: What?
Jimmy: Pop.
Clerk: I don't know what you're talking about.

Jimmy *(scornfully):* You never heard of pop?

Clerk: No, and neither did you!

Jimmy: Listen, it's that stuff that comes in a bottle—you shake it up, and it fizzes out?

Clerk: Oh! You mean a soda!

Jimmy: No! I don't want a soda! *(A "soda" where Jimmy lives is made with ice cream, flavoring, and soda water.)*

Clerk: Well, then, what *do* you want?

Jimmy: Never mind! You wouldn't have it anyway!

At this point, I partially reconciled the two antagonists by suggesting that they were both talking about the same thing. Jimmy, incidentally, finally got his "pop," "soda," "tonic," "minerals," "soft drink," or whatever it is called in your part of the country.

A particularly exasperating aspect of our language is that we have words which would appear to represent opposites, but in fact we use the words interchangeably:

> *Verbal Paradox*[2]
> *Inflammable and flammable*
> *Burn with an equal flame;*
> *Bested at chess, or worsted,*
> *My plight is just the same;*
> *Sleeves raveled and unraveled*
> *Are but a single kind;*
> *Both boned and deboned filets*
> *Are boneless cuts, I find.*
> *In short, what seems antonymous*
> *May really be synonymous.*
> *—Richard Bardolph*

Both types of bypassing (same word—different things and different words—same thing) have a common basis, of course. Both types involve people missing each other's meanings, and the consequences of both types are equally worthy of consideration.

SOME CONSEQUENCES

Bypassing can have a wide variety of consequences. It may be helpful to suggest something of their range.

---

[2] From "Pepper . . . and Salt," *The Wall Street Journal*, Oct. 29, 1981, p. 23. Reprinted with permission.

The Range of Consequences

Bypassing is certainly one of the most prevalent, costly, and dangerous patterns of miscommunication in organizations or virtually anywhere else. But it is not always serious, hazardous, or even important. Sometimes its results may be amusing or even hilarious. In fact, much of our humor is based on bypassing. A personal story makes the point. It happened on my first day of college teaching, years ago. Mustering as much dignity as was possible for a neophyte, I walked into the classroom and announced that I was going to seat the class alphabetically. I explained that I had difficulty in associating names with faces and that by seating them alphabetically, "I will get to know you by your seats." Of course the class bypassed me!

But I did not have the only red face that day, for 20 minutes later a young, innocent freshman woman rose to describe her initial campus impressions. She said that she was particularly fond of the serenades—when the fraternity men would come as a group to sing beneath the women's dormitory windows. "We girls love it so," she emphasized, "we wish the boys could stay all night!"

Unfortunately, not all bypassings end so delightfully (at least from the audience's point of view). Bypassings occurring every day in industry, in government, and in homes result in enormous wastes of time, money, effort, and tempers. History is full of examples of bypassings that have led to catastrophes. There is even disturbing evidence to suggest that a bypassing on a word in the Japanese response to the World War II Potsdam ultimatum may have led to the dropping of the atom bombs on Japan and to Russia's declaration of war on Japan—events that have had irrevocable effects upon world affairs.

Immediate Consequences

Before we leave this cursory review of bypassing, we should note that the immediate effects of this breakdown in communication generally fall into one or the other of two broad classifications.

Apparent Agreement. Many bypassings have apparent agreement as their immediate consequences. That is, the initial result of the bypassing was such that those involved felt that they were in harmony with each other. Jane Dover and her supervisor, for example, believed that they had had a mutual understanding. The bypassing, however, concealed an actual disagreement (i.e., the people involved differed on meanings).

It is the *acting* on the false assurance of agreement that so frequently leads us into trouble.

Jeannie, nine, called to her mother upstairs: "Mom, may I fix the Easter eggs?" "Yes, dear," mother called back, "We'll need three dozen eggs. Be sure to cook them for at least 15 minutes."

Jeannie placed the eggs in the largest kettle she could find and filled it with cold water. Then she set the kettle on the stove and turned on the gas.

After 15 minutes of eager clock-watching, Jeannie removed the eggs from the water (which had not yet begun to boil) and set them on the table.

While she was preparing the Easter egg dyes, her brother Tom, 14, walked into the kitchen and picked up an egg. "Are you sure you cooked these long enough?" he asked. "Sure. Exactly 15 minutes, just like Mom said." "Well, OK—say, want to see what a hard head I have?" And with that Tom cracked a very uncooked egg on his head!

Apparent Disagreement.   But bypassing can also conceal actual agreement while manifesting apparent disagreement. Jimmy and his "pop" illustrate this pattern of miscommunication.

Whether the immediate consequences of bypassing is an apparent agreement or an apparent disagreement, the subsequent effect *can* be unpleasant, unproductive, and even fatal. Let us now consider some of the factors that contribute to this often troublesome pattern of miscommunication.

THE UNDERLYING MECHANISM

Just what happens when people bypass? What kind of thought process occurs that often leads to dangerous and costly miscommunication?

Recall the DuFore-Dover incident? They bypassed each other, that is, missed each other with their meanings. But *why*? Let us presume that neither *intended* to miscommunicate. Certainly the supervisor did not use any big, foreign, or unfamiliar words. Why, then, did the communication go askew?

Suppose that we asked them what they thought went wrong in their communication. Their responses might follow this pattern:

Dover: I was sure I knew what Janet meant—finish up Elizabeth's work and do it before tomorrow morning. I never thought she was talking about Catherine and me doing the work the next morning.
DuFore: I was certain that Jane would understand what I was driving at. It never occurred to me that she would put a different interpretation on my remark.

"I was sure ... I never thought ..."; "I was certain ... It never occurred to me ..." These women are revealing the key assumption underlying their behavior—the assumption that *words mean the same to the other person as they do to me.*

That is an enormously pervasive assumption. Most of us act on that assumption much of the time. And more often than not people do interpret our words as we intend—and usually we decode their words appropriately as well. But consistent success may lead to overconfidence and complacency—the ideal attitudes for bypassing.

There are at least two additional reasons for the epidemic prevalence of the assumption. First, it is a highly enticing notion. We want to feel that we are understanding and being understood by the other person. Second, the assumption supports our basic egocentrism, as is suggested by this passage from Lewis Carroll's *Through the Looking-Glass*:

> Humpty-Dumpty said: "There's glory for you." "I don't know what you mean by 'glory,'" Alice said. Humpty-Dumpty smiled contemptuously. "Of course, you don't till I tell you. I meant, 'There's a nice knock-down argument for you.'" "But 'glory' doesn't mean a 'nice knock-down argument,'" Alice objected. "When I use a word," Humpty-Dumpty said in a rather scornful tone, "it means just what I choose it to mean, neither more nor less."

Few of us are as frank as Humpty-Dumpty, though we are frequently as arrogant. We would not call it arrogance (unless we were talking about the other individual) because we are largely unaware of the prevailing egocentrism which so frequently accompanies our use of words. If we were to watch our own language use scrupulously during a 24-hour period, we would almost certainly catch ourselves talking or listening (writing or reading) dozens of times with the Humpty-Dumpty attitude. We would find ourselves assuming, "I *knew* what the other person understood or meant simply because that was the way I used or would have used the words."

That assumption is not unfailingly valid—and we have already suggested the consequences of acting unconsciously upon it when it is false.

Digging more deeply, we find the assumption is supported by two pernicious fallacies. One is that words are used in only one way ("the way *I* am using them")—that words have mono-usage. The other is that words have meanings. I shall attack each of these fallacies, for they lie at the foundation of bypassing.

Fallacy That Words Have Mono-Usage

The first of the fallacies is the assumption of mono-usage. The notion that words are used to convey one and only one meaning is so patently ridiculous that it hardly appears necessary to refute it. Yet so much of our communication seems to be based on this misconception that I must comment on it.

To begin, let me ask a question: How many words are used in only one way? Except for certain technological terms, virtually all of our common words (as far as I have been able to determine) are used in more than one way. That is, the words we generally use in our day-to-day communications almost invariably have multiusage. In fact, for the 500 most commonly used words in our language there is an aggregate of over 14,000 dictionary definitions! Take the word *fast*, for instance:

A man is *fast* when he can run rapidly.
But he is also *fast* when he is tied down and cannot run at all.
And colors are *fast* when they do not run.
One is *fast* when s/he moves in suspect company.
But this is not quite the same thing as playing *fast* and loose.
A racetrack is *fast* when it is in good running condition.
A friend is *fast* when s/he is loyal.
A watch is *fast* when it is ahead of time.
To be *fast* asleep is to be deep in sleep.
To be *fast* by is to be near.
To *fast* is to refrain from eating.
A *fast* may be a period of noneating—or a ship's mooring line.
Photographic film is *fast* when it is *sensitive* (to light).
But bacteria are *fast* when they are *insensitive* (to antiseptics).

And note the versatility of *call* in this gripping narrative:

Jim *called* on Joe to *call* him out for *calling* him up at midnight and *calling* him down, but their wives *called* in friends who got the fight *called* off.[3]

If one recognizes the prevalence of multiusage in our language, one will anticipate that words can readily be understood differently by different people.

Neologisms

The prevalence of multi-usage in a language is directly related to the extent of the *neologizing* occurring in that language. When something new appears—an invention, a novel event, a new relationship or combination, and so on—how does it become named? Basically, there are two neological tacks: (1) invent a new word (word coinage), or (2) use an old word in a different way (usage coinage).

Word Coinage.   We acquire new words in a variety of ways. For example, words are coined when we:

---

[3] The sentence does not exhaust the multi-usages of *call*. Webster's Unabridged lists 40 different definitions for the word. Other kaleidoscopic words: *turn* (54 definitions), *fall* (50), *touch* (46), *use* (87), *run* (104), and *set* (194).

a. Combine the first letters of a number of words (acronyms):

AIDS: *Acquired Immune Deficiency Syndrome*

DINK: *Double Income; No Kids*

LASER: *Light Amplification by Stimulated Emission of Radiation*

LEM: *Lunar Excursion Module*

NIMBY: *Not In My Back Yard*

RAM: *Random Access Memory*

SCUBA: *Self-Contained Underwater Breathing Apparatus*

SIDS: *Sudden Infant Death Syndrome*

YUPPIE: *Young Urban Professional*

b. Combine parts of existing words:

acid rain	gridlock	multiplex
agribusiness	input	palimony
boom box	interface	phonevision
camcorder	lumpectomy	plastic money
exit poll	megamall	television
fanny pack		

c. Use part of or make a compression of existing words:

fan from *fantastic*
nincompoop from *non compos mentis*
rad from *radical*

d. Make a generic word out of a proper name:

Charles C. *Boycott*	Nicholas *Chauvin*	Gaston *Chevrolet*
Lord *Cardigan*	Lord *Chesterfield*	Earl of *Davenport*

Many flowers have received their names this way:

Michel *Bégon*	Anders *Dahl*	Leonard *Fuchs*
George *Camel*	William *Forsythe*	Alexander *Garden*

Women have been shortchanged, but not totally neglected:

Amelia *Bloomer*	Madame *Pompadour*	*Mae West* (life vest)
Marie *Curie*	*Shirley Temple* (drink)	

And to whom are we indebted for the first flushing toilet?

A Chelsea sanitary engineer, Thomas *Crapper*.

e. Make a generic name out of a fictional character:

babbitt	*mentor*	*Rambo*
gargantuan	*quixotic*	*robot*
malapropism	*pollyanna*	*serendipity*

f. Make a generic word out of a trade name:

aspirin	kleenex	scotch tape
cellophane	linoleum	shredded wheat
coke	milk of magnesia	yo-yo
dry ice	mimeograph	zipper
escalator	nylon	
fridgidaire	pogo stick	

g. "Borrow" from another language:

French: *ambience, liaison, rapport, rendezvous*

German: *blitzkrieg, kindergarten, wanderlust*

Spanish: *adios, fiesta, siesta*

"Loans" from less prominent contributors:

Algonquian (American Indian): *chipmunk, pecan, skunk, squaw*

Arabic: *admiral, almanac, hashish, mattress, sheikh*

Araucanian (Chile): *poncho*

Australian aborigine: *boomerang, kangaroo, koala*

Basque (Spain): *bizarre, jai alai*

Carib: *canoe*

h. Make common usage of a word or phrase invented and used by a specific group:

barf	freebee	pig out
chill out	geek	rouge
dorkmeier	gnarly	slob up
dudette	nerd	trekkie
dweeb		

Usage Coinage. The kind of neologism that is more germane to bypassing, however, is that which occurs when a new usage is made of an existing word. But in defense, were it not for usage coinage, puns, sad to contemplate, would be impossible. Thus, we would have been deprived of the delightful liberties taken by the suppliers of names for the colors of a certain auto a few years ago:

Anti-Establishment Mint   *Last Stand Custard*
Freudian Gilt   *Original Cinnamon*
Hula Blue   *Thanks Vermillion*

Marketers opted not to use:

Come-and-Get-Me Copper   *Statutory Grape*
Gang Green

Consider these words now being used in ways quite different from (and in addition to) the ways in which they were defined only a decade or so ago.

acid	freak	main
Apple	gas	malling
bad	gay	man
bag	generic	mashed
black	grass	matrix
blitz	gross	menu
boomerang	Guardian Angels	micro
bread	hackers	militant
brother	hang-up	moon
buff	hardware	pad
buns	hawk	oreo
coke	head	pig
crack	heavy	pot
crash	high	program
deep sixed	hijack	punk
demonstration	hip	ram
dove	hit	rap
downer	hog	rents
dropout	hunk	right on
dude	ice	rug
far out	into	score
fat cat	joint	scum
flake	kill	silo
flash	kinky	slim
flip	macro	smack

soul	stonewalled	turkey
speed	straight	turn off
split	streaking	turn on
squeeze	terminal	upper
squid	tool	video
stoked	transplant	vigilante
stoned	trip	

This constant piling on of usages moved one anonymous bard to express his or her frustration in verse:

Remember when hippie meant big in the hips,
And a trip involved travel in car, planes, and ships?
When pot was a vessel for cooking things in,
And hooked was what grandmother's rugs may have been?
When fix was a verb that meant mend or repair.
And be-in meant merely existing somewhere?
When neat meant well-organized, tidy, and clean,
And grass was a ground cover, normally green?
When groovy meant furrowed with channels and hollows,
And birds were winged creatures, like robins and swallows?
When fuzz was a substance, real fluffy, like lint,
And bread came from bakeries and not from the mint?
When roll meant a bun, and rock was a stone,
And hang up was something you did with the phone?
It's groovy, man, groovy, but English it's not.
Methinks that our language is going to pot.

The accumulation of usages occurs incessantly in a living language. And if we consider some of the special kinds of usage accumulation we will be alerted to some of the areas of potential bypassing. Among them are: *(a)* etymological shifts, *(b)* regionalisms, and *(c)* technical/common usage.

Etymological Shifts.   A great many of our older words have under-gone etymological shifts. That is, they have acquired new usages as they have been passed down through time. Some of the usages drop out after a while, but many remain, and the result is often a formidable accumulation of definitions, all of which are operating at present. The word *mess* is a good example. A Latin term, it originally stood for "something sent." This usage is still reflected in such words as *message, messenger, mission, missile, missive, missionary, emissary, emission,* and *remission.* Later, mess came to represent food sent from the kitchen to the dining table; then a quantity of soft food (mess of porridge); then a sufficient quantity of a certain kind of food for a dish or a meal (mess of peas). Still later, mess referred to the entire dining situation, including the people sitting at the dining table (the soldiers were at mess). Finally, mess came to denote the various dinnerware, glasses, and dishes, with the unfinished food still clinging to them, which were piled together in a heap after dinner, and thus to represent any general disorganization (what a mess!). We even speak of emotionally disorganized people in this way. (Is he a mess!)

We have a great knack for using old words in new ways. Incidentally, I have found that whether one approves of such new usages or not, it is generally wise to keep abreast of them. Recently, my office was chilly, and I walked into my young secretary's office to ask: "Are you cool in here?" "Crazy man!" she responded gleefully.

The rapidity of the etymological shifts is one reason why learning English is so difficult for foreigners. Although they may have mastered the grammar and the conventional usages (both of which remain relatively constant), they may have trouble keeping up with the ever-changing idiom. Not long ago a student from India enrolled at Northwestern University. On his first day at the university, an American student generously escorted him about the campus, helpfully pointing out the buildings in which the new student would be having classes, the cafeterias, the library, and so on. Finally, they returned to the Indian's dormitory room. When the American had seen that the newcomer was comfortably situated, he left with a cheery, "See you later!" The Indian stayed up until three o'clock in the morning, for he did not want to be so impolite as to retire when his new friend had obviously promised to return!

A Thailander enrolled at another midwestern university. He eagerly waited for an opportunity to meet the university's president, a renowned scholar. Finally, he was granted an appointment. With the utmost solemnity, he walked into the president's office, bowed humbly to the president, and said: "I am most honored to meet with you, sir. I know that you are a very wise guy."

Perhaps someone should have said something to the proprietor of a smart dress shop in Paris who felt that he would entice English-speaking patrons by advertising "Gowns for Streetwalking."

Sometimes the tables are turned. Copywriters for General Motors discovered that "Body by Fisher" became "Corpse by Fisher" in Flemish. Chevy's Nova sold poorly in South America until a name change. *No va* is *no go* in Spanish! And a sales vice president of a large American firm ended a talk to the firm's Spanish-speaking representatives in Colombia with an exuberant and (he thought) supportive declaration: "We at the home office are behind you all the way!" Unfortunately, the instantaneous translation was: "We at the home office are watching your every move!"

Regional Variations.   Word usages vary not only from time to time but from geographic region to region. In his quest for pop, Jimmy learned this the hard way. What a "sweet roll" is in some areas is a "bun" in others and a "Danish" in still others. "Evening" in some parts of the South is the period from noon through twilight. In the rest of the country, however, it generally refers to the period from sunset or from the evening meal to bedtime.

The Pennsylvania Dutch present a special communication problem. These good people speak English all right, but often using a Germanic-type grammar. The results are sometimes quite charming:

"Throw Papa down the stairs his hat."

Girl to her brother chopping wood: "Chonny—come from the woodpile in . . . Mom's on the table still . . . and Pop's et himself already."

But how would you respond to the pleasant chap, standing in front of you in a line at the Lancaster post office, who asks: "If a body goes quick out and comes right aways back in again, will he be where he was yet?" And no one will convince the American motorist that the English speak English.

British	American	British	American
Road Up	Road Repairs	Bump	Collision
Diversion	Detour	Double Bend	S-Curve
Corner	Turning	Dual Carriageway	Divided Highway
No Overtaking	No Passing	Halt	Stop
No Waiting	No Parking	Mews	Alley
Pavement	Sidewalk	Hackney Carriage	Taxi
Bonnet	Hood	Boot	Trunk
Caravan	Trailer	Petrol	Gas

And better carry a *torch* in case you have to change a *tyre* in the dark.

Small wonder that George Bernard Shaw described us as two great nations separated by the barrier of a common language.

It was this transatlantic rift that so effectively stymied a young man who, with his wife and infant son, was visiting England. The robust baby, who was bottle-fed, quickly demolished the supply of nipples that his mother had brought from the States.

Accordingly, father was dispatched to a nearby pharmacy where he asked a buxom clerk: "Do you have nipples?" The young lady stiffened and blushed profusely. Puzzled, my friend tried again: "You know, rubber nipples for a baby bottle?"

The clerk brightened: "Oh, I understand, sir—yes, I have teats."

Now it was the customer's turn to flush over what seemed a thoroughly unnecessary proclamation.

Technical/Common Usage. Specialists (and almost everyone is a specialist to some degree) tend to develop their own private language. Salespeople speak of *closure* (the completion of a sale); plumbers, of *wiping a joint* (applying molten lead with a pad to join pipes); publishers, of *fillers* (short items to fill out columns); television directors, of *stretching* (slowing up to consume time); and laundry personnel, of *mangling* the wash (smoothing it by roller pressure). Ordinarily, these specialists use such terms to good effect when communicating with fellow specialists. Many of these words and phrases, however, are also used by the general public, but in quite different ways. Let the technician forget that the outsider is not accustomed to these words in his specialized sense, and the results are more likely to be confusing at best.

> I learned something of the intricacies of plain English at an early stage in my career. A woman of 35 came in one day to tell me that she wanted a baby but that she had been told that she had a certain type of heart disease which might not interfere with a normal life but would be dangerous if she ever had a baby. From her description I thought at once of mitral stenosis. This condition is characterized by a rather distinctive rumbling murmur near the apex of the heart, and especially by a peculiar vibration felt by the examining finger on the patient's chest. The vibration is known as the "thrill" of mitral stenosis.
>
> When this woman had been undressed and was lying on my table in her white kimono, my stethoscope quickly found the heart-sounds I had expected. Dictating to my nurse, I described them carefully. I put my stethoscope aside and felt intently for the typical vibration which may be found in a small but variable area of the left chest.
>
> I closed my eyes for better concentration, and felt long and carefully for the tremor. I did not find it and with my hand still on the woman's bare breast, lifting it upward and out of the way, I finally turned to the nurse and said: "No thrill."
>
> The patient's black eyes snapped open, and with venom in her voice she said, "Well, isn't that just too bad? Perhaps it's just as well you don't get one. That isn't what I came for."
>
> My nurse almost choked, and my explanation still seems a nightmare of futile words.[4]

Miscommunication is also possible, of course, from specialty to specialty. The dentist's *closure* (the extent to which the upper and lower teeth fit together when the jaw is closed) differs from the salesperson's. And the parliamentarian's *closure* (a method for ending debate and securing an

---

[4] Frederic Loomis, M.D., *Consultation Room* (New York: Alfred A. Knopf, 1939), p. 47.

immediate vote on a measure) differs from both. Consider the machinist who ordered a tree. "What caliper size do you want?" inquired the nurseryman. "About three inches," said the machinist, whose calipers measure *diameters*. The tree man brought a sapling only one inch across, for his calipers measure *circumferences*.

Computers and Multi-Usage.   Because of the multi-usage of words in English (and in many other languages), it is unlikely that computers will replace human translators—at least in the near future. The very precision that the computer requires of its inputs severely limits its ability to cope with a highly ambiguous natural language.[5] For example, when asked to interpret the sentence "Time flies like an arrow," one computer gave several answers including: "Check the speed of flies as fast as you can," and "Certain flies have a fondness for an arrow."

And when computerized translation between natural languages is attempted, the problem is compounded. In one test, the computer received in English, "The spirit is willing, but the flesh is weak." This was translated into Russian as, "The liquor is still good, but the meat has gone bad." In an English-Japanese attempt, the output was "Invisible lunatic." The input? "Out of sight, out of mind."

Fresno Bee editors concede that their word processors are not the ultimate answer. Having pushed the "search-and-replace" key at the wrong time, they had to run the following correction.

> An item . . . made reference to . . . new taxes that will help put Massachusetts "back in the African-American." The item should have said "back in the black."

The Fallacy That Words Have Meanings

The persistent delusion that words have meanings stems from what the late Irving J. Lee called the container myth:

> If you think of words as vessels, then you are likely to talk about "the meaning of a word" as if the meaning were *in* the word. Assuming this, it is easy to endow words with characteristics. Just as you may say that one vessel is costlier or more symmetrical than another, you may say that one word is intrinsically more suitable for one purpose than another, or that, in and of itself, a word will have this or that meaning rather than any other. When one takes this view, he seems to say that meaning is to a word as contents are to a container.[6]

---

[5] In fact, artificial languages such as FORTRAN, ALGOL, COBOL, BASIC, PASCAL, C, C + +, PROLOG, and SQL had to be devised to accommodate the computer.

[6] Irving J. Lee, "On a Mechanism of Misunderstanding," in *Promoting Growth toward Maturity in Interpreting What Is Read*, ed. Gray, Supplementary Educational Monographs, no. 74 (Chicago: University of Chicago Press, 1951), pp. 86-90. Copyright, 1951, by the University of Chicago.

FIGURE 10.2

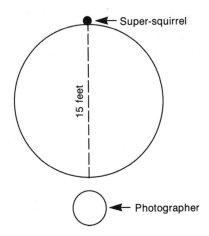

Lee suggested that when a person acts upon the unconscious assumption that words *contain* meanings, he is insidiously led to assume that when he talks (or writes), he is handing his listener (or reader) so many containers of meanings. If this is the case, the recipient is bound to get the correct meanings.

Words, of course, do not contain or have meanings. Apart from the people who use them, words are merely marks on paper, vibrations in the air, raised dots on a Braille card, and so on. Words really do not mean at all—only the users of words can mean something with the words they use. This is a sensible enough statement to accept—*intellectually*. Unfortunately, our *behavior* with words frequently does not abide by it.

But just what *do* words do—or, more precisely, what do people do with them? What happens inside people as they use words? By way of examining this internal verbal behavior, perhaps you will respond to the three questions below.

Question 1. In a redwood forest in northern California stands a huge tree—15 feet in diameter at breast-high level. Clutched to the bark at this level is Super-Squirrel. (Why *Super*-Squirrel will be clear in a moment.) On the opposite side of the tree is a photographer who would like to take Super-Squirrel's picture. (See FIgure 10.2.)

However, when the photographer walks to his right, Super-Squirrel senses the photographer's movement and does the same. When the photographer moves to his left, so does Super-Squirrel. No matter how fast or quietly the man moves, Super-Squirrel is a match for him and manages to keep the tree's diameter between them. The photographer decides to back off a mile or two and sneak in from behind, but the uncanny squirrel detects this as well.

A squirrel hunter would suggest throwing a stone or stick to one side of the tree to scare the squirrel around to the other side. And that might work with an ordinary squirrel, but this is *Super*-Squirrel! Super-Squirrel keeps the tree's diameter between itself and the photographer at all times.

Given: There is no elevation change, such as tree-climbing or mountain climbing, by either Super-Squirrel or the photographer.

The question: Can the photographer circle Super-Squirrel?

Question 2. Would you pay $25 for a slightly used but fully functioning Zalunk?

Question 3. Does $x + 3 = 5$?

I have no way of knowing your answers, but I can report the answers given by more than 5,000 people, including college students, business and government executives, police administrators, military officers, and hospital and medical personnel, distributed among 197 groups. Their answers were confined to three choices: "Yes," "No," and "I don't know."

	Yes	No	I don't know
Question 1 (Super-Squirrel)	61%	37%	2%
Question 2 (Zalunk)	8	31	61
Question 3 (x)	4	2	94

Note two aspects of the above figures:

1. The apparent controversy generated by question 1 in particular. (You might try the Super-Squirrel problem at your next party or coffee break—if you are willing to risk group disintegration!)
2. The rapidly mounting "I don't know" answers and, conversely, the decreasing assurance of answers as we move down through the questions—that is, 98 percent positive answers (yes or no) to question 1 but only 6 percent to question 3.

And yet the three questions share a basic feature. Each contains a key variable, and the question cannot be answered yes or no until that variable is fixed, that is, defined.

The clearest example is question 3. Obviously, the answer is yes, *if* one fixes the variable x as 2—or no, if it is fixed as other than 2. And perhaps that is why there were so few yes or no answers. Since the question-asker did not fix the variable for them, people recognized the active role that they would have to play in fixing it for themselves.

But this was also true of the other two questions. However, significantly fewer people seemed aware that *they* were the variable-fixers. To say yes to the Zalunk question, one (unless answering facetiously) would presumably have had to fix (define) Zalunk as something that was worth $25 to own, or at least to satisfy one's curiosity about. To answer no would require defining Zalunk as not worth $25 to own, and so on.

The question with which responders seemed *least* conscious of their roles as variable-fixers was the first. Many steadfastly held that the photographer could circle the squirrel, and others just as tenaciously claimed that he could *not*. Put these opposing camps in the same room, and observe the decibels rise!

The yes-responders argued that the photographer could walk all the way around the tree. That would cause the squirrel to scamper all the way around it too, so that the photographer's path would encompass the squirrel's route. And that, according to the "Yes-ers," is "circling the squirrel." (See Figure 10.3.)

"Hardly," the no-responders retorted. "Circling the squirrel requires that the photographer orbit the squirrel, with the latter as the orbit's axis—or at least pass around the back of the squirrel. Since the case prohibits the photographer from being on the same side of the tree as the squirrel (to say nothing of the photographer's passing *through* the tree!), this cannot occur. Thus, the photographer cannot circle the squirrel." (See Figure 10.4.)

So either answer is correct, depending upon whose definition we accept.

Now, why do people quarrel over silly, petty questions like this—and even sillier and pettier ones? Partly because they *think* they are disputing *facts*—but they are not. They are disagreeing about what *name* they will give to those facts. The issue is not physical but semantic.

FIGURE 10.3

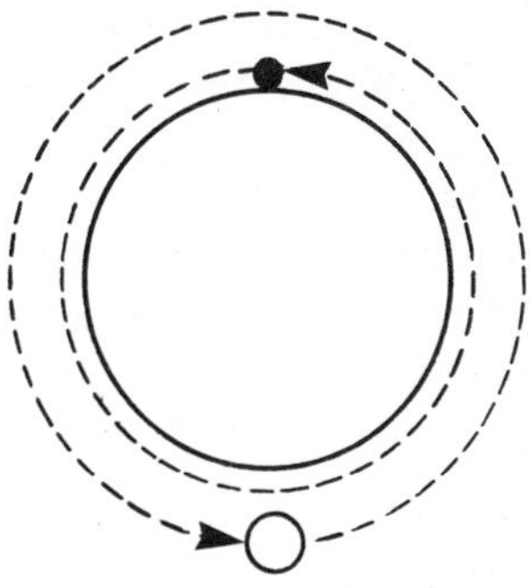

FIGURE 10.4

The cardinal delusion is their belief that words *have* meanings—*apart from the people using them*. Words are just so many meaningless variables—like *x* and *Zalunk*—until someone fixes the variable; that is, chooses to intend or interpret the words in a particular way.

When we assume that words *have* meanings, we fail to realize the active role that the communicator (sender or receiver) plays as a variable-fixer. The communication problem, then, is *not* that people fix variables (i.e., define words), for we could not communicate otherwise. The problem arises only when (1) the speaker (or writer) fixes a variable one way, (2) the listener (or reader) fixes the variable differently, and (3) each assumes that the other is or should be fixing it in the *same* way.

DELIBERATE BYPASSING

Up to now, we have been assuming that the communicators, regardless of their degree of success or failure, *intended* to understand each other. This is not always a warranted assumption. The speaker (or writer) may desire to be bypassed. Or the listener (or reader) may just as earnestly contrive to miss meanings. The motives of the communicators, therefore, must be considered in an analysis of a bypassing.

The story is told of the congressman running for reelection who was speaking before a group of constituents. At the conclusion of his prepared talk, a question came from the floor: "Congressman, you didn't say anything about Social Security. Just how do you feel about Social Security?"

Realizing that his audience was evenly and irreconcilably divided on the issue, he responded with a wink and a knowing smile: "Don't worry about that subject, my friend— I'm all right on that one!"

And *everyone* applauded!

And a certain used-car dealer used purposeful bypassing to his advantage with this advertisement: "Money cheerfully refunded in 24 hours if not satisfied." Some wishful-thinking buyers were convinced that they were being offered an unlimited guarantee on their purchase and that it would require only a day for the dealer to refund their money. Weeks (or days) later, when some of the secondhand autos began to break down, expectant owners approached the dealer, who reported: "The advertisement? Oh, that meant I was giving you a one-day guarantee!"

I nominate for first place among deliberate bypassers the international propagandists who make an art of misunderstanding—and of being misunderstood. Consider this example, which emanates from an international fair. It seems that the Russians were displaying their small car, the Ziss. In the U.S. display was an American subcompact. Someone thought of having an automobile engineer from a neutral nation examine each car carefully and decide which was superior.

"Reverend Benson says for you to call later. He just got into the bathtub."
Parade Magazine. Reprinted by permission.

"You told me to hang your mother's picture in the hallway."
HERMAN COPYRIGHT 1988, Jim Unger. Reprinted with permission of Universal Press Syndicate.

The engineer decided in favor of the American auto. However, the Russian news agency triumphantly reported the news to the home folks in these words: "In comparative tests of Russian and foreign automobiles, the Russian Ziss placed second while the American car was next to last."

My fond hope is that with the advent of *glasnost* that example will soon be obsolete.

I would award honorable (perhaps it should be dishonorable) mention for intentional bypassing to the pedestrian who was arrested in Washington, D.C., for walking on the "Don't Walk" sign. His alibi in court was that he thought the sign was an advertisement for the taxi company!

Purposeful bypassing can be used constructively as well. Take the case of a certain labor-management conciliator. The union contract had only a week to run. The union had adamantly refused to discuss terms with management and was preparing to strike. When the conciliator asked union officials why they had refused to bargain, he was told: "Why, we want a substantial increase [they told him confidentially that this meant $2 to $3 per hour], and we're dead sure management won't go along with us, so why waste time?" Nothing the conciliator could say would persuade them to meet with management. Finally, he turned to the company, where he was told in confidence that it was willing to give $1. "Would you say this would be a 'substantial increase' "? he asked. "It certainly would be," he was assured. He then returned to the union officials and reported that the company was willing to talk in terms of a "substantial increase." With that, he was able to coax the union's representatives to meet with the company's. With his guidance, the two parties were able to reach a compromise in time to avert a strike that neither side wanted.

Of course, the *receiver* of communication may bypass intentionally just as readily as the *sender*. Our legal system takes this into account by insisting that a law must be obeyed not merely in accord with its letter (words) but with its spirit (intent). The law recognizes that the letter of even the most cautiously written statute may be subject to willful misinterpretation.

Gobbledygook

Before leaving the topic of intentional miscommunication we should consider gobbledygook. This is the smoke-screen kind of communication which, through the use of technical jargon, involved sentences, and polysyllabic words, seems more calculated to obscure than to inform.

In the pursuit of total organizational flexibility and integrated management mobility, one must consider such factors as systematized transitional capability and synchronized logistical programming as well as parallel reciprocal contingencies. Perhaps, however, the most significant factor of all is the basic balanced policy concept. For after all without optional digital and incremental projections the network is by and large merely a functional second- or third-generation time-phase continuum.

If that has you reeling, it has served its purpose. Erudite, sophisticated—but utterly nonsensical. I composed it from the now famous (infamous?) Systematic Buzz Phrase Projector, which purportedly originated in the Royal Canadian Air Force. For aid in constructing your own esoteric prolixities and verbose amphibolies, here are the raw materials:

Column 1	Column 2	Column 3
0. integrated	0. management	0. options
1. total	1. organizational	1. flexibility
2. systematized	2. monitored	2. capability
3. parallel	3. reciprocal	3. mobility
4. functional	4. digital	4. programming
5. responsive	5. logic	5. concept
6. optical	6. transitional	6. time-phase
7. synchronized	7. incremental	7. projection
8. compatible	8. third-generation	8. hardware
9. balanced	9. policy	9. contingency

Simply think of a three-digit number, and select the corresponding buzz words from the three columns above. For example, 230 produces "systematized reciprocal options," an expression bound to bring instant impressiveness—and confusion.

The New Yorker has the delightful policy of reprinting material that has appeared elsewhere—then adding its own, usually acerbic, comment.

APPLIED THEOLOGY 142. Sociology of Religion and Teaching.

This is a macro/micro humanistic approach to the sociology of religion and teaching containing four components: (1) Examination of historical paradigms; (2) Field studies of radical sociological change in religious states; (3) Analysis of social-cultural continuities and discontinuities, derived and underived religious posturing, dimensions of tension, crisis confluence and synthesis in cross-cultural states; (4) A correlation of sociology and teaching enabling the student to distill transcendent processes as well as to develop a more cogent language of religion in the context of educational goals. *Harvard Divinity School* catalog.

The New Yorker's response? "Those who pass go straight to heaven."

Gobbledygook leads not so much to miscommunication as to noncommunication. It is often the refuge of insecure writers (or speakers). (If you can't say it clearly and simply, to paraphrase composer Jean Sibelius, you don't understand it.) Unsure of what they mean or of how their ideas will be received, they—like the proverbial cuttlefish—evade their enemies by disappearing in a cloud of ink.

But whether bypassing be purposeful or not, the pattern of miscommunication is essentially the same and the corrective measures are equally applicable.

CORRECTIVES

These techniques will not eradicate all harmful bypassing, but they can prevent a great deal of it:

1. Be person-minded, not word-minded.
2. Query and paraphrase.
3. Be approachable.
4. Use backup methods.
5. Sender: Employ the PTA.
6. Receiver: Practice the PRA.
7. Delay a day.
8. Get and provide the "telling" response.
9. Be sensitive to contexts.

Make these techniques habitual. Make them your conditioned response to a communication situation. Consider them as the finely tempered muscles of the athlete. Even after these habits have been established, they must be practiced and strengthened daily.

Be Person-Minded—Not Word-Minded

Communicators who habitually look for meanings in the people using the words, rather than in the words themselves, are much less prone to bypass or to be bypassed. They realize that the important issue in communication is not what the words mean, but what the *user* means by them. When alert communicators talk or write, they are aware that their listeners or readers may *not* necessarily interpret the senders' words as they mean them. When they listen or read, they are aware that the speaker or writer may have intended the words other than as they (the receivers) are interpreting them at the moment. They recognize that communication involves variable-fixing by the sender—and by the receiver.

To keep person-minded in your communications, frequently ask yourself:

This is what it means to me, but what does it, or will it, mean to them?

What would I mean if I were in another's shoes?

Does my interpretation of their words coincide with their viewpoint (as I see it)?

Are the sender and receiver fixing the variables in the same way?

Query and Paraphrase

Query the Speaker or Writer.   Some of the best parental advice children receive somehow becomes lost as they grow older. Almost everyone has been told: "If you don't understand your teachers, ask them what they mean." But as time goes on, something happens to us. We evidently become too inhibited or proud or embarrassed to ask others what they mean.

A common complaint among my colleagues in college teaching is that students do not ask enough questions in the classroom—the very place where questions should abound![7] It is almost as if we believed that asking a question of a speaker or writer (assuming that circumstances permit) would lead them to doubt our intelligence! Nothing could be farther from the truth. Professors and executives alike indicate that they respect a thoughtful question. To them it indicates interest and a sense of responsibility rather than stupidity.

To be sure, some managers (and teachers) resent questions from subordinates. But more about that later under the heading "Be approachable."

So, ask questions when:

---

[7] Business executives express much the same concern. "What do you have to do to get people to ask questions?" a vice president of a manufacturing firm asks. "If people would only make *sure* they got it straight, we'd save five hundred thousand dollars a year."

1. You don't understand or can't make sense of what you have heard or read.
2. You think there may be a legitimate interpretation other than the one which first occurred to you.
3. You sense something out of alignment—something that doesn't quite mesh with the rest of your knowledge of a situation.

A special suggestion for the boss: You can ask questions, too, but avoid closed-ended questions. They often begin with *do* or *is* and can be too easily answered with *yes* or *no*. Then you still don't know if your receivers have understood you or how they feel about your message. Ask the open-ended question that cannot be answered with the communication stopping mono-syllable. You encourage your people to give a fuller, more honest indication of their comprehension and feelings.

Closed-ended: Did you understand me? Is that clear?
Open-ended: How would you go about doing that?
    What's your reaction to that idea?

Paraphrase the Speaker or Writer. Putting a speaker's or writer's communication into your own words and asking if your paraphrasing is acceptable is one of the oldest, simplest, most useful, and most neglected techniques in communication.

I once observed a fascinating series of business meetings in which the technique of paraphrasing was put to a special use. The meetings involved the regular executive conferences of a certain firm, but a new touch had been added. An outsider was engaged to serve as moderator. The requirements were that the moderator be reasonably intelligent, have a good memory for spoken communication, and develop the knack of paraphrasing the statement of another without making embellishments, judgments, deletions, or additions.

This is how it worked. The agenda having been set up previously, the meeting began with the moderator stating, "Ladies and gentlemen, the meeting is convened. Who would like to begin?" Some of the participants raised their hands, and the moderator recognized, say, Executive A, who then made a statement. Then, before anyone else was permitted to speak, the moderator paraphrased A's remarks. A would now either accept the moderator's rephrasing as accurate (in which case the next person would be permitted to speak) or correct it. In the latter case, the moderator would then paraphrase A's correction, which A would either accept or correct, and so on, until A accepted the moderator's paraphrasing without qualification.

After A and the moderator agreed on A's communication, any other member was permitted to query or paraphrase what had been said if he or she were still in doubt about A's meaning.

The procedure sounds laborious, and indeed it was for the first few meetings. But soon, this group of executives was holding conferences (which had been notorious for their miscommunications) with startling equanimity and progress. I have never experienced group discussions with so few instances of bypassing; moreover, many potential bypassings were revealed by the moderator's rewordings. An additional benefit, according to the executives involved, was that with the moderator's paraphrasings, the speaker was assured that at least one other person in the room understood fully what was said—a very satisfying and previously infrequent experience!

The meetings, it is true, were somewhat longer[8] than usual, but who can estimate the amounts of time and the money, effort, and nervous tension saved by thus preventing miscommunications?

The simple techniques of the query and the paraphrase can be potent defenses against bypassing. But discretion must be exercised. Occasionally a person may go to absurd lengths, making the techniques an end in themselves rather than a means toward clarifying communication.

A "Peanuts" cartoon a few years ago made the point aptly. It showed Charlie Brown greeting Linus, who was making a snowman in his backyard. The dialogue, box by box, went approximately like this:

Charlie: Hi, Linus. Did you have a good Christmas?
Linus: What do you mean: "Did I have a good Christmas?"
Linus: Do you mean, did I get a lot of good presents?
Linus: Or do you mean did I have a good time with all my cousins who came to visit?
Linus: Or do you mean was it good in a spiritual sense?
Linus: Or do you mean . . .
Charlie: (*Sigh*)

Be Approachable

The Responsibilities of the Sender.   So far we have been discussing the techniques of querying and paraphrasing from the receiver's point of view; that is, how the listener or reader should use them. But communication is a two-way street, with responsibilities at both ends. Senders (speakers, writers) should do their utmost to make querying and paraphrasing possible. They should not only permit it or make themselves *approachable*—they should encourage it, invite it—even, on some occasions, insist on it.

But some people in positions of responsibility are threatened by feedback. They may feel so insecure or so poorly versed in their field that they

---

[8] Frequently, of course, B's reaction to A's statement was delayed by the moderator's interposition. For the special value of such delays, read, "Correctives," Chapter 18.

regard a question as a challenge that they must ward off. Ironically, such defensiveness often leads to even more destructive consequences than those feared.

For under the best of circumstances, most subordinates are somewhat inhibited in dealing with their superiors. Conditioned by past experiences with authority figures and regarding the boss as the reward-controller, the subordinate tends to be circumspect in communicating upward. So when a manager deliberately—or unwittingly—becomes unapproachable, the boss virtually assures the strangulation of the channel upward.

To the extent that communicating upward to the boss is perceived as dangerous, painful, embarrassing, or unpleasant, the upward flow of communication will be curtailed and filtered. The boss just won't get the bad news until it becomes so bad that it can no longer be concealed—until there is, indeed, a real problem.

Supervisors who thus contribute to an "approachability gap" between themselves and their people are doing a disservice to those people, to their organizations, and particularly to themselves. They are brewing their own poisons.

At the risk of appearing kindergartenish, I often urge people with responsibilities to paste a sign on their respective bathroom mirrors.

It simply asks:

> ## ARE YOU APPROACHABLE?

I hope it will trigger a daily self-examination.

Am I approachable?[9] Do my people[10] really feel free to query, paraphrase, and, in general, communicate with me? Have I done everything possible to make their channel to me free and clear—and do I *keep* it that way? Do I make an extra effort to be approachable to more timid, reticent people?[11] Am I *genuinely* receptive to feedback, and do I continually communicate my receptivity to others?

Strictly speaking, the admonition should be to *attain* and *maintain* approachability—two verbs. For approachability is a form of trust. And trust is a precious and fragile commodity, hard to build sometimes but

---

[9] Lest current or aspiring managers absolve themselves too readily—"My people really feel free with me"—let them consider the frequent discrepancy between the subordinate's perception of the freedom to communicate up to the boss and the boss's perception of that freedom.

[10] By "my people" I mean the manager's immediate subordinates—those who report directly to him/her. By no means am I advocating violating the chain of command.

[11] This emphasis on receptivity is not intended to retard the development and maturation of employees. The manager must use discretion to assure an open communication channel without inducing excessive dependence on the part of subordinates.

easily destroyed. And once trust is abused, it usually becomes singularly difficult to rebuild. So we have to work to achieve approachability and keep working to maintain it.

Use Backup Methods

I am frequently asked: "Which is the best communication method?" The best method depends upon the circumstances, of course, but there is no perfect method—each method has its limitations. A face-to-face conversation, for example, has many advantages. If you and I are sitting opposite one another over a coffee table, we have a good deal going for us. Beyond the language of words, we are also communicating with facial expressions, postures, gestures, and vocal inflections, to say nothing of subliminal clues that we may be sending and receiving. In addition, we have the immediate opportunity to assess one another's reception of our respective messages. If I say something and see a furrowed brow or a whimsical smile, I can ask for further feedback: "How do you feel about that?"

None of these extras would we have if I were, say, sending you a memo, letter, or a report. On the other hand, what we *don't* have is a *record* of our communication. And if it becomes evident a week later that, despite the advantage of our face-to-face chat, we bypassed, can you visualize the futile, irreconcilable debate that would be likely to follow: "Don't you remember? You said this!" "No, I didn't. I said that!"

Since no method is perfect, the obvious strategy is to shore up the inadequacies of one method with the strengths of another. Use multiple methods. In this case, how about having one or both of us jot down the salient points of our conversation and send a copy to the other? Sure, it takes time and effort—scarce commodities in most organizations. But when we consider that top administrative officers estimate that the cost of miscommunication ranges between 25 and 40 percent of budget, can we afford not to take the time and effort?

Sender: Employ the PTA

This stands for *pre-transmission audit*. It is applicable when you have the time to prepare a message in advance—such as a memo, a letter, a report, or an oral presentation. After you have composed the message but before you deliver it to your final recipient, get a third party—a friend, a secretary, your spouse—to check it for bypassing possibilities. Ideally, this auditor ought to be objective and ought to have the same relevant background as your final decoder. The point is that when we prepare messages, they frequently sound entirely intelligible and acceptable—inside our own heads. Some of this feeling could be wishful thinking—we would dearly want the receiver to interpret the message that way. The somber fact is that we are generally *not* the best judges of the adequacy of our own communiqués.

Receiver: Practice the PRA

This stands for *post-reception audit*. It is the same idea as the PTA, except that you get your auditor to check the message after you have received it but before you take action on it. Here again, the relative outsider might spot potential bypassings that had eluded you on first reading (or hearing).

Delay a Day

If the situation is emotional and if possible, delay a day before sending your message or before acting on a received message. Write it up and lock it up—for a day. The value of incubation is illustrated in Chapter 18, "Undelayed Responses (Snap Reactions)." Very often the quality of encoding and decoding can be improved if one takes the time to sleep on the message.

Get and Provide the "Telling" Response

If you are sending the message, it's up to you to get a "telling" response from your recipient—a response that tells you how the other person is decoding your message. What counts is not what was in your head or even what you said or wrote. The final arbiter in communication is how the receiver interprets the message. Conversely, if you are the receiver, then your primary responsibility is to *provide* that telling response to your sender. It takes two (at least) to communicate. Each has a mutual responsibility to make the communication succeed.

Be Sensitive to Contexts

In view of the incredible amount of ambiguity in our language, it is surprising that we communicate as well as we do. Our primary aid is *context*—the surrounding words (verbal context) and the surrounding circumstances (situational context). The context provides the prime body of clues that we use to interpret each other's messages.

Context \ 'kän-,tekst \ *n* [ME, weaving together of words, fr. L *contextus* connection of words, coherence, fr. *contextus,* pp. of *contexere* to weave together, fr. *com- + texere* to weave—more at TECHNICAL] (1568) **1** : the parts of a discourse that surround a word or passage and can throw light on its meaning [verbal context]**2** : the interrelated conditions in which something exists or occurs [situational context]: ENVIRONMENT, SETTING[12]

---

[12] From *Webster's Ninth New Collegiate Dictionary* (Springfield, Mass.: Merriam-Webster, Inc., 1986). Reprinted with permission.

This is how it works. (To get the best effect from this demonstration, cover up the remaining lines on this page and reveal one line at a time.)

A single word or short phrase is like a single piece of a jigsaw puzzle—difficult to understand until you combine it with other pieces. Suppose that I say simply: "one eighty-three." You might feel that you have no idea of what I mean. Actually, you probably have too many ideas. It may occur to you that I might mean:

- A bowling (hopefully not a golf) score.
- A street address.
- A price—$1.83 or $183. If a Realtor® says it, you might interpret the number as $183,000!
- A page in a book.
- A highway route.
- Miles per hour at, say, the Indianapolis Speedway.
- A temperature in Celcius or Farenheit.
- A length in inches, feet, yards, or miles. Or in millimeters, centimeters, meters, or kilometers.
- A post office box number.
- The atomic weight of a chemical element in the periodic table.
- A hotel room.

But suppose that I start adding a few words; that is, adding verbal context. Note how quickly you create a meaningful interpretation of "one-eighty-three" as you combine the jigsaw pieces:

First, *pounds of weight.*
Then, *woman.*
Then, *five feet tall.*
Then, *17 years old.*
Finally, *sitting in her doctor's office waiting for an appointment.*

Let us take a more detailed look at the role of verbal context.

Verbal Context.   Suppose that I overhear two men talking. However, they are so far away that the only word I pick up is *plufe.* What under the sun did they mean? The men are drawing closer, and now I hear: "Say, Ralph, could you plufe me a dollar? I'll pay it back tomorrow." Then later: "It was raining last night when I landed at O'Hare. So the stewardess plufed me an umbrella, to get from the plane to the terminal."

While I may wonder at that strange word, I am now reasonably confident that I understand what they are saying. But why? No one defined "plufe." No one said "This is what I mean by plufe . . ." I guessed at what the men meant by this term from the verbal context in which it occurred. Using the surrounding words as clues, I zeroed in from an almost unlimited number of possible interpretations to one—a synonym for lend.

Verbal context is not limited to the accompanying words in a sentence, but consists of the neighboring sentences, paragraphs, and so on, as well. If you hold up an object and ask: "What's this?" the appropriate response might be "off-white," "a shirt," "$17.50," or "broadcloth," depending upon whether we had been talking about colors, classifications of garments, prices, or fabrics.

It is largely the verbal context by which we deduce what others mean (how they are fixing the variables)—and how they interpret what we mean.

Sometimes, however, we are admonished to reduce the verbal context—"boil it down," "be concise," "don't camouflage your meaning with excessive verbiage." Pliny the Elder confessed: "I am writing you at length because I do not have time to write a short letter." The Lord's Prayer consists of 56 words and the Gettysburg Address has 266. But the Pentagon somehow needed 16 single-spaced pages of specifications for a plastic whistle used by military police and drill instructors and 18 pages for a recipe for a Christmas fruitcake!

Can you devise clearer and more economical expressions of the following sentiments?

> Do not, however disadvantageous the circumstances, permit yourselves to be forced into a position in which you must acquiesce in the transfer of ownership of this vessel to persons owing allegiance to a country whose interests are inimical to those of ours.
>
> I must be given maximum latitude to enjoy the benefits of our country, unfettered by degrading restrictions on my activities; if I am denied this privilege I would prefer to be permanently deprived of the exercise of my viable functions.
>
> "Don't give up the ship" and "Give me liberty, or give me death," respectively, would do very nicely.

Obviously, discretion must be exercised by the sender, who must avoid unnecessarily long and repetitious communications, for they can be as confusing as if they were intended to deceive.

Dr. George Russell Harrison recalled this incident:

> A plumber of foreign extraction wrote the National Bureau of Standards and said he found that hydrochloric acid quickly opened plugged drainage pipes and inquired if that was a good thing to use. A scientist at the Bureau replied that "the efficacy of hydrochloric acid is indisputable, but the corrosive residue is incompatible with metallic permanence."

The plumber wrote back thanking the Bureau for telling him that hydrochloric acid was all right. The scientist was disturbed about the misunderstanding and showed the correspondence to his boss—another scientist—who wrote the plumber: "We cannot assume responsibility for the production of toxic and noxious residue with hydrochloric acid and suggest you use an alternative procedure."

The plumber wrote back thanking the Bureau for telling him that hydrochloric works fine. Greatly disturbed, the scientists took their problem to the top boss. He broke with scientific jargon and wrote the plumber: "Don't use hydrochloric acid. It eats hell out of pipes."

But an equal if not greater danger lurks in *under*—communication which provides such scanty context that bypassing is virtually invited. This memorandum appeared briefly on a federal agency bulletin board:

> Those department heads who do not have the services of full-time secretaries may take advantage of the stenographers in the secretarial pool.

One wonders if that was an inadvertent invitation to bypassing, or do our federal friends have perks of which we are unaware?

Because of the necessity for conciseness, signs are particularly vulnerable targets for bypassing. Among my collection: Sign over a combination greasy-spoon diner and gasoline station:

> Eat Here And Get Gas

One wonders whether the proprietor was (1) obtuse, (2) banking on others sharing his sense of humor, or (3) issuing a fair warning.

Sign outside a church announcing a forthcoming sermon:

> Do You Know
> What Hell Is?
> Come hear our
> new organist.

Another church sign:

> If You're Tired Of
> Sin—Come In

Penciled beneath: "If you're not—phone 366-5619."

In the interests of sanitation and aesthetics this sign was posted in a University of Colorado cafeteria:

> ## Shoes Are Required To Eat In The Cafeteria

Added gratuitously was: "Socks can eat wherever they want."
This sign appeared at a dingy nightclub:

> ## Clean and Decent Dancing
> ## Every Night Except Sunday

The unsolicited addition: "You must do a big business on Sundays!"
If you visit Myrtle Beach, S.C., stop in at Dave's Bait and Tackle Shop.
In addition to the usual necessities for fishing, Dave's features sandwiches, beer—and a remarkable sign:

> ## DAVES
> ## EAT
> ## WORMS

Evidently, gentlemen there with a certain first name have unusual
dining habits. If you catch them at a meal it might make an unforgettable
part of your trip.

And while we're in the category, Harry's Fly, Bait, and Tackle Shop
(address mercifully withheld) was recently burned. The local newspaper
announced that repairs had been completed and Harry's Fly is now open.

And finally, this sign at a power station in Ireland:

> ## To Touch These Overhead
> ## Cables Means Instant Death
> Offenders will be prosecuted.

Which seems only just for such a shocking offense.

Classified advertisements are another fertile field for inadvertent
bypassing. The ad placer, keen on reducing costs, reduces his context:

Apartment for Rent, View takes in 4 counties, 2 bedrooms.
For Sale: 1979 Cadillac hearse. Body in good condition.
For Sale: Large Great Dane. Registered pedigree. Will eat anything.
  Especially fond of children.
Wanted: Dynamite handler. Must be prepared to travel unexpectedly.

Quoting out of Context. Lifting words or even sentences, paragraphs, and chapters out of context is a well-known ploy of propagandists and others who seek to distort communication. This is hardly a new deceit. Witness this circular used by Republicans in the campaign of 1928:

> They quoted an article from the presumably unbiased *Encyclopaedia Britannica* (11th ed., Vol. XXVI, p. 392), to show the corruption of Tammany Hall, and the danger of putting a member of the Tammany Society in the presidential chair. They quite failed, however, to quote the very relevant final sentence of the *Britannica* article, namely: "The power of the organization in the state and in the nation is due to its frequent combination with the Republican organization, which controls the state almost as completely as Tammany does the city."[13]

Quoting into Context. Wordsmiths are still using elections as opportunities to persuade the electorate to vote their way. The larger, if less glamorous, part of the Chicago area ballot in 1984 involved 35 incumbent judges of the Cook County Circuit Court. Voters were to decide which of them should be retained. For several days preceding the election, newspapers carried an advertisement.

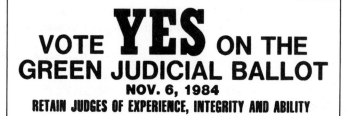

The judges were listed and each name was followed by **YES** and the candidate's ballot number. Also, three dignitaries were quoted:

> "I strongly urge all voters to retain qualified judges on the Judicial Retention Ballot." Governor James R. Thompson
>
> Mayor Harold Washington says: "It takes a YES vote of 60 percent to retain a judge on the bench. I HOPE AND URGE MY SUPPORTERS AND FRIENDS TO VOTE UNANIMOUSLY TO RETAIN THOSE GOOD JUDGES THAT ARE ON THE JUDICIAL RETENTION BALLOT."
>
> U.S. District Attorney Dan Webb says: "I personally know many of the judges that are running on this retention ballot. In my opinion, there are

---

[13] Edwin Leavitt Clarke, *The Art of Straight Thinking: A Primer of Scientific Method for Social Inquiry* (New York: Appleton-Century-Crofts, 1929), p. 348. Reprinted by permission of Appleton-Century-Crofts, Inc.

judges on this particular retention ballot that are among the finest jurists in our nation."

A quick impression of the overall context of the ad, highlighted by the large heading and the long and conspicuous columns of yeses, would lead the reader to believe that the governor, the mayor, and the district attorney had enthusiastically endorsed all of the candidates. But a more careful interpretation of the statements is that the endorsers had left it to the public to determine which were "qualified" and "good" and "finest."

Little wonder that Thompson et al. were cautious. The candidates had been evaluated by several interested organizations and some had been found wanting. Fifteen of the 35 received a "not recommended" or "not qualified" appraisal from one or more organizations. One judge was rejected by the Chicago Bar Association, the Chicago Council of Lawyers, the Cook County Bar Association, the Women's Bar Association of Illinois, and the West Suburban Bar Association!

Now, who devised this artful ad? Perhaps it was lack of pride of authorship, but you might need your magnifying glass to read Paid for by the 1984 Judicial Retention Committee at the bottom of the ad.

Did the ad work? Receiving a higher than average vote (77–84 percent) all 35 were retained!

Returning to the issue of inadvertent bypassing—an answer to the problem of insufficient verbal contexts is, of course, for the sender to provide and/or the receiver to obtain enough related information to determine the intent of the excerpt.

In conclusion, be sensitive to verbal contexts, the surrounding words and sentences that may help to determine the meaning of any word, phrase, or passage. Ask yourself: Is this word, phrase, and so on, taken out of its verbal context? Might I interpret it differently if I knew what went before or after it? Am I giving my receiver sufficient (but not too much) context to understand my communication?

Situational Context. What lies beyond the context of words and phrases? How does this communication fit into the larger framework of people and happenings? Make a habit of orienting yourself toward the situational context of the message.

Not to absolve Janet DuFore (see page 268), but if Jane Dover had been more aware of the overall situation she might have approached her supervisor with this paraphrasing:

My understanding is that Elizabeth will be out again tomorrow and that you want me to complete her bookkeeping before work begins tomorrow morning. Is that correct?

This would prompt DuFore to clarify her message and that bypassing could have been nipped in the bud. All of this presumes that DuFore would indeed have been *approachable* (see pp. 292–94).

If the situational context is clear and mutually understood, we may need very little *verbal* communication. The epitome of this was perhaps the exchange of messages between Victor Hugo and his publishers. In 1862, after completing his monumental *Les Misérables*, Hugo went on holiday. Anxious to know how the novel was selling, he wrote Hurst and Blackett. His letter consisted of simply "?" Knowing what was uppermost in the author's mind, the publishers responded with "!"

NONVERBAL AMBIGUITY

The focus of this chapter, and of the whole of Part Three, is on *verbal* communication. But nonverbal exchanges can be ambiguous, too, especially when we try to communicate interculturally. An intriguing book by Morris et al. lists 20 widely used gestures.[14] What is intended by the gesturer may vary greatly in different parts of the world. It may even be equivocal within a limited area.

For example, among other meanings, the thumb-up gesture can be perceived as: OK—all is well; simply one; a sexual insult; a hitchhike request; and a direction. The authors suggest hitchhikers avoid this gesture in northern Greece and southern Sardinia. It is likely to be interpreted as "get stuffed" and does not encourage drivers to stop, except to pick a fight. They recommend a loosely waved, flat-hand gesture as practiced by the local hitchhikers.

SUMMARY

Bypassing occurs when communicators miss each other's meanings. It may take place when they use the same word to mean different things or when they use different words to mean the same thing. The effects of bypassing may range from the trivial and humorous to the serious and even catastrophic. In general, the immediate consequence of a bypassing may be either an apparent agreement on meanings when a disagreement actually exists, or an apparent disagreement when an agreement actually exists.

---

[14] Desmond Morris, Peter Collett, Peter Marsh, and Marie O'Shaughnessy, *Gestures* (New York: Stein and Day, 1979), p. 195. See also, "The International Language of Gestures," *Psychology Today*, May 1984; and Roger E. Axtell, ed., *Do's and Taboos Around the World* (New York: John Wiley & Sons, 1987).

Basically a person bypasses because of the assumption, usually unconscious, that words mean the same to other persons. Underlying this assumption are two insidious fallacies. The first fallacy, that words have mono-usage, thrives despite the manifest multi-usage of so many words in our language. The second fallacy is that words *have* meanings. This fallacy obscures the fact that words are not containers of meaning but rather are variables to be fixed (defined) by those who use words in sending and receiving messages. In this sense, bypassing occurs when (1) the sender fixes a variable one way, (2) the receiver fixes it another way, and (3) each assumes that the other is fixing the variable in the identical way. Deliberate bypassing was acknowledged. It is relatively easy to misunderstand or to be misunderstood, if one intends to do so.

Several commonsense but uncommonly used techniques are effective in curbing bypassing. (1) Be person-minded—not word-minded; (2) query and paraphrase; (3) be approachable; (4) use backup methods; (5) employ the PTA; (6) practice the PRA; (7) delay a day; (8) get and provide the "telling" response; (9) be sensitive to contexts (verbal and situational). To be truly effective, these techniques must become deeply embedded habits which, in a sense, are on the alert even when we are not.

Discussion Questions

1. If you were looking for a church to join and were invited to a church that professed to be based on communistic beliefs, would you:
a. Refuse the invitation?
b. Report the group to the proper authorities?
c. Take some other action? If so, what?

2. Our Declaration of Independence states that "all men are created equal," but evidence clearly indicates that babies are born with great variations in mental and physical capacities. Discuss the apparent discrepancy.

3. During a discussion among friends, someone suggests that "more socialistic concepts should be incorporated into our federal government." Then he turns to you and says: "What do you think?" How would you respond?

4. Doing some research on differing socioeconomic classes, you spend a couple of weeks in a tiny and remote village in Appalachia. These people refer to their shoes as "holy bibles." How would you respond to this? Why?

5. Precisely what is entailed in bypassing?

6. What unconsciously held, fallacious assumptions contribute to bypassing?

7. Why might people find these assumptions attractive?

8. How can one prevent bypassing? As sender? As receiver?

9. How can you help others to avoid bypassing without insulting their intelligence?

10. "Our communication would be just as effective if the large sphere in the sky that shines at night were called 'the sun,' if children who wear dresses were called 'boys,' and if members of the Republican party were called 'communists.' " How do you respond to this assertion? Why?

11. "Words mean the same to the other person as they do to me." Why would communicators make this assumption?

12. The words *davenport, bloomers, boycott,* and *quixotic* have what in common?

13. What did G. B. Shaw mean when he defined England and the United States as "two great nations separated by the barrier of a common language"? Can you think of analogous situations?

14. What are the principal advantage and the principal limitation of computer languages compared to such natural languages as English?

15. Give an example of deliberate bypassing. Are there walks of life in which deliberate bypassing tends to be practiced? Is deliberate bypassing ever defensible ethically?

16. Discuss the techniques for reducing bypassing. Are there limitations to their use? Can you think of other preventives?

17. Regarding the "Product-Information Program," (Case 10.2) which pictures— Steger's or Robbins'—was more correct? Explain your answer.

18. Describe an incident, possibly involving yourself, in which bypassing occurred. Analyze specifically why it occurred, what might have been done to prevent its occurrence, and what measures would prevent its recurrence.

CASES

CASE 10.1

Was There a Noise?*

In Sweet Esther, Wisconsin, Bert Johnson and Fred Carter were hauled into court on a disorderly conduct charge. They had been picked up fighting in a drugstore. When the judge asked them for their story, Johnson replied:

"Well, your honor, we're neighbors, and Carter, here, told me he was goin' down to the drugstore—and did I want anything? I said I'd go along with him.

"Well, sir, on the way down Carter says, 'I got a puzzle I bet a dollar you can't figure out—now suppose lightning strikes a tree in the middle of the forest and the tree falls down. Now, there ain't no animals or birds or insects or people or instruments anywhere near the tree. So was there a noise when it fell?'

"Well, quick as a wink I says: 'Sure, there's a noise—it don't matter if people ain't there.' Then Carter gets on one of them superior grins of his and says: 'I guess you ain't as bright as you think you are—there ain't no noise if nobody can hear it.' "

The two men glared at each other, and Johnson continued: "Well, you know how it is, your honor—I'm sayin' there's a noise and Carter sayin' there ain't, and we start talkin' louder and louder—one thing leads to another—I guess I gave Carter a little shove—then he shoved me—and so on and so on—only by this time we were in the drugstore, and I guess we messed the place up a bit."

Discussion Questions

1. Was there a noise when the tree fell?

2. What must you do in order to answer yes or no to that question?

3. When groups discuss the noise question, there are often disagreements. Why? What assumptions to discussants often make?

4. What does this case have to do with bypassing?

---

* The case is fictitious, but hardly unrealistic.

CASE 10.2

The Product-Information Program*

The Meridian Corporation is a leading manufacturer of television and radio receivers, VCRs, camcorders, cellular telephones, and other electronic products. It had been the policy of the firm to hold an annual national convention to which its 200 district distributors were invited and which they attended at company expense. One of the more important events of the convention was the Product-Information Program. This program consisted of a speech coupled with whatever visual aids (videocassettes, motion pictures, sound-slide films, and so on) were appropriate. The purpose of the program was to introduce the new models and to explain their features.

Each distributor was given a duplicate set of materials (script, video or audiocassette, films, recordings, and so on) so that he or she could stage a similar Product-Information Program for the district salespersonnel.

To accomplish this, the materials were reproduced 200 times and shipped to the distributors' respective home addresses while they were still in conference. Thus, on returning home, they would be able to commence their own Product-Information Program meetings immediately. Beginning the meetings immediately was essential if the salespeople were to be able to capitalize upon the national advertising campaign conducted by the firm simultaneously with the conclusion of the convention.

Daniel Steger, merchandising manager of Meridian, was usually in charge of preparing and presenting the Product-Information Program at the national convention. He would write the script and ordinarily engaged the Raymond Company, an audiovisual aids firm in the city, to prepare his other materials. On this occasion he needed a rather lengthy sound-slide film. A month before the convention, Ted Robbins, a technician from Raymond, and Steger went over the plans for the film in detail. Robbins submitted sketches for each frame, which Steger approved.

Two weeks later, Steger phoned Robbins.

S: Say, Robbins, is it too late to add another frame to our film?
R: No, I don't think so—what do you have in mind?
S: Well, this comes between the 16th and 17th frames, so we'll call it frame number 16A. I would like a picture of a stationary core with three or four small dots circling around it—do you get what I mean?
R: Sure, no problem.
S: I was hoping you'd say that because our fax machine is down right now.

---

* All names have been disguised.

R: Well, then, don't bother. Any other changes?

S: None that I can think of.

R: OK, fine, we'll add 16A, and you'll have the finished product the day before the convention.

S: Can't make it any sooner?

R: 'Fraid not—we're swamped already.

S: OK then—make that change, and I'll see you in two weeks.

The sound-slide film was delivered on schedule on the day before the convention. Steger previewed it, and when frame number 16A appeared, he stared in amazement. This is what he saw:

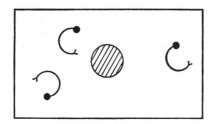

This is what he had in mind when he had phoned Robbins two weeks earlier:

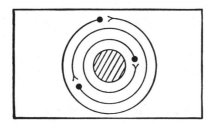

Steger jumped to the phone and demanded that the frame be changed. The Raymond Company assigned a double crew which worked the rest of the day, all of the night, and half of the next morning to replace the 200 sound-slide films and to deliver a copy to a badly shaken Steger, barely in time for him to make his appearance before the convention. The total cost of replacing the films was $6,250.

Discussion Questions

1. How do you analyze what happened?

2. Can you draw still another picture that would satisfy the "stationary core . . ." description?

3. Can you express Steger's picture in words that cannot be misinterpreted?

4. How could this costly error have been avoided?

5. Who should pay the $6,250?

CASE 10.3

Jack McGuire*

The company I work for is engaged in selling metals to industrial accounts. These metals are steel, aluminum, brass, copper, stainless steel, nickel, Monel and nickel alloys for foundry work, as well as for fasteners (machine screws, washers, nuts, and so on), pipe fittings, rivets, and other items, such as nails, studs, and so forth.

The policy of the company in regard to sales personnel is to hire people and train them in the plant for about a month to familiarize them with the products sold. The next step is to have them come into the office where they learn office procedures, basic facts about metals, pricing setup, company policy in regard to returned goods and other matters. An important step in this process is listening to a veteran salesperson handle customers on the phone, as well as observing how customers who come into the office are handled.

Jack McGuire, a personable young sales trainee, had recently gone through this procedure and was now handling customers by phone. Jack had joined the company immediately after his graduation from high school, where he had been an outstanding athlete.

In preface, it should be noted that during an average week, a salesperson receives about one or two calls wherein the customer has contacted the wrong company or the customer has a misconception about the products handled by the company.

One day McGuire received a call from the purchasing agent of one of our large industrial accounts.

> **Buyer** *(without announcing her company's name):* Do you have any track spikes in stock?
> **McGuire** *(with a little chuckle):* No, I am afraid you called the wrong place. You will have to try a sporting goods house like Dooner's.
> **Buyer** *(angrily):* Thank you for the information *(bangs down the receiver).*

One week later, our regular saleswoman, Fran Clifford, called on the account and was confronted by the buyer in an angry manner, "What are you hiring now, wise guys? I called up for track spikes to be used in our scrap metal yard, and your salesman told me to go to Dooner's."

Clifford explained that the man was new and that it probably was an honest error. Later, Clifford explained to McGuire that what the buyer

---

* All names have been disguised. Printed by permission of the author, whose name has been withheld by request.

had wanted were railroad track spikes which are used like steel nails where heavy timber is involved.

Discussion Questions

1. What is your analysis of this case?
2. How could Jack have avoided this unpleasantness?

CASE 10.4

Room 406*

It was 4:56 P.M. on Tuesday on the surgical floor of John Randolph Memorial Hospital. Nurse Rhoda Fleming, an efficient woman with 15 years' service in the hospital, was in charge of the floor that afternoon. She was making her final check of the rooms prior to the arrival of her relief, who came on at 5:00 P.M. In Room 406, she found that Mr. Henry Youstra, who had undergone surgery the week before, and who had not responded well, had finally died. Mentally, she began to review the procedure on expirations—call a doctor to pronounce death; notify various administrative departments, including Admissions and Reception; wrap body; and so forth. Suddenly recalling that she had a 5:15 P.M. dental appointment, she decided to ask her relief, who generally arrived early, to handle the procedure.

While depressed about death, she couldn't suppress a feeling of relief, for bed space was a critical problem at the hospital. She would tell her relief to prepare the room immediately for a new patient. She returned to the floor desk, which was located near the elevators. The night nurse, Ann Simmons, had already arrived and was waiting at the desk.

"Anything new, Rho?" she asked.

"406 just died, so that room's all set to go again. I hate to see them go that way, but we can certainly use the space. I'm pressed—will you take over?"

"Sure. How about 411, did you give her her shot yet?"

"No, and you'd better do that soon. Old Doc Anders might be up, and he'd have a conniption if she hadn't had it yet."

"Does the office know that 406 is ready?"

"No, you can tell them after you get things cleaned up."

Nurse Fleming then left, and Nurse Simmons gave 411 her shot and went about her other routine duties. At about 6:30 P.M. Nurse Simmons called the office and told them that room 406 was ready for occupancy, though she had not checked that room herself. She was told that a Mr.

---

* All names are disguised. Printed by permission of the author, whose name has been withheld by request.

Leopold would be down from emergency surgery later on and would be given that bed. She then carried on her other duties.

Visitors' hours began at 7:00 P.M. at Randolph Hospital, and as was her custom Mrs. Henry Youstra left home at 6:00 P.M. so as to arrive just at 7:00. Over the weeks of visiting her husband, she had acquired the habit of asking for her visitor's card by the room number, as the cards were issued by room number. The woman at the front desk gave her the card prepared for visitors of Mr. Leopold, and she took the elevator to the fourth floor. Nurse Simmons was at the fourth-floor desk when Mrs. Youstra arrived there. Nurse Simmons recognized Mrs. Youstra as a nightly visitor and smiled professionally at her, not recalling which patient she visited, nor looking at the name on the card. Nurse Simmons placed the card in the desk file, and Mrs. Youstra went down the hall.

At 8:00 P.M., the end of visiting hours, Nurse Simmons checked each room to see that all visitors had left. In Room 406 she found Mrs. Youstra dead on the floor beside the bed containing her husband's body.

Discussion Questions

1. Analyze in detail the critical exchange between Nurses Fleming and Simmons.
2. In summary, how do you perceive what has happened?
3. What patterns of miscommunication seem to have occurred here?
4. What measures will help to prevent a recurrence of this sort?

CASE 10.5

The Sturdy Corporate Homesteader*

In a happier time, so a U.S. Chamber of Commerce speaker tells us, the government used the public domain to "give every man a chance to earn land for himself through his own skill and hard work." This is the sturdy homemaker sob with which the air will presently resound when this gentleman's associates get to work on Congress. He may have been thinking of the California redwood forest. It was so attractive a part of the public domain that in this generation we have had to raise millions of dollars from rich men and schoolchildren to buy back a few acres of it here and there for the public.

Under a measure called the Timber and Stone Act, a homemaker who had his first citizenship papers could buy 160 acres of redwood forest from the government for $2.50 an acre, less than a panel for your living-room costs. Agents of a lumber company would go to a sailors' boardinghouse on the San Francisco waterfront. They would press a gang of homemakers and lead them to a courthouse to take out first papers. Then they went to a

---

* From Bernard De Voto's "The Easy Chair," *Harper's Magazine* (May 1953), pp. 57-58. Reprinted by permission.

land office and each filed claim to 160 acres of redwood: a quarter-section whose number the lumber company had supplied. At a lawyer's office, they transferred to the lumber company the homesteads they had earned by skill and hard work, received $50 for services rendered, and could go back to the boardinghouse. "Fifty dollars was the usual fee," a historian says, "although the amount soon fell to $10 or $5 and eventually to the price of a glass of beer."

Under this act, four million acres of publicly owned timber passed into corporate ownership at a small fraction of its value, and 95 percent of it by fraud. Under other acts supposed to "give every man a chance to earn land for himself," enormously greater acreages came to the same end with the sturdy homemaker's help.

The laws stipulated that the homemaker must be in good faith. Erecting a "habitable dwelling" on his claim would prove that he was. Or if it was irrigable land, he had to "bring water" to it, for a homemaker would need water. Under a couple of dozen aliases apiece, employees of land companies or cattle companies would file claim to as many quarter-sections or half-sections of the public domain and after six months would commute them, get title to them at $1.25 per acre.

The sworn testimony of witnesses would prove that they had brought water to the claim; there was no reason for the witnesses to add they had brought it in a can. Or the witnesses swore that they had "seen water" on the homestead, and so they had, having helped to throw it there cupful by cupful. Or to erect a "12 by 14" cabin on a claim would prove good faith. Homemaker and witnesses neglected to mention that this "habitable dwelling" was 12 by 14 inches, not feet. Alternatively, a "shingled residence" established that the homemaker intended to live on his claim; or could be created by fastening a couple of shingles to each side of a tent below the ridgepole. Sometimes a scrupulous corporation would build a genuine log cabin 12 by 14 feet, mount it on wagon wheels, and have the boys drive it from claim to claim, getting the homemaker a lot of public domain in a few hours. In a celebrated instance in Utah the efficiency of this device was increased by always pushing the truck over the corner where four quarter-sections met.

In six months the homemakers, who meanwhile had been punching cows or clerking in town, commuted their two dozen parcels of the public domain. They transferred them to their employers and moved on to earn two dozen more quarter-sections apiece by their skill and hard work. Many millions of acres of publicly owned farmland and grazing land thus passed economically into the possession of corporate homemakers. If the corporation was a land company it might get half a million acres convenient to a railroad right-of-way or within a proposed irrigation district. Or a cattle company could thus acquire a hundred thousand acres that monopolized the water supply for miles and so graze a million acres of the public domain entirely free of charge.

Lumber companies could operate even more cheaply. Their employees need not pay $1.25 per acre or wait to commute their claims. They could pay a location fee, say $16 per 320 acres, and the company could forthwith clear-cut the timber and let the claims lapse. At 20 cents an acre virgin stands of white or ponderosa pine, Douglas fir, or Norway or Colorado spruce were almost as good as some of the damsites which, our propagandist hopes, will presently be offered to the power companies.

These are typical, routine, second-magnitude land frauds in the history of the public domain out West—to describe the bigger ones would require too much space. Enough that in the golden age of landgrabs, the total area of the public domain proved up and lived on by actual homesteaders amounted to only a trivial fraction of the area fraudulently acquired by land companies, cattle companies, and lumber companies. Among the compelling reasons why the present public-land reserves had to be set aside was the headlong monopolization of the public domain that was threatening the West with peonage.

Those reserves were also made to halt the waste of natural resources which the United States had dissipated more prodigally than any other nation. They had to be made so that a useful part of our national wealth could be preserved, developed, wisely managed, and intelligently used in future times. They had to be made so that the watersheds which control the destiny of the West could be safeguarded. But no one should forget for a moment that they were, besides, necessary to prevent Eastern and foreign corporations from taking over the whole West by fraud, bribery, and engineered bankruptcy.

Discussion Questions

1. What is the relevance of this article to communication?
2. Could this egregious bypassing have been prevented?

CASE 10.6

Garnishment Policy*

The loose credit policies of many retail stores have created a serious problem for many employers. These policies have permitted their employees to extend their credit far beyond their budgeting capabilities. Thus, they become delinquent with their payment contracts. Creditors, to effect repayment of their contracts, resort to legal means of collection. They file wage assignments or garnishments with the individual's employer and by so doing make the employer a collector of indebtedness.

In the Glennon Company, the policy regarding garnishments had been to withhold the required amount from the employee's weekly

---

* The author's name has been withheld by request. All names have been disguised.

paycheck and send a separate check for this amount to the creditor. With delinquencies mounting, the Payroll Department became increasingly burdened by the policy.

Finally, Glennon's board of directors adopted a new policy that complied with the law yet promised to ease the work load of the Payroll Department. Accordingly, the president sent a memo to the department:

> Effective immediately. Honor assignments of wages but do not remit. Hold for full amount and make creditor prove claim.

Austin Horlick, a machine operator with an excellent work record, was a victim of the easy credit stores, and when he found it impossible to pay all of his obligations as contracted, he skipped payments and became a delinquent on the books of his creditors. It was just a question of time before one or more of them, failing to have their accounts brought to date by credit letters and phone calls, filed wage assignments with his employer.

The Quick Money Loan Company was one of these creditors. Tom Lederer, the Quick Money's manager, called Alan Curland, Glennon's paymaster, to inquire about the status of his assignment. The men were acquainted through many similar contacts.

Tom: Al? Tom, at Quick Money. What is the status of my assignment against Austin Horlick?

Al: Hello, Tom. Just a moment until I check his file. *(Pause).* You're first, Tom.

Tom: Thanks, Al. Paydays are still Friday, aren't they?

Al: Yes, Tom, but there has been a change in the company policy. I will not be able to send you a payment each week. The new policy is to hold for the entire balance.

Tom: That will be OK, Al. I'll mark my records up for a month and check with you at that time as to the amount you have on hand.

Al: OK, Tom, the plant is working a lot of overtime, so you will probably have about $30 a week held up.

Tom: Thanks, Al. The balance of the account is $171.23. At that rate it will take about six or seven weeks to wipe out the debt. Maybe Horlick will make other arrangements and get a release before then. Thanks again, Al, I'll be talking to you. Goodbye.

Al: Goodbye, Tom.

The following day, George Smith, a co-maker for Austin Horlick, called at the Quick Money Loan Company and made a payment of $100 in exchange for his release from the contract. This payment was made the day after Lederer had talked to Curland. Smith's payment reduced the debt so that the balance could possibly be liquidated by the wage assignment withholdings in three weeks. Lederer marked the record to call Curland again in two weeks to advise him of the correct payoff figure. When the time had elapsed, he called Curland.

Tom: Al, Tom Lederer.

Al: Hello, Tom. What's on your mind today?

Tom: The Austin Horlick case. I received payment on the account from the co-maker and I wanted to give you the payoff figure.

Al: Fine. How much do you need?

Tom: $80.46 will take care of it.

Al: Hold on a minute while I get the file. *(Pause)*. Say, Tom, I can't send you the money yet: we haven't withheld enough.

Tom: How much do you have?

Al: $92.

Tom: That's more than is necessary. I only need $80.46.

Al: The assignment is for $171.23 plus the accruing interest, and that is what I will have to hold for.

Tom: Why? I just told you that I had received a payment from the co-maker and I will only need $80.46.

Al: I'm sorry, Tom, but the policy now is to hold for the entire balance.

Tom: But, Al, the amount has been changed and you will be holding more than will be required.

Al: Can't help it, Tom. I have my orders, and I have to comply.

Tom: There is something wrong with that kind of thinking. Hadn't you better call your home office for clarification?

Al: No. They told me what to do, and that is what I'm going to do.

Tom: I thought that the company was trying to avoid trouble. This stand is going to cause you to be deluged with lawsuits.

Al: I know it, but it is out of my hands, and from what they have said to me in the past, I'm not going to cross them again. I told them that we would be spending more time in court than before, but they don't seem to care. Guess they want to give the legal staff something to do.

Tom: OK, Al, I'll check with you later to see if you can't work something out. I hate to send this to our attorney as it will increase the debt that Horlick has with me. I don't see any reason for him to be penalized because of this foolish misunderstanding.

Discussion Questions

1. Why was the garnishment policy issued?

2. How do you evaluate the policy and the manner in which it was issued?

3. How does this case resemble or differ from "The Product-Information Program" and "The Sturdy Corporate Homesteader"?

CASE 10.7

The Expensive Expense Accounts*

John Holland, controller of Lawton Pharmaceuticals, Inc., contacted Harry Triemstra, partner of Froehling, Winthrop, and Triemstra, public accountants. Holland wanted an audit of one of Lawton's divisions, and hopefully, because of a current profit squeeze, at the lowest possible fee. Triemstra assured Holland that the job would be done competently and inexpensively as possible.

Triemstra assigned Ellen Swenson, a capable and experienced senior, to the account, emphasizing Holland's concern about the fee.

"Let's make a good impression, Ellen," Triemstra said, "Lawton could be a big account for us."

Jeff Watkins, a bright but inexperienced young junior, was also assigned to the job, under Swenson's supervision. Swenson and Watkins began their examination on Monday, and despite the fact that this was Watkins' first audit, the work went smoothly. Swenson was eager to complete the assignment quickly, not only to please the client but to be free to attend a technical seminar in Chicago the following week. Late Friday afternoon she reviewed the work and determined that the examination had been completed except for analyzing a few small expense accounts.

"Jeff, it looks to me as if we've just about wrapped this one up except for vouching the expense accounts. So why don't you do those, and I'll be back from the seminar a week from Monday to review the work papers. And, incidentally, Jeff—you've done a very good job, considering this has been your first audit."

Jeff was obviously pleased with the compliment. "Thanks, Ellen, it was a pleasure working with you. I'll have those accounts ready when you get back."

The following Friday, Harry Triemstra received another call from John Holland.

Holland: Say, Triemstra, I thought we were in agreement that the costs on this job would be minimal.

Triemstra: Exactly. What's wrong?

Holland: Then why has this greenhorn accountant of yours been spending a solid week vouching all our expense accounts? I can tell you there's no way we're going to pay for those 40 hours of vouching work!

Triemstra: He's been vouching expense accounts all week? Frankly, this baffles me. I'll check with our senior, Ellen Swenson, and find out why she decided to extend their tests. I'll get back to you.

---

* All names have been disguised.

As soon as he finished his conversation with Holland, Triemstra buzzed his secretary: "Get hold of Swenson immediately. She's in Chicago at that [expletive deleted] seminar!"

Discussion Questions
1. How did this miscommunication occur?
2. Who was responsible and to what extent?
3. What were the consequences of this miscommunication?
4. How could it have been prevented?

CASE 10.8

"But I Thought You Said . . . ."*
David P. Mayer[†]

The daily pressures of the supervisor's job sometimes prevent him from communicating with his subordinates as well as he should. And he may also neglect the important job of training his subordinates to give him the information he should have. In the ensuing dialogue between a boss and his secretary, the reader will find some glaring cases of noncommunication on both sides. Probably nobody is this bad, but it's just possible that the reader may get some clues to where he could improve the effectiveness of his own communication and that of his subordinates.

Boss: Barbara, please type this cost report and let me have it by five o'clock.
Secretary: Right, Mr. Lohr, five o'clock.
Boss: And you better check my figures.
Secretary: OK. Will you want any extra copies?
Boss: Well, ah . . . oh, prepare the usual number.
  (Time passes—it is now five o'clock.)
Secretary: Here's the report, Mr. Lohr. I was afraid I wouldn't make it.
Boss: Do my figures check out?
Secretary: They add up.
Boss: Good. I didn't know if the last column checked out with the Accounting Department.
Secretary: Oh! . . . I didn't check with them.
Boss: I told you to.
Secretary: I'm sorry. You said to check your figures, so I just verified your totals.

---

* Reprinted with permission. *ETC.: A Review of General Semantics*, 33 no. 2 (1976), pp. 185–88.

[†] Former Chief of Personnel Program Management, U.S. Veterans Administration.

Boss: I ran those totals on a tape myself.

Secretary: There was no tape attached to your worksheets.

Boss: Well, check those last line entries with Mr. Adams in Accounting.

Secretary: Mr. Adams just left; it's after five.

Boss: What? After five! I wanted this report to go out this evening.

Secretary: You said you wanted it ready by five o'clock. You usually take this report home and review it.

Boss: I know, but it's due out this evening.

Secretary: It's not due till the 15th. We still have three days.

Boss: No, no. The due date was changed.

Secretary: It was?

Boss: Yes, you knew that.

Secretary: No, I didn't know it.

Boss: Didn't you check your reports-control card?

Secretary: I did, and it still shows the 15th due date.

Boss: Your card is wrong. The date was changed.

Secretary: This is the first I've heard of it.

Boss: It was changed in a recent letter from the home office.

Secretary: I don't see those instructional letters any more.

Boss: You don't?

Secretary: No. You told Betty to handle them so she could learn the office control system.

Boss: But you're still handling the reports-control cards. Didn't you ask her to keep you informed of any changes?

Secretary: No, I thought you did.

Boss: You should have done it yourself.

Secretary: I'm not her supervisor, and her boss is a little touchy about ...!

Boss: Now I wonder how many more control records are inaccurate.

Secretary: I don't know.

Boss: Well, that's another problem to look into tomorrow. . . . Will you check out those cards in the morning?

Secretary: Yes, but will you let her supervisor know that I'm following your orders?

Boss: Remind me in the morning.

Secretary: OK—now, what about mailing this report?

Boss: Call and see if Mr. Johansen is still here so we can get it signed.

Secretary: What about those figures ... ?

Boss: We'll just have to take a calculated risk.

Secretary: ... and by the way, Mr. Johansen left at two o'clock.

Boss: What?

Secretary: His secretary told me he was going to leave at two o'clock and anything needing his signature should be sent up to him before then.

Boss: Why didn't you tell me?

Secretary: You were out, so I left a note on your desk.

Boss: Your note said that Mr. Johansen wanted the outgoing mail before two.

Secretary: Well . . .?

Boss: Well, what? We're supposed to get all outgoing mail to him by two o'clock every day. I thought this was just a reminder that we've been slipping on this a little. Now I'll have to stop off at his house and. . . .

Secretary: He's not at home. He left to attend a meeting in Columbus.

Boss: Why doesn't someone *tell* me these things?

Secretary: He announced it at his staff meeting yesterday.

Boss: I wasn't here yesterday.

Secretary: It's in the minutes.

Boss: I haven't seen any minutes.

Secretary: There's a copy in your mail basket.

Boss: I haven't had time to check my incoming mail.

Secretary: You know, Mr. Lohr, I think you'd have more time if you let Mr. Covington do this report.

Boss: He doesn't know how; he's too new.

Secretary: We should train him—he's waiting for assignments.

Boss: I don't have the time to train him.

Secretary: You do too much yourself, Mr. Lohr.

Boss: I have to if I want things done right. Well, Mr. Johansen's assistant lives next door to me—I'll get him to sign the report.

Secretary: I'll call and tell him you're coming over.

Boss: Good, and don't forget to send the Accounting Department a copy of the report in the morning.

Secretary: Ah, I didn't make an extra copy.

Boss: And why not?

Secretary: You said the "usual number."

Boss: What I meant by the "usual number" was enough copies to distribute to all concerned.

Secretary: Well, I didn't know Accounting wanted a copy. We've never sent them one before.

Boss: For some reason or other they asked for one this time.

Secretary: You mean they sent us a request?

Boss: Last week. I thought you knew. Well, have Rachel make a copy for them in the morning.

Secretary: Rachel won't be in tomorrow.

Boss: She didn't mention anything to me about taking off.

Secretary: Sure she did.

Boss: When?

Secretary: The day before yesterday. She asked you right after your long-distance telephone conversation with . . .

Boss: Oh, yes, now I remember. I was so preoccupied about that call, Rachel's request just didn't register.

Secretary: You know, there doesn't seem to be too much communicating around here.

Boss: People just don't listen . . . that's the trouble.

Secretary: I agree.

Boss: Agree with what?

Secretary: That people just don't listen.

Boss: You're right. Tomorrow we're going to start a campaign to improve communication in the office.

Secretary: That's a wonderful idea.

Boss: And now I'd better get this over to Mr. Johansen's assistant.

Secretary: Don't forget you have a dental appointment at 10:30 tomorrow.

Boss: I canceled it.

Secretary: Oh, no! And I canceled your two office appointments for tomorrow morning.

Boss: But that's why I canceled the dental appointment—to keep those interviews. They're important.

Secretary: You didn't tell me.

Boss: Well, tomorrow we start that campaign.

Secretary: Right, good night—see you tomorrow.

Boss: Oh, that reminds me, I won't be in until ten tomorrow—have to take my wife to the doctor.

Discussion Questions

1. The author concedes he has telescoped a litany of miscommunications. However, as an exercise in communication analysis dissect this case speech by speech. What patterns of miscommunication are occurring here?

2. How might these patterns of miscommunication be prevented in the future?

3. Do the author and/or Lohr exhibit sexism?

CHAPTER ELEVEN

Allness
Arrogance and
Closed-Mindedness

❋
❋
❋

An employee: You can't get anywhere around here. What's the use of coming up with any new ideas? They won't listen to you anyway!

His supervisor: My people are automatons—no drive, no ambition, no initiative. They won't move unless I push them!

Motorist: Never try to reason with a cop. They're obsessed with their authority!

Police officer: I get fed up taking abuse from the typical idiot behind the wheel!

A father: I can't let my son use my tools; he'd ruin them in two seconds!

His son: I just *look* at those "precious" tools and Dad blows his cool!

Have you noticed the tone of finality and absoluteness in which people sometimes talk? When they speak in this way, it is almost as if they were declaring: "What I am saying is all there is to say about the subject—there is nothing more." It is hardly a rare characteristic. Stop in at your barber shop or beauty salon or unisex hair stylist and listen to the ease and dispatch with which the intricate problems of national and international affairs are neatly and conclusively solved. Listen to the talk of quarrelers, and you will find a similar note of arrogance, of unseemly assurance and know-it-allness—or *allness*, for short.

Underlying much of this dogmatic, unqualified, categorical, closed-minded thinking and communication are two assumptions—both are fallacious, and both are usually held unconsciously by the communicator.

TWO FALSE ASSUMPTIONS

(1) It is possible to know and say everything about something. (2) What I am saying (or writing or thinking) includes all that is important about the subject. These assumptions are so patently ridiculous that it seems pointless to refute them. And yet a considerable proportion of communications is apparently based upon them. Perhaps, as the late J. Samuel Bois said, we need to crack through the hard shell of the obvious.

We can go about it this way. Pick up a simple object, say, a piece of schoolroom chalk. Examine it; study it. What could you say about it? You might mention that it is white, small, lightweight, cylindrical, nonedible, inexpensive, a writing instrument, tasteless, hard, smooth, soluble in water, and related to our national economy. You might add that it is a mineral, usually calcium carbonate, capable of squeaking on a blackboard, brittle, a manufactured product, a schoolroom necessity, used in children's games, a domestic product, powdery when crumbled, likely to soil dark clothing, usually shipped in sawdust or in a protective box, inorganic, and so on.

While you might be quite willing to stop talking about the subject, you would not contend that you had said everything about it. But just how long would it take to say everything about it? A half hour? Two hours? A day? When we consider the origin of the material, its countless evolutions, and its dynamic atomic structure, it is evident that to say or know *all* about even the simplest object is impossible. This story about Agassiz, the great naturalist and teacher of scientists, is pertinent:

A scientist, he thought, was a man who sees things which other people miss. . . . One of his students has left an account of how he trained them:

"I had assigned to me a small pine table with a rusty tin pan upon it. . . . Agassiz brought me a small fish, placing it before me with the rather stern requirement that I should study it, but should on no account talk to anyone concerning it, nor read anything relating to fishes, until I had his permission so to do. To my inquiry 'What shall I do?' he said in effect: 'Find out what you can without damaging the specimen; when I think that you have done the work I will question you.' In the course of an hour I thought I had compassed the fish; it was rather an unsavory object, giving forth the stench of old alcohol. . . . Many of the scales were loosened so that they fell off. It appeared to me to be a case of summary report, which I was anxious to make and get on to the next stage of the business. But Agassiz, though always within call, concerned himself no further with me that day, nor the next, nor for a week.

"At first, this neglect was distressing; but I saw that it was a game, for he was . . . covertly watching me. So I set my wits to work upon the thing, and in the course of a hundred hours or so I thought I had done much—a hundred times as much as seemed possible at the start. I got interested in finding out how the scales went in their series, their shape, the form and placement of the teeth, etc. Finally, I felt full of the subject and probably expressed it in my bearing; as for words about it then, there were none from my master except his cheery 'Good morning.' At length, on the seventh day, came the question 'Well?' and my disgorge of learning to him as he sat on the edge of my table puffing his cigar. At the end of the hour's telling he swung off and away, saying, 'That is not right.'

"It was clear that he was playing a game with me to find if I were capable of doing hard, continuous work without the support of a teacher, and this stimulated me to labor. I went at the task anew, discarded my first notes, and in another week of ten hours a day labor I had results which astonished myself and satisfied him."

After this arduous assignment was over, Agassiz did not praise his pupil ... but gave him a more difficult task of observation and comparison. This was all the praise the pupil could expect, for it meant: "You are becoming a competent scientist."[1]

Obviously, we can never know or say all about anything. But we need to discuss how these fallacious assumptions arise and how we can cope with them.

THE PROCESS OF ABSTRACTING

The structure of our language contributes to the problem of allness. Just what do we do when we use language—when we talk, write, listen, read, think, and so forth? We abstract. Let me demonstrate this by first of all listing a few details about a certain person I know. Among many, many other things this person is a(n):

male	hater of soap operas,	possessor of civil
gardener	bridge, and tardy people	rights
husband	consumer	avid detective-story
veteran	son-in-law	reader
citizen	redhead	teller of droll jokes
tax exemption	salesperson	lover of music, rose
golfer	father	growing, and
Scout leader	cousin	swimming
moderate drinker	human being	student of current
registered voter	car owner	political campaign
churchgoer	taxpayer	issues
baseball fan	10 lb.-overweight	newspaper reader
Rotary member	person	son

---

[1] From Gilbert Highet, *The Art of Teaching* (New York: Alfred A. Knopf, 1950), pp. 242–43. Reprinted by permission.

Now what happens when I say something about this person? Suppose I say: "He is a good voter." What I am doing, in effect, is calling your attention and mine to some details about this person; perhaps to such details as a citizen, a registered voter, a student of political campaign issues and candidates, and so on. But, at the same time, I am neglecting and inducing you to negelect that he is redheaded, a husband, a father, a veteran, a car owner, a golfer, a churchgoer, and literally thousands of other details that we might have attended to.

This characteristic of language use—this process of focusing-on-some-details-while-neglecting-the-rest—is called *abstracting*. When we talk, write, listen, read, and so on, we are necessarily abstracting. However, this is often difficult to remember. And when we are unaware that we are attending to some details about a situation, a person, and so forth, while simultaneously overlooking a host of others, it becomes extremely easy to assume that what we know or what we say is all that we really need to know or say.

ALLNESS DEFINED

Allness, then, is the attitude of those who are unaware that they are abstracting and thus assume that what they say or know is absolute, definitive, complete, certain, all-inclusive, positive, final—and all there is (or at least all there is that is important or relevant) to say or know about the subject. Allness, as one wag paraphrased the above definition, is what people have "who think they know everything about everything—which is quite annoying to those of us who do!"

THE CRAVING FOR CERTAINTY

Just when the speaker convinces me
Of what he has brilliantly planned,
Just when I bow to his wisdom he says,
"On the other hand—"[2]

This bit of doggerel reminds us of the confortable feeling of knowing, of being sure. We may tolerate ambiguity and discontinuity to a certain extent, but conversely, in varying degrees, we crave certainty.

"The demand for certainty," wrote Bertrand Russell, "is one that is natural to man, but is nevertheless an intellectual vice."[3] On a doubtful day, propose an outing to your children and note how they insist that you

---

[2] Arnold J. Zarett, "Ambidextrous," *The Wall Street Journal*. Reprinted by permission.

[3] Bertrand Russell, *Unpopular Essays* (London: George Allen and Unwin, 1951), p. 26.

declare whether the day will be fair or foul—and their disappointment when you cannot give a firm answer. The same sort of dogmatism, Russell contended, is demanded, in later life:

> So long as men are not trained to *withhold judgment in the absence of evidence,* they will be led astray by cocksure prophets, and it is likely that their leaders will either be ignorant fanatics or dishonest charlatans. To endure uncertainty is difficult, but so are most of the other virtues. For the learning of every virtue there is an appropriate discipline, and for the learning of *suspended judgment* the best discipline is philosophy.[4]

But he warned against philosophy teaching no more than skepticism, for while the dogmatist may be dangerous, the skeptic is ineffectual.

> Dogmatism and skepticism are both, in a sense, absolute philosophies; one is certain of knowing, the other of not knowing. What philosophy should dissipate is certainty, whether of knowledge or of ignorance.[5]

Bacon expressed it more succinctly: "Learning teaches how to carry things in suspense without prejudice till you resolve."

The craving for certainty leads easily to oversimplification. Senator Patrick Moynihan said: "One of our greatest weaknesses as Americans is the habit of reducing the most complex issues to the most simplistic moralisms." As one historian put it, "The essence of tyranny is the denial of complexity."

Recognizing the increasing interrelatedness of business with its environment, James McSwiney, former president of the Mead Corporation, cited the urgent need for "complexifiers."

> Yesterday—so to speak—the man who could cut through the web of detail and get at the heart of the matter was the hero. He often moved to the top of the organizational ladder. He never seemed to be in doubt!
>
> ... But *today* we worry more about the person who is *too ready* to fire off an instant decision that solves one problem and creates *twenty* more.
>
> No one welcomes indecision in management. ... The need is not to *agonize,* but to really *analyze*—and to take *intelligent action.* ...
>
> The point is *intelligent action* today must include an understanding that a business decision can have political, social, cultural, technological, even religious, as well as economic ramifications. The complex problems of our society which once might have been considered peripheral to business are now *central* to making *intelligent* decisions.

---

[4] Ibid., p. 27.

[5] Ibid.

For some the craving for certainty seems essentially motivated by internal insecurities. Others, in fairness, have omniscience thrust upon them by the roles they play in society. We dearly *want* the doctors diagnosing our illnesses, the attorneys handling our cases, and the police officers protecting our lives and property to be *right*.

Is it any wonder that when constantly pressured to fulfill the roles of authority, people can sometimes be seduced by it? Internally generated or externally imposed, the need for certainty and simplicity often leads to elaborate defense mechanisms which assure that certainty and simplicity. The allness attitude, buttressed by its two enticing but false assumptions is such a mechanism.

MODES OF ALLNESS

More specifically, to what sorts of problems does allness contribute? The following suggest a few of the various manifestations of the allness attitude, and situations in which allness tends to occur.

1. *When we talk or write (or abstract in any manner)* unaware *that we are abstracting, and thus* assume *that we have covered it all.*

This attitude, which is exemplified by the paired statements at the beginning of this chapter, is epitomized by the expression "often in error—but never in doubt." This is not to suggest that close-minded people never change their minds but that with them it seems to be a process of moving from one state of certainty to another.

Now let us consider what may happen when such abstractors get together.

2. *When two or more people abstract different details from a given situation, are* unaware *that they are abstracting, and thus both* assume *that what they know is all.*

An almost inevitable consequence of this state of affairs is the rigid drawing of lines and unintelligent, destructive conflict. "Behind every argument," said Justice Louis Brandeis, "is someone's ignorance."

Letters-to-the-Editor columns of newspapers and magazines provide abundant examples of this mode of allness. Each letter is, of course, an abstraction—it represents a selection of some details and the omission of others. But so frequently letter writers seem unaware that they have abstracted—that they have not covered it all. Consider this series of reactions to a *Life* article:

Sexy Movies

Sirs:

You have published your all-time champion picture! Those seven women of Chadron! Good old-fashioned Americans mad as hell! More people like these ladies and we would soon be back to normal.

Sirs:

How vile, disgusting, vulgar and completely filled with sin! I refer to the small minds of certain people, a few of whom seem to reside in Chadron, Neb. as well as New York, London, Hong Kong. When will they learn that sex, in all of its many forms, is wholesome and normal in every respect?

Sirs:

What our area expected and what it got from *Life* were two different things. Once again the city slickers east of the Hudson have succeeded in labeling the ranchers and rubes of Nebraska as Rip Van Winkles to whom the 20th century may yet become obvious.

It's nice to see our area get national publicity, and maybe the ladies' approach to the sex movie problem could be copied elsewhere. I just wish that one time someone, somewhere would let the eastern seaboard know that out here on the Great Plains we do hold full membership in the human race. Otherwise, some future Barry Goldwater may do more than just threaten to saw off the Thirteen Colonies.

I had begun to fear that these readers would never reconcile their differences when a fourth writer seemed to settle the whole matter.

Sirs:

Thank God for those saviors of morality and decency in Chadron, Neb. It should be quite clear by now that there is a nationwide Communist-supported plot to encourage the moral decay of our youth through sex education in schools and lewd motion pictures featuring perversion and nudity. Besides, if the good Lord wanted us to be photographed running around without any clothes on, we would have been born that way.

How's *that* for unassailable logic!

When one assumes that only one viewpoint or abstraction is correct, it follows inexorably that all other perceptions become quite intolerable. Which recalls a cartoon of several years ago showing a driver and a companion. In front of their car—*six inches* in front of their car—is another car. And the driver is saying disgustedly: "Look at how close that maniac is driving ahead of us!" As Jonathan Swift said 300 years ago: "It is impossible to reason a man out of something he has not been reasoned into."

It is difficult under the best of conditions to concede points of view that are different from our own. Davis has an interesting diagram[6] showing how a production expert's perception of a problem tends to differ from that

---

[6] By permission from *Human Behavior at Work,* 8th ed., by Keith Davis and J.W. Newstrom. Copyright 1989, McGraw-Hill Book Company.

FIGURE 11.1

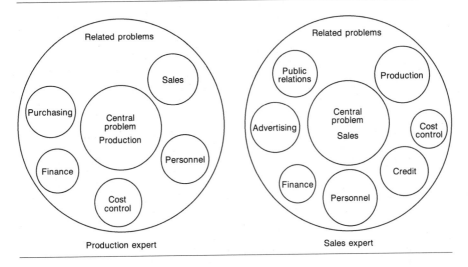

of a sales expert. We see our own bailiwick as the central problem area and others as only related problems.

When conducting management seminars, I sometimes ask the executives present to "please raise your hand if you do *not* work in *the key function* of your organization." I have seen very few hands over the years.[7] During a recent winter, Washington, D.C. suffered a heavy snowfall, and an emergency announcement was made on TV and radio that night: "Only essential personnel need report for work tomorrow morning." The next day the agencies reported one of the highest attendance records in history!

3. *When we evaluate a* group *on the unconscious assumption that our experience with one or a few members holds for all.*

This is still another form of reacting to the abstraction as if to the totality. Consider this letter to a newspaper's advice column.

Dear Ms. Landers:

You are wrong when you tell the girls that there is a man shortage. I am 29, have a successful law office and a car. For several years I have tried every conceivable place, including church, to find a girl

---

[7] My purpose here is not to discourage pride in or commitment to one's job or department. My concern is with destructive provincialism: preoccupation with one's own function to the exclusion of and possible detriment to others. A salesperson, for example, might hype sales with extravagant promises about the qualities and delivery of the product. The resultant customer complaints could wreak havoc in engineering, production, and service.

friend but have had no luck. Many girls marry when they are about 20. They marry men with whom they grew up. Most of the other girls are going steady. I can't even meet young women who are not married or going steady!

I am not quite average looking, so women have snubbed me for about 14 years. I now hate all American women and especially USO and Red Cross girls. USO girls snub any man who isn't handsome or doesn't meet their specifications. When Red Cross girls are not on duty they will have nothing to do with enlisted men and date only officers.

My hatred for women now is such that if I saw a woman dying I would not walk a step out of the way to help her. If I handle an eviction suit, a woman tenant gets no break from me. When it is a collection case, if a woman doesn't pay immediately, I have her wages garnished even though I know she will lose her job. Why shouldn't I? It looks as though I will have to go to Europe to get a wife.

HOMELY

Admittedly, Homely's letter does sound extreme—but then some people do talk, and think, this extremely on occasion. Supposedly here is a man who has had some unfortunate experiences with some members of the opposite gender. But these women can represent only an infinitesimal fraction of the group. However, Homely has apparently forged an all-embracing, unyielding generalization about females that may well constitute a self-fulfilling prophecy. Thus, his subsequent relationships with women are likely to continue to be unsatisfactory.

Sidney Harris wrote this article almost 40 years ago. Unfortunately, it still seems valid:

Some weeks ago, I presided as toastmaster at a large luncheon sponsored by the National Conference of Christians and Jews. A few hours later, I flew to New York to visit some friends living in Greenwich Village.

As I taxied into New York from the airport, the relationship between these two events suddenly struck me. To the average mind, the phrase "Greenwich Village" conjures up a definite set of images, most of them bad, and most of them false.

To the reader of sensational journals or to the casual tourist, Greenwich Village is a weird neighborhood in lower Manhattan, composed largely of ranting poets, crazy artists, ridiculous perverts and "Bohemians" of the lowest order of depravity.

Actually, this is only a part of the truth and not the larger part. Anyone who has stayed in the Village for more than a few weeks learns that the painters, the poets and the perverts are only the most obvious tenants of the neighborhood.

The great bulk of the population in the Village is made up of substantial citizens living in well-kept homes, with well-tended children, dogs, and back gardens. The houses along 10th St. are charming and almost austerely Early American. Washington Square is bursting with roller skates, softballs and all the springtime signs of bourgeois maternity.

Now, what the ignorant majority thinks of "Greenwich Village" is exactly what it thinks of other races and creeds. It is always the obvious undesirables that, in the public mind, characterize a group or a neighborhood. It is the deplorable habit of human nature to identify any object with its worst attribute.

If a man drinks, we describe him as a "drinker," never adding that he is kind, humorous, brave and truthful. The part we dislike becomes the whole—until we get to know the whole. And, until "brotherhood" among people becomes a reality, we will be as unfair toward other races and creeds as we are in our ignorant and partial judgment of Greenwich Village.[8]

The second to last paragraph smacks a bit of the all-inclusiveness that the author himself is condemning. However, the expression, "the part we dislike becomes the whole—until we get to know the whole," is poignant. If I don't like the part, am I likely to get to know the whole? Will I not tend to avoid it, to perpetuate my ignorance about it and thus my prejudice against it? Is it a case of knowing what we like—or of *liking what we know and disliking what we don't know?* After all, isn't prejudice, as the psychoanalyst Judd Marmor expressed it, "being down on something you're not up on"?

4. *When we become closed to the new or different.*

"I can't get *through* to them." "She simply won't listen." "His mind is made up, he refuses to be disturbed by facts." Familiar expressions? They are usually directed at people who appear to have *alled* themselves in. Their tolerance for the new or different is nil. They seem to have lost—or suppressed—one of the most distinctive characteristics of human beings: viability—the apparently unlimited capacity to learn, to grow psychologically.

Watch babies, and observe how natural it is for them to learn. They are constantly reaching, probing, grasping, fingering, testing, looking, tasting, listening. Later their insatiable curiosity, when they become agile enough to exploit it, may drive their parents up the walls. But it is graphic evidence of our deeply ingrained drive to know, to discover, to grow.

And yet often by the time we reach college, or well before, we have lost much of this viability. Why this occurs is too complex a problem to explore in detail here. But let me suggest one way of thinking about the progressive psychological arthritis that seems to afflict many of us.

As we grow older, more and more of what we learn is actually *relearning*. To learn something new or especially something different may

---

[8] "The Village Is Sadly Misjudged," *Chicago Daily News,* April 14, 1954. Reprinted by permission.

require that we relinquish something we already hold—that we discard certain accepted assumptions and cherished beliefs. This can be an unpleasant, uncomfortable experience. But some people find it a distinctly threatening state of affairs. And when we are threatened we often resort to some defense mechanism or other. Allness can be a particularly effective bastion at such times.

To the extent that I come to believe genuinely that I know all there is to know—or at least all I need to know—I really need not expose myself to novel, contrary, or disturbing experiences and ideas.

Unfortunately, I must pay a price for my insularity, comforting though it may be: I do not learn—I cease to grow. "It is impossible for anyone to begin to learn what he thinks he already knows." Epictetus' 1,900-year-old admonition is still valid. If we think we know—whether we do or not—we simply do not have the motive to expend the energy to do the growing—and it does take energy to grow psychologically.

And we must *will* to learn—for one cannot *be* taught. Kahlil Gibran, the Lebanese poet-philosopher, understood that learning was largely an act of the student's volition when he described the province of the teacher:

> *If he is indeed wise he does not bid you*
> *enter the house of his wisdom,*
> *But rather leads you to the threshold*
> *of your own mind.*[9]

All of which suggests that there is an inverse relationship between allness and viability (Figure 11.2).

When your viability is high, your allness is correspondingly low. The gap between them represents the potential for psychological growth. Note, however, that as the allness increases, the viability decreases and the growth potential diminishes until the allness exceeds the viability, and now the potential for nongrowth, for psychological stagnation, increases.

This is not to imply that you will live out your life at a fixed balance between a certain level of viability and a corresponding level of allness. Indeed, if you plot an average day on the above chart, you might find considerable variation. The key questions: How much gray area does one generate? And does it occur at critical times? Figure 11.3 shows what might be a typical day in the life of a hopefully atypical student. If he were to verbalize his fluctuating attitude, it might sound something like this:

> *"Marketing*—Now there's a field for you! I'm really fascinated by the ways they find out what the public wants to buy and what

---

[9] Kahlil Gibran, *The Prophet* (New York: Alfred A. Knopf, 1963, originally copyrighted by Gibran, 1923), p. 55.

FIGURE 11.2

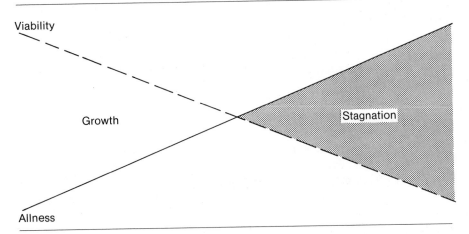

FIGURE 11.3

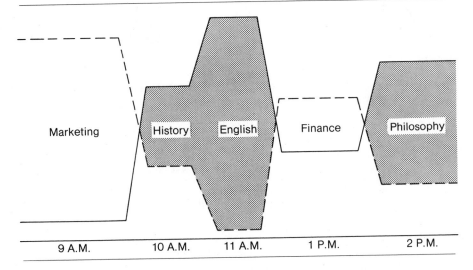

merchandising techniques are effective and so on. I'm going to be able to *use* this course.

"*History*—Frankly, this bores me. What good is it to know what happened so long ago? Times have changed. Life is different now, so why dig up the dead?

"*English*—I positively can't stand this! I've had this stuff drilled into me for 12 years. When will they let up? When I go into business, I'll have a secretary writing my letters.

"*Finance*—This is all right, but it's plenty stiff. Some of it is practical, but a lot of it I'll never use.

"*Philosophy*—Man, is this stuff up in the clouds! I just hope I can bull through the exams."

A college student with this much shaded area isn't getting his (or his parents') money's worth out of his education.[10] But there is a more subtle danger here. Aside from the possibility of flunking out, the student is cultivating a pernicious habit. Getting by and stagnating can become a way of life. His innermost feeling may be: "If I can just get through this horrible course—or curriculum—and get my diploma—then I'll be free—then I'll start to grow!"[11]

I wish him well, but I am not too optimistic about his prospects. Not infrequently, the young person who begins to vegetate habitually during college days—or earlier—continues to die psychologically more or less the rest of his life. "Anyone who is too old to learn," said Harry Hoskins, "has probably *always* been too old to learn." Our habit patterns can be insidious tyrants. God may forgive us our sins—but our nervous systems won't!

DELIBERATE DECEPTION

Abstracting, to recapitulate, involves simultaneously singling out some details while ignoring the remainder. When people are unaware that they are abstracting, they are in danger of unwitting, undesirable allness reactions such as those we have just examined.

However, the deliberate and judicious selection and suppression of detail can be a most cunning device for deception. The *Slovar Inostrannykh Slov* is the *Russian Dictionary of Foreign Words*. Here is one of its definitions:

> Boy Scout: A member of a bourgeois children's organization having a military-political character in capitalist countries.

A gross slander? Perhaps. But why is it difficult to refute? Let us dissect it.

> "bourgeois"?—admittedly most Scouts *are* middle-class kids—but that is because most of the population of "capitalistic countries" is middle-class. The definition gains additional leverage because *bourgeois* is an inflammatory word in Ivan's lexicon.
> "military"?—Granted, if being organized into "patrols" and "troops," and having rank, the close-order drill and saluting, and so forth, are "military."

---

[10] Employees with this much shaded area aren't giving their employers their money's worth.

[11] Lest these remarks be construed as pertaining only to college students, let us recognize that we are students all of our lives—or should be. An academic *commencement,* after all, is intended to designate a *beginning,* not an ending.

"political"?—Conceded, if pledging allegiance to their nation's flag and helping to get out the vote (without respect to party or candidate) on election day are "political."

Moreover, the "military-political character" suggests Hitler's youth movement of the 1930s, the Jugendbund, or Mao's teenage Red Guard of 1966-67.

The shrewdness of this fallacy lies not in what is said but in what is not said. Where does the definition include the essence of scouting—the character building, the good deed a day, the fitness of body, mind, and spirit, and so forth? These aspects are artfully omitted, for apparently they do not fit the predetermined purpose of the definer.[12]

This is skillful abstracting. If an out-and-out lie is told about us, we can combat it with the truth. But when a partial truth is insinuated as the whole. . . . How does one respond to "Is it true that you're not using coke now?" without leaving a residue of doubt?

SUMMING UP

Now for a review. The rationale of this chapter can be stated as follows:

1. We can never say or know everything about anything.

One of the most tantalizing truths we know is that there is so much we may never know. . . . We simply cannot overtake the coy horizons of the sea of unawareness that surround our modest island of perception. On this fact rests securely the conviction that humility is a vital part of wisdom.

—Wendell Johnson

2. Thus, when we talk, listen, write, read, think, observe, and so on, we necessarily abstract—that is, select some details while omitting the remainder.

Talking, for example, is an enormously selective process. No culture has created a way of talking that does not emphasize some things at the expense of others.

3. However, the very process of abstracting can conceal its own nature—that it is a selection-omission act.

---

[12] Let us hope that *glasnost* will prevail and that example, like the "Ziss" incident (p. 287), will soon be only a grim reminder of the prolonged cold war between the Soviet Union and the United States.

Consider the tone of the paired statements at the beginning of this chapter. Note the extent to which the speakers seem unaware that they were abstracting.

4. Thus the speaker, listener, and so on, has no warning that he or the other person is leaving out details, and oftentimes the more one leaves out, the harder it is to recognize that one has left out anything.

Bertrand Russell said: "One's certainty varies inversely with one's knowledge." And four centuries earlier Michel de Montaigne in *Of Divine Ordinances* had written: "Nothing is so firmly believed as what we least know."

5. To be unaware that one has abstracted, that one has left out details, that one has not covered everything, is the ideal condition for allness.

> The greatest of all faults is to be conscious of none.
> —*Thomas Carlyle*

CORRECTIVES

What, then, can we do about our abstracting to correct allness—or better, prevent it from occurring? Stop abstracting—or at least reduce the amount of abstracting we do? The first alternative is impossible—aside from breathing, digesting, and carrying on other autonomic nervous system processes, virtually everything we do involves abstracting in some fashion or other. The second alternative is possible, but it could be undesirable. Students, for example, do very little except abstract. They listen to lectures, participate in discussions, take notes, write research papers, give oral reports, read books and articles, take exams, choose a major, plan a career, interview employers. These activities and hundreds of others inside and outside the classroom require the ability to abstract. In fact, much of students' training is calculated to develop and refine their abstracting skills.

And consider people working in organizations. The chances are that their principal value to their employer is the special kinds of abstracting they do. For example, what do accountants do? They take myriads of individual, unorganized data and glean from them meaningful abstractions, such as a profit and loss statement, which they and others can use to make important decisions. Imagine carting 30 bushels of raw data into a board of directors' meeting and announcing: "OK, folks, here's the information you wanted!"

Generally, the higher people rise in an organization, the more critical their abstracting skills become. Indeed, often an extremely important factor leading to one's rise is that he or she had or was developing the abstracting skills required by the more responsible position.

How could a business firm, a government, or any kind of organization function if there were not people who could conceptualize, theorize, extrapolate, plan, organize, coordinate, categorize, catalog, codify, generalize, evaluate, analyze, synthesize, and carry on other abstracting processes?

No. The antidote for allness is not the *avoidance* but the *awareness* of abstracting. Some suggestions:

1. *Develop and maintain a genuine humility*[13]*—a deep conviction that you can never say or know everything about anything.*

The humility displayed by a witness in court while being sworn in is an example:

Bailiff: Do you swear to tell the truth, the whole truth, and nothing but the truth, so help you God?
Witness: Look, if I knew the truth, the whole truth, and nothing but the truth—I would *be* God!

Disraeli said: "To be conscious that you are ignorant is a great first step toward knowledge." Lawrence A. Appley, of the American Management Association, held a similar view with reference to management development:

Before the executive can communicate effectively or, in fact, handle any of the other tasks of management, he must first know that he doesn't know. When a man develops the humility to admit that perhaps he doesn't know all the answers after all, then he is ready to begin to learn. It's at this point that management training becomes a wise investment.

And doubting (of this sort) does not come easily, wrote Anatole France. It is . . . "rare among men. A few choice spirits carry the germ of it in them, but these do not develop without training." Nor without effort, we might add.

2. *Recognize that you inescapably abstract (i.e., select and omit details) when you talk, listen, write, read, think, and observe—for when you* **consciously** *abstract:*

   (a) . . . you are inclined to evaluate the quality of your abstractions more judiciously—and, if necessary, to upgrade their quality.

---

[13] Humility not in the sense of meekness and self-abasement but in the older usage of the word—*openness to truth*. As such, humility is an antonym for arrogance, close-mindedness.

Leo Rosten regards as shallow and shoddy the abstractions—not of young people in general—but of those who presume to speak for them:

> I have read a slew of articles by the young—about their (and our) problems. The writers are bright, articulate, unfailingly earnest. Their grievances, as distinguished from either their knowledge or their reasoning, are often legitimate and moving. . . .
>
> There *is* plenty wrong in this muddled, unjust, horrid world. But our problems are outrageously oversimplified by the glib (old *or* young), and by airy assumptions that money can solve everything, can solve it painlessly, can solve it swiftly. . . .
>
> What idealists ignore are the objective *consequences* of their reforms. (Southern farm labor thronged North, into already explosive metropolitan slums, when relief payments were raised there; minimum wage laws *created* unemployment among those unskilled, dropouts, minorities they tried to help.)[14]

The oversimplifiers notwithstanding, it has taken humanity thousands of years to acknowledge that no one has all the answers—that the best we can expect from many of our social problems with their subterranean complexities is to reach a shaky compromise which nobody really likes but with which the various interest groups can live.

This is a worn but serviceable kernel of knowledge that one generation should be able to pass along to the next. But so frequently the new generation (my own included, when it was new) seems to become infatuated with its own oversimplifications. And by the time its idealism and its realism finally become congruent, it has dissipated much of the irreplaceable zeal and energy of youth.

> (b) . . . *you tend to be more empathic—to sense that the other person may not be abstracting as you are.*

> "Tell me," said the blind man, "what is white like?"
> "It's like newly fallen snow," replied his sighted friend.
> "Lightweight and damp?"
> "No, it is more like paper."
> "It rustles then?"
> "No, no . . . well . . . it is like an albino rabbit."
> "I understand—soft and furry."

> (c) . . . *you are more prone to be exploratory and innovative; you are less tyrannized by habit, precedent, and tradition.*

---

[14] If you wish to evaluate the quality of Rosten's abstractions, see Leo Rosten, "Who Speaks for the Young?" *Look,* May 15, 1970, pp. 16 and 18.

Chapter 17, "Blindering," develops this aspect of conscious abstracting.

3. *Make a habit of adding or at least silently acknowledging the etcetera when you abstract.*

Adding the etcetera is an extensional device urged by general semanticists[15] to help keep ourselves aware that we never cover it all. "The word 'and,' " said William James, "trails along after every sentence. Something always escapes."

Alfred Korzybski went a step farther. He arbitrarily defined the period (punctuation mark) as etcetera. He said in effect, "When you see a period in my writing or hear one in my talking, please translate it as etcetera. It will remind both of us that I have not covered everything." Editor Leo Lerner expressed it thusly:

> The important thing about etcetera is that we should think it even when we don't say it. When we make a statement and think of the "and so forth" at the end of it, we show we realize that we have not said all that is possible to say about the subject, that we have uttered an approximation, a fragment, a partiality. The use of etcetera is an exhibition of the consciousness of ignorance, a humility, a sincere modesty.

The point is not to make a fetish of conspicuously "etcetering" every statement. This may suggest (sometimes correctly) that one is bankrupt of ideas or further examples.

"Buy my used car. First of all, its depreciation will be nil. Second, personal property taxes on it will be very low if not nonexistent. Third, if you buy this used car instead of a new car you won't agonize about getting that first dent. *Etcetera, etcetera, etcetera.*" The three etceteras translated: "I really can't think of a single additional claim for the rusty old hulk, but admitting this to you isn't likely to close the deal."

"Etcetering" can also be used as a ploy to conceal the audacity of the speaker's views. The king of *The King and I* was wont to make the most imperious assertions and then to attempt to disclaim any arrogance by vehemently ending the statement with "etcetera, etcetera, etcetera!"

4. *Frequently ask yourself: Do I have an "all-wall"?*

Do I find myself fending off the new or different? After all, I do have the power to protect myself in large measure from such "disturbing changes."

---

[15] So highly regarded is "etcetera" that it is the title of the professional journal published by the International Society for General Semantics.

Who is so deafe or so blinde as hee
That willfully will neither heare nor see.

—*John Heywood (1546)*

CHALLENGING A MYTH

The crux, once again, is the *awareness* of abstracting, not the *avoidance* of it. While extolling the virtues of viability, open-mindedness, and flexibility, in no way do I advocate a posture of indecision, diffidence, or vacillation.

Yet there exists a subtle but pervasive myth in our society—that the ability to decide and take action is fundamentally incompatible with the ability to learn, grow, and change. It is as if decisiveness and viability were polar opposites on a single continuum (see Figure 11.4).

Thus, according to this myth, one could become decisive only at the expense of an open mind. Conversely, one could become open and viable only at the cost of the capacity to act. This is the oversimplification which H. L. Mencken helps to perpetuate:

> *It is the dull man*
> *who is always sure.*
> *It is the sure man*
> *who is always dull.*

The epigram is cute, pithy, and quotable. But it is a fiction.

Why the myth came to be I shall leave to the historians and the anthropologists. Perhaps it has something to do with the action orientation of Western thought—as distinguished from the passive and contemplative Eastern mentality. Is it mere coincidence that so many of our folk heroes have been "men of action," "quick on the draw," "faster than a speeding bullet"?

Be that as it may, the single continuum is simplistic. I submit that decisiveness and viability are independent variables, that a more valid diagram would consist of two continua (see Figure 11.5).

At A we see the vegetable, at B the ineffectual intellectual, at C the impulsive menace. The myth suggests that D is impossible—and that is why it is a myth. The D type orientation is not only possible but mandatory for leaders in our complex organizations.

An old Arabic apothegm is roughly analogous to Figure 11.5 .

> *He who knows not and knows that he knows not,*
> *he is simple—teach him.*
> *He who knows but knows not that he knows,*
> *he is asleep—wake him.*

FIGURE 11.4

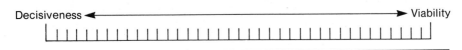

FIGURE 11.5

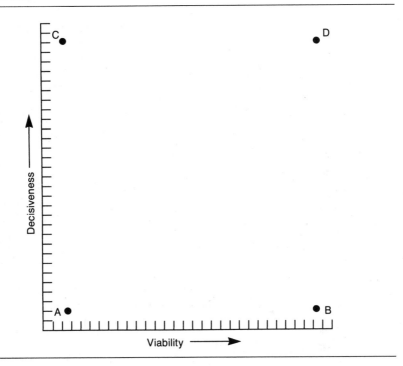

He who knows not but knows not that he knows not,
 he is a fool—shun him.
He who knows and knows that he knows,
 he is wise—follow him.

Action and Viability

The objective, then, is to be able and willing to resolve problems and take action while remaining open to experience. The goal is an attainable but difficult one. "It is hard to be strong and not rash," goes a Japanese proverb.

A leader, said Dwight D. Eisenhower, must constantly make distinctions. "One of his problems is to keep his mind open, to avoid confusing necessary firmness with stubborn preconception or unreasoning prejudice." G. K. Chesterton expressed the thought more trenchantly: "I am firmly convinced that the purpose of opening the mind as in the opening of the mouth is to close it on something solid."

George Counts confronted the paradox deftly.

There is the fallacy that the great object of education is to produce . . . the individual who adopts an agnostic attitude towards every important social issue, who can balance the pros against the cons with the skill of a juggler, who sees all sides of every question and never commits himself to any, who delays action until all the facts are in, who knows that all the facts will never come in, who consequently holds his judgment in a state of indefinite suspension, and who before the approach of middle age sees his powers of action atrophy and his social sympathies decay. With Peer Gynt he can exclaim:

> Ay, think of it—wish it done—will it to boot,—
> But do it—No, that's past my understanding.

This type of mind also talks about waiting until the solutions of social problems are found, when as a matter of fact there are no solutions in any definite and final sense. For any complex social problem worthy of the name there are probably tens and even scores, if not hundreds, of "solutions," depending upon the premises from which one works. The meeting of a social situation involves the making of decisions and the working out of adjustments. If we wait for a solution to appear like the bursting of the sun through the clouds or the resolving of the elements in an algebraic equation, we shall wait in vain. . . . society requires great numbers of persons who, while capable of gathering and digesting facts, are at the same time able to think in terms of life, make decisions, and act. From such persons will come our real social leaders.[16]

Profile of Viable People[17]

Viable—capable of living or developing, as viable seeds, physically and psychologically fit to live and grow.
I know some viable people.
They keep pushing beyond the horizons of what they already know.
They refuse to be stuck in yesterday. They won't even remain rooted in today.
They are teachable.

---

[16] George S. Counts, *Dare the School Build a New Social Order?* (New York: John Day Pamphlets, 1942), no. 11, pp. 20–22.

[17] This was written by Dr. Irving J. Lee shortly before his death in 1955. From Irving J. and Laura L. Lee, *Handling Barriers in Communication* (New York: Harper & Row, 1956), pp. 148–49. Reprinted by permission. The original title was "Profile of a Viable Man." It was written in an era when "men" or "man" was conventially used to represent humankind. I am confident that Irving, a truly viable man, and Laura, an equally viable woman, would have heartily approved of the literary license I have presumed.

They keep learning. They continue to see and listen. All their horizons are temporary.

They don't deny today's wisdom—rather, they add dimensions to it.

They have strong beliefs, faith, aspirations, but they know the difference between belief and bigotry—between knowledge and dogmatism.

They are acutely aware of the limits of what they know.

They are more likely to wonder and inquire than to dismiss and deny.

They know a great deal, but they also know that they do not know it all.

I also know some stunted, deadened people.

Their outlooks have been blighted—their interest diminished—their enthusiasm restricted—their sensitivity limited.

They are the old fogies, though they may be young in years.

They strive only to stay where they are.

They see only the dimensions of what has already been explored.

They search with their eyes only for what is old and familiar. They have frozen their views in molds.

They have narrowed the wave lengths.

They are imprisoned in the little community—the little dusty dungeons of their own minds.

They are the conflict carriers.

* * * * *

Not ignorance
But ignorance of ignorance
Is the death of knowledge.
   —Alfred North Whitehead

Discussion Questions

1. "The essence of tyranny is the denial of complexity." What is meant by this?

2. "Dogmatism and skepticism are both, in a sense, absolute philosophies; one is certain of knowing, the other of not knowing. What philosophy should dissipate is *certainty,* whether of knowledge or of ignorance."—Bertrand Russell. Do you agree? Disagree? Why?

3. "Prejudice is being down on something you're not up on."—Judd Marmor. Agree? Disagree? Why?

4. Why is it sometimes so difficult to accept or even tolerate viewpoints or abstractions that differ from our own?

5. How could you best teach nonallness to others? How might a supervisor help reduce the allness of a subordinate? Vice versa?

6. Precisely what is allness? Is it the same as abstraction? Explain.

7. What is the relationship, if any, between allness and viability? Between allness and decisiveness?

8. Are there any occupations in which allness is particularly difficult to avoid? Why?

9. Some people seem to equate nonallness and weakness. Discuss.

10. Some apparently single-minded leaders, such as Napoleon, Hitler, Stalin, and Mao, have been outstandingly effective for varying lengths of time. Discuss them in relation to the allness concept.

11. Describe an incident, possibly involving yourself, in which allness behavior occurred. Analyze specifically why it occurred, what might have been done to prevent its occurrence, and what measures would prevent its recurrence.

CASES

CASE 11.1

The Hayden Company*

The Hayden Company, headquartered in Dayton, Ohio, had numerous divisions in unrelated industries throughout the United States. These divisions for the most part were autonomous in their operations.

Guy Horton was attached to the personnel department in the headquarters office of the Hayden Company. He reported to the personnel director, Joyce Higgenson. He served in an advisory capacity and gave assistance in problems of office and laboratory personnel to the office managers in the various divisions of the firm.

These divisions did not have personnel officers as such, and all recruiting, selecting, and training were carried on through their respective office managers.

An acute problem had arisen in the Memphis division. Because of separations and expanded operations, several additional researchers would be needed within five to six weeks. The research these people would do would be in the field of farm chemistry and the application of farm products to industry.

Mr. Horton's search to find personnel to fill this need took him to several midwestern universities where he was permitted to look through alumni records and also to talk to graduating seniors who qualified. One of the schools he visited was the Rogers Institute of Technology, an institution with a high scholastic rating.

Horton sent the following report to Ms. Higgenson, relating his experiences at Rogers:

"I visited RIT yesterday morning and was permitted to interview several seniors and also to look at alumni records for candidates for the Memphis Laboratory. The students I talked to gave me a very unfavorable impression; their dress and speech could have been much better. After speaking to a number of them, I did not think it worthwhile to interview others. My next step was to seek out the alumni records, and believe me I did not get a great deal of cooperation on this. Some clerk showed me an enormous card file, and without further word he left. I leafed through this card file for a while but gave it up as a waste of time. I judged this school as being no more than a trade school, and it would be a waste of time to visit it in the future."

Discussion Questions

1. What do you make of the circumstances surrounding Guy Horton's visit to the Rogers Institute of Technology?

---

* All names have been disguised.

2. Is allness involved in Horton's judgment of Rogers? Any other patterns of miscommunication?

3. What advice would you offer Mr. Horton?

CASE 11.2

Aldermanic Election*

Allenshire, population 50,000, a suburb of a large city in New England, is largely Republican and predominantly Protestant. Many of its citizens are well-to-do executives and professional people. The per capita income of the suburb is well above the national average.

In an aldermanic election Martin J. Stewart, the incumbent alderman of the 3d Ward, was opposed by Ronald Green. Stewart's supporters distributed the leaflet shown in Exhibit 1 (p. 345), and Ronald Green's supporters distributed the leaflet shown in Exhibit 2 (p. 346).

Discussion Questions

1. What is the 3d Ward Young Republican Club trying to accomplish—and how?

2. What are Green's supporters trying to accomplish—and how?

3. What does this have to do with allness?

4. Are there other patterns of miscommunication involved here?

CASE 11.3

Interview with Miss Winkler*
Schuyler Dean Hoslett

This conversation takes place in the office of Mr. Zurch, director of personnel for an organization employing about 3,500 persons. Miss Winkler has been reported by her supervisors as doing unsatisfactory work; they ask that she be transferred on the basis of a list of charges outlined in a memorandum. Mr. Zurch has sent for Miss Winkler, who enters his office while he is talking to an assistant about another matter. Also present in the office at the time of the interview, but presumably not able to hear the conversation and doing other work, were Mr. Zurch's secretary, his assistant, and the recorder of the interview. Inasmuch as Miss Winkler spoke in a low tone, all of her comments were not audible to the recorder, especially as she became more emotional and finally tearful, but the conversation was substantially as follows (see p. 346):

---

* All names have been disguised.
* Reprinted from "Listening to the Troubled or Dissatisfied Employee," *Personnel* 23, No. 1 (1945), pp. 54–56, by permission of the American Management Association.

EXHIBIT 1

ALLENSHIRE YOUNG REPUBLICAN CLUB
COMPARE YOUR ALDERMANIC CANDIDATES
Then—VOTE for Alderman Martin J. Stewart—April 7

Alderman Martin J. Stewart   *Ronald Green*

Residence

212 Grey. Homeowner.   609 Wilson. Homeowner.
Allenshire resident 24 years.   Allenshire resident 8 years.

Family Status

Married. 2 children, 4 grandchildren.   Married. 2 children.

Occupation

Businessman. President,   Lawyer. Partner, law firm of Green,
 National Office Supplies Co.   Weisman, and Epstein.
                                          Former EPA lawyer.

Political Activities

Assistant secretary, Allenshire   Vice president, Allenshire Democratic
 Republican Club.   Club. Active in last November's
                                          campaign for Levine, Democratic
                                          nominee for sheriff.

Local Government Experience

Alderman the past two years.   None
12 years on Park District Board
 without salary. Now president.

Civic Activities

Deacon, First Methodist Church.   Member, Temple Beth Israel.
Charter member, Northwest   "Active participant in
Allenshire Community Club.   community and charitable
Air raid warden during the war.   activities."
Civilian Defense Chairman for
 Allenshire during the war.

Endorsements

Allenshire Young Republican Club.   Allenshire Democratic Club.
Allenshire Women's Republican Club.   3d Ward Independent Citizens for
3d Ward Young Republican Club.   Green.
3d Ward Women's Republican Club.   Committee of 100 Nonpartisan
Service as alderman rated very highly   3d Ward Neighbors.
 in poll of fellow aldermen and city
 department heads.
3d Ward Residents for Stewart.

3d Ward Young Republican Club

EXHIBIT 2

Biographical Sketch

of

RONALD GREEN

Candidate for ALDERMAN—3D WARD
Allenshire   Election: April 7

Born: [Nearby city], 1954

Married: One son, seven years old; one daughter, six months old.

Residence: 609 Wilson Avenue, Allenshire (own home). Allenshire resident 8 years.

Education: [Local university], 1976, School of Law, 1978 (Scholarship student— top student in class).

Community and charitable activities:
Participated in community activities such as factory zoning problem in south end of ward, Northwest Allenshire transportation problem, and represented community (without fee) in litigation concerning the Jackson School corner— gasoline station zoning problem. Member of several Allenshire civic, social, and religious organizations; lecturer on municipal, governmental, and legal problems; member, participant, and attorney for charitable organizations.

Experienced educator:
Member of faculty [local university, School of Law] since 1987. Presently serving as a member of that faculty.

Governmental experience:
Formerly Assistant Regional Attorney, U.S. Government Agencies (four New England states).

Professional experience:
Practicing attorney since 1978. Admitted to practice before state and federal courts, U.S. Court of Appeals, and U.S. Supreme Court.

Professional associations:
Member, Allenshire Bar Association; State Bar Association; Federal Bar Association; [list of national and honorary legal fraternities].

W: Did you send for me, Mr. Zurch?

Z: Yes, I did; I'll be with you in just a minute. *(Mr. Zurch continues to talk to his assistant for seven minutes. During this time there is considerable confusion in the office, with the telephone ringing* *often, and with Mr. Zurch becoming more and more concerned over some matter about which he talks loudly, interspersing his rather definite comments with considerable swearing. This, it may be noted, is his usual manner under stress. Mr. Zurch continues:)* Now, look, Miss Winkler *(takes several minutes to look over her file and to talk to his assistant about another matter)*, you remember we talked together in March and at that time B Division was not satisfied, and since then you have been with Mr. Newton, and he was not altogether satisfied.

W: He didn't tell me anything like that. *(Speaks in a low, courteous voice.)* He told me after I left that he wanted me back. . . .

Z: Now you have been in C Division and there is a report on your work there. Now Miss Winkler, we take each employee and try to fit her in where she can do the best job. We realize that people sometimes can't get along because of the supervisor, or fellow employees, and we try to make adjustments. *(This comment is given in Mr. Zurch's usual direct and belligerent manner.)* Now you have been in a number of positions. How many have you occupied?

W *(after thinking a moment)*: Four or five.

Z: Do you agree with the comments made in this report? *(Quotes from report before him on the desk.)* "Shows little interest in work and says she doesn't care for filing."

W: *(Miss Winkler's voice is growing husky now, and her response is almost inaudible, but she explains that she doesn't like filing and that she wasn't hired to do that kind of work. She was to be a stenographer.)*

Z: We don't have the work always to everyone's satisfaction.

W: But I wasn't told that was what the job would be.

Z: But we can't give everyone a job he wants. . . . *(Interview has turned into something of an argument at this point; Mr. Zurch presents next charge.)* "Deliberately slows down on the job."

W: No, I do not. *(Miss Winkler seems quite incensed at this charge.)*

Z: "Uses business hours to write letters."

W: I did that once.

Z: "Doesn't keep up to date with her work."

W: They put in a new system up there, and the supervisor asked me to help with it, and I said I would. But I couldn't keep up to date on my own work and do that too. The supervisor asked me to do this at the same time that I had more than enough work of my own to do. *(Though deeply disturbed at these charges, Miss Winkler's responses are direct; by this time, however, she is on the verge of tears.)*

Z: "Leaves 15 minutes before 12 and returns 20 to 25 minutes late."

W: If I went before 12, I returned earlier.

Z: "Uses rest room facilities on second floor instead of third as required by the rules."

W: They were dirty on the third floor.

Z: We can't be in those rooms every minute of the day. When I went in there *(apparently at an earlier complaint)*, it wasn't dirty—only a few papers thrown around. It wasn't like any bathroom at home, but it wasn't dirty.

W: I have seen it at times when you couldn't use it.

Z: Why didn't you report it?

W: I did—But that's a petty thing *(i.e., the complaint)*.

Z: Yes, but it means five to ten minutes more away from your desk. Listen, Miss Winkler, I think the supervisor doesn't have an ax to grind; maybe all of these things aren't true, but a certain amount is.

W: I did the work I was told to do, but some had to be left over. They expected me to get the mail out, and certain work had to be left.

Z: That's right, but there are those times when you were away from your work. *(Mr. Zurch explains the limitations on the number of persons the organization may hire; that each girl must do her work, or the organization will get behind.)*

W: I still think the charges aren't fair.

Z: Well, tell me, are there any differences between you and Jones *(her immediate supervisor)?*

W: I'd rather not say.

Z: Don't you get along?

W: Oh, sometimes.

Z: Please tell me the story. . . . *(When it is apparent that there will be no response)* Did you go over this with Miss Counce *(the counselor)?*

W: *(Miss Winkler replies that she did, but by this time she is crying softly, and the exact words were not heard.)*

Z: We have a reputation of being fair. We try to analyze every factor in a report of this kind. . . . You have been here two years, long enough to know the whole story. . . . Do you think you aren't in the right job?

W: I want to leave the job.

Z *(in a milder tone)*: Now that's not the right attitude. We won't get anywhere that way. Has Mr. Achen *(a higher supervisor)* ever talked to you?

W: Not once.

Z: Has the principal clerk of the department talked to you about it?

W: Yes, once. *(Two sentences not heard.)*

Z: Do you think your work too heavy?

W: I can keep it cleaned up at times, but not all the time. There are days when with dictation, etc., I can't.

Z: Well, why don't we have the job analyzed on a week's basis and see if there is too much for one person.

W: A week wouldn't be right; once I was behind for three weeks.

Z: Honestly, haven't you taken extra time off?

W: No, absolutely not. I've noticed other girls going out when they weren't supposed to, though.

Z: Are you getting along with other employees?

W: Yes.

Z: Well, I'll tell you, you go back upstairs after you get set (*i.e., after she has made repairs on her face because of the crying*). Do you have any other comment to make?

W: I feel he (*supervisor*) has been very unfair about my slowing down on my work.

Z: All right, OK, now you stay down until, let's see, it's 3:30 now, until 3:45. I'll call them to expect you at 3:45.

Mr. Zurch's comment after the interview: "This girl comes from a good family and environment and apparently feels that she has a better head than the other workers. Our problem is to get her adjusted. I disagree with this report that she purposely slowed down on the job. The fact that she didn't like filing is nothing against her; we have that trouble all the time. But there is no question that she takes time off. I think 50–60 percent of the charges are correct and the rest is put on for a good story. We'll find that the supervisor hasn't talked to her correctly. She would be a better employee under a girl who could handle her or a smart-looking man. You noted that she was especially indignant at charges of slowing down, but not so indignant on spending extra time out."

Mr. Zurch calls the immediate supervisor and the next higher supervisor into his office to discuss the situation.

Z: What is it all about, this Winkler case?

Mr. Achen: Her attitude is wrong. She wants to be a stenographer, and she was hired as a clerk-typist, and there isn't a 100 percent steno job up there. We give her some dictation, but can't give her full time. She doesn't want to do filing.

Jones: She gets behind. (*Telephone call interrupts.*)

Mr. Achen: She said to someone, "I'll let this filing pile up and just see what happens." I think for the good of the department she should be transferred. (*Another telephone call interrupts.*)

Z: But we can't transfer her all the time.

Mr. Achen: We spoke to her about the rest rooms, but she disregards the rules. We have given her a fair chance.

Z: OK, thanks a lot. (*Apparently the decision is to transfer Miss Winkler to another department. Mr. Zurch goes off to a meeting.*)

Discussion Questions

1. Why did Zurch call in Miss Winkler?
2. What do you think of his approach?

3. Why did he level the charges one after the other without developing Miss Winkler's replies—possibly without listening to her?

4. What did Zurch learn from this interview?

5. What did you think of the manner in which the problem was resolved?

CASE 11.4

The Kiss and the Slap*

In a railroad compartment, an American grandmother with her young and attractive granddaughter, a Romanian officer, and a Nazi officer were the only occupants. The train was passing through a dark tunnel, and all that was heard was a loud kiss and a vigorous slap. After the train emerged from the tunnel, nobody spoke, but the grandmother was saying to herself, "What a fine girl I have raised. She will take care of herself. I am proud of her." The granddaughter was saying to herself, "Well, grandmother is old enough not to mind a little kiss. Besides, the fellows are nice. I am surprised what a hard wallop grandmother has." The Nazi officer was meditating, "How clever those Romanians are! They steal a kiss and have the other fellow slapped." The Romanian officer was chuckling to himself, "How smart I am! I kissed my own hand and slapped the Nazi."

Discussion Questions

1. What does this story have to do with allness?

2. Why did the grandmother, granddaughter, and the Nazi officer perceive the situation so differently?

3. Could this case be analyzed in terms of other patterns of miscommunication?

CASE 11.5

Mickey Mouse in Gray Flannels
*Gerry Friedman**

I was a sales engineer for XYZ, Inc.—specifically, the New York City district sales office. Morale under our sales manager, Mr. Utley, was high. Apparently top management regarded him highly too, and promoted him to Product and Sales Service Manager and assigned him to the Chicago Divisional H.Q.

The following incidents concern the *new* NYC sales manager. They will be presented in two parts: (1) the description of the incident and (2)

---

* Alfred Korzybski, "The Role of Language in the Perceptual Processes," *Perception: An Approach to Personality,* eds. Robert R. Blake and Glenn V. Ramsey. Copyright 1951, The Ronald Press Co. Reprinted by permission.

* Gerry Friedman, 32, is a sales engineer in a midwestern city. He prepared this case for a course in organizational behavior that he took in conjunction with an evening MBA program. All names, including the author's, are disguised.

my interpretation of it. At the end of the case is an organization chart of the XYZ Corporation. (See Exhibit 1 on p. 357.)

Christmas Party

The Eastern Division had a Christmas party. Utley's promotion had been announced, but he was not to depart until his successor had been selected and oriented.

NYC salesman Gant remarked to the Regional Sales Manager, Heinze, "I hope you're not planning on promoting Kenton. If so, over half of the NYC sales staff will leave!" Heinze angrily replied, "Who the hell do you think you are to tell me who I can or can't promote!"

In early January, Heinze announced the promotion of Kenton to NYC District Sales Manager in spite of his Washington office performing under 75 percent of quota two years in a row.

Interpretation.   (Opinions stated in these interpretations are my inferences and are not presented as fact.)

Kenton was disliked by most of the NYC sales personnel. His business activities were unpalatable to most of us. He appeared more interested in selling his bosses than in selling his customers and us.

Gant's Christmas party prediction was not a guess. His opinion was firmly based on discussions we had among ourselves about potential new managers to take Utley's place.

Toll Receipts

Shortly after Kenton arrived, he began the policy of including toll receipts with our expense reports. Tolls varied from 25 cents to 75 cents each. The date and time of day were stamped on most of these receipts.

Interpretation.   This policy was not consistent with Kenton's advice that we make effective use of our time. The toll areas had automatic and manual toll booths. Only the manned booths gave receipts. It was common for us to wait from 15 seconds to over a minute for a manned booth, when we could have driven through an automatic booth in a few seconds. There are many toll areas in the NYC area (including New Jersey and Connecticut). At the end of a week it was common for me to accumulate 20 or more toll receipts. These receipts had to be stapled in chronological order. The total reimbursement on 20 toll receipts may be $5 to $8. The time required to handle these receipts was worth more than $10.

The only logical reason I see for his change of policy is that the dates and time of the day stamped on the receipts were a handy check so that Kenton could verify that his people were actually in the field.

Restaurant Receipts

It had always been the custom to obtain receipts for lunch and other entertainment when accompanied by a customer. If the receipts were included with the expense report, the salesperson would be reimbursed for the expense. One of our secretaries informed some of us that she overheard Kenton calling restaurants to verify that the receipts were not forged.

Interpretation.   Our secretaries were also displeased with Kenton. They would relay information when they thought it would be useful to us.

So far he had given us two messages—he didn't trust us, and it would be better to impress him and other XYZ personnel than to impress customers. So we started writing neater reports; we became more exact and effective at writing letters of which Kenton received a copy; we would not turn in toll receipts if the stamped times were not in our best interests. Because he didn't trust us, we began to follow his prophecy of us. For example, two salespeople would have a long lunch and turn in a receipt claiming that a customer had been along. I don't think he ever called customers to verify if they had been to lunch as claimed on the receipts.

Utley and Kenton had been in sales together in the NYC office several years ago. On a visit to New York, Utley told us that Kenton was a goof-off and apple-polisher at that time. He warned us that Kenton could not be trusted and that he would "poison his mother if it paid enough." Corporation management never seemed to ask employees for their opinion of their boss or fellow workers, so Kenton's unsavory characteristics were apparently unknown to his bosses.

Sales-Stimulation Program

We had a sales meeting each Monday. It began about 5 P.M. and ended anywhere between 7 P.M. and midnight. The corporation had a sales stimulation program which consisted of literature and cassette tapes sent to each of our homes—about one tape each month. Kenton played these tapes at the sales meetings.

Interpretation.   He clearly distrusted us and thought we would play these tapes on our own.

Cards and Beer

When Utley was manager, we would play cards and have a few beers at the office after the sales meetings. This practice stopped immediately after Kenton became manager. He would not allow card playing or drinking on company premises.

Interpretation. Kenton drank and gambled so his reason was not that he disapproved of these activities. I feel he feared reaction from his superiors if they learned of the activities.

These Monday night card games were replaced with a bull session by the salesmen at a local pub. The conversation inevitably led to the poor working conditions under Kenton. Morale was very low. We exchanged new job leads.

Utley respected our right to enjoy a card game and a few beers in the office. This increased our morale. His attitude was, "Let's work hard, but take time out for play, too." I interpreted Kenton's attitude as, "Let's work hard, and don't take time out for play."

The Heinzes' Cocktail Party

Mrs. Heinze sent invitations to each of us in sales and to each of our spouses to attend a cocktail party at the Heinzes'. The sales staff was delighted. This would be an opportunity to become acquainted with Kenton and Heinz and their wives on a social basis. The party was very disappointing. When Kenton talked individually and privately with each of our spouses, he was trying to find weaknesses in our selling habits, such as the amount of work done in the evening at home, arising time in the morning, and time spent at home during normal customer contact hours. He tried to encourage each spouse to interact with his or her mate in the best interests of the company.

Interpretation. I believe that Kenton read a book once that stressed the commitment of employees' spouses to company goals, but he apparently didn't learn how to apply the rules.

Shortly after this party, we—and our spouses—had another gathering and compared notes. It was apparent that Kenton's brainwashing attempt had backfired.

Meet the Veep

Several members of our top management were traveling to NYC for a trade show. Late Friday afternoon preceding the show, Kenton, who was out of town, phoned our office, leaving a message with one of the secretaries. Each of us was to meet one or more of the executives at the airport, escort them to their hotels, and have dinner or refreshments with them if they so desired.

I was to meet our vice president of research and development on Sunday at 11:00 P.M. at Kennedy Airport. This was the first and only information I had received on these plans. I explained to the secretary that I would be unable to comply.

At 2:00 P.M. on the Sunday afternoon preceding the show, we had a meeting at the Coliseum to learn the corporation plans for the coming week at the show. After the meeting was over, at 8:00 P.M., I explained personally to Kenton why I would be unable to meet the vice president.

He exclaimed that this was the first he had heard of it. Our secretary had not given him my message, nor had he asked her for any return messages. He expected his orders (even through our secretary) to be obeyed.

He had been in Washington, D.C. on business, and said that I should have contacted him there. I explained that the cost for a phone call to Washington would be more than a cab ride from the airport, and that my judgment indicated that no action was necessary.

He criticized my poor business judgment and said he would say more about this at a more convenient time for him. My reason for being unable to meet the VP that Sunday evening (even without alternate plans, I would have refused under the circumstances) was a meeting at our church in Hackensack, N.J. Even this was no justification to Kenton.

He coerced Wallace into meeting the VP. This, by the way, caused hard feelings toward me by Wallace, as he blamed me for his plight.

Interpretation.   Kenton apparently felt that we had no alternative but to follow his orders. His method of handling people typically had an adverse effect on those people. He felt that all of us were on duty 24 hours a day, and that we should drop all personal plans to work for him.

Kenton thought this was a good way for him to impress the home office. He expected top management to react something like this: "Wow, personalized taxi and guide service by one of Kenton's salespeople. Kenton must be a real good manager. He is very promotable. He will be the youngest vice president in XYZ history."

When I find that my boss expects me to devote five extra hours on a Sunday night so that he may gain a small favor in a VP's eyes, I'll refuse every time, regardless of any prearranged plans.

Kenton Writes His Own Fan Letter

Kenton prepared a typed letter and addressed it to Mr. Stein, our vice president of marketing, and gave it to salesman Stone and told him to sign it.

This letter to Stein complimented Kenton on a recent business transaction at one of Stone's accounts. Kenton's intent was to have Stein believe that Stone had written the letter himself. Stone did not agree with the contents of the letter; therefore, he did not sign it. Consequently, the letter was not sent as Kenton had intended.

Interpretation.   When Stone told me this, I could hardly believe him until he showed me the letter. I felt Kenton must be psychologically unsound. We felt he was definitely going overboard in trying to sell himself.

Gant's Territory Offered

Kenton took me to dinner one evening. I was shocked when I learned the reason for this dinner. He explained that Gant was doing an ineffective job and that he would have to let him go. Kenton was assigning me to Gant's territory. This would be a promotion for me since Gant's territory included the most important customer in our district. Gant was unaware that he was going to be fired. Kenton was unaware that both Gant and I were actively seeking employment elsewhere. Among the salesmen in our office, Gant was my closest friend.

Interpretation. Gant had been with XYZ for over five years and had an excellent sales record working for Utley in the NYC office and previously in the Albany office.

During my sales training three years earlier, I spent one week in the Albany office and made several sales calls with Gant. My personal opinion then and now is that he is an above-average salesman.

Gant's Christmas party remark had doomed him to early dismissal. True, Gant was not as effective working for Kenton as for Utley, but neither was I nor any of the other NYC sales staff.

Kenton had been able to work up a case against Gant so that he could be fired. But most of the rest of us could have been fired if Kenton had wanted to build a case against us.

I felt very uncomfortable when I knew about Gant's diismissal before he did.

No More Goof-Offs

At our dinner, Kenton said, "The NYC office has always been a bunch of goof-offs. I'm going to tighten the reins on these people."

Interpretation. This comment was a duplicate of Heinze's attitude. It appeared that Kenton was able to alter his behavioral pattern to match that of his boss. But an alternate theory is that his behavioral pattern was developed prior to working for Heinze. The question here is, What came first—his behavioral pattern or his boss?

This goof-off characterization is an overgeneralization. Heinze observed occasions when the NYC salespeople played hard. Apparently he was not aware of our work hard attitude during business hours.

Heinze did not completely approve of Utley as he was not molded in Heinze's image. It is my opinion that Heinze wanted Utley promoted out of his region.[1]

---

[1] Utley's promotion did not bring him up to Heinze's status on the organization chart.

The Youngest VP

Kenton also said: "I'm going to be the youngest vice president in the history of XYZ."

Interpretation.   Kenton was quite a thin man with a pretty face and wavy hair. He had about three years of college, but had not graduated. At 33, he had 12 years' experience with XYZ. Part of his success was due to the rapid growth of XYZ and part to political maneuvering.

The above points suggest why he had so much drive to succeed. He wanted to impress his brother, possibly by passing him on the organizational ladder. Perhaps, during his childhood, he was not successful in sports or in winning friends, and was known as a sissy. This early consideration by others may explain his almost totally dictatorial attitude and almost complete disregard for others' feelings. He did not intend to let anything stand in his way.

Exodus

Within one year of Kenton's promotion, Fox and Stone quit and joined competitive companies. Gant and Smith were fired. (Smith was newly hired to handle my territory in New Jersey.) They joined a competitor. Raymond and I both quit and moved to an unrelated industry.

Rath stayed because she felt she had a good chance to receive a promotion to district manager of a small office soon. Bolling looked for other work.

Wallace resigned (she had 12 years' experience with XYZ and was considered an excellent salesperson by top management). Stein, the F Division VP for marketing, finally intervened and persuaded Wallace to retract her resignation.

Gant's Christmas party prediction came true. Out of the eight original salespeople in the office, five had left, and the remaining three were unhappy with their jobs. In addition, the first person Kenton had hired was asked to leave within six months.

Interpretation.   As each of us left, we hoped someone from the home office would investigate, but nothing was done until Wallace resigned. I don't know what was disclosed during her discussion with Stein. Kenton is still NYC Manager, and Heinze is still Eastern Regional Manager.

Summing Up

I believe Kenton's contribution to XYZ profit, since he became NYC District Manager, was insufficient, even negative.

Four people were trained by XYZ, and this training expense is now benefiting competition. Everyone who was hired to replace us was given extensive and expensive training.

The most important account in the NYC area had four different people calling on it within one six-month period, resulting in some lost business and image.

What counts at XYZ is not how one does the job, but how his or her superiors *believe* he or she is doing the job.

EXHIBIT 1
Organization Chart for the XYZ Corporation

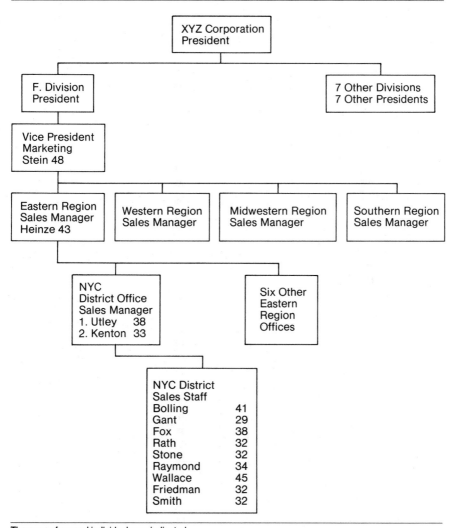

The ages of several individuals are indicated.

Discussion Questions

1. Why did Gerry write this case?

2. What is fact—and what is tint in this case?

3. What is the relevance of the self-image concept to this case?

4. Draw Johari Grids for some of the relationships in this case.

5. Suppose that Heinze acquires a copy of this case and confronts Kenton with it; how would Kenton respond?

6. What does this case have to do with allness?

CHAPTER TWELVE

Differentiation Failures:
1. Indiscrimination
Stereotyping

❋
❋
❋

The two accounts that follow may seem quite diverse, but they are alike in at least one important respect.

Grand Falls, N.B., Jan. 9 (AP)—The foamy white waste products of a starch factory looked like snow to Frederick Boucher, seven, so he jumped into an eight-foot ditch filled with it. Two classmates on their way home from school with Frederick called for help, but by the time the rescuers arrived the boy was dead.

The interview was going smoothly for George Ramsey,[1] a young black man who was soon to be graduated from a well-regarded midwestern university. Judy Novak, the assistant personnel manager, was highly impressed with him on every count—academic record (upper tenth of his class), extracurricular activities, employment experience, references, and so on. Her telephone rang. It was Fred Carleton, founder and president of the firm. He had seen Ramsey apparently being interviewed for a job and insisted that Novak "ease him out of here as soon as possible." Why? In Carleton's words, Ramsey was "clearly a radical—those people with the Afros are all alike!" Judy felt that she had no alternative but to terminate the interview, explaining lamely that Ramsey's qualifications were not appropriate for the currently available positions that the company had.

In each of the above cases, a person failed to discriminate—to separate like things from one another. Whether it was piles of white material or blacks, someone overlooked important differences and saw only similarities. The president, for example, seems to have had difficulty in differentiating

---

[1] All names have been disguised.

among young black men with Afros. To him they evidently appeared as indistinguishable as the proverbial peas in a pod.

We shall use the term *indiscrimination* to represent the behavior that occurs when one fails to recognize variations, nuances, differences; when one is unable or unwilling to distinguish, to differentiate, to separate apparently like things from one another. *Indiscrimination* may be defined, then, as *neglecting differences* while *overemphasizing similarities*. It is one of three forms of differentiation failure that we shall examine in this book. Two others, *polarization* and the *frozen evaluation*, are discussed in the next two chapters.

HARDENING OF THE CATEGORIES

One of the most troublesome consequences of indiscrimination is an evaluational disease that we might appropriately label "hardening of the categories." Most of us have a penchant for categorizing—for classifying. Show someone something that person has never seen before—an unusual butterfly, a peculiar tree leaf, a strange rodent—and one of the first questions is likely to be: "What kind is it?" We meet a new person, and we are uneasy until we can find a pigeonhole. What *is* she?—how is she classified? Is she a salesperson, plumber, farmer, teacher, painter? Is she Protestant, Catholic, Jew, atheist? Democrat, Republican, independent? Lower, middle, upper class?

Categorizing, per se, is not undesirable. Under some circumstances, as we shall examine later, it is essential. But we are concerned here with categorization when the categories become hardened, unyielding, when they tend to deter further analysis and investigation that would be desirable. Joe White,[2] for example, as an office manager for a meat-packing firm, has developed a category for women workers over 50 years old. "They're insecure, inefficient, ineffectual, and temperamental," he will tell you. Thus, when Mary Grey, 52, a widow, applied for a clerical position, Joe did not even bother to interview her. He knew "her kind." Fortunately, another manager of the company did interview her and hired her on the spot. She has since proved to be a stable, energetic, and intelligent worker.

Stereotypes

The word *stereotype* is a useful one for our purposes. Originally a printing term, it stood for a plate that printed the same picture, drawing, and so forth, over and over again. Thus a sociological or psychological stereotype is a fixed, conventional image or picture. One who stereotypes

---

[2] The names are fictitious, but the incident actually occurred.

applies the image of the group to all individuals assigned to that group. The stereotyper disregards, consciously or otherwise, any differences or distinctions that the individual may have that are different from those of the stereotyped group.

The journalist Tom Stacey depicted one group thus: "Politicians are like a bunch of bananas—they stick together, they're yellow, and there's not a straight one among 'em." That's clever and cute and—unjust. Admittedly, politicians are easy targets for satirists, and some of them richly deserve the darts. But in fairness, can we lump in with such politicians the high-minded, courageous men and women of integrity and ability who have literally given their lives in the political service of their nation?

Consider also the prevailing stereotype of poets in America. Such adjectives as thin, effeminate, meek, sensitive, delicate, and eccentric may come quickly to mind. The stereotype can exist only so long as the exceptions are suppressed. But the generalized image dissipates when one considers some of our late contemporary poets—for example, warm, wiry Carl Sandburg; barrel-chested former backwoodsman Lew Sarett; and rugged Robert Frost.

Of course, stereotypes can be expedient devices at times. Many television, pulp, and movie writers cherish them because they serve as shortcuts to characterizations. In the past, screenwriters merely depicted a lean, lanky, sad-faced black shuffling through a scene. They had tapped a familiar mold. The personality and behavior were completely predictable because the writers permitted no deviations from the established pattern.

This story is told of Metropolitan Opera Company prima donna Dorothy Kirsten's debut in motion pictures. Having always worn her hair down, Miss Kirsten was surprised when the studio requested her to change to an upswept coiffure. Reason: "They wanted me to look like a prima donna!" And the Hollywood actor John Wayne was given his first opportunity when the director Raoul Walsh decided that he measured up to the requirements: "To be a cowboy star you gotta be six feet three or over; you gotta have no hips and a face that looks right under a sombrero."

And so stereotypes can save time and effort. They obviate any additional analysis or investigation. There is no need to look for differences—a stereotype precludes them. Stereotyping permits us to set up neat, well-ordered, and oversimplified categories into which we can slip our evaluations of people, situations, and happenings.

THE BATTLE OF THE CATEGORIES

Few of us go very far in life without having to fight the battle of the categories. Try to change your line of work, to transfer from one subject major to another in college, to compete for a dramatic role in the school play when you have been classified as an athlete or a campus politician, and you invariably find people resisting your attempt to break through their categories.

One of the most widespread and anguished complaints from actors and actresses is that they were stereotyped early in their careers. Thus, they are now rarely offered roles other than the kind they had previously portrayed.

Basil Rathbone, the personification of Sherlock Holmes in many minds, was such a victim. In his recently rereleased autobiography, *In and Out of Character*, he claims that he was typecast more "than any other classic actor. . . . My 52 roles in 23 plays of Shakespeare, my years in the London and New York theater, my scores of motion pictures including my two Academy Award nominations, were slowly sinking into oblivion and there was nothing I could do about it."

Out of thousands, a few managed to evade such branding. These particular personalities come to mind:

Carol Burnett	Tom Cruise	Kathleen Turner
Glenn Close	Robert DeNiro	Joanne Woodward
Jamie Lee Curtis	Michael Douglas	Gene Hackman
Faye Dunaway	Richard Dreyfuss	Dustin Hoffman
Sally Field	Richard Gere	Jack Lemon
Jane Fonda	Marsha Mason	Paul Newman
Angelica Huston	Demi Moore	Jack Nicholson
Shirley MacLaine	Julia Roberts	Al Pacino
Alan Alda	Meg Ryan	Robert Redford
Marlon Brando	Sissy Spacek	Patrick Swayze
Kevin Costner	Meryl Streep	Lynn Redgrave

Those are some of the largest names in Hollywood, of course, which raises a question. Did these people reach stardom at least partly because they resisted typecasting? Or were they "big" enough to defy categorization and choose a variety of roles? Or both?

In a penetrating book about the Rockefellers, the great-grandchildren of John D. uniformly complain how they have been victimized by stereotyping. For example, Hope, daughter of John D. III, laments:

> In growing up a Rockefeller, I lived with a tag, just like a Jew or a black. I'm not by any means suggesting I suffered in the same way, but it is true that when people heard the name Rockefeller, there was no way they could see the person named Hope.[3]

As one hardens categories, and accepts stereotypes, one is progressively less able to search out the differences. The characteristic response

---

[3] Peter Collier and David Horowitz, *The Rockefellers* (New York: New American Library, 1979), p. 526.

to a new person, situation, thing, or idea is to find the proper category, to slip the new object into a pigeonhole. Some persons are terribly uneasy until they can tack on a label. Does this person belong to a union? Is he a Jew? A Democrat? A Sigma Sigma? An ex-convict? These people can only relax when they find the "right" tag.

A key danger with hardened categories is that the categorizer is prone to evaluate with faulty analogies. Situation (or person) A is new, but seems similar to situation (or person) B. Anxious to complete the pigeon-holing, the categorizer sweeps A into B's category with the dangerous assumption that the way to behave with respect to A is the way with respect to B.

When his outfit was deactivated, Sergeant Vincent Bonura[4] was reassigned to another camp. He reported to his new company commander, Captain Carl Barnes, and the men exchanged salutes.

"At ease, Sergeant, smoke if you like."

"Thank you, sir."

"Well, Sergeant, I want to get the best from every one of my men, so I'll want to check you on all your past experience so I can see best where I can use you. Let's see . . . Bonura. That's Italian, isn't it?"

"No, sir, I'm Sicilian."

"Ooooh, a Sicilian. . . . Well, Sergeant, I've had Sicilians in my outfits before, and I want to get one thing straight. I don't like any troublemakers in my company."

"Sir, I'm not a troublemaker!"

"Don't interrupt me, Bonura!"

"Sorry, sir."

"In Nam, I had this man . . . Mazzaro . . . Marzano . . . something like that, and from the time he came to me until I got rid of him he gave me nothing but trouble. Now I don't know why you got shipped out of your old outfit. . . ."

"Sir!"

"Sergeant! I don't know why you got shipped out, but if you're the hot-headed type, I'll make it plenty rough for you around here—and give you plenty of time for cooling off!"

CONTRIBUTING FACTORS

Why do people behave in these irrational, rigid ways? They do so because they neglect differences and overemphasize similarities. And why do they do that? Two of the major contributing factors are (1) self-serving emotions and (2) the structure of our language.

---

[4] The names have been disguised.

Self-Serving Emotions

I know a bright young man who also happens to be a college instructor. He's still paying off debts he accumulated in graduate school and, in the interests of economy, he purchased a motorcycle for transportation. But he hadn't foreseen the reactions of others. Here's his account:

> I never understood much about the nature of prejudice until last year, when I bought a motorcycle. In short order, I learned what it was like to be a member of a minority group.
>
> For the first time in my life, I knew I was being judged not for myself, but for what I stood for in the minds of some. I was no longer a separate and distinct individual, but a type. Or rather, a stereotype called a motorcyclist.
>
> Even though only a small fraction of the people who ride motorcycles are hoodlums or even roughnecks, perceptions of the whole class are influenced by the conduct of the worst element. Statistically, that perception is a very crude caricature of the average motorcyclist. We are all regarded with the same suspicion and uneasiness, if not downright hostility, as if we were all charter members of the Hell's Angels. Everywhere I rode, I felt the hot breath of prejudice on the back of my neck.

My friend evidently experienced what psychiatrists call paranoid projection—the tendency to displace one's fear or anger or aggressiveness on some group easily identifiable by race, religion, political persuasion, or lifestyle that deviates from society's norms. British psychiatrist Dr. Anthony Storr said, "There can be very few of us who do not unthinkingly entertain beliefs or prejudices about groups other than our own which will not stand the light of critical examination . . . for it is prejudices of this kind which serve to bolster our self-esteem."

By projecting from some small percentage of motorcyclists to the whole group, we legitimatize our irrational fears and transfer our own latent aggressive feelings to an alien group. In England, Storr points out, the Scottish, Irish, and Welsh were the victims of the same suspicion and defamation that blacks, Jews, Hispanics, and other minorities have experienced in the United States.[5]

Language Structure

There is another contributor to indiscrimination worthy of attention, not merely because it is important, but because it offers a remedial approach to the problem. It constitutes a factor that can be altered and thus can effect an important change in the outcome. I am speaking of *language*. We can demonstrate the point if you will study Figure 12.1. Now,

---

[5] William B. Helmreich, *The Things They Say Behind Your Back* (New York: Doubleday, 1982) is an insightful book on stereotyping.

FIGURE 12.1

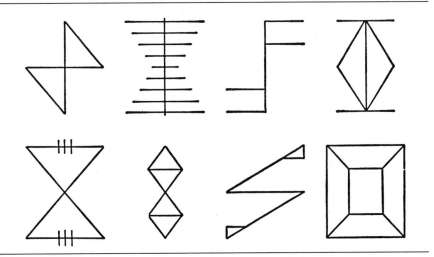

before you read any further, make a statement (write it down, speak it aloud, or simply say it to yourself) about what you see there.

If you responded without too much consideration, the chances are that your statement described how the items in the figure were *alike*. "Geometric figures," "straight-line drawings," "patterns," "forms," and so on, are common responses. Our little game illustrates what linguistic specialists have recognized for years, English-speaking persons find it relatively easy to perceive and to speak in terms of similarities. In other words, we are often more prone to generalize than to differentiate.

Our propensity to see similarities may be explained partly by the abundance of generic nouns and verbs in our language.[6] We may use the word *wood,* for example, to stand for a myriad of objects ranging from a sliver to a giant Sequoia. Consider the enormous variety of fabrics that *cloth* may be used to represent. Think for a moment of the almost infinite variations in form, size, shape, color, and so forth, that such words as *African, furniture, Catholic, student,* and *animal* may represent.

Here is a curious and revealing comparison. In English, we can use the word *snow* to refer to a snowflake, a snowball, a flurry, a blizzard, an avalanche, lightly or heavily falling snow, snow that is dry, wet, caked, loose, compact, shifting, still, and so on. But the Eskimo (Inuit), astonishingly, have no one word for all of these! To be sure, they have a large vocabulary of words for many specific forms of snow. For example, they

---

[6] We have no monopoly on general words (or on the ability to generalize). But our language is outstanding in this respect when compared with certain other languages, particularly those of some of the more primitive cultures.

have 26 specific expressions for textures of ice and snow. But they have no one general word, such as our *snow*, for all of them. This is fortunate, in a way, for the Eskimo. With their abundance of specific nouns and a dearth of general nouns, they are led to focus upon the differences in their environment. Take the case of snow, for example. The Eskimo have to be constantly on the alert for the differences in drift patterns, textures, crust strengths, and so on. If they do not attend to these, they may not provide a full dinner table for their families—they may not even get home to their families at all. And so their language, which encourages them to perceive differences, may be a definite boon in this respect.

Our preponderance of mass verbs is another case in point. We have a large number of verbs that represent, to many foreigners at least, a perplexing variety of actions. *Get, make, do, carry,* and *use* are just a few of these. *Go* is a particularly interesting example. We use this word for going on foot and also for being transported, as by vehicle. But the German has no comparable verb. When he or she goes on foot, *gehen* is appropriate. But traveling by vehicle requires an entirely different verb, *fahren*.

The language of the Navaho Indian goes much farther. When traveling by horse, the Navaho have no way to express the general notion of going by horseback. Their language requires that they specify the gait of the animal, whether it be, for example, at a walk, a trot, or a gallop. Moreover, the language insists upon another division of the generic process of going. The Navaho must distinguish among starting to go, going along, arriving at a point, returning from a point, and so forth. Such distinctions can, of course, be made in English, but they are not made consistently.

Conversely, it appears that the plethora of general verbs[7] (and nouns) in our language both reflects and encourages our inclination to see the relationships and similarities among phenomena.

The crux of this chapter is that the process of noting similarities generally involves the neglecting of differences. Recall your reaction to the drawings in Figure 12.1. When one says or visualizes: "They are all geometric designs, figures, drawings, and so on," attention is called to the ways in which the units are alike and suppressing recognition of their differences. One neglects, for the moment at least, that the second drawing,

---

[7] English certainly has no dearth of specific nouns and verbs, especially with respect to those aspects of our culture on which we place a great deal of emphasis. Sports is an example in point. These synonyms for the verb *defeat* were gleaned from just one week's scanning of newspaper sports pages:

bash	edge	overtake	slash	stifle	trounce
batter	mangle	scalp	slaughter	top	vanquish
best	massacre	scuttle	slip by	topple	wallop
blast	maul	shade	smash	trample	whip
crush	nick	sink	smother	trim	whitewash
down	nip	skin	squeeze by	trip	zap

top row, is similar to a row of telephone poles reflected in water; that the fourth drawing, bottom row, is the only rectangle, and so forth.

A language that prompts us to note similarities, then, may tend to discourage us from observing differences. And the failure to see differences, as we have discussed, may lead to the destructive and dangerous patterns of indiscrimination. Let us now examine some of the possible preventives and remedies that we may use in coping with indiscrimination.

CORRECTIVES

A difficult aspect in the treatment of hardened categories is that categorizers are usually unaware that stereotypes are affecting their behavior. They become so oblivious of their overemphasis on similarities and neglect of differences that they take the rigidly categorized world of their own making for granted.

Of course, we all carry our sets of categories around with us. You are a rare person if some sort of stereotyped image does not occur to you at the mention of at least some of these terms:

preppies	groupies	wife-abusers
doctors	rednecks	alcoholics
Southerners	gays	white-collar workers
addicts	straights	damn Yankees
union officials	jocks	management
blacks	yuppies	terrorists
feminists	couch potatoes	evangelists
professors	lawyers	artists
radicals	chauvinists	teenagers
bankers	the homeless	wetbacks
muggers	Satanists	punk rockers
homophobes	cops	ex-cons

But the mere occurrence of conventionalized images to you does not necessarily make you a chronic stereotyper. Joe may be quite aware that his generalized image is just that, and often with little or no basis in fact. He says to himself, in effect: "Sure, you mention 'professor,' and I think immediately of the pedantic, absentminded fuddy-duddy, carrying a rolled-up umbrella and wearing spats. But that's just the stereotype. Actually, very few of the professors I have known even approach this caricature."

The problem of indiscrimination arises when a person is unaware of or unwilling to recognize stereotypes as such—when, in other words, the categories become hardened. Thus an approach to the dissolution of stereotypes—to the softening of categories—is to work toward the awareness of them. What can we do to alert ourselves to the influences of stereotypes upon our evaluations and communications?

Become Sensitive to Differences

Recall that this chapter holds that the overemphasis on similarities and the corresponding neglect of differences frequently lead to stereotyping. In fact, stereotypes cannot exist without the neglect of differences. The moment we begin to take differences into account, our stereotypes begin to disintegrate. As we make a deeply ingrained habit of looking for differences, we approach a self-awareness which makes possible mature, intelligently discriminating behavior in dealing with people, situations, happenings, relationships, and so forth. "The more we discriminate among," Irving J. Lee said, "the less we will discriminate against."

Internalize the Premise of Uniqueness. Perhaps the first step toward developing a heightened awareness of differences is to disavow the erroneous notion of identicalness. No two things have ever been found to be exactly identical in all respects—or even in one respect. Those two peas in the pod are actually quite dissimilar, even to the naked eye, if one observes closely. "Nature," wrote Ralph Waldo Emerson, "never rhymes her children nor makes two alike." No two snowflakes, no two blades of grass, no two grains of sand—no two of anything—have ever been shown to be completely identical. An important technique of identification is based on the presumption that no two fingerprints are exactly the same. Consider that there are about 5 billion persons on earth with approximately 10 fingers each and add all the people who have gone before us and are yet to come—it is an astonishing presumption. Yet it has never been disproved.

Nor have we contrived two of anything that are completely identical. A machinist friend tells me that possibly the most precise manufactured objects are Johansson blocks. Jo blocks are used to check the accuracy of micrometers (extremely exact instruments in themselves). I have seen Jo blocks so precise that placing two of them together created a partial vacuum, so that a person found it impossible to pull them directly apart! You had to twist and slide them to separate them. Are Jo blocks identical, then? They are incredibly alike—machined within a tolerance of plus or minus two millionths of an inch! But note, these are tolerances—that is, even Jo block machinists must admit that they can only approach identicalness, never attain it.

Because no two of anything have been found to be absolutely the same, we have a useful premise: There is always uniqueness, never identicalness. If we are deeply convinced that there are always differences, we may not be so prone to overlook them. We will be less likely, in the words of A. B. Johnson, to "disregard the individuality of nature, and substitute a generality which belongs to language."

Index Your Evaluations. One simple device which has proved successful in developing the awareness of differences is the *index*. Indexing is hardly a new process. Cooks index their recipes, executives their correspondence, librarians their papers and books. Each is separating items according to the essential differences among them. The habit of indexing people, things, situations, and so on, is equally, if not more, useful. The salesperson who habitually indexes will react to purchasing agent$_1$ as if he or she were different from purchasing agent$_2$—they are different.

Make a habit of indexing. The next time you hear someone (or yourself) making statements such as these below, ask yourself *Which?*

"Union officials are corrupt!"	*Which* officials of *which* unions!
"Women shouldn't be allowed to drive automobiles!"	*Which* women drivers?—and might there be some men drivers you would ban from driving?
"Doctors are mercenary!"	*Which* doctors? Would you include your hometown physician? Those who contribute half their time to charity cases? Those who work in laboratories at a fraction of the income they could command?

Doctor$_1$ is different from doctor$_2$, of course, and doctor$_2$ is different from doctor$_3$, and so on. Use the little subscript as a mental exercise, as a habitual memory jogger to call your attention to the differences.

As the next two chapters will describe two other types of indexing, let's index the indexes. To distinguish them, this chapter advocates the use of the Which Index.

THE VALUES OF SEEING SIMILARITIES

To digress for a moment, I trust that I have not given the impression that one should focus on differences at the expense of similarities. The ability to note similarities is essential in generalizing, categorizing, codifying, organizing, classifying, arranging, cataloging, and so forth. These activities, in turn, are indispensable in learning, analyzing, problem solving, innovating, decision making, and so on. For example, children learn about fractions when their teacher shows how the parts of a pie, when put together, make a whole pie. From this they can generalize to (i.e., see the similarities with) fractions of a plot of land or fractions of a container of milk. They eventually generalize to the visualization of fractions as an abstract idea.

Take another case. Suppose that you plan to build a motel and want to find the optimal location for it. Your basic approach is to analogize—that is, you will look for similarities with respect to location among successful existing motels. You may find that these motels are usually located on major highways within easy access of motorists. Moreover, they tend to be situated on the outskirts of cities, far enough out to avoid high real estate taxes and competition from hotels, yet close enough in to utilize the inexpensive urban power and water, and so forth. Thus you may be able to make a wiser decision because you have been able to abstract key similarities out of a myriad of differences among the motels.

Categorizing, cataloging, and classifying (all based on seeing the similarities) are imperative in modern business. Imagine the chaos in the offices of the comptroller, the purchasing agent, the production control manager, and so forth, if they were somehow prevented from classifying and organizing the multitudinous data and details with which they deal.

Scientific advance (or progress on any frontier) is intimately related to the perception of similarities. We learn about the unknown largely on the basis of the known. Someone must have been able to generalize from perhaps a rolling log to the notion of a wheel, from a boiling kettle to a steam engine, and from a flying kite, bird, and so on, to the visualization of an airplane.

This chapter hardly proposes to minimize the value of seeing similarities. Our goal is to achieve better-balanced perceptions—to see differences as well as similarities. To accomplish this, most of us need training in looking for differences. Thanks to our formal education, language structure, and so forth, we are already adept at noting similarities.

SUMMARY

In life, there are differences as well as similarities. Our language structure, however, which subtly influences our evaluating and communicating patterns, encourages us to overemphasize similarities and to neglect differences. The frequent result is that we may behave in terms of stereotypes (neglect of differences) and react to essentially different and unique people, situations, and things as if they were identical with our self-manufactured stereotypes. We can develop a greater sensitivity to differences by internalizing the premise of uniqueness and by applying the Which Index in our evaluations of people, situations, and so forth. The deeply ingrained habit of asking "Which?" will diminish the tendencies to overgeneralize that so frequently lead to stupid, unsafe, and unsane behavior.

Remember, these are differences that make a difference—take them into account.

Discussion Questions

1. In primitive societies, such as those of the Eskimo, there tend to be fewer generic words and more specific words, especially for important aspects of life. The Trobriand Islanders, for example, have no single word for *yam* but many specific words to denote the yam at its various stages of growth. What are the implications of this? Is it good or bad that a language has many or few mass words—many or few specific words? Why?

2. "The more we discriminate among, the less we will discriminate against."— Irving J. Lee. Do you agree? If people lived by this motto, would it be an effective attack on bigotry, on racial, ethnic, and sexual inequities? What are the obstacles to promulgating this concept more widely?

3. A century and a half ago A. B. Johnson warned against the tendency to "disregard the individuality of nature, and substitute a generality which belongs to language." What did he mean? Specifically, what should we do to heed his warning?

4. This chapter seems to be mainly concerned with the tendency to overlook differences. But what about similarities? Is there not value in being able to abstract them from a situation?

5. What connection is there between the ability to perceive similarities and education? Business decisions? Scientific advance? Government?

6. Prepare a report on an incident, perhaps involving yourself, in which indiscrimination occurred. Analyze why it happened, what could have been done to prevent or correct this incident, what measures are likely to prevent its recurrence.

C A S E S

CASE 12.1

The Dixon Company*

The Dixon Company, a national restaurant chain, recently found itself short of the cash funds necessary to establish several new restaurants. Albert Bullock, the president, instructed Walter Green, the company's 60-year-old treasurer, to enter into negotiations with a local bank for a $1.6 million loan. The bank indicated that the loan would be granted provided the company submitted a satisfactory audit report by an independent public accounting firm.

Mr. Green requested the public accounting firm of Wilscher and Wunderlich to perform the audit. Edward Thorndike, a partner in W & W, assigned Tom Scott to supervise the audit. Scott, 26, had been with W & W for five years and had proven to be a highly capable certified public accountant, although inclined to be somewhat overconfident in his manner.

Within the first few days of the audit, Scott uncovered several company accounting policies that were not in agreement with generally accepted accounting principles. After lengthy discussions with Mr. Green, Scott was able to have these exceptions corrected.

During the final week of the audit, Scott took another apparent accounting principle variance to Green.

Scott: I've got another book adjustment for your approval, Mr. Green.

Green: All right, Tom, what is it?

Scott: As you know, accounting depreciation principles are based on the theory that certain assets purchased and used in the business produce income. If such an asset is usable over a period of more than one year, its cost should be systematically and consistently prorated over its estimated useful life. Thus, each year's income is charged with a proportional part of the cost of the equipment used to produce such income. I've discovered that while you follow this principle in regard to most assets, you do not consistently and systematically depreciate class 10 equipment (dishes, glassware, etc.). In the last three years, you charged off 5 percent, 8 percent, and 3 percent, respectively. If you had followed a correct policy, the percentages would all be the same.

Green (*smiling*): Well, Tom, I've gone along with all your other adjustments, but you're off base on this one. I guess you still have a little to learn about the restaurant business.

---

* All names have been disguised.

Scott (*suddenly flushing with anger*): Why, any elementary accounting textbook will tell you you can't vary your depreciation rate
policy.

Green: You go out and find yourself a modern, up-to-date book on
depreciation methods, young man. Then, you will realize you are
wrong.

The conversation grew more heated and finally Scott walked angrily
from Green's office, saying: "Well, I'm sorry if I can't make you understand this, but I'm going to report this to my supervisor, and I'm sure we'll
have to note this exception in our report to the bank."

Scott phoned Thorndike and reported his disagreement with Green.
Mr. Thorndike replied: "Tom, a dish does not *wear* out; its life ends suddenly with a crash. The normal depreciation principle often cannot be
applied to a restaurant's class 10 equipment. Variable depreciation rates
based on such factors as actual glassware inventory counts or current
glassware purchases are acceptable. These factors give some indication of
the rate of loss as the result of breakage."

When he had concluded the phone conversation with Scott, Thorndike
made this notation in his assignment files: "*If* we get the Dixon job next
year we will have to find someone else to handle the fieldwork. Scott
seems to have clashed with the company's treasurer."

Discussion Questions

1. How does this case relate to *indiscrimination*?

2. Why did Scott insist that he was correct in challenging the company's depreciation policy?

3. Scott flushed with anger. Why?

4. How should Tom Scott have behaved differently?

CASE 12.2

Tommie Sanders–A*

Sanders: Just for the record, my name's Tommie Sanders and I'm
assistant director of sales for a large hotel near Chicago's O'Hare
Airport. Well, since all of this is going to be disguised anyway, I'll
level with you. I was baptized as Tomasina Maria Sanchez
Sandoval.

Interviewer: You've changed your name?

Sanders: Yep. Legally. I went to court and everything.

Interviewer: Why the change?

---

* All names have been disguised. You may wish to compare this case with "Tommie
Sanders–B," Case 7.6.

Sanders: Prejudice. Look, I was born and raised in Mexico—Monterrey. I was very fortunate. My father is an engineer and an executive with a big steel firm in Monterrey. So he could afford to give me a top-notch education. I even have an M.B.A. from UCLA. Despite all that, up here the minute they learn you're from Mexico or Puerto Rico or anywhere in Central or South America, they put you down.

Interviewer: Hispanic stereotyping?

Sanders: Exactly. And I got tired of it and I fought it.

Interviewer: How?

Sanders: Well, I wasn't too smart at first. I'd get mad and then they'd pour it on all the more. Then I finally wised up.

Interviewer: How was that?

Sanders: Well, I did some thinking. No way was I going to change gringo thinking. So I decided to become a gringo myself—or gringa, if you want to be correct about it.

Interviewer: How did you do that?

Sanders: I'm kind of proud of the way I handled that. As I mentioned, I got the UCLA degree, I had my name changed, and I worked real hard on my English. Hear any accent?

Interviewer: Sure don't.

Sanders: And you won't unless I became very, very tired—or if I drink a little too much.

Interviewer: So you have to watch out sometimes?

Sanders: Yes, but I know when I'm approaching my limit so that's under control. Well, to continue—I became a naturalized U.S. citizen. And probably my biggest plus is that my skin is pretty light and I don't look very "Mexican," whatever that is. I even married a gringo guy. I met him at UCLA.

Interviewer: Does he know about your background?

Sanders: Oh, sure, I wouldn't keep that from him, but nobody else around here knows about it.

Interviewer: And you'd like to keep it that way?

Sanders: Precisely. Oh . . . (wistful) . . . I might eventually open up if the world ever grows up . . . or if I become more secure.

Interviewer: A number of Mexicans have become very successful and famous. Perhaps that will help.

Sanders: Maybe. But it's interesting that Anthony Quinn and Raquel Welch and Martin Sheen only admitted their Mexican origin *after* they became big movie stars. Oh, I forgot one thing. A lot of the people around here speak Spanish—you know, waiters, kitchen help, housekeepers, and so forth. Well, I can speak Spanish as well as they can. In fact, I can speak it better because a lot of those people don't have much education.

Interviewer: So?

Sanders: When I speak to them in Spanish I deliberately make mistakes so I don't tip anybody off.

Interviewer: That's something else you have to watch.

Sanders: Yep.

Interviewer: How about being a woman—any prejudices there?

Sanders: Oh, sure, and you have to take a certain amount of crap. But I don't let it bother me—I'm used to it. Actually, if I had stayed in Monterrey it would have been a lot worse. Where do you think that word "machismo" came from?

Interviewer: I'm a little confused with the chronology. You attended primary and secondary schools in Mexico?

Sanders: Right.

Interviewer: Then college?

Sanders: Yes, but at Southern Cal, I majored in psych. Then the M.B.A. at UCLA with a major in marketing. Then I took a job with a first-class hotel in Los Angles.

Interviewer: Did you experience ethnic prejudices at these places?

Sanders: Some, but not as much as I found in other parts of the country.

Interviewer: And yet the newspapers keep reporting about the shoddy treatment migrant workers receive in California.

Sanders: Well, yes—but they're working on the farms and ranches. From what I hear they're treated like dirt. It would be even worse if they didn't have people like Cesar Chavez sticking up for them. Of course, one of their problems is that a lot of them are still illegal so they're constantly worried that Immigration might swoop down on them and send them back across the border.

Interviewer: Didn't they take advantage of the Amnesty program back in the late 1980s?

Sanders: Well, a lot weren't even in the country back then. And those that were—well, they just didn't trust the government and come forth.

Interviewer: You can understand that?

Sanders: Sure. They never could trust the Mexican government so they weren't about to trust the gringo government.

Interviewer: Getting back—it wasn't too bad in the universities or at the hotel?

Sanders: No, and one reason for that is that there were a lot of sharp Mexicans in those schools and a gringo would feel pretty foolish to put down a straight A Mexicano when he's lucky to be pulling down Cs himself.

Interviewer: How about the hotel?

Sanders: Well, by the time I got to the hotel I had degrees from those prestigious schools behind me and also I started at the hotel with a pretty decent job and salary.

Interviewer: What did you do there?

Sanders: They put me on the fast track so I wound up doing just about everything at different times—front desk, food service, sales, catering, housekeeping. I was even a "bell boy" for a while. You name it—I did it.

Interviewer: How long did you stay there?

Sanders: Almost seven years. Then I got an offer from this hotel that I just couldn't refuse.

Interviewer: And by the time you came here, you were Tommie Sanders?

Sanders: That's right. I felt I could make a clean start on that front, and I have.

Interviewer: Everything else going O.K. here?

Sanders: Well, I've been here two years and I can't say I'm crazy about these Chicago winters! But Kenny and I have a nice home in Oak Park and he really enjoys his work.

Interviewer: And how about your work? How's that been going?

Sanders: For the most part it's been great. I've received a couple of pay raises and my responsibilities have increased. Frankly, there are a couple of clouds on the horizon.

Interviewer: What clouds?

Sanders: I knew you'd want to talk about those! But I can't do it right now. I've go to get to a meeting. Maybe we can talk about the "clouds" later.

Tommie Sanders excused herself.

Discussion Questions

1. What do you think of Tommie's decision to conceal her ethnic background?

2. Do you have any suggestions for her now?

3. Why is this case appended to this chapter?

CASE 12.3

Once a Hammersmith . . .

Kathy Schneider*

I'm a metallurgist with the Amerosa Steel Forge Company near Gary. My husband is a metallurgist, too, but he's with a competitor. I'm an innocent bystander in this case but I think it's an interesting situation.

I first met Chris Rodriguez when he was about 26. He had joined Amerosa when was 19. His initial job was as a floor sweeper in the production

---

* All names (including the author's) have been disguised.

department. He was a bright, personable young fellow so he won a number of promotions and finally he was offered the position of hammersmith.

Now, the pay for hammersmiths is excellent but the working conditions—well, they are incredible. The steel billets and blooms are brought in just below the melting point. The hammersmith positions the glowing hot metal on the press and triggers the automatic hammer.

Well, the jarring, the noise, the fumes and worst of all, the temperature—well, you wouldn't believe it. There's an old joke that hammersmiths never have to go to hell—they've already been there.

Oh, I should mention winter. Remember those fumes? You need fresh air to dissipate them. And also you have to have an enormous amount of fresh air for the heat treatment furnaces. So there is a tremendous draft from outside. Now in the winter it might be 10° below outside and that metal might be 700° above. So imagine how that would be—the hammersmith is roasting in the front and his butt is freezing. . . . But the industrial engineers say—this is a joke, by the way—they say that *on the average* he's comfortable!

The job pays damned well but those guys take a beating. I don't begrudge them their paychecks.

Well, anyway, Chris did fine. But after four or five years he got a little restless. It seems that hammersmithing at Amerosa is pretty much a dead-end job. All the foremen in production were only in their 30s and 40s and with the seniority system they have here there was no way Chris could move up where he was. So he went to management and asked if they would transfer him to sales.

Well, I don't blame him for that. Sales is a hell of a lot cleaner than working down there with the presses. And I think he would have been very successful in sales. As I said, he was smart, good-looking, knew how to talk to people. And by now he certainly had the technical background. I should add that in our business if you're in sales you have to know your beans. You're working with purchasing agents with the client companies and they won't tolerate dummies.

But management just dragged their heels and passed the buck and finally they just came out and told him: "You're in production and that's where you're going to stay."

He didn't take that too well. He didn't say anything but you could tell that it bothered him that they had turned him down.

So guess what happened two years ago? Chris just up and quit—no warning! Somehow he got some financial backing so he took his two younger brothers—both of whom worked for Amerosa—and went down to Kentucky and set up his own steel forge shop!

How's he doing? As far as I can tell—very well. He's handling sales, of course. Please don't mention this to anyone but they offered jobs to me and Fred—that's my husband—and we're thinking about going down there and joining them.

Discussion Questions

1. What has happened in this case?
2. Why was Chris refused a transfer to sales?
3. What does this case have to do with "indiscrimination"?

CASE 12.4

Wright Cleaners and Dyers, Ltd.*

Wright Cleaners and Dyers operated a number of retail branches throughout a large metropolitan area. Many of the older branches were located in neighborhoods that had become economically depressed. A few, such as the store established in Whitesdale six months earlier, were in upper middle-class communities.

Richard Clark, 35, an executive in a rapidly expanding firm, lived in Whitesdale with his wife and two young sons, 5 and 3. As Clark left for a short business trip on Monday, he asked his wife to take several of his shirts to Wright's. Mrs. Jackson, sole clerk at the Whitesdale branch, promised Mrs. Clark that the shirts would be ready by Wednesday.

Mrs. Jackson, 61, a widow, had been forced by the death of her husband to obtain employment. She had been working for Wright's for six months—her first job since her marriage in her early 20s. Except for a brief indoctrination period at Wright headquarters, she had spent all of this time at the Whitesdale store.

Clark arrived home late Wednesday night and wasn't expected in the office until Thursday noon. The next morning he drove with his sons to Wright's. He walked into the store with his boys at 8:30 A.M..

> **Clark:** Are my shirts ready yet?
> **Jackson:** Do you have your ticket?
> **Clark:** Ticket? No, I didn't know you had to have one.
> **Jackson:** Oh, yes—I can't find your laundry without a ticket number.
> **Clark:** Well, OK—I guess my wife has it at home.

Clark loaded his boys into the car, drove the mile back to his home, picked up the ticket, and returned with his children to Wright's.

> **Jackson** (after glancing at the ticket number): Oh, that's not in yet.
> **Clark:** But my wife said they were promised for yesterday.
> **Jackson:** Well, they may have come in this morning, but they would be in large boxes in the back, and it would take an hour to unpack them. You come back in an hour, and I'm sure I'll have them ready for you.

_____

* All names have been disguised.

Clark: Why don't you let me help you go through the boxes? This running back and forth is getting ridiculous.

Jackson: I can't do that—no one is allowed back of the partition.

At this, Mrs. Jackson walked behind the partition, leaving an exasperated Clark, who decided he could do no more with the situation at this point.

In an hour Clark returned.

Jackson: Here are the shirts—I got them out for you. I'm sorry about the delay.

Clark: If you're sorry, may I assume that you wouldn't like to have this sort of thing happen again?

Jackson: Why, yes, of course.

Clark: Well, whose rule is it that no one is allowed to help you sort out the laundry in an emergency?

Jackson: The supervisor's—that's a store rule.

Clark: Then I would suggest that you advise your supervisor, since you are closer to the situation, that this store is in Whitesdale— not in some blighted type of neighborhood. I think you can assume that people are honest here.

Jackson: Oh, it isn't a question of honesty. I had a woman in here a couple of weeks ago who went through the cleaning bags hanging on the racks—tearing them open—to find her cleaning.

Clark: I don't see the similarity—I had the ticket number—nothing would have had to be torn open.

Jackson: Well, no one is allowed behind the partition. That's a store rule.

Clark: I know, and most of the time it's probably a good rule—but don't you suppose there might be an exception—an instance when a rule might be broken?

Jackson: No, that's what rules are for. (*Mrs. Jackson quickly walked behind the partition.*)

Later in the day, Clark telephoned Wright's main office and spoke to Anthony Conti, supervisor of stores.

Clark: Mr. Conti, I didn't feel like doing you people a favor this morning, but I'm a little more mellow now. I'd like to tell you about a practice which may lose you customers. (*Clark recounted the incident with Mrs. Jackson.*)

Conti: Well, I'll tell you, Mr. Clark—I'll tell you why that happened. You see, we train our girls all alike because we may have to transfer them from one store to another, and so on. Now we tell them *never* and under *no* conditions to let anyone go back of the partition. And there are two reasons why we tell them this. Now we find that nine times out of ten whenever we get a customer back there fooling around with the cleaning, there's going to be confusion. And the second reason is the safety of the girls. You know what I mean—we can't let a man back there with the girls.

Clark: I know what you mean, but I don't think Mrs. Jackson should have been concerned. She's seen me several times in the store. And I don't exactly dress or look like an escaped convict—besides, I had my two little boys with me.

Conti: Well, you have to have a rule, though—you never know, and those things can happen.

Clark: Yes, but the probability of their happening in Whitesdale is pretty remote, don't you think?

Conti: Well, maybe—but rules are rules, and we make the girls live up to them.

Discussion Questions

1. How do you size up Mrs. Jackson? Why did she respond to Clark as she did?

2. How do you size up Mr. Clark? And why did he deal with Mrs. Jackson as he did? What motivated him to call Conti?

3. How do you size up Mr. Conti? Why did he favor standardized practices? He refers several times to "the girls." Does this suggest anything about Conti?

4. What does this case have to do with indiscrimination?

CASE 12.5

The Wayland Company*

The Wayland Company, a large ore producer with its headquarters offices in New York City, maintained numerous lead, zinc, and feldspar operations. One of its larger feldspar centers was located at Bixby, Utah. Early in the spring, Robert Harris, plant manager at Bixby, flew to New York for an annual meeting with Cal Douglas, production manager of the feldspar operations, and Fred Squires, chief cost accountant for Wayland's. Douglas and Squires were located in the New York offices.

The purpose of the meeting was to establish the standard costs[1] of the Bixby plant for the coming fiscal year. Predictions were to be made about the extent of such expenses as supplies, repair material, repair labor, fuel,

---

* All names have been disguised.

[1] "Standard costs are the costs that should be incurred under normal conditions to produce a given product or parts or to perform a particular service." From Kermit D. Larson, *Fundamental Accounting Principles*, 12th ed. (Homewood, Ill.: Richard D. Irwin, 1990), p. 1096.

and direct and indirect labor. Direct labor[2] costs were by far the largest expenditure in the plant. Direct labor is generally considered a variable cost[3] in that it varies directly with the quantity of production. Past experience at Bixby had shown, for example, that the direct labor required for producing one ton of feldspar was approximately one-half hour; for producing two tons, one hour, and so on. A measure of the efficiency of the operation could be determined by the extent to which the actual direct labor cost ran above or below this norm. It was the company policy, therefore, to hold the plant manager responsible for maintaining his variable costs, direct labor included, at the lowest feasible level. He was not held responsible, however, for fixed costs, which were beyond his control.

Cal Douglas called the meeting to order, and the three men began to go over the standard costs. As the conference reached the topic of direct labor, Fred Squires remarked: "According to our figures, the direct labor cost incurred at Bixby should be $1.98 per ton and it should be 100 percent variable cost."

Douglas: I don't think you're taking into consideration the fact that our Bixby plant has recently been organized. A clause in our contract with the union states that five men have to be paid for five hours a day regardless of production. In other words, if Bixby had 100 percent downtime, these particular men would have to be paid for five hours for every day of the downtime period, whether it is for one day or for six months! It's my thinking, therefore, that all costs incurred when the plant is not operating should be classified as fixed and not be charged to the plant manager.

Harris: Mr. Douglas is correct about our plant being organized and I've got to pay those five men no matter what the production situation is. If their time is classified as variable cost, then I would be held responsible for an expenditure over which I have no control. And I certainly agree with Mr. Douglas when he says these should be fixed costs.

Squires: Mr. Harris, you don't seem to realize that what you're asking us to do is contrary to all established cost accounting principles. If we classify any of your plant's direct labor as fixed costs we would incur some serious problems with respect to accounting terminology. Based on my 25 years as a cost accountant, this idea would certainly be a radical innovation, and in my opinion it just cannot be done.

---

[2] Direct labor is that directly related to the product.

[3] The obverse of variable cost, in accounting terminology, is fixed cost, i.e., cost incurred independently of the quantity of production, e.g., rent, property tax, depreciation, insurance, and so forth.

Cal Douglas, sensing that the meeting had reached an impasse, suggested that they break for lunch. After lunch the conference reconvened and the controversy grew more heated. Finally, Douglas commented: "Gentlemen, it's evident that we have reached a stalemate here. Frankly, we haven't the time to work it out. I think I can see both points of view, and I realize that we're asking Fred to act against some established accounting principles, but frankly I think we must make an exception in this case. We simply must adjust our cost accounting procedure to accommodate our labor problem."

Mr. Squires replied with repressed anger: "Do you realize what repercussions this would lead to? It would change accounting terminology and procedures we've been abiding by for years. Cost accounting, by its nature, has to be consistent from period to period. If we inaugurate this procedure we'll be harming the accuracy of our total plant costing."

Discussion Questions

1. What was the position of Douglas and Harris?
2. What was Squires' position?
3. What patterns of miscommunication do you see operating in this case?
4. What do you recommend to reconcile their differences?

CASE 12.6

On a Bus*
Ruth Lebow Cogan

I was doing industrial nursing at the time of this story, and if you have ever done industrial work you know you start to work at 8:00 A.M., not five minutes after, and you finish at 4:30 P.M., not five minutes earlier.

On this particular evening I had to go to school after work, so instead of going home my usual way I caught a Jackson Boulevard bus going east. It must have been about 20 minutes to five before I caught the bus, since I had to walk a block to catch the bus and had to wait a few minutes before it arrived. The bus reached State Street about five o'clock, and it was at this time that I transferred, or tried to, to a northbound bus.

I was carrying an armload of books and no other packages when I boarded the bus. I handed the driver the transfer and started to move to the back of the bus when the driver called me back. He said, in what appeared to me to be a very accusing voice, that my transfer was an hour overdue, that it was stamped for four o'clock. I told him the other driver must have made a mistake since I had not finished work till 4:30. At this point he accused me of lying and said I was shopping for an hour and tried

---

* Printed by permission of the author.

to get by with an old transfer. By this time he was shouting and all the people in the bus were intently watching and listening for the outcome. He asked for another fare, and seeing there was no future in arguing with him, I opened my purse and found that I had no change—only a $10 bill. I told the driver I only had $10 and asked if he could change it. His face was getting redder and redder, and he finally burst out with, "I'll change it and give you all your change in silver." By this time I was furious and told him I did not care how he changed it as long as he gave me my change.

At this point he really lost control and blared out that he knew people like me—always trying to cheat the bus lines out of a fare and that I didn't pull the wool over his eyes and that he could see through my act. He said he changed his mind, that he would not cash my $10 and that I would just have to get off the bus. Under fire of accusations I had no alternative but to get off, since technically he was within his rights to refuse to change a $10 bill.

Discussion Questions

1. Who is at fault?
2. What patterns of miscommunication seem to be involved in this case?

CHAPTER THIRTEEN

Differentiation Failures
2. Polarization
Going to Extremes

❋
❋
❋

Polarization may be considered as a special form of indiscrimination, but because of its relevance to what has been happening in our nation and, indeed, in many parts of the world, it warrants a separate chapter.

> A college professor may be either a top-notch researcher or an excellent teacher; he may not be either, but he certainly won't be both.
>
> Kids these days don't appreciate what they have. Either you sweat for what you get, or you'll take it for granted.
>
> The cops in this precinct are either honest and walking on their uppers, or they're grafting and living high.

Perhaps those statements seem a bit jarring. Are such statements less offensive if they are made by people of renown?

> *Life is either a daring adventure or nothing.*
> *—Helen Keller*

> *Each individual is either a Sinner or a Saint.*
> *There is no halfway business with God.*
> *—Aimée Temple McPherson*

> *There are but two objects in marriage, love or money. If you*
> *marry for love, you will have some very happy days, and*
> *probably many very uneasy ones; if for money, you will*
> *have no happy days and probably no uneasy ones.*
> *—Lord Chesterfield*

The world is divided into people who do things and people who get the credit.
—Harry Golden[1]

The latter statements may be more memorable, but they are still oversimplistic. Whether expressed by celebrities or not, each of the above quotations perpetrates a *polarization*.

DEFINITION

To define *polarization,* we must distinguish between two kinds of situations that apparently present two, and only two, alternatives. One of these is a genuine dichotomy; the other is a false dichotomy.

Contradictories

At any given time and place, you will either marry or you will not marry; you will either be arrested for speeding or you will not; you will either receive a pay raise or you will not; you will either make the varsity basketball team or you will not; and so forth. These are authentic dichotomies or contradictories. Note their characteristics: (1) one alternative must occur, but (2) both cannot.[2] Take this statement: "People are either over six feet tall, or they are not." Everyone, at any given time and place, (1) must be in one camp or the other, for there is not middle ground, and (2) cannot be in both camps.

It is quite safe, sound, and sane to make either-or statements about contradictories. But there is another type of situation about which either-or statements and evaluations can be quite misleading and dangerous.

Contraries

Examine this statement: People are either tall or short. It has the either-or form, but it does not involve contradictories, for there is middle ground—countless people are neither tall nor short. And this is the key distinction between contradictories and contraries. Contradictories involve no middle ground, no other alternatives; contraries do. Moreover, the middle ground may consist of gradations, shadings, degrees—an unlimited number of them in many cases. The temperature of the air around us is a good example—it isn't simply hot or cold. The temperature

---

[1] Publisher and author Golden also felt that there were two kinds of people in the world: Those who insist on dividing the world into two kinds of people and those who don't (!).

[2] Aristotle expressed these requirements as two of his laws of thought: (1) something must be either A or non-A, and (2) nothing can be both A and non-A at the same time and place.

varies by smooth, continuous changes that we express conveniently in arbitrary steps called degrees. Actually, there are an infinite number of gradations between 0 and 100 degrees Fahrenheit, or Celsius.

Indeed, it is as if nature abhorred contradictories. Contradictories appear to be largely human-made. Consider the computer. It operates on the contradictories of open and closed. A given circuit is either open or it is closed. To accommodate this limitation the binary numeral system was adopted. It consists of only two numerals—*0* and *1*—to represent opened or closed circuits. For those who may not be familiar with it the binary system looks like this:

Decimal	Binary	Decimal	Binary	Decimal	Binary
0	0	4	100	8	1000
1	1	5	101	9	1001
2	10	6	110	10	1010
3	11	7	111	11	1011

The decimal 2, then, is not read as 10, but as one circuit closed, another circuit open.

A simpler example of such contradictories are the go/no-go gauges used in industry to determine whether or not an object meets given specifications.

On the other hand, consider some of the contraries masquerading as contradictories.

Life or death. Precisely when does life begin and when does it end? With legalized abortion and organ transplants, these are no longer only philosophical questions. They have become vital physiological, legal, and moral issues. For example, when may a heart be transplanted from one person to another? When the donor dies is the over-simplified, black-and-white answer. But, *when* does he or she die? When no pulse or breath can be detected? When no reflex action can be elicited? When the heart and lungs cease to function? When an irreversible coma is recorded on an encephalograph? In a recent meeting of the American Academy of Neurology one conclusion was clear: There was *no* generally accepted conclusion as to when death comes.

Male or female. As disconcerting as it may be to male chauvinists or women's libbers, there apparently is no 100 percent male or no 100 percent female. Evidently there is maleness and femaleness in varying degrees in each of us. Again the issue is not merely academic. In a recent Olympics, 11 women athletes were disqualified because analyses revealed that they were insufficiently female to compete with other women. And recall the furor when, after a sex-change operation, Renee Richards née Richard Raskind sought to compete as a woman in tennis tournaments.

Animal or vegetable. As if the foregoing were not disturbing enough, here is yet another old, comfortable oversimplification under attack: the supposed contradictories of animal or vegetable. Where do you put the *euglena*, which digests food like an animal and photosynthesizes like a plant? Or where does the *ascidian* fit? It is classified as an animal, yet it produces cellulose, which has been considered a function unique to plants.

It seems fair to conclude that most of the important aspects of living involve *contraries*. Health-illness, wealth-poverty, war-peace, loyalty-treason, hero-villain, sanity-insanity, beauty-ugliness, conservative-liberal, intelligence-stupidity, bravery-cowardice, line-staff, investment-speculation, right-wrong, competence-incompetence, mind-body, good-bad, heredity-environment, true-false, honesty-dishonesty, guilt-innocence, and so on, are not simple, either-or matters. But people sometimes deal with these and other contraries in an irrational way. This behavior is called polarization.

Polarization

Polarization occurs when one, failing to differentiate, treats contraries as if they were contradictories; when one deals with a situation involving gradations and middle ground in strict, either-or contradictory terms. I recall the intense conflict in a certain midwestern town over the issue of fluorine in drinking water. Impressive scientific evidence had been presented to the effect that fluorine in proper proportion to the water markedly reduced dental decay, especially in children. But nothing could persuade the majority of the town's citizens that the fluorine would not be poisonous, and the health measure was voted down.

The fluorine issue involved contraries; it was a matter of gradations. But the majority of the citizens treated it as if they were dealing with contradictories. "Fluorine," they polarized, "is either poisonous or it's safe. We know it's poisonous, so we're not going to have anything to do with it!"

Fluorine is, of course, a deadly poison—*in sufficient quantities*. But medical and dental research had demonstrated that in minute amounts (as with other "poisons" such as iodine, chlorine, and arsenic) it was highly beneficial. It was the failure of some people to see the graded uses and effects of fluorine that cost the town a valuable health aid.

Another issue involves cyclamates, a type of sugar substitute. The federal Food and Drug Administration has banned them because studies indicated that ingesting certain quantities of cyclamates caused cancer in rats. However, the estimate is that one would have to consume daily 120 cases of soft drinks to have a comparable exposure. Saccharin, a sweetener which has aided diabetics and dieters for 90 years, and aspartame, the newest synthetic sweetener, are similarly in jeopardy. In an article just published in *Science,* Bruce Ames, professor of cell biology (University of California–Berkeley) states that tests in which rodents are fed massive doses of chemicals may be useless for calculating cancer risks in humans.

The question of just *how much* of these chemicals is dangerous to humans has never been answered.

CONSEQUENCES

Let us examine some of the manifestations and effects of polarization.

Deluding Ourselves

Not the least of the negative effects of polarization is that we may deceive ourselves. One psychiatrist described the obsessive (either-or) disability of one of his patients:

> . . . he revealed a classification of all women into contrasting classes—the thin and virtuous, the fat and vicious. He felt that he should marry, and the idea of marriage to any but a thin and virtuous woman was inconceivable. Nevertheless, he was attracted only by fat women, and his few would-be virtuous approaches to thin women had been signally unsuccessful.

As bizarre as this unfortunate man's perceptions may have been, are they really much different from the polarizations so many of us practice? I knew an aggressive young man who vowed while in college that his annual income at the age of 30 would be $100,000. Today he is 40—bitter and disillusioned, for he is making "only" $70,000. In his eyes he is a dismal failure.

> For several years the comptroller of a big firm, looking forward to his own retirement, had been grooming a man we'll call Smith as his successor. Smith was aware of this plan and worked so successfully toward the goal that he was also being considered as a candidate to step eventually from the comptrollership to the presidency. Then one day he went completely to pieces.
>
> The comptroller asked him sympathetically what was the matter.
>
> "I've just found out," Smith said after some coaxing, "that I've got diabetes."
>
> Examination by a specialist showed that he had only a mild case and that with insulin shots and reasonable care in his diet he would have no trouble. This enabled him to get to work with much of his old efficiency, but he insisted that he be dropped from consideration as the comptroller's successor.
>
> "Up to now," he explained, "I've hardly been sick a day in my life. Now I'll never again be able to think of myself as healthy."
>
> Smith destroyed his career because he saw health as an absolute. That is, he saw himself as formerly absolutely healthy and now absolutely unhealthy. He had completely obliterated from his mind the possibility of a middle ground.

Deluding Others

Polarization may, of course, be used to mislead others. In their famous debates on slavery, Stephen A. Douglas attempted to use polarization to his advantage when he threw apparent contradictories at Abraham Lincoln. Lincoln neatly sidestepped the horns of the false dilemma by exclaiming, "I protest against the counterfeit logic which concludes that because I do not want a black woman for a slave, I must necessarily want her for a wife. I need not have her for either. I can just leave her alone."

Polarization is also a favored ploy for getting out from under, as per Captain Queeg's (*The Caine Mutiny*) stock reply to those who criticized his unreasonably harsh treatment of subordinates: "Well, what do you want me to do—give him a commendation?"

And parents often use polarization on children for "their own good." A friend of ours thought she had mastered the technique when she would ask her four-year-old: "Which would you rather do first, Johnny, take your bath or brush your teeth?" Johnny, of course, didn't want to do either, but how can you say no to a question like that?

But Johnny learned to retaliate in kind. One day while shopping with his mother, he pulled her over to the toy department and demanded: "What are you going to buy me, Mom, a bicycle or an electronic game?"

Among the most effective polarizers in modern history were Adolf Hitler and his Nazi henchmen. "Everyone in Germany," declared Hitler, "is a National Socialist—the few outside the party are either lunatics or idiots." The thesis they so successfully inculcated was that an enemy of the National Socialist party was necessarily an enemy of Germany.

Unfortunately, polarizations still prevail. Ever since the 1983 election, the Chicago City Council has been sharply divided racially. At that time it was Mayor Harold Washington and 21 aldermen (all black) versus the remaining 29 aldermen (all white). The resulting "Council Wars" were often ludicrous. The "city that works" managed to do so despite rather than because of the Council.

Today, the names of the leaders have changed but otherwise the situation has scarcely altered. The current mayor (white) received 90 percent of the white vote. His nearest competitor (black) received 95 percent of the black vote.

Polarization in America

Of course, one needn't be a Chicagoan to experience divisiveness. Consider some of our current schisms. Some historians contend that our country has not been so polarized since the Civil War.[3] Vietnam is over, and so

---

[3] A war, incidentally, which cost 620,000 American lives—more than the carnage of World Wars I and II, Korea, and Vietnam combined.

is the Persian Gulf conflict (we hope). But debate continues to rage over ecological issues; abortion; poverty; racial, ethnic, and sexual inequities; S&L and bank bailouts; wife- and child-abuse; and terrorism.

How do such polarizations come to be? The answer would be encyclopedic but I will suggest just one contributor to these ruptures. It has to do with how some people use *language*—how they talk and write and think about the issues that divide them.

I submit that people tend to become polarized partially because they talk in polarized terms. Consider the ubiquitous bumper slogan "America—Love It or Leave It." That has a ring to it, and when uttered with sufficient fervor, it may tingle the spine. But unfortunately, regardless of the composer's intention, it could be an expression of a mindless retaliation against some of the equally mindless criticisms heaped upon our nation. When it is intended or interpreted thus, it becomes a rank polarization which seems to offer two, and only two, alternatives: (1) blind faith in and unquestioning acceptance of the status quo, or (2) give up—and get out.

This was essentially the sentiment expressed in Stephen Decatur's famous toast (Norfolk, Virginia—1816):

> *Our country! In her intercourse with foreign nations may she*
> *always be in the right; but our country, right or wrong.*

I prefer Carl Schurz's expression, given in an address to Congress (1872):

> *Our country, right or wrong.*
> *When right, to be kept right;*
> *When wrong, to be put right.*

So if we must sloganize, perhaps we could adorn our bumpers with a third alternative: "America—Stay and Improve It." That may not stimulate the adrenals as much, but it seems to me that it makes eminently better sense.

The Plight of the Moderate. But the more divided a society becomes, the more difficult it is to remain temperate. One remains silent, passive, and ineffectual, or one speaks out and risks being driven to either of the poles. The distinguished critic Joseph Wood Krutch once said: "From experience I have learned that you can't criticize anything without having it supposed that you favor the opposite extreme." Horace warned against this tendency 2,000 years earlier: "When I caution you against becoming a miser, I do not therefore advise you to become a prodigal or a spendthrift."

The plight of the moderate was depicted adroitly a few years ago in a cartoon showing two men talking. The gist of their conversation:

First man: Well, what's your choice—anarchy or repression?
Second man: What do I get if I choose anarchy?
First man: You get crime in the streets, riots, chaos.
Second man: What do I get if I choose repression?
First man: You get law and order, internment camps, censorship, and police brutality.
Second man: And what do I get if I choose peace, brotherhood among people, and an end to poverty?
First man: You get ignored. . . . So what's your choice—anarchy or repression?

America's Viability. Our nation's vitality historically has been its viability—its ability and willingness to self-examine, to adjust, to evolve. But we must protect that viability and the system that preserves it from destruction by the polarities of anarchy and suppression. Dwight D. Eisenhower wrote: "We must never confuse honest dissent with disloyal subversion."

The danger is that ideas, *per se,* will be suspect. Fear is ruinous. It compels the fearful to turn to authority, however oppressive, for security. And for the oppressors fear is the fundamental means of control.

Ramsey Clark, a former attorney general, once told the National Students Association that "people who fear dissent will not know the truth." It is, after all, the truth, not fear, which will set us free.

Clearly, our vitality is our viability. Our Constitution is a remarkable document, but even it has been amended 26 times!

The Vicious Pendulum Effect

The most destructive consequence of polarization is the escalating conflict, or the vicious[4] pendulum effect.

The pattern is a familiar one. Two persons—or two groups or two nations—with perhaps only moderately differing views on a given issue begin to discuss that issue. Emotions rise, and the discussants start to swing farther and farther apart. Soon their positions become polarized and rigid. No middle ground appears possible, and they are engaged in a heated and seemingly irreconcilable dispute. When superpowers arrive at this "You're nuts!"—"No, you are!" stage, fingers reach nervously for nuclear missile buttons.

---

[4] *Vicious* in the dual senses of savage and self-energizing (akin to the *vicious circle*).

Assumptions.   At the root of this dangerous escalation are two erroneous and unconsciously held assumptions. One is the aforementioned polarization—the oversimple either-or thinking that leads us to treat contraries as if they were contradictories. The second assumption has also been examined earlier—the fallacious but attractive notion that "the world is as I experience it" or, in short, the "I-know-reality" assumption (IKR).

Chapter 4, "Perception and Communication: The Process of Perception," argued that our contact with reality is only indirect—that which we experience is not reality but our perceptions of it. And our perceptions are likely to be influenced, indeed distorted, by our past perceptual experiences—by our psychoprogramming.

Visualize a person who assumes, albeit unconsciously, that he or she knows reality—has direct and valid contact with it—the perceptions, therefore, are undistorted by prior programming. This person is almost certain to be a threat to and to be threatened by others who make similar assumptions about themselves but do not share this particular programming.

Underlying this threat is fear. Anger, profanity, physical threats, and violence notwithstanding, the primary emotion is fear of loss of contact with reality. This dread can sometimes be warranted, as those who have endured certain mental illnesses can readily attest. But the IKR fallacy evokes the fear needlessly. Indeed, it virtually guarantees it. It does so by setting up within a person a thoroughly unrealistic and unreasonable expectation that is bound to be thwarted.

One's usual response to fear, real or unfounded, is defense—often an overreaction. Basically, then, it is a perceived threat to one's contact with reality leading to a defensive overreaction that energizes the pendulum to swing in escalating arcs.

The Pendulum Effect.   Consider how the polarization and IKR fallacies combine to contribute to the pendulum effect. Let a pendulum (Figure 13.1) represent an individual's perception—especially a point of view, value judgment, opinion, or any other expression of how this person *values* or *feels* about something ("Your tie is nauseating!") rather than a *factual* description of that something ("Your tie has orange and purple stripes with pink and yellow polka dots"). And let *X* represent reality or sanity or intelligence or justice or honor or rationality or morality . . . or any other virtue that seems relevant to the situation. And let *Y* stand for the antonyms of these respective perceptions—unreality, insanity, stupidity, injustice, and so on.

Let's use *reality* and *unreality* to illustrate. And let's assume that when the pendulum is at dead center (see 1 at *X* in Figure 13.1) it most closely approaches *reality*. Thus this viewpoint, opinion, and so on, is considered quite realistic (or sane or intelligent, and so forth). To the extent

FIGURE 13.1

"Unreality," etc.

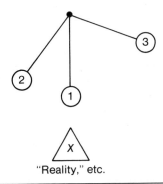

"Reality," etc.

that the pendulum is off center—either left or right of X (see 2 and 3 in Figure 13.1)—it is away from reality and toward unreality, and thus is regarded as *less* realistic, *less* sane, and so on.

There can be and there frequently is a discrepancy between where one's pendulum is objectively and where one perceives it to be. But it seems fair to assert that many people (especially when they are in conflict with others) perceive their respective pendulums as permanently anchored at X. This, of course, is consistent with the IKR fallacy, and smugness is usually the hardest of all qualities for anyone to detect in oneself.

Suppose that Jones and Smith are about to discuss a topic on which their views are actually quite similar and, assuming objective standards, quite close to reality. Jones's view, which is slightly liberal, is at A', and Smith's slightly conservative view is at A—the two views are a scant two units apart, and each view is only one unit removed from X (see Figure 13.2).

Smith speaks first and, operating under his IKR assumption, states his A position as though it were at X—for he truly believes it to be there. Now since Smith and Jones are two units apart, and Smith is seemingly at X, it follows that to maintain the two-unit discrepancy, Jones's pendulum is displaced to B'—two units from *reality*! (See Figure 13.3.) This poses a perceived threat to Jone's IKR. His feelings at the moment, if he could understand and verbalize them, might well be: "This man says he knows reality. What he says differs from what I know. Therefore, if he is right, I am wrong. If his position is realistic, mine is not. He is challenging my contact with reality—my sanity!"

Jones feels compelled to defend—more likely to overdefend—his sanity by attacking Smith's. Jones may overreact with a somewhat more vehemently liberal view, say at C'—two units from his original position, A', and three units from Smith's. Consistent with his IKR, Jones will express his view as if it were at X. This has the effect of bumping Smith from X to C (see Figure 13.4).

Now it is Smith's turn to be threatened. He is likely to retaliate—probably to *over*-overreact—counterattacking Jones's contact with reality (see Figure 13.5).

At this pace, it won't be long before the men, alternating between bumper and bumpee roles, progressively ram each other into unreasoning, polarized positions ignoring the middle ground (see Figures 13.6 and 13.7)—positions that neither would have supported had they not been psychologically frightened into them.

CONTRIBUTING FACTORS

Polarization, ranging from innocuous either-or fallacies to the dangerous and destructive pendulum effect, is basically the confusing of contraries for contradictories. We shall now examine some of the reasons for this misevaluation.

Similar Grammatical Form

Contraries and contradictories are often stated in a similar grammatical form:

You either had coffee this morning or you didn't. (Contradictories)
You are either a coffee fiend or a complete abstainer. (Contraries)

That both contradictories and contraries are frequently expressed in the either-or pattern probably accounts for some of the confusion between them.

Neglect of the Middle Ground

A more complex and important reason for polarization is the disregard or avoidance of the shadings and gradations between the extremes. The tendency to neglect the middle ground may be attributed to a number

FIGURE 13.2

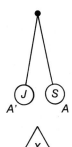

FIGURE 13.3

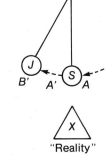

FIGURE 13.4

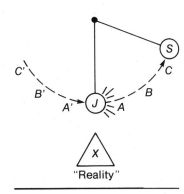

FIGURE 13.5

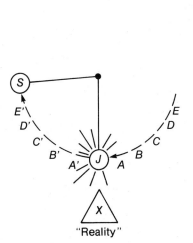

FIGURE 13.6

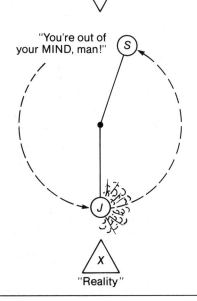

FIGURE 13.7

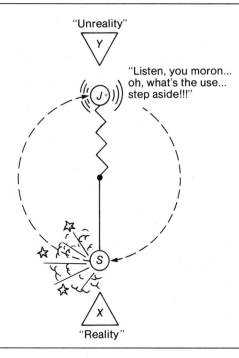

of factors. Most of the important ones fall under the headings of conditioning and expediency.

Conditioning. All through life we are conditioned to polarize. It is altogether possible that our training in this respect begins even prenatally. Note the role of simple motor activities in our conditioning. We have extensor and flexor reflexes. We can contract a muscle and relax it. We can inhale and exhale.

Consider, too, our linguistic conditioning. Let me illustrate the point by inviting you to take a little test. First of all, give the opposites of the following words:

        white— _____
        good— _____
        polite— _____
        honest— _____
        success— _____

Simple, wasn't it? Opposites come very readily to mind. But now try the second part of the test: fill in the gradational terms between the extremes:

```
white—_____—_____— gray —_____—_____—black
 good—_____—_____—_____—_____—_____—bad
polite—_____—_____—_____—_____—_____—impolite
honest—_____—_____—_____—_____—_____—dishonest
success—_____—_____—_____—_____—_____—failure
```

You probably found this part much more difficult. Actually, the cards were stacked against you. There are comparatively few intermediate terms in our language. Of course, we have the imprecise, quantifying adjectives and adverbs such as *slightly, fairly, medium, average, very, extremely,* and so on, but using them requires extra thought and effort, and we frequently neglect them.

The paucity of middle terms tends to encourage polarization. If we cannot say that someone is entirely honest, it is easier to classify that person at the opposite pole as dishonest. We disregard the infinite gradations of honest between the poles partially because we lack the quantifying substantive words to express them. A young high school graduate was reported to have hanged himself because he had failed by a slim margin to be elected to the National Honor Society. It seemed to make little difference to him that he had been president of his class, that his parents had given him a new automobile as a graduation gift, that he had been awarded a college scholarship, and that he had been accepted by one of the foremost universities in the nation. In his stage of depression, it was impossible to conceive of anything short of complete successs as other than total failure.

There are many other factors in the environment that condition us to polarize with ease and alacrity. Here are a few of them.

a. *The Two-Sided Question.* It seems as if someone is always attempting to temper a heated argument by admonishing: "Now remember, there are two sides to every question!" Our well-meaning friend may actually be more misleading than helpful, for few questions of any importance have only two sides—most such questions are multisided. Are the problems of public school integration, nuclear weapons control, street crime, or poverty simple pro and con affairs? Or, for that matter, can the problem of choosing a vocation or a mate, of raising children, or earning a living be solved by a categorical yes or no? The reporter-columnist Nicholas Von Hoffman stated: "The illusion of objectivity is dead. The old criteria for objectivity are that there are two sides to an argument and both must be reported. This defies the realities of today, where there are 30 or 40 sides to a story."

And yet the two-sided question myth is a prevailing one. "Did you hear about the Smiths' breakup? It was all his fault." "No, she was to blame." Could not both of them have contributed to the strife, and could there not have been factors beyond the control of both—inability to have children, financial difficulties, inlaw interference?

To be sure, there are legitimate two-sided questions—in law and in debate, for example. But the charges or resolutions are scrupulously phrased and defined in order to permit positions of guilty and not guilty (note the avoidance of the contraries guilty and innocent), affirmative and negative.

b. *Cheap Fiction.* Whether it occurs in the form of paperback novels, slick magazines, television, or the movies, cheap fiction is replete with polarization. The beauty is breathtaking, while the beast is grotesque; the rich are fabulously so, and the poor are penniless; the paragon of honesty invariably clashes with the despicably deceitful.

If there is anything adult about the current rash of adult movies, television dramas, stage plays, and novels, it is the avoidance of depicting the good guy as insufferably virtuous and the bad guy as unrelievedly evil.

c. *Restrictive Laws.* Laws are sometimes written in either-or, blanket terms. Several years ago, the Food and Drug Administration was required to forbid the use of coal-tar dyes in lipsticks. Under an archaic law, an ingested product (women sometimes consume minute amounts of their lipstick) containing any amount of any toxic material had to be banned. Cosmetics industry representatives claimed that a woman would have to eat 100 lipsticks a day for 90 days to suffer any ill effects. Even the FDA admitted that the amount of dye seemed completely harmless, but its hands were tied until the law was changed.

Police officers are often faced with the necessity of modifying the letter of the law. With limited resources they must use discretion in determining the *level* of enforcement that is desirable and feasible.

Expediency. It is much easier to think of a person as either intelligent or stupid rather than rating that individual more precisely along a continuum of mental ability. It might be considerably simpler for a teacher to pass or fail students. But rating them along the range of A–B–C–D–F, percentages, and so on, requires a good deal more consideration and judgment.

And, too, we are often pressured for decisions. We feel that we haven't had the time to investigate and analyze. And we are uncomfortable with the uncategorized, the unresolved—so "if it ain't this, it's gotta be that."

CORRECTIVES

To prevent polarization, habituate these techniques:

1. Detect the contrary.
2. Specify the degree—apply the How-Much Index.

3. Separate the double contraries.
4. Guard against the *vicious pendulum* effect.

Detect the Contrary

The first step in combating polarization is to detect the contrary. But how can one quickly, yet dependably, distinguish it from the contradictory? Aristotle's laws of thought are 23 centuries old, but so far as they apply, they are still valid and practical.

1. Something must be either A or non-A.
2. Nothing can be both A and non-A at the same time and place.

Use these laws to test an either-or situation.

An employer: "The biggest problem with secretaries is initiative. Some, when they see a job to be done, will always go right ahead and do it without having to be told. But the others—you literally have to lead them by the hand—especially if it involves anything outside of their regular routine."

Which are involved—contraries or contradictories? To qualify as a contradictory, the situation must measure up to both of Aristotle's requirements. Must a secretary either always go right ahead and do it or be led by the hand? Hardly; there is abundant middle ground. The situation fails on the first criterion of the contradictory, and it is therefore a contrary.

Specify the Degree—Apply the How-Much Index

Having determined that one is dealing with a contrary, the next step is to specify the degree between the extremes. In other words, it is no longer a question of either-or but of how much.

If a person steals a 29-cent stamp from the office postage supply, we might describe the action as dishonest—or at least as not honest. If a person steals $100,000, we could say the same thing. But would we not have had an obligation to quantify—to distinguish the degree of dishonesty involved? Do other circumstances influence the degree of honesty? Is there a difference between stealing a given amount from a rich person and stealing from a poor one? Does stealing with the intent of repaying make a difference? What about stealing for a worthy cause?

To a great extent, the method of applying the How-Much Index depends upon the nature of the contrary and upon the availability of terms to denote the degrees.

Use a Quantitative Index When Possible.   Some objective contraries (e.g., tall-short, light-heavy, hot-cold, large-small) lend themselves to a quantifying index. *Time* magazine writers, for example, often use a telling detail in parentheses to specify: "The boy was tall (5 feet 11 inches) for his age (13) . . ."; ". . . has the largest undergraduate enrollment (28,000) in the state."

Use Substantive Middle Terms When Available.   Many contraries, of course, cannot be quantified. One cannot describe a person as 89 percent patriotic, 2.3 times more friendly than a neighbor, or ¼ ill. But some contraries do have a supply of substantive middle terms that may be helpful in specifying approximate degrees between the poles. The following adjectives, by no means as precise and as nonoverlapping as inches, pounds, or miles per hour, still may suggest some of the gradations and nuances along the beautiful-ugly continuum:

agreeable	frightful	ordinary
attractive	ghastly	passable
beauteous	glamorous	piquant
becoming	good-looking	plain
beguiling	gorgeous	pleasing
bonny	graceless	presentable
captivating	grisly	pretty
charming	grotesque	radiant
coarse	gruesome	ravishing
comely	handsome	repugnant
cute	heavenly	repulsive
dazzling	hideous	resplendent
devastating	homely	revolting
divine	horrible	stunning
drab	horrid	uncomely
dreadful	ill-favored	unprepossessing
elegant	loathsome	unseemly
exquisite	lovely	unsightly
fair	monstrous	well-favored
fetching	nondescript	winsome

Use Quantifying Terms.   Certainly, such words as *very, slightly, moderately, extremely, generally, seldom, average, fairly, often, medium,* and so forth, do not approach the specificity of the numerical indexes, but they are obviously superior to the *absence* of quantification. Remove the quantifying terms *most* and *generally,* from the statement below, and note how much more harsh, unyielding, and "either-or-ish" it becomes:

Most American educators agree that the elective system in our colleges and high schools leads generally to an aimless nibbling at knowledge, or to excessive specialization.

Separate the Double Contraries

The compound polarization merits special consideration. Actually, it involves mistaking double (or multiple) contraries for single contradictories. This bit of doggerel epitomizes a common compound polarization:

Girls at college
Are of two strata:
Those with dates
And those with data.[5]

The old beautiful-but-dumb cliché. The counterpart for males: All brawn and no brain. Not only are both notions fallacious, but some evidence indicates that if there is a correlation between physical and intellectual superiorities, it is a positive rather than a negative one.

But let us return to the double contraries—how can we deal with them? The first step is to cut them down to size—to separate the contraries and work on them individually. Suppose we take the brawn-brain fable. Expanded, it would appear: People are either brainy (and puny) or brawny (and stupid). It is immediately clear that there are two continua involved—intelligence and strength. We can now proceed to specify degrees on each of them with the How-Much Index as before. Graphically, our double values might be expressed as shown in Figure 13.8.

Lest the foregoing treatment appear a bit frivolous, consider this compound polarization:

There are two kinds of doctors: Those who are dedicated; those who are dollar conscious.[6]

Is it not more likely that most doctors are some degree of both?

Combining Contraries. Compound contraries, then, are misleading when (1) they are treated as contradictories and (2) they are falsely correlated. But sometimes contraries are related—and useful information can be expressed by combining them, provided that they are dealt with as contraries rather than as contradictories.

---

[5] Richard Armour, *Reader's Digest*. Reprinted by permission.

[6] Attributed to a high-ranking officer of a national service and fraternal organization.

FIGURE 13.8

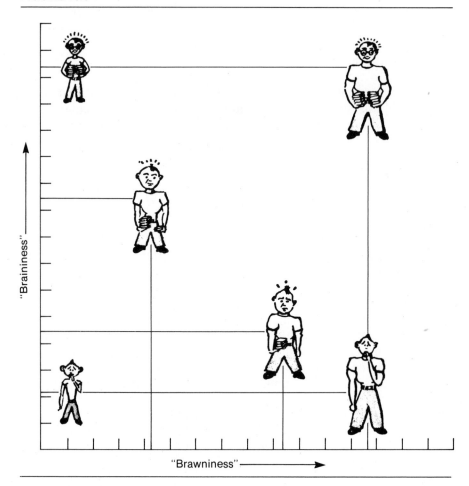

"Braininess" →

"Brawniness" ⟶

The Weather Bureau's temperature-humidity index (THI) does this. What is important to most of us is not how cold or hot or how humid or dry the weather will be, but how *comfortable* we will be. A temperature of 85 degrees Fahrenheit sounds warm, but the THI tells us that at a 25 percent relative humidity, the day will be reasonably comfortable. The THI also tells us that a more moderate 75 degrees will be rather unpleasant if it is accompanied by a humidity of over 60 percent.

The bureau has also combined the contraries of temperature and wind velocity to give us the wind-chill index. Ten degrees above zero coupled with a brisk breeze can be decidedly more uncomfortable and dangerous than 10 degrees below zero on a calm day.

Guard against the Vicious Pendulum Effect

We can minimize the pendulum effect if we are mindful of two key factors: (1) controversial issues are usually complex, and (2) our perceptions of such issues are programmed by prior experiences.

Complex Issues. Controversial issues are generally highly complex. Because they are multifaceted, it is highly unlikely that any one viewpoint will be 100 percent valid. Be wary, therefore, of blanket statements. One can prevent or ameliorate the pendulum effect by analyzing the issues, carefully selecting aspects to be conceded, and specifying the nuances and gradations between the polarities.

Programmed Perceptions. We have observed how polarizers progressively frighten each other, with a succession of overreactions, toward the extremities. Such people would not be so inclined to overdefend if they were not so frightened, and they would be less threatened if they were relieved of the burden of the IKR fallacy.

The IKR fallacy is their undoing. It is this fallacy that provides the psychological fuel that propels disputants' pendulums in ever-widening arcs. When a person expresses an opinion or a value judgment, regardless of how vehemently, that person is not, contrary to belief and desire, talking about reality but describing inner feelings. And that description need not frighten another person whose personal view happens to be different.

The chief antidote for the IKR fallacy, then, is to eradicate it by conscious, humble acknowledgment that no one knows reality—that no one has direct and valid contact with reality—that what we experience is not reality but our perception of it, which in turn is inevitably biased by our past experiences.

To the extent that you genuinely accept and internalize these premises, you will be impervious to threat by another person's disagreeing with your views on politics, religion, culture, art, morals, music, or any other value-judgment area. Your armor consists of these insights:

You recognize that the other person is only talking about the programmed feelings inside his or her head.

You recognize that you are only talking about the programmed feelings inside your head.

You recognize that neither of you stands to lose contact with reality because you concede that neither of you had direct and valid contact to begin with.

Unthreatened, you are unlikely to counterattack and threaten the other person. Thus neither the other person's pendulum nor yours receives the initial impetus that sets it swinging.

Some specific suggestions for countering the *IKR* fallacy:

1. Determine whether you and the other party are disagreeing on facts or on your respective feelings about those facts. If the former, get out the yardstick, measuring cup, bathroom scale, speedometer, odometer, thermometer, micrometer, or whatever other standardized measuring device is appropriate and available. If the latter, try to discover and understand the underlying assumptions, needs, motives, and programmings that led to those feelings, value judgments, and attitudes.

2. Try role reversal. If the discussion seems to be degenerating into a futile and heated dispute—the pendulums start to swing—strike a bargain with each other. Promise that for the next 15 minutes you will express the other person's point of view as persuasively as you can—provided that the same is done with yours. Prediction: For the first few minutes both of you will feel awkward and artificial. But gradually, as each of you exercises discipline, and speaks convincingly from the other person's frame of reference, you will begin to realize that, astonishingly enough, there is some value, some intelligence, even some sanity in the other person's position. Role reversal will not guarantee a total resolution of conflict, but it does tend to keep the discussion on the real points in contention and to restrain the pendulum's momentum.

3. Don't get personal. Escalating pendulum effects are usually those that grow not only progressively vehement but progressively personal as well. Try to stay on the issue and off the individual.

Say: "I can't really agree with that idea."
Not: "That's a ridiculous idea!"
Worse: "You're an idiot!"

4. Keep your cool. It takes two to tango—and also to fight. When attacked, resist the temptation to overreact—to counterattack. Unthreatened, the other person will find it unnecessary to be defensive. You can disagree without being disagreeable.

5. Without making a fetish of it, try to label your opinions, feelings, and value judgments as such—not as objective, unassailable facts. Helpful phrases: "I believe . . ."; "I think . . ."; "It's my feeling that . . ."; "In my opinion . . ."; "According to my value system . . ."; "As I see it. . . ."

6. Acquire the *to-me-ness* and *to-the-other-ness* habits. Preface your value judgment statements with "to me."

Not: "The Church is no longer relevant."
But: "To me, the Church is no longer relevant."

Substitute "appears to me to be" for "is" when linking a noun with an adjective with the verb *to be*.

Not: "Pornography is harmful to children. . . ."
But: "Pornography appears to me to be harmful. . . ."

Similarly, when listening to the other person's opinion, add (silently) "to that person" or "appears to that person to be" to his or her declarations.

Someone says: "Those oil-rich sheiks are greedy beyond belief."
You interpret: "(To that person,) those oil-rich sheiks . . . or "Those oil-rich sheiks (appear to that person to be) greedy. . . ."

These word additions and substitutions not only render value-judgment statements more temperate but more accurate as well—for they denote more explicitly that the speaker is not speaking about the facts out there but about the feelings inside.

7. Resist absolutes; they are a telltale sign of the desperate disputant.

"You *never* listen to me . . .!"
"You're *always* late in submitting your reports. . . ."
"*All* the kids have one, Mom. . . ."

Absolutes fail on at least three counts: They tend to provoke retaliatory antonyms by the other party, thus accelerating the swings of the pendulum.

"You *never* consult me anymore!"
"What do you mean? I *always* ask for your advice first!"

They make a graceful retreat difficult. Having committed oneself to an absurdity—"*No one ever* appreciates *anything* I do in this department!"—how does one back down without losing face?

Third, they weaken your case. They render your position vulnerable and easily challenged.

"You say you *never* receive information from headquarters. I believe you did receive the May 15 general directive and the June sales forecast. And did you not receive the revised list of corporate objectives last Thursday?"

The indiscriminate use of all-inclusive terms, such as *all, everywhere, always,* and *everyone,* often reveals one's failure to be selective. Confronted with a controversial issue, I may fail to distinguish among its components—to differentiate those aspects that I consider genuinely valid and important from those that are dubious and trivial. Rather I imprison myself with all-embracing defenses of my position and blanket indictments of my opponent's. My unconscious assumption appears to be that to concede anything weakens my case. Lord Acton's advice seems more to the point—accede in everything you can, for this strengthens the part that remains.

SUMMARY

Polarization tends to occur when contraries (situations involving graded variations, middle ground) are treated as if they were contradictories (strictly either-or affairs).

Moreover, we may be misled not only by our own polarizations but by the purposeful or unintentional polarizations of others.

One of the most destructive forms of polarization is the vicious pendulum effect—the escalation of conflict. It thrives on overreactions. Regrettably, the easiest, the most dramatic, and the most infantile response to opposition is absolute counteropposition. Such polarization has become a commonplace in America, but it is nonetheless a clear and present threat. Whether suppression or anarchy or sanity will prevail is yet to be seen. However, one cannot but agree with William Buckley's admonition: "Reason may not save us; but the absence of reason will not save us."

The factors contributing to polarization include the similar grammatical form of contradictories and contraries and, more important, our propensity to neglect the middle ground. Conditioning and expediency are among the influences accounting for the latter.

Polarization tends to be reduced when one develops habits, first, of distinguishing contraries from contradictories and, second, of specifying the degree (applying the How-Much Index). In the case of compound polarizations, the initial step is to separate the contraries. Then the gradations on each continuum can be specified.

The vicious pendulum effect can be dampened if we can recognize different perceptions as products of different conditionings and if we can acknowledge that in complex issues literally no one (including ourselves) has the one complete and unassailable viewpoint.

Discussion Questions

1. "Faced with significant decreases in applicants, should colleges lower admissions requirements or contract facilities?" How do you feel about this?

2. What cases in this chapter as well as in other chapters seem to involve the vicious pendulum effect?

3. Give five examples of true contradictories and five involving contraries.

4. "Modern logic has abandoned one of Aristotle's most basic principles: the law of the excluded middle, meaning that a statement must either be true or false. In

the new system a statement may have three values: true, false, or indeterminate. A close analogy to this system in the legal field is the Scottish trial law, which allows three verdicts—guilty, not guilty, or not proven."—John Pfeiffer *(Scientific American)*.

How do you react to the above?

5. Precisely what is polarization? What contributes to it? How can it be prevented?

6. What is the vicious pendulum? What are its mechanics—that is, how does it occur? Remedies?

7. Was polarization involved in the case "General Patton and the Sicilian Slapping Incidents" (Chapter 9)?

8. Does the "Craving for Certainty" discussed in Chapter 11 have any bearing on polarization?

9. "Be contented, and you'll live longer."
"Don't be contented—or you'll stagnate."

"War is coming—because there have always been wars."
"War isn't coming—because neither side can win it, and both sides know it."

"Think big—for you have to spend money to make money."
"Watch your pennies—and the dollars will take care of themselves."

"An objective test doesn't let you express yourself."
"An essay test is so vague you don't know what's expected."

Your reaction?

10. "What we tragically fail to recognize is that extremism is always a symptom of failure in the feedback process of an institution, and not a cause of anything in itself."

—Sydney J. Harris

How do you feel about the above statement? Why?

11. "I divide all readers into two classes: those who read to remember, and those who read to forget."

—William Lyon Phelps

How do you react to this statement? Why?

12. What vicious pendulum effects do you see occurring today in your community? In our nation? In the world?

13. "In nature and in the id, there are no opposites which exclude each other."

—Eric Berne

Do you agree?

14. List and discuss contraries masquerading as contradictories. For example: mind or body, heredity or environment.

15. What is the plight of the moderate? Can one be a centrist and still be effective?

16. Dr. Martin Luther King, Jr., wrote: "To retaliate in kind would do nothing but intensify the existence of hate in the universe. Along the way of life, someone must have sense enough and morality enough to cut off the chain of hate."—*Stride*

toward Freedom. Bayard Rustin, a leading civil rights leader, stated: "As you get black backlash in response to white backlash, the intensity of the white backlash increases. We're in trouble because one backlash reinforces the other."
Your reaction to these statements?

17. In addition to the THI and the wind-chill index, what other combinations of contraries are useful?

18. Describe an incident, possibly involving yourself, in which polarization occurred. Analyze specifically why it occurred, what might have been done to prevent its occurrence, and what measures would prevent its recurrence.

To underscore the urgency for coping with the vicious pendulum effect, I cite a recent confrontation:

To stem a tide of shoplifting, a college bookstore in the Northwest began to require that students check their bags and outer coats. In retaliation a group of students, male and female, entered the store and checked *everything*!

The bare facts speak for themselves.

CASES

CASE 13.1

Deadly Force*

The use of deadly force in effecting the arrest of an alleged felon is a serious problem to the police officer, who is in the position of judge and jury. In a split second, the officer must at times decide the guilt or innocence of a person, which ordinarily could take a court months of contemplation to decide.

Ralph Rogers, a police officer for less than a month, was patrolling on foot. Suddenly he saw a man sprinting from a store with a woman chasing after him, screaming, "Stop that robber!" The man was running toward an idling automobile. Another man was at the wheel, evidently waiting for the runner. The officer realized that he could not possibly overtake the fleet runner and considered for a moment his terrible dilemma. He decided against shooting, and the man scrambled into the car, which was already starting to move—a screech of tires, and the car turned a corner and was out of sight.

The woman, breathless, ran up to the officer. She was furious. "Why didn't you stop him!" she snarled. "You could have shot him easily! He stole $700 from me!"

The officer's face grew crimson. "Look, lady," he choked, "what could I do? If I had shot and killed him I could have been tried for murder or manslaughter."

"But he robbed me of $700! Don't you have the right to shoot a robber?"

"Yes—but I didn't *know* he was a robber when I was chasing him. Maybe you don't know this, but if he had stolen less than $15, that would be petty larceny, and he would not be classified as a felon. That means that if I had killed the guy I could be tried for murder or manslaughter.

"So, do you see the position I'm in? If I shoot and possibly kill a man I am liable for a serious offense. If I let him get away I'm the goat. Don't worry, lady, you won't be the only one I get hell from. The chief is going to have plenty to say, and so are the newspapers! What a law we have when you're damned if you do—and damned if you don't!"

Discussion Questions

1. What do you think of Officer Rogers' dilemma? Were there alternatives?
2. What could Officer Rogers do to deal with similar situations more effectively?

---

* All names have been disguised. Printed by permission. The author's name has been withheld by request.

CASE 13.2

Evans and Borne*

Evans and Borne were a partnership with branches in four cities— New York, Chicago, Boston, and Los Angeles. Each branch was supervised by a vice president. The firm was an investment banking firm that participated in securities underwritings and also acted as a dealer and agent in the sale or purchase of securities. The company had been rapidly increasing its business volume during the last five years and currently employed 400 persons.

Due to this expansion, the accounting department had been responsible for an ever-increasing amount of record-keeping. (The department also maintained an interoffice account, necessary because each branch office kept its own accounting records.) Management decided that a consulting firm ought to look into the possibility of a basic change in procedure. Such a firm was engaged, and after a study of several weeks it submitted the following recommendation:

> Evans and Borne has arrived at a point in its operation where a decision must be made as to whether to continue operations under the present system or to install an electronic accounting system. We recommend the latter.

The consulting firm was discharged and the president, James L. Borne, called in his executive committee (the four vice presidents) to discuss the recommendation. After about an hour's discussion of the pros and cons of the two alternatives, Mr. Borne, well known for his decisiveness, rose and spoke enthusiastically:

> Judging from our talking here, we are just about unanimously agreed that the electronic system is for us. I feel the same way. The growth of our business alone convinces me that a year from now we will have no choice. The size and complexity of our operation will force us into electronic accounting. And so I firmly feel that not only should we go into the new system but that we should do so immediately. As you know, these new machines are a tremendous investment, and I want them to start paying off just as soon as possible. So, what do you say? Shall we get into electronics as soon as possible?

The system was installed within three months. It was quite evident within the first month that the company was in over its head. There had not been time to train personnel adequately, and tempers flared continuously.

The turmoil in the accounting department was such that management was seriously considering discarding the system. But by this time

---

* All names are disguised. Reprinted by permission.

the company had been irrevocably committed to it; there would be no turning back. It was almost a year before the department was restored to order.

Discussion Questions

1. What does this case have to do with polarization?
2. Were there any other patterns of misevaluation operating here?
3. How should Evans and Borne have gone about the system changeover?

CASE 13.3

Preston Lee, CPA*

It was a cold day even for February, but the sky was cloudless and sunlight streamed through the window of Professor Robert Dillon's study. Dillon was entertaining two old friends, Wallace Borden and June Compton.

"When you review a situation like we went through with Preston Lee, you are never sure you did the right thing," said Borden. "It just makes you sick when a promising young man leaves you for a routine job as a payroll auditor in an insurance company."

Wallace T. Borden was the partner in charge of the Oklahoma City office of J. D. Rodman & Co., CPAs, the headquarters of which was in Fort Worth. There was also an office in Austin, Texas. The firm enjoyed an excellent reputation and was particularly well-known in the oil industry, which provided a majority of its clients. The Oklahoma City office was opened 20 years ago with Borden in charge, and since that time had grown slowly but steadily. June Compton, an outstanding member of the professional staff, became the second resident partner in Oklahoma City, 13 years ago. Presently, there were four men and two women on the professional staff in that office.

Preston Lee was 22 when he joined the firm five years ago at a salary of $29,000. He had been graduated from the University of Oklahoma. A good-looking young man over six feet tall and weighing over 200 pounds, Lee had earned a B+ average on his major, accounting, and a B- average overall.

He had taken the CPA examination while still in college, and secured a condition. He took the examination again and passed it. When he resigned a year ago, his salary was $39,500 and he was due for a raise.

Wallace Borden Tells His Story

Professor Dillon paused briefly. Then he turned to Borden:

---

* All names have been disguised.

Dillon: How did all of this happen?

Borden: Let me begin with some related matters. In my opinion, salaries paid by the Oklahoma City office are comparable to those paid by other CPA firms here. The University tells us that most of their graduates are going out at higher than our starting salary. But most of them are going out of Oklahoma—many of them to the East—so it is hard to compare.

It is our policy to hire right out of college and develop them, so of course it is rare for them to have the CPA when hired. Press Lee was an exception. He was the only person on the staff who actually had the CPA, but today they all have it. I am talking about staff, of course, not partners.

Preston Lee: The First Year

Lee had been with us only a few months when I had to send him in on a tough job. The accounting department of one of our clients broke down, and our other people were tied up, so Lee went in under my supervision. A key person had left the client's employ, and the records were messed up. Press moved right in, and every time I checked he was on top of it, so I began to relax my supervision. He brought the job out in good shape. Naturally we developed confidence in him and began pushing him along.

Shortly after that job, another client called. The comptroller is a CPA, and he has strong ideas about being audited by a non-CPA. In spite of the fact that Press Lee was just out of college, he and this comptroller got along fine, and he was the only one who was permitted to do the audit. Naturally, this puffed him up.

A Difference of Opinion

In his second year with us, Press began to feel that our firm was lacking in aggressiveness; that we were self-satisfied and didn't hustle to expand the practice. He thought the firm should be more active in social affairs, particularly at country clubs—giving parties to drum up more business. He also thought he should have an expense account to cover the cost of lunches and drinks for clients' personnel and others. He mentioned that some of the Oklahoma City offices of the big national firms were doing just that and that one had started a new office and in six years it had grown to a professional staff of about 50.

Dillon: Was that so?

Borden: Well, yes, we see the partners of that firm in the clubs and hotels talking to our clients. They are putting ideas in people's heads about the wonderful job they are doing, giving them brochures such as the one on the federal income tax—tips for oil companies.

We discussed the question of professional ethics with Press, and his feeling seemed to be that they were doing it, and no one was telling them they couldn't, and if we didn't do it too, we would lose out.

We were at a client's Christmas party and Press was talking to a business associate of the client. This fellow hit it off real well with Press. They both got pretty high and started talking about auditing, and Press said to him, "Why the hell don't you bring your audit over to our firm and let us take care of you?" and the man said, "Well, I am just going to do that."

Well, this man's auditor is a good CPA and a friend of ours. So we discouraged Lee from talking to the guy anymore, and he was pretty unhappy, I'll tell you. Here he had some business all lined up, and we threw cold water on it. He was really upset.

So we weren't about to give him an expense account. We didn't think it was the proper thing to do with such a young man. We had serious reservations about whether we could control it adequately, or his behavior either. And then there was the effect on the other staff men. From Press's standpoint we were just old fogies.

By the end of the year, we rated Lee as having more potential than either Condon or Burke, who were many years his senior. Our problem was to get his attitude straightened out. Press was too concerned with selling himself to the client. But in this, his success was outstanding.

We suggested that he take on some community work, and he joined some Jaycee committees. He always did everything with a lot of enthusiasm—or with none; when he went flat, he went really flat. What with one thing and another, I think he might have been president if he had kept pushing, but he didn't. His interest cooled off, and he dropped it. Press is like that; hot one minute, cold the next.

Just before New Year's, Press married an attractive young lady named Charlotte.

The Next Summer

We were really surprised at what happened in our counseling interview in July. We review our staff people twice each year, try to assess their progress, and look at their salaries.

So that July, we talked with Press and told him that from our point of view, he was making progress, that we had no particular comments to make at that time about strengths or weaknesses, and that we were raising his salary $200 a month. He sort of leaned back in his chair and said: "Same old raise, huh? There is no progress."

Dillon: How do you account for his reaction?

Borden: June thinks it was outside influence. Press knew a union official who believed that employers took advantage of their employees. I understand that he said that staff people should receive substantially all of the net fees which they generated and that partners should get their compensation from the fees from their own work. He favored more holidays, longer vacations, and more fringe benefits. I think Lee was influenced by this fellow.

We were very surprised. We had just raised him to $36,500, against Condon and Burke at $37,000. He was raised $7,500 in three years. At the same time that we had given him a raise, we had given them none, but he didn't know that, at least not then. After the interview, he walked out into the staff office and, in typical Press Lee fashion, said to Condon and Burke: "Well, I got a $200 raise. How much did you guys get?"

As they hadn't been raised, this caused some difficulty.

I suppose he thought his rate should go up to the same level as Condon and Burke, in spite of the big difference in age and experience. He said he thought he was better than they were. His attitude was what bothered me, not his competence. He was handling responsible jobs well, but we felt his relations with the clients were a bit immature. He was always kidding with them; he seemed to us to be a bit shy on professional attitude. But we thought he needed to mature a bit.

In the conference, he said that he didn't feel that he should be asked to work under Condon and Burke any more; that he was doing as good work as they, and carrying as much responsibility, and that he was a CPA and they weren't.

When we had put him on a job with Burke in charge he hadn't cooperated very well. It was obvious that he didn't intend to take direction from Burke. We never had this particular difficulty with him before. During the first two years he took supervision well.

Not long after the interview, he went out and interviewed the local office of a national CPA firm. I have a good friend who interviewed him. Apparently Press felt he had a lot of specialized tax knowledge about the oil industry that he wanted to sell to them. He made some remarks about J. D. Rodman being a nonaggressive, dead-end firm and was rather taken aback when my friend told him that they had the highest respect for us. They said they had no opening in Oklahoma City, but might be able to get him a job in Kansas City, but he didn't want to move to Kansas City, so that was that.

New Office in Stillwater

We had been wanting for some time to open an office in Stillwater. Finally, one of our clients built a new building there with space in it planned for us, so we had a partners' meeting and agreed to do it, with

Robert Golden, a younger partner from the home office in Fort Worth, in charge.

At the firm picnic, in August, Bob Golden's wife, Gloria, was talking to the other wives and said that she had no desire to move to Stillwater. Gordon Campbell, our managing partner in Fort Worth, heard of this. Here he had an office, and nobody to put in it. For various reasons, none of the other partners in Fort Worth could move and there was no staff person that seemed appropriate.

Campbell phoned me and asked whether Condon or Burke would be interested in going to Stillwater. I said they had the capacity all right but they didn't have their CPAs, and so that was dropped. So I said that it seemed to me that Preston Lee was a possibility, that he had the personality and drive to make a new office go, and would do a good job if someone stood behind him to keep him from going off the deep end. I pointed out that he felt himself at a dead end in Oklahoma City and he might welcome the opportunity. We kicked the idea around a bit, and Gordon said: "Why don't you check with Lee and see if he's interested?"

I said I didn't want to mention it to him unless it was pretty sure that he would get the opportunity if he wanted it, and Gordon said that of course he understood that.

Dillon: So then you talked with Lee?

Borden: Yes, we took him to lunch. We told him that the firm definitely was going to open an office in Stillwater and that Bob Golden was the logical man to go, but apparently he didn't want to. Would he be interested? We said we didn't know for sure that it would develop for him but that he was a strong candidate among others.

Press asked about compensation and we told him that this hadn't been discussed but that we were sure consideration would be given to the expenses involved in moving, that he would have an opportunity to grow and that his compensation would grow accordingly. We told him that he wouldn't be a partner and that we wouldn't guarantee that he would ever be a partner, but that the opportunity was definitely there.

So he talked to his wife, and they decided it would be great. She had gone to school in Stillwater and hadn't finished, so she would go back to school, and they made plans bang, bang, bang. I called Gordon, and he said, "Fine. Send him down here to talk and send his wife with him."

But the next morning Gordon called, and he was really upset. He had gone down to the office early, and Bob Golden came in and said he was looking forward to going to Stillwater and his wife was very enthusiastic about it, too. So of course the only thing he could do was call me and say he was sorry and that there was no point in Press coming to Fort Worth.

So June and I got Press in and explained to him about Golden: that he was the logical one to go and that after further consideration he had decided to go. We expressed to Press the thought that his having been so strongly considered was a great compliment, as most of the others were older than he was, with more experience. We told him that another opportunity would come along and that we thought he had a great future with the firm.

Gordon Campbell was in town a few weeks later, and he and I took Lee to lunch, and Gordon told him he was sorry about the way things had worked out, but that he had had to make the decision on the basis of the welfare of the firm as a whole, that Lee had received very careful consideration and had been a strong candidate, and that in a few years, with a bit more experience, he would be an even stronger candidate. Gordon told Press he had a big future with the firm.

The Last Three Months

Dillon: What happened then?

Borden: Three weeks later Press came into my office and told me he had considered the situation every way he knew how and he had arrived at the conclusion that there was no future for him in the firm and that there was no alternative for him but to resign.

So we asked him: "Well, what do you have in mind?"

And he said, "Nothing. I'm going out and get a job."

June and I spent a good deal of time, jointly and separately, with Press. We both told him quite bluntly that he was just plain wrong and making a mistake. There was a future for the firm, and he was a part of that future. We told him that we were not proposing to hand him a big job or a partnership on a silver platter, but he could earn one through his own efforts. We weren't going to divide up the present situation and just hand him a slice, but he could build a share for himself, in time. You don't become a partner because you are a nice guy; you become a partner because you earned it.

I think that he had hoped to pressure us into a substantial raise or a junior partnership or something. Communication broke down, and I'm guessing, but I think when he said he was quitting that he didn't intend to leave, but was applying pressure.

He wanted a rating equal or superior to Condon and Burke. He wanted equal money. He didn't want them telling him what to do. If we had given this to him, I really don't know if we would have had problems with Condon and Burke. But I don't give in to that kind of pressure. Anyway, it's against the firm's policy.

The upshot was that we didn't offer him anything—except advice that he was being premature. Then he talked around that he could get a better job somewhere, where there was more opportunity. He made a trip to Billings, with his wife, and they didn't welcome him with open arms the way he expected. The man's wife was in the hospital, and he kept the Lees waiting around and in the end didn't offer him the comptrollership that Press thought he would get, and that was a blow. Another company offered him $16,000 for six months as an internal auditor, but that was temporary, and it wasn't a vice presidency, and Press was insulted.

In the meantime he had done a great deal of talking about the wonderful job he was going to have and then, when he had more trouble than he expected, he talked to everyone about his troubles. I guess he was getting rather desperate.

So finally, the California Insurance Company offered him $40,000 as a payroll auditor in San Francisco, and they told him that, with his CPA and all, it was a wonderful opportunity for him to move into an executive spot, and he took it and moved out of town. Up to the time that he actually gave notice, Fran and I kept trying to convince him to stay.

Comments by June Compton

Compton: The two senior men, Graham and Corcoran, who left us two years ago may have influenced Lee's behavior. During his first six months on the job, Lee worked closely with them and under their supervision. They seemed to have a lot of personal problems. Both were rather negative toward their work and apparently believed that the firm owed them opportunities which it failed to provide. Both had a strong dislike for Condon. Lee was never able to reconcile their adverse opinion of the firm and what they regarded as their inability to progress in such a firm, with our enthusiasm for its potential.

I had several talks with Lee about his negative attitude, which seemed to be focusing on Condon. Just before he told us he was leaving the firm, he said that he could not work with Condon and therefore could not be in the same organization.

I talked with him about attitude and the need to be able to work with most anybody—whether a fellow employee, or client, or client's employee—and what it meant to be part of an organization. I suggested that some problems take patience to work out in fairness to everyone. He agreed to reconsider, but later, he decided that it was unnecessary.

We thought Press had a big future ahead of him, with us. But, obviously, he didn't think so.

Incidentally, after he resigned but before he left town, he often came into the office and had coffee with us, or just talked. Early in January, after Condon gave notice, Press was having coffee with me and he mentioned the news about Condon leaving and said: "Maybe I shouldn't have quit."

Borden: So that's the story, Bob. One always thinks, maybe if we had done it differently . . .

Memo from Borden

Two days later Dillon received a note from Borden:

Dear Bob,
Just to round out the Press Lee affair, here's the gist of a phone call I had with California last month. June and I would be quite interested in your views on this situation after you've had a chance to mull it over.

Sincerely,
Wallace

Enclosure: Mr. Davis, personnel manager of the California Mutual Insurance Company, called to ask about Preston Lee. They are considering hiring him as an internal auditor. I told Mr. Davis that:

Lee's reputation for honesty and integrity is excellent. Clients have complimented us on his ability to work with their employees. There is some resistance to supervision. His judgment needs maturing but overall is good. He is dependable; has no bad work habits, apparently handles his finances and family affairs well. He has an excellent record on committee work in the Junior Chamber of Commerce and seems to have leadership qualities.

Mr. Davis asked if we would hire him back. I said no, that our experience is that a man who quits for a supposed advancement does not possess qualities necessary to become a partner and usually is not a satisfactory employee.

W. T. Borden

Discussion Questions

1. What is the principal problem of this case?

2. What was Preston Lee's frame of reference?

3. What was Wallace Borden's frame of reference?

4. Regarding Borden's comment: "Maybe, if we had done it differently," what should have been done differently, in your opinion?

5. What does this case have to do with polarization?

CASE 13.4

Two Factions*

A problem of undeniable importance lies within the confines of the police department for which I work. I think that I can safely say that it has

---

* Printed by permission. The author's name has been withheld by request.

directly involved a large percentage of the members of this department and, moreover, its effect has been felt by every citizen of our city.

The problem originated years ago, but instead of diminishing with time, it has grown to be a complex and difficult situation. This problem is now evidenced by open dissension and strife within the ranks of those employed around me.

Approximately 10 years ago, the city's police administration tolerated gambling and the illegal sale of liquor to a considerable extent. In all probability, this tolerance was the result of some political pressures plus the desires of a few corrupt people who were interested, not in better government, but in building large bank accounts.

This state of affairs continued unchallenged for several years, until a group within the department began to develop. About 25 or 30 officers, headed by four or five recognized leaders of no great rank, held a few informal meetings. They decided that all illicit forms of entertainment in the city should be closed. It was clear that some of the officers were motivated largely by public spirit while others joined the group because they had been excluded from the group receiving graft money and privileges.

Thereupon, this group (with the exception of a few who agreed in theory but would not shoulder direct responsibility) began to act. In groups and simultaneously, they entered establishments, effected some arrests, and closed the doors to further operation. These officers, for the most part, made these raids and arrests while on off-duty time.

Immediately, attempts were made to conciliate the two factions, but they failed. The consequences were not long in coming. The leaders of the Vigilante group were fired on the grounds that they had been acting without authority, due to the fact that they were not actually on duty, nor did they have their supervisor's consent to act.

Within the police department, the remaining Vigilantes were met with both hatred and sympathy and a wide crack soon appeared within the organization.

Almost at once, the dismissed members began suit to regain their positions, and after a year's legal debate, full reinstatement plus salary reimbursement was ordered. All men resumed their positions with the department.

Perhaps this solved their respective problems, but it certainly was of no value with respect to the enmities created in the rank and file. In fact, the flames were fanned to the point where everyone was placed in an impossible situation—one must either associate with one group or the other or be disliked by both.

These two factions, the "Vigilantes" and the "Anti-Vigilantes," have been at great odds since that date. They refuse to speak to one another, and open condemnations are the rule. Politics play a larger and larger part in the organizational structure of the department. The Public Safety Commissioner (an elective position), if favorable to one faction, will immediately upon taking office assign favored positions to his group and thus relegate the out-group members who had been holding these positions to more or less menial stations. It should be quite evident how this constant displacement of key personnel depreciates the value of our organization and also should show quite clearly that the breach in the ranks grows deeper with each change.

Many new men have been added to our department since the trouble originated, and a large percentage of them have been drawn into the struggle. I cite my own experiences as an example: One of my best friends in the city happens to have been an active leader of the Vigilante group. Our friendship is based almost entirely on mutual interests outside our field of work, namely fishing and hunting, but because of my association with him, many say I am a sympathizer of the Vigilante faction. I have lost several friends who say that because I enjoy this man's company, I am a believer in his theories and a backer of his principles.

Upon the completion of my probationary period, I was told that it would be impossible for me to be a fence-sitter, in other words, that I would be forced to declare my sympathies for one group or the other. I laughed then because I could not see why my choice of friends should be based on such damned foolishness. But I am no longer laughing, for it has affected my working conditions and even threatens any future chance for advancement or promotion. This much has happened to me, and of a certainty it is happening and has happened to many others.

Discussion Questions
1. How do you analyze what had happened in this police department?
2. What should the author do?
3. What should the Public Safety Commissioner do?

CASE 13.5

For Men Only*
Randall Beckman

Tom DiRicco and I are managing partners of a small legal firm in a Pittsburgh suburb. We have been expanding slowly but satisfactorily, and about six months ago we decided that I should go to our local university law school to recruit one or two additions to our professional staff.

With scheduling assistance from Dean Coleman, I interviewed a dozen or so candidates and was especially impressed with two of them. Checking with the dean I learned that both had received several job offers and were probably on the verge of making a decision. Ordinarily I would have consulted with Tom, but he was out of the city, and "unreachable." I

---

* All names have been disguised.

felt that I had to act fast, so I made a firm offer to both students. They promised to consider it and let me know by the end of the week. The next day, Wednesday, Tom returned to the office.

Tom: Any luck at the university?

Randy: Two hot prospects—both graduating in June—I think we have a good chance with both of them because they indicated that they would like to stay in this area.

Tom: What are their names?

Randy: Charles Timmons and Mary Klein. They're both—

Tom: Mary?

Randy: Yes, do you know her?

Tom: No—but where did you get the idea that we want a woman in here?

Randy: Why not? She's sharp as a tack—upper 10 percent of her class. She already has a CPA, so she would strengthen us in tax accounting. Plans to take the bar exam in September, and I'm betting she'll pass with flying colors.

Tom: Well, let her fly her colors somewhere else.

Randy: What kind of attitude is that?

Tom: It's sanity—that's what kind of attitude it is. Have you ever worked with a female attorney before?

Randy: No, have you? *(I'll admit I was getting a bit miffed at this point.)*

Tom: That's beside the point. Let me tell you what to expect of Miss Stein—

Randy: Klein!

Tom: What?

Randy: Klein—her name is Klein!

Tom: OK, take it easy. Miss Klein will require a minimum of two years before she can pull her weight here.

Randy: You can say the same thing about a man.

Tom: Yes, but in two years Miss Klein will be *Mrs.* somebody, and then what happens?

Randy: You tell me.

Tom: She will either be "with child" or moving elsewhere when her husband has his job transferred.

Randy: Aren't you making some gigantic assumptions?

Tom: You made a gigantic assumption offering this broad a job.

Randy: She's no "broad"!

Tom: Let's say none of the other things happen. How do we know what will happen when she starts working with our men? Suppose she *is* pretty good—is she going to be promoted over some of the men? We don't need a battle of the sexes here.

Randy: Why shouldn't she be promoted if she's good enough?

Tom: And another thing, how will our clients react if we assign her to them? Won't they feel they're getting second-class service?

Randy: Why, you male chauvinist pig! Maybe Gloria Steinem has a point!

Tom: She's got a point all right—her pointed head! And so do you for committing us to this girl!

Randy: I *had* to—if you'd let the office know where to reach you on your junkets, I could have talked it over with you before making a decision.

Tom: What do you mean "junket"? Since when is driving to Harrisburg for a trust seminar a "junket"?

Randy: Forget it. What are we going to do about Miss Klein?

Tom: *We* aren't going to anything about Miss Klein! *You* will withdraw the offer.

Randy: I'll do nothing of the kind. If you'll cut out the bigotry crap and listen to reason—!

Tom: Will you listen to the idiot who's talking about reason?!

Our so-called conversation was interrupted at this point by a call from, as luck would have it, Mary Klein. She was regretful because she felt sure that she would have been happy working for us, but another job offer was just too good to turn down.

DiRicco and Beckman were off the hook, but it's fully six months later and the relations between Tom and me are still strained.

Discussion Questions

1. What miscommunications do you see occurring in this case?
2. How could the communications have been improved?

CHAPTER FOURTEEN

Differentiation Failures
3. The Frozen Evaluation
Neglecting Change

✳
✳
✳

This chapter deals with a third form of failure to differentiate. The previous two chapters were concerned with necessity for indexing on a horizontal basis—that is, with the need for differentiating among people, circumstances, attitudes, objects, and so forth, at a given time. The present chapter calls for a vertical sort of indexing, to take into account the way a person, a situation, a thing, and so on, changes with time.

THE CASE OF FRANK

I want to tell you about a personable man you would probably like and respect. Frank, to give him a name, began life with two strikes against him. To make a long, sordid story short, an alcoholic, violent-tempered father, the frequent absence of a mother who was forced to work away from home, and the influence of a gang of young toughs which Frank joined at 13 were sufficient to turn him into a brash, cynical, externally callous adolescent. After numerous scrapes he finally got into serious trouble in 1941. Caught stealing a car at 18, he was sentenced to two years in prison. Actually, the sentence was a fortunate development for Frank. The grimness of prison life quickly dissolved his brashness. Under the skillful guidance of the prison chaplain and a social therapist, Frank was beginning to gain insights about himself at the time of his release. With 11 months off for good behavior, Frank felt that he had paid his debt to society—but there were those who did not agree. On his return home, his drunken father cursed him and forbade him at first to enter the house, ironically for bringing shame to the family's name. Some of the neighbors openly mocked him as he walked down the street; others pointedly ignored him. He tried to find work, but, even with an abundance of war-time jobs, no one would hire anyone with his record. Frank was understandably relieved when he was drafted two months later.

He sank gratefully into anonymity, but even in the Army there were incidents, as, for example the time an officer's footlocker was burglarized. Frank, though innocent, was the first to be called in for questioning. But, on the whole, Frank's three years in the Army were helpful. They gave him time to think. He could now see how his environment helped drive him into crime. He began to go to church, where he found solace and encouragement and firmly resolved to salvage the rest of his life.

When the war ended, Frank received an honorable discharge and returned home. His father had died during the war. His brother and three sisters had all married, and the sisters had moved away. The brother lived in the family house with his wife and two children, and Frank's mother lived with them.

It was now over five years since Frank had stolen the car, but many had still not forgotten. There was no more open taunting, but many of the neighbors seemed cool and distant. Finding a job was difficult too. It became painfully clear that his record still followed him. Once he lied about his prison sentence and was hired—only to be fired under embarrassing circumstances a week later when he was found out. Police drove up to his home twice during his first month at home to take him to headquarters for questioning about auto thefts.

Finally, Frank moved to another section of the city, and life began to improve. A kindly man hired him as a mechanic's apprentice in his garage. Three years later, with steady pay increases, he married. Today, he is the likable manager of the garage. He has a lovely wife, and their two children are college graduates. He still visits his elderly mother from time to time, but, he much prefers to have her come to his home. The old neighborhood hasn't forgotten the old Frank.

Frank has been the victim of a special form of failure to differentiate: the *frozen evaluation*. Some people made evaluations about the Frank of 1941. The Frank of 1992 is virtually another person, but the evaluations have remained unchanged—frozen.

Not all frozen evaluations, of course, are as poignant and enduring as those concerning Frank. I was recently the delighted[1] target of one. Hurrying for an appointment, I was fortunate enough to find the one remaining curb parking space in the area. The space was the one nearest to the corner. When I returned 30 minutes later, the car in the space behind mine had left and a woman was trying energetically but ineptly to park between my car and the one in the third space from the corner. As I unlocked my door, the woman leaned out and proceeded to upbraid me

---

[1] Delighted only because I felt that the incident would be an apt illustration for this chapter.

most indecorously for failing to park in the second space, thus depriving her of the corner space, a much easier space in which to park! In her frustration she had unconsciously frozen her evaluation of the parking situation. She had assumed that the now-vacant second space was also empty at the time that I had parked!

The parking incident was an example of an evaluation made in the present and frozen to apply inappropriately to the past—a sort of retroactive frozen evaluation. The obverse—evaluations that are indiscriminately spread over the future without respect for change, as in the case of Frank—can also have undesirable consequences. Universities, hospitals, and other institutions that receive stipulated bequests and gifts are sometimes hamstrung by this kind of frozen evaluation. Several decades ago, an Eastern college was willed $400,000—a very considerable gift, especially in those days. The donor, an ardent railroader, decided that the industry would always flourish, as indeed it did at the time he wrote his will. Thus he stipulated that his gift was to be invested in 10 particular railroad stocks in prescribed amounts. The investment was to remain undisturbed. Only the dividends were to be used by the college. A foolproof plan, reasoned the benefactor: the college would have a continually increasing endowment with commensurate dividends. Unfortunately, his prediction was faulty. As the years passed, most of the railroads on the list met with difficult times, and several failed. The college, unable to react to changing economic conditions, could only sit by helplessly and watch the investment shrink to a fraction of its original value.

But, in fairness, some wills have been admirably apt. Shah Muhammed I (1740-97), regarded as one of history's cruelest tyrants, instructed that his remains be interred in the city sewer!

When I unconsciously (or perhaps deliberately) spread an evaluation over the future and/or over the past, disregarding changes in whatever I am judging (a person, group, situation, and so on), I have frozen my evaluation. Some of our most destructive frozen evaluations are those we make about *ourselves*. Take this case of self-imposed torment, for example, as reported by a psychotherapist.

His client was an attractive young woman, aged 17. She had been brought to him by her parents, who were concerned with the extreme shyness she exhibited in the presence of young men or boys. With girls her own age she seemed arrogant, and with older women she appeared self-confident. But she could not even discuss young males without stammering and blushing profusely.

Investigation ruled out medical and home environmental factors. The therapist began meeting with the girl, gradually gaining her confidence. She was finally able to recount this event:

Three years earlier she had attended a children's party where a number of boys were also invited. A door accidentally closed on her fingers. The pain was excruciating, and the girl became ill and vomited. The incident was quickly forgotten by all except the girl, to whom it remained an overwhelming mortification. Although she tried not to think of it, the bitter memory was always reinstated by the presence of boys.

THE ASSUMPTION OF NONCHANGE

The frozen evaluation seems to occur most frequently when one somehow assumes nonchange. Suppose that John Brown, as a freshman, failed one of my courses, mainly through negligence and irresponsibility. And suppose that someone comes to me four years later and asks my appraisal of Brown, whom I have neither seen nor heard of since. I can very confidently say, "Oh, Brown is a poor student," if I assume that John has not changed. But how reliable is this assumption? I think you will agree that I might be doing Brown a great disservice with my obsolete evaluation.

I have frequently been impressed by late bloomers—students who started their academic careers quite unprepossessingly but then found themselves and graduated with honors that one might not have dreamed possible from their work years earlier.

Consider, for delayed maturers, this lackluster trio:

A as a tyke roamed San Francisco streets, sometimes visiting saloons with his father. The father died (can San Francisco saloons be lethal?), and the boy's family moved back East. Here the young man enrolled at Dartmouth, soon quit, and took a job in a mill. Then he entered Harvard, and again quit. But now things began to look up. He married and taught English (extraordinarily well) at a high school, then at a normal school. But despite having embarked on a successful career, our friend suddenly chucked it all, packed up his family, and headed for England. Is there no hope for this nomad?

B candidly states in his autobiography: "[I was] considered by all my masters and by my father as a very ordinary boy, rather below the common standard in intellect. To my deep mortification my father once said to me, 'You care for nothing but shooting, dogs, and ratcatching.' . . . As I was doing no good at school, my father wisely took me away at a rather earlier age than usual, and sent me to Edinburgh University. . . . During the three years I spent at Cambridge my time was wasted, as far as the academic studies were considered." Another inauspicious beginning.

C's early scholastic career was described by Liam Hudson: "At sixteen he failed the entrance examination to the Zurich Polytechnic. He . . . eventually took a good degree, although not good enough to gain him a post in research. One of his professors really did describe him as a lazy dog, and his professor of physics did recommend him to try biology or medicine instead." Another loser, no doubt.

Fortunately, none of these people heeded their early press notices. They refused to freeze their self-evaluations, and they went on to great creative accomplishments. Their names? Robert Frost, Charles Darwin, and Albert Einstein. Incidentally, as children, Einstein along with Thomas Edison and Winston Churchill, would have been termed *learning disabled* had that classification been available then.

Laws, rules, and regulations are another area rife with the premise of permanence. Structures that may be justified *when* they are initially imposed tend to remain on the books long after the conditions that gave rise to them have changed.

> In Tacoma, Washington, the law says that drivers must stop outside the city and inform the chief of police that they wish to enter Tacoma.
>
> In Tennessee it is illegal to drive along a highway without having a herald precede you.
>
> Dress up proper in Hamilton, Ontario. The law decrees that anyone appearing on the streets after midnight without a full-dress suit can be arrested.
>
> In Idaho it's quite all right to buy a chicken after dark—*provided* that you have a permit from the sheriff!

Ordinarily these relics do no more harm than to clutter up statute books, but occasionally archaic regulations can be troublesome. Early in World War II, Britain had to use every available weapon, even 15-centimeter guns that dated back to the Boer War. A time-and-motion expert found that the manual called for Gunner No. 6 to stand smartly at attention during the entire operation of the gun. "Why is this man doing nothing?" No one knew. Finally, the expert located a veteran of the Boer War who explained: "G-6 is holding the horses."

This leads to a much broader question: How valid is the general premise of nonchange—the assumption that appears to underlie so many of our frozen evaluations? Actually, the notion that there is rest, pause, cessation, and so on, is a pernicious fallacy.

On every level we can observe, or at least presume, process. Everywhere about us we can see evidence of incessant change—of aging, wearing out, growing, eroding, regenerating, decaying, and so forth. Even the solid earth undergoes perpetual change. Considering the dramatic changes, such as earthquakes and volcanic eruptions; the slower ravages of wind, rain, glacial movements; and the even slower migrations of massive tectonic plates, the surface of the earth is in continuous motion.

The land surfaces of the world are no more in a state of absolute quiet than are its water surfaces. Minute waves called *microseisms* are continuously moving through the rocks over the entire surface of the earth, as can be seen by examining a sensitive seismograph record obtained in any part of the world.

Geometricians tell us that, although imperceptible to us, the Atlantic widens, the Pacific narrows, the Alps grow higher, the Red Sea broadens to an ocean, Los Angeles slides northward, and Africa splits apart.

And modern-day physicists postulate that on submicroscopic levels there is never-ceasing change. The inert book you are reading is presumed to be composed of infinitesimal particles whirling about at the speed of light—the "mad dance of electrons," as Alfred Korzybski called it.

On the macroscopic level, consider the exponential rate of techno-logical changes that we have experienced. Consider the last 50,000 years—roughly 800 current lifespans. Thus 800 people living end to end could represent the entire period. Of these 800, 650 lived in caves or less. Only the last 70 had any effective means of communication. Only the last six saw a printed word or could measure heat and cold. Only the last four could measure time with any accuracy. Virtually everything in our material world was invented during the lifetime of the very last person. And more technological progress will probably be made during the first half of the 801st person's life span than during the lifetimes of the previous 800! It has been estimated that knowledge has multiplied eight times since 1850 and that 80 percent of what we know today was discovered in the last 15 years! Hence, the oft-told story of the alumnus who visited his old physics professor. After glancing at a current exam, the former student remarked: "Why, these are the same questions I answered ten years ago!" "Yes," explained the professor, "but the answers are all different now."

Future Change

These have been past changes. How about the future? Can we expect a slowdown, a tapering off? Hardly. The pace will quicken, says the 30,000-member World Future Society. Here are a few of the predictions they recently made:

By 2000, 100,000 people in the United States will be above the age of 100 and the 85-and-older group will grow faster than any other population segment.

By 1995, due to the destruction of tropical forests, animal and plant species will become extinct at the rate of one per hour!

By 2020, soil erosion will be rampant. Most of the soil of southern Iowa, for example, will be gone and each acre will require 38 per-cent more fertilizer and 38 percent more fuel for tilling.

Blue-collar workers will constitute only 10 percent of the U.S. work force by 2000.

By 2050, unless there is a drastic downturn in population growth, more people will be born in *one year* than in the 1,500 years following Christ.

On the brighter side, we may have only 10 percent of the current auto accidents. Sweden is experimenting with microcomputer technology controlling sensors buried in the highway to guide traffic.

Finally, robots are multiplying like rabbits, about 30 percent a year. There should be 35,000 of them installed in the United States by 1995. To replace those missing blue-collar workers?

Currently 200,000 new chemicals are developed every year, and that number will be doubled by the 21st century.

Most of those prophecies were fairly long-range. According to the American Association of Retired People these changes will occur in the 1990s:

The proportion of people aged 20–29 in the United States will fall from 18 to 13 percent.

More than 21 million new jobs will be created.

Genetic mapping will allow the identification of 4,000 inheritable disorders among people of all ages.

There will be new drugs to cure or prevent "killer" diseases such as heart disease, hypertension, and some cancers, and chronic diseases such as Alzheimer's.

Fiber optics, interactive video, and teleconferencing will enhance the use of nontraditional settings for learning and other purposes.

Products such as emergency response systems, portable heart monitoring devices, and home robot/computers will be widespread.

Driving a car will be easier, and safer, what with ultraviolet headlights to reduce glare; alarms to alert drivers starting to doze off; displays in windshield showing the car's speed and gas situation; fast-acting windshield defrosters; collision-avoiding sensors such as radars beaming down a darkened highway to detect oncoming obstacles, and so forth.

And be on the lookout, says forecaster Kim Long, for the "smart toilet." In addition to its usual indispensable functions, it will register weight, analyze urine, and measure temperature, blood pressure, and pulse.

In the face of such manifest transformation—past, present, and future—it seems incredible that some people remain impervious to the realization of change. When the first atom bomb exploded, Albert Einstein said: "Everything has changed—except the thinking in men's minds."

CHANGES IN PEOPLE

And people, despite the perceptions of some, change too—often very slowly, sometimes markedly. Infants become children, adolescents, young adults, middle-aged, and finally elderly people, experiencing gradual and sometimes abrupt changes beyond enumeration.

Humorist Erma Bombeck underscores her own transformations as she records her three daughters discussing Mom:

"This is weird," said the oldest child. "Are we talking about the same Mom? The thin, bright-eyed, dark-haired girl who used to read me stories, bake cookies, paste my baby pictures in the album and giggle a lot?"

The middle child said, "The somber-looking blonde who used to put me to bed at 6:30 and bought me a dog to save on napkins?"

The baby said, "The grayish lady who falls asleep during the six-o'clock news and is going to show me my baby pictures when we finish shooting the roll at my graduation?"

I knew I should have raised 'em in separate parts of the house[2]

The periods in which people live change too. Consider the attitude shifts of the public. In 1922, for example, *Good Health* published an article that typified current public opinion about smoking:

Tobacco benumbs all the finer sensibilities. That's why men smoke. A man who loves his wife and children is lonely when away and misses the home folks. He smokes, and at once his loneliness is gone. Tobacco fills the place of home and family. It kills the fine sentiment that made him long for the home fires and the familiar faces.

The smoker's business is not prospering. He is worried. He ought to find out the cause and remove it. He smokes instead. He is no longer worried. All is well. But the business fault is not corrected. More business enterprises have run aground in a fog bank of tobacco smoke than have been wrecked by hard times or business panics. Tobacco is an enemy of business as well as of morals. . . .

The college "Smoker" is a devil's den, a snare which has lured many thousands of promising young men to mental and moral ruin. The smoking room is sister to the saloon and must be eliminated along with its iniquitous

---

[2] Erma Bombeck, "They Remember Mama . . . in Three Different Versions," *Albany Times—Union*. Reprinted by permission.

relative, if civilization is to be saved from the demoralization which threatens it.[3]

Contrast that with the the the public's attitude 40 years later. In 1962, with 8 out of 10 men and 1 out of 3 women smoking, the nonsmoker was almost an oddity! Now the public's sentiments are changing again. The American Heart Association reports that the mixture of chemicals in cigarette smoke kills 350,000 Americans yearly through heart disease, cancer, and emphysema.

Increasingly, the smoker is being considered not as a moral leper but a witless self-destructionist—even a threat to those who inhale secondhand smoke. In a conflict between smokers and nonsmokers, whose rights should prevail? Of 10,000 recent visitors to the Epcot Center, 77 percent sided with the nonsmokers and only 3 percent with the smokers. The remaining 20 percent felt both should receive equal consideration.

For some time, being thin has been fashionable. Cases of anorexia nervosa and bulimia are increasing. Overweight is a dirty word. But this has not always been so. Note this admonition from *The Lady's Realm* of February 1906:

> Angularity of form is invariably ugly, and is best remedied by very careful dieting. Fattening foods of all kinds should be eaten. Farinaceous foods, rice and tapioca, taken in the form of milk puddings, are excellent. Potatoes, butter and beans should be eaten freely. Sweets and pastry are useful in encouraging the development of adipose tissue. Cream also forms a delicious food with fattening properties.

Our attitudes about dress are equally transient. This mandate on beach apparel was rigorously enforced in 1925 by the Wilmette (Illinois) Park District:

> For women, blouse and bloomer suits may be worn, with or without skirts, with or without stockings, providing the blouse has one-quarter arm sleeve, or close-fitting arm-holes, and providing the bloomers are full and not shorter than four inches above the knee.
>
> Men's suits must have skirt effect or shirt worn outside of trunks, except when flannel knee pants with belt are worn. The trunks must not be shorter than four inches above the knee, and the shirt must not be shorter than two inches above the bottom of the trunk.

Try posting *that* on today's beaches!

Our appraisal of marriage has certainly been changing. In 1955, the median age at first marriage was 22 for men and 20 for women. Now, it's

---

[3] "The Immorality of Smoking," *Good Health,* December 1922.

432   P A R T   T H R E E   Patterns of Miscommunication

26 for men and 23 for women. Fewer of us seem to be taking that big step. In 1946 the annual rate was 118.1 marriages for 1,000 eligibles. Currently, it's 57. And *staying* married isn't the imperative that it used to be. The divorce rate in 1970 was 47 per 1,000. Today it is 133.

But attitude changes concerning smoking, anatomy, dress, and marriage seem almost tortoiselike compared to our fickleness regarding what is—or is not—*IN*.

According to the latest evaluation:

In	Out
Discount warehouses	Designer boutiques
Personal saving	Conspicuous consumption
Timex	Rolex
"Roseanne"	"Dynasty"
Personal saving	Consumer borrowing
Fried chicken and mashed potatoes	Sun-dried tomatoes and goat-cheese pizza
Honda and Hyundai	Porsche and BMW
$25 Keds	$100 Nike Air Jordans
Casual cookouts	Catered dinners
Fighting about the check	Fighting for the check

Of course, by the time you read this, the ins will be outs and the outs will be ancient history. So if you want to keep up to date you might be guided by this nostrum: "When the TV weatherman wears it, does it, says it, or eats it, it's probably on its way out."

CHANGES IN BUSINESS

One of the more dynamic aspects of American life is business. Fluctuation is the rule. Booms and busts, sellers' markets and buyers' markets, inflations and deflations—nothing stands still for very long. The television market is a dramatic example. Forty years ago, 7- and 10-inch black-and-white sets were being snapped up at high prices. Thirty years ago, dealers in TV-saturated areas were driven to considerable lengths to move their merchandise. One offered a 21-inch set for $100, no down payment. He did a brisk business, but only because of his special enticement: a no-interest $500 loan went with each set! His advertisement: "Pay off your doctor and grocer bills; buy shoes for the kids; make payments on your house, car, and appliances—and have TV too!" Twenty years ago, *color* TV manufacturers found it impossible to keep up with the demand. Today the industry is swamped with foreign imports—principally Japanese. And tomorrow?

Today only 2 percent of our population are involved in agriculture. Only a hundred years ago only 2 percent were *not* in agriculture.

The automobile market is another example of change. As late as the 1950s, U.S. manufacturers produced 80 percent of the world's cars. By 2000, according to industry analysts, Detroit's market share will probably be less than 30 percent.

Is there any product more American than Good Humor ice cream bars, Alka-Seltzer, or Thermos bottles? And how about firms such as Brooks Brothers, Smith-Corona, Pillsbury, General Electric, Wilson Sporting Goods, and Carnation? They've recently all been sold to non-Americans. Last year foreign investors bought nearly 400 U.S. companies for $60 billion. That's a 61 percent increase over the previous year and represents a marked acceleration of foreign purchases. Non-Americans now control more than 12 percent of U.S. manufacturing assets and employ 3 million Americans.

Change is virtually synonymous with our economy. The value of money is a case in point. A dollar is a dollar, right? Wrong! Not with inflation ravaging it. A recent article in *The Wall Street Journal* projected the value of the dollar assuming that the current rate of inflation, 6 percent, remains constant. Other factors being equal, your salary will double in 12 years, triple in 7 more years, and quadruple in another 5 years. That's the good news. The bad news is that prices would escalate as well.

Few aspects of organizational experience have changed as dramatically as the manner of supervising employees. The following were office rules insisted upon by Zachary U. Geiger, a California carriage and wagon maker, a century ago:

> Office employees will sweep the floors, dust the furniture, shelves and showcases. Each clerk will bring in a bucket of water and a scuttle of coal for the day's business. Make your pens carefully. You may whittle nibs to your individual taste.
>
> This office will open at 7 A.M. and close at 8 P.M. except on the Sabbath, when it will remain closed. Every employee should lay aside from each pay a goodly sum of his earnings for his benefit during his declining years, so that he will not become a burden on the charity of his betters.
>
> Any employee who smokes Spanish cigars, uses liquor in any form, gets shaved at a barbershop or frequents pool or public halls will give me good reason to suspect his worth, intentions, integrity and honesty. The employee who has performed his labors faithfully and without fault for a period of five years in my service, who has been thrifty and attentive to his religious duties, and is looked upon by his fellow man as a substantial and law-abiding citizen will be given an increase of five cents per day in his pay, provided a just return in profit from the business permits it.

In summary, "The only thing constant in life," as La Rochefoucauld wrote, "is change."

A DURABLE FALLACY

Subtle Changes

It seems odd that such a palpable fallacy as the notion of nonchange should persist. Among the reasons for the fallacy's durability is that some changes occur so gradually that we are insensitive to them. We often fail to keep abreast of the changes in the people closest to us (friends, spouse, children, subordinates). Because we are with them so constantly, their incremental alterations may be imperceptible to us.

Tolerance for Change

Another factor that protects the fallacy of nonchange is that change is generally less comfortable than nonchange. Indeed change can be downright terrifying, especially if it involves the unknown, the unpredictable, the unexplained, and thus, the *un*-understood. Alvin Toffler's title for his best-seller, *Future Shock*, was most apt. The accelerated changes that he and Naisbitt & Aburdend (*Megatrends 2000*-published in 1990) anticipate can be quite disturbing.

Thomas Holmes[4] has been studying the cumulative effect of change upon people. His overall conclusion is that we seem to have a certain tolerance for the changes we experience in a given period. If we exceed that tolerance, we increase our chances of becoming ill. "If it takes too much effort to cope with the environment, we have less to spare for preventing disease," says Holmes.

Accordingly, he has assigned numerical values to various kinds of changes. Here are the top ten on his Social Readjustment Rating Scale:

Life Event	Value
1. Death of a spouse	100
2. Divorce	73
3. Marital separation	65
4. Detention in jail or other institution	63
5. Death of a close family friend	63
6. Major personal injury or illness	53
7. Marriage	50
8. Fired at work	47
9. Marital reconciliation	45
10. Retirement	45

---

[4] See Thomas E. Holmes and Ella M. David, *Life Change Events Research, 1966-1978* (New York: Praeger, 1984).

Here's how it works—suppose in a 12-month period, a person has a marital separation (65); then a reconciliation (45); then a divorce (73); and then gets fired (47). That racks up 230 points. Holmes contends that that person has better than a 50 percent chance of becoming ill in the near future.

Some of us might become ill with far fewer points, and that is part of my uneasiness with the numbers and the change categories. I believe different people value a given change quite differently. A divorce for one person might be devastating; for another, it could be relatively unimportant.

However, there are several aspects that strike me as valid and helpful:

1. The notions of changes *piling up* on us seem authentic. What may be a minor irritation on one day may become a major stress on another day when one is oversaturated with change.

2. Notice that good as well as bad changes can be stressful. Marriage and reconciliation and, later in Holmes' list, outstanding personal achievement, vacation, and Christmas may be positive, but they are still changes.

3. Holmes is constructive when he suggests that if we can anticipate life changes and plan for them, we can reduce their stressful impact.

The Language Factor

Language is another important perpetuation of the insidious assumption of nonchange.

When we trace back to the roots of our language, we discover many clues as to why we talk—and behave—as we do. The basic form and structure of the English language were laid down in ancient Greece. Now consider what life must have been like then—comparatively slow, static, and unchanging. Not much written history to give a sense of process. To us the average Athenian's life would seem extraordinarily placid—one day very much like any other.

Consider, then, that our language was spawned by this relatively constant society. Is it any wonder that the Greeks created a language that reflected their static existence? The result is that, although we live in an enormously more dynamic environment, we still use a language that strongly implies nonchange, rest, and permanence—and thus are seduced to overlook change.

Note how incredibly easy it is in our language to speak or write (or listen or read) without taking time into account. Read each of the paragraphs that follow, and decide the date line of each.

(A)

Prompted by widespread fears that new weapons of mass destruction might wipe out Western civilization, the Pope today issued a bull forbidding their use by any Christian state against another, whatever the provocation.

Date _____

(B)

We need law and order. Yes, without law and order our nation cannot survive. Elect us, and we shall restore law and order.

Date _____

(C)

The earth is degenerating these days. There are signs civilization is coming to an end. Bribery and corruption abound. Violence is everywhere. Children no longer respect and obey their parents.

Date _____

(A) could have been a plea by Pope John Paul II, but it was actually Pope Innocent in 1139, and the weapons had nothing to do with nuclear or biological warfare.

(B) could have been contemporary campaign rhetoric, but it was Adolph Hitler in Hamburg in 1932.

(C) was from an Assyrian tablet, circa 3000 B.C.

And therein lies an important inadequacy of our language system—the prevailing failure to specify time.

CORRECTIVES

The two preceding chapters described the need for discriminating among people, qualities, traits, and so forth, without regard for time differences. The current chapter calls for time differentiation. Let me say this a little differently.

The frozen evaluation was defined as a judgment set in concrete—an evaluation that remained constant and inflexible despite changes in its object. It seduces us to see now as forever. The basic problem, therefore, is to keep our evaluations in pace with past and future changes in the person or situation—whatever it is that we are evaluating. When the object changes, then the evaluation ought to change correspondingly. How can we accomplish this? How can we keep from freezing our evaluations, and how can we thaw those already frozen?

Internalize the Premise of Change

Substitute the conscious premise of change for the unconscious notion of nonchange. Believe firmly in the process nature of people, of situations, of things, and so forth, and you will be more likely to keep your evaluations up to date.

Apply the When Index

A very simple, yet effective, device for implementing the awareness of change is the When Index. Using the When Index is simply assigning a date. For example, the following Associated Press release appeared in 1950:

Williams Signs with Red Sox for Record Baseball Pay of $125,000

Boston, Feb. 7 (AP)—Ted Williams, the Red Sox slugger, today signed the highest salaried contract in baseball history—for an estimated $125,000.

Babe Ruth's $80,000 salary in 1930 and '31 was tops in the old days.[5]

At first glance, Mr. Williams seems to have fared considerably better financially than did Mr. Ruth. But the Foundation for Economic Education, Inc., made a revealing analysis by When-Indexing (i.e., dating) the purchasing power of the take-home dollar. See Figure 14.1.

FIGURE 14.1

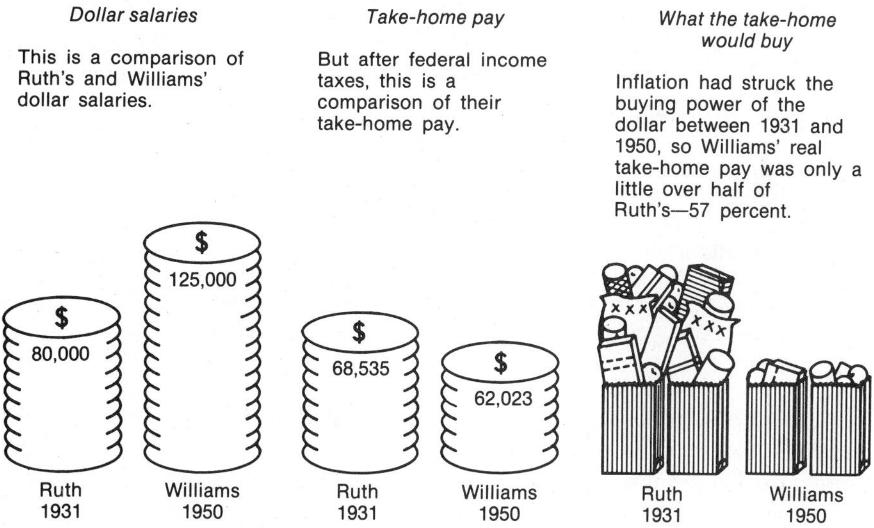

Dollar salaries

This is a comparison of Ruth's and Williams' dollar salaries.

Take-home pay

But after federal income taxes, this is a comparison of their take-home pay.

What the take-home would buy

Inflation had struck the buying power of the dollar between 1931 and 1950, so Williams' real take-home pay was only a little over half of Ruth's—57 percent.

| | $80,000 | $125,000 | $68,535 | $62,023 | | |
| Ruth 1931 | Williams 1950 | Ruth 1931 | Williams 1950 | Ruth 1931 | Williams 1950 |

If Ted Williams were to have as much buying power in 1950 as Babe Ruth had in 1931, he would have had to be paid $327,451.

---

[5] *The New York Times,* February 8, 1950. Reprinted by permission of the Associated Press.

To update this illustration: As of this writing, 32 major league baseball players annually receive in the neighborhood of $3 million (or more) for their services.[6] This, of course, is a very nice neighborhood. Their purchasing power, if not their talent, clearly exceeds that of the legendary Sultan of Swat. But it's different for the "average" big leaguer. That poor soul makes *only* $891,188 a year, which—given the ravages of inflation, taxes, and the cost of living index—represents only *half* of Ruth's purchasing power!

The advent of cryogenics has spawned a poignant joke concerning the relevance of When-Indexing. It seems that a rich man with a terminal illness was nearing death. He decided that he would have his body frozen in the hope that if sometime in the future a cure would be found he could be thawed and restored to health. Sure enough, 20 years later his dream was fulfilled and he recovered. His first act was to get to a pay phone and call his brokerage house. "How's my IBM stock?" he asked. "$35,000 a share," was the response. "That's marvelous!" he exclaimed. Just then the operator interrupted. "Your time is up. Please deposit $500 for another three minutes."

That story no longer seems quite so funny—not with serious economists such as John McCarthy extrapolating that if prices change in the next 40 years as they have in the last 40, then the average family's income will be $124,000, a college president's salary will be $600,000, homes will sell for $300,000 to $500,000, and bread for $7 a loaf!

The When Index (which may be expressed as a mental or even an explicit superscript; for example, the United States^{1992} is not the United States^{1986} is a reminder of the constant flux that characterizes the world in which we live. The following brief cases suggest its usefulness.

The Case of Earl Wood[7]

Earl Wood, 40, fell 25 feet to his death from a second-story fire escape door in the Ellington Company.

Police believed that Wood, an assembler, was unaware when he stepped from the door that the fire escape had been removed for repairs. Employees said that Wood frequently spent his rest break on the fire escape.

Even a structure as seemingly unchangeable as a fire escape is not always the same. Fire escape^{yesterday} is not fire escape^{today}. Had Wood engrained the habit of When-Indexing, he would have been prompted to look before stepping out onto a fire escape that was not there.

---

[6] In 1991, pitcher Roger Clemens (Boston Red Sox) reputedly made over $5 million. Some anonymous statistician calculated that he thus received more than $2,500 *per pitch*— whether or not it crossed the plate!

[7] The names are disguised. Otherwise the account is accurate.

The Case of David

Six-year-old David had had his experiences with innoculations, so his mother was not too surprised that he protested vigorously when she told him that he was to receive a polio shot the following afternoon.

"David," she countered, "I know how you feel, and I am willing to make a bargain with you. Now, the shot is not going to hurt you today or tomorrow morning, is it?" "No," he admitted. "And it isn't going to hurt when we leave the house and while we are driving to the doctor's office?" "No." "And it isn't going to hurt when we are sitting in the waiting room, reading the comic books?" "No." "Or when the doctor rubs your arm with alcohol and gets the hypodermic ready?" "No." "Then there would be no sense in crying or yelling at any of these times, would there?" "No, I guess not." "But it *will* hurt when he sticks the hypodermic into your arm, right?" "Yes!" "Well, young man, at *that* time you may yell your head off!"

David agreed, and when the inoculation actually occurred, a relaxed David considered the prick hardly worth yelling about, and his When-Indexing had spared him needless anxiety.

Try this sort of When-Indexing on yourself the next time you make a dental appointment or anticipate some other unpleasant experience. As Seneca wrote, "There is nothing more miserable and foolish than anticipation." A wise old professor of mine realized this as he viewed the self-imposed anxiety associated with tardiness: "I'm never late until I get there."

The Administration of Change

So much for the individual's coping with change. What about organizations? So often organizations must adapt to changes if they are to compete successfully, or even survive. Here are a few suggestions[8] for the manager who is required to administer changes:

1. *Involve your people in planning for changes.* It will help them understand rather than fear the change. Planning will allay possible concern that management is "trying to pull a fast one." The involvement may generate useful ideas from people closest to the affected activity.

2. *Use feedback so people can express their resistance.* Letting people get it off their chests usually reduces resistance. At least it will give you a more accurate conception of why they are resisting.

---

[8] Gordon L. Lippitt, Jack Mossop, and Petter Langseth, *Implementing Organization Change* (San Francisco: Jossey-Bass, 1985). See also Allan R. Cohen, Stephen L. Fink, Herman Gaden, and Robin D. Willits, *Effective Behavior in Organizations*, 4th ed. (Homewood, Ill.: Richard D. Irwin, 1988), Chapter 14: "The Manager as the Initiator of Change in the Organization," pp. 405–53; Paul Hersey and Kenneth H. Blanchard, *Management of Organizational Behavior*, 5th ed. (Englewood Cliffs, N.J.: Prentice-Hall, 1988), Chapter 15, "Planning and Implementing Change," pp. 333–63.

3. *Consider group aspects.* Will change break up congenial work groups? Disrupt commuting schedules and carpools? Affect vacation plans? Assign people to a group with incompatible standards of conduct?

4. *Build a trusting work climate.* Mistrust and distrust occur when people have incomplete or incorrect information. They often feel helpless and impotent, sensing they cannot influence the situation.

> To build a trusting climate, tell the truth. It's been proven time and again that people would rather have bad news than no news. Given the facts, they feel they can do something about a problem.

5. *Be certain that your people know the real goals or reasons for the change.* Be sure people do not create erroneous assumptions and circulate false rumors regarding the change.

6. *Use problem-solving techniques.* (See Chapter 17, "Blindering.") Identify the *real* problem. You may think: "If only I could get Sam to retire, the morale of the group would improve greatly." It's unlikely, however, that deep-seated attitudes are caused by a single individual in a group.

7. *Be sensitive to timing.* It's generally better to get people favorably disposed toward the advent of, say, automated data processing before rather than after the installation is made.

SUMMARY

A frozen evaluation is one that is spread unconsciously (or perhaps deliberately) over the future and/or over the past, without regard for change. The frozen evaluation may take on a great variety of forms, not the least serious of which are those that have to do with our evaluations of ourselves. Underlying most frozen evaluations is the assumption of nonchange—a fallacious and often unconsciously held notion that there is rest, permanence, constancy. The When Index reminds us to take change into account in our evaluations—to distinguish among time^1, time^2, time^3, and so on.

Discussion Questions

1. What do indiscrimination, polarization, and frozen evaluation have in common? How are they distinguished?

2. The Case of Frank is about a man who found it difficult to live down his past. Do you know other people who have resigned themselves to others' frozen evaluations of them? Under what conditions is this most likely to happen?

3. "But always we begin by speaking as we think, and end by thinking as we speak. . . ."—Lester Sinclair. What are the implications of this statement? If we were to improve our language system, would this improve our thinking?

What are the practical limitations on improving or changing a language system?

4. "No man dies in the world into which he was born."—Margaret Mead. What did she mean? Do you agree? How does this statement bear on this chapter?

5. Why is it possible in English and in many other languages to talk and write datelessly—that is, to make declarative statements, for example, without specifying the time to which those statements apply?

6. The Case of David suggests a way of using the When Index to minimize anxiety over future events. What do you think of this notion? Is there positive value in worry—especially if such concern helps us to prevent or avoid or cope with a problem?

7. Report upon an incident, perhaps involving yourself, in which frozen evaluations played a role. Why did the incident occur? What could have been done to prevent or correct the situation? What measures could prevent a recurrence of such frozen evaluations?

C A S E S

CASE 14.1

Apex Forgings*
Stan Liska

This is going to be a little hard to believe, but I swear it's true. I'm the industrial relations manager for our plant, Apex Forgings. Under Section 7, Article 17, of our basic agreement with the union, employees may bid on permanent job vacancies. These vacancies are posted on the company bulletin board. Such jobs are awarded solely on a seniority basis—the man with the longest service gets the job, regardless of his background. I don't agree with it—but that's the contract.

So, naturally, the man who gets the job often has to be trained for it. Sometimes the training is done by the lame duck who is on the job but will be released from it as soon as the new man can take over.

Last summer a job vacancy occurred in Department 23, the Axle Machining Department. Accordingly, an End Face Operator vacancy was posted. George Morales, 27, a Puerto Rican, was awarded the job, and since he had no prior experience on that job or in that department, he was to be trained by the incumbent, Fred Meister, 32. Morales' English was none too good but I wasn't concerned. He had done a good job in Department 14, and I felt he would learn quickly.

At the end of the first day Morales filled out his production record card exactly as Meister had completed his. I'm still not clear as to whether Fred knew what George was doing. Anyway, the next day Fritz Heinsohn, 55, the foreman of Department 23, really chewed out Morales.

> **Heinsohn:** What the hell do you think you're doing? The way you filled out your card there would be twice as many axles turned out as possible. We don't need any wise guys around here. You don't put nothin' on this card, is that understood?

Morales had received no previous instruction on filling out the time card, but he sensed that Heinsohn was in no mood for discussion, so he just said he understood. Morales thought Heinsohn had uttered some racial slur under his breath as he walked away, but George couldn't be sure, so he let it go.

Two weeks later Morales was considered trained, so Meister left for greener pastures and Morales was left alone. On the morning of the next day, Heinsohn appeared again and laced into George.

---

* All names have been disguised.

Heinsohn: What do you mean by not putting anything on your damned card? How the hell are we supposed to know how many axles you're turning out? Do you think we're mind readers around here?

Morales started to explain, but Heinsohn interrupted.

Heinsohn: Hell, you spics are all alike—if they're not punks, they're dummies. Now, you keep a record of how many axles you run and put it on the card. And don't let me hear no more crap from you.

At that, Heinsohn turned and walked away. To make a sad story short, Morales fell off a little in his production that first week and Heinsohn kept jumping on him. George finished out the week—and just never came back. My honest opinion is that we lost a good man.

You might wonder how Heinsohn is regarded by Al Mayer, our superintendent. The answer is highly. Heinsohn gets the most product out the back door. Mayer simply ignores Fritz's turnover, low department morale, scrappage, and giving a bad example to the other foremen.

Discussion Questions
1. What patterns of miscommunication seem to be involved in this case?
2. How could these patterns of miscommunication have been prevented?

CASE 14.2

"We're Better than Orange"*

Blue versus Orange!!!

Orange is the number-one team in the country according to a poll of those who know. They do not rate Blue within the top 20. Conclusion: Blue cannot possibly beat Orange next Monday night at Orange.

We must concede that the odds are against Blue. Orange is undefeated this year, and is invincible at home, having won 130 games or so in a row on its home court. Looks bad, doesn't it?

Before I go any farther, let's look at some of the records. Tuesday evening, we played Green here. The score was 88 to 55 at the end of the game, Blue on the long end of the scoring.

Earlier this year, Green played Red at Red. It lost to Red by only four points. The amazing bit in this comparision is that Red held the aforementioned Orange squad to a four-point spread on a neutral court. Figuring a home floor edge of 10 points, Red is only 4 points worse than Orange, but

---

* The colors stand for various colleges and universities. Otherwise this article is a reprint from Blue U's student newspaper.

is worse than Green by 6 points. Therefore, Orange is two points worse than Green. Seeing that we beat Green by 33 points at home, I subtract 10 points, which shows me that we are 23 points better than Green. Since Green is 2 points better than Orange, I have come to the conclusion that Blue is 25 points better than Orange on a neutral court and 13 points better than Orange at Orange.

This makes for an interesting twist in the records, which will show you that nothing is impossible in this game called basketball. So there you are.

So, c'mon Blue, we know you can do it! We're with you!

[According to this reasoning, Blue will defeat orange by 13 points. Blue actually lost by 21.]

Discussion Questions

1. What does this case have to do with frozen evaluations?
2. What was the author's motive for writing this piece?

CASE 14.3

Ice Cream and Advertising*

James Clifford, an account executive with a Detroit advertising firm, had learned through a friend that a certain Michigan manufacturer of ice cream had developed a revolutionary process for packaging ice cream. He reasoned that the president of the ice cream firm might be a good prospect for an advertising program designed to capitalize on the packaging innovation. He asked his friend, who was also an acquaintance of the president, to arrange an interview for him. He had hoped to meet with the president, Mr. Shepherd, before the innovation became common knowledge among the agencies. Clifford's friend made the appointment with Shepherd's secretary.

Meanwhile, Clifford set about preparing a brochure containing a detailed plan of demonstrations in Michigan and the Midwest and several illustrations of displays for stores.

Unfortunately, Shepherd's secretary had forgotten to notify her employer of the appointment. When Clifford arrived, she suddenly recalled her error and with great embarrassment admitted her mistake to Mr. Shepherd. The president, a kindly man in his 70s, remarked; "Oh, I don't think any harm's been done. Since the error has been on our end, he shouldn't suffer. I'm not too busy now anyway, so you can have him come in. But I think it would be best to explain the slipup to him so he will know that he'll have to start from scratch with me since I know nothing about him or the purpose of his visit."

---

* All names have been disguised.

The secretary explained her error to Clifford and showed him to Mr. Shepherd's office.

Shepherd: I'm terribly sorry this happened, Mr. Clifford, but I'm sure it won't hamper our meeting.

Clifford: That's perfectly all right, sir. Your secretary explained the situation to me, and we all slip up once in a while. (*Smiling*) After all, they're still putting erasers on pencils.

Shepherd (*smiling*): Well, it's nice of you to be so gracious. Now, what did you have in mind?

Clifford began to discuss the company's new packaging process and the desirability of setting up an advertising campaign. He was taking the brochure from his briefcase when Shepherd interrupted:

Shepherd (*sadly*): Young man, I'm afraid my secretary's error was more costly than I had thought.

Clifford: How is that, sir?

Shepherd: Why, you've made your trip for nothing.

Clifford: I don't understand.

Shepherd: Why, if I had known you were going to talk about advertising I could have saved you a trip.

Clifford: You mean you've already signed with another agency?

Shepherd: Not at all. I simply don't advertise—never have and never will.

Clifford: You've never advertised?!

Shepherd: Never. My grand-dad founded this company 80 years ago on the theory that a good product will sell itself—and he was right. My dad followed his practice, and so do I. So you see, I'm not about to waste any money now on advertising. I just don't believe in it.

Clifford made a few vain attempts to dissuade the old man, but it was obvious that Shepherd was unalterably opposed to advertising his product. In resignation Clifford returned to Detroit, where he reported to his supervisor:

Clifford: I simply don't understand the man. He's the kind of guy who wakes up in the morning to his GE electric clock; brushes his teeth with Crest; puts on his Arrow shirt, Kuppenheimer suit, and Florsheim shoes; eats his Kellogg's corn flakes; drives his Cadillac to work, and then says, "I don't believe in advertising"!

Discussion Questions

1. Are there any frozen evaluations going on in this case?
2. Is Mr. Shepherd a lost cause insofar as progress is concerned?
3. How could this evaluation be corrected?

CASE 14.4

The Frozen Andy*

William Lyon

Phil entered my office as my stomach ascended to my throat. His crimson face warned me that I was in for another unpleasant encounter. A fleeting thought reminded me that I should have better control of my inner response by now—this was not the first time.

"Why did you put Andy on the Green job?" screamed Phil with uncontrollable anger. I motioned for him to close the door. The slam echoed down the corridor.

"Why?" was my inept response.

"Why? You know damn well he's immature as hell. He doesn't know when to be serious. He'll run Tom up a tree. Just like last fall on the packing job."

I looked out the window to compose myself. The coloring of the leaves was impressive.

"But Phil, that was a year ago. Andy has advanced significantly and has had favorable reports in the last six months. I felt he could handle the job and in fact feel we have to give him something more challenging so he can grow."

"He's not going to grow on my accounts!" Phil was again at the screaming level. "I was against hiring him in the first place. He just doesn't have it—and never will!"

"But what about his favorable reports?" I queried.

"I don't give a damn what others say or feel about him. I don't want him on my jobs. It's just too big a risk. Don't you see?" he pleaded with authority. "Get him off!" The door opened, and a red neck disappeared through it.

Evidently Phil had been in personnel and seen the long-run schedules that I had been working on. I proceeded to review the matter with Simon, the managing partner. After several minutes of discussion, he suggested that he should talk with Phil to correct the situation. I left his office somewhat relieved, feeling that Si would stand behind Andy (and me).

That afternoon my phone rang. It was Si. He said that he had had a long discussion, somewhat heated, with Phil. He told me that it didn't

---

* All names have been disguised.

appear that Phil was going to change his mind and that I should make the necessary changes in the schedule.

Discussion Questions
1. What patterns of miscommunications do you see in this case?
2. How could they be prevented in the future?

CASE 14.5

Money Troubles*

The money market can be treated the same way as any commodity market. In general, when the supply of money is plentiful, its price (which is the rate of interest) will be lower than when its supply is short. This, however, is only part of the story, since it is widely known that federal controls on the money supply are in force. The following incident arose out of the changing price of money.

As a farm loan appraiser for an insurance company's mortgage loan department, I am charged with several duties. Perhaps the most important of these are the recommendations of new loan business.

Not long ago, the money supply was diminishing significantly and mortgage money was becoming scarce. Those of us in the field were aware of the tighter money market, but no policy change in regard to the interest rate was issued from the home office. In my own case, I had two farm loan applications on my desk, to be submitted at the then prevailing interest rate. These were to be sent to the home office for approval as soon as the appraisal report was completed and as soon as proper credit checks were made. The following day, I mailed these cases to the home office and assured the applicants that their cases would be approved.

In that same day's mail, I received a memorandum stating that "all farm loan applications must be submitted at a 1/2 percent higher interest rate, effective as of the date of this memorandum."

The two loan applications that were submitted at the old rate were committed and mailed to the applicants at the new rate. Both applicants were very unhappy about the change in their applications. They felt that they had been double-crossed. There is no question that the company and I lost considerable goodwill not only with these people but with many of their friends to whom they complained about our treatment of them.

Discussion Questions
1. Who is responsible for the loss of goodwill described by the author?

---

* Printed by permission of the author, whose name has been withheld by request.

2. What does this case have to do with the frozen evaluation?

3. What measures could have prevented or ameliorated this incident?

CASE 14.6

John Lundy*

John Lundy, 40, had been a press operator with the Romaine Company for over 15 years. For the past four years, he had operated mechanical forming presses. His most frequent job was making top and bottom caps for water heater jackets. His raw material was a sheet of 18–20 gauge cold-rolled steel. The sheet was eight feet long and two feet wide, and it weighted about 10 pounds. The procedure was to grasp the sheet with a suction cup and to slide it on rollers to a stop at which the first two feet of the strip were properly positioned under the press. He would then press two buttons simultaneously, which caused the machine to press down with a force of 100 tons, forming the cap.[1] The press would rise automatically, whereupon John reached under with both hands and lifted and removed the cap and placed it on his stack of finished pieces. He then moved the next two feet of sheet under the press and repeated the process. Thus, he made four caps from each strip.

One day the press suddenly malfunctioned. John had pressed the buttons, the press descended and rose, and he started to reach for the cap. Without warning, the press descended a second time and Lundy narrowly escaped serious injury. Cautiously he tried the machine again, and it double-hit again. He called Frank Torgeson, his foreman, and complained about the press. Torgeson immediately ordered the machine shut down and called maintenance. In the meantime, he assigned Lundy to a similar press nearby.

Three hours later two maintenance men arrived, briefly discussed the machine with the foreman, and set to work. They suspected that a faulty connection in the machine's electrical system permitted a second cycle. Accordingly, they climbed to the top of the press, about 18 feet above the floor, and called to John: "Hey, Lundy, do you want to come over here and go through an operation so we can see what's happening from up here?"

"OK," John replied, and he walked to the press. He cupped the sheet, slid it into place, and pressed the buttons. The press descended, and John reached under for the cap—the press recycled, and his right hand was severed at the wrist.

---

* All names have been disguised.

[1] The buttons were positioned at eye level and spread apart in such a way as to require the use of both hands to operate them, thus protecting the operator's hands from injury as the press descended.

Discussion Questions

1. How do you account for this tragedy?
2. What patterns of miscommunication appear to be involved in this case?
3. How could this accident have been prevented?

CASE 14.7

Be a Millionaire!

In 1978, the U.S. Congress created the National Commission of Social Security. The Commission's objective was to study options in the financing of retirement. Chaired by Milton Gwirtzman, an attorney, the Commission reported its recommendations to the Congress in 1981. The report included the suggestion that virtually all individuals be allowed to invest in Individual Retirement Accounts (IRAs) and that the maximum annual amount of contribution be sizable. The proposal became law and the modified IRAs became available in 1982.

Anyone could now invest up to $2,000 of earnings or the entire amount of earnings, whichever was less, in an IRA. A married couple could invest up to $2,250. If both spouses were working, each could contribute up to $2,000 for a total of $4,000. Investors could deduct the amount of their contributions from reportable income on their federal income-tax returns. Thus all investments and any appreciation of funds in the IRAs would be tax-deferred until withdrawal, normally retirement, at which time one's taxable income would presumably be lower.

Banks, savings and loans, and other thrift institutions, and many other financial organizations began to compete aggressively for customers to open IRA accounts.

This advertisement of a certain savings and loan association was fairly typical:

BE A MILLIONAIRE!

Open an IRA with us.

Your money is insured up to $100,000 by the Federal Savings and Loan Insurance Corporation.

Your investment will be compounded DAILY at 12 percent.

Invest $2,000 a year for 30 years and you will retire with $652,000!

A couple investing $4,000 a year will have more than a
MILLION DOLLARS!

Mr. Gwirtzman objected strongly to such advertising in a letter to Paul Volcker, chairman of the Federal Reserve Board.

Discussion Questions

1. What was Mr. Gwirtzman complaining about? What is wrong with the ad?
2. What does this case have to do with the frozen evaluation?

CASE 14.8

The New Salesman*

Our company was in the process of adding a dairy route truck service to their operation. Manager Rita Stevens had finished her planning and began to act so that this service could be initiated prior to October 1. One of the tasks confronting her was the hiring of a dairy route salesman. It was obvious that none of her present employees qualified for the job and she decided to advertise in the local paper. After interviewing many candidates, she hired Norm Alquist, whom she considered extremely well qualified. Alquist was hired prior to the deadline of September 15, which allowed the new salesman to attend the training school and begin route work on October 1. Stevens was extremely busy setting up the new service was tardy in forwarding the paperwork that was necessary with newly hired employees.

On October 15 these papers arrived in the personnel office and the bonding information proved to be most interesting. Alquist, now an employee for one month, had been convicted of embezzling and had served out a sentence in jail five years ago. He had been a lawyer and was now barred from practice. Glen Forbes, personnel manager, had the responsibility, according to policy, to notify the company's insurance office of the risk so that they in turn could contact the insurance company.

Predictably, the insurance company denied bond for Alquist, and Forbes called Stevens.

Forbes: Say, Rita. You got yourself a dilly this time.

Stevens: What do you mean?

Forbes: Why, Alquist, of course. The insurance company turned thumbs down.

Stevens: What does that mean?

Forbes: He can't be bonded and he must be terminated.

Stevens: Well, I figured he couldn't be bonded but I don't see why I have to fire him. He's doing a damn good job for us and I'm trying to get this truck service off the ground.

Forbes: I can understand your concern for the new business, but what possessed you to hire the guy in the first place? Didn't you know about his record?

---

* All names have been disguised. The author's name has been withheld by request.

Stevens: Sure I did—he came right out and laid it on the line. I checked with the police and he's been clean ever since. But he's had a tough time of it—his references unanimously state that he was an excellent salesman but that it was just against company policy that he be retained.

Forbes: Well, I guess he's going to collect another reference, because we're in the same boat.

Stevens: Are you saying I can't keep him?

Forbes: I'm saying you can't keep him on any bonded job. Make a file clerk out of him if you want to but he can't handle money for us.

Stevens: That's ridiculous. I don't want to lose a top-notch salesman. Besides, what kind of money are we talking about? He starts off with $25 in change in the morning and because most of his accounts are charged, he's unlikely to collect more than $100 a day.

Forbes (*growing impatient*): I don't care if it's 100 *cents*—he can't handle money!

Stevens: Look—I'll be accountable for any loss on his part.

Forbes: No dice—it's against policy.

Stevens (*exasperated*): I never heard of anything so stupid!

Forbes: Look, Stevens—don't talk to *me* about stupidity—*I* didn't hire this con!

Stevens: He's *not* a con—he's served his time. Do you want to crucify the guy for the rest of his life?

Forbes (*clenching his teeth and suppressing his anger*): This is getting no-where—you do what you want to—(*deliberately*) *but the guy can't handle money*—goodbye! (*Hangs up.*)

Discussion Questions

1. What has occurred in this case?
2. What are Stevens' perceptions? Forbes'?
3. What do you recommend be done now?
4. What does this case have to do with "Frozen Evaluations"?

CASE 14.9

Tom Rollins*

My name is Tom Rollins. I'm 28 and single. I earned a Ph.D. in marketing from a prestigious university in New England two and a half years ago.

Now I'm teaching in a large state university in the Southwest. The Dean of the School of Business Administration here told me the criteria

---

* All names have been disguised.

for promotion before I took the job. He said every faculty member is graded on teaching, research, and local citizenship.

I asked him if that was the priority—the order in which he listed them. He wouldn't commit himself, saying all three were important.

Well, I believe I'm measuring up on all three counts. My teaching is going well. I received an award for Excellence in Teaching when I was a T.A. and now I'm one of 10 nominees for Teacher of the Year here. I love teaching and really try to help the students—and they like me, too.

My publication is fine. I've had four articles published in professional journals and two more accepted. I have a textbook about one-half written.

My "local citizenship" has been good, too. I've been appointed to two committees and so far this year I've missed just one meeting with one of the committees. And, of course, I always contribute in every meeting.

Incidentally, I'm black but I can say honestly that I've experienced no prejudice here. Oh, there are a couple of older men on the faculty who aren't exactly crazy about me. But I don't think that's a race thing. It's just jealousy. Those guys would probably have their noses out of joint about any young person who's moving up faster than they are. They haven't published anything for years.

I've been told unofficially and confidentially that I've got a lock on associate professor next year assuming I don't mess up.

Now, maybe you feel my head is swelled from all these early successes and you might be right. But something happened two weeks ago that brought me back to earth in a hurry.

The spring semester had just begun. The event occurred in my 10 A.M. class. My course was heavily overenrolled and the room was simply too small for the class. So I did some inquiring and there wasn't an available room on campus at that time—at least not one that would accommodate my group.

Then I hit on an idea. There's a classroom in another building, Merriam Hall. The room's normally used only for the Executive Development Program the school conducts in the summer. At other times it's usually vacant. It's a really neat room—large, well lighted (indirect lighting), ventilated, carpeted, comfortable chairs, nice pictures on the walls, a drinking fountain, a closet to hang coats, even bookcases and a fireplace.

Well, I turned on the charm and got permission to use that room for my class. I felt like a hero—I was sure none of the students knew about the room. So when they showed at Merriam would I ever be the big cheese who gets the ear of the powers that be!

So in the next class session, which happened to be on a Friday, I walked into the classroom and proudly announced that, "beginning next Monday the meetings of this course would be held in Merriam 107!"

I expected a cheer. Instead all I got was silence. Somehow I had laid an egg but I couldn't figure out why.

I decided not to pursue it then and there and went on with the class—and what a long 50 minutes that was!

Finally, the bell rang and the students got up to leave. I cornered a few of them and tried to find out why Merriam 107 went over like a lead balloon.

At first the kids were reluctant to speak, but then they began to tip me off—and what a barrage of complaints I heard!

"It's going to take me two minutes longer to get to my next class!"

"I signed up so that all my classes met here in this building. Now, I'm going to have to go outside!"

"And how about bad weather? We have plenty of it here in February and March!"

"I originally arranged to meet my boyfriend after class but this will make that impossible!"

It was a long weekend, but I did gain back a few points when the group met in Merriam 107 on Monday and realized what a fine room it was. I kept hoping the group would gradually come to like it, but now it's two weeks later and the strain is still there. I really don't know what to do about it.

Discussion Questions

1. How do you size up Tom Rollins?

2. What were his motives in acquiring Merriam 107 for his class?

3. What do you think of the manner in which Rollins handled that situation?

4. How should Rollins have handled it?

5. How should Rollins have reacted to the silence which followed his "lead balloon" announcement?

6. How should Rollins have handled the situation after two weeks?

7. Why is this appended to the "Frozen Evaluation" chapter?

CHAPTER FIFTEEN

Intensional Orientation
1. A General Statement
Going by Maps Rather than by Territories

❋
❋
❋

This chapter will not deal with a specific pattern of communication difficulty. The purpose here is to describe and discuss a general orientation toward the relationship between words and what we use them to stand for—between the map and the territory.[1] In the two following chapters, we shall examine a number of forms of misevaluation and miscommunication to which this orientation can lead.

One way to define the *intensional* (the s is intentional) *orientation* is to show it in action.

THE GRAHAM UNIVERSITY TAX CASE[2]

Graham is a large private university located in Allyn, a pleasant suburban community. For years, town-gown relations had been quite amicable except for one point of friction—taxation.

Graham held two types of exemption from real estate taxation. Exemption$_1$ concerned its educational property, that is, property used directly for educational purposes, such as classrooms, libraries, administration buildings, dormitories, and athletic fields. No one quarreled over this exemption, however, for it was granted to all schools and colleges.

Exemption$_2$, on the other hand, covered Graham's investment properties. These were real estate holdings that were not directly used for educational purposes, although the income from them was. It was around this

---

[1] See the map-territory analogy on p. 226.

[2] The names have been disguised; otherwise the details are factual.

exemption that the friction revolved. Interest in the issue waxed and waned, but there was always an underlying current of resentment among many of the townspeople. It was generally believed that the university's exemption had removed a sizable portion of the suburb's real estate from the tax rolls, thus increasing the taxation on the individual's property.

The debate became especially heated during election years. One aldermanic candidate, for example, published a statement in the *Allyn Times* to the effect that Graham's exemption$_2$ was depriving Allyn of tax revenue from 6 percent of its area and 10 percent of its assessed value. Other published statements, letters to the editor, and so on contended that the exemption covered as much as 50 percent of Allyn's real estate.

And there were citizens who supported the exemption. "So what if we have to pay more taxes," they argued, "isn't it worth it? Graham has put Allyn on the map, made us a cultural center. Moreover, Graham's thousands of students contribute to the economic health of the community with their purchases in Allyn."

And so the discussing and the contending and the arguing continued until the *Times* decided to do something about it. It hired competent real estate taxation specialists to determine the status of tax exemptions in Allyn. After a comprehensive survey, the specialists submitted their report: 16 percent of the total of Allyn's real estate was tax exempt. This included not only Graham's property, educational and investment, but that of the other colleges, the private and public schools, the churches, the municipal buildings, the libraries, the hospitals, the parks, and so forth. The subject of debate—Graham's investment property—constituted only one half of 1 percent of Allyn's real estate!

The friction disappeared almost immediately. Even the most ardent disputants admitted: "If that's all it amounts to—it's hardly enough to fuss about."

INTENSION AND EXTENSION

The Graham case involved a problem that was approached in two vitally different ways. For years people had been verbalizing, theorizing, speculating about Graham's exemption$_2$. They talked, they discussed, they disputed. The more they talked about the problem, the farther they seemed to move away from it. They became so absorbed in their personal maps of the territory that it became increasingly difficult for them to examine the territory itself. They were intensionally oriented—more concerned, that is, with the feelings, thoughts, suppositions, beliefs, theories, and so on, inside their skins than with the life facts outside.

Finally, the *Allyn Times* took a radically different tack. "Look," said the publisher, "all this talking about the problem has only succeeded in aggravating the situation. Let's quit talking for once and go out and do some looking—let's go out and see just what this exemption amounts to." The publisher's stop-talking and start-looking approach is characteristic of the extensional orientation.

We are oriented intensionally when we are predisposed to become absorbed with the map and to neglect the territory. This tendency is epitomized in this charming fable.

A Man Lived by the Side of the Road . . .
. . . and sold hot dogs.
He . . . had no radio.
He had trouble with his eyes, so he had no newspaper or TV.
But he sold good hot dogs.
He put up a sign on the highway, telling how good they were.
He stood by the side of the road and cried: "Buy a hot dog, mister." And people bought.
He increased his meat and bun orders, and he bought a bigger store to take care of his trade.
He got his son home from college to help him. But then something happened.
His son said: "Father, haven't you heard the news? There's a big depression on. The international situation is terrible, and the domestic situation is even worse."
Whereupon his father thought: "Well, my son has been to college. He listens to the radio and TV and reads the papers, so he ought to know."
So, the father cut down his bun order, took down his advertising sign, and no longer bothered to stand on the highway to sell hot dogs.
His hot dog sales fell almost overnight.
"You were right, son," the father said to the boy. "We are certainly in the middle of a great depression."[3]

Extensional orientation, on the other hand, is the predisposition to inspect the territory first—and then to create verbal maps to correspond with it. One of the greatest extensionalists in history was Galileo. Time and again he refused to be governed by the revered maps—the theories and postulates—of his time and went instead to observe the territory for himself. The Aristotelian law of falling bodies was one of these unquestioned maps. Postulated more than 19 centuries earlier, it held that the velocity of falling bodies was directly proportional to their weight—a notion consistent with the prevailing theory of gravitation. But Galileo had to see for himself and proceeded to the Leaning Tower of Pisa, where he exploded the law and started the world thinking about a new theory of gravity.

Philip Chapnick, in the September 1988 issue of *AI Expert* (a leading journal in the hi-tech field of artificial intelligence), wrote:

---

[3] From a Quaker State Metals Co. advertisement.

Alfred Korzybski, the eclectic Polish semanticist, coined the aphorism "the map is not the territory" over 50 years ago to remind us that the world is always richer in detail and different than any symbolic representation we can construct. Many implications can be drawn from this suggestive phrase. For instance, the features of territories portrayed by maps are necessarily refracted. We should use maps without confusing them with the real thing.

INTENSIONALITY: SOME MANIFESTATIONS

Basically, we behave intensionally when we respond to our maps (our feelings, imaginings, visualizations, formulations, attitudes, theories, preconceptions, evaluations, inferences) as if we were responding to the territory (objects, people, happenings, relationships, things, and so on). Trouble tends to come when the map is an inadequate representation of the territory. Take the case of a young soldier in the Vietnam conflict. Seriously wounded and unconscious, he desperately needed a transfusion, but blood of his unusual type was unavailable, and there was scant hope of acquiring some in time. Fortunately, a black soldier in his battalion heard about the boy's condition and volunteered for a transfusion. His blood type was suitable; the transfusion was made, and the soldier's life was saved. On the road to recovery several days later, the young man was told of the man who had given his blood. The boy became almost uncontrollable with fear and rage. He was overwhelmed by a lifelong delusion that having the black man's blood in his veins would change the color of his skin and even alter the shape and size of his lips and nose, the texture of his hair, and so forth.

Instead of reacting to the territory, a situation in which he was generously given lifesaving blood, the young soldier responded in terms of his fallacious map.

Consider another kind of map. What is your image of a prison? According to studies, most people, including most prisoners, visualize stone walls, iron bars, and armed guards. So imposing is this perception, conclude some authorities, that the vast majority of inmates never even try to break out. Therefore, reasoned prison officials in Northern Ireland, in these taut economic times, could we not reduce the cost of incarceration without reducing the effect? The walls and bars are already here so let's reduce the guards. Dummies were manning the observation posts when 38 men broke out of Maze Prison recently!

To a greater extent than most of us are aware, we are conditioned to react intensionally by our environment. Society's customs, traditions, norms, mores, and so on, are maps—sometimes spurious ones—which become so ingrained in us that we often treat them as territories.

I can still recall the hubbub that occurred a few years ago when a college professor married a woman who had attended one of his courses a year before. The professor, an exceptional scholar and teacher, was 40, and his lovely and intelligent bride was 32. The two were obviously well suited to each other, and their marriage has since proved eminently successful.

This was the territory, but some people paid more attention to their specious maps. One newspaper headlined the wedding story with a cradle-snatching implication: "Teacher Marries Pupil." Many readers, largely ignorant of the facts of the situation, raised their eyebrows and clucked their tongues, and some readers even wrote letters of protest to the college president. They had become so distraught at the imagined violation of a social taboo that they were hardly able or willing to examine the territory behind their fallacious maps.

Sometimes we behave intensionally because we want to. It is a relief, occasionally, to escape to our inner self-made worlds. There is value in daydreams, movies, television, novels, and so forth, when these serve as temporary safety valves. There is danger, however, when the world of make-believe becomes accepted as real. Children are perhaps the most susceptible. A mother caught her seven-year-old son pouring ground glass into the family stew. He wanted to find out whether it would really work, as it had with the characters in a television play he had seen. Another youngster accidentally hung himself while attempting to free himself from a trick knot from which a comic book hero had escaped. And still another boy caused a $100,000 warehouse fire by using a clever incendiary made of a burning cigarette inserted in a book of matches. He had learned the trick from a movie.

But some adults seem as prone to delude themselves—to react to faulty or fictional maps as if they were the actual territories. Milton Caniff, originator of the comic strip "Terry and the Pirates," tells of the time that one of the characters, Hot Shot Charlie, was sent to the United States for a period. Always a precisionist, Caniff depicted him as quartered at an actual apartment in Boston. One day the strip showed Hot Shot receiving a cable with the apartment's address clearly visible on the wire. The next panels showed him packing and leaving for overseas.

A day or so later Caniff received an urgent request from the apartment-house owner. "Please print a block in your comic strip," the owner pleaded, "and explain that there is no vacancy at _____ Street!" The poor man had been deluged with eager inquiries about Hot Shot's vacant apartment!

Another powerful and often unsuspected purveyor of specious maps is the popular song. Sometimes their approach is not to *solve* problems but to *escape* from them, usually via self-delusion.

Years ago we uncritically absorbed such lines as:

"I'd rather have a paper doll . . . than a real live girl."

"I'm gonna sit right down and write myself a letter and make believe
it came from you."

"Wrap your troubles in dreams and dream your troubles away."

I'm no connoisseur of contemporary lyrics but our kids and their
friends tell us that with today's music, problem-escape is still a frequent
theme. And, in the case of heavy metal rock, the advocacy of escape is
often with the aid of chemicals.

There is increasing concern that violence, so pervasive in movies and
television, has a most dangerous influence on children. Saturated with
media mayhem, some children seem to consider it with insouciance—as
normal. One young man freely admitted slaying an elderly woman. His
defense, albeit unsuccessful, was simply that he had watched too much
violence on TV!

But the most pathetic victims of the celluloid chimera are perhaps
some of the stars themselves. Living in the fanciful world created by press
agents and celebrity worshipers, their maps become tragically out of
phase with life facts. The too frequent results are emotional breakdowns,
broken marriages, and suicides.

Generally speaking, intensionality is most likely to lead to undesirable consequences (1) when one's map inadequately represents the territory and (2) when one is unaware of responding to a map rather than to
the territory.

Every medical student knows that the length of the small intestine is
22 feet or thereabouts, for the textbook said so. But Dr. Betty Underhill
has revealed this map to be a dangerous fallacy. In 100 autopsies, she
found that men's intestines ranged in length from 16 feet to 25 feet, 9
inches; women's, from 11 feet to 23 feet, 6 inches. Differences such as
these, she asserted, can be life-and-death matters in surgery.

Not a few women are incensed with a particular map known as
male chauvinism. They are understandably angered and exasperated
with the dependent roles to which they have been traditionally confined. They firmly denounce, for example, the rank inequity of receiving less pay for comparable work than their male counterparts. I do
not presume to explore the origin of this particular map. But I can
make an observation on just one way in which it has been reinforced
and perpetuated.

In Chicago, Chuck Schaden, an old-time radio buff, conducts a nightly
radio program. He plays transcriptions of Golden Oldies, soap operas and
serials: "Suspense," "Inner Sanctum," "The Shadow," "The Whistler,"
"The Green Hornet," "Gang Busters," "Jack Benny," "Fred Allen," "Bing
Crosby," "Amos and Andy," "Easy Aces," "Myrt and Marge," "Vic 'n'
Sade," "One Man's Family," "I Love A Mystery," and so forth.

Especially fascinating are the kid shows: "Jack Armstrong," "Captain Midnight," "Terry and the Pirates," "Dick Tracy," "Tom Mix," and so on. Almost invariably in these radio serials, the female role is a subservient one. While Jack Armstrong, Billy Fairfield, and Uncle Jim are fighting evil in far-off lands, Betty (Billy's sister) is generally tucked out of harm's way. Captain Midnight and his teenage sidekick, Chuck Ramsey, take considerable risks. But Patsy Donovan is consistently treated as a fragile incompetent—"You stay here, Patsy, it might be dangerous."

Admittedly, there was one exception—"Little Orphan Annie." But even she had to rely frequently on male stalwarts such as the Asp, Punjab, and the incredibly rich and powerful Daddy Warbucks.

Now visualize the 1930s and 1940s and the millions of little boys and girls transfixed by their families' radios night after night after night. The message—sometimes subtle, often blatant—was constant: Girls are inferior to boys.

And the kids soaked up that message without question, challenge, or reservation. That was one way myriad mental maps were formed and solidified.

A DEFECTIVE TOOL

Language, broadly speaking, is a map . . . and a map is a tool, of sorts. Now if a tool were damaged, you might repair or replace it. I obviously regard English as a defective tool—the last six chapters and the next two focus on specific deficiencies. So why not simply replace or repair the language? Unfortunately, changing a language is usually anything but simple. Let's examine a few aspects of the problem.

Replace the Language

In theory, a truly international language sounds like a good idea. It probably wouldn't cure all of the world's ills, but it would be a step in the right direction. Certainly there have been efforts to create such a language—over 100 in the last century and a half. And some of these artificial languages are considered superior to English as a communication instrument. Yet not one of them, including the relatively popular Esperanto, has really succeeded. Why?

People tend to be very touchy about their language . . . something they are beginning to learn long before they are aware they are learning anything. Perhaps they feel, consciously or otherwise, that language is a repository of their culture. In a sense, it is. But in any event, people generally resist language replacement with remarkable tenacity. Consider a few examples:

Note the animosity that exists between some English-speaking Canadians and some French-speaking Canadians. The former insist on an all-English-speaking Canada. The latter periodically threaten to secede.

A much older rift exists in Belgium between the Flemish (similar to Dutch)-speaking Flemings and the French-speaking Walloons.

The national language of the Republic of Ireland is English. Yet there are those who persist in the teaching and perpetuation of Gaelic, even though it is an archaic language elsewhere.

We still hear of riots and loss of life in certain provinces of India because of attempts to install a national language.

France is desperately trying to preserve the purity of French. A fast-food restaurant chain was recently fined $300 for advertising "hamburger" instead of "steak haché." Other Franglais words to avoid when you are in Paris: "Le drugstore," "le walkie-talkie," "le jumbo jet," "le hot stuff," and "le 5 o'clock shadow."

And lest we feel too smug, let us remind ourselves that a serious debate is rapidly heating up over the issue of bilingualism in the United States.

The irony is that in spite of all the rancor and even bloodshed, we will probably eventually have an international language anyway. Which one? English . . . with all its warts! And why? Simply because its speakers have spread it throughout the world by trade, colonization, conquest, and achievements in science and the arts.

Evidence? Half the world's scientific literature is published in English. It is the official language of international aviation. Major international meetings are conducted in English, or have provision for simultaneous translation into English of speeches in any other language.

English is the standard language in some countries in every continent. Schoolchildren in Germany, France, Japan, and many other nations learn English as their second tongue.

So we are moving inexorably toward English as a common language. But which English? What they speak in London or Edinburgh or Swansea or Sydney? The best bet is American English largely because of the globe-circling influence of, among other things, American movies and television.

Caution: If this discussion has led you to consider dropping the foreign language you're studying, don't. Given our vaunted resistance to change, neither American English nor any other tongue will become a universally used language in the 20th century, nor in the 21st, according to some authorities. So let's examine a less drastic approach for improving the tool.

Repair the Language

Repairing the language is obviously less extreme than replacing it. But we haven't fared too well in the mending department, either.

Here's a simple example: "Ain't" used to be an acceptable contraction of *am not*. Unfortunately, it began to be used by some in lieu of *isn't* or *aren't*. "He ain't going to the ball game," or "they ain't as clever as they think they are." Accordingly, the word fell into ill repute and is no longer used in *"polite"* society. So what do we say instead? *Aren't,* as in "I'm going to have to lose some weight, aren't I?" We prefer to overlook the fact that the contraction uncontracted is "are not I." So join my crusade for restoring *ain't* to its former and needed usage. But let's not hold our breaths until it's re-accepted.

A far more serious illustration of resistance to linguistic change concerns phonetic spelling, spelling a word the way it sounds. English orthography is ridiculously inconsistent. Why doesn't *tomb* rhyme with *comb*? Why does neither of them rhyme with *bomb*? Or why does *tomb* rhyme with *room, comb* with *home,* and *bomb* with *mom*? Why can *ough* be pronounced so differently as in *dough, through, ought, hiccough, trough, tough,* and *bough*?

How do you pronounce *whales*? Well, it could be the name of the great sea mammals. But this word could also be utterly silent, provided we take the *w* from *wreck*, the *h* from *honesty*, the *a* from *loafer*, one *l* from *will*, the *e* from *hypocrite*, and one *s* from *dress*.

If we converted to phonetic spelling, we would have to make some provision for a few homonyms *(bore* and *boar, bell* and *belle)* but think of the advantages. It has been estimated that elementary education could be reduced by two full years! What a savings in time and energy and dollars and drudgery! It would spare kids from the labor of having to learn our ludicrous spelling irregularities by rote. Perhaps then education, which is supposed to be exciting, would have a chance to be just that.

Has phonetic spelling been tried for English? Many times in many places with uniformly lackluster results. The *Chicago Tribune* tried going modestly phonetic many years ago. They started using *tho* for *though* and *thru* for *through* and *nite* for *night,* and a few others; and they lost subscribers! People feel very strongly about their language and don't care for change even if the objective is eminently sensible.

Here's another example of needed but resisted change. Our language is loaded with sexist words, references, and images.

Frequently this language ignores or even excludes women. *Manslaughter—* could killing a woman be a less serious matter? *Man overboard* might refer to a woman. *Workman's compensation—*obviously women don't qualify. Politicians concern themselves with the *man on the street* and the *common man—* never mind that women vote, too. *All men are created equal,* but not women?

We write *Dear Sir* to women. We carefully note a *woman* doctor or a *female* lawyer performed professional work lest others automatically think the professional was a man.[4]

A more subtle example is that we simply don't have a generic pronoun to refer to both sexes simultaneously. Traditionally, we say *he* and *him* and *his* when we refer to a male and female together. "When the human being is attacked, *he* tends to run or fight."

Some contend that when you use these pronouns in a general sense, everyone will interpret them as referring to males and females equally. But research doesn't support this.

Janet Hyde studied groups of first, third, and fifth graders and college students. Subjects were presented with a pronoun in a sentence and asked to create a story about it. When cued with *his*, only 12 percent of the stories were about females. When cued with *his* or *her*, 42 percent of the stories concerned females. Another finding: Elementary schoolchildren were far more likely to interpret the generic *his* as masculine than college students.

We often say or write *man* when we mean men and women—"Man does not live by bread alone," and "The nuclear bomb threatens the survival of mankind."

So how can we begin to balance the scales—to strive for a sexually inclusive language? Here are a few suggestions;[5] when referring to both women and men, we can:

1. Use gender-free words such as *police officer* instead of *policeman; fire fighter* instead of *fireman; mail carrier* instead of *mailman.*
2. Substitute *person* for *man* as in *salesperson, chairperson,* and *spokesperson.* Discretion is advised, though—*personhole* cover, *personagement,* and *penpersonship* are a little much.
3. Use plurals because they won't require singular pronouns later. For example, "people like to use *their* own discretion. . ." rather than "a person likes to use *his* own discretion. . . ."
4. (The grammarian in me cringes at this one.) Use the plural *they, them,* and *their* with singular antecedents. Examples: "everyone to rest themselves"; "it's enough to drive anyone out of their senses";

---

[4] *Cleaning up Sexist Language* (Chicago: 8th Day Center for Justice, 1980), p. 4. See also: Dale Spender, *Man Made Language* (London: Routledge and Kegan Paul, Ltd. 1980); "Sex-Role Stereotypes" in Robert Kreitner and Angelo Kinicki, *Organizational Behavior* (Homewood, Ill.: Richard D. Irwin, 1989), pp. 119–21; and "Sexism in Organizations," in Robert Lussier, *Human Relations in Organizations* (Homewood, Ill.: Irwin, 1989), pp. 437–42.

[5] See "Avoid Sexist Language" in Grethen N. Vik, Clyde W. Wilkinson, and Dorothy C. Wilkinson, *Writing and Speaking in Business*, 10th ed. (Homewood, Ill.: Richard D. Irwin, 1990), pp. 48–50.

"nobody likes a mind quicker than their own." So use that one if you must—many do—at least you'll be in good company. The statements are, respectively, from Shakespeare, Shaw, and F. Scott Fitzgerald.

5. Use doubles such as *he-she, he and/or she,* and *s/he.* Unfortunately, they still look and sound ungainly.

6. Resort to the use of *one*—but with restraint: "When one eats one eventually becomes sated; at which point one usually ceases to eat." (One more *one* and one might regurgitate.)

7. Create a unisex third person singular pronoun. This is the most sensible of the suggestions, but given the resistance against deliberate language change (which is the main point of this section), it is the least likely to be successful. *Se,* as a combination of *she* and *he,* has been suggested, but don't hang by your eyelashes until it comes into conventional usage.

So much for a few of the imperfections in our language. If we can't do much to replace or repair it, at least we can be aware of its flaws and misdirections and treat them accordingly. That is the purpose of this chapter. In fact, it is the basic thrust of the whole of Part Three, "Patterns of Miscommunication."

CORRECTIVES

As the problem of intensional orientation has been stated only generally, at this point we can offer only general advice for dealing with it. We shall reserve for the next two chapters the task of defining intensionality in more specific forms and of offering techniques for preventing or diminishing its consequences.

The basic advice is to get extensional. Develop the show-me or let-me-see attitude. Develop a healthy distrust of preconstructed maps. Go to the territory, look, observe, explore, probe, examine—*then* make your maps. This is the tenor of the homey advice World Court Justice John Bassett Moore once gave the late radio-television commentator Edward R. Murrow: "When you meet men of great reputation, your judgment of them will be greatly improved if you view them as though they were in their underwear."

Extensionality is the *sine qua non* of scientists. They make hypotheses (tentative maps), yes, but usually on the basis of previous observation of the territories, and then they check those maps against the territories again—and again—and again. If a map matches the territory, well and good; but if it does not, one alters the map or discards it and builds another, and another, until one has a map that adequately represents the territory. And be careful not to form the map too early. This is the caution that Arthur Conan Doyle (a scientific man, himself) has Sherlock Holmes express in *A Scandal in Bohemia*:

Dr. Watson: What do you imagine it means?
Holmes: I have no data yet. It is a capital mistake to theorize before one has data. Insensibly, one begins to twist facts to suit theories instead of theories to suit facts.

This is the scientific attitude, the territory-first-then-map approach; but surely there is great need for that approach beyond the confines of the laboratory.

SUMMARY

Intensional orientation is a general term for the tendency to be guided primarily, if not exclusively, by one's maps rather than by the territory. Trouble, confusion, and danger are most likely to occur (1) when the map inadequately represents the territory and (2) when the individual is unaware that he or she is dealing with a map rather than with the territory.

The basic technique for preventing or minimizing the injurious effects of intensional orientation, simply stated, is to develop an extensional orientation—a readiness to seek out the territory rather than a willingness to be mesmerized by one's often fallacious maps. Extensionality, in short, is the propensity to look first—then talk.

Discussion Questions

1. Intensional orientation can sometimes lead to harmful, unintelligent, even self-destructive behavior. However, are there not circumstances when such an orientation would be harmless—even desirable?

2. What are the conditions in which intensional orientation would be considered undesirable?

3. If people resist linguistic change, why does slang seem to change so rapidly?

4. What does this chapter have to do with communication?

5. Report on an incident, perhaps involving yourself, in which intensional orientation played a role. Why did the incident occur? What could have been done to prevent or correct the situation? What measures could prevent a recurrence of similar incidents?

C A S E S

CASE 15.1

The Continental Electric Company*

The following statement is by Howard Teal, manager of the Mandota plant of the Continental Electric Company, regarding a problem he had had with an assembly line. The line consisted of 35 people working on precision electrical parts.

Two years ago, during the summer, five workers at about the middle of the assembly line began to complain of severe itching and of welts on their arms and legs. The welts resembled mosquito bites, but the employees insisted these were not mosquito bites. They said that bugs were crawling from the assembly table and biting them. They sat at the assembly table with their backs to heavily screened windows. No mosquitoes could possibly have come in from the outside.

Well, we finally called in an exterminator, who spread all sorts of insecticides around the room. Things were fine for a few days, but then the workers began complaining again. The exterminator came back every three weeks, but that didn't seem to help. By the end of the summer, 11 people had registered complaints. The unrest subsided in the fall.

With the coming of hot weather last year, the complaints began once more. This time, 15 employees insisted they were being bitten. Finally, in July, they threatened to walk off the job. I immediately called in a dermatologist, who examined the employees. He told them that they were not being bitten and that the whole thing was in their imaginations.

The workers became angry, and the complaints became more pronounced. So back came the exterminators. After a few days, the complaints began anew.

The employees claimed they had seen little green bugs crawling around their work areas. There were a few insects, small enough to get in through the screen—the things one finds on trees during the summer. I know they don't bite, but I wasn't going to argue. Instead, I had the exterminators back a few more times until the fall season started.

Then, as before, the complaints ceased.

This year, the hot weather set in about May 15, and so did the unrest in the assembly room. Some 20 to 25 employees were now convinced that they were being bitten by insects around the assembly table. Even my supervisor began to itch.

I then visited Dr. Jay, an entomologist at the university. He suggested that I have the employees collect insects from the assembly room, put

---

* All names have been disguised. Printed by permission. The author's name has been withheld by request.

them in jars, and send them to him for analysis. Many employees in the assembly room collected insects with zeal. I might add that assembly line efficiency dropped somewhat. When the collection had been completed, I delivered our specimens to Dr. Jay. After a careful analysis, he concluded that none of the insects brought to him for analysis would bite human beings. But the complaints continued.

Dr. Jay decided to visit the plant. Upon arriving, he took off his shirt, rolled up his trousers, and sat at the assembly table for a long time. He was not bitten once. He then interviewed several complaining employees. He suggested that they might themselves be bringing in insects from the outside. The workers insisted that they were being bitten at work because the symptoms occurred only in the plant.

Dr. Jay then submitted a highly technical report with the scientific terms for each type of insect he had analyzed. The report suggested that these insects did not normally bite and listed various physiological causes of itching. He suggested that the welts could have been caused by intense scratching due to itching sensations brought about by perspiration or by psychological causes. I posted his report on the bulletin board for all the employees to read.

At Dr. Jay's suggestion, I painted two ordinary 150-watt bulbs purple and secured them to the floor at each end of the assembly line. The lights gave the appearance of ultraviolet ray. As far as the employees were concerned, that was exactly what they were. They were and are still unaware of what I did.

Throughout June, July, August, and September, after installation of the lights, we had only two minor complaints of employees being bitten while on the assembly line.

Discussion Questions

1. Why did the workers suffer from itching and welts?
2. What does this have to do with intensional orientation?
3. Why were the employees angered by the dermatologist's conclusions?
4. Why did the purple lights seem to work?
5. What do you think of the purple lights ploy?

CASE 15.2

The Water-American*

At my first admission into this printing-house I took to working at press, imagining I felt a want of the bodily exercise I had been us'd to in

---

* From *The Autobiography of Benjamin Franklin* (Lexington, Mass.: D.C. Heath, 1908). Reprinted by permission.

America, where presswork is mix'd with composing. I drank only water; the other workmen, near fifty in number, were great guzzlers of beer. On occasion, I carried up and down stairs a large form of types in each hand, when others carried but one in both hands. They wondered to see, from this and several instances, that the *Water-American,* as they called me, was *stronger* than themselves, who drank *strong* beer! We had an alehouse boy who attended always in the house to supply the workmen. My companion at the press drank every day a pint before breakfast, a pint at breakfast with his bread and cheese, a pint between breakfast and dinner, a pint at dinner, a pint in the afternoon about six o'clock, and another when he had done his day's work. I thought it a detestable custom; but it was necessary, he suppos'd, to drink *strong* beer, that he might be *strong* to labor. I endeavored to convince him that the bodily strength afforded by beer could only be in proportion to the grain or flour of the barley dissolved in the water of which it was made; that there was more flour in a pennyworth of bread, and therefore, if he would eat that with a pint of water, it would give him more strength than a quart of beer. He drank on, however, and had four or five shillings to pay out of his wages every Saturday night for that muddling liquor; an expense I was free from. And thus these poor devils keep themselves always under.

Discussion Questions

1. In what way do the workers display intensional orientation?
2. How would you classify Franklin's orientation?

CASE 15.3

"Get Off Route 25, Young Man"*
Charles F. Kettering

My home is in Dayton, Ohio, and I was a friend of the Wright family and learned to fly on the very early Wright airplanes. Their first flight was on the 17th of December, 46 years ago. Everyone was perfectly sure that it was a crazy thing to try. The undertakers moved into Kitty Hawk with a number of caskets because they thought the Wrights would kill themselves.

When they made those first three flights on December 17, 1903, they wired their sister that they had succeeded, that they were very happy, and that they should be home for Christmas.

She thought it was a world-shaking event, so she very excitedly called a Dayton newspaper on the telephone. She rang and rang and rang. The newspaper boys were playing pinochle, but finally one of them answered.

He said, "Yes?"

---

* *Collier's,* December 3, 1949, pp. 13–14. Reprinted by permission.

She said, "This is Katherine Wright speaking," and very excitedly read the telegram.

He said, "Good. Glad to hear the boys are going to get home for Christmas," and hung up the telephone.

The newspaperman said to the others: "Nobody's going to catch me on that, because it has been proved mathematically that a heavier-than-air machine can't fly."

* * * * *

I had a friend who was the research and development man for one of the British railroads. He came to this country to deliver a commencement address at a technical university. After the address he came to Detroit to see our laboratories.

"Ket," he said, "when you were over in London last year you told me some things you fellows were doing with Diesel locomotives and you lied to me."

I said, "Not intentionally."

"But," he said, "you told me you were running these locomotives about a hundred miles an hour."

I said, "We are."

"And that you were taking power on the front wheels; that is, the wheels that are ahead."

I said, "We are."

He said, "I have the formulas in my portfolio that say you can't do that."

I said, "For Heaven's sake, don't let the locomotive know about it."

I said to him, "I won't argue with you at all." I took the telephone, called Chicago and got him transportation from Chicago to Denver, and flew him to Chicago to make the connection. He made the trip to Denver, where I had him ride partway on the Diesel engines.

He stopped in to see me on his way back. He was returning to England. I said, "I didn't expect to see you again. Did you ride that locomotive?"

"Yes," he said.

"Did it go a hundred miles an hour?"

"It did."

"Well," I said, "that's the reason I didn't expect to see you back. Maybe you forgot to take the portfolio with the equations in it."

He said, "The thing that amazes me is why we could be so 100 percent wrong."

I said, "You weren't wrong. You didn't start in right."

The two of us got out his formulas. He wasn't talking about our locomotive at all. Our locomotive uses an ordinary truck like a streetcar's. He was talking about a locomotive with a rigid frame which would normally have a small-wheel lead truck in front of it.

I said, "What's the use of using mathematics on one kind of thing and then applying it to another which is in no way related? It isn't even a second cousin to it."

* * * * *

When we first put self-starters on automobiles, I attended a meeting of the American Institute of Electrical Engineers. They asked me if I would make a little talk on the self-starter, and I did.

One fellow got up and said, "No wonder you made your self-starter work; you profaned every law of electrical engineering."

I didn't profane any fundamental laws of electrical engineering. All I did was make the starter work. Those laws had nothing whatever to do with self-starters; they were written for something entirely different.

* * * * *

As I said before, my home is in Dayton, and we have had our laboratories for years in Detroit, which is several hundred miles away. I keep my home in Ohio and drive back and forth weekends.

Some of the people who work with me also drive between Dayton and Detroit. One said, "I understand you drive from here to Dayton in 4½ hours."

I said, "I can do that once in a while, depending on traffic."

He said, "I don't believe it."

I said, "But I do it."

He said, "I'm a much better driver than you are, and I can't do it."

I said, "I'm going down Friday. Why don't you ride along with me?"

So we rode into Dayton in about 4½ hours, or a little more, and he said, "Hell, no wonder you can do it. You didn't stay on Route 25!"

Now, Route 25 is the red line that is marked on all the maps between Detroit and Dayton. If you are a stranger, that's the road you should take. It never occurred to my colleague that you could take any other road on either side of Route 25. There's a lot of country on either side of it; in fact, half the earth is on each side of it.

Discussion Questions

1. What do the four incidents have in common?

2. How do the incidents differ?

3. What patterns of miscommunication seem to be involved here?

4. What preventive measures do you recommend for these patterns of miscommunication?

CASE 15.4

The Trials of Galileo

Galileo is perhaps most widely known and remembered for his astronomical studies. Early in life he became a convert to the Copernican ideas, ideas that conflicted with the medieval conception of the universe as established by Ptolemy. Ptolemy declared that the earth was an immovable sphere, fixed in the center of the universe, with the sun and the stars revolving about it. For many centuries the Ptolemaic system was almost undisputedly accepted. Not only did it seem to agree with the perception of the senses but it was also in harmony with the homocentric doctrine of theology, which recognized man as the principal object of divine concern. The entire universe was conceived as having been created to serve man's needs. Hence it was but natural to regard the earth, the abode of man, as the center of the universe. . . .[1]

It was not until he made a number of discoveries by means of the telescope that he boldly championed Copernicanism. Apprised that a contrivance had been invented in the Dutch Netherlands by which distant objects could be made to appear much nearer and larger, he set to work and soon constructed a telescope, becoming the first scientist to apply it to astronomical observation. With the new instrument Galileo made a number of important discoveries. He found that the moon, instead of being self-luminous, owed its light to reflection; also he proved its surface was deeply furrowed by valleys and mountains. The latter discovery shattered the Aristotelian idea that the moon was a perfect sphere, absolutely smooth. Especially noteworthy was Galileo's discovery of the four satellites of Jupiter, whose revolutions confirmed by analogy the Copernican explanation of the solar system. Galileo also perceived movable spots on the disc of the sun, inferring from them the sun's axial rotation and by analogy the rotation of the earth on its axis.

After making his discoveries with the telescope, Galileo could not restrain his enthusiasm for the Copernican system. So persistent were his activities in behalf of it and so unsparing was his ridicule of its opponents that the Church, which still adhered to the Ptolemaic theory, became alarmed. In 1615 he was ordered by the Inquisition to desist from further advocacy of the doctrine "that the earth moves around the sun and that the sun stands in the center of the world without moving from east to west." Galileo submitted, and for the next 16 years remained silent. Meanwhile, however, he was writing the great work of his life, which he published in 1632 under the title *Dialogue concerning the Two Chief*

---

[1] Robert Ergang, *Europe from the Renaissance to Waterloo* (Lexington, Mass.: D.C. Heath, 1954). Reprinted by permission.

Systems of the World. The main reason for his choice of a dialogue between three persons as the medium for his thought was probably a desire to avoid committing himself openly. The work presented overwhelming proof of the Copernican theory. When it was examined by the ecclesiastical authorities, Galileo was immediately summoned to appear before the Inquisition at Rome. Near 70 and broken in spirit, he was forced in the presence of the full Congregation to abjure on his knees the doctrines defined as contrary to the Holy Scriptures. The oath of recantation read in part, "I Galileo Galilei . . . swear that with honest heart and in good faith I curse and execrate the said heresies and errors as to the movement of the earth around the sun and all other heresies and ideas opposed to the Holy Church; and I swear that I will never assert or say anything either orally or in writing, that could put me under such suspicion." A story has it that after he recited the abjuration Galileo muttered under his breath, *"Eppur si muove* (But it [the earth] does move)." Though the legend is unsupported by historical evidence, it indicates the value of the renunciation, which was obtained under duress, and expresses the general belief as to what went on in Galileo's mind.

The last years of his life Galileo devoted to the study of dynamics, publishing in 1636 his famous *Dialogues on Motion,* a consolidation of his earlier work on the subject. This book not only laid the foundation for the study of mechanics but specifically served as the preliminary work for Newton's laws of motion. Soon after publishing it, Galileo became blind and also partially deaf. Yet he continued to work until his death on January 8, 1642, at the age of 78. Many historians of science regard Galileo as the founder of experimental science. His investigations of nature discredited dependence upon accepted authority, particularly upon Aristotle. Galileo's fight for the Copernican system did much to promote its acceptance and win supporters for it.[2]

Discussion Questions

1. Why did the Church find it necessary to silence Galileo?

2. Why do inventors sometimes have great difficulty in having their innovations accepted by others?

3. What is the relationship between intensional orientation and experimental science?

---

[2] Ibid. Reprinted by permission.

CASE 15.5

"They Don't Do It Our Way"*
Dr. Ina Telberg

* * * * *

One Man's Meal . . .

One of the most deeply rooted, and largely unconscious, features of any culture is what the psychologists call the *time perspective*. Within the United Nations, at least three different time perspectives operate.

"Gentlemen, it is time for lunch, we must adjourn," announces the Anglo-Saxon chairman, in the unabashed belief that having three meals a day at regular hours is the proper way for mankind to exist.

"But why? We haven't finished what we were doing," replies—in a puzzled manner that grows rapidly more impatient—an Eastern European Delegate, in whose country people eat when the inclination moves them and every family follows its own individual timetable.

"Why, indeed?" placidly inquires the Far Eastern representative, hailing from a country where life and time are conceived as a continuous stream, with no man being indispensable, with no life process needing to be interrupted for any human being, and where members of electoral bodies walk in and out of the room quietly, getting a bite to eat when necessary, talking to a friend when pleasant; but where meetings, theater performances, and other arranged affairs last without interruption for hours on end, while individuals come and go, are replaced by others, meditate or participate as the occasion requires, without undue strain, stress, or nervous tension.

As one or the other group persists in its own conception of the time perspective, as the Anglo-Saxons demand that the duration of meetings and conferences be fixed in advance and that meals be taken regularly at fixed hours, and as the Russians sit irritated and the Latins puzzled and the Secretariat frantic—as this condition continues, mutual friction grows, murmurs of "unreasonableness" are heard around the room; and, when the issue under discussion is an important one, overt accusations are hurled across the room of "insincerity," "lack of a serious approach to the problem," and even "sabotage."

Irony Or Poetry

Another frequent source of irritation, rooted deeply in the cultural differences among nations, is the *length and the style of oration*.

The Latins are usually accused of unnecessary length and of equally unnecessary flights of poetic fancy. The Russians are disliked both for the

---

* Reprinted by permission from *UNESCO Courier*, May 1950.

length of their speeches and the irony and sarcasm of the speeches' content. The utilization of irony in political speeches is a long-standing tradition of *public oratory in Russia*. It has nothing to do with the Soviet Government. . . . I was flown . . . from [Europe]. I was tired, sleepy, and a stranger to the United Nations. . . . Vishinsky was delivering his now famous veto speech in the Political Committee. . . . A regular interpreter failed, and I was rushed to the microphone in the middle of the speech. I remember how my voice trembled when I first began to speak. I knew that I was on the air, and that many of my friends in America and England were listening. In a few minutes, however, I lost every trace of self-consciousness as Mr. Vishinsky's Russian carried me away by its sheer beauty, force, and richness of expression. Latin quotations, Russian proverbs, even Shakespearean poetry, were utilized for the purposes of his attack on the British and the American positions.

Next day I was startled by the press reactions. I myself even received some fan mail: a couple of letters that denounced me as a Communist for having interpreted the speech with such fervor, and another one that praised me for same. I realized then how unnecessarily vitriolic, aggressive, and offensive the address was when translated: in fact, how ill-adapted was the Russian oratorical style to delivery in a foreign tongue. It was not the language itself, however, that was the obstacle. It was the tradition behind the language; what I have since learned to call *speech etiquette*.

Settling a Grave Issue

The Latins, on the other hand, far from employing sarcasm, prefer to sprinkle their speeches with a liberal amount of poetic imagery, metaphysical expressions, and literary allusions.

During the General Assembly meetings in Paris, a Latin-American delegate pleaded for the inclusion of the phrase "from the cradle to the grave" in the Article of the Declaration of Human Rights dealing with social security. He wanted to ensure that a worker, or rather, a citizen, should be covered by measures of social protection in just that manner: from the cradle to the grave. He meant precisely, literally, what he said.

"Such phrases have no place in a serious document," pronounced a Western European Delegate.

"But the Declaration should be beautifully worded," argued another Latin Delegate.

"It's a legal document—not a poem," muttered a Benelux member.

A member of the United States Delegation whispered darkly into a neighbor's ear:

"Why not 'from womb to tomb'? At least it rhymes!"

Before the final text of the Article was settled upon, several other poetical versions were suggested. Some others, quite unprintable, shortly made the rounds of the corridors outside the conference rooms. . . .

The Origin Of Life

Life itself is prized differently in different cultures. To die of peaceful old age is the ideal life pattern in some parts of the world. Death for a country or an ideal is the desirable social behavior in others. Nowhere have these differences been made so manifest as in the drafting of the Declaration of Human Rights.

"Man is of divine origin, endowed by nature with reason and conscience," argued several Latin-American delegates.

"All life is of divine origin, not only human life," a representative of a Buddhist state murmured gently. *"Is it not vanity to attribute divine origin to human life alone?"*

"Man is not divine. He is rooted in the very land he tills, in the soil that bred him," stated an Eastern European Delegate from a proponderantly agricultural area. The Soviets suggested tactfully that science had reservations on the whole subject. The Anglo-Saxon bloc, evidently not quite definite on the subject of human divinity, kept still.

Confusion over China

Humor relief is not infrequently provided by the very cultural differences that are usually so productive of misunderstandings.

On one occasion, a misunderstanding was particularly startling:

"Gentlemen, gentlemen, let us not act in this matter like an elephant in a china shop!"

As this remark was being rendered from the Russian into English, a language in which the Chinese Delegate was following proceedings, he promptly raised his hand.

"Mr. Chairman, I should like the Soviet Delegate to explain just what China has to do with his objections."

"Mr. Chairman, I said nothing whatever about China. The Chinese Delegate must have misunderstood."

"Mr. Chairman, I distinctly heard my country mentioned. I request an explanation." . . .

Discussion Questions

1. In terms of the *intensional orientation* concept, what do Dr. Telberg's illustrations have in common?

2. In addition to language differences, what else contributes to miscommunication within the UN?

3. The United Nations has been criticized from some quarters as an ineffectual body for solving the world's problems. How do you feel about the objectives and accomplishments of the UN?

4. Compare "Cultural Pitfalls" with "They Don't Do It Our Way."

CASE 15.6

The Flag, the Anthem, and the Four-Letter Word

The Flag

Note: The U.S. flag has been in the news again. In the spring of 1989, student Scott Tyler of the School of the Art Institute of Chicago spread an American flag on the Institute's floor in front of a registry book and solicited comments. He titled his exhibit: "What Is the Proper Way to Display a U.S. Flag?"

Veterans' groups turned out in force to protest. The U.S. Senate, the Chicago City Council, and both houses of the Illinois General Assembly passed measures barring "such flag abuse."

Supporters of the artist, calling themselves the "No Mandatory Patriotism Committee," reported that Tyler had received death threats and other warnings from anonymous critics.

All this recalled a protest at the 1984 Republican Convention in Dallas. Gregory L. "Joey" Johnson, a member of the Revolutionary Communnist Youth Brigade, was convicted of burning a flag.

In June 1989, in a 5-to-4 vote, the U.S. Supreme Court overturned Johnson's conviction. Chief Justice William Rehnquist, President George Bush, and Senator Robert Dole, among others, sharply contested the Court's ruling, which struck down laws that prohibited flag desecration as a form of peaceful political protest.

Controversies involving flag treatment have flared throughout our history. The following is a relatively unemotional event of a few years ago.

Eugene B. Colin, 46, a Skokie, Illinois, advertising executive, was teaching a semantics course at a local high school. He held a small U.S. flag for about 30 minutes while he explained to his students that the real value of the flag was in terms of what it meant to them. Otherwise, it was just a cloth made up of stripes and stars of various colors.

Then he put the flag on the floor in front of him. That, he admitted, was a bad move. "If anything, it certainly was a case of poor judgment," he said later. "I don't think I'm second to anyone in my reverence for everything this country stands for. I just wanted to illustrate that the value of a thing is what we impute to it."

Somehow word reached the Skokie police, who obtained a warrant and arrested him. Colin, who lives in Skokie and receives no pay for his teaching, stated that he didn't know he had done anything wrong.

According to school officials, most of Colin's 15 students (all adults) wanted him to continue teaching.

The Anthem[1]

On a Saturday evening in December 1941, shortly after Pearl Harbor, I had a dinner date with another graduate student. We went to a restaurant that had a small dance floor at the end of the room farthest from the

---

[1] By Alma Johnson Sarett. Reprinted by permission.

entrance and that employed a small orchestra on weekends. We sat at the table next to the dance floor.

During an intermission three young men in Navy uniforms, who occupied a table near us and who had each downed several drinks from the bar since our arrival, went out on the dance floor and began an impromptu floor show. Their horseplay included several apparently unintentional sprawls on the floor, and the "emcee's" speech came out as "Laszh'n'szhen'lemen" etc. Suddenly one of them seized a trumpet from the deserted orchestra stall and began playing a wavering but recognizable version of "The Star-Spangled Banner." With his two companions following, he began a stumbling parade up and down the dance floor. By the time the trumpeter had reached the second or third bar of the anthem, everybody in the restaurant had risen to his feet—except my escort. When I realized that he had remained seated, I sank back down into my own chair. One of the men in uniform stopped, looked at us, and called "Shtan' up! Shtan' up!" but we remained silent and seated. After they had returned to their table, my escort said, "I will not take part in dishonoring a symbol of my country." Shortly afterward, we rose to leave. As we made our way the length of the room to the door, it seemed to me that all talk ceased and that the eyes that followed us were filled with hostility and suspicion.

The Four-Letter Word[2]

In a suburban courtroom just north of Detroit last week, a high school teacher named Nancy Timbrook clutched a shredded Kleenex as she defended her actions before a judge. She admitted that she had, as charged, written a four-letter variant of the word *to copulate* on her classroom blackboard.

> **Prosecutor:** Didn't you know that it was an unfit word to use in front of children?
>
> **Mrs. Timbrook:** That's what I was trying to teach—that it was indecent and immoral. It's always made me sick every time I've seen it. I've seen it every day in the [school] john. I wanted to stop it.
>
> **Prosecutor:** Did you know that writing that word was a crime?
>
> **Mrs. Timbrook:** I didn't know I was doing anything that would send me to jail.
>
> **Judge:** Ignorance is no excuse.
>
> **Mrs. Timbrook:** Perhaps I should have studied law instead of literature.

While the four-letter word under discussion has become commonplace in the works of many modern novelists, its use is far from accepted

---

[2] "English Lesson," *Time*, March 28, 1969, pp. 69 and 72. Reprinted by permission.

in high school English classes. Any teacher who makes it the theme of a classroom exercise can expect a strong reaction—if not from the students themselves, at least from their parents. Which is what happened to Mrs. Timbrook, 36, a truck driver's wife and the mother of nine children, who teaches at Lamphere High School in Madison Heights, Michigan.

Led by God. The incident took place last month after Patrick Eady, 32, a social studies teacher at Lamphere, invited two college-age youths who are members of a local left-wing group called the White Panthers to address his students. Their talk was freely sprinkled with the provocative verb (or noun, or adjective, depending on how it is used). News of the highly unusual lesson spread quickly through the school. Annoyed by the students' snickering, Mrs. Timbrook decided to discuss the word in class the very next day. She printed the word on the blackboard for each of her four English classes and asked each what it meant. "I was led to do that by God," Mrs. Timbrook, a deeply religious woman, later recalled. "I didn't know what I was going to do until I walked into the classroom."

For the most part, the students merely giggled and answered that the word meant sexual intercourse. But many of the 42,000 residents of the town questioned Mrs. Timbrook's divine inspiration. She insisted that her lecture's purpose was to prove that the word was "devoid of life and love." Nevertheless, parents besieged the superintendent of schools with irate phone calls and, at hastily convened meetings, vilified Mrs. Timbrook as a "whore" and a "disgrace to womankind."

Eady was fired from his job. When Mrs. Timbrook was given non-teaching duties in the superintendent's office, other teachers boycotted the school for a full day. Then one father, Police Lieutenant William Sloan, brought criminal charges against Mrs. Timbrook and Eady. Both were arrested on a state charge—"depraving the morals of children." Mrs. Timbrook was also charged with violating a local ordinance that forbids the writing of "indecent and immoral language."

In court, Judge Edward Lawrence conceded that her motive had been a moral one. But he was not inclined to minimize her offense. "People may commit murder in the heat of passion," he said, "but that doesn't excuse murder. People may write obscenity for various reasons, but that doesn't excuse obscenity." While the state charge against her was dropped, Mrs. Timbrook pleaded guilty to violating a local ordinance. She faces penalties of up to 90 days in prison and a $500 fine at her sentencing next month. Eady, who comes to trial next month, is not likely to get much more sympathy.

Discussion Questions

1. What do these incidents have in common?
2. What do these incidents have to do with *intensional orientation?*

3. How do you analyze the incident of the flag?

4. How do you analyze the incident of the anthem?

5. How do you analyze the incident of the four-letter word?

CASE 15.7

Reification Can Kill Us*
Sydney J. Harris

You may never have heard of the word *reification,* or know what it means. But it may kill you, and me, and millions more around the globe, as it has many times in the past.

To *reify* means to treat an abstraction as though it were real and personal and existent. *Russia* is such an abstraction. *America* is another. If we go to war, these two reified abstractions will be seen as fighting one another.

Of course, no such things exist. Russia is made up of millions of individuals, and so is America. The people in Russia have nothing against the people in America, and the same is true the other way around.

If you were to walk the streets of Russia—as more than 100 Americans recently did on a Fellowship of Reconciliation tour—you would find not only no personal animosity among the ordinary citizens, but also a passionate craving for peace and a dread fear of atomic warfare.

They, just like us, want a tranquil and secure future for their children; like us also, the average citizen has little to say about his government's stance in world affairs; and, of course, they are even worse off than us, for they cannot vote out of office a regime they dislike or oppose.

The true tragedy of the current confrontation between our two countries is that it has so little to do with the ordinary citizen, and so much to do with power politics at the highest level. But it is not the generals and politicians who will be slaughtered if we go to war; it will be the rest of us, like it or not, want it or not.

The danger in reification is that it forces us to think—and to feel—in terms of these abstractions rather than in terms of flesh-and-blood human beings; that it depersonalizes the conflict and transforms it into a battle of slogans and flags and symbols that have only a tenuous relationship to the reality beneath them—the suffering, the dying, the desolation beyond belief that nuclear war will leave in its wake.

This is not to equate the Soviet system with ours; for ours, with all its imperfections, is vastly more desirable than theirs. But it is not *systems* that are going to kill and be killed, it is people—and people far more like

---

* Formerly, "The Process of *Reification* Makes Doom a Reality," *Chicago Sun-Times,* December 20, 1982, p. 35. From *Strictly PERSONAL* by Sydney J. Harris (c) by and permission of News America Syndicate.

us than unlike us, as we would see if we had the opportunity to get to know them better.

A *country,* like a *government,* is an abstraction. There is no such thing, except on paper, or in the mind.

It is governments that start wars, or renew them, for reasons that may not have anything to do with the basic welfare of their own populace. Now it has reached the point where *no* nuclear conflict can protect or advance the welfare of any civilian population. Everything has changed except the minds of those who lead us, in nearly every part of the world.

Confucius told us long ago that all reform must begin with the reform of language. And the first thing that must go is the *reification* of words like *Russian* and *American* when we mean men and women and children of God.

Discussion Questions
1. What do you think of the title of this case?
2. Do governments start wars?
3. What do you think of the Confucian advice?
4. What does this case have to do with intensional orientation?

CHAPTER SIXTEEN

Intensional Orientation
2. "Pointing" and "Associating"
Ignoring Emotionality in Language

❋
❋
❋

A department store manager received a shipment of high-quality handkerchiefs and, in an adventuresome mood, placed half of them in a pile at one end of a sales counter with a sign: "Fine Irish Linen—$1.00 Each." He stacked the other half at the opposite end of the counter with a sign: "Nose Rags—3 for 50¢." The Irish linens outsold the nose rags five to one!

A delicatessen operator performed the same sort of experiement with some first-rate cheese. She cut two large wedges from the same wheel and placed them in her showcase. She labeled one wedge, "Imported English Cheddar," and the other, "Smelly Cheese." The former, at twice the price, far outsold the latter.

And Haldeman-Julius, publishers of the little five-cent Blue Books, discovered years ago that changing titles could have an effect on sales:

Title	Number of Copies Sold*
Markheim	100
Markheim's Murder	7,000
The Mystery of the Iron Mask	100
The Mystery of the Man in the Iron Mask	11,000
The Art of Controversy	100
How to Argue Logically	30,000
Fleece of Gold	600
Quest for a Blond Mistress	50,000

*During equal periods of time.

It is obvious that the way we react to the *words* by which things are called can affect very considerably the way we react to the *things* themselves. You will recall from Chapter 8 that the students in Dr. Lee's classes responded quite differently to the foods they were eating after they were told that the foods were dog biscuits and grasshopper cookies.

One way of understanding how our response to words can affect our evaluations of things is to recognize the versatility of language use. Among other uses, we employ and react to words as *pointers* which call attention to something. We also use and react to words as *evokers* of associations.

Suppose that you and I are riding through the country and I see a small pool of water and say, "Look at that swimming hole over there." My words may serve the purpose of a pointing finger and call your attention to a pool that you might otherwise have missed.

But if you happen to associate certain memories, experiences, and feelings, pleasant or otherwise, with the term *swimming hole,* then it is entirely possible that my words would stir you up a bit. Moreover, they might suggest to you a great deal beyond the physical pool to which I was referring.

For convenience, we will use the terms *pointing* and *associating,* respectively, to represent these two functions of language. However, we must guard against the view that words are used *either* as pointers *or* as associators. They are ordinarily used and reacted to as both. The situation is a case of double contraries.

Take the term *sulfuric acid.* (See Figure 16.1) For A, who has never studied chemistry and is not especially familiar with the term in any other context, the words may have little pointer or associator value; for B, whose hand was once badly burned when someone threw sulfuric acid at him, the words might usually have great associator value but perhaps comparatively little pointer value; C, a chemist, may ordinarily use and react to the term with largely pointer value and practically no associator value; and so forth.

Theoretically, depending upon the individual, the time, the place, the verbal context, and other circumstances, one may use or react to a given word or phrase with values anywhere along the infinitely graded double continua.

Even though our terms *pointers* and *associators* imply a fallacious polarization, they provide a useful distinction for describing and coping with serious patterns of miscommunication. I shall henceforth use the words in quotes to underscore the multivalued and interrelated sense in which I am intending them. Let the quotation marks remind us also that people (not words) do the "pointing" and "associating" with words.[1]

---

[1] The reader has probably assumed that I am deliberately refraining from using the words *denotations* and *connotations*. These terms have come to suggest so strongly a polarized view of language use that it seemed advisable to avoid them.

FIGURE 16.1

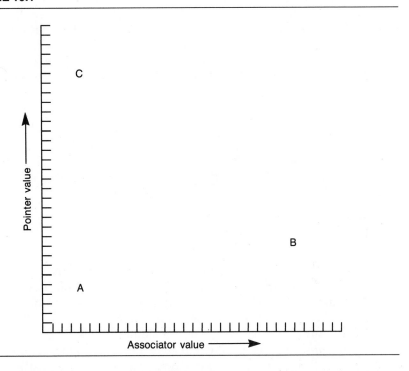

It is clear that when people send and receive them, words may have many functions; "pointing" and "associating" are prominent among them. The crux of this chapter, then, is that confusion, misunderstanding, and other kinds of trouble may readily occur when communicators forget or are unaware that both "pointing" and "associating" are usually involved in communication.

The failure to recognize the "pointing-associating" duality of language may lead to several patterns of miscommunication. Three prevalent and troublesome forms are the "pointing-associating" confusion, name-calling, and "associative" bypassing.

THE "POINTING-ASSOCIATING" CONFUSION

We delude ourselves with words when we confuse the "associating" and "pointing" functions. We often react to the associations evoked in us by the label as if we were reacting to what the label was "pointing" to—the object itself. Most Americans shudder at the prospect of eating rattlesnake meat or French fried grasshoppers. Is it because they dislike the taste? Hardly, for most of them have never eaten these foods, which, incidentally, are regarded as delicacies in some parts of the world. It is obvious that they are reacting not to the foods themselves but to their names and to the associations that they have for the names. Consider whether you would not be somewhat more favorably disposed toward a sirloin steak than toward a slice of dead cow, even though both labels can be used to point to the same piece of meat.

Juliet understood the "pointing-associating" confusion when she pleaded with Romeo in one of literature's most quoted expressions:

> *'Tis but thy name that is my enemy. . . .*
> *What's in a name? that which we call a rose*
> *By any other name would smell as sweet.*
>   *—Romeo and Juliet, Act 2, Scene 2*

Euphemisms and Dysphemisms

To euphemize is to substitute an inoffensive, mild, or pleasant "associator" for one that may produce an opposite reaction. To euphemize is to put, literally, a "good face" on something. Calling a liquor store a "package store" or "party store" does not change the store, its contents, or its function, but it may soften the impression for many. I have coined the word *dysphemism* as the antonym of *euphemism*. It puts a "bad face" on the thing. Calling the same establishment a "booze store" still doesn't change the store, but it may change the way some people feel about it.

There are many occasions on which euphemisms or dysphemisms, used judiciously, may serve good purposes—or at least expedient ones. When consoling a friend who has just lost someone near, you would almost certainly use "passed away" rather than "croaked" or "kicked the bucket." And surely it is kinder to refer to a thin person as "on the slender side" than as "skinny" or "spindly." More appealing titles for people's jobs may also have their value:

Yesterday	Today	Tomorrow
Handyman	Repairman	Customer engineer
Typewriter	Stenographer	Visual transcriptionist
Bookkeeper	Comptroller	Tax avoidance researcher
Garbageman	Sanitary engineer	Excess materials manager
Telephone girl	Switchboard operator	Audio connection supervisor
Head clerk	Office manager	Coffee break coordinator

On the other hand, a person running for election might not be reluctant to use dysphemisms in describing a liberal intellectual opponent as "that stubborn, radical egghead." Your children and mine may be equally energetic, but if I don't happen to like you, I may prefer to describe yours as "wild" and my own as "active." Your wife may be a "gabby gossip," but mine is an "enthusiastic conversationalist." And while my home may have that "lived-in look," yours is just "shabby."

Paradise Island, in the Bahamas, which relies heavily on the tourist trade, underwent a needed name change. One wonders how many vacationers would book an idyllic two weeks on Hog Island—its former name.

Sensitive to public criticism, the U.S. Congress no longer takes "recesses." These are now called *district work periods* by the House and *nonlegislative periods* by the Senate.

Nor is the executive branch insensitive to "how it will play in Peoria." "Reagan changed the name of the MX dense pack to 'the Peace-keeper,' " cracked Johnny Carson, "because he figured 'the World-ender' wouldn't go over so well." Rear Admiral Eugene J. Carroll (ret.) added: "Calling the MX a peacekeeper is like calling the guillotine a headache remedy."

Our present administration has clearly mastered the ploy. If an individual is paying more to Uncle Sam these days it is not because of a "tax increase"—rather it is due to a new policy of "revenue enhancement."

Such verbal gymnastics are officially recognized by the Committee on Doublespeak (National Council of Teachers of English).[2] The annual Doublespeak Award goes to those who have used the most misleading, self-contradictory, or evasive language. Here are a few of the recent "winners":

Term	Translation
Strategic misrepresentation	Lie
Inventory shrinkage	Employee theft
Negative patient care outcome	Death
Learning resources center	Library
Impact attenuation device	Sand-filled oil drum
Poorly buffered precipitation	Acid rain
Therapeutic misadventure	Malpractice
Combat emplacement evacuator	Shovel
Incontinent ordinance	Bombs that fall on schools
Tactical redeployment	Retreat
Ballistically induced aperture in subcutaneous environment	Bullet hole
Portable, hand-held communications inscriber	Pencil

Our State Department earned a special Doublespeak Award when it announced that it would no longer use "killing" in official reports on the status of human rights in countries around the world. Hereafter, it would be the "unlawful or arbitrary deprivation of life."

---

[2] William Lutz, chairman of the committee, regards such obfuscations as "corruptions of what language is supposed to do—communicate." See his delightful book, *Doublespeak* (New York: Harper & Row, 1989).

The current upheaval in the Middle East is replete with doublespeak. Saddam Hussein, whose Iraqi troops invaded Kuwait, explained that he was only responding to an "invitation" from "revolutionary elements" in Kuwait. As for the foreigners in Iraq who were forced to serve as shields against air attacks—they were termed (after Hussein tired of calling them "guests") "detainees" or "restrictees" but never "captives" or "hostages."

In fairness, the interruption of Iraqi shipping in the Persian Gulf may have looked like a "blockade." But it wasn't, said President Bush. It was not even a "quarantine" but merely an "interdiction."

One of the most acute dangers of euphemisms-dysphemisms and, in general, of reacting to "associators" as if they were "pointers" is that we tend to lose sight of the things being represented. We become so mesmerized by the *name* that the *thing* becomes obscured. On some campuses the name of one's sorority or fraternity looms very large in extracurricular matters. Fraternity men have told me that the dating of sorority women of other than the "better" houses is frowned upon by their brothers. Ironically, the "Eta Byta Pi" label on a young woman sometimes seems a more important criterion for date selection than the unique characteristics and qualities of the woman herself. But is this behavior less rational than voting a straight party ballot without any apparent concern for the qualifications of the individual candidates? Speaking of politics, have you heard of the Democratic nomination for treasurer in a Michigan county a few years ago? The Democrats discovered that they had nominated a T. Edward Aho, 52, an inmate of a state mental hospital! Aho, an unemployed worker, was not prominent, but his Finnish name had vote appeal in the Finnish-dominated county. Similarly, a certain city ward, predominantly Scandinavian, voted a Mr. Jensen into a minor office. It was only after the election that most of the voters realized that Mr. Jensen was a black man.

One-time Vice President Fritz Mondale was embarrassed a couple of years ago when an excerpt of his book, *The Accountability of Power,* appeared in *Genesis,* "a magazine for sophisticated men." The issue in which Mondale's byline appeared also featured such articles as "Erotic Diary of a Nympho Cheerleader." How had it happened? Mondale's publisher gave the reprint permission because "judging from its plain little letterhead and its title, the magazine sounded kind of religious."

Mr. Mondale, of course, suffered a much greater blow—a decisive loss in his bid for the presidency. Many of his supporters may have deserted him ... but his sense of humor didn't. His post-election appraisal: "I wanted to run for the presidency in the worst possible way—and I did!" Michael Dukakis probably felt the same way.

There are many who readily capitalize upon our tendency to react to "associators" as if they were "pointers." Some of the most skillful of these people write advertising copy. With deft pens poised, these word-magicians sift through hundreds of words to find the term or phrase that is most likely to elicit quickly the desired response to their products. They overlook few possibilities for word appeal. In the automobile industry, for example, even the car's colors are verbally glamorized. It is no longer possible to buy a black or a red or a green or a blue auto. But you can get one in Morning Mist, Carnival Red, Fern Mist Green, Ginger Glow, Calypso Coral, or Burgundy Fire. My personal prize goes to the inventor of the name for a certain yellow color that one manufacturer used a few years ago. To me the color was a bilious gray-yellow, reminiscent of dusty mustard. Its name—the stroke of a master—was Sunglo!

Classified advertisers are generally not as adept as their distant cousins in the agencies, but they too contrive studiously to find the "right word." The favorite terms for describing a house for sale, according to a survey of 8,000 ads in eight major U.S. daily newspapers, were "cute," "a cutie," "adorable," "exquisite," "elegant," "a dandy," "magnificent," "glamorous," "spic and span," "clean as a pin," "a rare find," and a "real bargain." A farm was seldom a "farm" but a "rural hideaway," a "rustic retreat," or a "secluded estate." There were few "jobs" in the Help Wanted columns, but "openings" and "positions" were plentiful. Dogs for sale were advertised variously as "love that money can't buy," "darlings," "cuddlies," and "swell pets." Possibly the most refined touch of all was the term for a bitch with a litter of pups—she was listed as a "matron."

Even the farmer who was busily building an unusual structure on his east forty had a flair for "associators." "What's it going to be?" asked a neighbor. "It all depends," was the reply. "If I rent it, it's a pastoral lodge— if I don't, it's a cowshed." And if you happen to write restaurant menus, you had better watch your "associators," for they determine to some extent how much you can charge for the food.

Hamburger	$1.75
Salisbury Steak	$4.00
Chopped Tenderloin Steak	$7.50
Charcoal-broiled Chopped Tenderloin Steak	$9.00
Prime tenderloin Steak, Charcoal Grilled (chopped)	$11.50
Du Boeuf Haché Grillé au Charbon de Bois	$18.50

And make certain your dining establishment has *ambience*—if it's only *atmosphere*, you'll have to reduce your menu prices.

Parents have naming responsibilities, too. They name their children. So if that obligation is in the near future for you, you may want to consider a study conducted by Deborah Linville. She asked seniors and graduate students at the Rensselaer Polytechnic Institute to rate 250 female names in terms of sexiness.

According to her group, among the sexiest names were Alicia, Adrienne, Candace, Cheryl, Christine (highest rated), Dawn, Gail, Heather, Holly, Jacqueline, Jennifer, Julia, Kathy, Maria, Marilyn,

Melanie, Michelle, Renae, Susan, Tamara, and Tina. Among the lowest rated: Alma, Cornelia, Doris, Edna, Elvira, Ethel (lowest), Esther, Florence, Magdalene, Myrtle, Rosalind, Silvana, and Zelda.

But there's more. Linville mixed a few of the top-rated names with a few of the lowest rated. Then she asked a second group of students to rate the names as job applicants. The nonsexy names were chosen by male raters (far more than by female raters) for employment and promotion over the sexy counterparts.

All of which seems to leave parents in a fix. They may opt for a name in the middle of the list hoping to find a reasonably attractive one which at the same time would not be a burden in their daughter's climb to the firm's (or nation's) presidency. In the middle list: Anne, Audrey, Barbara, Betsy, Betty, Carolyn, Catherine, Charlotte, Elaine, Ellen, Faith, Hope, Jean, Jill, Joanne, Joyce, Laura, Linda, Marcia, Marian, Mary, Patricia, Priscilla, Ruth, Shirley, Viriginia, Wendy, and Yolanda.

Humorist Art Buchwald, on reviewing the Linville study, suggested that it might be invaluable evidence in a job discrimination suit. "If an Ethel gets promoted over a Christine, although Christine has been in the organization far longer, Christine has got one heck of a case."

Lest it appear that euphemizing and dysphemizing are merely playing with words, I submit that a key issue in a continuing controversy is whether an abortion should be regarded as "killing a human being" or "terminating a pregnancy."

NAME-CALLING

There is a species of the "pointing-associating" confusion that merits special attention. It concerns the "associating" labels that people apply to one another and to themselves. The names we call others or by which we are called can profoundly influence our evaluations and behavior.

The Double Burden

The child's retaliation, "Sticks and stones may break my bones, but names can never hurt me," is unfortunately only half correct. Names can hurt us, even more grievously, on occasion, than sticks and stones.

Consider the youngster who survived polio with a withered leg. The physical pain of walking and the psychic pain of watching other children run may be as nothing compared with the burden of a thoughtlessly imposed nickname such as Limpy or Gimpy. Or consider the youngster scarred by acne. A disfigured face is a sufficient trial, but a label such as Scarface may well double the burden.

Adults are not exempt from carrying a double burden. A psychologist who serves as an employee counselor with a manufacturing firm recently described the case of a young, intelligent, and attractive woman who came to him for help. Until recently she had been considered by her supervisor to be a superior employee, but during the last few months she had grown nervous and irritable. Her work began to deteriorate, and her supervisor finally recommended that she speak with the counselor. He learned that the young woman had been divorced three years previously but seemed to have made a satisfactory adjustment. In recent months, however, her social life was more than she could bear. Breaking down, she sobbed: "I've dated four men in the last year, and in each case things were going fine until my boyfriend found out I had been married. Two of them dropped me like a hot potato, and the other two began taking such liberties that I had to drop them. Why don't men give divorcées a chance to start over? Look, I'm decent and I intend to stay that way, but they make it pretty rough."

Living Up to the Labels

This young woman was resisting her label, but this is not always the case. People, often unconsciously, tend to live up to their labels. I shall never forget an experience in a group dynamics course in college. There were about 20 in the class, and we met twice weekly in two-hour discussion sessions. Our basic purpose was to study group dynamics by observing the dynamics of our own group. Along about the sixth week, one member of the group made a statement to this effect: "It has occurred to me that certain people in this group tend to play certain roles. I have noticed that whenever someone is being picked on, Kathy will step in to defend him—she's sort of a protector of the underdog. And when we begin to argue and the tension begins to build, have you noticed that it's often Bill who tries to relax us with a comical remark? And Don usually backs anyone who wants a change—he's 'Mr. Progressive'!" He continued to categorize three or four other members. The group responded with some chaffing of the "underdog protector," "the jokester," and so on, and the subject was forgotten—apparently. But as the weeks went on, it became obvious that some of those labeled were portraying their "roles" in and out of season! Kathy was defending underdogs more vehemently than ever; Bill was joking more than ever—even when there were no tensions to be broken; and so forth. In fact, their role-playing became so restrictive that this was the only kind of behavior they were able or willing to portray.

Unhappily, living up to one's labels can have far graver consequences. Consider this statement from a social worker's file:

> I got a reputation as the town's bad girl. Sure, I did some of the things they said I did. But not until I had been blamed for a lot of things not my fault. After that I didn't care.

The double burden has become so oppressive for adolescents in trouble that authorities have been moved to speak out against such incriminating labels as "juvenile delinquent." Joseph Lohman, a sociologist and for four years sheriff of Cook County, Illinois, has said: "The name juvenile delinquent . . . sets the young person apart and may motivate further misbehavior." Mrs. Newton P. Leonard, president of the National Congress of Parents and Teachers (PTA) a few years ago, exhorted her nearly 9 million members to discard the label. "Juvenile delinquents, so-called, are children in trouble, children in conflict—with the law, with society, with themselves," she said. "The last thing they need is to be branded with a dehumanizing label and a matching set of attitudes from members of the community."

Living Down the Labels

Living up to one's labels may result in irrational and tragic behavior, but the consequences of living them down can be equally foolish and dangerous. For instance, a Claremont, California, youth became so embarrassed when he failed his driver's license test that, to prove himself to his ridiculing friends, he stole a car and drove it—to Philadelphia! But for a more poignant example, consider the case of a 17-year-old who stabbed a 14-year-old boy to death. A typical attack-by-bully incident? If you were to look behind the glaring headlines, you would find a very different kind of explanation. You would discover the story of a life in torment—the story of a boy pathetically small for his age, frail since infancy, a boy prevented by malnutrition from entering school until he was 8, a boy now 17 who weighed only 90 pounds and stood 4 feet 11 in his shoes. You could see the image of a lad taunted by his playmates with the stinging labels of Half-Pint, Short-Stuff, and Peanut.

On the fateful day, Adrian encountered two boys—each three years younger but 50 pounds heavier than he. The boys began the usual "runt" diatribe, and the conflict escalated. "Mickey started for me," testified Adrian, "and Tommy went to the side. They were bigger than me, and I thought they were gonna beat me up. I hadda use something to protect myself. He [Mickey] kept coming, and I stabbed him." The weapon was a knife that Adrian used to open boxes in the grocery store where he worked. Adrian's face clouded as he recalled that his tormentors had also called him an imp, a weasel, and Wimpy.

Positive Labels

These sobering illustrations of the possible consequences of living up to or of living down one's labels should not suggest that such behavior is necessarily negative and destructive in its effect. On the contrary, labels may sometimes have definite positive influence. I am firmly convinced that a fair share of the good in people is derived from the good that was expected of them as children. Many children, I am confident, became honest, responsible, generous adults partly, if not largely, because others, notably their parents, teachers, and play-mates, *expected* such qualities of them and communicated their anticipations to them. By making clear to children that you believe they are truthful and that you genuinely trust them, you are implic-itly, if not explicitly, labeling them as "truth-tellers," and the chances are that they will live up to the label. It is the genuine high expectation (which implies trust, confidence, respect) of the other which, after all, is the cornerstone of Theory Y (see Chapter 3).

But even positive labels may be dangerous. Unrealistic positive labels may entice one to overreach one's capabilities and thus lead to frustration, disillusionment—even tragedy. Consider the case of the young man described in Chapter 13, "Polarization" ("Contributing Factors" section), who, on the eve of his high school graduation, was found hanged in his attic. An outstanding personality, the boy had been president of his class, active in school affairs. He had just been accepted for enrollment by one of the nation's leading universities and had been given a new convertible by his proud parents. What could conceivably have driven him to suicide? Authorities uncovered a probable reason: He had missed being elected to the National Honor Society by a fraction of a point. His self-image (his self-labels, if you will) and this overwhelming failure were evidently irreconcilably polarized in his tortured mind.

"ASSOCIATIVE" BYPASSING

This fallacious "pointing-associating" duality of language offers still another possibility for communication difficulty. Chapter 10 described bypassing as the miscommunication pattern whereby people miss each other with their meanings. We were concerned there with words that were being used and reacted to primarily as "pointers." Let us now examine the tendency of people to miss each other's "associative" meanings.

"Associative" Bypassing Becomes Possible

This type of bypassing becomes possible in the following situations:

1. When the sender (speaker, writer, and so on) assumes that, because his or her words are intended to be merely "pointers," they will necessarily have little or no "associative" value for the receiver (listener, reader, and so forth):

> In the earlier years of commercial aviation a cabin attendant would warn passengers: "We're flying through a *storm*. You had better fasten your *safety* belts; it will be less *dangerous*." He or she might have intended nothing more than merely "pointing" with those words, but you may be sure the novice passengers "associated" a great deal more. Today, flight personnel are trained to elicit pleasant and secure associations with: "We're flying through some turbulence now; please fasten your *seat* belts—you will be more comfortable."[3] Even so, perfection is still ellusive—not long ago a vivacious young flight attendant strayed from the script to announce gaily that we were to land soon: "Folks, please fasten your seat belts; we'll be hitting the ground in just a few minutes."

2. When the receiver interprets words as largely or solely "pointers," whereas the sender intended them to be "associative."

> If you have ever complained: "Oh! You take things so literally," you have probably been involved in this sort of *"associative"* bypassing. It is the pathetic miscommunication which occurs when the young lady vainly tries to encourage her shy date with "Johnny, I'm cold." Whereupon her gallant escort whips off his jacket and slips it around her shoulders. She had wanted the jacket, all right, but with Johnny's arms still in the sleeves!
>
> This is the pattern, too, of sarcasm which fails. A sales manager was busily preparing for a trip which was to take him away from the office for the day. He called his filing clerk, pointed to a small pile of correspondence, and instructed: "Please file these letters." And, hoping to jar him from his usual lethargy, the manager added wryly: "Be sure to take all day with the job!" He did.

3. When the communicator (sender or receiver or both) assumes that words have the same "associative" value for the other person as they have for oneself.

> Illustrative is the case of the hospital patient who was awaiting major surgery the next day. He was toying with breakfast as he worried about the operation. Suddenly a nurse appeared at his door, noticed the barely touched food, and blithely said: "Better eat—*while you can!*" The poor man immediately assumed the worst. But the nurse had only meant to imply that the food service attendant would soon pick up the breakfast tray!

---

[3] When you fly you may be told that there is *open seating*. That sounds delightful—sit anywhere you wish—like owning your own airliner. You do indeed have your option, provided that someone is not already seated there! So if you don't get reasonably close to the head of the line of onboarding passengers, you may find yourself seated opposite the lavatory wedged between two corpulent riders.

A POSSIBLE MISUNDERSTANDING

I hope I have not given the impression that "associators" are bad or that they are to be avoided or abolished. In the first place, "associating" is not a thing that can be destroyed. It is a function of words, and it has no existence apart from people using and reacting to words. As long as people have imaginations, as long as they have the agility to leap beyond the immediate objects of their senses, there will be "associating." And let us be everlastingly grateful for it. The world would be unbearably prosaic without humor (an enormous portion of which is based upon association) and without poetry, drama—literature in general—which is designed to elicit rich associations from us. "I love you" (among the most highly "associative" phrases in our culture) would be just so many flat, commonplace words if the sender and the receiver were not able to transport themselves beyond mere "pointers."

Are we not sometimes the poorer for having cast out "associators"? Consider that in Victorian times only horses *sweated,* men *perspired,* and women—why they merely *glowed*!

No, this chapter has not been calculated to annihilate "associators" (even if that were possible). And certainly there has been no intention of debasing or minimizing their value and usefulness. On the other hand, it is clear that there are occasions when it is important, even imperative, to be *aware* of when "associators" are being used and to know how to cope with them. It is for these purposes that the following corrective measures are offered.

CORRECTIVES

It is the major thesis of this chapter that words can be used and reacted to both as "pointers" and as "associators." When communicators forget, ignore, deny, or, for any reason, are unaware of this duality, patterns of miscommunication become possible which may lead to confusion and trouble. Among these patterns are the "pointing-associating" confusion, name-calling, and "associative" bypassing. The suggestions which follow should be helpful in recognizing and dealing with these patterns.

The "Pointing-Associating" Confusion

Make a Habit of Distinguishing between Labels and Things. Living and communicating with labels as we do, we are frequently enticed to accept them as the things they represent. Communicators must be wary of reacting to labels as if they were more than representations (and often misleading representations at that). In this vein, give Mrs. Haney credit for a sensible adjustment to what had been a distinctly distasteful task for her. As a child, she was occasionally required to fish out of the sink the potato peelings, carrot scrapings, and assorted remains from the dinner dishes. This was referred to in the family as "cleaning out the garbage," a chore (and phrase) which distressed her to the point of nausea. At Girl Scout camp a year or so later, she gained an insight. There the girls were instructed to scrape the "leftover food" off their plates. On returning home, she discovered that she could remove the "garbage" from the sink with scarcely a qualm as long as she reminded herself that it was "leftover food" she was touching.

Remember, the map is *not* the territory; words are *not* that which they are being used to represent. Ask yourself: "Am I responding to the *object* or to the *association* I have for its *name*?"

Don't Permit the Label to Obscure the "Product."   Develop the extensional habit of looking behind labels to see the product more clearly. Manufacturers who assume that consumers usually look beyond the labels have sometimes paid for their overconfidence. Several years ago a new chocolate dessert topping came on the market. The product was tasty and inexpensive, but many customers adamantly refused to try it, apparently because they were unable or unwilling to look beyond its rather colorful name—Goop!

Others have also learned the lesson painfully. "Mrs. Japp's Potato Chips" had been distributed throughout greater Chicago for sometime before World War II. But shortly after Pearl Harbor sales began to sag. It didn't take Mrs. Japp (a Danish name) long to find the answer and change the name to "Jay's Potato Chips." The product has prospered ever since. Similarly, "Mikado" wooden pencils became "Mirado."

It came as no great surprise to the sports world that the National League Cincinnati Baseball Club changed its name from "Reds" to "Redlegs" in the era of congressional investigations of Communists. This, incidentally, was the same wordwise organization which felt that "bleachers" was a somewhat unattractive name for its uncovered stands. Since then the stands have been known as the Sun-Deck, and its patrons are permitted to wear beach costumes. For night games—miracle of miracles—it becomes the Moon-Deck!

Another convincing illustration of the role that a label plays in the acceptance of labeled products occurred in Shawnee Mission, Kansas. The Home Economics course offered to 7th-grade boys was suffering considerable absenteeism. Those who did attend were assaulted with "sissy," "pantywaist," and "wimp." The course's name was changed to Cooking—no change in attendance. The name was changed again to Bachelor Survival. The school can't satisfy the demand for enrollment!

Remember that, despite your intentions, your words can affect other people. Buddha recognized this 25 centuries ago when he admonished:

"Whatever words we utter should be chosen with care, for people will hear them and be influenced by them for good or ill."

Name-Calling

The basic advice is to recognize names for what they are—merely tags, often inaccurate, and always incomplete representations of the flesh-and-blood persons to whom they are appended. Remember that the labels in themselves are utterly powerless and meaningless. It is our reactions to the labels of others (and to our own) that can have profound effects on our evaluations and behavior. It is tempting for those who do the labeling and for those who are labeled to assume that the labels are valid and complete.

More specifically, if the labels assigned to you are negative and unfavorable, refuse to live up to them, to resign yourself to them. Resist them, contradict them with your behavior (actions are usually more convincing than words). But, on the other hand, avoid overreacting to them and assuming a manner or characteristic which is as bad as or worse than the trait originally labeled. If your labels are positive, recognize that they may serve as a beneficial stimulant, but be wary of *overreaching* your capacities.

If you are doing the labeling, if label you must, be careful in your selection of tags. Negative labels are seldom useful and often dangerous, whereas positive labels are often, but not invariably, beneficial. If you want someone to be honest, let the person know that you genuinely trust him or her.

"Associative" Bypassing

"Associative" bypassing occurs when communicators miss each other with their "associative" meanings. Such bypassing is similar to bypassing (the missing of "pointer" meanings), and the reader is encouraged to review the correctives section in Chapter 10, "Bypassing."

But, in addition, remember:

1. Words to which you "associate" little or nothing may be highly "associative" for the other person.

Labor contract negotiators have learned to be alert to some of the redflag words which upset the other party. In meeting with company representatives, union negotiators, for example, refrain from mentioning the union "demand" and substitute union "proposal" when softer associations seem in order. They find, too, that discussions with management in terms of what "your employees want" rather than what "the union (or 'we') wants" are often carried on with more equanimity and objectivity.

2. Words "associating" a great deal to you may "associate" little or nothing to the other person—they may merely "point" for others.

Before making his final decision on a proposal to move to new offices, the head of a large company called his top executives together for a last discussion of the idea. All were enthusiastic except the company treasurer, who insisted that he had not had time to calculate all the costs with accuracy sufficient to satisfy himself that the move was advantageous. Annoyed by his persistence, the chief finally burst out:

"All right, Jim, all right! Figure it out to the last cent. A penny saved is a penny earned, right?"

His intention was sarcastic. He meant for the treasurer to stop being petty. But, unfortunately, the latter interpreted "penny saved, penny earned," quite literally.

He put several members of his staff to work on the problem and, to test the firmness of the price, had one of them interview the agent renting the proposed new quarters without explaining whom he represented. This indication of additional interest in the premises led the agent to raise the rent. Not until the lease was signed did the agency chief discover that one of his own employees had, in effect, bid up its price.

3. Your receiver (or sender) may not be "associating" as you are.

Employed by a tool and die works, a young engineer was assigned to study the plant's production procedures in general and to devise improvements. Tool and die people are the aristocracy of factory workers, and their foremen are of correspondingly high standing. The engineer was aware of this and took great care to show respect.

When he found one department where he thought he could make considerable improvement, he first set about making friends with the workmen and their foreman. Once he had gained their acceptance he got the foreman to call the men together so that he could outline his plans to the whole group. Because he thought that several of the men might resist change, he sought to allay their fears by saying:

"Of course, at this stage what I'm proposing is only an experiment."

The men not only dragged their heels but actively sabotaged his attempted innovations. Finally, the foreman went to the production manager. The gist of his complaint was that the engineer was trying to use him and his men as "guinea pigs."

You may be tempted to dismiss this as an unthinking reaction on the part of the men. But it was the engineer who sought to communicate something to them, not they to him. He wanted to make them feel that he was proposing only tentative changes which would not become permanent unless they proved successful.

This chapter is not a blanket indictment of euphemisms and dysphemisms, but Ben Franklin probably wouldn't be so fondly remembered if he had said, "Nothing is so certain as negative patient care outcome and revenue enhancement."

Discussion Questions

1. Euphemisms and dysphemisms are sometimes used to deceive others. What can be done to combat such forms of misrepresentation, since they are usually not direct contradictions of truth?

2. On the other hand, what should be the rights of advertisers, public relations people, editorialists, lawyers, salespersons, writers, and others who rely largely upon words to accomplish their purposes?

3. Do you agree that only half of the sticks-and-stones expression is true? Why?

4. Recalling the illustration of students living up to their labels in the group dynamics course: What can be gained or lost by such labeling?

5. What are the pros and cons of positive labeling?

6. What are the pros and cons of "associators"?

7. Report upon an incident, perhaps involving yourself, in which "pointing-associating" confusion (or name-calling or "associative" bypassing) was involved. Why did the incident occur? What could have been done to prevent or correct it? What measures would tend to prevent its recurrence?

C A S E S

CASE 16.1

Galvanized Sheets*

Some years ago the manufacturers of galvanized sheeting were experimenting with new methods of galvanization. The object was to develop a process that would be quick and inexpensive, and yet would coat sheeting in such a manner that it could be bent sharply without the galvanizing peeling off. One firm, the Ewell Company, finally developed a process that met these qualifications.

Their method was to manufacture sheeting in a continuous roll so that it could be galvanized as as it rolled through the galvanizing pit. The sheeting was then cut to specifications.

The company felt that it had a superior product but decided upon a marketing test as a precautionary measure. A few salesmen in certain pilot territories were instructed to begin selling the new products to their customers; that is, sheet metal shops, ventilating firms, and so forth. Since no trade name had as yet been selected, the salesmen were told to refer to the new product as "continuous roll galvanized sheets."

Customer reaction ranged from apathy to resistance. The salesmen returned to the plant and complained that the average customer had a firm conviction that the rolling process[1] would flatten out the galvanizing to such an extent that it would be too thin to withstand severe bends without peeling.

The salesmen tried in vain to explain that the "continuous roll" of their new galvanizing process didn't really involve rolling in the thinning sense at all. The reports were disturbing, but Ewell, convinced of the superiority of its product, decided to gamble. The continuous roll process was adopted throughout the plant. The product was trademarked Flex-tite in the hope that this would offset prejudices. Production began in full swing while management crossed its fingers and waited.

Within two years it was obvious that the gamble had paid off. The company, now producing Flex-tite exclusively, had doubled its total sales of galvanized sheeting.

Discussion Questions

1. Why was the original label for the new product objectionable?

---

* All names have been disguised.

[1] *Rolling* in the metals industries generally referred to the process of thinning strips of metal as they passed between sets of rollers. The rollers exerted great pressure on the strips and literally squeezed them down into thinner gauges.

2. Give other examples of production-oriented labels which other organizations use in connection with their products or services. If *your* organization (educational institution, business firm, government agency, and so forth) guilty of this?

3. What relevance does this case have for this chapter?

CASE 16.2

Sticks and Stones . . .*

Despite the child's defiant jingle, names hurt more than sticks or stones: a man can more easily bear an attack on his body than an offense to his feelings, and will remember an insult long after he has forgotten an injury.

—*Sidney Harris*

Live Wire. In Christchurch, New Zealand, hauled into court on a charge of using foul language to a telephone operator, an angry subscriber countercharged that the girl just laughed and laughed after he obliged her by spelling his name: Montmorency de Villiers.

Any Other Name. In Calgary, Alberta, George and Rosie Big Belly asked the provincial secretary what could be done for them under the provisions of The Change of Name Act.

Typo. In Philadelphia, when *Inquirer* columnist Frank Brookhouser reported that Hubert B. Wolfeschlegelsteinhasenbergerdorff had registered to vote in the November elections, Hubert wrote in indignantly to say that a *u* had been left out: his name was Wolfeschlegelsteinhausenbergerdorff.

In New Haven, Connecticut, Yale graduate student Edmund D. Looney petitioned the superior court for permission to change his name, claiming that it might interfere with the practice of his future profession—psychiatry.

Tired of Living in Snake Den. Johnston, Rhode Island, residents of Snake Den Road complained to the City Council of the frightful name of their street. The council ordered the name changed to Belfield Drive.

Southern Hospitality. In Birmingham, Alabama, when the judge asked him what the initials stood for, juryman W. J. Weaver recalled: "My mother and daddy had 11 daughters in a row. They decided to call me Welcome John."

Maiden Name. All through school, Mary Hooker had been embarrassed. Her mother's solace: "Don't worry, dear. One day, you'll marry a fine young man and that will be the end of the name problem." Unfortunately, Mary fell in love with and married Elmer Tramp.

---

* All items except the Harris quote and *"Maiden Name"* are from *Time* and are reprinted with permission.

CASE 16.3

The Manatee

The manatee is excellent eating—and this is its trouble. It has been in danger of being hunted out of existence in Florida. Kirk Monroe, a state senator, sought to protect the animal with a $500 fine for killing one. He introduced a bill in the state legislature in which he omitted the mammal's common name but used only its scientific name, *trichecus latirostris*.

The bill seemed tabled for posterity until on the last day of the legislative session one senator rose and opined: "If there is a beast with any name as that in the state of Florida it ought to be protected." The bill passed unanimously.

Discussion Question
1. Why did the bill pass?

CASE 16.4

"The Four Goals of Labor"

Fortune conducted an interesting test. A cartoon entitled "The Four Goals of Labor" was clipped from a union newspaper and duplicated. *Fortune* deleted the union appellation and indicated that the cartoon had come from an NAM Newsletter. Twenty union members (who were unaware of the reattribution) were asked whether they thought the cartoon was a fair representation of labor's goals. Four reluctantly conceded that it was. Two were undecided. The other 14 roundly condemned the cartoon, describing it as patronizing, loaded, or paternalistic. One said, "Makes me want to spit."

Discussion Questions
1. What does this experiment prove?

2. How would a group of managers respond to something that had been falsely attributed to the AFL-CIO?

CASE 16.5

Prestige Foods*

Prestige Foods—attractively packaged fruits, fowl, meats, and so forth—have found widespread favor as business gifts. The foods are generally of high quality and even more highly priced. The gift is invariably accompanied by a piece of sales literature. The following were sent with a smoked pheasant and a box of apples, respectively.

---

* All names have either been disguised or omitted.

Smoke Dreams Come True

Rembrandt stewed over his canvas—a regular fussbudget about deep, rich browns. Stradivari swooned over a violin, working for a tone of pure gold. But they weren't in it with the way we toil, turning out our smoked bird masterpieces.

Wild life is pampered on our rolling wooded acres. Birds are urged to gorge on the fat of the land. To the plumpest we award the great adventure of the smokehouse and the great wide world, where they make mouths water and gladden hearts.

This succulent creature is ready to eat. It's been slowly smoked over fragrant hickory embers. Lazy little plumes of smoke sealed in the sweet juices, turned the outside crackly brown. We firmly believe you can't get such happy flavor anywhere else.

This bird will keep approximately two or three weeks in the refrigerator. (Hsst! Or a year in a freezer with the wrapper left on. But who's that Spartan?)

Hints for Serving

How to Slice. With any smoked bird it's gourmet-wise (not stingy) to slice it wafer thin. That lets your lucky palate savor every delicious smoky morsel. A good sharp knife will do the trick.

Getting Het Up, Whole. If—instead of eating your bird cold, just as it comes—you have a yen to try it hot, here's how. Put it in a roaster with some good strong chicken broth or consommé. Use a moderate oven and baste conscientiously.

Wonderful Canapés. Here's where a smoked bird really preens itself. Try slivers of the tender smoked meat on little squares of fresh buttered toast—goldly brown and fragrant. Top with a dab of horseradish, or better yet, our very own Dippin' Gravy.

Or mince some of the smoked meat and add to softened, well-seasoned cream cheese. Spread on crisp crackers.

Or serve thin slices of smoked meat with snowy rings of Bermuda onion on rounds of buttered rye.

Or carry out your own inspirations. This bird can't *help* being delicious!

Fancied Up

Smoked Bird à la King. And we really mean regal. Use your favorite Chicken à la King recipe, substituting whatever smoked bird you're blessed with. Just before serving, add a good stiff dose of Sherry or Madeira.

Smoked Bird Rarebit. Nestle slices of smoked bird between pieces of hot buttered toast. Cover with strips of brisk sharp cheese and slide under the broiler till the cheese starts to burble and run. Serve at once.

Smoked Bird and Scrambled Eggs. Mince the meat and add to slightly beaten eggs. Cook in double broiler, stirring thoughtfully.

Smoked Bird Salad. Toss some savory bird shreds in with your favorite mixed salad—crisp greens, dewy tomatoes, shivery cucumbers. Let it glisten with good French dressing and rejoice in a mite of Roquefort.

Glorious Leftovers

, Never, *never* throw out that precious carcass till it's worked magic! Would you toss out platinum? Would you discard diamonds?

'Tis wonderful—that carcass—in soup, beautiful soup. And that goes for the glittering white bones of the most greedily denuded. Try simmering that exposed frame in a kettle of Split Pea Soup. Serve in man-size soup plates, spiked with Sherry. O tempora! O mores! And the same for Black Bean or Lentil.

Greetings From Sparkling Brook, California

Dear Epicure:—

These Golden Globe Apples were sent to you at the request of the person whose name appears on the address label.

They are grown solely by me, in a little hidden valley in the Sierra Nevada Mountains of California. Your donor is able to send them to you through having acquired a Preferred Share in the fruits of my orchard.

When I first found this valley, over 20 years ago, it was an abandoned homestead—so forlorn that folks poked fun at me, and said: "What are you going to raise, Joe—sagebrush or rabbit weed?"

But here I had found one old apple tree, with a heavy crop on it. And a native of these parts told me that every fall, for 25 years, he had helped himself to apples from it. "Hmm," I thought, "a natural apple spot if there ever was one."

So here I planted a dozen different kinds of apples—including a new one, recently discovered growing wild on a mountainside. And this new one turned out to be just the apple this little valley was waiting for.

Here our golden California sun gives its flesh and skin a golden tinge. Here our cold mountain nights develop its fruit sugars, and make it so crisp that every bite crackles. Here the volcanic ash in the soil gives it a tang no other apple has. And here the pure mountain springs from which its growth is watered fill it with a ciderlike juice which is nature's true champagne.

Because this "Golden Globe" Apple is a luxury fruit which can be gotten nowhere else, apple lovers all over America now send to me for it. If, after eating these, you would like information on my various packs, and Preferred Rights to them, I will be glad to send it.

Sincerely yours,
Joe Wilson

CASE 16.6

Flight from Scorn—A Tale of Two Boys

These two accounts, with only the names disguised to prevent further embarrassment, are factual.

Thirteen-year-old Danny detested his schoolmates calling him Fatty. Five months ago, he weighed 105 pounds—seemingly not excessive for his height, 5 feet 5 inches. But by Danny's own perception he was a bit too chubby. So he began to diet—with a vengeance. His parents were not alarmed at first but when his weight dropped to 62 pounds they took him to a hospital. Doctors ruled out glandular problems and ordered tube feeding. He gained 10 pounds in five days. Finally, he divulged his secret—he'd been worried about the teasing. Now at 74 pounds he's been discharged for another crack at Mom's good home cooking.

Eleven-year-old Larry was a different target for ridicule: he has one brown eye and one blue eye. Classmates began calling him "old brown and blue eyes." Larry decided he could stand it no longer and ran away from home. But two nights of sleeping under porches proved even worse so he turned himself in to police who in turn returned him home.

Discussion Questions

1. Why did Danny and Larry behave as they did?
2. Can you give examples of older people who overreacted to name calling?
3. How can we protect ourselves against the double burden of name calling?

CASE 16.7

McCall College*

McCall College is a small eastern liberal arts college. For many years its theater department had enjoyed an excellent and well-deserved reputation among the student body and faculty and among the community in which the college was located. The theater department presented eight or nine plays yearly, the season beginning in October and ending in May. Each play was presented for six performances—one each night from Wednesday through Sunday and a matinee on Saturday. The average attendance over the years had been gratifyingly high, 85 percent of capacity, ranging from 65 percent to frequent standing-room-only audiences.

Last year the theater's director, Doug Lawson, decided that for one of the midseason productions he would present a collection of excerpts from several plays rather than one single play. The theme was to portray the changes in theatrical production from classic Greece up to the 20th century. He titled the production, accurately enough, *Theater Styles Review,* and chose excerpts from Euripides' *Hippolytus,* representing the classic Greek theater; *Everyman* (medieval morality play); Shakespeare's *Midsummer Night's Dream* (16th century); Molière's *The Would-Be Gentleman* (17th century); Sheridan's *School for Scandal* (18th century); Stowe's *Uncle Tom's Cabin* (19th-century melodrama); Ibsen's *Ghosts*

---

* All names have been disguised.

(19th-century realism); and Wilde's *The Importance of Being Earnest* (19th-century comedy of manners).

Lawson designed the sets and carefully rehearsed the cast. After several weeks of hard work, everyone from Lawson to the student curtain-puller eagerly anticipated the audience reaction.

Finally, on opening night Lawson peeked through the act curtain to count the house. The auditorium was virtually empty! It seemed incredible. The weather was typically unpleasant for February, but audiences had turned out on much more inclement nights. No one could think of a competing attraction in town that night, and yet there they were—or weren't—an audience of only 20 percent capacity!

But the show must go on—and so it did, admirably. The sparse audience thoroughly enjoyed the presentation, and Lawson, despite his disappointment with the size of the audience, was justifiably proud of his company. He had rarely seen an opening night at McCall so brilliantly and flawlessly executed.

After the performance the director, cast, and crew sat down together to ponder. The only possible answer, everyone agreed, must lie in freakish chance. It just happened, someone offered, that everyone decided, for one reason or another, that he would attend on some night other than the first. But just wait, some promised bravely, we'll have overflow crowds the rest of the week!

But there were no overflow crowds. To be specific, the audiences ranged between 20 and 35 percent of capacity. Lawson was stunned. Didn't people like the excerpt format? He had had good audience reactions to it on several previous occasions. Were the performances poor? Certainly his own judgment and the demonstrably appreciative audiences precluded this as a reason. What then? Lawson called his company together and began:

> As you all know, we have just had the greatest attendance flop in the 15 years I have been here. Now why? Don't tell me the audiences, what there were of them, didn't love it. And you people did marvelously. Now the purpose of this meeting is to decide what went wrong, correct it, and run the show again in May. I gambled with it once and lost, but I'm just stubborn enough, and confident enough of my product, to gamble again. Now, what went wrong?

Several suggestions for minor changes in dialogue, business, and sets were made. Someone suggested that the title might be changed. Lawson invited the troup to think of a better name. Some suggestions: *Lagniappe, Grease Paint Review, Sex through the Ages, Euripides Goes Wilde, 2600 Years of Grease Paint*. Finally, *Athens to Broadway* was selected, and the production was repeated during a week in May.

The attendance soared to the old standard. The audiences ranged from 70 to 85 percent of capacity during the six performances.

Discussion Questions

1. How do you account for Lawson's "greatest attendance flop"?
2. How could this miscommunication have been prevented?

CASE 16.8

The Bright Young Man

Bob Elgin, a district manager, had long considered the company's management training program inadequate and felt that he had a responsibility to supplement company-sponsored trainees by developing people with management potential from the ranks. Such was the case when he hired Bruce Gorman, recently discharged from the Army, for an office position in one of his plants.

Bruce immediately asserted himself and was not hesitant about offering suggestions for improvement and criticism of areas that he felt were not up to par. Bob took an immediate liking to Bruce and proposed him for acceptance into the company-sponsored management training program. Bob's request was denied, primarily because Bruce lacked a college education and because of the personnel interviewer's evaluation of Bruce as having a cocksure attitude.

Exercising his prerogative, Bob decided to put Bruce through the training program at the district's own expense.

Bob and Bruce developed considerable rapport, and with the management trainer's guidance Bruce progressed rapidly. When the opening arose, Bob was able to sell Bruce to higher management as a plant manager.

Bruce was so elated that he told Bob that in his new assignment he would break all existing records—and proceeded to do so. One of the boasts Bruce made to Bob was that he would reach a credit currency of 70 percent his first month. The plant under the previous manager had never exceeded a credit currency of 55 percent. Bruce's credit currency for his first month was 68.9 percent.

Bob was delighted. He immediately dispatched a congratulatory memo to Bruce, inserting a good-natured needle about his missing his prediction by a hair:

To: B. N. Gorman
From: R. L. Elgin
Subject: Credit Currency Report

68.9 percent is not 70 percent, but what else can I expect from a green manager? Here's hoping you do better this month.

A week later Bob visited Bruce's plant for the first time since the credit currency report. He entered Bruce's office to find him hard at work at papers strewn about his desk.

Bob said jocularly, "That's a mighty fine impersonation of a hard worker!"

Startled, Bruce looked up and retorted sharply, "I thought I'd have more than one month to prove my worth!"

Discussion Questions

1. What were Bob Elgin's perceptions regarding himself and Bruce up to the moment Bruce gave his sharp retort?

2. What were Bruce Gorman's perceptions regarding himself, his job, and Bob Elgin up to and including Bob's remark: "That's a mighty fine impersonation . . ."?

3. What does this case have to do with "pointing" and "associating"?

4. What should Bob do now?

CASE 16.9

Leonard Who?

Would Fred Astaire and Ginger Rogers have been as light on their feet had they remained Frederick Austerlitz and Virginia Katherine McMath? Would Jack Benny, Eddie Cantor, and Rodney Dangerfield have been as hilarious if they hadn't changed from Benny Kubelsky, Edward Israel Itzkowitz, and Jacob Cohen? Would Boris Karloff have been as menacing as William Henry Pratt? And would Natasha Gurdin, Doris Kappelhoff, Frances Gumm, Raquel Tejada, Alexandra Zuck, and Norma Jeane Baker have been as glamorous as Natalie Wood, Doris Day, Judy Garland, Raquel Welch, Sandra Dee, and Marilyn Monroe? We may never know the answers to these crucial questions but Nicholas Aloysius Adamshock, Reginald Truscott-Jones, Alexander Archibald Leach, Eugene Maurice Orowitz, Leonard Slye, and Spangler Arlington Brough were likely better off being known as Nick Adams, Ray Milland, Cary Grant, Michael Landon, Roy Rogers, and Robert Taylor. And Charo (kootchy, kootchy!) is easier to remember than Maria Rosario Pilar Martinez Melina Baeza.

Many newer stars have eschewed pseudonyms. Anka, Baez, Cosby, DeNiro, Fonda, Gere, Hawn, Jagger, Lauper, Manilow, McCartney, Minnelli, Nugent, Pacino, Richie, Ronstadt, Sedaka, Spacek, Springsteen, Streep, Streisand, Travolta—those names don't seem particularly lyrical. But they are originals and they don't seem to have hampered their owners' careers.

And finally the old joke:

I wonder if anyone ever needled Big John Wayne about his name originally being Marion Morrison.

I know of one fellow who did.

Really? I'd sure like to meet him!

So would I, but I don't think they'll dig him up just for that.

Discussion Questions

1. Why does this case appear in this chapter?

2. Most of the pseudonyms seem euphemistic compared to the originals. Roy Rogers sounds more attractive than Leonard Slye. But what about Boris Karloff?

3. What do you think of the apparent trend of performers to retain their original names?

CASE 16.10

A New Witch Hunt

We used to call them cold sores. Now they have a new name, and thereby hangs a tragic tale.

Doctors now refer to the common childhood ailment as *herpes—herpes simplex* I, to be more exact. But that's close enough to *herpes simplex* II, the dreaded genital herpes that has contributed to a great deal of anguish and downright unsane behavior.

As of this writing, the most notorious victim—or villain, depending upon your point of view—is three-year-old Johnny Bigley of Anne Arundel County, Maryland.

Johnny contracted the virus at birth, and cold sores periodically break out on his hands and back. That condition plus its ominous label have terrorized the Pasadena Elementary School since Johnny enrolled.

His teacher immediately asked for and received a transfer to another school. The parents of Johnny's classmates have steadfastly refused to permit their children to attend classes when Johnny is present. Lawyers representing the school and the teachers sought an injunction to keep Johnny out of school except on days on which there are no sores whatsoever anywhere on his body.

The judge decided that Johnny would submit to a daily examination by a doctor and that he would be kept home on days when there were sores on his hands. Johnny could come to school if he had sores on his back, provided he wore a one-piece jump suit—and if the school took precautions originally calculated as a protection against hepatitis.

None of these rulings have dissuaded parents or teachers who demand more stringent restrictions. The 10-day injunction has now expired and Susan Russell, attorney for the parents and teachers, argues: "You have to weigh one child's right to an education against the risks to all the other children—and there is a slim risk of infection."

The rancor continues despite the fact that the risked infection is simply to cold sores to which, according to doctors, up to 70 percent of the children get anyway.

Dr. Ward Cates of the National Center for Disease Control states: "The likelihood of these children getting the virus from him [Johnny] is much smaller than of their getting it from kids without any symptoms at all." And Dr. Andre Nahmias of Emory University's medical school stresses that the herpes simplex I virus is "so ubiquitous [more than 70 percent of the adult population now carry it] that it is virtually impossible to avoid exposure."[1]

Such authoritative comments ought to be calming but they are not. Some parents can't back down even if they want to. According to attorney Russell, one parent was warned that if her child attended class with Johnny, he would not be allowed into his after-school day center.

The upshot is that young Johnny continues to arrive at an empty school, carrying all the grown-up sexual stigma associated with "herpes."

> The sobering lesson is an old one: that words are amazingly powerful. We jeer at the idea that people might once have believed in spells, or proved their innocence by reciting complicated oaths without a slip.
>
> But confronted by a word that conjures up a reality we can't control—a disease we can't cure or don't understand—we shy away as if Johnny Bigley had the black plague. Grown-ups can, and should, behave better.[2]

Discussion Questions

1. Why do the parents refuse to let their children attend class with Johnny Bigley?

2. What do you think of the judge's ruling?

3. What else can be done to ameliorate the matter?

4. Assuming the affair can be resolved, what is the possible long-range effect upon Johnny?

CASE 16.11

Résumé Expansion

A highlight of *The Official M.B.A. Handbook* or *How to Succeed in Business without a Harvard M.B.A.* is résumé expansion. That seems a very modest expression for the highly creative reconstructive surgery the authors propose.

The basic idea is to "transform the insipid into the inspired, the mundane into the magnificent, the illegal into the entrepreneurial." While

---

[1] "Herpes Hysteria in the Classroom," *Newsweek,* January 22, 1985, p. 38.

[2] Morton Kondracke, "Doublespeak and the Witch Hunt," *Chicago Sun-Times,* February 2, 1985, p. 13.

EXHIBIT 1

Education
High School: Scarsdale High, Scarsdale New York
College: North Western U., September 1977–
June 1981
· *Made Dean's List*
· *So did 82% of the class*
· *Babysat a couple of times for my*
Philosophy prof. when he and spouse
went to Chicago
· *Dealt a little marijuana to friends to*
work my way through school after
the Old man cut me off.

Graduate Work: Harvard Business School, Septem-
ber 1981 – M.B.A. expected in June
1983 (God willing!)
· *Grind in library six days a week*
· *Organized Saturday Night parties*
to meet local college women with
chicks appeal.

Work Experience
Cook: Kentucky Fried Chicken, summer 1981
· *Biggest one in Westchester*
· *Cooked on swing shift*
· *Took home extra chicken if I cooked*
too much
· *Taught high school kids how to*
cook chicken, and told them to hustle.

Caddy: Greenview Country Club, summer 1980
· *Found golfer's Balls*
· *Replaced divots*
· *Told members off when they*
undertipped
· *Tended the pin*
· *Arranged member's betting pools*
· *Stepped on opponents balls in the*
rough

Other Experience: Won $50,000 in McDonald's
"Build a Big Mac" contest summer
1981
· *Spent $18,000 of winnings on new*
Corvette
· *Totalled car into front window of*
local Teamster's union hall while
coming home blotto from party
· *Sold car to pay repair bills and*
settle with Teamsters
· *Used remaining $21,000 to pay for*
business school

they don't advocate outright lying, they do advise that you "repackage
your achievements in terms that give them dignity and importance."
They offer this illustration:[3]

Prentiss Robert Jackson was a business student who used this technique.
Born of humble stock in Scarsdale, New York, he had an academically successful but otherwise nondescript four years at a well-known midwestern college. On the face of it, he was afraid that his lack of serious work experience
would doom him to a decade of penal servitude in somebody's personnel
department. Instead, by careful application of résumé expansion, P.R. was
able to turn his meager summer experience into a corporate recruiter's
dream. Follow along as we trace the evolution of Jackson's résumé from
scribbbled work sheet (Exhibit 1) to finished product (Exhibit 2).

---

[3] Jim Fisk and Robert Barron, *The Official M.B.A. Handbook,* pp. 107-9. Copyright ©
1982 by 82 Corporation. Reprinted by permission of Wallaby Books, a division of Simon &
Schuster, Inc.

EXHIBIT 2

Career Objective: A position offering
challenge, personal growth,
and serious *dinero*

Résumé of
PRENTISS ROBERT JACKSON

Home address:
12 Spruce Lane
Scarsdale, N.Y.

School address:
27 Gallatin Hall
The Business School
Boston, Mass.

Education

1981–1983   **HARVARD GRADUATE SCHOOL OF BUSINESS ADMINISTRATION**
Worked my way through school by winning $50,000 special
construction contract from national restaurant chain. (Was forced to
dispose of major asset, however, after run-in with local Teamsters
organization.) Founding member, Aflu-American Association.

1977–1981   **NORTHWESTERN UNIVERSITY**
B.A. received June 1981. Dean's List. Established primary day-care
service for faculty children. Paid for tuition and expenses last three
years by founding a small business that marketed a complete line of
leisure products to students, achieving return on investment of 2,048
percent. Summa cum laude thesis: *David Bowie: The Last Existential
Man.*

Work Experience

Summer
1982   **GOLF COORDINATOR, GREENVIEW COUNTRY CLUB**
Responsible for revitalization of golf course to achieve improved
playing characteristics. Tripled player through-put by utilizing batch
processing. Provided professional assistance and financial consulting
services to members. Helped ensure members' strategic success by
repositioning them vis à vis their competitors.

Summer
1981   **SPECIAL ASSISTANT TO FRANCHISER, KENTUCKY FRIED
CHICKEN, HARRISON, NEW YORK**
Senior production officer during high-volume evening shift. Audited
inventory stocking levels and instituted control systems to prevent
exceeding storage capacity. Conducted initial employee orientation
and instituted employee motivational seminars.

Discussion Questions

1. What are the differences between the pre- and post-expansion versions of Jackson's résumé?

2. What patterns of miscommunication did the expanded résumé attempt to exploit?

3. Do you advocate the Fisk-Barron résumé-expansion approach?

CASE 16.12

Good News and Bad News

The previous case focused on the employment résumé, usually a key factor in finding a position. For those who are anticipating a full-time job, there is good news—and bad news.

First, the good news: YOU WON'T BE FIRED.

Unfortunately, however, you can be "nonretained," "nonrenewed," "de-hired," "selected out," "outplaced," or "released." You can also be subjected to "a work force adjustment," "a head-count reduction," "a negative employee retention," or "a corporate downsizing." Or you may be an unwilling participant in a "career alternative enhancement program."

But keep thinking of the bright side—you will never be fired.

Discussion Questions

1. Why does this item appear in this chapter?
2. Is it better to be "outplaced" than to be "fired"?

CHAPTER SEVENTEEN

Intensional Orientation
3. Blindering
Defining Over-Restrictedly

❋
❋
❋

A good way to get the essence of this chapter under your skin is to make an earnest effort to solve the following problem.

Objective: To draw through all nine of the spots, with these restrictions:

1. Start with your pencil on any of the nine spots.
2. Draw four straight lines without removing your pencil from the page.
3. You may cross over lines, but you may not repeat them, that is, trace back on them.
4. Some readers may already know the solution. Congratulations! Their reward is a further challenge: Do the problem in three lines! (That will teach them to be so clever!)

Most people have difficulty with the problem because they unconsciously add a fourth restriction—one that renders the problem insoluble.

Did you perceive the nine spots as a *square?* (See Figure 17.2 on p. 514.)

Most people in our culture would see it as such[1] But did you then restrict your drawings of lines to the boundaries of your square: Did you assume that you could not draw beyond?

If you did (and most of us would), you were severely hampering your progress toward a solution. Once you remove the *self-imposed restriction,* the solution comes easily (Figure 17.2).

---

[1] People in some cultures, such as the Trobriand Islanders, fail to perceive such connecting lines and would see, in this case, simply an aggregate of isolated spots.

FIGURE 17.1

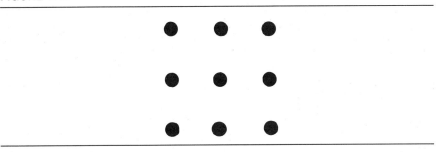

The nine-spot puzzle illustrates one of the key difficulties in problem solving—the tendency to *restrict* one's view of the problem. Clearly, one of the most important reasons why one has a limited perception of a problem grows out of the *definition* of the problem. (Most people define or think of the problem above as the nine-spot *square*.)

A pertinent example of a restrictive problem definition occurred in a certain family I know. The wife complained that "the powder room was cold" during the winter. The husband unquestioningly accepted his wife's articulation of the problem, and together they began to work on it. Their first attempt was to cover the window and its frame with a large piece of plastic. This approach was not only unsightly but ineffective—the powder room seemed as cold as ever. The next action was to install a storm window. Since the window's dimensions were atypical, a tailor-made one had to be ordered—cost: $48.50. That helped, but not much. Now the couple began to contemplate construction overhauls. She favored having the furnace people install another radiator in the room. He argued for tearing into the outside wall and inserting more or better insulation. Either plan would have run into hundreds of dollars.

Before taking either step, the couple, fortunately, began to reconsider the *definition* of the problem. "Let's face it," they jointly concluded, "our problem is not a cold powder room. It's a cold (and uncomfortable) *toilet seat!*" A fuzzy cover ($4.95) now adorns the seat, and the problem has been solved.[2]

In sum, the *words* we use to define a problem or situation can act as *blinders* (not unlike a horse's blinders or blinkers that prevent distractions from the side and limit its field of vision) and thus restrict us in our approach to the problem or situation.

Incidentally, the key to solving the nine-spot problem with *three* lines is to note that the challenge was simply to "draw through all nine of the spots." There was no requirement that the lines pass

---

[2] Ordinarily, to establish the authenticity of this illustration, I would cite the name of the family involved—but my wife would kill me!

FIGURE 17.2

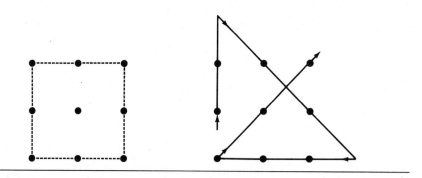

FIGURE 17.3

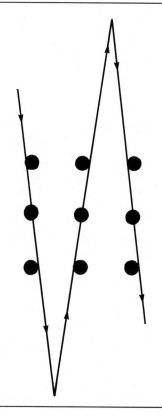

through the *centers* of the spots. Given the leeway of slicing through the peripheries of some of the spots, the problem can be readily solved, as shown in Figure 17.3.

SOME CONSEQUENCES

Roughly speaking, blinders may lead to two broad kinds of consequences. Blindering may (1) delay or impede desirable solutions and (2) lead to undesirable solutions.

Delayed Solutions

If you are still in the mood for puzzles, try this one. Two cyclists are separated by 30 miles of straight, flat road. They begin pedaling toward each other simultaneously. At the same time, a fly takes off from the handlebars of one of the cyclists, flies to the second, turns instantaneously, flies back to the first, and so on. The fly continues to make these alternating flights as the cyclists continuously decrease the distance between themselves. Finally, the fly is smashed between the cyclists as they collide. Both cyclists were traveling at 15 miles per hour, and the fly at 40—all at constant rates of speed. The problem: What is the total distance of the fly's flight, that is, how far did the fly fly? (Don't read farther until you have tried to work out the problem for yourself.)

If you arrived at an incorrect answer, or at no answer at all, or at the correct answer in more than 15 seconds, something must have impeded your progress. Examine the assumptions you made about the problem. Did your reactions resemble one or more of these?

1. "The problem is difficult. It requires computation—paper and pencil work."
2. "The problem is incomplete. I don't have all of the necessary data."
3. "The problem is silly. I won't waste my time and energy."
4. The technicality finder: "A fly couldn't fly that fast." "How could the fly turn instantaneously—it would lose some speed."

Probably underlying each of these expressions (though only the first admits it) is the assumption that the problem is complex. Once we define a problem as complex, we are more likely to search (if we search at all) for an answer by using complex techniques, for example, by computing the sum of the decreasing distances of the fly's individual flights.

The problem, however, is quite simple—*if* one defines it as such. The cyclists are 30 miles apart and pedaling at 15 miles per hour. They will thus collide in one hour. The fly that travels at 40 miles per hour will thus have flown 40 miles.

I admit that I may have helped blinder you by asking "How *far* did the fly fly?" thus focusing attention on distance and away from time. Had the question been "How long did the fly fly, and therefore how far?" the correct answer would probably have come much more rapidly and easily.

The phenomenon of blindering as a factor in impeding progress is suggested by M. W. Ball:

> Oil men, through some queer quirk of herd psychology, have been great respecters of political boundaries. When oil is found in a state they are likely to search that state with enthusiasm and thoroughness, ignoring areas of equal promise just over the state line. Perhaps this explains why no oil was produced in New York until five years after its discovery in Northern Pennsylvania. . . .[3]
>
> Down in Texas, close to the southeast corner of New Mexico, the year that saw Maljamar discovered saw the discovery of the Hendricks field, one of the great fields of the West Texas Permian basin. The field was scarcely more than a stone's throw south of the New Mexico border, on a structural feature that obviously extended into New Mexico, yet for nearly three years the state line stopped the oil men cold.[4]

The Electra Story.   It would be difficult to find a more poignant example of blindering contributing to a tragic delay in problem solving than that of the ill-fated Electra.

On September 29, 1959, a Lockheed Electra flying over Buffalo, Texas, crashed, killing all 34 aboard. Why it crashed was a mystery. The weather had been clear and calm. No planes or rockets were reported in the region. The pilot had reported no difficulties a few minutes previous to the crash.

The tragedy touched off one of the greatest aviation accident investigations in history. Before it was over, the investigation had involved hundreds of engineers, pilots, and government investigators.

The investigation was intensive, extensive, expensive—and for six months almost completely futile. The Lockheed and Civil Aeronautics Board investigators had made the blindering assumption "that the Electra was a sound mechanism and had presumed that the Buffalo crash was caused by some inexplicable distortion of a basically solid plane."

A terrible price had to be paid for this blindering—for this delay in solving the problem. On March 17, 1960, another Electra with 63 aboard plummeted into soft earth near Tell City, Indiana.

The circumstances of the crash suddenly made it impossible to continue to assume that the Electra was a basically sound plane.

Now, the investigators concentrated on the design of the plane itself. And finally an answer came.

> As long as the Electra's outboard nacelles retained the stiffness for which they had been designed, the plane was safe and sound. But *if* the struts and

---

[3] From *This Fascinating Oil Business*, by Max W. Ball, copyright 1940, used by special permission of the publishers, The Bobbs-Merrill Co., Inc., p. 342.

[4] Ibid., pp. 358-59.

braces inside the nacelle structure cracked or otherwise loosened, and *if* the wing was jolted hard by air turbulence or by a sudden pull-up, and *if* the plane was moving at high speed at the time, a curious chain-reaction effect could be induced. Both the Electra's big, square-bladed propeller and its turbine engine turn at high speeds—the prop makes 1,280 revolutions and the turbine 13,820 revolutions a minute. Thus, when running, they comprise a huge gyroscope with all the same odd reactions to disturbance that children discover in toy gyroscopes at Christmas. When the sudden jolt caused the wing to flex and agitated a nacelle, this whole package of spinning metal, which projects far out in front of the leading edge of the wing, would begin wobbling in its mount, like a pointed forefinger with its tip describing a small circle.

The odds against this motion doing anything more than dampening or soothing the initial movement of the wing itself were enormous. But in the Electra the oscillating wing and the swirling power plant suddenly began "exchanging energy." Each deformation of the flexing wing forced the turbine to wobble more wildly. Every increase in the engine's wobble, in turn, fed new violence back into the fluctuation of the wing. As the wing's leading edge was twisted alternately upward and downward by this process, airflow added still more impetus to its movement. In a very few seconds, with all these tremendous forces working on it in lethal rhythm like a fat man jumping harder and harder on a springboard, the wing would snap off as though it were made of glass. The mystery—in the opinion of Lockheed, of the FAA, and of the airlines involved—was finally solved.[5]

Yes, finally solved, but what a horrendous price for a blindered delay.

More recently, there has been a rash of air crashes. Some of them involved the DC-10. This time, however, governmental, manufacturing, and carrier authorities have taken relatively swift remedial action. With the approximately 400 DC-10s in use worldwide, the cost ($10,000) per modification will be $4 million. But that seems trifling compared to the sparing of untold lives. Let's hope that this time they're right.

We can also hope that the dread Legionnaires' Disease (which killed 36 people and hospitalized 151 at an American Legion convention in Philadelphia in 1976) has been finally, if tardily, explained. The cause, according to Dr. Joseph McDade, a microbiologist with the U.S. Public Health Service Center for Disease Control, is apparently a new bacterium.[6]

The breakthrough occurred only when McDade, having ruled out other bacteria, decided upon a new approach—to look for a strange organism rather than a familiar one. The irony is that the deadly bacterium had

---

[5] "Brilliant Detection in Jet-Age Mystery," *Life*, July 25, 1960, p. 88. Reprinted by permission.

[6] Peter Gorner, "Legionella—the Rare Killer That Almost Got Away," *Chicago Tribune*, Section 2, May 31, 1982, pp. 1-2; and Allan Buckheim, M.D., "Legionnaires' Disease . . . ," *Chicago Tribune*, Section 5, February 8, 1990, p. 5.

been known to science as early as 1947, but only as a curiosity. No one knew it then as *pneumophilia* (grisly translation, lung-loving). It surfaced again in 1959. And then in 1965 an outbreak of a pneumonia-like disease killed 16 at St. Elizabeth's Hospital in Washington, D.C. The surmise now is that the lethal culprit was again pneumophilia—but it was not recognized as such.

Had blindering prevented the discovery of the cause then? Could the 187 Philadelphia casualties have been averted?

Blinder Names.   One cannot help wondering how long progress has been retarded by the assigning of inappropriate names. How much time was lost and how many lives were squandered by the term *malaria?* Contracted from the Italian word *mala aria* (bad air), the term perpetuated the erroneous notion that the disease was caused by the bad air of the swamps. And how long were the properties of *oxygen* concealed by its misleading name? Oxygen stems from the Greek term for *acid-producer*—but unfortunately oxygen does not produce acid! And how many bright and willing scientists were inhibited from even dreaming of the possibility that the *atom* (from the Greek for *indivisible*) could be split, largely because its *name* said that it could *not* be divided?

A compound blinder term is *guinea pig*, often a synonym for an experimental subject. First, it is not from Guinea (West Africa) but South America. Second, it is not a pig but a rodent. Third, it is not even the favored experimental animal, ranking only fifth following, respectively, the mouse, the rat, the chick, and the rabbit.

Perhaps the most dramatic blinder-busting in athletics occurred on May 6, 1954. That was the day Roger Bannister ran the mile in under four minutes. Until then, it seemed to have been carved in granite that the magical four-minute mile was simply beyond mere mortals. Bannister clearly opened the floodgates because in the next two years the four-minute mile was bettered 317 times! The record is now 3:46.31 minutes and the sub-four mile is the standard for world-class runners.

Gloria Steinem in *Advertising Age* alerts us that "working women" is a blinder term. It excludes homemakers. Instead, she says, we should talk about work outside the home or work inside the home and put an end to the semantic slavery of homemakers being classified as women who don't work.

The common cold continues to elude medical science, but at least a significant semantic breakthrough may have occurred. Dr. Martin Colburn of the University of Illinois has concluded from his studies that the common cold and cold weather have only the word *cold* in common. He has ascertained that cold weather *alone* does not cause colds. His explanation for the higher incidence of respiratory illnesses during cold weather is that we spend more time indoors in closer and more frequent proximity with people who bear the cold virus.

Undesirable Solutions

Blindering may not only retard or prevent the finding of appropriate, constructive solutions, but it may steer us toward improper, unintelligent, even dangerous solutions. As a young man, the renowned anthropologist Benjamin Lee Whorf served for some time as an analyst for an insurance company. He was solely concerned at first with the physical factors in fires and explosions, for example, defective wiring and the presence or lack of air spaces between metal flues and woodwork. But he soon began to notice certain human factors as well. He found that the way people defined or labeled a situation greatly influenced their behavior toward it. For example, he found that people tended to be extremely cautious around what they called "gasoline drums." Great care was taken to prevent smoking or striking matches in their vicinity. But when the drums were emptied and were thus now labeled "empty gasoline drums," caution was thrown to the winds. Cigarettes were smoked with abandon because the situation was now defined as safe. Ironically, the "empty" drums were *full* of gasoline vapors, and one spark could be sufficient to explode them—an enormously more dangerous circumstance than when they contained the liquid gasoline.[7]

Among other similar incidents, Whorf cited the case of the tannery drying room:

> A drying room for hides was arranged with a blower at one end to make a current of air along the room and thence outdoors through a vent at the other end. Fire started at a hot bearing on the blower, which blew the flames directly into the hides and fanned them along the room, destroying the entire stock. This hazardous setup followed naturally from the term "blower" with its linguistic equivalence to "that which blows," implying that its function necessarily is to "blow." Also its function is verbalized as "blowing air for drying," overlooking that it can blow other things, e.g., flames and sparks. In reality a blower simply makes a current of air and can exhaust as well as blow. It should have been installed at the vent end to draw the air over the hides, then through the hazard (its own casing and bearings) and thence outdoors.[8]

CORRECTIVES

It is obvious that blindering can be a serious hindrance in business, education, government, science, and even in our personal lives. How,

---

[7] From "The Name of the Situation as Affecting Behavior," by B. L. Whorf. Published in "The Relation of Habitual Thought and Behavior to Language," in *Language, Culture, and Personality: Essays in Memory of Edward Sapir*, ed. Leslie Spier et al. (Menasha, Wis.: Sapir Memorial Fund, 1941). This article, with the exception of the following incident involving the "blower," is reproduced in Case 17.3.

[8] Ibid.

then, can we cope with it? How can we eliminate it or at least minimize its destructive influence? The following suggestions are offered.

Remember, Defining = Neglecting

Blindering is the process of narrowing one's perception, of channeling one's vision of a situation, problem, phenomenon. These restrictions are frequently introduced by the verbal (and nonverbal) definitions that one assigns to the situation, and so on. To define is "to mark the limits or boundaries of." Thus, when I define the chair I am sitting on as a piece of office furniture, I am setting up certain restrictions. I am calling attention to those attributes that my chair has in common with other office furniture, such as that it is usually found indoors, in offices (rather than in homes or on lawns), that it is largely utilitarian (as opposed to decorative), and so forth. At the same time, however, my definition is neglecting a host of other aspects which my chair does not share with office furniture in general. My definition distracts attention from a myriad of details unique to my chair—among them its specific color, its weight, the textures of its plastic and steel surfaces, the tensile strengths of its various materials, its style, its molecular structure, its cost, its resale value, and the origins of its materials. In short, the process of defining inevitably involves the excluding of some (actually, most) details.

The crux is that, although definitions unavoidably neglect some aspects, it is nevertheless essential that we do define, delimit, categorize, classify, organize our data and experience. The practical implication, therefore, is that it is dangerous to *forget* that defining is necessarily a process of restricting and neglecting. Remember, in other words, that you are abstracting.[9]

Does My Definition Blinder Me?

Consider this experiment conducted with college students. One group was confronted with the problem of removing a ping-pong ball from the bottom of an upright rusty pipe. The students were not to change the position of the pipe in any way. In the room were a hammer, pliers, rulers, soda straws, pins, and a bucket of dirty water. After several futile attempts to fish the ball out with the various "tools," the group struck upon the idea of pouring the dirty water into the pipe and floating the ball up.

A second group of students was given the same problem, but with one change. Instead of the bucket of dirty water, a large pitcher of clean ice water, surrounded by crystal goblets, and set on a clean tablecloth, was placed in the room. These students never solved the problem. In this case

---

[9] The overly restrictive definition is likely to be the key hindrance in the problems of Case 17.1.

FIGURE 17.4

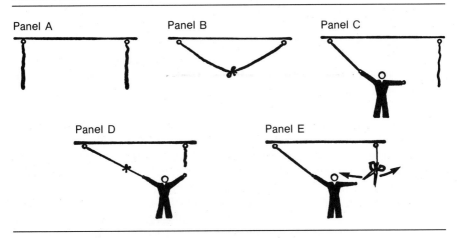

Panel A Panel B Panel C

Panel D Panel E

they defined the water as *drinking water*—and their definition blindered them from other possible uses.

The same phenomenon is illustrated by the popular scissors and strings experiment shown in Figure 17.4. The experimenter hangs two strings from the ceiling, as in panel A. The objective is to tie the two ends together, as in panel B. The strings are so far apart, however, that the subject cannot quite reach the second string while holding the first string, and vice versa (panel C). The subject is now given one instrument with which to solve the problem—a pair of scissors. Some individuals promptly snip off a length from one string and tie it to the other. The addition permits them to move closer to where the end was, but, alas! they find that the shorter string is now too high for them (panel D).

Their definition of scissors as a "cutter" inhibits their thinking of it as anything else. A pair of scissors, after all, is also a length, and tying it to the end of one of the strings might have given the additional length necessary to reach the second string. A pair of scissors is also a weight, and tying it to a string which could then be set in motion as a pendulum would be an effective solution to the problem (panel E).

It may be exceedingly helpful on occasion to ask oneself: "Am I blindering myself, restricting my approach to the problem by my definition, my sizing-up of the problem?"

How to Recognize Your Blinders

This is the crux, of course. How can we cope with our blinders if we do not recognize that we are being blindered in the first place? We scoff at the old wives' tales of yesteryear, but is it not possible that unwittingly we still accept a good many chimeras as valid?

Here are several practical, day-to-day techniques which will help us to uncover and eliminate our blinders.

Talk with an Outsider.   There are times when we have difficulty seeing the forest for the trees. We become so immersed in a problem that we become quite unable to see it from other vantage points. One of the chief values of outside consultants to a business institution is the freshness of outlook they bring. As dispassionate observers, unencumbered with the minutiae of problems, they are often able to suggest views and insights that have eluded those closer to the situation. Bell Telephone Laboratories deliberately assigns a new person to a research team from time to time in order to get the benefit of his or her naiveté. The newcomer is often able to stir up the thinking of the scientists who have been at the problems longer, and thus to prompt them to arrive at new and better approaches.

But the outsider need not always be a professional or even well versed in a particular problem area. Often a spouse, a friend, a parent, even a child, can help one see a problem in a new light. And not infrequently, as in nondirective counseling, the very process of explaining the problem to another, of making the effort to get someone else to see one's problem, helps one to break through self-created encasements.

Emotional problems are particularly vulnerable to blindering. Often individuals are too close to such problems to perceive them objectively. Here is a letter to an advice columnist from a clearly distraught wife—and the columnist, as the outsider, provides, happily, the obvious solution:

My husband is a minister. He does everything on a scheduled basis. And I mean *everything*.

Sunday is our night for lovemaking. I am not complaining, because I enjoy it as much as he does. But he is very big and strong and very physical. He's not rough or abusive, but he's very affectionate and puts a lot of enthusiasm into everything. To get to the point, on Monday morning I'm exhausted, and that's the morning I do my wash.

Any suggestions?

Tired on Monday

Dear Tired: Yes. Wash on Tuesday.

Kill "Killer" Phrases.   This apt coinage is by Charles H. Clark of Autonetics, Inc., who has compiled a list of phrases that squelch a new idea before it has a chance to be examined. "Let's be practical," "We've never done anything like that," "We've always done it this way," "It'll cost too much," "The boss won't like it," "It can't be done," "We're doing the best we can," and "The customers won't stand for it" are examples. Granted, some suggestions prove to be worthless or worse. But some, ridiculous or impractical at first hearing, may have a gold nugget in them—something which, if combined with other ideas, might prove exceedingly useful. The point is that the killer phrase will decapitate the infant idea before anyone has had the opportunity to dig for its gold, to give it a fair appraisal.

Brainstorm with a Group. Brainstorming, an idea-generating technique that swept the nation some years ago, has definite blinder-finding potential. The rules of the game are quite simple. A group of people meet to make suggestions relevant to a given problem area. The goal is quantity, not quality—the more ideas, the better. At first, no one evaluates the worth of the ideas. Only afterward are the ideas sifted through for possible pearls. The key antiblindering feature of brainstorming is the interpersonal excitement and stimulation generated among the group. A may say something that sets off B and C, who in turn mention something that triggers ideas from D, E, and F, and so on. Participants are urged to build upon or modify one another's ideas. The upshot is that ideas may appear that might never have occurred to the same people if they had been working as solitary thinkers.

However, brainstorming is not without its own blindering dangers. Without skilled leadership, the flow of ideas may get started down one relatively narrow channel—one idea merely pressing another deeper into this specialized rut. Good leadership can guide the ideas through a more comprehensive and useful area.

The next two suggestions also involve groups but with lessening degrees of interaction.

Use the Nominal Group Technique. The group in this approach exists largely in name only—thus, nominal group. True, the members are physically present and they are addressing the same problem. But, unlike brainstorming, there is relatively little interaction.

First, a problem is articulated and individuals independently list as many solutions as they can conceive. Next, in round-robin fashion, each person expresses a solution. Someone adds the idea to a master list. The process continues until all of the generated solutions have been recorded. The next phase is to clarify and evaluate (cite pros and cons) each solution, but not to arrive at a decision. Next, each member privately rank-orders the solutions. These individual priorities are tabulated and the aggregate evaluation of the solutions is revealed to the group.

Among its strengths, this method balances participation and influence of members. It produces a large number of creative ideas and a good deal of member satisfaction without exposing individuals to personal confrontation. Its prime limitation is that it can handle effectively only one problem at a time. Furthermore, the problem to be addressed should be quite specific and well-defined.

Use the Delphi Technique. This approach is useful when people cannot or for any reason do not meet face-to-face. The first phase is for the chairperson to send a statement of the problem to each participant. Each records potential solutions and returns them. The chairperson now summarizes them and sends a copy to each participant for appraisal and additional suggestions. These are again summarized and the process continues until a clear consensus appears, or a vote is taken.

This technique allows for the participation of a large number from a wide geographical area. Although not eliminated, social pressures are certainly reduced. The prime disadvantage is time; it generally takes a good deal of time to gather data from a widespread group. Perhaps with intercomputer capability, the intervals can be shortened. Any values of social interaction, however, are probably irretrievable.

Since the chairperson interprets and summarizes the individual inputs, that role is critical.

Start Anywhere—But Start.   How many times have you tackled a creative project and had difficulty in beginning? Perhaps it was a term paper, an essay, or a report, and the main heading or the lead sentence simply did not come, regardless of your efforts to grind it out. I have wasted hours, I am embarrassed to say, because I could not begin a chapter or an article or even a paragraph in a way that satisfied me. I finally discovered what others have known for years—that it is rarely necessary to begin at the beginning. The important thing is to start—start anywhere, but start. Often when I start where I can make a start, I come back to the beginning, and the chapter title or the lead line, or whatever it was that had me blocked, falls into place.

Try the Reversal Technique.   If your initial and seemingly normal reaction to a problem does not work, you might try just the reverse. Dr. Edward de Bono, director of the Cognitive Research Trust at Cambridge University, offers this illustration:

> An ambulance speeding along a narrow country road is suddenly confronted with a flock of sheep completely blocking the road. The "normal" response would be to try to drive through the sheep. Because the sheep would tend to walk away from you, that approach would be difficult and slow, as well as dangerous for the sheep. So, suggests de Bono, do just the reverse. Stop the vehicle, get out, and drive the sheep past your stationary vehicle.

The reversal technique can be an excellent blinder-buster because it frees one from the old and possibly fixated ways of looking at the problem. That in itself can be helpful—even if the reversal doesn't make immediate sense. But frequently an apparently ridiculous solution works brilliantly.

> A conscientious young couple I know found their lives alarmingly changed after the birth of their first child. The baby, it seemed, needed very little sleep.

Long past the age at which most infants settle into an acceptable nighttime routine, she continued to call for attention—at midnight, 2 A.M., 4 A.M., and so on. Her parents took turns walking the floor with her. ("We can't stand to hear her cry.") When, at 15 months, she still didn't sleep for more than two hours at a stretch, the pediatrician suggested a sedative. Both parents disliked the idea of drugging a baby. I proposed reversal—that the parents take the sedative—and they laughed . . . but they tried it. The very first night they slept soundly from 10 P.M. to 6 A.M. "If the baby cried, it couldn't have been for long," her mother said sheepishly. "I certainly didn't hear her." After three nights they gave up sedatives and discovered that their baby slept like an angel.

My favorite example of reversal comes from a used-car salesman who loathed his job because it sometimes involved unloading questionable cars on ignorant buyers. He longed to quit, but the only thing he knew was cars. In a moment of pure inspiration he jumped the fence: He set up a used-car locating-and-inspecting service to guide the innocent. For a modest fee he helps prospective buyers locate possible cars, lists the cars' present and potential problems with repair estimates and negotiates with the owner on price. As part of his service he guarantees that if certain components fail he will replace them, and if the car proves a total loss, he offers to buy it back. Not surprisingly, he makes more now than he did as a salesman—and is a lot happier.[10]

Redefine the Problem. Defining the problem too narrowly can lead to limited solutions—or poor solutions—to wit, the celebrated toilet seat case previously described. Dr. de Bono cites this example: The apartments in a certain high-rise building are being changed to offices. A key problem arises—the elevators are inadequate for the greater number of people using them. Visitors and employees are complaining of long waits. De Bono suggests that if you define the problem as "How can we reduce the waiting time?" the tenable solutions are few. Installing new elevators would be quite expensive. Speeding the elevators up might be dangerous. Staggering working hours could be very complex and might create more problems than it solves. However, if you state the problem as "How can we diminish visitor and employee impatience?" many more alternatives arise. For example, provide comfortable chairs and couches near the elevators; install snack food vending machines nearby; put up a bulletin board with interesting information (suggestion box questions and answers, news about employees and organizational tenants, social notices); provide mirrors—a sure focus of interest. The broader definition of the problem permits moving freely beyond the problem's initially apparent boundaries.

---

[10] Fredelle Maynard, "How to Solve Problems like an Expert," *Woman's Day,* April 1976, p. 171. Excerpt reprinted by permission of *Woman's Day Magazine.* Copyright © 1976 by CBS Publications, Inc.

"Most people," states one management consultant, "formulate the wrong questions. It's the difference between asking, 'How can I build a better mousetrap?' and 'How can I get rid of mice?' The first question limits you; the second frees you to explore new, offbeat solutions."

The Namibian Directorate of Nature Conservation a few years ago had need of a redefinition. The African black rhinocerous had been hunted almost to extinction. The traditional conception of the problem: How can we prevent poachers from killing the rhinos? The standard remedy was to keep predators and prey separated from each other. That approach was usually costly as well as ineffective.

But they asked a new question: *Why* are poachers killing the animals? Answer: In some quarters, powdered rhino horn is a highly prized aphrodisiac. To the poacher, the black rhino was a gold mine on the hoof.

This led to another problem redefinition: How can we eliminate the poachers' incentive for killing the rhinos? Answer: Surgically remove the horn, without harming the animal, before the poacher gets there.

And it's working! Authorities are delighted that the black rhinos are surviving—even thriving. Tourists are bringing in badly needed capital to see the beasts in their native habitat.

Even the rhinos seem content. Admittedly, they didn't take kindly to the surgery and had to be tranquilized. But the amputation has had no apparent bad aftereffects. The only ones unhappy with the situation are frustrated poachers and amatory potion consumers.

Conservationists are considering the use of this tactic to save other animals. The idea probably has limitations, though, unless someone can find a way for leopards, zebras, crocodiles, snakes, and so on to fare without their respective skins.

Use Results-Oriented Planning. The Center for Constructive Change (Durham, New Hampshire) devised this technique. Its essence is to resist focusing on personalities and methods, but to define clear goals and then work backward.

Dr. Thomas Marshall, CCC vice president, illustrates the center's approach with an explosive situation recently faced by a Pittsburgh labor relations manager. A foreman—a steady, honest, hardworking employee of 30 years— wanted to fire a young black whose performance and absentee record were unsatisfactory. The union steward charged racial prejudice and a meeting was set up. Ordinarily, Dr. Marshall suggests, the procedure would have been "Let's get the facts," followed by a shouting match of accusation and counteraccusation. Whatever the eventual decision, it would seem arbitrary and unfair to the loser.

The labor manager, a CCC graduate, avoided this trap. He began by addressing the young black: "The purpose of this meeting is to help you

Well, yes. Then, to the foreman, he said: "It's your job to help him become an efficient worker, right?" Sure. "All right," the manager continued. "Now if everything in your department were going the way you'd like it, what would be happening?" The foreman was happy to elaborate: This young fellow would get to work every day on time; he would produce a certain number of spark plugs, a certain maximum of scrap (unusable parts). Once the goal was defined, the manager moved backward. Are the workers informed of their production record daily? No? Well, wouldn't it help if they had this information?

Then it was the worker's turn. How often had he been absent in the past month? Could he improve that record? How about making a plan for the next few weeks—a quota of so many spark plugs per day the first week, a maximum of one absence per month. The end result was a plan workable because it has built-in controls and checks, has been accepted by both parties—and doesn't depend for its success on changing individuals. (The foreman doesn't have to get over his prejudice against blacks, if indeed he has one.). . . .

. . . The CCC approach would be to set aside the immediate disagreement—or, rather, to see the "problem" as an opportunity for creative planning. "Don't focus on people, problems or on the present environment," Dr. Marshall says, "but on *where you want to be.* Instead of blaming the other person, concentrate on setting up objectives together, then work out strategies to promote those objectives."[11]

Break a Set.   A set, in the psychological sense, is the readiness of the organism to respond in a particular way. Breaking a set, then, frees one of habitual ways of perceiving and coping. It liberates one from culturebound and unchallenged assumptions. This vignette usually discloses one such assumption:

The scene is an office; one of the secretaries is dying. Her water carafe has been poisoned. Three executives—Archer, Baxter, and Cummings—are looking on helplessly. The police arrive. Just before she expires, the young woman, without looking at or pointing at any of the executives, gasps: "He did it!" Why was Baxter arrested?[12]

Breaking this kind of cultural set opens up new avenues for problem-solving. My housecleaner, the most efficient I've ever had, is a vigorous 25-year-old male. Laid off from a sandblasting job that he hated, he was without work a long time. But then he noticed the number of want ads for domestic help and wondered why domestic help was considered female. Men should be especially good at washing floors, putting up storm windows, cleaning garages and basements, he thought. This enterprising fellow now has a truck, two male assistants and a business that occupies him seven days a week.[13]

---

[11] Ibid., p. 173.

[12] Because Archer and Cummings are women. If this answer doesn't immediately occur to the problem-solver, could the culprit be our culture, which has conditioned us (up till now, at least) to think of executives as men?

[13] Maynard, "How to Solve Problems," p. 174.

List and Analyze the Components.   This technique was originally developed to promote the invention and improvement of products. It consists of examining the individual parts of a situation or an object with a view to determining how each part could be improved. A screwdriver, for example, traditionally consists of a wooden handle, a round steel shank, and a wedge-shaped end that is inserted into a screw slot. To produce a better screwdriver, we could consider how to improve each component. Could the wooden handle be replaced by plastic or rubber? It would be less likely to split, perhaps cheaper to produce, and so on. Would a square or hexagonal shank allow for the application of greater torque with a wrench or a pair of pliers? And so forth.

Capitalize upon Apparent Disadvantages.   The key to this technique is to focus not on "How can I minimize the liability?" but on "How can I make the most of it?" A producer of jams, jellies, and so on, did this admirably well: "With a name like Smuckers, it's got to be good."

I know a high school teacher whose classes were demoralized by drugs. Her students were much more enthralled with marijuana supply sources and prices than with homework. More often than not, they came to class stoned. Instead of ignoring the drug problem, the teacher made it the focal point of the year's work. She had the students do research on the history of marijuana laws and on the effects of amphetamines, cocaine, and LSD; conduct interviews at a halfway house; and write pro and con letters concerning drug laws to the news media and lawmakers. The teacher feels that she never had a better class.

A young woman who had just graduated with a major in advertising also used a disadvantage to her advantage. She wanted to join a top New York firm. Her friends tried to discourage her. Better join a small company first and get some experience, they said—no major would hire a neophyte. Undaunted, she applied to the firm of her choice. As predicted, one of the first questions put to her was: "What experience do you have?" Her forthright answer: "Absolutely none. I want to learn this profession from a top-notch company. Hire me, and train me *your* way. I won't have to unlearn a lot of things I learned with other organizations." She got the job.

Break the Tension Cycle.   Sometimes you find yourself working on a problem, making reasonable headway, when suddenly there's a brick wall. You are blocked, stymied. Most people back off a few feet and run headlong at the wall to butt it down. It doesn't give, so they try it again—and again—and again. Ironically, the more frustrated they become in attacking problems, the tenser they become. The more tense, the more fixated, the less insight—the less likelihood of noticing that there may be other ways of dealing with a brick wall, perhaps going over, under, or around it. And thus the *tension cycle,* one of the most effective deterrents to problem solving, takes over.

There are several ways to break the tension cycle—among them, leaving the area of frustration, learning to relax physically the individual members of the body, participating in an unrelated activity, and so on. The last is my favorite. If I find myself stymied in my work and beginning to grow tense, I shift to another area of the same work. If this is not effective, I pull out of my desk a list of previously planned short-term and reasonably agreeable tasks. Then I spend 20 minutes, say, taking a book to the library—or out of the library, or answering a letter, or reorganizing my bookshelves, or just taking a walk around the block. When I return to my original work I am invariably more relaxed, and quite often I can now see a solution to the problem that I had not noticed before. Regardless of what you call it—intuition, the subconscious, what-have-you—there does appear to be something working inside us even if we are not fully aware of it, and often it works more efficiently when we are not consciously holding the reins.

Distinguish among Your Deadlines. One of the greatest sources of personal tension in our modern world is the well-known deadline. But the relationship between deadline tension and blindering is not always clear. How is it that some people seem to work well under deadline pressure while others go to pieces? Part of the confusion may lie in the ambiguity of the term *deadline*. There are at least three types of deadlines.

1. *Those that are externally imposed and unavoidable.* Some people, especially those involved in the news media, work with heavy deadlines hanging over them constantly. Evidently they accommodate themselves to the pressure of time, and work with great efficiency and surprising ease. For most of us, however, unavoidable deadlines are rare occurrences. Most of our deadlines are of the following two kinds.

2. *Those that are self-imposed.* Among individuals who tend toward perfectionism there is the inclination to set up arbitrary deadlines for themselves. Before long, the deadlines seem to become quite demanding, and the tension cycle is likely to set in. Self-imposed deadlines may be helpful stimulators and guides, so long as we recognize them as such; but if we let them take on the guise of externally imposed unavoidable deadlines, we are inviting tension and blindering.

3. *Those that are created through procrastination.* There are probably some students who do not procrastinate, but by and large they have avoided my classes. These deadlines actually exist, of course, but better planning could have made them less formidable. But advice of this sort is usually futile, for procrastinators usually rationalize that they work better under pressure anyway—and perhaps they do. They certainly have had a great deal of experience under these conditions!

Perhaps the best overall antidote for blindering is expressed by the motto of the Air University, *Proficimus more irrenti*, usually translated as

"Progress unhindered by tradition." Major General M. K. Deichelmann phrased it more pragmatically as "Stay loose, boy—stay loose."

Discussion Questions

1. Precisely what is blindering? How does it occur? Why? What are its potential dangers? What measures help to prevent or correct it?

2. How many blinder names or phrases can you think of?

3. The tension cycle was described as a cyclical process of frustration leading to direct attack on the blockage, which in turn increases frustration, which in turn leads to more fixated attacks, and so on. How can we know when we are withdrawing gracefully or giving up too easily?

4. Does blindering seem to be related to other concepts in the book?

5. Report upon an incident, perhaps involving yourself, in which blindering occurred. How and why did it occur? What could have prevented it or ameliorated its consequences? What measures could prevent its recurrence?

CASES

CASE 17.1

Puzzles to Ponder

Here are some conundrums to contemplate. Caution: You may encounter a trick in each of them. But the trick is likely to be a *self-imposed limitation—a blinder*. You may unconsciously assume that you *must* (or must *not*) solve the problem in a certain way. So give yourself a pat on the back if you not only solve the problem but spot the key *blinder*—the false assumption which hampers solving the problem. (If your time is short or your morale is low or your will is weak, you will find the answers following Case 17.7, on pages 544–45.).

1. George Carson and his son, Mike, were speeding along Route 30 one rainy evening when suddenly their car skidded off the road. George was killed instantly, but Mike, though seriously injured, was still alive when the police arrived. He was rushed to the hospital and immediately wheeled into the emergency room. The old surgeon looked at the patient and gasped: "My God! I can't operate—he's my son!"

    How could the surgeon be correct about Mike's identity? (Hint: Mike has two parents and no stepparents.)

    Answer: _____

    Blinder: _____

2. Move one of these coins once so there are five coins in each row.

    Answer: _____

    Blinder: _____

3. The numbers below are in this order for a reason. What is it?
   8—5—4—9—1—7—6—10—3—2—0

   Answer: _____

   Blinder: _____

4. O—T—T—F—F—S—S—E—N—T— — — — —
   What are the next three letters?

   Answer: _____

   Blinder: _____

5. Three men checked in and paid $30 for a hotel room. Later the clerk discovered that he had overcharged them $5. He gave Jake, the bellman, five one-dollar bills to return to them. Jake, resentful that the men had failed to tip him for carrying their luggage, pocketed $2 and gave a dollar to each of the men. Thus, the men had paid $27 for the room. However, $27 plus the $2 Jake kept equals $29.
   What happened to the extra $1?

   Answer: _____
   _____

   Blinder: _____
   _____

6. Ten gumball machines, each with a glass globe loaded with gumballs, are mounted on a heavy table. You have it on good authority that nine of the machines dispense balls weighing one ounce each. The remaining machine dispenses half-ounce balls. The appearance (size, shape, color) of the balls from all the machines is identical.

   Using a spring scale (not a set of balances) such as is found in the grocery store, how can you determine which machine is giving the half-ounce gumballs? There are some restrictions:

   1. You *must* use the scale to *solve* the problem, not merely to *verify* a solution.
   2. Only *one* use of the scale—that is, one registration of the dial—is permitted. Each time you add or subtract a gumball is considered a separate weighing.

   Answer: _____
   _____

   Blinder: _____
   _____

7. What do these letters have in common: A—E—F—H—I—L—M—N—O—R—S—X? What do these letters have in common: B—C—D—G—J—K—P—Q—T—V—W—Y—X? Why could U belong to either group?

   Answer: _____

   _____

   Blinder: _____

   _____

8. What number comes next in this mathematical sequence?
   769 378 168 48 32

   Answer: _____

   Blinder: _____

9. What did Attila the Hun and Felix the Cat have in common?

   Answer: _____

   Blinder: _____

CASE 17.2

The Rawley Company*

The Rawley Company, manufacturers of custom-made metal-forming machinery, had been in business for over half a century. It was located in a large midwestern city and employed approximately 100 persons. Executives of Rawley had become aware that their company's sales had fallen considerably short of its production capacity. Stimulated by the company's president, James Howe, a dynamic man with an inquiring mind, the firm decided to approach the problem through the cooperative efforts of a group of persons to be known as the Sales Council.

The Sales Council was to be composed of representatives of various departments of the firm, some of which were not conventionally concerned with sales. The representatives and their departments included:

James Howe, *president* (designer, engineer, sales)

Donald Brewster, *vice president* (assistant general manager, manager of sales)

Ramona Prescott, *vice president and treasurer*

Clifford Carlin, *assistant vice president* (production manager)

Ralph Goodwin, *assistant vice president* (warehouse manager)

_____

* All names have been disguised. Printed by permission of the author, whose name has been withheld by request.

Arthur Howard, *assistant sales manager*

Chester Green, *Eastern sales*

Fred Lemec, *in charge of machinery orders*

Russell Thurston, *engineer and salesman*

The Sales Council was to operate on the assumption that ultimately every employee was directly or indirectly related to the sale of the company's products. Consequently, the combined thinking of representatives of these various sections might produce helpful suggestions for their common objective, increased sales.

In order to expedite the meetings of the Sales Council, a professor of interpersonal communication from a local university was called in to act as moderator. It was felt that he should act as a disinterested chairman whose primary responsibility was simply to help the members of the group to understand one another as clearly and as accurately as possible. Specifically, he was to repeat and/or paraphrase the statement of each speaker immediately after the speaker had finished making it. This was to give the speaker the feeling that at least one other person understood what he or she had tried to communicate. Furthermore, all other members of the Sales Council were to have the opportunity to agree or to disagree with the accuracy of the moderator's restatement of the speaker's statement until, theoretically, each person present was satisfied that he or she and the moderator had understood the speaker.

Shortly before the first Sales Council meetings were to be held, some of Rawley's executives and the professor met for an orientation session in a conference room in a nearby restaurant. The meeting was to explain to the professor what the Sales Council was, what its objectives were, and what the professor's role as moderator was to be.

After each executive present had expressed his or her view of these points, the professor, David Wilson, asked to have the floor.

Wilson: Gentlemen, I'd like to try to sum up what I think you have been saying about the Sales Council so that you can tell me if you think I understand you. As I get the picture, you are proposing an experiment in group problem solving. Casting this approach in my own frame of reference, this going to be essentially a group—something like the conventional classroom situation—in which the lines of communication are directly between teacher and students and only indirectly from student to student. . . .

Howe *(acting as chairman, breaks in):* I see heads shaking in disagreement, Dave. Ralph?

Goodwin: Dave, I don't like your analogy. This is not going to be a classroom situation at all. The moderator isn't supposed to act as an autocrat. He's trying to achieve the cooperation and communication of the group at a high level. . . .

Wilson: I think you're right about the analogy being a poor one, but I only used it to describe the direction of the communication lines as I see them in the Sales Council. . . .

Carlin: No offense meant, Dave, but you can't presume to act the role of a teacher, the subject-matter expert. You don't have the company background for it.

Ten minutes later:

Wilson: Now, getting specifically to the role of the moderator. . . . The way I get it, he is to listen to Speaker A, filter through his own personality and background what he thinks A has said, and express it to the group. . . .

Goodwin: You don't filter anything. Your job is to repeat what A has said.

Carlin: Well, he's to *paraphrase* what A has said so that A will know that at least one person has understood him.

Wilson: I get that, but how can I possibly relay a man's statement, other than through the sheer repetition of his exact same words, unless I interpret, size up what he has said? In other words, isn't it inevitable that I filter what comes to me through my own nervous system, my personality, my background?

Goodwin: Filtering is changing the substance you are conveying—that isn't your job.

Carlin: You don't *filter*—you *reflect* what has been said.

Wilson: Perhaps "filter" has been a bad figure of speech, but even in reflecting the other fellow's statement, must I not determine his meaning for myself—and how can I size up the meaning unless I relate his words to my own unique frame of experience?

At this point, dinner was announced and the subject was dropped.

Discussion Questions

1. What do you think of the conference communication technique proposed by the Sales Council?

2. Speech by speech, how do you analyze the communication occurring in this case?

3. Who is responsible for this wheel-spinning?

4. What does this case have to do with *blindering?*

CASE 17.3

The Name of the Situation as Affecting Behavior*
B. L. Whorf

There will probably be general assent to the proposition that an accepted pattern of using words is often prior to certain lines of thinking and forms of behavior, but he who assents often sees in such a statement nothing more than a platitudinous recognition of the hypnotic power of philosophical and learned terminology on the one hand or of catchwords, slogans, and rallying-cries on the other. To see only thus far is to miss the point of one of the important interconnections which Sapir saw between language, culture, and psychology. . . . It is not so much in these special uses of language as in its constant ways of arranging data and its most ordinary everyday analysis of phenomena that we need to recognize the influence it has on other activities, cultural and personal.

I came in touch with an aspect of this problem before I had studied under Dr. Sapir, and in a field usually considered remote from linguistics. It was in the course of my professional work for a fire insurance company, in which I undertook the task of analyzing many hundreds of reports of circumstances surrounding the start of fires, and in some cases, of explosions. My analysis was directed toward purely physical conditions, such as defective wiring, presence or lack of air spaces between metal flues and woodwork, etc., and the results were presented in these terms. Indeed it was undertaken with no thought that any other significances would or could be revealed. But in due course it became evident that not only a physical situation *qua* physics, but the meaning of that situation to people, was sometimes a factor, through the behavior of the people, in the start of the fire. And this factor of meaning was clearest when it was a *linguistic meaning,* residing in the name or the linguistic description commonly applied to the situation. Thus around a storage of what are called "gasoline drums," behavior will tend to a certain type, that is, great care will be exercised; while around a storage of what are called "empty gasoline drums" it will tend to be different—careless, with little repression of smoking or tossing cigarette stubs about. Yet the "empty" drums are perhaps the more dangerous, since they contain explosive vapor. Physically the situation is hazardous, but the linguistic analysis according to regular analogy must employ the word *empty*, which inevitably suggests lack of hazard. The word *empty* is used in two linguistic patterns: (1) as a virtual synonym for "null and void, negative, inert," (2) applied in analysis of physical situations without regard to, e.g., vapor, liquid vestiges, or stray

---

* From "The Relation of Habitual Thought and Behavior to Language," in *Language, Culture, and Personality: Essays in Memory of Edward Sapir,* ed. Leslie Spier et al. (Menasha, Wis.: Sapir Memorial Fund, 1941), pp. 75-77. Reprinted by permission.

rubbish, in the container. The situation is named in one pattern (2) and the name is then "acted out" or "lived up to" in another (1); this being a general formula for the linguistic conditioning of behavior into hazardous forms.

In a wood distillation plant, the metal stills were insulated with a composition prepared from limestone and called at the plant "spun limestone." No attempt was made to protect this covering from excessive heat or the contact of flame. After a period of use the fire below one of the stills spread to the "limestone," which to everyone's great surprise burned vigorously. Exposure to acetic acid fumes from the stills had converted part of the limestone (calcium carbonate) to calcium acetate. This, when heated in a fire, decomposes, forming inflammable acetone. Behavior that tolerated fire close to the covering was induced by use of the name "limestone," which because it ends in "stone" implies noncombustibility.

A huge iron kettle of boiling varnish was observed to be overheated, nearing the temperature at which it would ignite. The operator moved it off the fire and ran it on its wheels to a distance, but did not cover it. In a minute or so the varnish ignited. Here the linguistic influence is more complex; it is due to the metaphorical objectifying (of which more later) of "cause" as contact or the spatial juxtaposition of "things"—to analyzing the situation as "on" versus "off" the fire. In reality the stage when the external fire was the main factor had passed; the overheating was now an internal process of convection in the varnish from the intensely heated kettle, and still continued when off the fire.

An electric glow heater on the wall was little used, and for one workman had the meaning of a convenient coat-hanger. At night a watchman entered and snapped a switch, which action he verbalized as "turning on the light." No light appeared, and this result he verbalized as "light is burned out." He could not see the glow of the heater because of the old coat hung on it. Soon the heater ignited the coat, which set fire to the building.

A tannery discharged waste water containing animal matter into an outdoor settling basin partly roofed with wood and partly open. This situation is one that ordinarily would be verbalized as "pool of water." A workman had occasion to light a blowtorch nearby, and threw his match into the water. But the decomposing waste matter was evolving gas under the wood cover, so that the setup was the reverse of "watery." An instant flare of flame ignited the woodwork, and the fire quickly spread into the adjoining building. . . .

Beside a coal-fired melting pot for lead reclaiming was dumped a pile of "scrap lead"—a misleading verbalization, for it consisted of the lead sheets of old radio condensers, which still had paraffin paper between them. Soon the paraffin blazed up and fired the roof, half of which was burned off.

Such examples, which could be greatly multiplied, will suffice to show how the cue to a certain line of behavior is often given by the analogies of the linguistic formula in which the situation is spoken of, and by which to some degree it is analyzed, classified, and allotted its place in that world which is "to a large extent unconsciously built up on the language habits of the group." And we always assume that the linguistic analysis made by our group reflects reality better than it does.

Discussion Questions

1. What was the central point of this article?
2. What does it have to do with *blindering?*

CASE 17.4

The Roberts Machine Company*

The Roberts Machine Company was a medium-sized firm which produced various types of shop machines—lathes, punch presses, drill presses, milling machines, and so forth. The sales department held a dinner meeting every other month. After dinner, in a hotel private dining room, Gordon Swift, sales manager, conducted a business meeting. The October meeting was attended by Swift, Al Rockland, assistant sales manager, and 11 salesmen, 6 of whom had more than 15 years of service with Roberts. Also present was James Jacobs, sales manager of Electro-Products, Inc., manufacturers of electrical components for home appliances. Jacobs was a personal friend of Swift and known to most of the men. He had been invited to observe the meeting. Swift had previously sat in on one of Jacobs' sales conferences.

The purpose of the meeting was to review a proposed new method for communicating product information to Roberts' dealers, using an audiocassette tape to accompany the firm's catalog. The dealer, in his own shop or home, could play the tape as he leafed through the Roberts catalog. Swift felt that the pictures and copy of the catalog alone did not communicate adequately the sales appeal of their product line. The tape, in his words, "added another dimension to product communication."

Swift opened the meeting by explaining the purpose of the catalog-tape technique and asked each salesman to play the role of a dealer as he listened to the record. The salesmen leafed through the catalog as the tape called attention to the advantages of each item.

When the tape ended, Swift asked for comments. Most of the men contributed to the informal discussion which followed. Mr. Jacobs did not participate.

Pros and cons of the technique were discussed; most seemed to agree that the catalog-tape idea was basically sound—a way of communicating

---

* All names and organizational designations have been disguised. Published by Northwestern University. Reprinted by permission.

to the dealer in two media, visually and aurally. A few wondered whether it might be too difficult for a man to listen, look at pictures, and read text at the same time.

There was some disagreement about whose voice should be used on the cassette. Several felt that a professional announcer should do the job; the majority preferred Mr. Swift as narrator. One of the salesmen suggested that the sales manager's voice would add a note of warmth and make the process seem more personal than the colder media of catalogs, pamphlets, and newsletters.

Some thought that the tape increased the accuracy of the communication—the emphasis and inflection of the narrator's voice would help convey information more precisely than the written word alone. One man wondered whether the average dealer would have facilities for playing the cassette. Others felt that virtually every home had a tape player these days.

After the discussion had continued for some 30 minutes, one of the younger salesmen, Ed Knoll, commented: "As long as we're talking about dealer communication, I think we could capitalize on the visual angle, too. I wonder if we couldn't take some pictures of several of our machines in action. You know, motion pictures of them."

There was an audible groan from several other salesmen—one of them quickly brought up another topic.

Jacobs was puzzled about the apparent indifference and negative reactions to Knoll's idea.

Although it was not strictly relevant to the catalog-tape proposal, Jacobs thought that the idea might have potential value for Roberts' overall sales program. The Roberts machines were intricate. Motion shots of machines in action could show what words and still pictures could not possibly convey. Moreover, Jacobs had always considered Knoll a bright, hardworking young man, who had shown drive and imagination during his three years with the firm. But Jacobs remained silent as the meeting continued for another hour.

At nine o'clock, Swift began to conclude the discussion.

Swift: Well, gentlemen, I think we've kicked this around long enough, and I appreciate your comments. Al and I will get our heads together next week, and we'll let you know whether or not we decide to go ahead with the catalog-tape idea.

But right now, I'd like to hear what our friend, Jim Jacobs, has to say about the performance we put on for him. He's been sitting here soaking it all in. Any reactions, Jim?

Jacobs: You're right, Gordon, I have been soaking it all in, which is a bit unusual for me. I'm usually running the show rather than watching it—and I certainly appreciate your invitation. I'd like to do this more often.

Now, if you don't mind, Gordon, I wonder if I could impose upon you and your men for about three minutes.

Swift: Go right ahead, Jim. Got something cooked up?

Jacobs: Well, in a way. You men all know how enthusiastic Gordon is about the subject of communication. And most of you know that I feel pretty much the same way. Gordon and I have spent hours at a stretch talking about the problems of communication in business. Heaven only knows, we've got them in our plant—and in my own department, too. Now, there was one point in this meeting that particularly interested me. You all recall that remark of Ed Knoll's about pictures of some of your machines in action? Well, I wonder if you'd oblige me by writing a short sentence or two about your reaction to Ed's comment. Don't bother to sign your name.

Each salesman wrote a brief note and passed it to Jacobs, who said: "Thank you very much, gentlemen. You might be interested in what I'm up to. Frankly, it's just a little experiment I thought of while I was sitting with my ears open for a change—instead of my mouth. I really don't know what to expect from it.

"But Gordon is giving me a lift home, so I imagine you'll be getting a feedback through him."

"Fine, Jim," Swift replied, "this might be interesting at that. And now, unless anyone has anything else to add, let's adjourn the meeting."

Swift began talking with several salesmen at the door while others were collecting their papers and getting their coats. Jacobs walked over to Knoll and said: "Ed, I wonder if you would tell me just what you had in mind with your idea?"

Knoll: Well, Mr. Jacobs, I thought we could shoot a short film on our own—probably wouldn't run more than $10. I have a VHS camcorder, and if the company would buy the videotape and let me rig up a few lights—

Jacobs: Were you suggesting that the videotape would be coordinated with the audiotape?

Knoll: Oh, no—it would be entirely apart from the catalog and audiotape. It would be just another way of communicating with our dealers and their customers, too. It could be placed on a regular VCR. Our machines are too big, too expensive, and there are too many models for our dealers to stock the complete line. The videotape would be a way of showing our machines in actual operation.

Jacobs thanked Knoll and joined Swift, who was waiting to drive him home. As they rode, Jacobs read the statements aloud. There were 11 of them:

Cost!!!![1]

Oh, no! Not the movie boys again!

That isn't the kind of thing we can afford to do now.

Coupled with the tape and review of the catalog, the film would be a sharp idea.

Necessity of having a projector and screen besides a tape player—too much apparatus.

Completely irrelevant in terms of a critique of the tape idea.

The idea is for catalogs and tapes to be sent out and heard. If they are going to show movies, you don't need catalogs.

Vision with the tape sounded like a good idea.

A sound film would be better than a film with a separate tape.

Book, voice, and pictures—too much to absorb.

That's all we need—another unusable film!

Discussion Questions

1. Is there any significance in the fact that the videotape suggestion came from Knoll?

2. Assuming the idea had merit, what do you think of how Knoll expressed it?

3. How do you analyze the various reactions to Knoll's suggestion?

4. What connection, if any, does *blindering* have with this case?

5. Are other patterns of miscommunication involved here?

6. Jacobs seemed to be on Knoll's wavelength from the outset. Why?

CASE 17.5

Flies, Typhoid, and Publicity*

It was while I was working at the Memorial Institute that an opportunity came for me to bring my scientific training to bear on a problem at Hull House. (My efforts in the baby clinic could not be called scientific.) This was in the fall of 1902, when I came back from Mackinac to find Chicago in the grip of one of her worst epidemics of typhoid fever. At that time the water, drawn from the lake, was not chlorinated; the only precaution taken against dangerous pollution was to make daily cultures of samples from the different pumping stations and the next day, when the cultures had had time to develop, publish the results and tell the pulic whether or not to boil water. It was assumed that housewives would look up these instructions every day, and act accordingly, but the actual result was that

---

[1] Swift told Jacobs that the Roberts Company had had an unpleasant, costly experience with a product motion picture film prepared by a professional firm. The film had cost $30,000 and for various reasons had never been used.

* From Alice Hamilton, M.D., *Exploring the Dangerous Trades.* (Boston: Little, Brown, 1943). Reprinted by permission.

typhoid was endemic in Chicago and periodically it reached epidemic proportions. On this particular occasion Hull House was the center of the hardest-struck region of the city—why, nobody knew. Miss Addams said she thought a bacteriologist ought to be able to discover the reason.

It was certainly not a simple problem. The pumping station which sent water to the 19th Ward sent it to a wide section of the West Side; the milk supply was the same as that for neighboring wards. There must be some local condition to account for the excessive number of cases. As I prowled about the streets and the ramshackle wooden tenement houses I saw the outdoor privies (forbidden by law but flourishing nevertheless), some of them in backyards below the level of the street and overflowing in heavy rains; the wretched water closets indoors, one for four or more families, filthy and with the plumbing out of order because nobody was responsible for cleaning or repairs; and swarms of flies everywhere. Here, I thought, was the solution to the problem. The flies were feeding on typhoid-infected excreta and then lighting on food and milk. During the Spanish-American War, we lost more men from typhoid fever than from Spanish bullets. Vaughan, Shakespeare, and Reed had made a study of conditions in camps—open latrines, unscreened food—which led them to attribute an important role in the spread of typhoid fever to the house fly. That was what started the "Swat the fly" campaign.

Naturally, my theory had to be put to the test, so, with two of the residents to help me, Maude Gernon and Gertrude Howe, I went forth to collect flies—from privies and kitchens and filthy water closets. We would drop the flies into tubes of broth and I would take them to the laboratory, incubate the tubes, and plate them out at varying intervals. It was a triumph to find the typhoid bacillus and I hastened to write up the discovery and its background for presentation before the Chicago Medical Society. This was just the sort of thing to catch public attention: It was simple and easily understood; it fitted in with the revelations made during the Spanish War of the deadly activities of house flies, and it explained why the slums had so much more typhoid than the well-screened and decently drained homes of the well-to-do.

I am sure I gained more kudos from my paper on flies and typhoid than from any other piece of work I ever did. Even today I sometimes hear an echo of it. In Chicago the effect was most gratifying; a public inquiry resulted in a complete reorganization of the Health Department under a chief loaned by the Public Health Service, and an expert was put in charge of tenement-house inspection. But unfortunately my gratification over my part in all this did not last long. After the tumult had died down I discovered a fact that never gained much publicity but was well-authenticated. My flies had had little or nothing to do with the cases of typhoid in the 19th Ward. The cause was simpler but so much more discreditable that the Board of Health had not dared reveal it. It seems that in our local pumping station, on West Harrison Street, near Halsted, a break had occurred which resulted in an escape of sewage into the water pipes, and for three days our neighborhood drank that water before the leak was discovered and stopped. This was after the epidemic had started. The truth was more shocking than my ingenious theory, and it never came to light, as far as the public was concerned. For years, although I did my best to lay to rest the ghosts of those flies, they haunted me and mortified me, compelling me again and again to explain to deeply impressed audiences that the dramatic story their chairman had just rehearsed had little foundation in fact.

Discussion Questions

1. Supposedly, blindering is involved in this case. How?

2. How does this case compare with "The Electra Story (pages 516-17)?

CASE 17.6

The Windy City

Chicago's nickname is "The Windy City." Many people, especially visitors, think of Chicago as being a very windy city.

The U.S. Weather Bureau's National Climate Center lists Chicago as *16th* in windiness among America's cities. Chicago's average wind speed is 10.4 mph. The top five on the center's list:

City	Mph
1. Great Falls, Montana	13.1
2. Oklahoma City, Oklahoma	13.0
3. Boston, Massachusetts	12.9
4. Cheyenne, Wyoming	12.8
5. Wichita, Kansas	12.7

Discussion Question

What does the above combination of statements have to do with this chapter?

CASE 17.7

A Very Clean Job*

When the time came for the annual audit of the Bronson Company, Mort Smith was pleased to receive the assignment again. Smith, senior auditor for McKinley, Karten, and Steiner, public accountants, had handled the Bronson audit for nine years and was very familiar with the company's system. As he explained to his superior, "It's a joy to do the Bronson

---

* All names have been disguised.

job. Their controller, Barry Revsine, is a CPA himself, and you can always count on his giving you a very clean job."

When Smith and Scott Petersen, a new junior on his first job, arrived at the Bronson Company, Revsine handed them a 30-page trial balance. During the course of the audit, approximately 20 adjusting journal entries were made. When the audit work was completed, Smith instructed Petersen to extend the trial balance, foot it, and finalize it.

Sometime later Petersen hesitantly approached Smith and said: "It doesn't balance." Smith replied curtly: "Check the footings and extensions and so forth."

Two hours later an anxious Petersen reported: "I'm sorry, but it still doesn't balance." "Listen, Scott," snapped Smith, "this is no practice set you're working on. Check your entries. See if they are posted correctly. See if they balance individually. Make a net income summary. You've done *something* wrong!"

Four hours later, a thoroughly frustrated Petersen tried a new approach. He checked the client's beginning balance and found it to be in error. Scott pondered how he would inform Smith that the client had made the mistake.

Discussion Questions

1. What kind of miscommunication was involved here?
2. How could this situation have been prevented?
3. How should Petersen deal with the situation?

Answers to Case 17.1: Puzzles To Ponder

1. *Answer:* The old surgeon is Mike's *mother.*

   Blinder: Assuming that all old surgeons are males.

2. *Answer:* Place the far-right coin on *top* of the corner coin.

   Blinder: Assuming that the problem must be solved in only two dimensions.

3. *Answer:* The numbers are arranged alphabetically: Eight—five—four—nine—and so forth.

   Blinder: Assuming some sort of mathematical series rather than considering the *spelling* of the numbers' names.

4. *Answer:* E—T—T for Eleven—Twelve—Thirteen. The letters are the initials of the spelling numbers: One—Two—Three—and so forth.

   Blinder: Assuming that the letters represent a mathematical series of the ordinal positions of the letters in the alphabet (e.g., 0

= 15th; T = 20th) rather than simply representing initials for the names of the numbers.

5. *Answer:* $27 *minus* the $2 Jake kept equals $25. And $30 minus the $25 room charge equals the $5 the clerk *tried* to return to the men.

   Blinder: The question posing the problem is misleading.

6. *Answer:* Arbitrarily label the machines as machine #1, machine #2, machine #3, and so on. Take one ball from machine #1, two balls from Machine #2, on up to 10 balls from Machine #10. You now have 55 balls. If all the machines dispensed one-ounce balls, the 55 balls would weigh 55 ounces. Place all of the balls on the scale. Fifty-five ounces minus the balls' combined weight in *half* ounces will give you the *number* of the culprit machine. For example, say the balls weigh 51½ ounces. 55 − 51½ ounces = 3½ ounces = 7 *half* ounces. Thus, machine #7 is the villain.

   Blinder: Assuming that you can take only one ball from each machine.

7. *Answer:* When you *spell* the letters, those on the top line begin with a vowel—for example, *eff, ell, ess*. Those on the bottom line begin with a consonant. *U* would fit with the first group if you spell it *ewe*—or the second group if you spell it *you* or *yew* or *yoo* (as in "yoo hoo").

   Blinder: Assuming some commonality among the letters other than the *spelling* of them.

8. *Answer:* 6. Each number is the product of the digits of the preceding number.

   Blinder: Assuming a mathematical series other than the one described.

9. *Answer:* The same middle name, "the."

   Blinder: Assuming (and hoping) that your author had higher standards for humor than he has.

CHAPTER EIGHTEEN

Undelayed Responses
Snap Reactions

✳
✳
✳

Game for another little test? OK. You will have exactly four minutes to complete it. All set? Just follow the instructions.

Name _____

Date _____

Test on Following Instructions

(Read all of the following directions before doing anything.)

1. Print your name, last first, on the top line following the word "Name."

2. Underline the word "print" in direction number 1.

3. In direction number 2, draw a circle around the word "underline," and in the above statement which appears in parentheses, cross out the word "anything."

4. Now, draw a circle around the title of this paper.

5. Circle the numbers of sentences 1, 2, 3, 4, and 5, and put an X over number 6.

6. Draw a circle around the word "all" in the above statement which appears in parentheses.

7. In sentence number 5, circle the even numbers and underline the odd numbers.

8. Put a circle around the number 2 in the third sentence.

9. Write "I can follow directions" above the title of this test. Start directly above the word "Test."

10. Underline the sentence you have just written.

11. Draw a square about one-half inch in size in the upper left-hand corner of this paper. Draw a circle around the square.

12. Cross out the numbers through 12. Now circle the same numbers.

13. Put an X in the square inside the circle in the upper left-hand corner.

14. Immediately beneath Instruction #14, copy neatly, in writing, the statement above that appears in parentheses.

15. Now that you have read all of the directions as stated in parentheses above, follow Instruction #1 only. Do not follow any of the other directions; omit them entirely.

16. If you failed to follow the instructions, you are entitled to some serious suspicions about the legitimacy of your author's ancestry.

That was diabolical, and if you fell for it, and most of us do, I hope you will forgive me. But what was the prime culprit? Was it not our reaction to time pressure? And we Americans seem especially susceptible. In some cultures where I have conducted seminars, such as in parts of Africa, Asia, and South America, people appear to be less vulnerable and the Instruction Test often flops—that is, fewer are caught by it. We have been programmed from childhood on to respect those who are quick on the draw, decisive, and "men of action." It is as if we had been taught to shoot first and ask questions later. I was an offender of the first order. When I had something new to assemble—such as a wagon for the kids—I would read the instructions as a last resort—after all of my actions had failed!

And, to be sure, there are circumstances when the snap decision is to be desired over the delayed response or no action at all. On the other hand, the consequences of some undelayed, unreasoned reactions have ranged from mild embarrassment to some of the greatest catastophes in history. Consider the tragic phenomenon of panic. Take the famous Iroquois Theatre fire (Chicago, 1903), for example. It is generally conceded that a considerable portion of the terrible death toll (almost 600) could be attributed to the crush of fear-crazed persons who jammed the exits.

> Doors, windows, hallways, fire escapes—all were jammed in a moment with struggling humanity, fighting for life. Some of the doors were jammed almost instantly so that no human power could make egress possible. Behind those in front pushed the frenzied mass of humanity. Chicago's elect, the wives and children of its most prosperous business men and the flower of local society, fighting like demons incarnate. Purses, wraps, costly furs were cast aside in the mad rush. Mothers were torn from their children, husbands from their wives. No hold, however strong, could last against that awful, indescribable crush. Strong men who sought to the last to sustain their feminine companions were swept away like straws, thrown to the floor and trampled into unconsciousness in the twinkling of an eye. Women to whom the safety of their children was more than their own lives had their little ones torn from them and buried under the mighty sweep of humanity, moving onward by intuition rather than through exercise of thought to the various exits. They in turn were swept on before their wails died on their lips—some to safety, others to an unspeakably horrible death.[1]

---

[1] *Chicago's Awful Theatre Horror* by Survivors and Rescuers (Chicago: Memorial Publishing, 1904), p. 36.

The veteran writer Ben H. Atwell, an eyewitness, testified to the senseless loss of lives:

> Piled in windows in the angle of the stairway where the second balcony refugees were brought face to face in a death struggle with the occupants of the first balcony, the dead covered a space 15 or 20 feet square and nearly 7 feet in depth. *All were absolutely safe from the fire itself when they met death,* having emerged from the theatre proper into the separate building containing the foyer. In this great court there was absolutely nothing to burn and the doors were only a few feet away. There the ghastly pile lay, *a mute monument to the powers of terror. . . .*
>
> *To that pile of dead is attributed the great loss of life within.* The bodies choked up the entrance, barring the egress of those behind. Neither age nor youth, sex, quality or condition were sacred in the awful battle in the doorway. The gray and aged, rich, poor, young and those obviously invalids in life lay in a tangled mass all on an awful footing of equality in silent annihilation.[2]

If that calamity seems remote, consider the Cocoanut Grove nightclub fire (Boston, 1942):

> To a week already overcrowded with gruesome news pictures from the war, Boston added a terrible climax of civilian tragedy on Saturday night (Nov. 28) when more than 400 people[3] lost their lives in a fire at a midtown night club. It was the worst U.S. disaster of its kind since the 1903 Iroquois Theatre fire in Chicago.
>
> A thousand merrymakers were packed in the Cocoanut Grove celebrating football victories and "getting away from the war" at 10:15 P.M. when the floor show was scheduled to start. A bus boy struck a match to see how to screw a light bulb back into its socket. A tinsel palm tree nearby caught fire and havoc took the stage. The guests' mad headlong rush for the two inadequate exits ended by completely clogging all escape. *More than the flames and stifling smoke, it was the hysteria and panic of the screaming, clawing crowds which piled up the dead like a dam.* One chorus boy kept his head in the pandemonium, directing entertainers to the safety of an adjacent roof through a second story window.[4]

Those are rather ancient examples. Aren't we finally beginning to learn a lesson? Regrettably, there is little evidence that we have. Indeed, I have three sets of news clippings in front of me that suggest quite the contrary.

---

[2] Ibid., pp. 41-42. Italics are author's.

[3] A subsequent article ("After Cocoanut Grove," *Atlantic Monthly,* March 1943, pp. 55-57) totaled the fatalities at just under 500, the hospitalized at 250.

[4] "Boston Holocaust," *Life,* December 7, 1942, © Time Inc., p. 44. Reprinted by permission.

One set depicts the infamous Sheffield (England) soccer tragedy—95 people were crushed to death; over 200 were injured.

Another concerns a fire in the Happy Land Social Club in the Bronx— 87 dead; only 4 escaped.

A third set describes the tunnel stampede in Mecca (Saudi Arabia)— 1,426 deaths; untold hundreds injured.

All three disasters occurred within recent years, and *panic* was clearly the major factor in each of them.

Panic, of course, is not exclusively a group phenomenon. The individual may experience solo panic that can lead to destructive consequences. Not long ago, a businessman was dozing as his commuter train sped home. The train stopped at the station just before his own and started up again, awakening the man. Startled and thinking that he was missing his station, the man dashed out of the forward door of the coach. He stumbled and fell under the train, and its wheels cut off his feet at the ankles.

Riots, lynchings, and many other forms of mob or individual violence or inaction (frozen panic)—unsanity, in any case—are almost invariably earmarked by irrational, impulsive behavior.

THREE CLASSES OF BEHAVIOR

The question is: How is it possible that normally civilized, law-abiding, peaceful, sane, and adult persons sometimes act like fear-crazed or enraged animals? How can humans, collectively or individually, lose their heads, or fly off the handle and, as a consequence, effectively contribute to the harm and destruction of themselves and others? Compare three broad classifications of human behavior:

Reflex Responses

Shine a light into someone's eyes, and watch the pupils contract. Draw a pointed instrument across the sole of a foot, and note the reaction of the toes. Tap the knee just below the patella, and watch the lower leg jerk. These simple reactions are called *reflex responses*. Involving no thinking, they are uncontrolled (and largely uncontrollable), direct, and immediate responses of the organism to stimuli.

Voluntary Responses

Now ask the same person to spell New York backward, to multiply 43 by 9, and then to estimate your weight. Assuming that this person had had no special preparation for these tasks, the responses will have characteristics opposite to those of reflexes. They will involve some thinking; they will be delayed, controllable (and controlled) responses.

Reflexlike Responses

Compare these two forms of behavior with a third:

We enlisted men were playing baseball with our officers. I had walked and had visions of stealing second. Unfortunately, their pitcher caught me leaning and threw to first base. Now I was in a rundown between the lieutenant playing first and the bird colonel playing second. I was a sure out, but just as the lieutenant threw to the colonel, I snapped to attention and saluted. The colonel promptly returned the salute and muffed the catch, and I scampered on to second!

The colonel's reaction appears to be a cross between a reflex response and a voluntary response. Like a reflex, his reaction was undelayed, uncontrolled, and apparently involved little or no thought. On the other hand, it resembled a voluntary response, in that his action was controllable (albeit largely uncontrolled in this instance). In short, his response could have been delayed, controlled, and premeditated—in other words, it *could* have been a voluntary response, but years of conditioning and habit militated against this. A reflexlike response, then, may be considered a potential voluntary reaction which, through habit, panic, conditioning, surprise, and so on, resembles a reflex.

Useful Reflexlike Responses.   Reflexlike responses often begin as conscious, voluntary actions. One *learns* to drive a car, play a musical instrument, type, throw a baseball, and so forth, quite consciously and perhaps laboriously at first. But with repetition, these actions become so habituated that they may be carried on with virtually no conscious control. Our capacity for learning these resposes is invaluable to us. Consider driving an automobile. If you had to maintain conscious control of your steering, braking, accelerating, and so on, you might have considerable difficulty in coping with, say, the added complexity of having the car in front stop quickly. You simply do not have the time, under these conditions, to decide with due premeditation that you must slow up or stop your car, that you must take your foot off the accelerator, that you must put it on the brake, that you must press the brake pedal hard enough to stop in time but not hard enough to skid your car into oncoming traffic, that you must be looking for possibilities of steering around the stopped car, that you must take into account the actions of the drivers behind and beside you, and so forth. If you are an experienced driver, you have so thoroughly habituated many of these actions that you will perform them without prethought and therefore will have time and concentration for coping with the less familiar aspects of the situation. Good typists, for example, are unaware of the specific movements of their fingers. In fact, if they began to *will* that certain fingers strike certain keys, the rate would fall off markedly and the errors would probably increase. If a punch press operator had to make conscious decisions before stamping each piece, you can imagine the decreased productivity.

There is perhaps no more relevant application of appropriate reflexlike responses than in sports. Thinking is often a handicap here. The athlete who has to *think* about throwing a punch, fielding a ground ball, or returning a serve is likely to flub it. Instead the athlete reacts with a lightning-fast conditioned reflex.[5]

In short, there is a great deal to be said for properly trained reflexlike responses.

Dangerous Reflexlike Responses. There are occasions, however, when reflexlike responses can lead to trouble. Take the rookie police officer who was assigned to night duty in a downtown shopping district. He was making his rounds, checking the rear doors of the shops, when he found the door of a furniture store unlocked. He swung the door open and noticed with a start that the figure of a man loomed in the darkness inside. The officer quickly went for his gun and was dismayed to see the "other man" go for his. The policeman immediately pulled his revolver and fired—and the "man" disappeared amid the sound of shattering glass. Upon investigating, the young officer discovered that he had destroyed a $400 mirror!

Most of us might argue that we would have done the same thing as the embarrassed rookie—and so we might, for we would have been rookies, too. But veteran police officers tell us that the situation could have been handled more skillfully. They say that they have learned from experience to suspect immediately the possibility of a mirrored image. They say that there are ways of weaving, ducking, and dodging—*while* reaching for one's gun—which (1) make one a difficult target if the "man" should actually turn out to be there and (2) permit a check on the suspected mirror. Of course, if the other "man" doesn't weave, duck, or dodge as you do, you may have a problem on your hands! But, the veterans insist, you are usually in a better position to cope with it.

Happily, not all inappropriate reflexlike responses end negatively. Once when Lauritz Melchior was in the finale of *Die Walküre*, a fire broke out in the stage light trough. Fortunately, a fireman was present, as required by law. Unfortunately, he had fallen asleep in the warm wings. Awakened by the clamor, he dashed onstage and threw a bucket of water on Melchior! Realizing his error, he promptly retreated and returned with a second bucket and doused the flames. The tenor took eight curtain calls; the fireman took ten!

---

[5] Perhaps it is primarily because there is so much time to think that golf can be so difficult. For what could be easier than to hit a *stationary, teed-up* ball? Almost anything, answers the exasperated duffer.

However, unthinking reponses can sometimes have far graver consequences than minor property damage and embarrassment. The ironic label for the following similar tragedies could be "The Quick and the Dead":

In Albany, Texas, two sisters were walking on a railroad trestle when a freight train bore down on them. Margie Dell Macon, 12, panicked and started to run. She stumbled, and the train killed her. Barbara, 14, remained where she was, crouched on the edge of the trestle. The train didn't touch her.

In Arlington Heights, Illinois, two brothers were walking on the shoulder of a busy road. They suddenly spotted a snake. Romeo Ramos, 6, ran onto the road into the path of an oncoming car. Roel, 11 stayed on the shoulder, unharmed. The reptile? An innocuous garter snake.

Destructive undelayed reactions are not confined to such specific situations. Consider Nystrom's analysis of extremist thinking and behavior. "Fanaticism," she wrote in a striking statement, "is a triumph of reflex over reflection."[6] She went on to explain: "It [fanaticism] differs from the more primitive reflexes in that it is conditioned . . . but it is reflex nonetheless: an absolute, fixed, undifferentiated, *immediate* response of the organism to a set of self-selected signals."[7]

THE PROBLEM OF UNDELAYED REACTIONS

The problem of undelayed reactions does not, of course, involve true reflexes, which for the most part consist of harmless and often self-protective behavior. Nor does it concern properly trained and habituated reflexlike actions which increase one's efficiency in repetitive tasks and facilitate the handling of unusual situations, as in driving an auto- mobile.

The undelayed reactions that are of concern here are those that can and ought to be delayed, controlled, and premeditated. The correctives which follow, then, apply to the reflexlike responses which, in the interest of saving tempers, time, energy, money, and lives, could and should be delayed, conscious, voluntary responses.

---

[6] Christine Nystrom, "Immediate Man: The Symbolic Environment of Fanaticism," *ETC.*, March 1977, p. 19.

[7] Ibid.

CORRECTIVES

Instantaneous Action Rarely Necessary

First of all, let us recognize that very few emergencies require an immediate action. This chapter has cited numerous examples of critical circumstances ranging from a policeman's reflection in a mirror to the unforgettable Iroquois Theatre fire. In no case was immediate, unthinking response necessary. In fact, in every case, had those involved delayed their reactions for even a moment to size up the situation, the consequences might have been a good deal happier.

The Habit of Delay

In the aftermath of the Iroquois Theatre catastrophe, Bishop Samuel Fallows wrote:

> Let every safeguard that human ingenuity can devise be furnished and yet there always remains the personal element to be taken into account. Habitual practice of self-control in daily life will help give coolness and calmness in times of peril. Keeping one's head in the ordinary things prevents its losing when the extraordinary occurs.[8]

The "habitual practice of self-control in daily life" is precisely what is advocated here. Frequently practice the technique of delaying your response, if only for an instant. It is especially helpful to discipline oneself under semiemergency circumstances. If, for example, someone makes a remark that seems offensive, resist the impulse to respond—instead, let you initial reaction be *delay*. Give yourself time to size up the situation: Did she really mean that? Will it be wise to retaliate in kind? What are his reasons for saying it? Could she only be joking? Hadn't I better give him a chance to clarify this? Chances are that your delayed reactions will be appreciably more intelligent, mature, and, in the long run, effective than your impulsive response would have been. The point is not simply to count to ten but *to size up* the situation—to analyze, detect the inferences, get more data, remember the etcetera, look for other alternatives, which-index, how-much-index, and when-index,—while doing so.

Since many of our harmful, overquick responses are vocal, a friend has developed the habit of clenching a pen or pencil crosswise between his teeth when the urge to "shoot from the lip" comes on. While the wear and tear on the writing instrument may be considerable, this little technique is a good reminder of the wisdom of delaying and rather effectively inhibits the verbal outburst.

---

[8] *Chicago's Awful Theatre Horror*, p. xv.

One Hour at a Time

For repetitive undelayed reactions, one might copy the one-step-at-a-time principle that has worked wonders for Alcoholics Anonymous. This technique could be used, for example, by harried executives with the habit of losing their tempers at the slightest provocation. By resolving repeatedly not to shout for the next hour, they can probably short-circuit the anger pattern and build some confidence in their ability to retain composure. When capitalizing on behavioral modification findings, it would also help if one's secretary or colleague would occasionally commend successful restraint.

Humor

Your sense of humor can be a marvelous tension-breaker for yourself as well as others—and a deterrent to self-defeating impulsive behavior. In the India-Burma theater during World War II, the forces of British Field Marshal Viscount William J. Slim had just suffered a resounding defeat. Searching for a way to relax his desperate staff, he remarked, "Things could be worse." "How?" came a disbelieving voice from the rear. "Well," replied Slim, "it could be raining."

Advance Preparation for Emergencies

The best general provision for emergencies is the deeply ingrained habit of delay-while-sizing-up, but more specific preparation is often possible. Generally speaking, an emergency is an emergency because it involves circumstances that are unexpected and unfamiliar and with which we feel unprepared or unable to cope. To the extent that the circumstances are anticipated and made familiar and to the extent that we are equipped to cope with them, they are no longer overwhelming crises. Training for combat is an excellent example of this. The recruit spends weeks going through many of the activities of warfare, firing various weapons, throwing grenades, taking forced hikes with full field pack, participating in bayonet drill, crawling through the infiltration course,[9] and so on. The object is to acquaint the soldier with as many of the aspects of combat as possible so that the actual experience will not seem overpoweringly complex and terrifying.

Speech training is another good example of advance preparation for emergencies. The beginning speaker is advised to become familiar in

---

[9] The infiltration course is a simulated battlefield. The trainee crawls 50 yards or so under barbed wire, with a brace of machine guns firing real bullets a few inches overhead. As an added feature, charges explode sporadically throughout the field, throwing showers of grit or mud everywhere.

advance, insofar as possible, with the components of the speaking situation. One is urged, for example, to master the speech (in many cases this will require committing the ideas and their connectives, though not the exact wording, to memory); to learn in advance what one can about the audience (size, age, sex, interests, prejudices, and so on); to know the purpose of the occasion; the topics of any previous and subsequent speakers; and the role one's own talk will play; and to acquaint oneself with the physical aspects (acoustics, arrangement of the audience, position of the speaker's stand, lighting, and so forth). In short, one becomes able to cope with difficult and critical situations to the extent they have been predicted, prepared for, and controlled in advance.

This has perhaps never been demonstrated more eloquently than when our astronauts dealt with the various dangers that confronted them. Recall that when the automatic aids to bring in his craft failed, Gordon Cooper calmly took over the manual controls and achieved a highly accurate reentry. Having practiced repeatedly for every conceivable emergency maneuver, Cooper could justifiably say: "I was not overly concerned. We had checked, checked, and double-checked. I felt right at home in the bird." He had done his homework well.

Hostage-taking, no doubt stimulated by the takeover of the American Embassy in Teheran, has become an increasingly prevalent phenomenon. Accordingly, a number of U.S. police departments are taking special preparatory training. Typically, personnel are informed that a simulation is about to occur—blanks will be used instead of real bullets. Otherwise they have no idea of what they will be up against.

The situation might involve a crazed gunman who has commandeered a business office and taken several hostages. If the officers perform well as a team, they may resolve the situation without injury or loss of life or even property damage. If they don't, they will be given explicit feedback so they can improve their performance the next time around—even if it turns out to be real.

Anticipating the Undelayed Responses of Others

So far, we have been concerned with measures to take that encourage *our* delayed reactions. Let us now consider how to deal with the harmful undelayed responses of *others*. First of all, it should be recognized that the tendency to react quickly varies from individual to individual, and within a given individual, from time to time. In other words, *which-index* and *when-index* the other person's propensity to fly off the handle. While Sam seemed to stand up under pressure last week, there is no guarantee that he will be as serene now.

Second, if you anticipate a potential flare-up, use the most snap reaction-proof medium of communication possible. For example, it is extremely easy for a person who becomes angry on the telephone to cut you off in an instant and proceed to act foolishly and destructively. Under some circumstances, a memo or letter, with no chance of immediate feedback from the other person and no possibility for control on your part, may be even worse. But a face-to-face communication gives you a chance to see the storm clouds forming and to forestall them. And even if the other person does "blow his top," you are there to help him regain his composure.

Third, and most important, don't match the other person's undelayed response with one of your own. Sorely tempting as they may be at times, mutual overquick reactions may make reconciliation considerably more difficult. And, after all, if you are right, you can afford to keep your temper; if you are wrong, you can't afford to lose it.

A Group Technique

In the chapter on *bypassing* I described a special conference technique. Although the clarification of communication among the participants was the prime objective, an important by-product emerged. The executive meetings of this particular firm had been characteristically marred by frequent angry exchanges among the conferees. But not long after the installation of the moderator system, it became evident that something had happened—the outbursts had disappeared. In fact, the meetings moved along with amazing tranquillity. The reason was soon apparent. The system required the moderator to paraphrase a speaker's remark before anyone else was permitted to respond. It was clear that this necessary delay, plus the likelihood of clarifying the communication, forced the quick responder to delay, to reconsider the response! And the other person, when finally allowed to speak, was invariably more cool-headed and objective than would have been the case had the individual been permitted to respond immediately.

And perhaps there is a moral in this experience for the individual as well as for the group. If you feel that you disagree with or disapprove of what someone has just said, take the time to make sure you understood correctly. This can have at least three salutary effects. You may find that you have misunderstood and are not actually in disagreement; your attempt to understand will tend to communicate respect for the other person, and the speaker is likely to return the consideration; and, finally, the delay may have given both of you time to be more intelligent and reasonable in your differing.

Finally, in a chapter on undelayed reactions there ought to be a reference to losing one's temper—a most pervasive human frailty. I can do no better than to quote a sagacious person whom I am proud to call a friend.

Temper
When I have lost my temper
I have lost my reason, too.

I'm never proud of anything which
  angrily I do.
When I have talked in anger and
  my cheeks were flaming red.
I have always uttered something
  which I wish I hadn't said.
In anger I have never done a kindly
  deed or wise,
But many things for which I felt
  I should apologize.
In looking back across my life
  and all I've lost or made,
I can't recall a single time
  when fury ever paid.
So I struggle to be patient, for
  I've reached a wiser age;
I do not want to do a thing or
  speak a word in rage.
I have learned by sad experience
  that when my temper flies
I never do a worthy thing, a
  decent deed or wise.

—John Charles Redmond

EPILOGUE

In a sense, this is the most important chapter in Part Three, "Patterns of Miscommunication." It is the chapter that promises to make the other chapters *work*. In the prior chapters you were repeatedly offered recommendations such as:

- Be aware when you are inferring and calculate the risk.
- Use the nine techniques for avoiding bypassing.
- Be aware that you inevitably abstract and remember the etcetera.

The idea is to substitute one set of reflex-like responses for another. I hope this chapter will help you do that.

Discussion Questions

1. Our culture tends to place a premium on the person of action, the quick thinker. Do you agree with that assertion? If so, why is it so? Do you feel that other cultures are similarly action-oriented?

2. Regarding the group technique: Will this delaying technique have any undesirable effects upon the group's activity? Might it slow progress to the point of boredom and apathy? Will any creativity be lost in the process? Will discussants be less candid if they realize that they are going to be paraphrased? On the other hand, what are the positive features of the technique?

3. This chapter promises to make the other chapters in Part Three *work*. How?

4. Report on an incident, perhaps involving yourself, in which an undesirable, undelayed reaction occurred. How and why did it occur? What were its consequences? How might it have been prevented? What measures might prevent its recurrence?

CASES

CASE 18.1

The Fateful Knob*

Any doctor, old or new, would have been glad to be called to this house, one of the most beautiful old homes in the city. I felt that my standing in the community was at stake and that it was an important moment.

At the conclusion of the examination I wanted to talk privately with the stiffly starched and immaculate nurse who was in attendance, who, too, was apparently making every effort to be perfect in her professional attitude. I wanted to give some instructions to the nurse and asked the family to excuse us for a moment while I talked to her privately. The nearest and most obvious place was the old-fashioned bathroom adjoining, and I asked her to go in. I closed the door.

"Sit down," I said, pointing to the bathroom stool, and then, as she took it, I noticed that the only place left for me was the indispensable one in any bathroom, which was covered by a gold and white lid.

I seated myself and talked for several minutes while the family waited anxiously outside for the verdict. Finally she rose and as I, too, rose, my hand automatically grasped the ornate pear-shaped knob at the end of the chain hanging beside me—and I pulled.

Why I pulled the cursed thing I'll never know. Instantly the place resounded with the familiar screeches and hisses of flushing water.

"Oh, doctor!" she gasped, "what will they think?—And the door shut!—What can I do?"

"Hell, woman," I said, my dignity ruined, "Don't ask me what you can do. I don't even know what I can do!"

I was never asked to return.

Discussion Questions
1. What is the principal pattern of miscommunication in this case?
2. Could this misevaluation have been prevented?

CASE 18.2

You Can't Outrun a Grenade
William A. Daniels

I recently finished basic training in the infantry, and I have to report that our platoon of recruits fell for the oldest trick in the Army.

---

* Frederic Loomis, M.D., *Consultation Room* (New York: Alfred A. Knopf, 1939), pp. 29–31. Reprinted by permission.

It was the first day of live hand grenade practice. Our sergeant, an apparently live grenade in hand, was instructing us. He emphasized several times: "When you are on the receiving end of a grenade, fall to the ground immediately and present as small a target as possible. *You can't outrun a grenade.*" These admonitions were greeted with the usual smirks and *sotto voce* wisecracks.

Then, suddenly, while attempting to show how to move a live grenade safely from hand to hand with the pin pulled, the grenade slipped from the sergeant's grasp and fell sputtering to the ground. Sixty men rose as one, and scrambled, and fought, and ran to escape the grenade which would explode in five seconds.

Five seconds passed, and no explosion occurred. The men sheepishly realized that the grenade was a dummy and that the sergeant had used this as an example of the damage and injuries that could result if panic were allowed to take control.

Discussion Questions
1. Why did the sergeant drop the grenade?
2. Why is this case appended to this chapter?

CASE 18.3

The Logan Company*

The Logan Company, a manufacturer of television and radio receiver sets, employed some 2,000 persons. The firm, which had been privately owned for over 30 years, had been sold to a large electronics holding corporation four years earlier, but retained substantially the same management after the sale. Following three unsatisfactory years, the president of Logan retired. The holding corporation installed Eric Stone as general manager; he was from outside the firm but within the holding company. Stone was given the rank of vice president, although he carried out the functions of the president, an office now vacant. He made many changes in the upper and middle management levels, including the product-line managers. The current situation, then, may be said to be one of flux and readjustment.

Among the responsibilities of the industrial engineering department was the supervision of the installation of production lines as new products or changes in products were introduced. One of these was a new conveyor assembly line for television tuners. Formerly the tuners had been assembled by conventional bench assembly methods, with workers compensated

---

* All names have been disguised. Printed by permission of the author, whose name has been withheld by request.

on an individual incentive basis. Many employees had expressed dissatis-
faction with the new methods, complaining that their take-home pay had
been markedly reduced.

Ray Edwards, 35, six years with Logan, was the industrial engineer in
charge of installing the tuner conveyor line. He found on Tuesday that it
was necessary to adjust the pace of the conveyor in order to train assemblers. He realized that the product-line manager, Fred Peterson, who had
joined the firm two months earlier, was under considerable pressure to
increase tuner production. So he phoned Peterson at 11 A.M. to discuss the
intended adjustment but was unable to reach him. As he waited for Peterson to return his call, Edwards reviewed four alternatives for timing the
change:

1. Have Logan's maintenance men make the adjustment after work
hours that day. To Edwards this did not appear to be a happy choice, since
it would require overtime pay at time and a half for the maintenance
workers. This pay would be charged against the industrial engineering
department. The department's budget for such expenses was already
strained for the fiscal period.

2. Wait until Saturday (a nonworking day) and have maintenance
people make the installation. Their overtime pay would then be charged
to the miscellaneous budget. While this would entail no loss of production
time or employee pay and would relieve the industrial engineering
department of overtime charges, the delay in installing the change would
interfere with operator training.

3. Have the salesman of the adjustment equipment make the change
during work hours. Since he would be paid by his own firm, the expense
would not be charged to the industrial engineering budget. However,
tuner production would be shut down, and workers would not be paid during the shutdown period.

4. Have the salesman start to make the change during the lunch
period. Edwards favored this plan because it would not only remove the
burden of overtime pay from his department's budget, but would require a
minimum shutdown time and loss of worker pay. However, Edwards
wanted to inform Peterson that the change might take longer than the
lunch period.

Peterson had spent the morning in conference in the office of the vice
president in charge of manufacturing, Roy Sheldon. Also present was Tom
Flynn, manager of the industrial engineering department, to whom
Edwards reported. Flynn, 38, had 13 years of service with the company.
At 12:45 P.M., as Peterson left Sheldon's office, he was stopped by Miss
Larson, Sheldon's secretary, who gave him Edwards' message, which had
been relayed to her by Peterson's secretary.

Peterson immediately picked up the phone on Miss Larson's desk and called Edwards.

Peterson: Ray, I understand you called—just got the note.

Edwards: (*The fourth alternative was now no longer possible, because the assemblers' lunch period had ended.*) Yes, Fred—we're going to have to regulate the tuner line. As you know, it has been going too fast for the workers.

Peterson: Yeah? (*Suspiciously.*)

Edwards: Well, we've purchased some new gearing that should do the trick of slowing down the line. Now, as to who to have make the change, I have a few ideas to sound out with you.

Peterson: Shoot.

Edwards: First, we could have the maintenance men do the job tonight. Frankly, I'm opposed to this, and so is Flynn. Their time would be charged to us, and we're up to the hilt right now in overtime charges. I don't think Tom would stand for it. So I thought. . . .

(*Click!*) Peterson had hung up. He charged angrily back into Mr. Sheldon's office and, in Sheldon's presence, proceeded to upbraid Tom Flynn for trying to shut down his production line in order to avoid overtime costs.

Discussion Questions

1. How would you describe the organization climate at Logan?

2. What was Edwards' frame of reference before the telephone conversation with Peterson?

3. What was Peterson's frame of reference before the telephone conversation with Edwards?

4. How do you analyze the phone conversation?

5. How should Edwards have handled the situation?

6. How should Peterson have handled the phone call?

7. Sheldon has now had the situation drop into his lap. What should he do?

CASE 18.4

The Mid-Western Telephone Company*

The general staff of the Mid-Western Telephone Company decided upon a revision in the company's billing procedure. Formerly, billing machine symbols had appeared on four portions of the bill. The change

---

* All names have been disguised. Printed by permission of the author, whose name has been withheld by request.

EXHIBIT 1

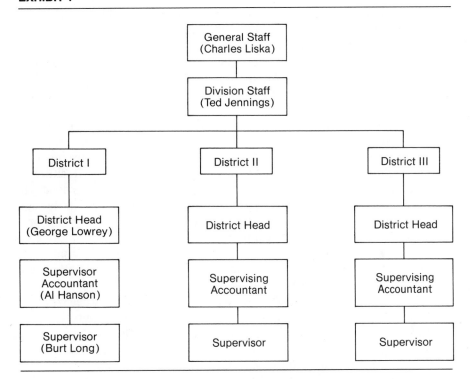

consisted in using these symbols on only one section of the bill. Thus, it was necessary to have three sets of symbols removed from each of the firm's billing machines.

Late Friday afternoon Charles Liska of the general staff requested the United Office Machine Company, which serviced the machines, to send out a repairman at the beginning of the week to remove the unneeded symbols. Liska then instructed Ted Jennings of the division staff to notify the district heads and the supervising accountants of each district of the change. Each of the supervising accountants was to have relayed the information to the supervisor under him (see Exhibit 1).

Jennings tried to contact George Lowrey, the district head in District I, and was unable to reach him. Jennings then called Al Hanson, the supervising accountant in District I, and gave the message to him and requested that he notify Burt Long, the supervisor whose unit was involved.

At the time he called, Hanson was wrestling with a production problem and was several hours behind schedule. He did not take any notes and forgot to contact Long.

Monday morning the repairman walked into Long's unit and told him that he was there to remove something, but he was hazy on whether he was to remove all the symbols or only some of them from the machines. Long, who had not been contacted about the matter, tried to call Hanson, but Hanson was not at his desk. Long then called Lowrey to ask him what to do. Hanson happened to be in Lowrey's office when Long's call came in. Lowrey, knowing nothing of the situation, told Hanson that Long was asking what to do about symbols on the billing machines. He asked whether Hanson could handle the situation.

Hanson flushed with embarrassment as he suddenly recalled his failure to convey Jennings' message to Long. He vaguely remembered something about the removal of symbols, but because he felt that Lowrey was already holding him responsible for his current production problem he dreaded admitting his error in the presence of his superior. He clutched the phone and told Long that all of the symbols were to be removed. He silently resolved to stop the repairman and check with Jennings as soon as he left Lowrey's office. Unfortunately, the district head began a prolonged discussion of Hanson's production difficulty. Hanson became so preoccupied with Lowrey's remarks that the symbols matter slipped his mind. Meanwhile Long relayed Hanson's instruction to the repairman, who proceeded to remove all of the symbols.

Sometime later in the morning, Jennings, following up to see whether the work had been done, discovered what had happened. Upon checking with the United Office Machine Company, he was told that the correct symbols could be replaced at $95 per machine and that the machines would have to be brought into the shop for the replacement.

The end result was that the ten machines of the unit were taken out of production for several days and that a cost of $950 ws necessary to replace the symbols.

Discussion Questions
1. Who contributed to this cacophony of errors and how?
2. How could this costly error have been prevented?
3. What patterns of miscommunication seem to be involved in this case?

CASE 18.5

Your Eyes Can Deceive You*
Arthur Bartlett

George Smith got home from a date with his girl about midnight. His mother was not at home. Probably she was out playing cards with friends, George thought. That had been her favorite recreation ever since her divorce, when George was six. Working all day in the candy factory, she

---

* Reprinted by permission from the *American Weekly,* Hearst Publishing Company, Inc.

liked to relax in the evenings. Now that George was 20, and working, and had a girl to occupy his attention, she often stayed out fairly late. So George went up to his own front room, undressed, got into bed and lay there reading the newspaper.

A bus stopped across the street, and George pulled aside the window shade and looked out. Under the street light, he could see his mother descending from the bus. A tall, heavy-set man got out behind her. The bus moved on. George was about to drop back on his pillow when his startled eyes stopped him. The man was reaching for his mother, trying to put his arms around her. George saw her push at him and try to step back off the curb; saw him grab her again and start pulling her toward him.

George leaped out of bed, pulled on his trousers and rushed down the stairs to the front door. Across the street, the man was still attempting to embrace his mother and she was struggling against him. George dashed to the rescue. Clenching his fist as he ran, he leaped at the man and punched with all his strength, hitting him squarely on the jaw. The man toppled backward and uttered a groan as his head hit the sidewalk. Then he lay there, still.

What happened next filled George with utter confusion. Dropping to her knees beside the unconscious man, his mother looked up at him with anguish in her eyes. "George," she cried, "what have you done? This is Howard Browser. . . . Howard, the candymaker at the factory . . . the man who asked me to marry him . . ."

The boy stared at his mother across the crumpled figure on the pavement. "He wasn't attacking you?" he demanded, dully.

"Of course not," she told him. "We'd been out together all evening. He brought me home. He wanted a good-night kiss, that's all. I was just teasing him."

An ambulance took Howard Browser to the hospital, but he never regained consciousness. He died the next day. George Smith spent that night in a jail cell.

The authorities finally decided not to prosecute. George, the investigation proved, didn't know Browser, had never seen him before. He had honestly thought that what he saw was a man attacking his mother.

Take the case of Matthew J. Flaherty, a Boston policeman, some years ago. Shortly after being appointed to the force, Matt Flaherty took a bride and they moved into their own home on Newcastle Road. Eleanor Flaherty loved the house, but she was nervous about being alone in it at night, waiting for Matt to come home from his late tour of duty. Every little noise make her think that there was someone in the house or trying to get in. When Matt got home she was usually so upset that he would search the whole house, from cellar to attic, though smiling at her fears.

"No burglars," he would assure her, "except in your pretty little head."

Still, he couldn't help feeling anxious. If anyone really were prowling around his house while he was away nights. . . .

One night—they had been living in the house about two months then—he made the usual fruitless search and went to bed. But he had hardly dropped off to sleep, it seemed, when we woke with a start. What had awakened him? Naturally, his first thought was of a prowler. Listening tensely, he heard a sound—the creaking of a floor board—on the other side of the closed bedroom door. Quietly, he reached for his gun and eased himself up in bed.

Sure enough, the door began to push open. Somebody was coming right into the room.

"Who's there?" Matt Flaherty yelled taking careful aim. There was no answer but a startled gasp, and he started shooting. It was too dark to see the figure beyond the half-opened door, but whoever it was fell with a thump to the floor.

Then Matt turned on the light. That was when he realized, for the first time, that Eleanor was not there in the bed beside him. She was lying just outside the door, dead.

Discussion Questions

1. How does the title of this article strike you?
2. Is there any similarity between the two incidents?
3. How could these tragedies have been prevented?

CASE 18.6

Torment in a Neighborhood*
Walter B. Smith

What made James Lee, the Chinese laundryman, go berserk?

Why did he shoot three men, two of them police, then try to fight off 150 more cops before falling with a bullet wound through the skull?

Lying Saturday in County Hospital, his head throbbing and his left ankle shackled to the bed frame, Jimmy Lee gave his explanation of why he did it.

"I was scared," he said.

He was scared, he said, because he thought the three men had come to beat him up and perhaps take his money because he had slapped a boy.

And he slapped the boy, Lee said, because he finally had become fed up with the way neighborhood kids in general tormented him with squirt guns, name-calling, door-banging, and other mischief.

The furious gun battle took place just a week ago in Lee's laundry at 2705 W. Diversey.

---

* *Chicago Daily News*. Reprinted by permission.

The city was shocked—the more so because such violence is so rare among Chicago's law-abiding Chinese.

Today two of Lee's victims are dead—detectives Jeremiah Lucey and Roman C. Steinke.

The third victim, truck driver Steven Malenk, 40, father of the slapped boy, has recently been discharged from a hospital.

Lee has a sewed-up hole in his head where a bullet went right through. Doctors expect him to recover, but he may be paralyzed for life.

Lee started the shooting when the two policemen went to the laundry with Malenk to arrest Lee on a warrant charging asault.

The warrant stemmed from an incident three nights earlier when Lee had slapped Malenk's son Steve Jr., 11.

For months, Lee said, neighborhood kids had badgered him. Sometimes they spit on the floor, sometimes they threw things, sometimes they called him obscene names.

On the evening of February 3, Lee said, the Malenk boy and a companion were heckling him. (The boys say they were just looking in the window.)

Lee chased them and caught Steve, slapping him.

Soon afterward Steve came back to the laundry with his father. Lee said the truck driver threatened him and they struggled. The laundryman admits he batted Malenk with a flatiron, breaking his wrist.

Malenk went to the Shakespeare police court next day and got the warrant charging Lee with assault.

Lee said he did not know about that when the officers came to get him last Saturday. Why didn't he go along peacefully to the police station?

"I was scared," Lee said. "All I knew was that these three men were coming to get me and wanted me to pay them $125. I thought they were going to beat me up."

He said he did not know that the men with Malenk were police. They wore civilian clothes.

"All I could think of was to shoot first."

The mention of $125 apparently was a misunderstanding of the policemen's statement that Lee would have to post $125 bail at the police station.

Lee said he kept the pistol and shotgun with which he fought the police as protection against burglars.

He lived alone at the laundry. He has no relatives in Chicago.

Lee told his story twice. First it was in halting English to a *Daily News* reporter. Then it was in Chinese to the Rev. Philip Lee, no relation, who was pastor of the Chinese Christian Union Church at 23d Street and Wentworth.

The wounded man's chief worry was about his laundry. The Rev. Mr. Lee assured him that arrangements would be made with a Chinese friend to see that the customers got back their shirts.

The clergyman said Chinese welfare organizations were making plans to give Lee the help he needs.

Lee said he was brought to America in 1934, at the age of two. After three years in New Jersey he was brought to Chicago, where he has lived ever since.

He said he had had his laundry at the Diversey address for six years, but that the trouble with the youngsters did not start until last September.

An inquest into the death of Detective Lucey has been continued to March 9.

* * * * *

James Lee died 2½ months later from his wounds. A newspaper account included the following:

> Lee said he went berserk because he was afraid the officers were going to beat him up. However, a fingerprint check showed Lee was sought as an Army deserter, and police said that might have been the reason he feared arrest.

Discussion Questions

1. How is this case similar to the two incidents described in "Your Eyes Can Deceive You," Case 18.5?

2. Does this case differ from those incidents?

CASE 18.7

Dyer Public Relations, Inc.*

Ralph Stewart, staff writer for a business magazine with a large national circulation, was talking with Robert Dyer for the second time in early March. He had already recorded Mr. Dyer's account of the formation and development of Dyer Public Relations, Inc., as well as Mr. Dyer's personal history. Now, to round out his prospective article, he needed further information about others in the firm.

Mr. Dyer was cooperative and said, "If you uncover anything constructive about how our communications and human relations are functioning, we'd be grateful—especially me. If it doesn't come up naturally, I suggest you probe and hear what we now call the 'Office Boy Incident.' Our people know you're here, and I've requested them to be frank in their interviews with you."

Dyer Public Relations, Inc., had been founded 14 years earlier in a large West Coast city by Robert Dyer—a driving, ambitious, dynamic young man with seemingly inexhaustible energy. The company became a

---

nationally recognized firm, grossing over $8 million annually. Dyer, Inc., employed approximately 40 persons. A partial organization chart appears in Exhibit 1.

In addition to Mr. Dyer, the following persons were involved in the "Office Boy Incident":

Mark Taylor—47, treasurer, had joined Dyer 13 years before. Taylor also maintained a private accounting practice. He had a working agreement with Mr. Dyer that he would spend approximately half

EXHIBIT 1

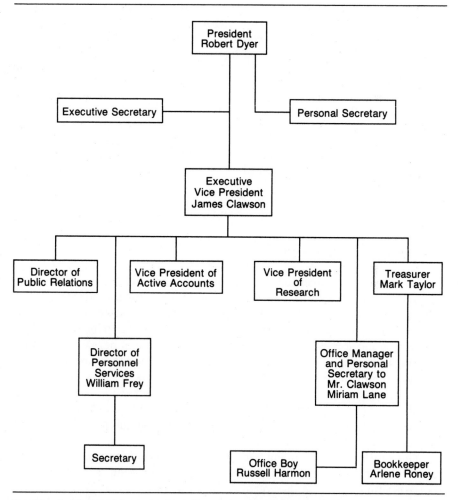

Note: The chart does not fully express the working relationships within the firm. Dyer frequently communicated directly with Taylor, the two vice presidents, and Lane. Each of these also communicated directly with Dyer. Dyer also worked directly with Frey and the public relations director. These two men, however, rarely initiated direct relations with Dyer.

his time on the Dyer accounts and the other half on his own practice. These percentages were never adhered to rigidly. Some months, Taylor spent more than 50 percent of his time on Dyer affairs; some months, less. This had been an established arrangement between the two men, and both seemed satisfied with its operation.

William Frey—27, held a Ph.D. in industrial psychology. He was in charge of personnel services, including testing and placement for clients and the Dyer staff. Frey had been with the Dyer firm for two years. His predecessor, Kenneth Elson, had served as director of personnel services and as office manager. When Frey assumed the personnel responsibilities, Miriam Lane became office manager.

Miriam Lane—26, was office manager of the firm and personal secretary to James Clawson, executive vice president. She had six years' service with Dyer and had been office manager for the past two years. The firm's general clerical work flowed across her desk. She asigned it to secretaries who were not already busy with duties for their immediate supervisors. She had direct responsibility for the work of Russell Harmon, office boy.

Russell Harmon—21, office boy, a university student majoring in business management, had been working approximately 30 hours per week with Dyer for the past year. He was hired as a clerk-typist, but it was understood that he was also to do all of the reproduction work, run errands, make deliveries, and so on.

Arlene Roney—23, bookkeeper, reported to Mark Taylor. She had been on the job only three days when the incident occurred.

The Office Boy Incident

Over the past several months, because of tax deadlines and other financial problems, Mark Taylor had been devoting considerably more than 50 percent of his time to the Dyer firm. He was attempting to clear up a few personal affairs before leaving on a business trip for Dyer.

One of those tasks was to send a letter to the members of his professional fraternity. He wrote it in longhand and handed the sheet to Arlene Roney, the new bookkeeper. "Arlene," he said, "this needs to be typed up and I'll need 25 copies. Give it to Russell."

She was a bit surprised because her duties did not include typing. However, Taylor was obviously pressed for time so she assumed he was asking her to type the letter.

She said later that no one had told her of Russell Harmon's responsibilities, although she had heard that he handled all the firm's reproductions.

Accordingly, she found a conventional typewriter and rather laboriously typed the letter. She finished just as Harmon was passing by so she handed the sheet to him. "Mr. Taylor would like 25 copies right away."

Glancing at the letter with its poor centering and ragged right margin, he realized he would have to reformat it using his PC. And then, for a really neat job, he would use the firm's laser printer to make the 25 copies.

"OK," he said, "except that I can't do it right now. I've got to run an errand. If I get back in time, I could do it before closing time, but I doubt if I can make it that soon. Guess it'll have to wait until tomorrow."

Roney felt that she could do no more about the situation and placed the letter on her desk. A few minutes later, Taylor approached her. "Did Russell do that letter job yet?"

Roney answered, "No, he said he didn't have time now and probably couldn't do it until tomorrow."

Taylor, visibly angered, rushed to Dyer's office. "Say, Bob, I know this is my personal work, but I would think I could get a little cooperation from the personnel around here—especially when you consider the amount of time I've been putting in for you."

Dyer: What do you mean? What kind of cooperation?

Taylor: Why, Harmon just refused to do a personal letter for me.

Dyer (*considerably disturbed*): Where is he? We'll just see what the hell's going on here!

Dyer walked to Miriam Lane's desk in the main office and demanded loudly, "Where is Harmon?"

Lane: Why—I don't know. I imagine he's out on an errand for Dr. Frey (*pointing toward Frey's office*). He's been sending Russell to the Weber Building, on the other side of the city.

Dyer turned and strode into Frey's office. "Why can't Harmon do this work for Mark?"

Frey was nonplussed. This was the second time that day that Dyer had appeared to hold him personally responsible for the conduct of persons over whom, in his opinion, he had no authority. Earlier in the day, Dyer had come to him with complaints about errors in the work of the secretaries. Moreover, Frey had noticed through the glass partition of his office that Lane had apparently directed Dyer to him. He was suddenly angered with Dyer's accusations and Lane's "buck-passing" and snapped, "I don't know! Harmon doesn't work for me! He works for Lane!"

Dyer stamped out of Frey's office and headed for his own. As he passed Lane's desk, he shouted, "When Harmon comes back, tell him I want to see him!"

Lane was incensed with Frey. She assumed that he had sent Dyer back to her. She got up and followed Dyer into his office. "Do you have to make a scene about this?" she asked. Dyer slammed his office door behind Lane and himself and said, "Who in the hell does Russell Harmon think he is? If Harmon refuses to work for Mark Taylor, he can just get his rear end out of this office!"

Lane: What's this all about?
Dyer: Mark brought something to Harmon to do and Harmon refused to do it. I want to see this kid now!
Lane: I'll find out from Russell about this.
Dyer: *I'll* ask him!

Lane returned to her desk. Shortly afterward Dyer, who had an outside appointment, left the office for the day. Harmon returned just before quitting time. When told of the incident, Harmon was bewildered. He felt betrayed by Frey, who had not, in his words, "stuck up" for him by telling Dyer that he was on an errand. He remarked about Roney to a friend, "I was never even introduced to the girl, and it looks like she's trying to shaft me. Why, I don't even know her!"

Mrs. Lane questioned Harmon about the affair and said she would explain everything to Dyer in the morning.

By coincidence, Frey, Lane, and Russell Harmon were scheduled to work overtime that evening. Harmon was still disturbed. Frey saw him talking to Mrs. Lane at the water cooler and went out to join them.

Harmon: What I can't understand is why Mr. Taylor didn't come to me. I could have explained everything, and the whole thing could have been prevented. But, boy! I guess I'm in the soup now. I want to see Mr. Dyer. It doesn't seem fair that he should hear only one side of the story.
Frey: Speaking about "sides of the story," maybe you would be interested in mine. (*Frey proceeded to recount how Mr. Dyer had charged into his office and upbraided him for Harmon's conduct.*)
Lane: If you ask me, I'm the one with the responsibility. I've got to see Mr. Dyer first thing tomorrow morning.

The three continued to compare their versions of the "Office Boy Incident." Frey and Lane were able to allay their suspicions of each other, although neither offered a formal apology to the other. Harmon, however, still felt upset. He told the others that nothing could clear up the situation until he had had a chance to explain the matter directly to Dyer, which he planned to do the first thing the following day.

Early the next morning, Lane explained the confusion to Dyer. At first, he became angry with Taylor for not giving him the complete account of the affair and said, "That's poor communication. If Mark is having trouble with his girl, I'll give him a pamphlet on how to communicate!"

Later he grew aggravated with himself, and finally he became contrite: "I'm sorry—that's one of my failings. I should be able to control myself." Stewart was told that Dyer frequently made this sort of statement after a flare-up.

When Russell Harmon reported to work, he walked to Lane's desk.

Harmon: Is Mr. Dyer in yet?

Lane: Well, yes, but the situation is all cleared up.

Harmon: Would it be all right if I saw him? I'd like to explain the thing to him.

Lane: Russell, I don't think you should do that. He knows that you weren't to blame, and I really think you should let the thing blow over.

After assurances from Lane that he was "in the clear," Harmon decided to let the matter drop.

Several employees told Stewart that Clawson was out of town at the time of the incident. One of them added, "It probably wouldn't have made any difference if he had been here."

Discussion Questions

1. What do you make of Dyer's candor in opening his firm to Stewart?

2. Step by step, how do you analyze the series of miscommunications which occurred in this case?

3. What do you think of the organizational structure of Dyer Public Relations, Inc.?

PART FOUR

Overview

❈
❈
❈

CHAPTER NINETEEN

Overview
Chapter Digests

✳
✳
✳

We have been examining human communications (the encoding and decoding phases, in particular) as they are influenced by assumptions held by the communicators involved. Some of these assumptions are destructive and troublesome because (1) they are false and imply an inadequate, distorted view of the world, and (2) communicators are usually unaware that their evaluations and communications are being influenced by these assumptions. Under these conditions, patterns of misevaluation and miscommunication are prone to occur and recur. Before summarizing those patterns, let us review Chapters 1 through 8, which laid the foundation for our examination of communication.

INTRODUCTION

Chapter 1 emphasized that human communication is a vital but complex and challenging process. Despite prodigious progress in the technical aspects of message transmission and reception and information gathering, processing, storage, and retrieval, we still have much to learn about what happens *inside people* as they engage in communication.

The book's focus is on these latter aspects—the subtle, subjective, internal phenomena of human communication.

The organization of the book is also described in this chapter, and the cases appended to the chapters are recommended for internalizing the contents of the chapters.

TRUST AND COMMUNICATION

Chapter 2 focused on the achievement of organizational objectives. In *interdependent* organizations the organization's human components (individuals and groups) are asked to *pull together*. They must avoid that very special and destructive form of competition that pits organizational members or groups of members *against* one another in win-lose (often eventuating in lose-lose) contests.

To accomplish genuine *collaboration,* mutual *trust* is critical. And to initiate and perpetuate trust, *communication* excellence is vital.

ORGANIZATIONAL CLIMATE AND COMMUNICATION

In Chapter 3, we began with a brief discussion of some of the major trends occurring within our present-day organizations. Among other changes, organizations are growing more complex. They are challenged to respond to ever greater demands from society and especially from their own members. In consequence, the organization requires greater communication competence on the part of its managers and key personnel than ever before in history.

This chapter then examined the overall climate of the organization, suggesting that a high-trust–high-performance cycle was desirable in the interests of both the individual and the organization. Conversely, a low-trust–low-performance cycle was to be prevented or, if already in effect, broken. McGregor's Theory Y (including some of the more recent developments such as situational leadership, goal setting, MBO, OD, Theory Z), with a policy of appropriate trust coupled with personal development, seemed a tenable approach. The integration of individual and organizational goals appeared to be a sound objective.

PERCEPTION AND COMMUNICATION

The next three chapters focus on the individual.

1. The Process of Perception

The central premise of Chapter 4 is that what we experience is not reality but our perception of reality. Our unwillingness or inability to internalize this truism can readily lead us into defensive and self-destructive behavior. Thus we are challenged to recognize that our "reality" is subjective, partial, unique, and subject to bias—and to ascertain accurately the perceptions of others.

2. The Frame of Reference and the Self-Image

The frame of reference concept, as discussed in Chapter 5, is offered to meet the above challenges. The frame of reference was likened to a stained-glass window in one's solitary confinement cell. The major lens of this window is one's self-image. A valid self-concept is essential if one is to deal effectively with others.

3. The Exceptionally Realistic Self-Image (ERSI)

Chapter 6 discusses some of the advantages that a person with an ERSI enjoys: the liberation of energy that would otherwise be required for self-image protection, the ease of maintaining an ERSI, the prerequisites for developing skills for reading others and screening inputs, and the selection of realistic personal goals.

This game plan for attaining an ERSI was recommended:

1. Make an earnest commitment to discover yourself.
2. Recognize and reduce your defenses against valid feedback.
3. Receive and evaluate the external and internal cues.

External feedback includes the cues that we may receive from others (hence, the Johari Window and the transactional analysis concepts) and from psychometric instruments and also the insights that we may derive from readings. Internal feedback can be acquired from, among other modes, psychotherapy, empathic listening, videotape playback, and personal stocktaking methods, such as the Personal Inventory and the Crisis Journal.

MOTIVATION AND COMMUNICATION

In Chapter 7, concern with the individual is the main theme, but this time as a need-satisfying organism whose needs influence perceptions and thus, behavior. I agree with Demosthenes: "The easiest thing of all is to deceive oneself; for what a man wishes he generally believes to be true." The chapter explores several motivation theories in order to determine a basis for understanding and predicting the behavior of others—mandatory skills for effective communicators.

THE PROCESS OF COMMUNICATION

Chapter 8 focuses on an individual's communication behavior and presents a model of the communication process—encoding, transmitting, medium, receiving, decoding. Encoding and decoding are the most subtle, least understood, and most neglected phases of the process. The insidious role of fallacious, unconsciously held assumptions is underscored. Such assumptions contribute to recurrent patterns of miscommunication; a consideration of some of the most troublesome of these patterns constitutes the remainder of the book (Chapters 9 through 18).

THE INFERENCE-OBSERVATION CONFUSION

The inference-observation confusion occurs when one somehow acts upon inference as if it were observation. (See Chapter 9.) In essence, we sometimes risk without being aware that we are doing so and are off guard, therefore, against the possibility that the inferences are erroneous. The situation is not unlike that of walking downstairs in the dark—of striding off the last step, certain that you had reached the floor level!

One of the key reasons that we often find it easy to substitute inference for observation is that our *statements* of inference can be readily confused with *statements* of observation. That is, there is nothing in the nature of our language (grammar, spelling, pronunciation, syntax, and so on) that inescapably distinguishes between the two types of statements. Thus the habit of differentiating statements of inference from statements of observation should go far in training one's acuity in distinguishing between inferences and observations on nonverbal levels.

Accordingly, a four-step procedure for coping with the inference-observation confusion was suggested:

1. Detect the inference.
2. Calculate the probability that the inference is correct.
3. Get more data—if the risk is a poor one.
4. Recalculate the risk.

Finally, it was argued that creativity and decisiveness are not incompatible with inference awareness. Creativity can be facilitated when one is conscious of inferring. And the quality of decisions can be enhanced by inference awareness. The issue is not the avoidance of inferring (risk-taking) but the awareness of it.

BYPASSING

Bypassing (Chapter 10) occurs when communicators miss each other with their meanings—either by using the same word while meaning different things or by using different words while meaning the same thing. Resulting in false disagreements (or agreements), bypassings can sometimes be innocuous, even humorous. But on other occasions, they can be significantly more costly and destructive.

Immediately underlying bypassing is the supposition that words mean the same to the other person as they do to me. This belief, in turn, is supported by two insidious fallacies: that words have *mono-usage*; that words *have meanings*.

To guard against unintentional bypassing (deliberate bypassing was acknowledged), the communicator can supplant these assumptions with two others that represent much more adequately the relation between words and meanings: (1) most words, with the exception of some technical terms, are used in more than one way; (2) meanings exist not in words but only in the people who speak, hear, write, and read them, the people who fix the variables—that is, assign meanings to words.

Querying, paraphrasing, being approachable, using backup methods, practicing pretransmission and postreception audits, delaying, and remaining alert to contexts, verbal and situational, are some of the ways of implementing these premises.

ALLNESS

Allness is a sort of evaluational disease. (See Chapter 11.) It occurs when one unconsciously assumes that it is possible to know and to say everything about something; that what one is saying (or writing or thinking) covers *all* there is (or all that is important) about the subject. The assumption is manifestly fallacious, and yet it is an extremely difficult one to dislodge if we do not recognize that we are inevitably and continuously abstracting.

To abstract is to select some details of a situation while neglecting others. We abstract when we observe (see, hear, smell, and so on), talk, listen, write, read, think, and so forth.

When we fail to realize that we are abstracting, that is, leaving out details, we are in distinct danger of believing that we have left out nothing—nothing of consequence, at any rate. Arrogance, intolerance of other viewpoints, and closed-mindedness are frequent consequences of such false assurance.

Allness is encouraged by the craving for certainty—the intolerance of uncertainty, if you will—which afflicts all of us to some degree.

To intensify our awareness of abstracting and thus avoid allness, we should:

1. Cultivate the humility to concede that we can never say or know everything about anything.
2. Recognize that abstracting is inevitable when we talk, listen, and so on, for then we would be more likely . . .
   a. To assess and perhaps improve the quality of our abstractions.
   b. To be empathic.
   c. To be creative and less inhibited by past practices.
3. "Remember the etcetera," a simple, yet effective device.
4. Free ourselves from the insularity of an "all-wall."

The essence of this chapter is not the *avoidance* but the *awareness* of abstracting. Accordingly, it was asserted that decisiveness and viability *are* compatible.

DIFFERENTIATION FAILURES

1. Indiscrimination

Indiscrimination occurs when one fails to recognize differences among the similarities. The frequent result is that one reacts to blacks, police officers, politicians, business executives, Jews, and so forth, as if they were all identical—or at least enough alike to preclude any important differences. But people, situations, happenings, things, theories, and so forth, are unique. No two of anything are totally identical. And often there are differences that make a difference. The basic device for warding off dogmatic, unreasonable indiscriminations is the Which Index—black$_1$ is not the same as black$_2$, and so on. (See Chapter 12.)

2. Polarization

Chapter 13 states that polarization is the result of the confusion of *contraries* (situations involving graded variations, middle ground, alternatives) for *contradictories* (strict either-or, no-middle-ground affairs). It is the tendency to evaluate and communicate in black-and-white terms when shades of gray would be more appropriate.

An escalating conflict (the vicious pendulum effect) occurs when polarizers drive each other into extreme positions. This pattern of miscommunication is dangerous enough on the interpersonal level, but on the national and international levels, it can be catastrophic.

Polarization can be prevented, or at least diminished, if we learn to distinguish contraries from contradictories and to apply the How-Much Index.

To cope with the pendulum effect, it is helpful to regard differing perceptions as the consequence of differing conditioning and to concede that in complicated problems no one (including ourselves) has the one complete and incontestable solution.

3. The Frozen Evaluation

The frozen evaluation generally occurs when one assumes nonchange (Chapter 14). It tends to occur when one unconsciously believes that the way it (a person, a process, a situation, an object, and so on) is now is the way it has always been—or always will be. This can be a troublesome and dangerous premise because literally nothing (especially human beings) remains the same. Perhaps the only constant aspect about the world in which we live is its inconsistancy.

We can keep ourselves alert to the process nature of life by habitually When-Indexing (dating) out thoughts and statements. Person[1982], after all, is not the same as Person[1992].

INTENSIONAL ORIENTATION

1. A General Statement

This first chapter on intensional orientation (Chapter 15) does not deal with a specific pattern of miscommunication but rather with a general approach to reality. We are intensionally oriented when we go primarily, if not solely, by our maps (verbal and otherwise) of the territory rather than by the territory itself. An intensional parent, for example, might be guided by hazy memories from childhood, by the theories in Sunday supplement articles, and by various childrearing notions and nostrums of one's generation to the virtual exclusion of one's firsthand observations of the behavior of the child.

Intensional orientation invites trouble, confusion, and conflict (1) because often our maps (one's child-care theories and notions, for example) inadequately and fallaciously represent the territory (the flesh-and-blood child's feelings and behavior) and (2) because we may be unaware that we are dealing primarily with these maps and not with the respective territories that they represent. We may thus be led to react to the territory inappropriately, unintelligently, and even dangerously.

The basic remedy for diminishing the destructive effects of intensional orientation is to "get extensional." That is, develop a readiness to go out and examine the territory rather than be content to be deluded by one's often spurious maps. The byword of extensionality is to look first— then talk.

2. "Pointing" and "Associating"

As discussed in Chapter 16, among the ways we use words are these: (1) simply to point to, or call attention to, what we are representing by the words and (2) to evoke associations (memories, feelings) for what we are referring to. "Jail," for example, may be used to point, figuratively, to the physical structure in which prisoners are housed. But it may also be used to elicit an emotional response, as when one is threatened with "jail."

When one is unaware that words may be used for these dual purposes, there is the possibility of a number of miscommunication patterns, including the "pointing-association" confusion (the tendency to respond to the associations evoked in one by words *as if* one were responding to what was being represented by the words); name-calling (the tendency for one's evaluation of a person to be influenced by the "associative" labels that have been applied to that person); and "associative" bypassing (the tendency for communicators to miss each other's "associative" meanings).

3. Blindering

My definition (i.e., my interpretation, size-up, perception, appraisal, and so on) of a problem greatly influences my attempts at solving the problem (see Chapter 17). But a definition is inevitably an abstraction, a leaving out of details. If, then, in defining a problem, I am *unaware* of leaving out details (especially if they are important or vital details), I am in danger of becoming blindered—of unconsciously permitting a narrowed perception to restrict my attack on the problem. The basic correctives are (1) to remember that definitions inevitably involve the exclusion of details (perhaps crucial ones) and (2) to recognize and remove the blinders.

UNDELAYED RESPONSES

Chapter 18 points out that some undelayed reactions, such as reflex responses, are largely unavoidable, harmless, and even self-protective. Others, such as many reflexlike responses, may be highly useful when they have been properly conditioned and employed—the numerous actions of driving an automobile, for example. But some reflexlike responses—for instance, those manifested in fear and rage—are often destructive. It is the latter that should be controlled if we are to avoid contributing to the harm of ourselves and others.

In some respects, Chapter 18 is the key chapter of Part Three, "Patterns of Miscommunication." Whereas the other chapters recommend various techniques, habits, and devices for avoiding and correcting the patterns of misevaluation and miscommunication, this chapter urged the basic setting for using them—the habit of delay-while-evaluating before action.

SUMMARY

The basic corrective methods for these patterns of miscommunication, then, have been to suggest techniques, first, for becoming (and remaining) aware of the insidious assumptions that influence our evaluation and communication and, second, to recommend the substitution of new, more adequate premises.

To implement these premises, I have suggested a number of evaluational habits as substitutes for, or modifications of, some existing habits. Let the reader be cautioned, however. The firm, enduring acquisition of these deceptively simple habits will not come easily. They will require practice and persistence. The experience will not be unlike that of a person who for years has typed with two fingers and is now learning the touch system of 10-finger typing. The individual may become discouraged, for efficiency may actually decrease at first. But eventually, the benefits—the ease and speed of touch typing—outweigh the temporary discomfort.

With cultivation, then, these evaluational habits (which, when, and how-much indexing; remembering the etcetera; querying and paraphrasing; distinguishing inference from observation; and so forth) can become second-nature conditioned responses that will pay handsome rewards in terms of more intelligent, safe, productive, and mature communicative behavior.

A Bibliography on Communication, Interpersonal Relations, and Related Areas

COMMUNICATION, INTERPERSONAL RELATIONS, MANAGEMENT

Adair, John. *Management Decision Making*. Brookfield, Vt.: Gower Pub. Co., 1985.

Adler, Ronald. *Communicating at Work*. 3rd ed. New York: McGraw–Hill, 1989.

Adler, Ronald, and George Rodman. *Understanding Human Communication*. 3rd ed. New York: Holt, Rinehart and Winston, 1988.

Ailes, Roger, and Jon Kraushar. *You Are the Message*. New York: Simon & Schuster, 1988.

Anderson, James A., ed. *Communication Yearbook*, vol. 12. Newbury Park, Calif.: Sage Publications, 1989.

Argyris, Chris. *Integrating the Individual and the Organization*. New Brunswick, N.J.: Transaction Publications, 1990.

Austin, Larry M., and James R. Burns. *Management Science*. New York: Macmillan, 1985.

Baker, Kenneth R., and Dean H. Kropp. *Management Science: An Introduction to Decision Models*. New York: John Wiley & Sons, 1985.

Barker, Larry L. *Communication*. 5th ed. Englewood Cliffs, N.J.: Prentice Hall, 1987.

Bateman, David, and Norman Sigband. *Communicating in Business*. 3rd ed. Hinsdale, Ill.: Dryden Press, 1988.

Beer, Michael, et al. *Managing Human Assets: The Groundbreaking Harvard Business School Program*. New York: Free Press, 1985.

Bergen, G. L., and W. V. Haney. *Organizational Relations and Management Action*. New York: McGraw-Hill, 1966.

Berko, Roy M., et al. *This Business of Communicating*. 4th ed. Dubuque, Iowa: Wm. C. Brown, 1990.

Blanchard, Kenneth; Patricia Zigarmi; and Drea Zigarmi. *Leadership and the One Minute Manager.* New York: William Morrow, 1985.

Borden, George A. *Human Communication Systems.* 2nd ed. Boston: American Press, 1989.

Brakel, Aat, ed. *People and Organizations Interacting.* New York: John Wiley & Sons, 1985.

Budd, Richard W., and Brent D. Ruben, eds. *Beyond Media: New Approaches to Mass Communication.* New Brunswick, N.J.: Transaction Publications, 1988.

Cascio, Wayne F. *Applied Psychology in Personnel Management.* 3rd ed. Englewood Cliffs, N.J.: Prentice Hall, 1987.

Catt, Stephen E., and Donald S. Miller, *Supervisory Management and Communication.* Homewood, Ill.: Irwin, 1985.

Chase, Stuart. *Power of Words.* New York: Harcourt Brace Jovanovich, 1954.

―――――. *Roads to Agreement.* New York: Harper & Row, 1951.

Cohen, Allan R.; Stephen L. Fink; Herman Gadon; and Robin D. Willits. *Effective Behavior in Organizations.* 4th ed. Homewood, Ill.: Richard D. Irwin, 1988.

Communicontents. Abstracts of communication books. Vol. 1. 1970–.

Cox, Charles, and John Beck, eds. *Management Development: Advances in Practice and Theory.* New York: John Wiley & Sons, 1984.

Cummings, L. L., and Randall B. Dunham. *Introduction to Organizational Behavior.* Homewood, Ill.: Richard D. Irwin, 1980.

Cushman, Donald P., and Dudley D. Cahn, Jr. *Communication in Interpersonal Relationships.* Albany, N.Y.: State University of New York Press, 1984.

Cutlip, Scott M., et al. *Effective Public Relations.* 6th ed. Englewood Cliffs, N.J.: Prentice Hall, 1985.

Davis, Keith, and J. Newstrom. *Human Behavior at Work.* 8th ed. New York: McGraw-Hill, 1989.

DeCenzo, David A., and Stephen P. Robbins. *Personnel/Human Resource Management.* 3rd ed. Englewood Cliffs, N.J.: Prentice Hall, 1988.

Dessler, Gary. *Management Fundamentals.* 4th ed. Reston, Va.: Reston Publishing, 1985.

Diebold, John. *Managing Information: The Challenge and the Opportunity.* New York: AMACOM, 1985.

Dittrich, John E., and Robert A. Zawacki. *People and Organizational Behavior.* 2nd ed. Homewood, Ill.: Irwin/BPI, 1985.

Donnelly, James H., Jr.; James L. Gibson; and John M. Ivancevich. *Fundamentals of Management: Functions, Behavior, Models.* 6th ed. Homewood, Ill.: Irwin/BPI, 1987.

Downs, Cal W., ed. *Communication Audits.* Glenview, Ill.: Scott, Foresman, 1988.

Drucker, Peter F. *The Effective Executive.* New York: Harper & Row, 1967.

―――――. *Management: Tasks, Responsibilities, Practices.* Abridged and rev. ed. New York: Harper & Row, 1985.

―――――. *Managing for Results.* New York: Harper & Row, 1986.

―――――. *The Practice of Management.* New York: Harper & Row, 1986.

Dunham, Randall B. *Organizational Behavior: People and Processes in Management.* Homewood, Ill.: Richard D. Irwin, 1984.

Dunham, Randall B., and Jon L. Pierce. *Management.* Glenview, Ill.: Scott, Foresman, 1988.

Eisenberg, Abne. *Communicating Effectively at Work*. Prospect Heights, Ill.: Waveland Press, 1984.

Erickson, Steve. *Management Tools for Everyone*. Princeton, N.J.: Petrocelli Books, 1985.

Flaherty, John E. *Managing Change: Today's Challenge to Management*. New York: Irvington Pubs., 1984.

Flippo, Edwin B., and Gary M. Munsinger. *Management*. 5th ed. Boston: Allyn & Bacon, 1982.

French, Wendell L., and Cecil H. Bell. *Organizational Development: Behavior Science Intervention for Organizational Improvement*. 4th ed. Englewood Cliffs, N.J.: Prentice Hall, 1990.

Fruehling, Rosemary T., and Roy W. Poe. *Business Communication: A Problem-Solving Approach*. New York: McGraw-Hill, 1984.

Fulk, H Janet, and Charles W. Steinfield, eds. *Organizations and Communication Technology*. Newbury Park, Calif.: Sage Publications, 1990.

Geneen, Harold S., and Alvin Moscow. *Managing*. New York: Doubleday Publishing, 1984.

Gibson, James L.; John M. Ivancevich; and James H. Donnelly, Jr. *Organizations: Behavior, Structure, Processes*. 6th ed. Homewood, Ill.: Irwin/BPI, 1988.

_____. *Organizations Closeup: A Book of Readings*. 6th ed. Homewood Ill.: Irwin/BPI, 1988.

Goldhaber, Gerald M. *Organizational Communication*. 4th ed. Dubuque, Iowa: Wm. C. Brown, 1986.

Goldhaber, Gerald M., and George A. Barnett, eds. *Handbook of Organizational Communication*. Norwood, N.J.: Ablex Pub., 1988.

Greene, Carles N.; Everett E. Cedam, Jr.; and Ronald J. Ebert. *Management for Effective Performance*. Englewood Cliffs, N.J.: Prentice Hall, 1985.

Greenwald, Howard H.; Susan A. Hellweg; Joseph W. Walter and Associates. *Organizational Communication: Abstracts, Analyses, and Overview*, 10. Beverly Hills, Calif.: Sage Publications, 1985. See also 5 (1980), 6 (1981), 7 (1982), 8 (1983), and 9 (1984).

Greenwood, James W., III, and James Greenwood, Jr. *Managing Executive Stress: A Systems Approach*. Tenafly, N.J.: Burrill-Ellsworth Assoc., 1984.

Gregson, Shaun, and Frank Livesey. *Management and the Organization*. Pomfret, Vt: David & Charles, Inc., 1984.

Halpern, Jeanne W. "Differences between Speaking and Writing and Their Implication for Teaching." *College Composition and Communication* 35 (October, 1984), pp. 345–57.

Haney, William V. "A Comparative Study of Unilateral and Bilateral Communication." *Academy of Management Journal* 7, no. 2 (June 1964), pp. 128–36.

_____. "Serial Communication of Information in Organization." In *Concepts and Issues in Administrative Behavior*. Eds. Sidney Mailick and Edward H. Van Ness, pp. 150–65. Englewood Cliffs, N.J.: Prentice Hall, 1962. Reprinted in *ETC: A Review of General Semantics* 21, no. 1 (March 1964), pp. 13–29.

Heneman, Herbert G. III, et al. *Personnel/Human Resource Management*. 4th ed. Homewood, Ill.: Richard D. Irwin, 1989.

Hersey, Paul. *The Situational leader*. New York: Warner Books, 1985.

Hersey, Paul, and K. H. Blanchard. *Management of Organizational Behavior*. 5th ed. Englewood Cliffs, N.J.: Prentice Hall, 1988.

Higgins, James M. *The Management Challenge: An Introduction to Management.* New York: Macmillan, 1991.

————. *Organizational Behavior.* New York: Random House, 1985.

Hoffman, W. Michael, et al. *The Ethics of Organizational Transformation.* Westport, Conn.: Quorum Books, 1989.

Howard, Ann, and James A. Wilson. "Leadership Is a Declining Work Ethic." *California Management Review,* vol. XXIV, no. 4 (Summer, 1984), pp. 33–46.

Huse, Edgar F., and Thomas Cummings. *Organization Development and Change.,* 3rd ed. St. Paul, Minn.: West Publishing, 1985.

Huseman, Richard C., et al. *Readings and Applications in Business Communication.* 2nd ed. Hinsdale, Ill.: Dryden Press, 1985.

Huseman, Richard C., and James M. Lahiff. *Business Communication: Strategies and Skills.* 3rd ed. Hinsdale, Ill.: Dryden Press, 1988.

Ivancevitch, John M., and Michael T. Matteson. *Organizational Behavior and Management.* Homewood, Ill.: Irwin/BPI, 1987.

Jamieson, Harry. *Communication and Persuasion.* Dover, N.H.: Croom Helm, Ltd., 1985.

Johnson, Wendell. "The Fateful Process of Mr. A Talking to Mr. B." *Harvard Business Review* 31 (January 1953), pp 49–56.

Kirkpatrick, Donald L. *No-Nonsense Communication.* 3rd ed. Elm Grove, Wisc.: K & M Publishers, 1983.

Koontz, Harold D., and Heinz Weirich. *Management.* 9th ed. New York: McGraw-Hill, 1988.

————. *Essentials of Management.* 5th ed. New York: McGraw-Hill, 1989.

Kotter, John P., et. al. *Organization.* 2nd ed. Homewood, Ill.: Richard D. Irwin, 1986.

Kreitner, Robert, and Angelo Kinicki. *Organizational Behavior.* Homewood, Ill.: Irwin/BPI, 1989.

Lau, James B., and A.B. Shani. *Behavior in Organizations.* 4th ed. Homewood, Ill.: Richard D. Irwin, 1988.

Lawrence, Peter. *Management in Action.* Boston: Routledge & Kegan Paul, 1984.

Leavitt, Harold J., and Homa Bahrami. *Managerial Psychology.* 5th ed. Chicago: University of Chicago Press, 1978.

Leavitt, Harold J., et al, eds. 4th ed. *Readings in Managerial Psychology.* Chicago: University of Chicago Press, 1988.

Lee, Irving J. *Customs and Crises in Communication.* New York: Harper & Row, 1954.

————. *How to Talk with People.* New York: Harper & Row, 1952.

————. "Procedure for 'Coercing' Agreement," *Harvard Business Review* 32, no. 1 (January 1954), pp. 39–45.

Lee, Irving J., and Laura L. Lee. *Handling Barriers in Communication* 2nd ed. San Francisco: International Society. In General Semantics, 1978.

Lee, Mary D., and Rabindra N. Kanugo. *Management of Work and Personal Life: Problems and Opportunities.* New York: Praeger Publishers, 1984.

Lee, Sang M., et al. *Management Science.* 3rd ed. Needham Heights, Mass.: Allyn & Bacon, 1989.

Lesikar, Raymond V. *Basic Business Communication.* 4th ed. Homewood, Ill.: Richard D. Irwin, 1987.

Level, Dale A., Jr. *Managerial Communications.* Homewood, Ill.: Irwin/BPI, 1988.

Lewis, Phillip V. *Organizational Communications: The Essence of Effective Management.* 2nd ed. Columbus, Ohio: Grid, 1980.

Liggett, Sarah. "Speaking/Writing Relationships and Business Communication." *The Journal of Business Communication* 22, no. 2 (Spring 1985), pp. 47–54.

Lippitt, Gordon, et. al. *Implementing Organizational Change.* San Francisco: Jossey-Bass, 1985.

Llevada, E. Jerry. *Management of the Quality Function.* Reston, Va.: Reston Publishing, 1985.

Lussier, Robert N. *Human Relations in Organizations.* Homewood, Ill.: Richard D. Irwin, 1990.

Luthans, F. *Organizational Behavior.* 4th ed. New York: McGraw-Hill, 1985.

Maidment, Robert, and William Bullock. *Meetings, Meetings, Meetings: Accomplishing More with Better and Fewer.* Reston, Va.: National Association of Secondary School Principals, 1984.

March, James G. *A Handbook of Organizations.* Skokie, Ill.: Rand McNally, 1965.

March, James G. A., and H. A. Simon. *Organizations.* New York: John Wiley & Sons, 1958.

Maslow, Abraham. *Toward a Psychology of Being.* 2nd ed. Princeton, N.J.: D. Van Nostrand Co., Inc., 1968.

Massie, Joseph L., and John Douglas, *Managing: A Contemporary Introduction,* 4th ed. Englewood Cliffs, N.J.: Prentice Hall, 1985.

McCoy, Charles S. *Management of Values: The Ethical Differences In Corporate Policy and Performance.* Marshfield, Mass.: Pitman Pub., Inc., 1985.

McFarland, Dalton E. *Managerial Imperative: The Age of Macromanagement.* New York: Harper Brothers, 1985.

McGregor, Douglas. *The Professional Manager.* New York: McGraw-Hill, 1967.

McGregor, Douglas. *The Human Side of Enterprise.* New York: McGraw-Hill, 1960.

McLuhan, Marshall. *Understanding Media.* New York: McGraw-Hill, 1964.

Mellor, D.H., ed. *Ways of Communicating: The Darwin College Lectures.* New York: Cambridge University Press, 1989.

Mescon, Michael, et al. *Management: Individual and Organizational Effectiveness,* 3rd ed. New York: Harper & Row, 1988.

Meyer, John W., and W. Richard Scott. *Organizational Environments.* Beverly Hills, Calif.: Sage Publications, 1983.

Micheli, Linda McJ.; Frank V. Cespedes; Donald Byker; and Thomas J. C. Raymond. *Managerial Communication.* Glenview, Ill.: Scott, Foresman, 1984.

Milkovitch, George T., and John W. Boudreau. *Personnel/Human Resource Management.* 5th ed. Homewood, Ill.: Irwin/BPI, 1988.

Mintzberg, Henry. *Mintzberg on Management: Inside Our Strange World of Organizations.* New York: The Free Press, 1989.

Morgan, Gareth. *Creative Organization Theory.* Newbury Park, Calif.: Sage Publications, 1989.

Newman, Wm. H. Summer, and E. Kirby Warren. *The Process of Management.* 5th ed. Englewood Cliffs, N.J.: Prentice Hall, 1982.

Odiorne George. *The Effective Executive's Guide to Managerial Excellence.* Westfield, Mass.: MBO, Inc., 1983.

Oncken, William, Jr. *Managing Management Time: Who's Got the Monkey?* Englewood Cliffs, N.J.: Prentice Hall, 1984.

Organ, Dennis W., and Thomas Bakman. *Organizational Behavior*. 3rd ed. Homewood, Ill.: Irwin/BPI, 1986.

Pace, R. Wayne, and Donald Faules. *Organizational Communication*. 2nd ed. Englewood Cliffs, N.J.: Prentice Hall, 1989.

Parker, Frederick. *Management Techniques for Top Executives*. Pompano Beach, Fl.: Exposition Press of Florida Inc., 1984.

Peter, Laurence. *The Peter Prescription*. New York: Bantam, 1984.

————. *The Peter Principle*. New York: William Morrow and Co., 1969.

Peters, Thomas J., and Nancy K. Austin. *A Passion for Excellence*. New York: Random House, 1985.

Peters, Thomas J., and Robert H. Waterman, Jr. *In Search of Excellence: Lessons from America's Best-Run Companies*. New York: Harper & Row, 1982.

Peterson, Brent D.; Gerald M. Goldhaber; and R. Wayne Pace. *Communication Probes*. 3rd ed. Chicago: Science Research Associates, Inc., 1982.

Pigors, Paul, and Charles A. Myers. *Personnel Administration*. 9th ed. New York: McGraw-Hill, 1981.

Pugh, D. S., ed. *Organization Theory*. Rev. ed. New York: Penguin Books, 1985.

Putnam, Linda L., and Michael E. Pacanowsky. *Communication and Organizations*. Beverly Hills, Calif.: Sage Publications, 1983.

Randolph, W. Alan. *Understanding and Managing Organizational Behavior*. Homewood. Ill.: Richard D. Irwin, 1985.

Raymond, H. Alan. *Management in the Third Wave*. Glenview, Ill.: Scott, Foresman, 1985.

Reitz, H. Joseph. *Behavior in Organizations*. 2nd ed. Homewood, Ill.: Richard D. Irwin, 1981.

Robbins, Stephen P. *Training in Interpersonal Skills*. Englewood Cliffs, N.J.: Prentice Hall, 1989.

Rockey, Edward. *Communicating in Organizations*. Lanham, Md.: University Press of America, 1985.

Roethlisberger, Fritz J. "Barriers to Communication between Men." *Northwestern University Information* 20, no. 25 (April 21, 1952).

Roethlisberger, Fritz J., and William J. Dickson. *Management and the Worker*. Cambridge, Mass.: Harvard University Press, 1950.

Scanlon, Burt K. "Creating a Climate for Achievement." *Business Horizons* (March/April 1981), pp. 5–9.

Schermerhorn, John R., Jr. *Management for Productivity*. 2nd ed. New York: John Wiley & Sons, 1989.

————. *Managing Organizational Behavior*. 3rd ed. New York: John Wiley & Sons, 1988.

Schrage, Michael. *Shared Minds: The New Technologies of Collaboration*. New York: Random House, 1990.

Schramm, Wilbur, and Donald F. Roberts. *The Process and Effects of Mass Communication*. Rev. ed. Urbana: University of Illinois Press, 1971.

Schramm, Wilbur. "How Communication Works." In *The Process and Effects of Mass Communication*, ed. W. Schramm. Urbana: University of Illinois Press, 1954.

Sears, Woodrow H., Jr. "Redefining HRD: Let's Cast Our Lot with Management." *Training* (May 1984), p. 120.

Sereno, Ken. *Notes of Human Communication Theory*. Dubuque, Iowa: Kendall-Hunt, 1989.

Shields, et al. *Effective Communication for Professionals*. Dubuque, Iowa: Kendall-Hunt, 1989.

Siegel, Lawrence, and Irving M. Lane. *Personnel and Organizational Psychology*. 2nd ed. Homewood, Ill.: Richard D. Irwin, 1987.

Sigband, Norman B. "Proaction, Not Reaction, for Effective Employee Communications." *Personnel* (March 1982), pp. 190–92.

Simon, H. A. *Administrative Behavior*, 3rd ed. New York: Macmillan, 1976.

Smeltzer, Larry R., and John L. Waltman. *Managerial Communication: A Strategic Approach*. New York: John Wiley & Sons, 1984.

Smith, Dennis L., and Keith Williamson. *Interpersonal Communication: Roles, Rules, Strategies, and Games*. 3rd ed. Dubuque, Iowa: Wm. C. Brown, 1985.

Smith, Peter B., and Mark F. Peterson. *Leadership, Organizations, and Culture*. Newbury Park, Calif.: Sage Publications, 1988.

Stam and Bowes. *The Mass Communication Process: A Behavioral and Social Perspective*. Dubuque, Iowa: Kendall-Hunt, 1988.

Steers, Richard M.; Gerardo R. Ungson; and Richard T. Mowday. *Managing Effective Organizations: An Introduction*. Boston: Kent Pub. Co., 1985.

Tayeb, Monir H., *Organizations and National Culture*. Newbury Park, Calif.: Sage Publications, 1988.

Terry, George R., and S. G. Franklin. *Principles of Management*. 8th ed. Homewood, Ill.: Richard D. Irwin, 1982.

Thayer, Lee, ed. *Organization-Communication: Emerging Perspectives I*. Norwood, N.J.: Ablex Pub., 1986.

————. *Organization-Communication: Emerging Perspectives II*. Norwood, N.J.: Ablex Pub., 1988.

Tosi, Henry L., and W. Clay Hammer. *Organizational Behavior and Management*. 4th ed. Columbus, Ohio: Grid, 1985.

Watson, Kittie, and Larry L. Barker. *Interpersonal and Relational Communication*. Scottsdale, Ariz.: Gorsuch Scarisbrick, 1989.

Weick, Karl E. "Misconceptions about Managerial Productivity." *Business Horizons* (July/August 1983), pp. 47–52.

Whyte, William F. *Men at Work*. Homewood, Ill.: Richard D. Irwin, 1961.

Wiener, Norbert. *The Human Use of Human Beings*. Boston: Houghton Mifflin, 1950.

Wiksell, Wesley. *Do They Understand You?* New York: Macmillan, 1960.

Williams, John W., and Steven A. Eggland. *Communication in Action*. Cincinnati: South-Western Publishing, 1985.

Wilson, Gerald L., et al. *Interpersonal Growth through Communication*. Dubuque, Iowa: Wm. C. Brown, 1984.

Winfield, Ian. *People in Business*. North Pomfret, Vt.: David and Charles, Inc., 1984.

Wolf, Morris P., and Shirley Kulper. *Effective Communication in Business*. 8th ed. Cincinnati: South-Western Publishing, 1984.

Wood, Donald N. *Designing the Effective Message: Critical Thinking and Communications*. Dubuque, Iowa: Kendall-Hunt, 1989.

Zeimer, Rodger, and William Tranter. *Principles of Communications*. 3rd ed. Boston: Houghton-Mifflin, 1990.

PERCEPTION

Allport, F. H. *Theories of Perception and the Concept of Structure*. New York: John Wiley & Sons, 1955.

Appelbaum, David. *The Interpenetrating Reality: Bring the Body to Touch*. New York: Peter Lang, Pubs., 1988.

Beaumont, J. Graham. *Brainpower: Unlocking the Secrets of the Mind*. New York: Harper & Row, 1990.

Berkeley Neuroscience Series. *Comparative Perception: Discrimination, Vol. 1*. New York: John Wiley & Sons, 1990.

————. *Comparative Perception: Communication Perception, Vol. 2*. New York: John Wiley & Sons, 1990.

Blake, R. R., and G. V. Ramsey, eds. *Perception: An Approach to Personality*. New York: Ronald Press Co., 1951.

Boudin, Don. *Ears to Hear, Eyes to See*. Nashville: Broadman, 1987.

Broadbent, D. E. *Perception and Communication*. New York: Oxford University Press, 1987.

Brouwer, Paul J. "The Power to See Ourselves." *Harvard Business Review*, vol. 42 (November 1964), pp. 156–62.

Carlsen, G. Robert. *Perception*. 4th ed. New York: McGraw-Hill, 1985.

Caws, Mary A. *Perspectives on Perception: Philosophy, Art, and Literature*. New York: Peter Lang, Pubs., 1989.

Combs, Arthur W., et al. *Perceptual Psychology*. Lanham, Md.: University Press of America, 1988.

Coren, Stanley, and Lawrence M. Ward. *Sensation and Perception*. 3rd ed. San Diego: Harcourt Brace Jovanovich, 1989.

Elsedoorn, Ben, and Herman Bouma, eds. *Working Models of Human Perception*. San Diego: Academic Press, 1989.

Gear, Jane. *Perception and the Evolution of Style: A New Model of Man*. New York: Routledge Chapman & Hall, 1989.

Gibb, Jack R. "Defense Level and Influence Potential in Small Groups." In *Leadership and Interpersonal Behavior*, eds. L. Petrullo and B. M. Bass. New York: Holt, Rinehart & Winston, 1961, pp. 66–81.

————. "Defensive Communication," *Journal of Communication* 11, no. 3 (September 1961), pp. 141–48.

Gifford, Don. *The Farther Shore: A Natural History of Perception, 1798–1984*. New York: Atlantic Monthly, 1990.

Goldstein, E. Bruce. *Sensation and Perception*. 3rd ed. Belmont, Calif.: Wadsworth Press, 1989.

Heuer, Herbert, and A. F. Sanders. *Perceptives on Perception and Action*. Hillsdale, N.J.: Lawrence Erlbaum Assocs., Inc., 1987.

Horney, Karen. *Neurosis and Human Growth: The Struggle toward Self-Realization*. New York: W. W. Norton, 1950.

Jongeward, Dorothy, and Dru Scott. *Women as Winners: Transactional Analysis for Personal Growth.* Reading, Mass.: Addison-Wesley Publishing, 1976.

Mackay, D. G. *The Organization of Perception and Action.* New York: Springer-Verlag, 1987.

Maclachlin, D. L. *Philosophy of Perception.* Englewood Cliffs, N.J.: Prentice Hall, 1990.

Marko, H., et al., eds. *Processing Structures for Perception and Action.* New York: VCH Pubs., 1988.

Matlin, Margaret. *Sensation and Perception.* 2nd ed. Needham, Mass.: Allyn & Bacon, 1988.

Polinski, Roth. *Psychology of Perceptions: Index of Modern Information.* Annandale, Va.: ABBE Pubs. Assn. of Washington, D.C., 1989.

Rogers, C. R. *Client-Centered Therapy.* Boston: Houghton Mifflin, 1951.

_____. "Communication: Its Blocking and Its Facilitation." *Northwestern University Information* 20, no. 25, pp. 9–15.

Schiffman, *Sensations and Perception: An Integrated Approach.* 3rd ed. New York: John Wiley & Sons, 1990.

Stauch, Ralph. *The Reality Illusion: How You Create the World You Experience.* 2nd ed. Tarrytown, New York: Station Hill Press, 1989.

Watzlavick, Paul, ed. *The Invented Reality: How Do We Know What We Believe We Know?* New York: W. W. Norton, 1984.

_____. *How Real is Real? Confusion, Disinformation, Communication.* New York: Random House, 1977.

MOTIVATION

Archer, Earnest R. *Influence and Motivation: A Managerial Perspective.* Duluth, Ga.: Wesley, Cabot & Keith Pub., 1987.

Archer, T., and L. G. Nilsson, eds. *Aversion, Avoidance & Anxiety: Perspectives on Aversely Motivated Behavior.* Hillsdale, N.J.: Lawrence Erlbaum Assocs., 1988.

Beck, Robert C. *Motivation: Theories and Principles.* 3rd ed. Englewood Cliffs, N.J.: Prentice Hall, 1989.

Blake, Robert R., and Jane S. Mouton. *Managerial Grid III.* 3rd ed. Houston: Gulf Publishing, 1984.

Bower, Gordon H., ed. *The Psychology of Learning and Motivation.* Vol. 20. San Diego: Academic Press, 1986.

_____. *The Psychology of Learning and Motivation.* Vol. 22. San Diego: Academic Press, 1988.

Brody, Nathan E., ed. *Motivation.* San Diego: Academic Press, 1983.

Brown, D. R., and J. Verloff, eds. *Frontiers of Motivational Psychology.* New York: Springer-Verlag, 1986.

Buck, Ross. *Human Motivation and Emotion.* 2nd ed. New York: John Wiley & Sons, 1988.

Carlisle, Kenneth, and Sheila Murphy. *Practical Motivation.* New York: John Wiley & Sons, 1986.

Diel, Paul. *The Psychology of Motivation.* Claremont, Calif.: Hunter House, 1990.

Epstein, Eugene, and William C. Freund. *People and Productivity: The New York Stock Exchange Guide to Financial Incentives and the Quality of Work Life.* Homewood, Ill.: Dow Jones-Irwin, 1984.

Evans, Phil. *Motivation and Emotion.* New York: Routledge, Chapman & Hall, 1989.

Ferguson, E. D. *Motivation: An Experimental Approach.* New York: Holt, Rinehart & Winston, 1976.

Fershleiser, Russel. "Toward Wholistic Approach to Job Satisfaction." *MBA Society Journal* III, no. 1 (1983), pp. 19–28.

Festinger, Leon A. "The Motivating Effect of Cognitive Dissonance." In *Assessment of Human Motives,* ed. G. Lindzey. New York: Holt, Rinehart & Winston, 1958, pp. 65–68.

————. *A Theory of Cognitive Dissonance.* Stanford, Calif.: Stanford University Press, 1962.

Goldberg, Joel A. *Manager's Guide to Productivity Improvement.* New York: Praeger Publishers, 1985.

Grant, Philip C. "Motivation, Myths, and Misnomers." *Management World* (June 1982).

Gorlitz, Dietmar, and Joachim Wohwill, eds. *Curiosity Imagination & Play: On the Development of Spontaneous Cognitive and Motivational Processes.* Hillsdale, N.J.: Lawrence Erlbaum Assocs., 1987.

Hacker, W., et al., eds. *Cognitive and Motivational Aspects of Action.* New York: Elsvier Science Pub. Co., 1983.

Herzberg, Frederick. "One More Time: How Do You Motivate Employees?" *Harvard Business Review* 46, no. 1 (January-February 1968) pp. 53–62.

————. *Work and the Nature of Man.* Cleveland: World Publishing Co., 1966.

Herzberg, Frederick; B. Mausner; and B. Snyderman. *The Motivation to Work.* 2nd ed. New York: John Wiley & Sons, 1962.

Higgins, E. Tory, and Richard Sorrentino, eds. *Handbook of Motivation and Cognition.* Vol. 2. New York: Guilford Press, 1990.

Houston, John P. *Motivation.* New York: Macmillan, 1985.

Losoncy, Lewis. *Motivating Leader.* Englewood Cliffs, N.J.: Prentice Hall, 1985.

McClelland, David C. *Motives, Personality, and Society.* New York: Praeger Publishers, 1984.

————. *Human Motivation.* New York: Cambridge University Press, 1988.

Maslow, Abraham H. *Motivation and Personality.* 2nd ed. New York: Harper & Row, 1970.

Quick, Thomas L. *Manager's Motivation Desk Book.* New York: John Wiley & Sons, 1985.

Shapero, Albert. *Managing Professional People: Understanding Creative Performance.* New York: Free Press, 1985.

Thompson, Ross A., ed. *Nebraska Symposium on Motivation and Socioemotional Development.* Lincoln: University of Nebraska Press, 1990.

Thurow, Lester C., ed. *Management Challenge: The Japanese View.* Cambridge, Mass.: MIT Press, 1985.

Weihrich, H. *Management Excellence: Productivity through MBO.* New York: McGraw-Hill, 1985.

COMMUNICATION PROCESSES

Speaking

Adams, Artie; Annette N. Shelby; and Jerry L. Tarver. *Speaking Up Successfully: Communication in Business and the Professions.* New York: Holt, Rinehart & Winston, 1984.

Applebaum, Ronald L., and Karl W. Anatol. *Effective Oral Communications in Business and the Professions.* Chicago: Science Research Associates, 1982.

Applebaum, Ronald L., and Roderick Hart. *Business and Professional Speech.* Chicago: Science Research Associates, 1984.

————. *Persuasive Speaking.* 2nd ed. Chicago: Science Research Associates, 1984.

Atkins, Martha A. *Fundamentals of Public Speaking.* Dubuque, Iowa: Kendall-Hunt, 1989.

Ayers, H. Joseph, and Janice M. Miller. *Effective Public Speaking.* 3rd ed. Dubuque, Iowa: Wm. C. Brown, 1990.

Barker, Larry L. *Communication.* 3rd ed. Englewood Cliffs, N.J.: Prentice Hall, 1984.

Barrett, Harold, *Practical Uses of Speech Communication.* 6th ed. Troy, Mo.: Holt, Rinhart & Winston, 1987.

Bell, Cary B. *Speaking in Business: A Basic Survival Guide.* Dubuque, Iowa: Kendall-Hunt, 1984.

Bock, et al. *Communication.* Dubuque, Iowa: Kendall-Hunt, 1989.

Brooks, William D. *Speech Communications.* 4th ed. Dubuque, Iowa: Wm. C. Brown, 1981.

Capps, Randall, and J. Regis O'Connor. *Fundamentals of Effective Speech Communication.* Lanham, Md.: University Press of America, 1984.

Chapey, Geraldine. *Developing Speaking Skill.* New York: McGraw-Hill, 1989.

Cook, Scott J. *The Elements of Speech Writing and Public Speaking.* New York: Macmillan, 1990.

Dance, Frank E., and Carol Zak-Dance. *Public Speaking.* New York: Harper & Row, 1986.

Dodson, R. J. *Guide to Speaking in Public.* 2nd ed. Salem, Wis.: Sheffield Pub., 1990.

Doolittle, Robert J. *Professionally Speaking: A Concise Guide.* Glenview, Ill.: Scott Foresman, 1984.

Glenn, Ethyl C., and Sandra H. Forman. *Public Speaking.* Englewood Cliffs, N.J.: Prentice Hall, 1990.

Hanson, et al. *The Practice of Public Speaking.* Dubuque, Iowa: Kendall-Hunt, 1990.

Lagerstrom and Cooper. *Strategies and Approaches to Public Speaking.* Dubuque, Iowa: Kendall-Hunt, 1989.

Miles-Brown, John. *Speech for the Speaker.* Chester Springs, Pa.: Dufour Editions, 1990.

Minnick, Wayne C. *Public Speaking.* 2nd ed. Boston: Houghton Mifflin, 1983.

Mississippi State University Staff. *Participating in Public Speaking.* 3rd ed. Dubuque, Iowa: Kendall-Hunt, 1989.

Nelson, Robert B. *Making Effective Presentations*. Glenview, Ill.: Scott, Foresman, 1989.

Phillips, Gerald M.; Kathleen M. Cougl; and Lynne Kelly. *Speaking in Public and Private*. New York: Bobbs-Merrill, 1985.

Reinhart, Susan H., and Ira Fisher. *Speaking and Social Interaction*. Englewood Cliffs, N.J.: Prentice Hall, 1985.

Samvar, Larry A., and Jack Mills. *Oral Communication*. 7th ed. Dubuque, Iowa: Wm C. Brown, 1989.

Tacey, William S. *Business and Professional Speaking*. 4th ed. Dubuque, Iowa: Wm. C. Brown, 1983.

Van Oosting, James. *The Business Speech: Speaker, Audience, and Text*. Englewood Cliffs, N.J.: Prentice Hall, 1985.

Verderber, Rudolph. *The Challenge of Effective Speaking*. 7th ed. Belmont, Calif.: Wadsworth, 1988.

Wilson, John F., et al. *Public Speaking as a Liberal Art*. 6th ed. Needham Heights, Mass.: Allyn & Bacon, 1990.

Writing

Adelstein, M. E., & W. K. Sparrow. *Business Communications*. New York: Harcourt Brace Jovanovich, 1983.

Adelstein, Michael. *Business of Better Writing Series*. Lexington, Ky.: KET, 1984.

Arnold, Vanessa Dean. "A Twenty-Five Year Perspective on the Pedagogy of Business Communication." *The Bulletin of the Association for Business Communication* 52, no. 3 (1989), pp. 3–6.

Baird, J. W., & J. B. Stull. *Business Communication: Strategies and Solutions*. New York: McGraw-Hill, 1983.

Bateman, D., & N. B. Sigband. *Teaching Business Communications Effectively*. 3rd ed. Glenview, Ill.: Scott, Foresman, 1989.

Baxter, C. McF. *Business Report Writing: A Practical Approach*. Boston: Kent Publishing Company, 1983.

Biddle, A. W. *Writer to Writer*. New York: McGraw-Hill, 1984.

Bonner, W. H. *Communicating in Business: Key to Success*. 6th ed. Houston, Tex.: Dame Publications, 1990.

Bovee, C. L., & J. V. Thill. *Business Communication Today*. New York: Random House, 1986.

Bowman, Joel P., and Bernadine P. Branchow. *Business Report Writing*. 3rd ed. New York: Dryden Press, 1988.

Brown, Leland. *Communicating Facts and Ideas in Business*. 3rd ed. Englewood Cliffs, N.J.: Prentice Hall, 1982.

————. *Effective Business Report Writing*. 4th ed. Englewood, Cliffs, N.J.: Prentice Hall, 1985.

Brownell, Judi. "The Radial Model: An Integrated Approach to In-House Communication Training." *The Bulletin of the Association for Business Communication*, vol. 52, no. 1 (1989), pp. 3–10.

Buschini, J., & R. R. Reynolds. *Communicating in Business*. Boston: Houghton Mifflin, 1986.

Davis, D., & R. M. Cosenza. *Business Research for Decision Making*. Boston: Kent Publishing Company, 1985.

DuFrene, Debbie D., and Beverly H. Nelson. "Selecting Word Processing Software for Business Communication Classes." *The Bulletin of the Association for Business Communication*, vol. 52, no. 4 (1989), pp. 6–8.

Dulek, Ronald E., and John S. Fielden. *Principles of Business Communication*. New York: Macmillan, 1990.

Dumont, R. A., and J. M. Lannon. *Business Communications*. Boston: Little, Brown and Company, 1985.

Ewald, Helen Rothschild. "The Me-in-You-Attitude: Business Communication as Transaction," *The Bulletin of the Association for Business Communication*. vol. XLVIII, no. 1, March, 1985, pp. 7–11.

Ewing, Jan. *Writing for Results in Business, Government, the Sciences, & the Professions*. 2nd ed. New York: John Wiley & Sons, 1985.

Figgins, R., et al. *Business Communication Basics: Application and Technology*. New York: John Wiley & Sons, 1984.

Frew, Robert M., ed. *Writer's Workshop: A Self-Paced Program for Composition Mastery*. 3rd ed. Sunnyvale, Calif.: Peek Publications, 1984.

Fruehling, Rosemary T., and Sharon Bouchard. *Business Correspondence Essentials*. 4th ed. New York: McGraw-Hill, 1986.

Fruehling, Rosemary T., and Neild B. Oldham. *Write to the Point! Letters, Memos, and Reports That Get Results*. New York: McGraw-Hill, 1988.

Gieselman, Robert D. *Readings in Business Communication*. 3rd ed. Champaign, Ill.: Stipes Publishing Co., 1986.

_____. "Research in Business Communication: The State of the Art." *The Journal of Business Communication*, vol. 17 (Summer 1980), pp. 3–18.

Glathorn, Allan A. *Writing for Success*. Glenview, Ill: Scott, Foresman, 1985.

Golen, S. P., et al. *Report Writing for Business and Industry*. New York: John Wiley & Sons, 1985.

Greene, Beth G. "ERIC: Computer Technology and Business Communication." *The Bulletin of the Association for Business Communication*, vol. 52, no. 4 (1989), pp. 36–39.

Haggblade, B. *Business Communication*. St. Paul, Minn.: West Publishing Company, 1982.

Halpern, Jeanne W., and Sarah Liggett. *Computers and Composing: How the New Techniques Are Changing Writing*. Carbondale, Ill: Southern Illinois University Press, 1984.

Harrison, Nancy. *Writing English: A User's Manual*. Dover, N.H.: Croom Helm, Ltd., 1985.

Henze, Geraldine. *From Murk to Masterpiece*. Homewood, Ill.: Richard D. Irwin, 1984.

Himstreet, W. D., and W. M. Baty. *Business Communications*. 9th ed. Belmont, Calif.: Wadsworth, 1990.

Huseman, Richard; James Lahiff; and John D. Hatfield. *Business Communication Strategies and Skills*. 3rd ed. Hinsdale, Ill.: Dryden Press, 1985.

Iacone, Salvatore, J. *Modern Business Report Writing*. New York: Macmillan, 1985.

Journal of Technical Writing and Communication. 1971–.

Journet, Debra, and Julie L. King. *Readings for Technical Writers.* Glenview, Ill.: Scott, Foresman, 1984.

Keithley, Erwin M., and Margaret H. Thompson. *English for Modern Business.* 5th ed. Homewood, Ill.: Richard D. Irwin, 1986.

Lahiff, J. M. "Effective Research—The Route to Good Reports." *American Business Communication Association Bulletin* 37, no. 1 (1974), p. 25.

Lesikar, R. D. *Basic Business Communication*, 3rd ed. Homewood, Ill.: Richard D. Irwin, 1986.

Lesikar, Raymond V. and John D. Pettit, Jr. *Business Communication: Theory and Application.* 6th ed. Homewood, Ill.: Richard D. Irwin, 1989.

————. *Report Writing for Business.* 7th ed. Homewood, Ill.: Richard D. Irwin, 1986.

Locker, Kitty O. *Business and Administrative Communication.* Homewood, Ill.: Richard D. Irwin, 1989.

Locker, Kitty O., and Francis Weeks. *Business Writing Cases and Problems.* Champaign, Ill: Stipes Publishing Co., 1984.

Mansfield, Carmella E., and Margaret Hilton Bahniuk. *Writing Business Letters and Reports.* Indianapolis, Ind.: Bobbs-Merrill, 1981.

Meyers, Alan. *Writing with Confidence.* Form B. Glenview, Ill.: Scott, Foresman, 1990.

Murphy, Herta A., and Herbert W. Hildebrandt. *Effective Business Communication.* 5th ed. New York: McGraw-Hill, 1988.

Murray, Donald M. *Writer Teaches Writing.* Boston: Houghton Mifflin, 1984.

Nixon, R. *Practical Business Communications.* San Diego, CA: Harcourt Brace Jovanovich, 1989.

Oliu, Walter; Carles Brusaw; and Gerald Alred. *Writing that Works.* 3rd ed. New York: St. Martin's Press, 1988.

Pearce, C. Glenn. "Business Communication: Forging the Future." *The Bulletin of the Association for Business Communication*, vol. 52, no. 1 (1989), pp. 42–44.

Pearce, C. Glenn; Ross Figgins; and Steven P. Golen. *Principles of Business Communication: Theory, Application, and Technology.* New York: John Wiley & Sons, 1984.

Podis, Leonard A., and Joanne M. Podis. *Writing Invention, Form & Style.* Glenview, Ill.: Scott, Foresman, 1984.

Robinson, P. A. *Fundamentals of Technical Writing.* Boston: Houghton Mifflin, 1985.

Roundy, Nancy. "A Program for Revision in Business and Technical Writing." *The Journal of Business Communication* 20 (1983), pp. 55–66.

Schell, John, and John Stratton. *Writing on the Job.* New York and Scarborough, Ontario: New American Library, 1984.

Schley, Jim, ed. *Writing in a Nuclear Age.* Hanover, N.H.: University Press of New England, 1985.

Sigband, Norman B., and David N. Bateman, *Communicating in Business.* 2d ed. Glenview, Ill.: Scott, Foresman, 1984.

Sigband, Norman B, and Arthur N. Bell. *Communication for Management and Business.* 5th ed. Glenview, Ill.: Scott, Foresman, 1989.

Sorrells, B. D. *Business Communication Fundamentals.* Columbus, Ohio: Charles E. Merrill Publishing Company, 1984.

Starzyk, L. J., & J. R. Jewell. *Effective Business Writing*. New York: Macmillan, 1984.

Strunk, W., and E. B. White. *The Elements of Style*. 3rd ed. New York: Macmillan, 1979.

Stultz, Russell A. *Writing & Publishing on Your Microcomputer*. Plano, Tex: WordWare Pub., Inc., 1984.

Sturgis, David L. "Business Communication Writing and Computer-Aided Small Group Interaction." *The Bulletin of the Association for Business Communication*, vol. 52, no. 4 (1989), pp. 12–15.

Swenson, D. H. *Business Reporting: A Management Tool*. Chicago: Science Research Associates, 1983.

Timm, P. R., and C. G. Jones. *Business Communication: Getting Results*. Englewood Cliffs, N. J.: Prentice Hall, 1983.

Treece, M. *Effective Reports*. Boston: Allyn Bacon, 1985.

Varner, I. *Contemporary Business Report Writing*. New York: Dryden Press, 1987.

Vik, Gretchen N.; Clyde W. Wilkenson; and Dorothy C. Wilkenson. *Writing and Speaking in Business*. 10th ed. Homewood, Ill.: Richard D. Irwin, 1990.

Walpole, Janey, *Writer's Grammar Guide*. New York: Simon & Schuster, 1984.

Walvoord, Barbara F. *Writing Strategies for All Disciplines*. Englewood Cliffs, N.J.: Prentice Hall, 1985.

Weeks, Francis; Daphne Jameson; and Robert D. Gieselman. *Principles of Business Communication*. 3rd ed. Champaign, Ill.: Stipes Publishing Co., 1984.

Weiner, E. S. *Writing: A Diagnostic Approach*. Elmsford, N.Y.: Pergamon Press, 1984.

Wells, Walter. *Communication in Business*. 5th ed. Boston: Kent Publishing Co., 1988.

Wilkinson, C. W., et al. *Communicating through Writing and Speaking in Business*. 9th ed. Homewood, Ill.: Richard D. Irwin, Inc., 1986.

Wolf, M. P., and S. Kuiper. *Effective Communication in Business*. 9th ed. Cincinnati, Ohio: South-Western Publishing, 1988.

Listening

Bell, George R. "Listen and You Shall Hear." *Secretary*, vol. 47, no. 9 (November-December 1987), pp. 8–9.

Bone, D. *The Business of Listening*. Los Altos, Calif.: Crisp Publications, 1988.

Bostrom, R. N. *Communicating in Public: Speaking and Listening*. Edina, Minn.: Burgess Publishing, 1988.

Bozik, M. "Critical Thinking/Critical Listening" (paper presented at the International Listening Association Convention, San Diego, California, March 15, 1986).

Brown, J. I. "Listening—Ubiquitous Yet Obscure." *Journal of the International Listening Association* 1 (Spring 1987), pp. 3–14.

Brownell, J. *Building Active Listening Skills*. Englewood Cliffs, N.J.: Prentice Hall, 1986.

————. "Listening: A Powerful Management Tool." *Supervisory Management* (October 1984) pp. 35–39.

_____. "Perceptions of Listening Behavior: A Management Study" (paper presented at the International Listening Association Convention, Scottsdale, Arizona, March 12, 1988).

Buttery, T. J., and P. J. Anderson. "Listen and Learn!" *Curriculum Review*, vol. 19, no. 4 (1988), pp. 319–22.

Coakley, C. G. *Teaching Effective Listening*. Laurel, Md.: Carolyn Gwynn Coakley, 1988.

DiSalvo, V. S. "Listening Needs in the Work Force" (paper presented at the International Listening Association Summer Conference, St. Paul, Minnesota, July 12, 1984).

Erway, E. "Listening as a Communication Competency" (paper presented at the Speech Communication Association Convention, Denver, Colorado, November 9, 1985).

Floyd, James, J. *Listening: A Practical Approach*. Glenview, Ill.: Scott, Foresman, 1984.

Forestieri, M. C. "Listening Instruction." *Speech Communication Teacher* 1 (Spring 1987), pp. 14–15.

Galvin, Kathleen. *Listening By Doing*. Lincolnwood, Ill.: National Textbook Company, 1985.

Glatthorn, Allan A., and Herbert R. Adams. *Listening Your Way to Management Success*. Glenview, Ill.: Scott, Foresman, 1983.

Gunn, James E. *Listeners*. New York: Ballantine Books, 1985.

Harris, Thomas E. "Effective Teaching of Business Communications: Responding to Reported Business Needs" (paper presented at the Meeting of the Eusbeen Regional Conference of the American Business Communication Association, 1983).

Hulbert, Jack E. "Barriers to Effective Listening." *The Bulletin of the Association for Business Communication*, vol. 52, no. 2 (June 1989), pp. 3–5.

Hunsacker, Richard. *Understanding and Developing the Skills of Oral Communication: Speaking and Listening*. Englewood, Colo.: Morton Pub. Co., 1983.

"Is Anybody Listening? Business Must Start Doing More Listening Itself." *Fortune* 42 (September 1950), pp. 77–83.

Johnson, Wendell. "Do You Know How to Listen?" *ETC.: A Review of General Semantics* 7, no. 1 (Autumn 1949).

Kerman, Joseph. *Listen*. 2nd ed. New York: Worth Publishing Co., 1976.

Lewis, Carol R. *Listening to Children*. New York: Jason Aronson, Inc., 1985.

Lucas, S. "Skills: Learning Is a Learned Art." *Working Woman* (August 1983), pp. 34–39.

Lundsteen, Sara. *Listening: Its Impact at All Levels on Reading and the Language Arts*. 2nd ed. Urbana, Ill.: National Council of Teachers of English, 1979.

Murphy, Kevin. *Effective Listening*. New York: Bantam Books, 1987.

Nichols, R. G. "Listening Is a 10-Part Skill." *Nation's Business* (September 1987), p. 40.

Niehouse, O. L. "Listening: The Other Half of Effective Communications." *Management Solutions* 31 (August 1986), pp. 26–29.

Nixon, Judi C., and Judy F. West. "Listening: Vital to Communication." *The Bulletin of the Association for Business Communication*, vol. 52, no. 2 (June 1989), pp. 15–17.

_____. "Listening—The New Competency." *Balance Sheet* (January/February 1989), pp. 27–29.

Papa, M. J., and E. C. Glenn. "Listening Ability and Performance with New Technology: A Case Study." *Journal of Business Communication* 25 (Fall 1988), pp. 5–15.

Reed, Warren H. *Positive Listening: Learning to Hear What People Are Really Saying*. New York: Franklin Wells, 1985.

Roach, Carol A., and Nancy J. Wyatt. *Successful Listening*. New York: Harper & Row, 1988.

Sayre, J. M. *How to Listen*. Danville, Ill.: The Interstate Printers and Publishers, 1987.

Shermis, Michael. "ERIC FAST Bibliograph No. 19: Listening Skills in Business." *The Bulletin of the Association for Business Communication*, vol. 52, no. 2 (June 1989), pp. 47–49.

Steil, Lyman K. *Secondary Teacher's Listening Resource Unit*. St. Paul, Minn.: Communication Development Inc., 1982.

_____. *Listening: It Can Change Your Life*. New York: McGraw-Hill, 1985.

Steil, Lyman K.: Larry Barker; and Kittie Watson. *Effective Listening: Key to Your Success*. Reading, Mass.: Addison–Wesley Publishing, 1983.

Whiteman, G. "Effective Supervisory Listening" [audiocassette]. Guilford, Conn.: Interdependence Associates, Inc., 1986.

Wilhelm, Kate. *Listen, Listen*. New York: Berkley Pub. Corp., 1984.

Wolvin, Andrew, and Carolyn Gwynn Coakley. *Listening*. 3rd ed. Dubuque, Iowa: Wm. C. Brown, 1987.

Reading

Adams, W. Royce. *Preparation: For Better Reading*. 3rd ed. Troy, Mo.: Holt, Rinehart & Winston, 1988.

Adams, W. Royce, and Jane Brady. *Reading Beyond Words*. 3rd ed. Troy, Mo.: Holt, Rinehart & Winston, 1987.

Atkinson, Rhonda, and Debbie Longman. *Reading Enhancement and Development*. St. Paul, Minn.: West Publishing, 1985.

Bailey, Richard W., and Robin M. Fosheim, eds. *Literacy for Life: The Demand for Reading and Writing*. New York: Modern Language Association of America, 1983.

Blanchard, Jay S., et al. *Computer Applications in Reading*. 3rd ed. Newark, Del.: International Reading Association, 1987.

Britton, Bruce K. *Executive Control Processes in Reading*. Hillsdale, N.J.: Lawrence Erlbaum Associates, 1987.

Brown, James I. *Efficient Reading*. 6th ed. Lexington, Mass.: D.C. Heath, 1984.

Carter and Booher. *Reading in the Real World*. Dubuque, Iowa: Kendall-Hunt, 1989.

Flemming, Laraine M. *Reading for Results*. 4th ed. Boston: Houghton Mifflin, 1990.

Greene, Beth G. "A Brief Overview of the ERIC Clearinghouse on Reading and Communication Skills." *The Bulletin of the Association for Business Communication*, vol. 52, no. 2 (June 1989), pp. 42–44.

Herr, Selma E. *Read with Understanding.* Ontario, Calif.: Piequet Press, 1985.

Leslie, Lauren, and JoAnne Caldwell. *Qualitative Reading Inventory.* Glenview, Ill.: Scott, Foresman, 1990.

Maggart, Zelda R., and Miles V. Zintz. *Corrective Reading.* 6th ed. Dubuque, Iowa: Wm. C. Brown, 1989.

May, Frank. *Reading as Communication: An Interactive Approach.* 3rd ed. Columbus, Ohio: Merrill, 1990.

Ormerod, Jan. *Reading.* New York: Lothrop, Lee & Shepard Books, 1985.

Perfetti, Charles A. *Reading Ability.* New York: Oxford University Press, Inc., 1985.

Schmelzer, Ronald V., and William L. Christen. *Reading and Study Skills, Book II.* 2nd ed. Dubuque, Iowa: Kendall-Hunt, 1989.

Spache, G. D. *The Art of Efficient Reading.* 4th ed. New York: Macmillan, 1984.

Weiner, Harvey, and Charles Bazerman. *Reading Skills Handbook.* Boston: Houghton Mifflin, 1977.

Witty, Paul A. *How to Improve Your Reading.* Chicago: Science Research Associates, 1963.

RELATED AREAS

Allport, Gordon W. *Pattern and Growth in Personality.* New York: Holt, Rinehart & Winston, 1961.

Applebaum, Ronald. *Group Discussion.* Chicago: Science Research Associates, 1988.

Applebaum, Ronald, and Roderick Hart. *MODCOM: Communication and Conflict.* 2nd ed. Chicago: Science Research Associates, 1984.

Asante, Molefi K., et al., eds. *Handbook of International and Intercultural Communication.* Newbury Park, Calif.: Sage Publications, 1989.

Aitchison, Jean. *Language Change: Progress or Decay.* London, England: Fontana Paperbacks, 1981.

————. *Words in the Mind: An Introduction to the Mental Lexicon.* Oxford, England: Basil Blackwell, 1987.

Berman, Sanford I. *Understanding and Being Understood.* San Diego: International Communication Institute, 1965.

Boardman, Phillip C. "Beware the Semantic Trap: Language and Propaganda." *ETC.: A Review of General Semantics* 35, no. 1 (March 1977), pp. 78–85.

Bols, J. Samuel. *The Art of Awareness.* Dubuque, Iowa: Wm. C. Brown, 1966.

Boorstin, Daniel. *The Discoverers: A History of Man's Search to Know His World and Himself.* London: Penguin Books, 1986.

Brown, Eric D. *Writing with a Word Processor: Communication in the Computer Age.* Reston, Va.: Reston Publishing, 1984.

Bryson, Bill. *The Mother Tongue: English and How It Got that Way.* New York: William Morrow and Co., 1990.

Burchfield, Robert. *The English Language.* Oxford, England: Oxford University Press, 1986.

Callahan, Joseph. *Communicating: How to Organize Meetings and Presentations.* Danbury, Conn.: Franklin Watts, Inc., 1984.

Chase, Stuart. *Danger! Men Talking*. New York: Parent's Magazine Press, 1969.

_____*Guides to Straight Thinking*. New York: Harper & Row, 1956.

Collier, R. M. "The Word Processor and Revision Strategies." *College Composition and Communication* 34 (1983), pp. 149–55.

Condon, John C. *Semantics and Communication*. New York: Macmillan, 1966.

Condon, John C., and Fathl S. Yousef. *An Introduction to Intercultural Communication*. New York: Bobbs-Merrill, 1975.

Crystal, David. *The English Language*. London, England: Penguin Books, 1984.

Dewey, John. *How We Think*. Boston: D. C. Heath, 1933.

Douglass, Merrill E., and Donna N. Douglass. *Manage Your Time, Manage Your Work, Manage Yourself*. New York: AMACOM, 1985.

Dutton, William H.; Janet Fulk; and Charles Steinfield. "Utilization of Video Conferencing." *Telecommunications Policy* (September 1982), pp. 164–78.

Ekman, Paul. *Telling Lies*. New York: W. W. Norton, 1985.

ETC.: A Review of General Semantics. Quarterly. San Francisco: International Society for General Semantics, San Francisco State College.

Fleishman, Alfred. *Sense and Nonsense: A Study in Human Communication*. San Francisco: International Society for General Semantics, 1971.

Froman, Robert. "How to Say What You Mean; Business Communication." *Nation's Business* 45 (May 1957), pp. 76–78.

_____. "Make Words Fit the Job." *Nation's Business* 47 (July 1959), pp. 76–79.

_____. "Prevent Short Circuits When You Talk." *Nation's Business* 51 (January 1963), pp. 88–89.

_____. "Test Your Judgment." *Nation's Business* 50 (January 1962), pp. 66–69.

_____. "Words Can Block Success." *Nation's Business* 49 (September 1961), pp. 36 ff.

General Semantics Bulletin. Periodic publication. Lakeville, Conn.: The Institute of General Semantics.

Haney, William V. "The Uncalculated Risk" (motion picture). Beverly Hills, Calif.: Rank–Round Table Films, Inc., 1971.

_____. "The Uncritical Inference Test: Research and Applications." *General Semantics Bulletin*, nos. 28 and 29 (1961).

Harris, Amy Bjork, and Thomas A. Harris. *Staying OK: How to Maximize Good Feelings and Minimize Bad Ones*. New York: Harper & Row, 1985.

Hayakawa, S. I. "How Words Change Our Lives." *Saturday Evening Post* (December 27, 1958), pp. 22–23.

_____. *Language in Thought and Action*. 2nd ed. New York: Harcourt Brace Jovanovich, 1964.

_____, ed. *Our Language and Our World*. New York: Harper & Row, 1959.

_____. *Symbol, Status, and Personality*. New York: Harcourt Brace Jovanovich, 1963.

_____. *The Use and Misuse of Language*. New York: Fawcett World Library: Crest, Gold Medal & Premier Books, 1962.

Heidinger, Virginia A. *Analyzing Syntax and Semantics*. Washington, D.C.: Gallaudet University Press, 1984.

Hinckley, Dan. *Writing with a Computer: Using Your Word Processor for a New Freedom and Creativity in Writing*. New York: Computer Books/Simon & Schuster, 1985.

Howard, Philip. *The State of Language*. London, England: Penguin Books, 1986.

Johnson, Alexander Bryan. *The Meaning of Words*. New York: Harper & Row, 1854. (Now available in an edition published by John Winston Chamberlin, Milwaukee, Wis.)

Johnson, Wendell. *People in Quandaries*. New York: Harper & Row, 1946.

_____. *Your Most Enchanted Listener*. New York: Harper & Row, 1956.

Korzybski, Alfred. "General Semantics." *American People's Encyclopedia,* vol. 9. Chicago: Spencer International Press, 1948.

_____. *Manhood of Humanity* (1921). Lakeville, Conn.: Institute of General Semantics, 1950.

_____. "The Role of Language in the Perceptual Process." *Perception: An Approach to Personality*. Eds. R. R. Blake and G. V. Ramsey. New York: Ronald Press Co., 1951.

_____. *Science and Sanity: An Introduction to Non-Aristotelian System and General Semantics* (1933). Lakeville, Conn.: Institute of General Semantics, 1948.

_____. *Time-Binding: The General Theory* (two papers, 1924–26). Lakeville, Conn.: Institute of General Semantics, 1949.

Korzbski, Alfred, and M. Kendig. *Foreword: A Theory of Meaning Analyzed*. General Semantics Monographs, no. 3. Lakeville, Conn.: Institute of General Semantics, 1942.

Lee, Irving J. *How Do You Talk about People?* Freedom Pamphlet. New York: Anti-Defamation League of B'nai B'rith.

_____. *Language Habits in Human Affairs: An Introduction to General Semantics*. 3rd ed. Westport, Conn.: Greenwood Press, 1979.

_____, ed. *Language of Wisdom and Folly*. 3rd ed. San Francisco: International Society for General Semantics, 1977.

Lee, Irving J., and Laura L. Lee. *Handling Barriers in Communication*. 2nd ed. New York: Harper & Row, 1978.

McLuhan, Marshall. *Understanding Media: The Extensions of Man*. New York: McGraw-Hill, 1965.

Martinez, Benjamin, and Jacqueline Block. *Perception, Design, and Practice*. Englewood Cliffs, N.J.; Prentice Hall, 1985.

Menninger, Karl A. *The Human Mind*. New York: Alfred A. Knopf, 1945.

Morain, Mary, ed. *Bridging Worlds through General Semantics*. San Francisco: International Society for General Semantics, 1984.

_____, ed. *Classroom Exercises in General Semantics*. San Francisco: International Society for General Semantics, 1980.

_____. *Teaching General Semantics*. San Francisco: International Society for General Semantics, 1969.

Ogden, C. K., and I. A. Richards. *The Meaning of Meaning*. New York: Harcourt Brace Jovanovich, 1952.

O'Neill, William F., and George D. Demos. "The Semantics of Thought Reform." *ETC.: A Review of General Semantics* 34, no. 4 (December 1977), pp. 413–30.

Oxford Guide to the English Language. London, England: Guild Press, 1986.

Penrose, John M. "Computer Software Review." *The American Business Communication Bulletin* (September, 1984), pp. 22–24.

Rapoport, Anatol. *Fights, Games, and Debates*. New York: Harper & Row, 1960.

Rowan, T. G. *Managing with Computers*. North Pomfret, Vt.: David and Charles, Inc., 1984.

Russell, Bertrand. *Human Knowledge*. New York: Simon and Schuster, 1948.

Sekuler, Robert, and Randy Blake. *Perception*. New York: Alfred A. Knopf, 1985.

Stevenson, Victor, et al. *Words: An Illustrated History of Western Languages*. London, England: MacDonald & Co., 1986.

Thayer, Lee O., ed. *Communication: General Semantics Perspectives*. New York: Spartan Books, 1970.

Weinberg, Harry L. *Levels of Knowing and Existence*. New York: Harper & Row, 1959.

Westcott, Malcolm R. "Creative Communication: Constructs, Associations, and Metaphors." *ETC.: A Review of General Semantics* 34, no. 4 (December 1977), pp. 433–42.

Wiener, Norbert. *The Human Use of Human Beings*. Boston: Houghton Mifflin, 1950.

Zinsser, William. *Writing with a Word Processor*. New York: Harper & Row, 1983.

Index to Cases

Index

❋
❋
❋